Apple Pro Training Series

Final Cut Pro X, Second Edition

Diana Weynand

Apple Pro Training Series: Final Cut Pro X, Second Edition
Diana Weynand

Published by Peachpit Press. For information on Peachpit Press books, go to:
www.peachpit.com

To report errors, please send a note to errata@peachpit.com. Peachpit Press is a division of Pearson Education.

Apple Series Editor: Lisa McClain
Editor: Bob Lindstrom
Production Coordinator: Kim Elmore, Happenstance Type-O-Rama
Contributors: Brendan Boykin, James Alguire, Lisa Hendricks, and Susan Merzbach
Apple Project Manager: John Signa
Apple Reviewers: Christopher Phrommayon
Technical Reviewer: Klark Perez
Copy Editor: Darren Meiss
Proofreader: Darren Meiss
Compositor: Cody Gates, Happenstance Type-O-Rama
Indexer: Jack Lewis
Cover Illustration: Kent Oberheu
Cover Production: Cody Gates, Happenstance Type-O-Rama
Media Producer: Eric Geoffroy

ISBN 13: 978-0-321-91867-3 ISBN 10: 0-321-91867-3
9 8 7 6 5 4 3 2 1 Printed and bound in the United States of America

Acknowledgments My deepest gratitude to all who provided footage for this book: for the *Fairly Legal* footage, thanks to Sarah Shahi and Gerald McRaney (http://www.usanetwork.com/series/fairlylegal/) and the folks at NBC-Universal; for the *Zero to Hero* footage, Stephen Pullin (www.pullin.tv) and Tom Compton, President of NHRA (www.nhra.com); for the *Delicious Peace Grows in a Ugandan Coffee Bean* footage, Curt Fissel and Ellen Friedland (www.deliciouspeacethemovie.com); for the short film, *I Think I Thought* (http://tinyurl.com/3asgbbk), Matthew Modine, Terence Ziegler, Adam Rackoff, and the Cinco Dedos Peliculas production company; to GoPro® (www.gopro.com) for their car-racing image; and to 2nd Side Adventures for the Baja Whales still images (www.2ndside.com).

I would like to gratefully acknowledge the tireless efforts of my first edition team—James Alguire, Lisa Hendricks, Susan Merzbach, and Hubert Krzysztofik—for their contributions to this book. And huge thanks to Brendan Boykin for his ongoing collaboration and for sharing his passion for Final Cut Pro, and also his Alaska images.

Special thanks to the Peachpit editorial and production staff for producing this book: Lisa McClain, Bob Lindstrom, Darren Meiss, Kim Wimpsett, Cody Gates, and Eric Geoffroy. I see your hard work throughout these pages. And thanks to Klark Perez for his careful attention to dotting I's and crossing T's during the technical review for this edition.

At Apple, special thanks to Christopher Phrommayon for reviewing this edition, Anne Renehan for her support and editorial advice during the first edition, and to Steve Bayes, Liza Patnoe, John Signa, and the developers who created this extraordinary software. And to Kent Oberheu for the cover art.

Finally, to my business partner, Shirley Craig (www.revuptransmedia.com), my grateful thanks for all you do.

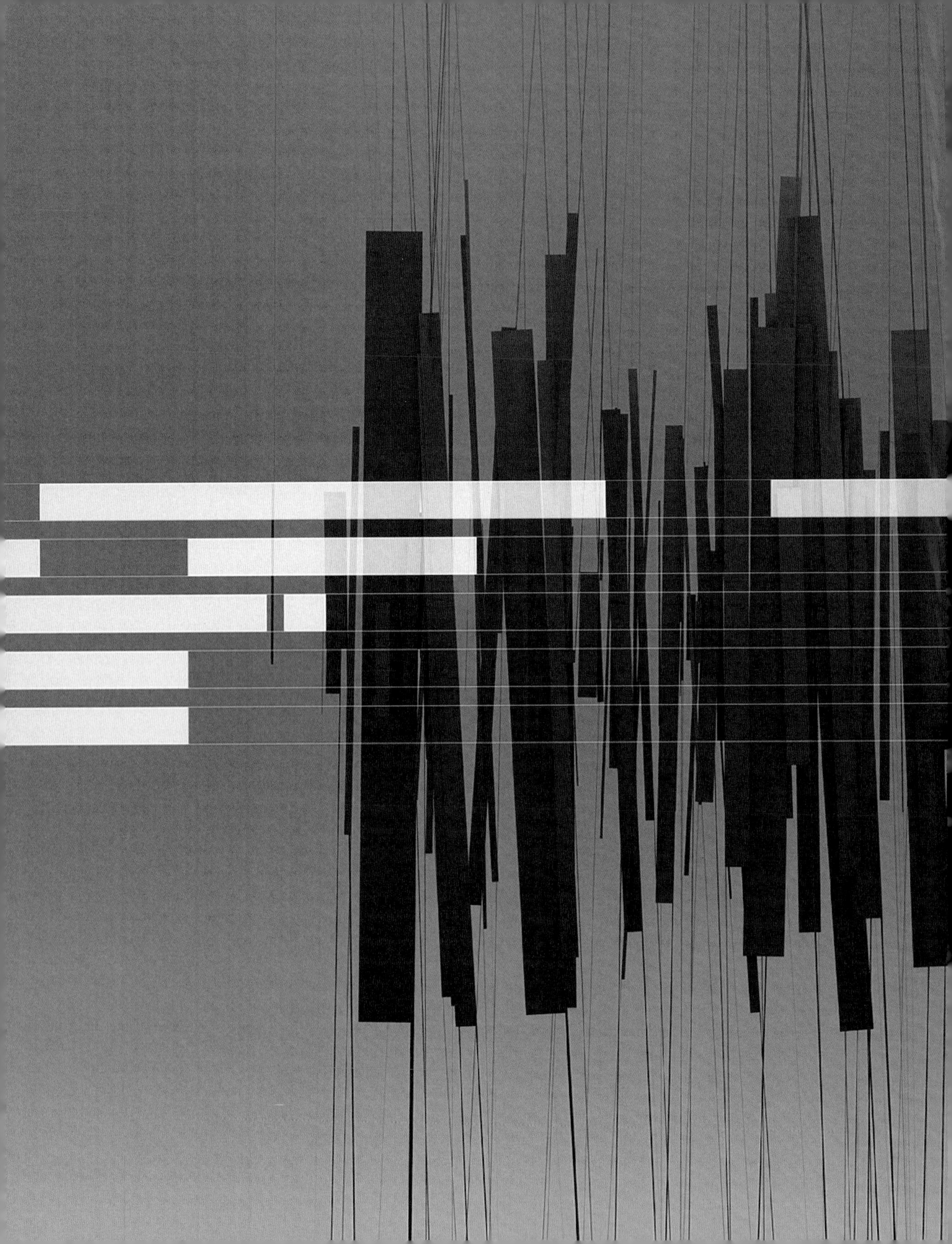

Contents at a Glance

Table of Contents

Getting Started

Welcome to the official Apple Pro Training course for Final Cut Pro X.

This book is a comprehensive guide to editing with Final Cut Pro. It uses exciting real-world footage from the USA Network series *Fairly Legal*, the award-winning documentary *Delicious Peace Grows in a Ugandan Coffee Bean*, exciting *Zero to Hero* racing footage from Pullin TV, and Matthew Modine's short film, *I Think I Thought*, all to demonstrate both the features of the application and the practical techniques you'll use daily in your editing projects.

For those who have edited on earlier versions of Final Cut Pro, or who edit on other NLE (nonlinear editing) platforms, you may ask yourselves: why make the jump to Final Cut Pro X? The answer lies not only in what Final Cut Pro X has the power to do, but what it has eliminated: many of the stumbling blocks that slow down the editing process. So let's start by taking a closer look at how that power will affect you as an editor.

The Power of "X"

Final Cut Pro X is not an upgrade, but a completely new application integrating some of the best of the latest OS X technologies. What this means for the editor is significantly better performance, workflow improvements, and the ability to perform many tasks simultaneously. For example, gone from Final Cut Pro X is the wait time for rendering and ingest. In the past, these activities halted the editing process. Now, rendering and importing, even analyzing and fixing, go on in the background as you continue to edit.

Another powerful aspect of the Final Cut Pro X technology is the Magnetic Timeline, which keeps audio and video locked in sync so it's virtually impossible to separate the two accidentally. The Resolution Independent Playback System allows you to handle and smoothly play all formats, from standard definition to 5K resolutions, regardless of the origin of media. Final Cut Pro X can automatically control the quality and color of images during ingest, while at the same time performing audio cleanup tasks. And you don't have to wait to begin organizing your footage. Metadata-based Keyword and Smart Collections begin during the import process, organizing files based on people and shot detection. Keywords will help you organize and locate clips within Final Cut Pro X with unprecedented speed, and unlimited undos and never having to save will provide a level of protection you've never known.

Bundled together, the many new developments in Final Cut Pro X will make your workflow faster, smoother, and easier so that you can spend more time in the creative decision-making process. And isn't that what editing is really about? But before you begin to explore the new interface or jump into the editing lessons in this book, let's take a more detailed look at what's "under the hood" of Final Cut Pro X to get a better understanding of this powerful and intuitive editing application.

The Technology of "X"

You may have heard some of the geeky buzzwords like 64-bit processing and memory management, Grand Central Dispatch, and OpenCL. But what do those terms mean, and how do these features matter in the day-to-day drama of video editors? Here's a brief look at these technologies, what they are, and why they make a difference when editing with Final Cut Pro X.

The 64-Bit Question

In order to utilize and support the new 64-bit processing in computer technology, Final Cut Pro X had to be completely re-engineered. You might be asking, "2-bits, 4-bits, 64-bits, a dollar. . . how many bits do I really need?" Typically, more bits means you can crunch bigger numbers—and crunch them faster—with more memory at your service.

Each central processing unit (CPU) is composed of different parts (registers, arithmetic units, controllers) working together to carry out an application's instructions. CPUs (and their components) are built to handle a specific number of bits (8, 16, 32, 64, and so on), like different cars' transmissions have different numbers of gears. Just as the number of gears in a transmission determines how fast a car can go, the bit depth—or number of bits the processor can manage—determines the largest number the processor can handle per clock cycle, and the maximum amount of memory that can be accessed.

Speed

The clock rate is how fast a CPU executes instructions. A 64-bit processor can move twice as much data as a 32-bit processor at the same clock rate, significantly improving performance. A 2 GHz processor can perform two billion instructions per second.

More Memory

A 32-bit processor is limited to using 4 GB of RAM, but a 64-bit processor can enable applications to address a theoretical 16 billion gigabytes of memory, or 16 exabytes. The more RAM you have, the faster your applications run because more data is kept in very fast physical RAM instead of on slower hard drives.

All this means that Final Cut Pro X runs faster than previous versions, can handle video formats from DV to 5K, can color correct video in an instant, can pitch correct audio on the fly while scrubbing through it, and can handle larger than ever project and sequence sizes.

Core Strengths

The Intel central processing units that Apple currently uses in its desktop and laptop computers are actually made up of multiple processor cores. It's like a two-for-one deal at your favorite store. In older, single-processor computers, each step of a task had to be performed in sequential order. Consider a task like mailing a letter. You fold the letter, place it in an envelope, address and stamp it, and then drop it in the mailbox. If you're the only one working on the task, and there are hundreds of letters, it takes some time to complete the task. With modern CPUs that have more cores (current Mac CPUs have between two and six cores), the Mac does more things at the same time, improving overall performance. Looking at that same mailing task, think of it as having one person per stage of the task. So a processor with four cores is like having three more people helping you: one to fold the letter, one to place it in the envelope, one to address and stamp it, and one to drop it in the mailbox. With more help tasks get done more quickly.

Following the Thread

One method applications use to take advantage of multiple processors or cores is through multi-threading, a programming technique allowing processors to work on different parts of a program at the same time. Multiple threads make applications more responsive by allowing them to perform different tasks at the same time, like a mail program being able to send and receive email simultaneously. But threading is complex, and implementing it is difficult to program.

Now Arriving at Grand Central Dispatch Workstation

Grand Central Dispatch (GCD) is the technology Apple has developed to help software developers write programs that let the operating system divide up jobs and schedule them to run on different processor cores as an alternative to application threads. GCD is the system services OS X uses to manage tasks, breaking them up into chunks, assigning the chunks to different processors or cores, and integrating the results. It's a lot like juggling, but instead of balls or bowling pins, OS X is juggling code, making sure the right piece gets to the right place at the right time. Programs that support GCD are multi-processor aware and can do more work faster when more cores are available to do the work.

Because Final Cut Pro X supports GCD and is multi-processor aware, functions like background rendering, analyzing and correcting video on ingest, editing while still importing video, and instant color correction are not only possible but fast. Think of more cores as more hamsters spinning those wheels inside your Mac to make it work faster.

Come In, It's OpenCL

Today's modern video cards sport powerful graphical processing units (GPUs) capable of performing trillions of calculations per second. But unless you're running games or high-end 3D software, much of that power languishes, unused. OpenCL (Open Computing Language) is an open standard set of routines, developed in part by Apple, that allows application developers to harness the power of those GPUs. With OpenCL support, Final Cut Pro X can use the video card's GPU as another processor to analyze or render video, perform instant color correction, or stabilize shaky footage.

Finish with a Cup of Cocoa

The magic behind all these powerful modern new features of both OS X and Final Cut Pro X is the Cocoa application development environment. Cocoa is a suite of object-oriented software libraries, runtime systems, and integrated development environments for creating software for both the OS X operating system and iOS. Originally released as NextStep in the late 1980s, Cocoa is a powerful set of object-oriented tools for creating almost any kind of software for the Mac and iOS devices that can take full advantage of Mac or mobile device hardware.

Together, all these elements form the incredible Power of X.

Downloading Final Cut Pro X

Final Cut Pro X is available from the Mac App Store. Since installation can begin immediately after purchase, you should read Apple best practices (http://support.apple.com/kb/HT4722) *prior* to installing to ensure the best performance. The exercises in this book are based on Final Cut Pro version 10.0.7. If you have an earlier version, you should download this free update or some exercises may not work as described.

The Course Methodology

This is, first and foremost, a hands-on course. Every exercise is designed to enable you to do professional-quality editing in Final Cut Pro as quickly as possible. Each lesson builds on previous lessons to guide you through the program's functions and capabilities.

If you are new to Final Cut Pro, start at the beginning and progress through each lesson in order. If you are familiar with an earlier version of Final Cut Pro, you can go directly to a specific section and focus on that topic, because every lesson is self-contained.

> **NOTE ▶** Due to individual preferences settings, your screen may not match all screen shots exactly as they appear in the book.

Course Structure

The book is designed to guide you through the editing process as you learn Final Cut Pro.

You will begin by learning to import and organize media, create metadata in the form of keywords and Smart Collections, edit clips into a project, and then refine your project by trimming and adjusting edit points and clip location.

After working on several projects, you'll complete them by mixing the audio and adding transitions and titles. Finally, you'll add effects, color correct your project, and then prepare it for delivery.

The lessons are grouped into the following categories:

- Lessons 1–3: Preparing to Edit in Final Cut Pro X
- Lessons 4–6: Crafting the Story
- Lessons 7–9: Completing the Cut
- Lessons 10–12: Applying Effects and Finishing

In addition to the exercises, each lesson includes "Take 2" scenarios that present real-world challenges for you to practice what you've learned before moving on to new material.

At the end of every lesson, you will have an opportunity to hone your skills as you apply your own creative touches to an "Editor's Cut" project, which is designed to review everything you learned in the lesson.

Using the DVD Book Files

The *Apple Pro Training Series: Final Cut Pro X* DVD (included with the book) contains the project files you will use for each lesson, as well as media files that contain the video and audio content you will need for each exercise. After you transfer the files to your hard disk, each lesson will instruct you in the use of the project and media files.

NOTE ▶ If you have purchased this volume as an eBook or your Mac lacks a DVD drive, you will find the URL to download the files following the book's index. If you purchased the eBook, you will also find a "Where Are the Lesson Files?" page located at the end of the book.

Installing the Final Cut Pro X Lesson Files

On the DVD, you'll find a file named APTS FCP X.sparseimage. This is a special file that operates like a virtual disk. You will use the contents of this virtual disk for the exercises in the book. Exercise care while installing these files (as with anytime you are performing media management functions) to ensure that the projects and media on the virtual disk are available within Final Cut Pro.

1. Insert the Apple Pro Training Series: Final Cut Pro X DVD into your DVD drive.

   Depending on which version of OS X you are using and the Finder's preferences, you may not see the DVD on your desktop. A quick look in a Finder window will display any mounted volumes (such as hard disks or DVDs) available to you.

2. In the Dock, click the Finder icon.

3. In the Finder window that appears, select the *APTS FCP X* DVD listed in the sidebar under Devices.

4. With the DVD selected, drag the APTS FCP X.sparseimage from the DVD to your desktop to copy it.

   Alternatively, you may drag the sparseimage to any locally connected hard disk such as an external FireWire or Thunderbolt hard disk. Whichever destination you choose, Final Cut Pro must have access to the sparseimage, and you must have Read and Write privileges. The DVD contains about 4 GB of data.

5 After the DVD is copied, eject it.

Before you begin a lesson in this book, you must mount the sparseimage to give Final Cut Pro access to the project and media files for the lesson.

6 On your desktop (or other location to which you copied the file), double-click the APTS FCP X.sparseimage file.

A virtual disk labeled APTS FCP X appears under Devices in the Finder window's sidebar.

NOTE ▶ Depending on which version of OS X you use and the Finder's preferences, you may not see the APTS FCP X disk on your desktop.

Each lesson will explain which files to open for that lesson's exercises. You should not disturb the contents of the Final Cut Events or Final Cut Projects folders on the APTS FCP X virtual disk.

Connecting Media to Project Files

The DVD's APTS FCP X virtual disk links the projects and media files within itself. If for some reason project clips appear as offline media files, you can reconnect to the Events that contain the media.

1 In the Project Library, select the project containing the offline clips.

2 In the Inspector, select the Properties tab. At the bottom of the Inspector, click the Modify Event References button.

3 If the media is available, click the Event referenced on APTS FCP X in the dialog that appears and then click OK.

The clips appear and play back. You may skip the remaining step.

4 If the application is unable to find the media, click OK and quit the application by choosing Final Cut Pro > Quit Final Cut Pro. Proceed with the steps in the previous section "Installing the Final Cut Pro X Lesson Files" to reinstall the projects and media files.

Using Final Cut Pro on a Portable

Some of the keystrokes identified in this book for desktop use work differently if you are using a MacBook or Apple Wireless Keyboard. Specifically, you'll need to hold down the Function key (fn) when using the Left and Right Arrow keys to access the Home and End keys, respectively.

About the Media

Four sets of media are used throughout this book. Together they represent different types of projects and media formats. The exercises instruct you to edit the media in a particular way, but you can use any part of this footage to practice editing methods. Techniques you learn using one set of media in a lesson can be practiced with a different set of clips to create a new project.

> **NOTE ▶** Due to copyright restrictions, you cannot use this footage for any purpose other than executing the exercises in this book.

The media, as it appears in the book, includes the following:

Delicious Peace Grows in a Ugandan Coffee Bean—An award-winning documentary narrated by actor Ed O'Neill, produced by Ellen Friedland, and directed by Curt Fissel. This documentary film tells the uplifting and inspiring story of how a group of Christian, Jewish, and Muslim Ugandan coffee farmers overcame historical and economic hurdles to build harmonious relationships and increase economic development. The footage was shot as HDV 1080i60.

Fairly Legal—This footage is from the USA Network television series that starred Sarah Shahi as Kate Reed. In this episode, "Bridges," which was directed by Peter Markle, veteran actor Gerald McRaney guests stars as Judge Nicastro. Thanks to her innate understanding of human nature, thorough legal knowledge, and wry sense of humor, Kate is a natural when it comes to dispute resolution. Except, it seems, when it comes to conflicts in her personal life. This episode was shot using the RED MX camera at 1920 x 1080 and 23.98 fps.

Zero to Hero—This exciting racing footage was produced by Pullin Television, in partnership with the National Hot Rod Association. The series, which was produced and directed by Stephen Pullin, highlights different drag car racing stars and showcases their backgrounds, their passions, and their commitment to racing. Broadcast on Fox Television as well as distributed over the Internet, each episode was created using a variety of camera sources, including Sony EX3, Panasonic P2, and GoPro for live events, interviews, and field production, as well as additional footage from ESPN broadcasts that was mastered on DVC Pro.

I Think I Thought—Matthew Modine wrote, directed, and starred in this sardonically humorous short film about Joe—a thinker in a world that no longer tolerates analytical thinking. The film was co-produced and shot by Adam McClelland and edited by Terence Ziegler. It was released in 2008 and is available to download from the iTunes Store. It was shot on the Panasonic AG-HVX200 camera.

System Requirements

Before using *Apple Pro Training Series: Final Cut Pro X*, you should have a working knowledge of your Mac and the OS X operating system. Make sure that you know how to use the mouse/trackpad and standard menus and commands and also how to open and close files. If you need to review these techniques, see the printed or online documentation included with your system.

For the basic system requirements for Final Cut Pro X, refer to the technical specifications at www.apple.com/finalcutpro/specs/.

About the Apple Pro Training Series

Apple Pro Training Series: Final Cut Pro X is both a self-paced learning tool and the official curriculum of the Apple Pro Training and Certification Program.

Developed by experts in the field and certified by Apple, the series is used by Apple Authorized Training Centers worldwide and offers complete training in all Apple Pro products. The lessons are designed to let you learn at your own pace. Each lesson concludes with review questions and answers summarizing what you've learned, which you can use to help prepare for the Apple Pro Certification Exam.

For a complete list of Apple Pro Training Series books, see the ad page at the back of this book, or visit www.peachpit.com/apts.

Apple Pro Certification Programs

The Apple Pro Training and Certification Programs are designed to keep you at the forefront of Apple digital media technology while giving you a competitive edge in today's ever-changing job market. Whether you're an editor, graphic designer, sound designer, special effects artist, student, or teacher, these training tools are meant to help you expand your skills.

Upon completing the course material in this book, you can earn Apple certification. Certification is offered in all Pro Applications, including Aperture, Final Cut Pro, Motion, and Logic Pro. Certification gives you official recognition of your knowledge of Apple professional applications while allowing you to market yourself to employers and clients as a skilled user of Apple products.

Apple offers three levels of certification, **Apple Certified Associate**, **Apple Certified Pro - Level One**, and **Apple Certified Pro - Level Two**. Certification exams do not require class attendance. Students who prefer to learn on their own or who already have the necessary skill set in the chosen application may take an exam for a fee.

Apple Certified Associate status validates entry-level skills in a specific application. Unlike an Apple Certified Pro exam, you can take Associate exams online from the comfort of your own home or office. Apple Certified Associate status is appropriate for students, for someone who is preparing for a first job out of school or a college-level program, or for anyone interested in validating entry-level credentials. Instructions on how to take the exam are included later in this book. For details on what the exam covers, please visit training.apple.com/certification/proapps.

An **Apple Certified Pro** is a user who has reached the highest skill level in the use and operation of Apple Pro Applications as attested to by Apple. Students earn certification by passing the online certification exam administered only at Apple Authorized Training Centers (AATCs). Apple Certified Pro status is appropriate for industry professionals.

For those who prefer to learn in an instructor-led setting, training courses are taught by Apple Certified Trainers at AATCs worldwide. The courses use the Apple Pro Training Series books as their curriculum and balance concepts and lectures with hands-on labs and exercises. AATCs are carefully selected to meet Apple's highest standards in all areas, including facilities, instructors, course delivery, and infrastructure. The goal of the program is to offer Apple customers, from beginners to the most seasoned professionals, the highest-quality training experience.

For more information, please see the page at the back of this book, or to find an Authorized Training Center near you, visit training.apple.com.

Resources

Apple Pro Training Series: Final Cut Pro X is not intended as a comprehensive reference manual, nor does it replace the documentation that comes with the application. For comprehensive information about program features, refer to these resources:

- Final Cut Pro Help: Accessed through the Final Cut Pro Help menu, the Reference Guide contains a complete description of all features. You can also access the help at http://help.apple.com/finalcutpro/.
- For a list of other resources, please visit the Apple website at www.apple.com/finalcutpro/resources/.
- For details on the Apple Training and Certification programs, please visit training.apple.com.

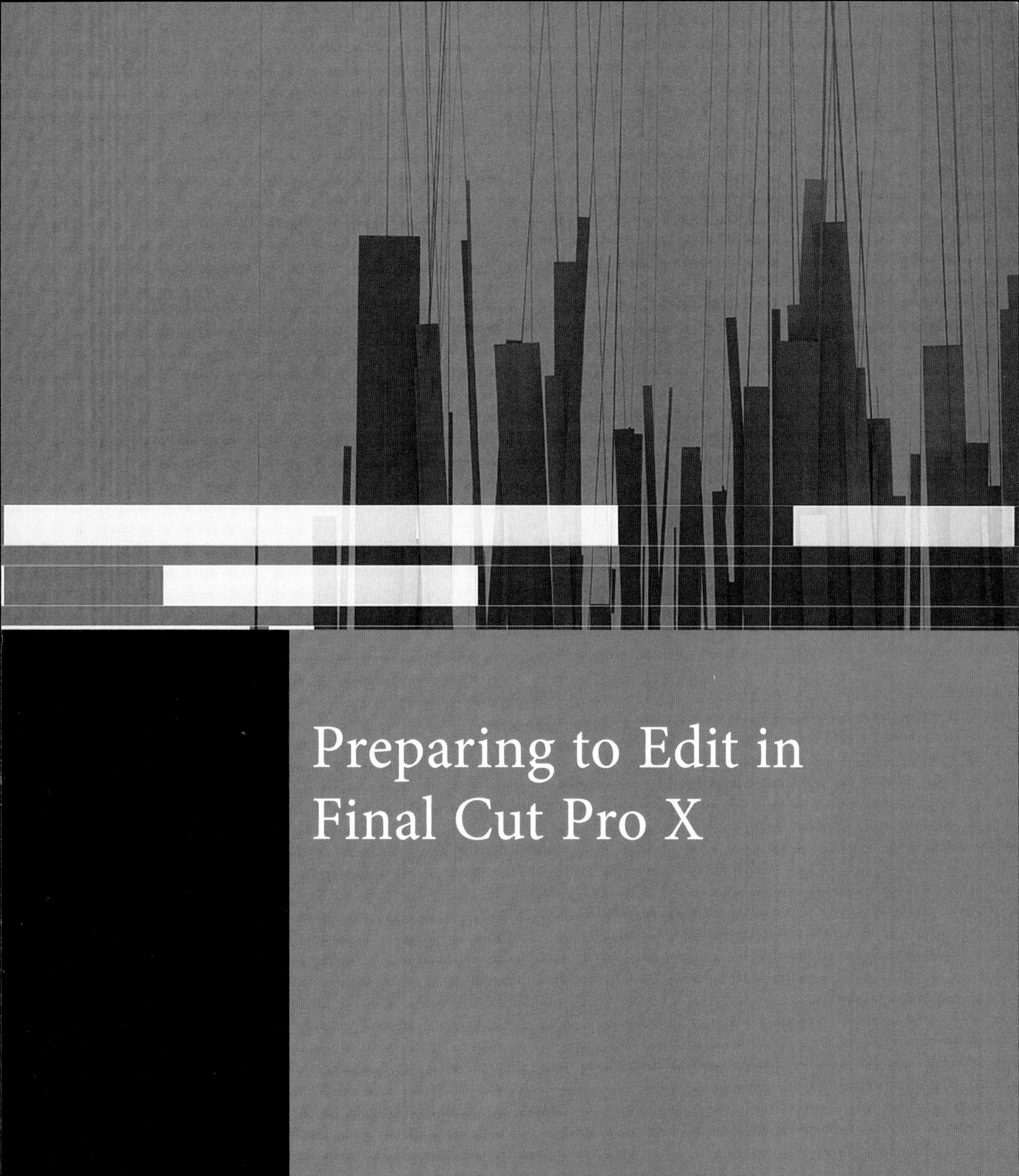

Preparing to Edit in Final Cut Pro X

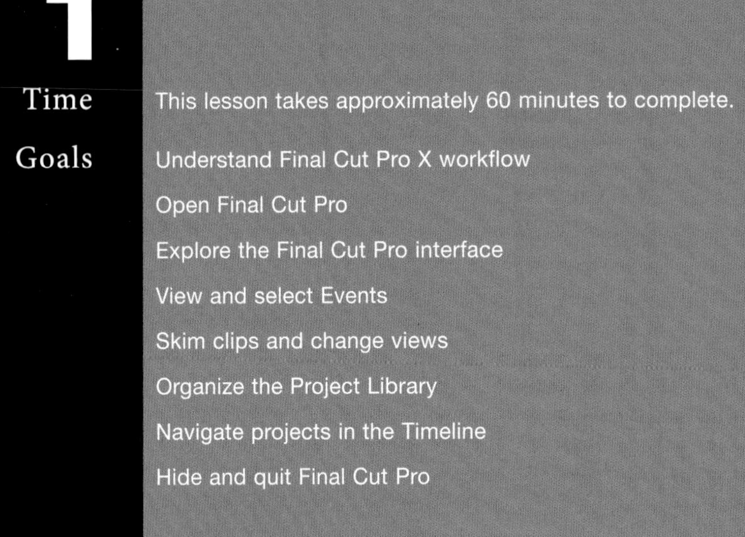

1

Time This lesson takes approximately 60 minutes to complete.

Goals

Understand Final Cut Pro X workflow

Open Final Cut Pro

Explore the Final Cut Pro interface

View and select Events

Skim clips and change views

Organize the Project Library

Navigate projects in the Timeline

Hide and quit Final Cut Pro

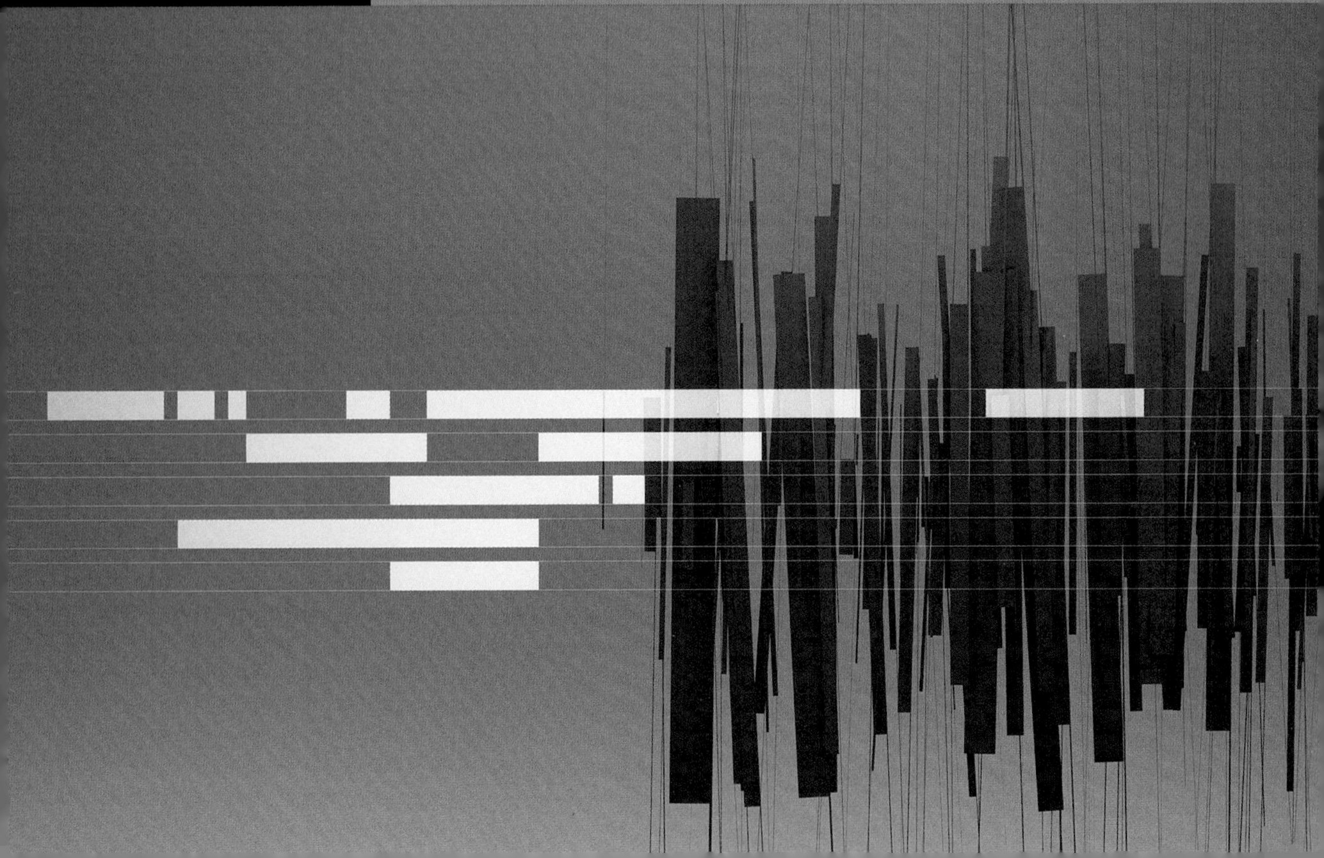

Lesson 1

Exploring the Interface

You are about to embark on an exciting journey in video editing. With each new technological development, applications evolve to anticipate the challenges of tomorrow. Final Cut Pro X harnesses the power of advanced technology to create new possibilities for today's video editors.

For newcomers, this book provides a step-by-step guide through an entire editing workflow. If you've used an earlier version of Final Cut Pro, you will discover many new approaches to your current workflow along with vastly improved processing power.

As you work through this book, you will practice each stage of the editing process. This first section focuses on preparing to edit in Final Cut Pro.

In this lesson, you will work with the Final Cut Pro interface, play source media, and view projects. You will also learn about menus and shortcuts. In the following three lessons, you will explore the Final Cut Pro interface, import content, and organize your files.

The world of the new Final Cut Pro X awaits you.

Following a Workflow

If you've ever been in a Hollywood editing room, you have seen the editor who cuts together the finished piece. But you may not have seen the assistant editor who imports media into the editing system and organizes the clips and media files, making them ready for the editor to do her creative work.

From the USA Network dramatic series, "Fairly Legal," starring Sarah Shahi (Lesson 6)

The procedure editors use to move through the editorial process is their workflow. Workflows can vary depending on the show format and genre. A reality show may have a dozen editors assembling media shot with 25 cameras in 15 different locations around the world. That show will require a much different editorial workflow than a dramatic television series, which is shot in a studio with only two or three cameras.

Today's editor has to deal with more formats and content than ever before. No matter the number of cameras, size of editorial staff, or amount of media, the editing system is the nucleus of a workflow. You use it to import media files and then organize those files by naming and tagging them. You preview content as clips and select those portions you want to include in a project. You edit, trim, refine, add effects and transitions, and eventually share the results by exporting or posting the movie you create. And depending on the project, you could be the entire editing team, so it's a good idea to master as many aspects of Final Cut Pro as you can so you're ready for any workflow. Final Cut Pro X helps you handle it all with ease, offering dynamic new ways to organize your media and find just the clips you need.

GoPro® HD HERO® Camera on race car used in Zero to Hero (Lesson 4)

As you work with Final Cut Pro, you will refine your own workflow and apply options and features to serve your projects. You will also begin developing a personal style and approach to editing with Final Cut Pro. Yet no matter what workflow you develop or style you follow, you will be seeking the same result as every other editor: to tell a really great story.

Opening Final Cut Pro X

Before you begin, you must install Final Cut Pro X onto your Mac. To work through the hands-on steps in these lessons, you also will need to transfer the project and media files from the included DVD to your computer. Directions for installing the software and book files can be found in Getting Started. After those two tasks are completed, you are ready to move forward with this lesson.

NOTE ▶ In Getting Started, you will find a link to the Apple installation best practices. If you have not already installed Final Cut Pro X, you may want to review those suggestions to maximize your system's performance.

You can open Final Cut Pro in one of three ways:

- In the Applications folder on the hard disk, double-click the Final Cut Pro application icon.
- If you're using OS X Mountain Lion, from Launchpad, click the Final Cut Pro icon.
- In the Dock, click the Final Cut Pro icon. This is the most common method.

1 If the Final Cut Pro icon does not already appear in your Dock, find the icon in your hard disk Applications folder and drag it to the Dock.

2 In the Dock, click the Final Cut Pro icon to open the program.

If this is the first time you've opened Final Cut Pro, an empty interface appears, with buttons that guide you in creating a new project and importing media. (You will learn how to import media in Lesson 2.)

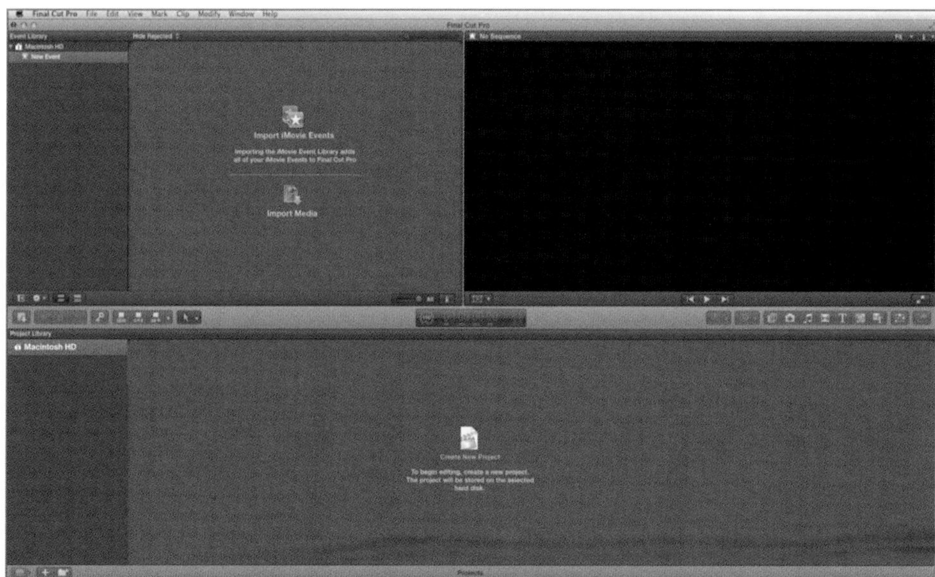

NOTE ▶ If you've already imported files or created a project in Final Cut Pro X, that content may appear here if the drive on which the media and projects were created is connected to your computer.

Exploring the Final Cut Pro Interface

Three primary areas make up the Final Cut Pro interface: the Event Browser, Viewer, and Timeline. The most basic functions of these windows can be divided into three activities:

- Event Browser—Access and organize source files
- Viewer—Play clips and projects
- Timeline—Edit projects

1 In the Event Library, select the APTS FCP X volume.

Every editing workflow begins with gathering and organizing your source media files. Final Cut Pro utilizes powerful media management through deep metadata handling, and the process starts at the point of importing clips into an Event. An Event in Final Cut Pro is simply a container that organizes imported source clips just as a folder holds documents. Available Events are displayed in the Event Library.

If you followed the directions in the Getting Started section, the Event *Delicious Peace* and several other Events appear under the APTS FCP X icon because the media files were imported for you. You'll get to practice creating these Events in Lesson 2.

TIP Depending on the work you've already done in Final Cut Pro and the external disks connected to your computer, you may see only a few Events or several. You can click the disclosure triangle next to a disk icon to hide that volume's Events.

2 To view the source content in the *Delicious Peace* Event, click its icon.

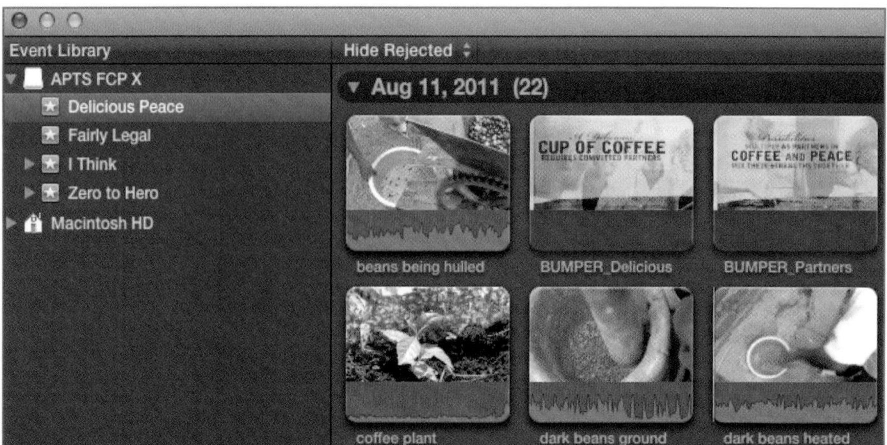

Selecting an Event displays its clips to the right in the Event Browser.

TIP Your clips in the Event Browser may not appear like those shown in the figure. Don't worry—you will learn how to adjust the appearance options later in this lesson.

3 To create more room to display clips in the Event Browser, close the Event Library by clicking the Show/Hide Event Library button.

The Event Browser is where you can quickly screen clips, tag clips or portions of clips for use, and sort source clips for use in your project. Final Cut Pro allows you to organize and retrieve desired clips from hundreds of source clips using complex, metadata-based searches.

In the lower portion of the interface you can see the Timeline where you edit your clips into a finished product. The trackless Timeline allows frame-accurate, fast editing without cumbersome technical barriers. And with features such as the Magnetic Timeline, editing is faster as you easily rearrange Timeline clips to find the right flow for your story.

As you will be telling different stories for various projects, you will need to bounce to the left side of the Timeline window to look at the Project Library.

4 In the lower-left corner of the Timeline window, click the Show/Hide Project Library button, if necessary to view the Project Library.

In the Project Library, you can view the list of available projects, sorted by connected hard disk. As you will see throughout this book, creating and managing your projects is simple. Attach a hard drive, create a project on that drive, and Final Cut Pro will manage it for you.

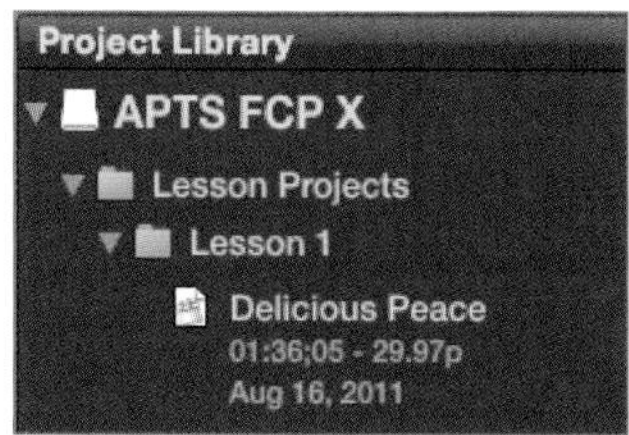

Using Menus, Shortcuts, and the Mouse

In Final Cut Pro, some editors use keyboard shortcuts to choose editing functions. Others prefer choosing menu items or clicking buttons or objects within the interface. Final Cut Pro also has a context-sensitive pointer. As you move the pointer over the interface, it may change to allow you to perform a specific function. Let's use this feature to create more room for clips in the Event Browser.

TIP ▶ To reset the Final Cut Pro interface to match the following figures, choose Window > Revert to Original Layout.

1 Position the pointer over the border between the Event Browser and Viewer. When the pointer changes to the vertical resize pointer, drag right to increase the size of the Event Browser window.

As you drag the border, the Viewer becomes smaller, creating a larger Event Browser and allowing you to see more clip thumbnails.

NOTE ▶ You can drag the horizontal resize pointer over the toolbar to make the upper windows larger or smaller during your editing process.

2 Position the pointer over the green star icon at the left end of the toolbar.

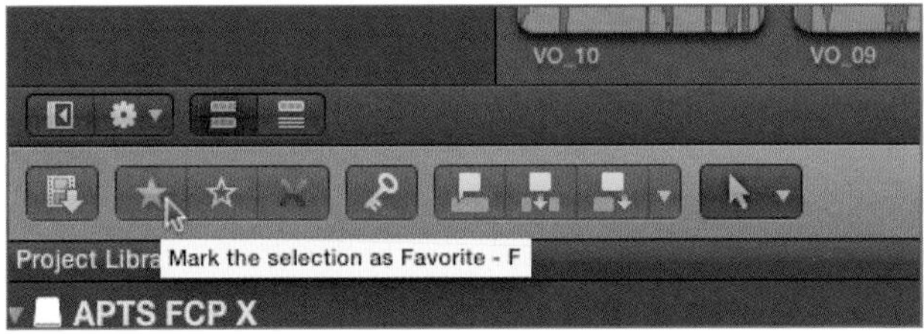

A tooltip explains that this tool marks a clip as one of your favorites. You will use this function in Lesson 3 to add keywords and tags to clips in an Event. The keyboard shortcut to access this function is F.

In addition to clicking the buttons in the toolbar, you can access tools to edit a project in the Timeline from a pop-up menu.

3 In the toolbar, click the Tools pop-up menu. Move the pointer over the first tool in the Tool palette. If it's not already the active tool, click to select it.

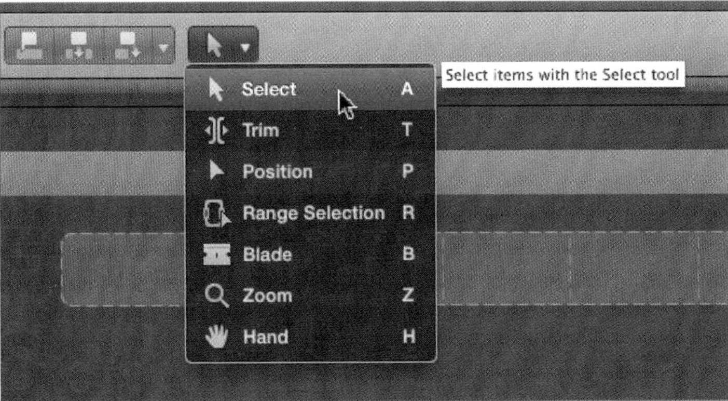

The Select tool, also known as the Arrow tool, is the default tool that you will use most frequently. Its keyboard shortcut is the A key, as shown in the menu. Throughout the editing process, you will access other items in the Tools menu to trim and divide clips, zoom in, and so on.

TIP As you finish using tools while editing, get in the habit of returning to the Select tool (by pressing A) because it's the tool you use almost all the time. You can easily remember the A keyboard shortcut because A is for Always, and the letter looks like the Select tool arrow.

4 In the menu bar of the interface, click Window.

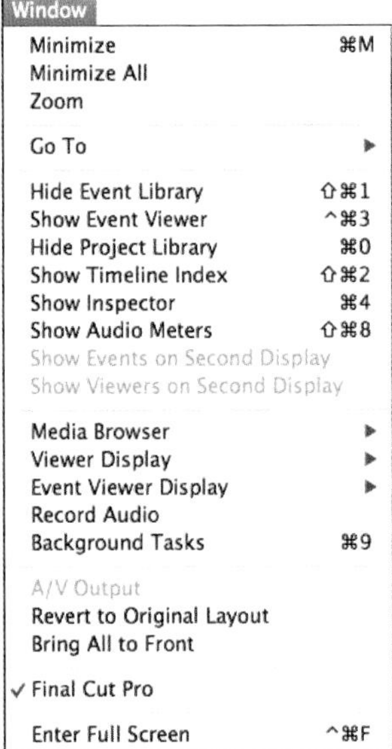

The Final Cut Pro menu bar organizes topics by categories such as View, Mark, Modify, and so on. Within each menu, specific functions that share a similar purpose are grouped together. In the Window menu, the "Go to" functions are grouped together, as are the Show/Hide functions. As in all Apple menus, black menu options can be chosen but dimmed options cannot.

NOTE ▶ In this book, when you're directed to choose an item from a menu—such as choosing "Go to Viewer" from the Window menu—it is written as "Choose Window > Go To > Viewer."

Many menu items can be chosen by pressing a keyboard shortcut. Shortcuts are either a single letter or a combination of a letter and one or more of the modifier keys: Shift (⇧), Control (^), Option (⌥), and Command (⌘). These keyboard shortcuts are often displayed next to the item in its menu.

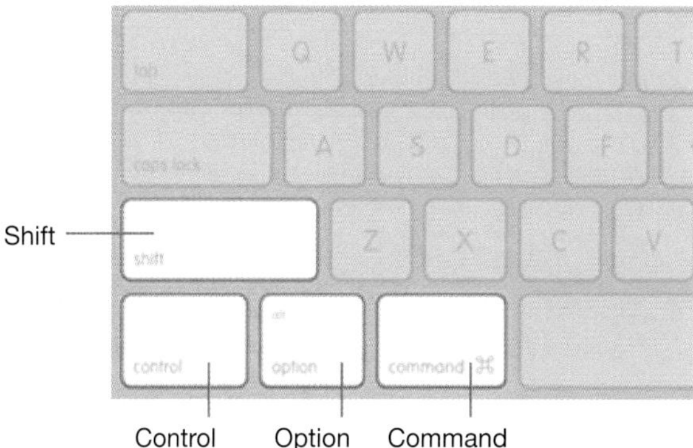

TIP ▶ In a later lesson, you will customize the keyboard layout (by choosing Final Cut Pro > Commands > Customize) to implement keyboard shortcuts you may already use on another editing system. But while you are learning Final Cut Pro, it's a good idea to first become familiar with its default shortcuts.

5 Choose Window > Media Browser. Move the pointer into the submenu and choose Effects. Notice that the keyboard shortcut for this option is Command-5.

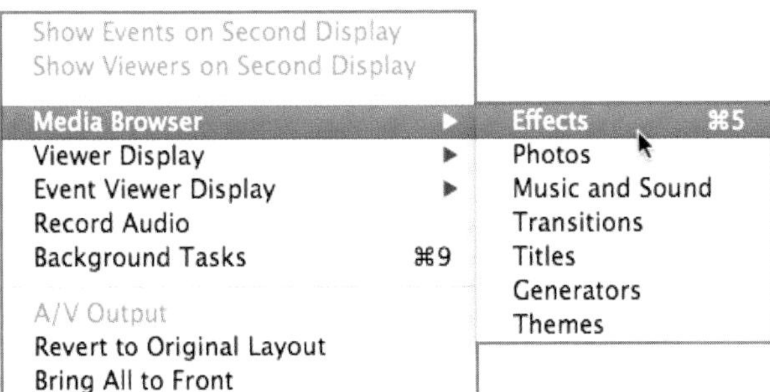

Two things happen when you open the Media Browser. In the lower right of the Timeline, the Media Browser window displays Final Cut Pro effects. In the toolbar above the Browser, the Effects icon is highlighted in blue.

Next to the Effects icon you can see additional media icons that appear in the Media Browser when selected. You will work with these options in a later lesson.

6 To close the Media Browser window, click the close button (X) in the upper-left corner, or click the highlighted media icon.

In addition to those options in the menu bar, you can access others using the Control key or a Multi-Touch device.

7 Move the pointer into the Event Browser and Control-click (or right-click) any thumbnail image.

A shortcut menu appears displaying a list of options specific to the selected item or area of the interface. In this case, the shortcut menu shows options available when a single source clip is selected. Control-clicking various areas of the Final Cut Pro interface will display shortcut menus from which you can choose context-sensitive options.

Viewing and Sorting Events

In the Final Cut Pro workflow, you import media files into Events, which are displayed in the Event Library. Remember, an Event is a container for imported media files. Events can be grouped and viewed in various ways, for example by date, disk, most recent, and so on. Once you create an Event and import source media into it, it will be listed in the Event Library as long as the drive containing the original media is accessible from your computer. Each Event appears as a white-starred purple Event icon. Again, the only way you can import a media file into Final Cut Pro is by adding it to an Event.

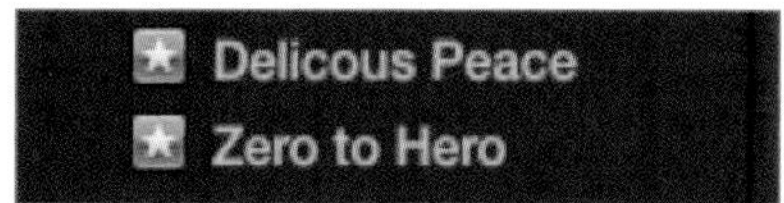

The more projects you edit in Final Cut Pro, the more Events you accumulate. In this way, the Event Library becomes a true library housing all the media you've ever imported. Therefore, it's important to know how to navigate, organize, and find the Event you want when you need it.

1 To reopen the Event Library, click the Show/Hide Event Library button.

2 In the Event Library pane, click the disclosure triangle next to the APTS FCP X icon several times to hide and reveal the Events on that disk.

When the disclosure triangle is closed, or when no Event is selected, no Event clips appear in the Event Browser. Instead a message directs you to select an Event from the Event Library.

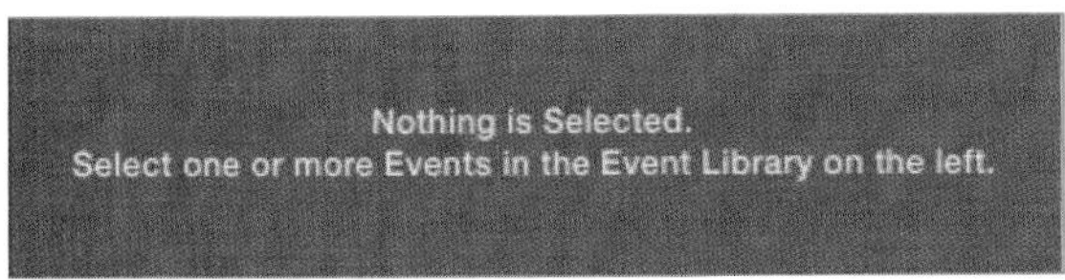

3 In the Event Library, select the *Delicious Peace* Event, if necessary.

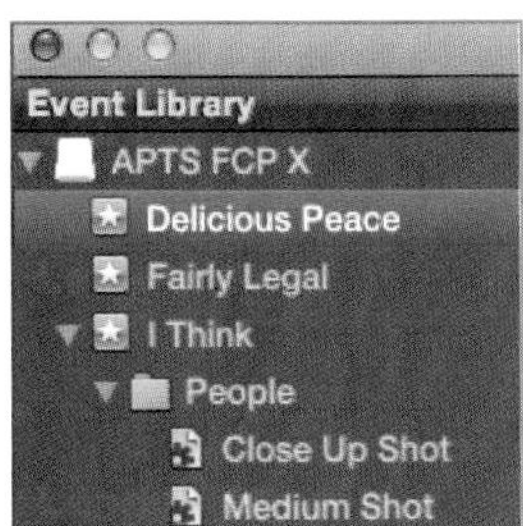

The files from this Event appear in the Event Browser. In Lesson 3, you will learn how to tag, sort, and filter individual files in an Event. In the Viewer window, you can see an image from one of the clips.

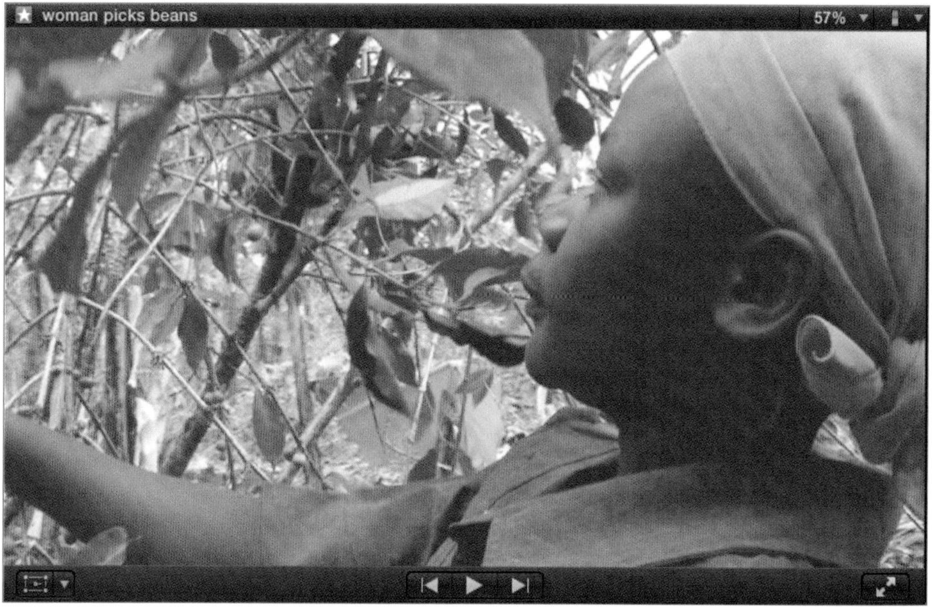

4 Beneath the Event Library, click the Action pop-up menu, which looks like a tiny gear.

Action pop-up menu

In the upper part of this menu, you can group Events in several ways. These options affect the display of Events in the Event Library. At the bottom of the menu are options to group clips in the Event Browser.

By default, Events are sorted by the date on which the content was created. Sorting by creation date may be a perfect way to find an Event on your computer and in your workflow. For this exercise, however, the date that the content was shot isn't valuable information and, in fact, could be distracting.

5 From the Action pop-up menu, choose Group Events by Date, and look at the submenu options.

Events can be sorted by year or even by year and month. If necessary, choose Don't Group Events by Date.

A common workflow for professional editors is to organize media onto external disks and connect the appropriate disk only when editing that project. But if you're using just one hard disk, you can choose not to display disk icons.

6 From the Action pop-up menu, if Group Events by Disk is selected, click it to deselect the option.

In the Event Library, the disk icons no longer appear, leaving just a list of available Events from any disk connected to your computer.

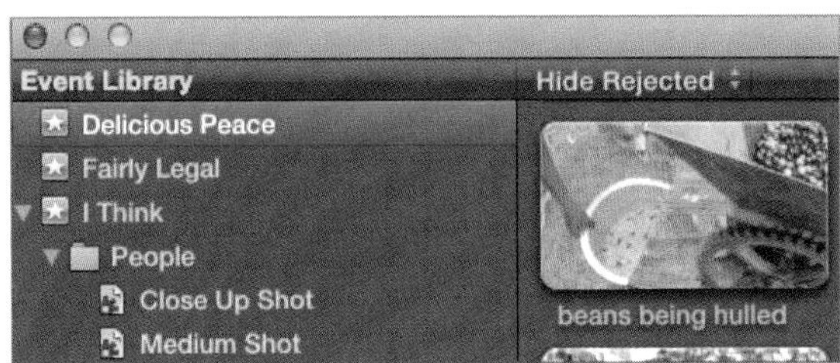

To reinforce the location of the Events used in these lessons, let's display the drives again.

7 From the Action pop-up menu, choose Group Events by Disk. Then click the disclosure triangle to display only the APTS FCP X disk where your lesson Events are located.

NOTE ▶ If some Event names are too long to read in the Event Library, you can make the library wider by dragging the boundary between it and the Event Browser to the right.

About the Delicious Peace Media

Throughout this book, you will work with content that represents several genres—documentary, drama, promotional, and television ad. The media you'll screen in this lesson is from the award-winning documentary, "Delicious Peace Grows in a Ugandan Coffee Bean," produced by Jemglo Productions, Director of Photography Curt Fissel, producer Ellen Friedland, Post-Production Supervisor Shannon L. Hartman, and narrated by actor Ed O'Neill (www.deliciouspeacethemovie.com). Living in the lingering wake of the Idi Amin regime of terror and intolerance in Uganda, Christian, Jewish, and Muslim coffee farmers challenged historical and economic hurdles by forming the Kawomera (Delicious Peace) Cooperative. Their mission was to build harmonious relationships and increase economic development, and they are succeeding. Partnering with a Fair Trade USA roaster, the farmers' standard of living is improving, peace is flourishing, and their messages of peace and fair wages are spreading to their coffee customers in the U.S. This documentary film tells the farmers' uplifting and inspiring story. The video was shot as HDV 1080i60. You can purchase coffee from this cooperative from the Thanksgiving Coffee Company in Fort Bragg, CA (www.thanksgivingcoffee.com).

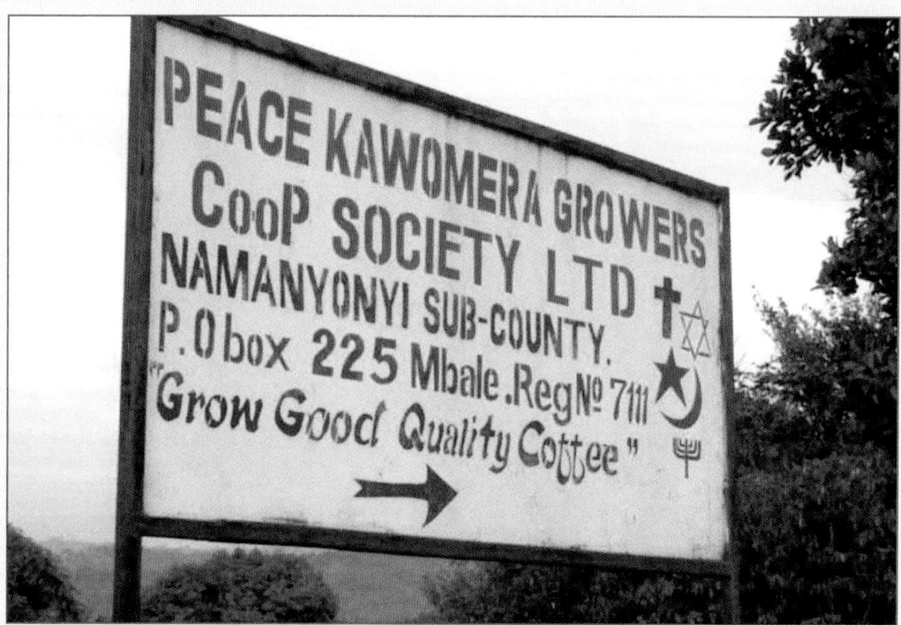

Skimming Clips and Changing Views

The lion's share of editing can often be devoted to the preparation and familiarization of content shot in the field. Unless you personally shot that media, you will need to take some time to view the clips in an Event and think about how you might want to use them in the project. In Lesson 3, you will learn how to input data that will help organize your clips for easy access and retrieval. In this exercise, you will learn how to select clips in the Event Browser and play them in the Viewer. You will also sort the clips and change clip views.

Viewing clips in the Event Browser can be approached in several ways. Often it's more productive to quickly skim through clips to search for a particular person or action. Other times, you may want to play the clip in real time to get a sense of timing or content in a scene. As you work with Final Cut Pro, you will develop a feel for its multiple viewing options and incorporate some of the keyboard shortcuts into your workflow.

1 In the Event Library, click the *Delicious Peace* Event to display those clips in the Event Browser. To make sure you're seeing all the clips in this Event, from the Event Browser Filter pop-up menu, choose All Clips.

TIP The default option in Final Cut Pro is to display the name of each clip beneath its thumbnail. If the names do not appear, choose View > Show Clip Names, or press Shift-Option-N.

You can also change how you group clips *inside* an Event, just as you group Events in the Event Library.

2 From the Action pop-up menu, choose Arrange Clips By > Name, and Group Clips By > None.

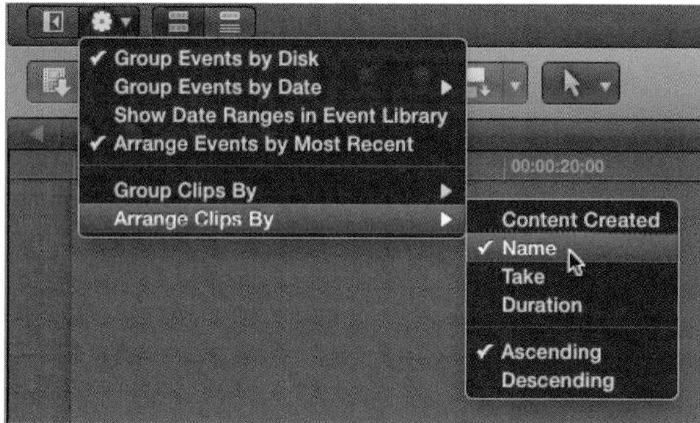

All the clips appear alphabetically in the Event Browser. Now let's look at the ways you can view clip thumbnails.

3 Beneath the Event Browser in the lower-right corner, verify that the Duration slider is at the far right so the duration amount reads All.

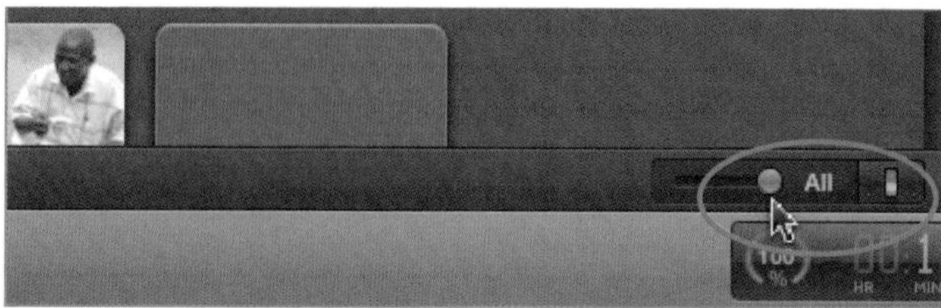

TIP If you can't see all the clips in this Event, scroll down.

When the Duration slider is set to All, a single thumbnail represents the entire clip. This is a great way to see more clips in the Event Browser at one time and get an overview of your clip options.

If you want to display a clip in the Viewer window, you can click it or *skim* through it.

4 Click the first clip, **beans being hulled**. To skim its content, move your pointer—now a hand icon—from one side of the clip thumbnail to the other.

Notice that the skimmer (thin pink vertical line) travels with you as you skim through the thumbnail, and a large view of the clip appears in the Viewer.

TIP For this exercise, make sure skimming is turned on in the View menu. If the digital audio sound is distracting as you skim, you can turn off audio skimming in the View menu. If you want to practice keyboard shortcuts, press S to turn skimming off or on, and press Shift-S to turn audio skimming off or on.

5 In the **beans being hulled** clip, click a frame in which a bean is coming out of the chute in mid-flight. Now move the pointer to another frame to find a different flying bean, and then skim back to the playhead.

The playhead is a white vertical line that appears when you click in a clip. While the pink skimming line travels along as you move your pointer, the playhead stays in place when you click, as if you were placing a bookmark at that location to identify a specific frame or action to which you may want to return.

NOTE ▶ The skimmer will snap back to the playhead location as long as the snapping function is toggled on. If your skimmer is not snapping to the playhead, choose View > Snapping. You will work more with snapping in another lesson.

6 Select the **man picks beans** clip, and skim through it. Click where the camera zooms into the tree branch to set the playhead at that location. Then move the pointer into the previous clip.

When you move the pointer from one clip to another, the thumbnail of the clip you were just viewing returns to the first frame of that clip. In this case, you would never know that the camera zoomed into the tree branch by looking only at this representative frame. You can change the thumbnail view by adjusting the Duration slider.

7 Drag the Duration slider to the left until the duration reads 2s, representing two seconds. Now scroll up and down to see the new display of clip thumbnails.

In this view, one thumbnail appears for every two seconds of media in each clip, and the thumbnail at the end of the **man picks beans** clip reflects the camera zoom into the coffee tree branch.

NOTE ▶ If a row of clips ends with a jagged edge, it indicates that that clip continues on the next line.

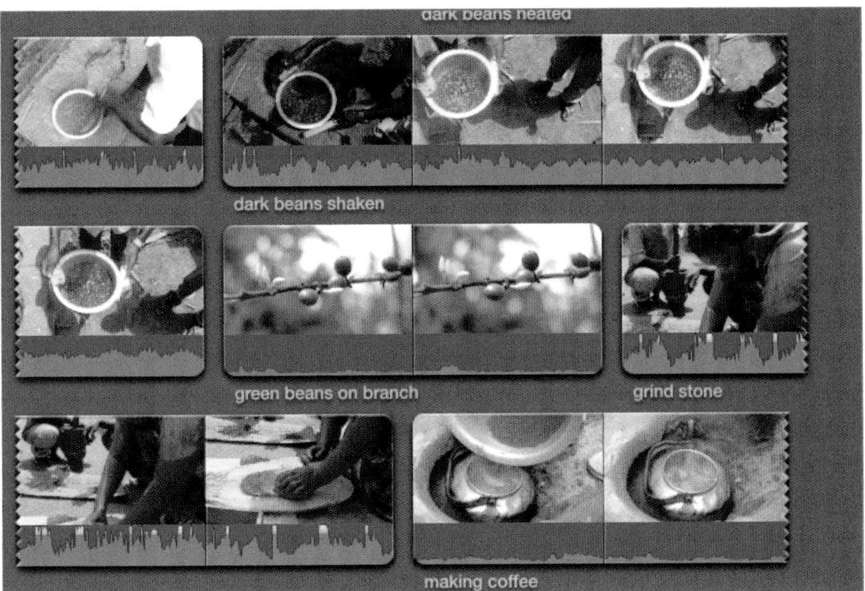

8 To select the **grind stone** clip, press the Up Arrow seven times, or until the clip is selected. To play this clip, press the Spacebar and then press the Spacebar again to stop playing the clip. As you start and stop, watch the toolbar above the Timeline to see the numbers change in the Dashboard.

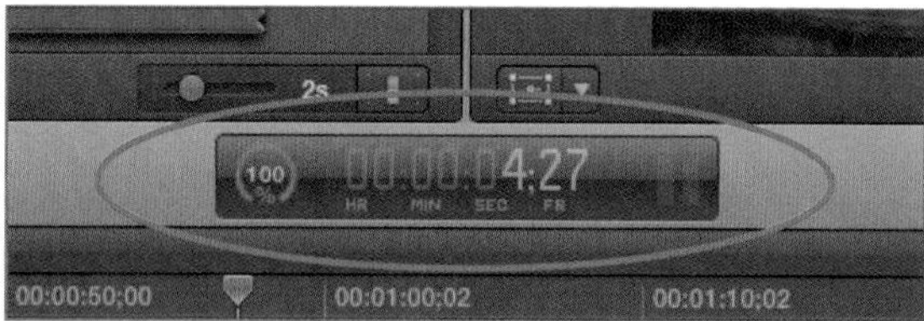

The numbers in the middle of the Dashboard are the timecode of the selected source clip. As you play a clip, the timecode changes. You will work more with timecode and the Dashboard in future lessons.

NOTE ▶ Timecode is an eight-digit number—representing hours, minutes, seconds, and frames—that identifies individual video frames. The computer uses timecode to find specific locations within a clip.

You can also use keyboard shortcuts to play a clip.

9 In the **grind stone** clip, press L to play the clip forward. Listen to find the point at which the woman says, “It has a nice smell.” Then press K to stop playback. Press the J key to play backward to a point before the woman’s statement, and then press L to play through the clip again.

TIP ▶ You can play backward by holding down the Shift key and pressing the Spacebar. To play forward from the beginning of a selected clip, press Control-Shift-I.

If you prefer to see more clips in the Event Browser, you can reduce the size of the clip thumbnails. You can also choose whether or not to display an audio waveform on the clip.

10 Next to the Duration slider, click the Clip Appearance button, which looks like a tiny light switch. In the Clip Appearance pop-up menu, deselect Show Waveforms. Then drag the Clip Height slider to the left to reduce the size of the thumbnails and display more clips in the Event Browser.

Another display alternative when working with clips is to view them as a list.

11 To the right of the Action pop-up menu, click the List View button. In the Event Browser, click the Name column to sort the clips by name. Then scroll through the list and click the **map of Africa** clip. Skim through the filmstrip at the top of the window.

Many editors prefer viewing their clips in a list because it allows them to visually focus on one clip while having access to several other clips at the same time.

All Clips
map of Africa
Name
Start
End
Duration
Content Created
man picks beans 00:00:00;00 00:00:06;15 00:00:06;15 Jun 28, 2011 8:37:11 PM
man roasts beans 00:00:00;00 00:00:08;29 00:00:08;29 Jul 3, 2011 6:43:05 PM
map of Africa 00:00:00:00 00:00:09:28 00:00:09:28 Jun 27, 2011 4:44:51 PM
map of Uganda 00:00:00:00 00:00:15:13 00:00:15:13 Jun 27, 2011 4:42:09 PM
OPENING_TITLE_alpha 00:00:00:00 00:00:20:28 00:00:20:28 Jun 27, 2011 4:43:20 PM

NOTE ▶ In the Viewer, filmstrip sprocket holes appear on the left side of the image area when the skimmer is on the first frame, or head, of the clip. They appear on the right when the skimmer is on the last frame, or tail, of the clip.

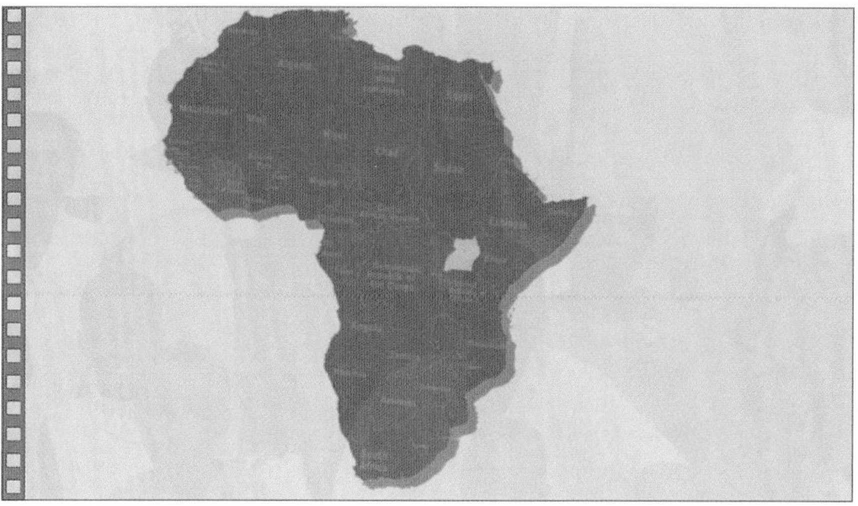

Take 2

Although the role of an editor may vary from production to production, one thing never changes—the editor is always a popular person. Why? Because the editor brings the project together. Sometimes the edit bay—or cutting room—is the first place that documentary team members see what's been shot. After shooting is completed, postproduction is when the director and producer focus their attention on the editorial possibilities. Exploring and shaping those possibilities is your job as an editor. And just as a director might shoot a "Take 2" to get a better performance from an actor, the Take 2 scenarios throughout this book allow you to practice and improve your editorial skills in Final Cut Pro.

For this Take 2, imagine that the director has just walked into your editing room and is asking to see a few of the Delicious Peace clips—now! Take a minute to review the various ways to select a clip, skim through it, and play it in the Viewer.

Working in the Project Library

During the editing process, you combine selected video and audio clips, or portions of clips, into a project that tells your story. You add music and sometimes narration, photos, titles, and anything else that brings your story to life. As with Events in the Event Library, any project you create on your Macintosh HD, or on a connected external disk, will appear inside Final Cut Pro. The more time you spend editing in Final Cut Pro, the more projects you will collect. And the more projects you have—the longer it will take you to search for the project you want. As with any good filing system, you can make retrieval easier by using a few folders to separate your projects into categories and even subcategories.

1 To open the Project Library, if it's not already open, click the Project Library button in the lower-left corner of the Timeline, or press Command-0.

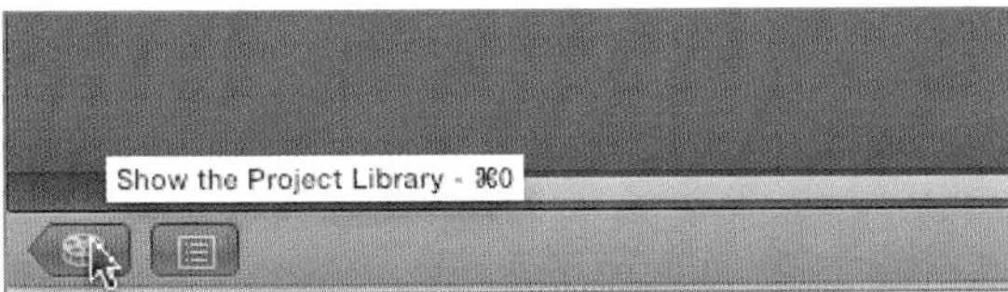

TIP Although it's pretty obvious, an easy way to tell whether you're looking at the Project Library is to look at the icon in the lower-left corner of the window. If the icon is blue, the Project Library is open for business! In fact, throughout Final Cut Pro, a blue icon means that window is open or that function is active.

If you've already created projects inside Final Cut Pro X, you will see them listed if the disk they were created on is connected. If you haven't created projects, or don't have other disks connected, you may see only the projects that are contained on the APTS FCP X disk.

2 Click the disclosure triangles to hide the contents of the individual lesson folders. These are the lessons you will work with throughout this book.

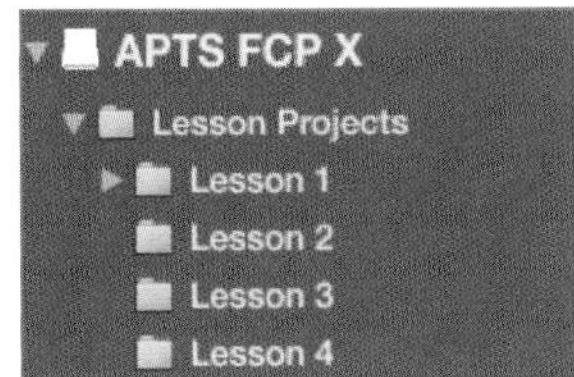

Each lesson has its own folder. In some lessons, you will create new projects, and in others you will work with projects prepared for you. You can perform one more step to further narrow your focus on the Lesson 1 project folder.

3 Drag the Lesson 1 folder from the Lesson Projects folder to the APTS FCP X icon. Then click the disclosure triangle of the Lesson Projects folder to hide the other lesson projects.

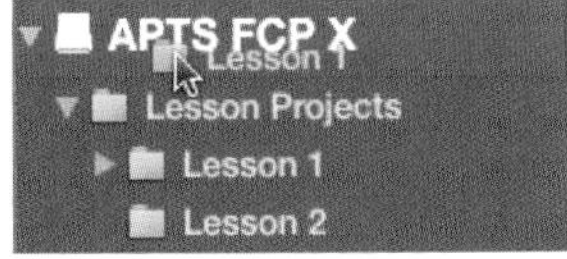

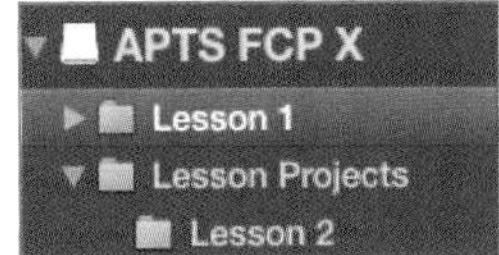

To bump up the level of a folder, drag it to the APTS FCP X icon

Now that you've organized your Project Library, let's prepare to view the project in the Lesson 1 folder.

4 Click the disclosure triangle next to the Lesson 1 folder to reveal its contents.

Two projects are included in the Lesson 1 folder. Beneath each project name you will see information about the project, such as the project length, frame rate, and the date it was last changed or edited. You can also skim a project in the Project Library just as you can skim a clip in the Event Browser.

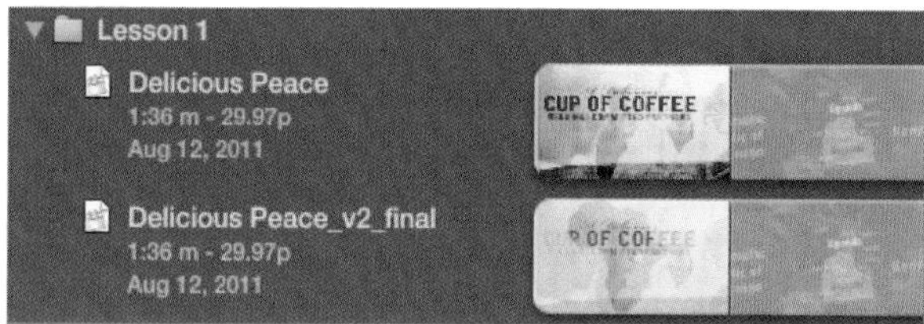

5 Click the *Delicious Peace* project to select it, and then skim through the thumbnails to preview the project. Then click the *Delicious Peace_v2_final* project, and preview it.

If you skim through the first few clips of the second project, you will see dissolve-type transitions between the graphic opening and the maps. You will learn to apply transitions to complete your cut in Lesson 7.

6 To open the *Delicious Peace* project in the Timeline, double-click its project icon.

TIP You can also open a project by selecting it and pressing Return.

The window changes to a Timeline window that displays a graphical representation of your project. Notice that video clips are colored blue and audio clips are colored green.

Viewing Projects in the Timeline

You view projects as a list in the Project Library, but play and edit those projects in the Timeline. In the Timeline window, you can view and edit one project at a time. You view a project in the Timeline by applying the same navigation techniques that you used to preview a clip in the Event Browser. And just as a clip from the Event Browser indicates a first and last frame filmstrip, indicators are placed in the Timeline to show when you are viewing the first and last frame of an edited clip.

Using shortcuts to navigate through a project can save you time during the editing process.

1 To play the *Delicious Peace* project in the Timeline, press the Home key and then press the Spacebar. As you play the project, the white playhead moves through the clips.

TIP If you are using a laptop computer or an Apple Wireless Keyboard, hold down the Fn (Function) key and press the Left Arrow key for the Home key, and hold down the Fn key and press the Right Arrow for the End key.

TIP As with clips, you can skim through a project to find a particular clip or section. You can also click the playhead to temporarily bookmark a specific frame or location.

2 To return to the beginning, or *head*, of the project, press the Home key. Press the End key to move the playhead to the end of the project, and then press Home again to return to the beginning.

3 Press the Down Arrow a few times until you see the brown close-up Uganda map in the Viewer.

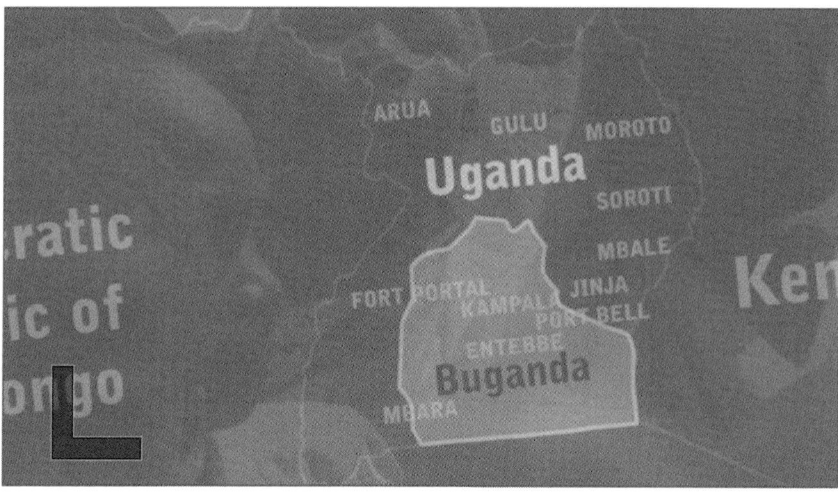

An L-shaped symbol in the lower-left corner of the Viewer indicates that the playhead is positioned on the first frame of the edited clip.

You can press the Left and Right Arrows to move one frame back or forward, respectively.

4 Press the Left Arrow once to move the playhead one frame left in the Timeline.

Now the playhead is positioned on the last frame of the preceding clip. In the Viewer, the reversed L-shaped symbol is in the lower-right corner of the image area, indicating that you are viewing the last frame of the edited portion of the clip.

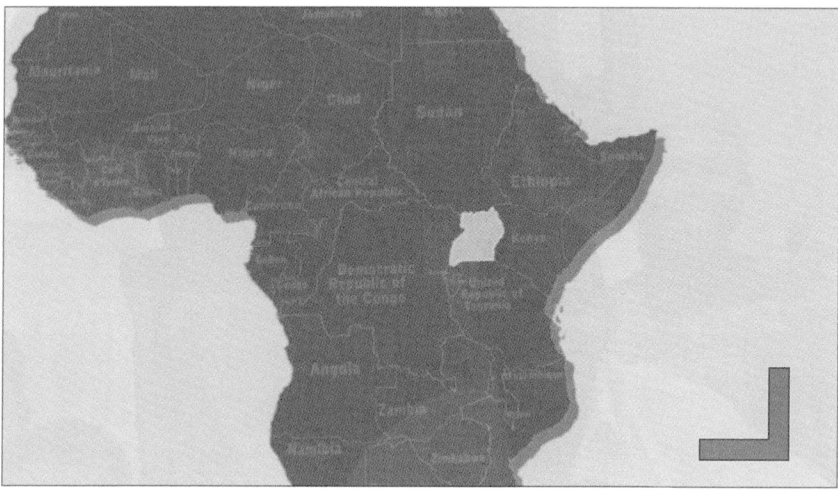

Beneath the Viewer's image area are transport buttons that you can click to play and navigate in the Timeline.

5 In the Viewer transport controls, click the Play button to play the clip for a few seconds. Then click the Previous Edit button a few times to return to the brown Uganda map.

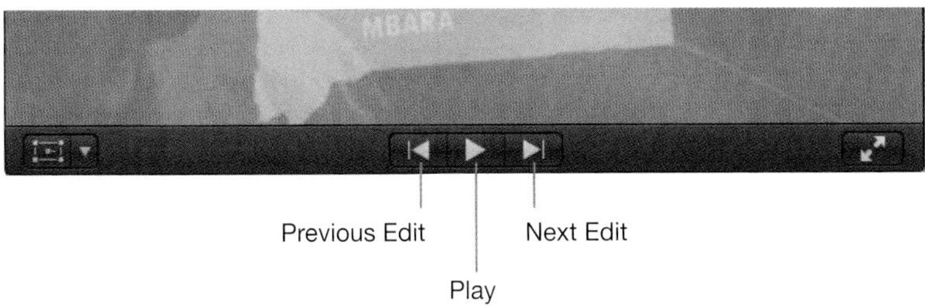

As you work in a project, you may want to zoom into an area for a closer look to see a clip name or view more thumbnails representing the clip. You can apply a few keyboard shortcuts to zoom in and out of a project, and to make all the clips fit in the Timeline window.

6 Click the Timeline to make it the active window, and press Command-= (equals) two times to zoom into the skimmer or playhead location. To scroll forward through the project, drag the scroll bar at the bottom of the Timeline to the right. You can also use the scroll feature on your mouse or trackpad.

TIP You can also zoom in and out by dragging the Zoom control in the lower right of the Timeline.

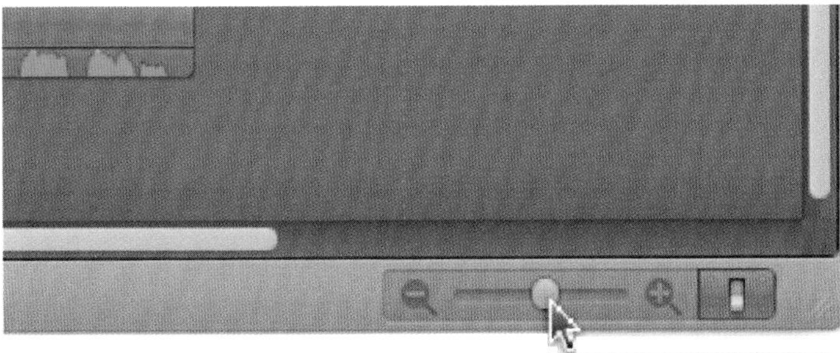

7 Now that you can read the clip names more easily, find and select the **dark beans ground** clip. Press the L key to play through this clip.

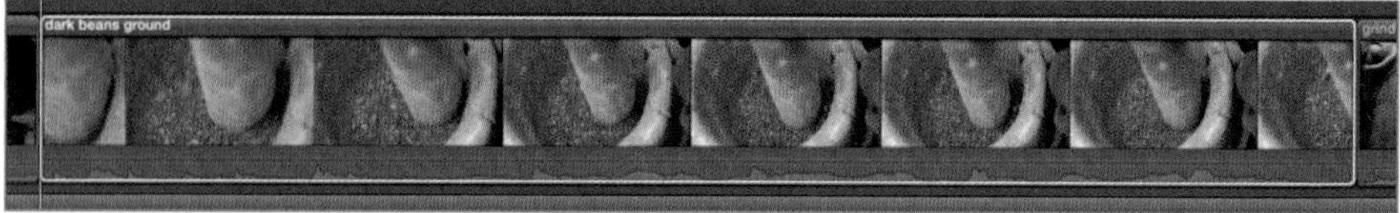

You can press the J, K, and L keys while in the Timeline as a convenient method to locate a specific action. By pressing combinations of these keys, you can play a clip slow or fast, forward or backward, or frame by frame.

8 Hold three fingers over the J, K, and L keys, and try the following key combinations to find and isolate each bang of the grinding stone in the **dark beans ground** clip:

- Press L two or three times to play quickly through the clip. When you press L repeatedly, the clip speed incrementally increases.
- Press K to stop, and then press J several times to play backward at incrementally faster speeds.
- Hold down both K and L to play forward in slow motion.
- Hold down both K and J to play backward in slow motion.
- Hold down K and tap L to move forward one frame at a time.
- Hold down K and tap J to move backward one frame at a time.

TIP You can also play a clip backward by pressing Shift-Spacebar.

9 To zoom out, press Command--(minus) several times until you see blank space to the right of the project clips. To fit all the clips in the Timeline window, press Shift-Z.

When viewing clips in the Event Browser, the Dashboard in the toolbar reflects the timecode of individual source clips. When the Timeline window is active, the Dashboard reflects the project time.

10 Press the Home key to move to the beginning of the project. Look at the Dashboard, and then play and stop the project while noting the time change. Press Shift-Right Arrow to move forward 10 frames and note the time again.

Press the Left and Right Arrow keys to step one frame back or forward respectively. Hold down Shift while pressing an arrow key to step the playhead in 10-frame increments.

TIP If you have a Multi-Touch trackpad, you can use a variety of multi-finger swipe gestures for navigating. You may need to disable or change the OS X shortcuts for your mouse or trackpad to utilize gestures within Final Cut Pro.

Take 2

The director liked the way you reconfigured the clip thumbnails in the Event Browser, making them smaller or larger, and hid the audio waveforms. But the display of a little knowledge can be dangerous. Now the director wants to know if you can make similar changes to clips in the Timeline. You can say "Yes" (because you almost always say "Yes" to the director). The Timeline has its own Clip Appearance pop-up menu in the lower-right corner of the window. To impress the director—or yourself—click the Clip Appearance (light switch) button to reveal the options and then take a moment to experiment with them.

Editor's Cut

You learned quite a bit in this lesson about screening your source media, changing Event and clip viewing options, and performing project management. You've even practiced those skills while serving the needs of others when editing a Take 2. While those efforts might help produce the finished director's cut you see on the big screen, in the Editor's Cut you'll apply you're newly gained knowledge to serve your own creative vision.

To review what you've learned in this lesson, take a moment to open the *Delicious Peace_v2_final* project that's in the Lesson 1 project folder. In this version, dissolves were added to help smooth some of the edits.

You will learn to add transitions in a later lesson. For now, take a moment to play that sequence and review some of the navigation techniques you learned in this lesson.

TIP To view a clip or project in full screen mode, click the Full Screen button in the lower right of the Viewer. To return to the interface, press the Escape key.

To review, you can navigate a project using any of the following steps:

- Click the navigation buttons and controls in the Viewer.
- Press keyboard shortcuts such as Up Arrow, Down Arrow, Left Arrow, Right Arrow, Shift-Left Arrow, and Shift-Right Arrow.
- Press the J-K-L keys to move backward or forward at different speeds.

Hiding and Closing Final Cut Pro

If you work with Aperture, you know that you never have to press Command-S to save imports, Events, color corrections, or anything else related to an image. It's all done automatically.

The same is true in Final Cut Pro X, which saves constantly in the background. When you quit the application, all your editing preparations and decisions are preserved, so you can feel secure knowing that all your work has been captured and saved. If you want to save a version of your project—with or without duplicate media—select it in the Project Library and choose File > Duplicate Project.

If you're a multi-tasker and need to quickly hide Final Cut Pro to get to another document or application, you can easily hide the interface and bring it back just as you would in any other Apple application: by choosing from the menu or by pressing a keyboard shortcut.

1 To hide the interface, choose Final Cut Pro > Hide Final Cut Pro, or press Command-H.

   The interface is hidden, and you can see your desktop or any other applications you may have opened.

   TIP With a Multi-Touch device, try out the multi-finger swipe gestures for revealing the desktop and, in OS X Mountain Lion, Mission Control.

2 Restore the Final Cut Pro interface by clicking the Final Cut Pro application icon in the Dock.

   A small indicator below or next to the Final Cut Pro icon in the Dock indicates that the application is still open, even if it is hidden.

   TIP Another way to move from one open application to another is to hold Command and press Tab repeatedly until the desired application is selected.

3 If you are finished working, quit the program by choosing Final Cut Pro > Quit Final Cut Pro, or by pressing Command-Q. If you are not finished working, leave the program open and continue with the next lesson.

TIP To keep your project folders organized, at the end of each lesson, click the disclosure triangle to hide the current folder's contents, and then drag it into the Lesson Projects folder in the Project Library.

Lesson Review

1. Describe three ways to open Final Cut Pro.
2. Which four modifier keys are often used in conjunction with keyboard shortcuts to initiate functions or commands?
3. How do you access a shortcut menu?
4. What is an Event?
5. How do you skim through a clip in the Event Browser?
6. How do you set the Event Browser display so that a single thumbnail represents each clip?
7. In addition to clicking the Play button, which keys on your keyboard can you press to play a clip or project forward?
8. Which keys do you press to move the playhead forward or backward in one-frame increments in the Viewer and Timeline?
9. What indicator in the Viewer window indicates that the playhead is on the first or last frame of an edited clip in the Timeline?
10. In the Event Browser, how do you toggle a clip's audio waveforms on or off?
11. What keyboard shortcuts are used to hide and quit Final Cut Pro?

Answers

1. Double-click the application in the Applications folder; click the icon in the Dock; or from Launchpad, click the Final Cut Pro icon.
2. The Shift, Control, Option, and Command keys
3. Control-click or right-click an item.
4. An Event is similar to a folder that holds video clips, audio clips, and still images. Each Event in the Event Library refers to a folder on a connected disk that contains the original source media files, any related render files, and a database file that tracks where everything is. When you import or record into Final Cut Pro, the source media files are stored in Events.
5. In the Event Browser, move your pointer from one side of the clip thumbnail to the other. The skimmer travels as you move through the thumbnail, and the clip appears in the Viewer.
6. Set the Duration slider to All, or with the Event Browser active, press Shift-Z.
7. The Spacebar and the L key
8. The Left Arrow and Right Arrow keys
9. An L in the lower left means that you're on the first frame of the edited clip, and a reverse L in the lower right means you're on the last frame.
10. In the Event Browser, click the Clip Appearance button. In the Clip Appearance pop-up menu, deselect Show Waveforms.
11. Press Command-H to hide the application, and press Command-Q to quit the application.

Keyboard Shortcuts

A	Choose the Select tool
F	Label clip or selection as a Favorite
Shift-Option-N	Show/hide clip names
J	Play a clip or project backward
K	Stop a clip or project
K tap J	Move playhead one frame to the left
KL	Play forward in slow motion

Keyboard Shortcuts

K tap L	Move playhead one frame to the right
L	Play a clip or project forward
S	Turn skimming off or on
Shift-S	Turn audio skimming off or on
KJ	Play backward in slow motion
Shift-Z	Fit the project within the Timeline or, in the Event Browser, display one thumbnail per clip
Command-0	Show/hide Project Library
Command-5	Open the Effects Browser
Control-click (or right-click)	Open shortcut menu
Spacebar	Play a clip in the Event Browser or project in the Timeline
Shift-Spacebar	Play clip or project in reverse
Home	Position the playhead at the head of the project
End	Position the playhead at the end of the project
Down Arrow	Move the playhead forward in the Timeline to the head of the next clip or edit point, or in the Event Browser, select the next clip
Up Arrow	Move the playhead backward in the Timeline to the head of the previous clip or edit point, or in the Event Browser, select the previous clip
Left Arrow	Move the playhead backward 1 frame
Right Arrow	Move the playhead forward 1 frame
Shift-Left Arrow	Move the playhead backward 10 frames
Shift-Right Arrow	Move the playhead forward 10 frames
Command-H	Hide Final Cut Pro
Command-Q	Quit Final Cut Pro

2

Time This lesson takes approximately 90 minutes to complete.

Goals

Create a new Event

Import files

Import folders as Keyword Collections

Analyze video and audio during import

Import from a camera or camera card

Create a camera archive

Import from the Finder or other applications

Lesson **2**

Importing Media

The number of cameras and other devices capable of shooting high-definition (HD) video has exploded in the past several years. No longer the exclusive domain of expensive camera rigs, HD video can be acquired by devices that fit in your pocket.

But an abundance of HD cameras ultimately creates an overabundance of HD video. At some point, you will need to funnel massive amounts of high-def media into your computer for editing. Like a capable assistant editor, Final Cut Pro X helps you conquer that video mountain using import functions.

From still photos and MP3 audio files, to digital SLRs and 5K resolutions, Final Cut Pro can import media from a variety of devices and a host of media formats. In fact, Final Cut Pro natively supports more formats than ever, with a *resolution independent* approach to editing that gives you an unprecedented choice of project content that you can mix and match.

Although the content you want to import has increased, the steps for importing that content have decreased, as Final Cut Pro now takes over many of the tasks previously required of you. Simply make selections on what you want to import, and how you want to import it, and Final Cut Pro goes to work in the background to organize, repair, and optimize media, freeing you to get started on the most important task of all—viewing and editing the story you want to tell.

In this lesson, you will use selected files to explore the different import options. You will import some clips from individual files, and others from pre-existing folders. Along the way, Final Cut Pro will, if requested, analyze the clips to detect people and shot composition, while at the same time correct common problems such as incorrect color balance and background noise. Once analyzed and corrected, Final Cut Pro organizes and stores everything in a way that makes it easy to find your imported files.

Importing Media into an Event

As you learned in Lesson 1, Final Cut Pro collects imported media into an Event. However, you can choose whether to actually copy the media or simply reference it in that Event. Allowing Final Cut Pro to fully manage the media files by copying leaves you to focus on the creative side of editing rather than micro-managing your media.

In this exercise, you will import media from the USA Network television series, "Fairly Legal." This import will copy those clips to a newly created Event.

1 If the Event Library is not visible, click the Event Library button beneath the Event Browser.

A good rule of thumb is that "all related media needs their own Event." So let's create an Event in the Library on your own hard disk before importing the media for this exercise.

2 In the Event Library, hide the APTS FCP X Events if necessary, and then click the Macintosh HD icon to select the internal hard drive as the destination for the new Event. Then choose File > New Event, or press Option-N.

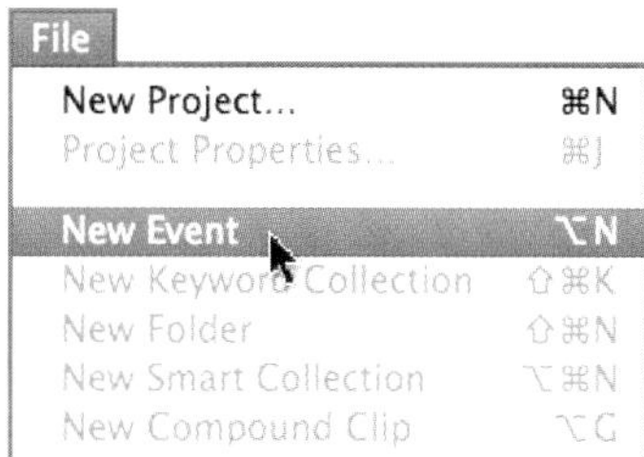

A new Event appears beneath the Macintosh HD icon in the Event Library. The default Event name is the current date and is already highlighted awaiting its new identity.

TIP When you want to create an Event on another hard disk, select that disk before you create the new Event. Also, you may already have an empty Event on Macintosh HD. You may delete a blank Event by Control-clicking (or right-clicking) the Event, and choosing Move Event to Trash from the shortcut menu.

3 In the name field, enter *Fairly Legal*, and press Return.

TIP To keep your Events well organized, give each Event a name that accurately describes the Event's contents. This description could be the name of the production, the video shooting location, or the client. Final Cut Pro Events flex to fit a variety of production genres.

Final Cut Pro provides several ways to import media files into an Event. You can click the Import Media button in the Event Browser, choose File > Import > Media, use a keyboard shortcut, or Control-click (or right-click) the Event in the Event Library. For this exercise, let's use the Import Media button.

4 With Fairly Legal selected in the Event Browser, click the Import Media button.

The Media Import window appears with a sidebar displaying all attached cameras, volumes, and camera archives. You'll learn more about these options throughout this lesson.

5 In the Media Import dialog's sidebar, select the APTS FCP X volume. Navigate to FCPX Book Files > Fairly Legal by double-clicking each folder. Select the first clip **4A-1_110(A)**.

The Media Import Viewer shows the selected clip. Below the Viewer is a filmstrip of the selected clip that is similar to the filmstrips you saw previously in the Event Browser. For this exercise, you'll import all of the *Fairly Legal* clips.

6 Press Command-A to select all of the *Fairly Legal* files, and then click the Import All button.

A dialog appears with several import options. Because Final Cut Pro needs to know the Event in which you'll store the imported clips, you'll choose your newly created Event from the pop-up menu.

7 Select "Add to existing Event" and make sure "Fairly Legal on Macintosh HD" appears in the Event pop-up menu.

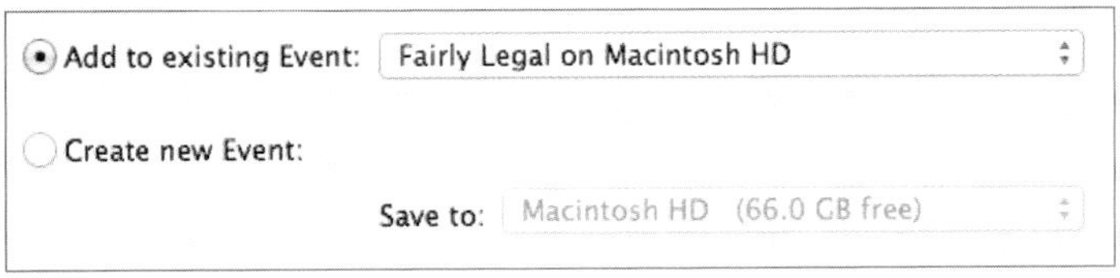

Add to existing Event: Fairly Legal on Macintosh HD
Create new Event:
Save to: Macintosh HD (66.0 GB free)

In the dialog, you can create an Event if one was not previously created. When you create an Event, you can save the new Event to a connected volume by using the "Save to" pop-up menu.

NOTE ▶ The notation "on Macintosh HD" is added to the Event name while working with this training media because the same Event appears on the APTS FCP X disk.

8 In the Organizing section, make sure that "Copy files to Final Cut Events folder" is selected. Deselect "Import folders as Keyword Collections." (These options are selected by default.)

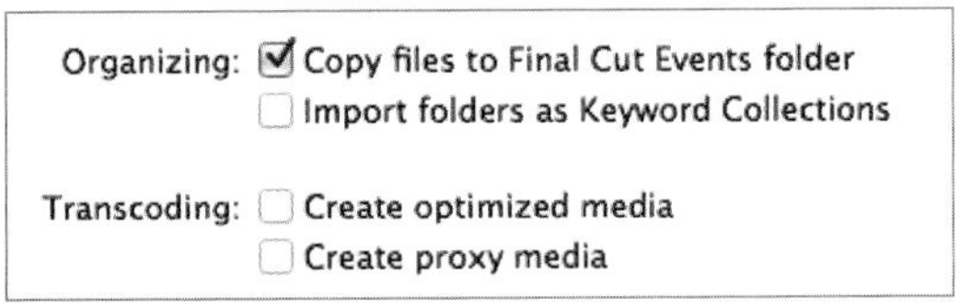

Organizing: Copy files to Final Cut Events folder
Import folders as Keyword Collections
Transcoding: Create optimized media
Create proxy media

When you copy files, the original files are physically duplicated in the Events folder to create new source files.

When you deselect "Copy files to Final Cut Events folder," Final Cut Pro creates only alias reference files in the Event that point to the original files in their original storage locations.

"Import folders as Keyword Collections" creates a Keyword Collection for each media folder you import. Although this is the default option, you will deselect it for the current exercise and apply it in the next exercise.

NOTE ▶ If you create alias files and later remove the disk containing the original files (or worse, delete those original files), those referenced clips in the Event will not play.

9 Deselect all other options in the dialog. Click the Import button.

The Media Import window automatically closes when the import process begins.

TIP ▶ You will not need to transcode media for the exercises in this book. However, see the sidebar on transcoding later in this lesson for more information on video formats.

10 With the *Fairly Legal Event on Macintosh HD* selected in the Event Library, click the Filmstrip view button.

In the Event Browser, the *Fairly Legal* clips begin to appear almost immediately. As the thumbnails appear, you can skim through the clips for a closer look. You can also adjust the height of the clip thumbnails as you did in Lesson 1 and change the duration of each clip's filmstrip.

NOTE ▶ When you change an Event's display options, those changes are applied only to that Event. While one Event might display tall thumbnails with short filmstrip durations, another might have short thumbnails and long filmstrip durations.

Because you decided to copy the media during import, the clips are now managed by Final Cut Pro.

TIP If you already have a well-organized collection of stock footage, images, and sound effects on an external drive, you can choose to work with the files from their original locations without copying them.

About the Fairly Legal Media

"Fairly Legal" is a USA Network television series starring Sarah Shahi, Michael Trucco, Baron Vaughn, and Virginia Williams. The series revolves around character Kate Reed (Sarah Shahi), who is a firm believer that justice can always be found—even if it's not always in the courtroom. Once a lawyer at her family's esteemed San Francisco firm, Kate's frustration with the legal system led her to a new career as a mediator. Thanks to her innate understanding of human nature, thorough legal knowledge, and wry sense of humor, Kate is a natural when it comes to dispute mediation. Except, it seems, when it comes to conflicts in her personal life. In this episode, "Bridges," which was directed by Peter Markle, veteran actor Gerald McRaney guest stars as Judge Nicastro.

Importing Folders as Keyword Collections

Now that you have imported files into an Event, you're ready to discover even more about the powerful media management tools in Final Cut Pro.

The *Fairly Legal* Event contains only a few clips, so finding the desired clip for editing isn't difficult. But what happens when you have several hundred clips in an Event? To solve this organizational challenge, Final Cut Pro provides several powerful features, including Keyword Collections. A Keyword Collection is a container of clips. When you select a Keyword Collection in an Event, the clips tagged with that keyword appear in the Event Browser.

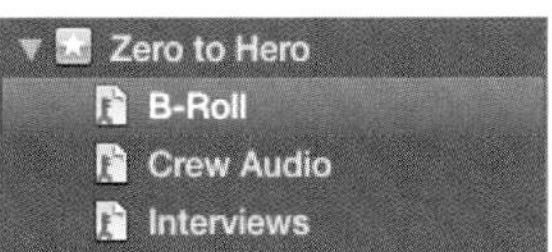

This metadata feature organizes a collection of similar clips. You'll learn how to manually assign and create Keyword Collections in Lesson 3. For now, you will discover how Final Cut Pro automatically creates Keyword Collections based on the source file folders imported into an Event.

If you've taken time to organize source media—such as interviews, exteriors, music, still images, and so on—into folders on your computer, you can create Keyword Collections based on that folder structure. When you import a folder of material, Final Cut Pro can recognize that a collection of related media is inside the folder. Final Cut Pro then *tags* the clips with the name of the folder and creates a Keyword Collection in your Event. Since the original folder and Keyword Collection share the same name, you can maintain the same organizational structure inside a Final Cut Pro Event that you created on your computer.

For this exercise, you will create a Event in the Media Import dialog, import another set of files, and watch Final Cut Pro automatically create Keyword Collections.

1 In the Event Library, Control-click (or right-click) the Macintosh HD icon and choose Import Media from the shortcut menu. You can also press Command-I.

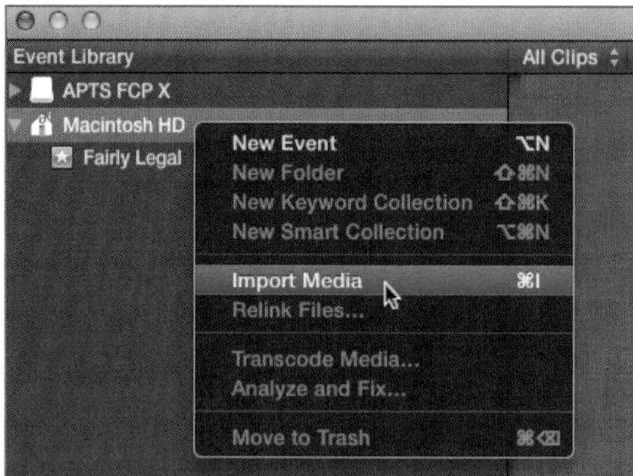

Before importing the next item, let's take a moment to add the FCPX Book Files folder to the Favorites section of the sidebar. You can include several folders as Favorites when you need frequent access to the same locations.

2 Above the file list, click the current folder pop-up menu, and choose the APTS FCP X disk.

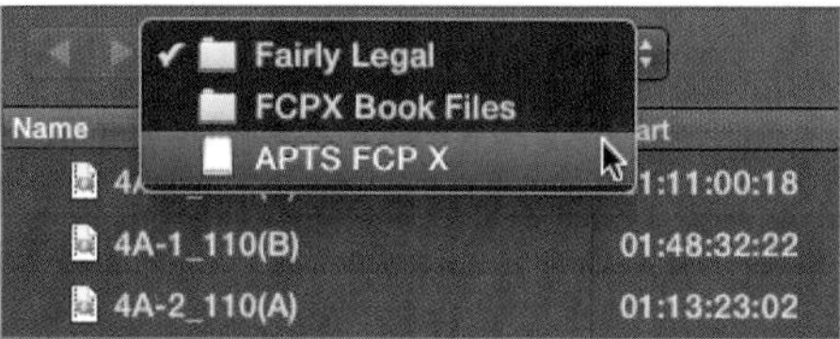

3 From the file list, drag the FCPX Book Files folder to the Favorites header in the sidebar.

4 In the Media Import window's sidebar, select the FCPX Book Files folder. Open the Zero To Hero folder in the file list, and then display the contents of the Interviews subfolder. Do not select the files inside the folder.

This folder contains four interview files. Having Final Cut Pro tag these clips as interviews during the import process will save you time by preserving your current organizational structure within the Event.

NOTE ▶ The four subjects in these interviews are NHRA (National Hot Rod Association) racers. You will learn more about them and this media in a later lesson.

5 With the Interviews folder selected, click Import Selected. In the options dialog, do the following:

- Select "Create new Event."
- Enter *Zero to Hero* in the "Create new Event" field. Make sure the "Save to" location is Macintosh HD.
- In the Organizing section, make sure that "Copy files to Final Cut Events folder" is selected.

- Select "Import folders as Keyword Collections."
- Click Import.

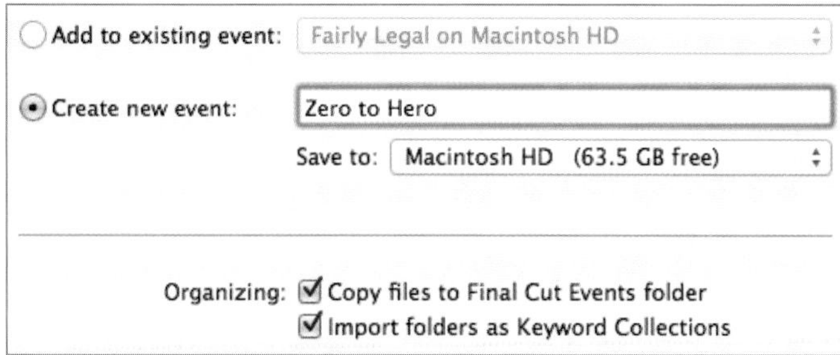

In the Event Library, select the *Zero to Hero* Event, and notice the entry named *Interviews*. This is a Keyword Collection, and its icon is a blue key. When you chose the "Import folders as Keyword Collections" option in the dialog, Final Cut Pro used the name of the Interviews folder as the name of the Keyword Collection.

In the Event Browser, notice the thin, horizontal, blue line at the top of each clip. This blue line indicates that a keyword (*Interviews*) has been assigned to the clip. In the next lesson, you will learn to sort and search by keywords, and manually add keywords to clips.

6 To import another folder into this same Event, Control-click the *Zero to Hero* Event in the Event Library and choose Import Media from the shortcut menu.

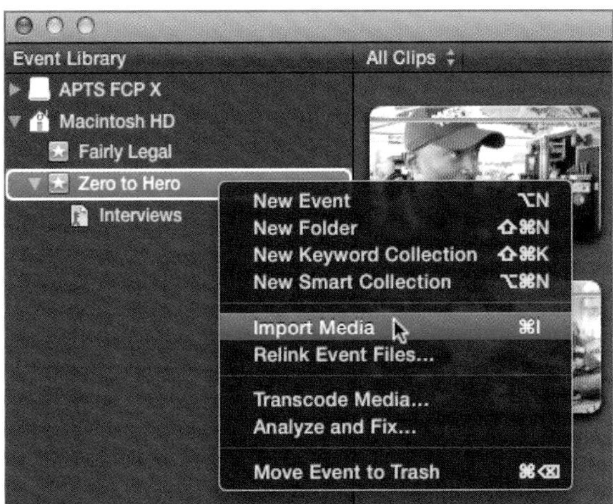

7 In the Media Import window, navigate to FCPX Book Files > Zero to Hero > B-Roll, and select that folder. Click Import Selected.

While interview material is often the basis of a project, additional material called B-roll helps visualize the story by adding important highlights, such as shots of the racers preparing for a race, crowd reactions, excerpts from the race itself, and so on. This would be good media to add to the *Zero to Hero* Event and integrate with the interviews, but it would also be helpful to organize these clips into their own Keyword Collection called B-Roll.

8 To direct these clips, select "Add to existing Event" and make sure "Zero to Hero on Macintosh HD" is selected from the pop-up menu.

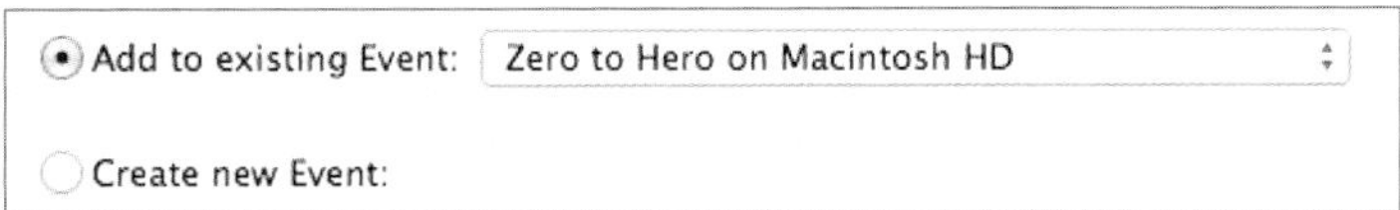

Since you initiated the import by Control-clicking the *Zero to Hero* Event, Final Cut Pro defaults to this Event.

9 In the Organizing section, make sure that "Copy files to Final Cut Events folder" and "Import folders as Keyword Collections" are selected. Then click Import.

In the Event Library, a second Keyword Collection called *B-Roll* appears under the *Zero to Hero* Event.

10 Select the *B-Roll* Keyword Collection and skim through some of the clips.

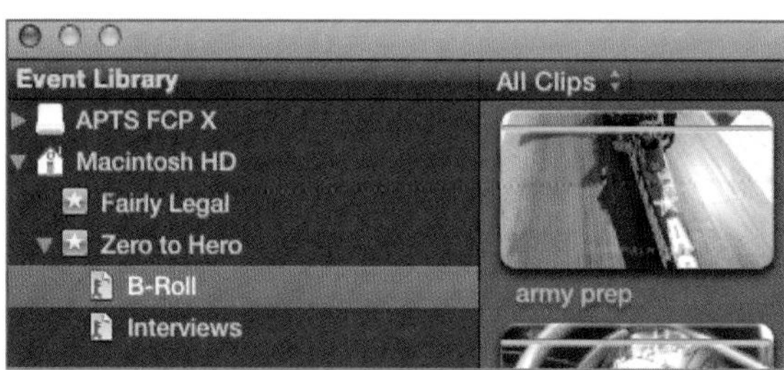

In the Event Browser, each clip is marked with a blue horizontal line indicating a keyword has been added to the clip.

TIP To speed the importing process, you can import all the relevant folders from a specific location at one time. You can also import a folder that contains other folders. The name of each folder is used as a separate Keyword Collection, and the parent folder name is also assigned as a keyword to tag the individual clips in that collection.

11 In the Event Library, click between the *Interviews* and *B-Roll* Keyword Collections, and then select the *Zero to Hero* Event.

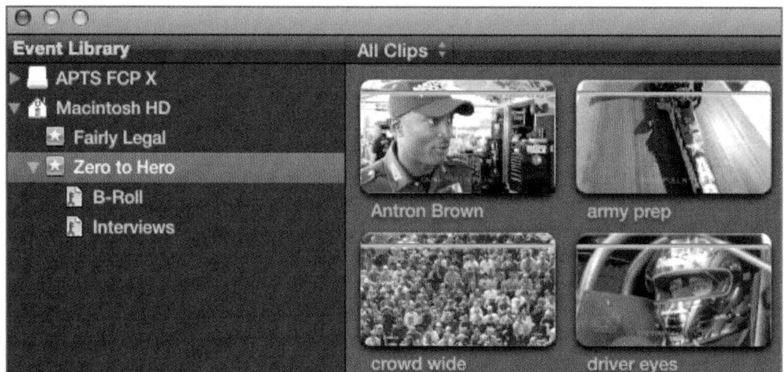

When you select the *Zero to Hero* Event, you see both sets of clips mixed together. When you select a specific Keyword Collection, you see just the clips that were in that original folder.

Analyzing and Correcting Imported Clips

Even with superb preproduction planning, the very nature of the digital, mechanical, chemical, and human elements interacting during a project's production phase means that not all your media will be free from defects. Fortunately, Final Cut Pro employs powerful algorithms to analyze many important aspects of your video, audio, and still image media files.

For example, Final Cut Pro can recognize common problems such as camera shake, color balance, shutter roll, audio hum, and background noise. It can also determine aspects regarding the content of your shots, including the number of people in a particular scene and the type of shot used (close-up, wide shot, and so on). Auto-analysis can be performed during or after import.

For this exercise, you will import and copy a new set of media from the FCPX Book Files folder, and have Final Cut Pro analyze the clips as it imports them.

1 In the Event Library, Control-click the Macintosh HD icon and choose New Event from the shortcut menu. Name the new Event *I Think*. In the Event Browser, click the Import Media button.

NOTE ► This set of media is from a short film called "I Think I Thought" produced by and starring Matthew Modine.

2 In the Media Import window, choose the FCPX Book Files folder from the current folder pop-up menu above the list view, and then select the I Think folder.

3 Click Import Selected and do the following:

- Select "Add to existing Event" and from the pop-up menu, choose "I Think on Macintosh HD," if it's not already selected.
- In the Organizing section, make sure that "Copy files to Final Cut Events folder" is selected.
- Deselect "Import folders as Keyword Collections."

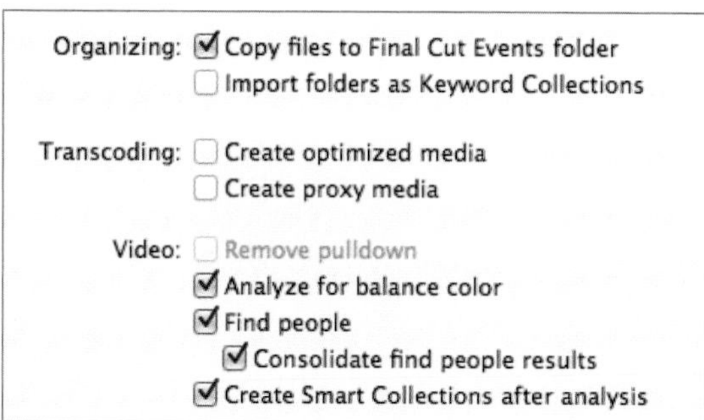

For this exercise, you will instruct Final Cut Pro X to analyze the video content to find errors, count the number of people in a clip, and identify shot types.

"Analyze for balance color" examines the color balance of each clip by measuring the contrast of the shot (comparing the highlight and the shadow areas) and spotting any color casts or tints in the image. This very handy analysis automatically fixes errors that are so easy to make during shooting (and would otherwise take you a long time to locate and repair).

4 Select "Analyze for balance color."

The "Find people" option looks for the number of faces within a clip and identifies the shot type or shot framing. Does the clip contain one or two people? Is the clip a close-up or wide shot? Final Cut Pro applies keywords to each clip that reflect the results of this analysis.

NOTE ▶ To reduce clutter, when "Consolidate find people results" is selected, "Find people" analysis will apply keywords based on the most prominent image information in every two-minute range. So if a shot contains a single person who moves in and out of frame, the entire two-minute range receives a single long, continuous keyword rather than several short, interrupted keywords.

5 In the Video section, select both the "Find people" and "Consolidate find people results" options.

The last Video option, "Create Smart Collections after analysis," helps you manage your Event. Earlier in this lesson, you learned that Keyword Collections group similar clips together. Another collection type aimed at organizing clips is a Smart Collection, which you will learn more about in Lesson 3. At present, be aware that Smart Collections group the results of stabilization, rolling shutter, number of people, and shot type analyses into Event collections.

6 Select "Create Smart Collections after analysis," leave all Audio options deselected, and then click Import.

NOTE ▶ You will learn more about audio analysis and repair in Lesson 8.

As the files are being imported into the *I Think* Event, Final Cut Pro immediately begins to analyze these clips as a background task, allowing you to continue working.

7 To see the analyzing progress, click the Background Tasks button in the Dashboard above the Timeline, or press Command-9.

When Final Cut Pro is performing a task, the Background Tasks indicator in the Dashboard displays a blue circle around a percentage of completion. When that task is complete, a green circle appears around 100%.

Background tasks 50% complete

Background tasks 100% complete

In the Background Tasks window, several tasks are listed. The tasks currently being processed display a progress bar.

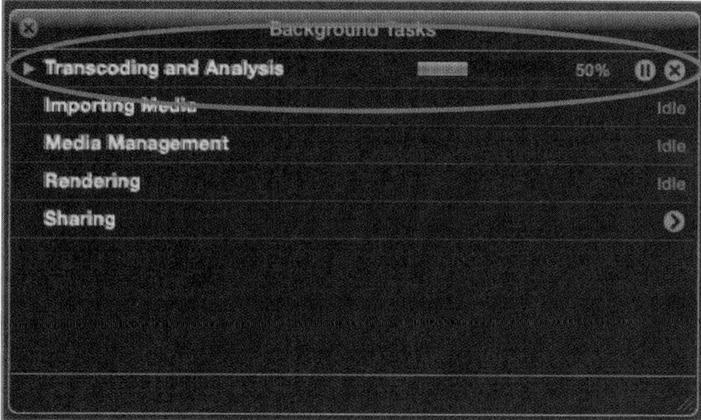

TIP To stop a task, simply click the X to the right of that task's progress bar. You can also pause a task by clicking the Pause button next to the X.

8 To close the Background Tasks window, click the close button in the upper-left corner. Or with the window active, press Command-W.

In the Event Library, the *I Think* Event contains a People folder with several purple-icon entries, notated with a purple gear icon. These are the Smart Collections Final Cut Pro created to organize the selected clips according to camera framing and number of people in the shot.

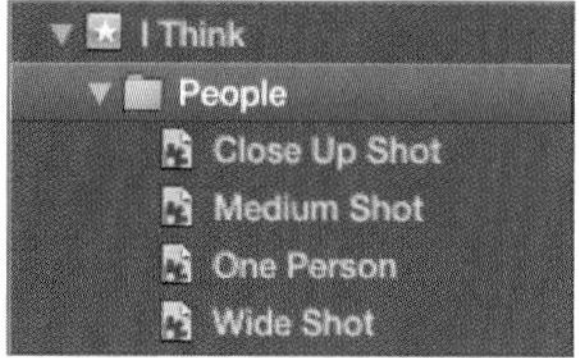

9 Select the People folder, and then select the different Smart Collections. And finally select the *I Think* Event.

Notice that some clips appear in more than one Smart Collection, but all people-oriented clips appear in the People folder. When you select the *I Think* Event, you once again see all the clips in this Event.

TIP If your clips are grouped by date, from the Action pop-up menu, choose Group Clips By > None.

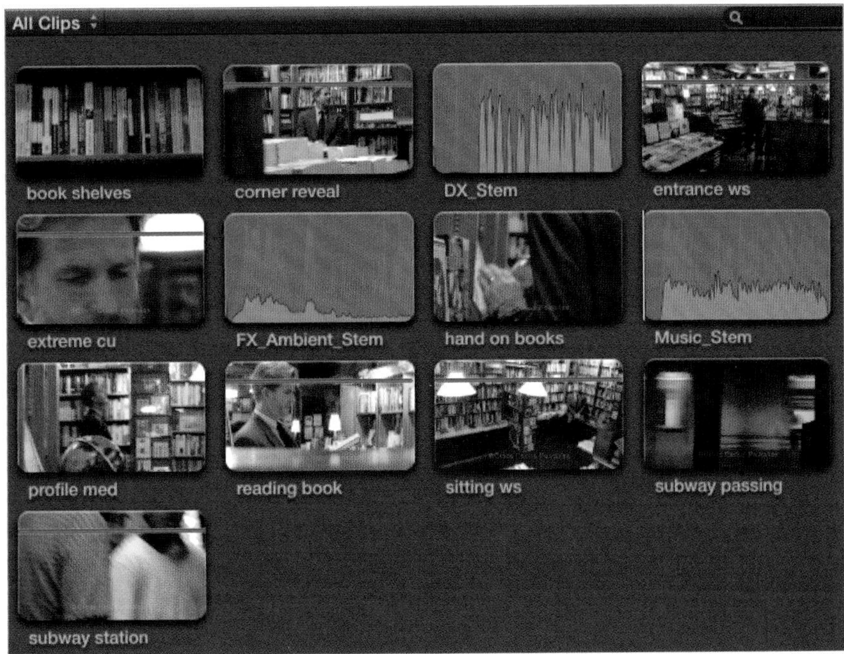

In the Event Browser, Final Cut Pro places a purple horizontal line (indicating an analysis keyword) at the top of those clips where it detected people in the shot. If you look closely or skim through these clips, you can see that Final Cut Pro made some pretty good choices. For example, it did not mark the people-less **book shelves** clip or the **subway passing** clip.

Now focus on the color balance adjustment you requested. Currently, the clips still look yellowish. This is because during analysis, color balance effects are applied to the clips but not automatically enabled.

10 In the *I Think* Event, skim through the **extreme cu** clip and notice the yellowish tint of the clip. As a reference point, click where the camera zooms out to a medium shot of Matthew reading a book.

This clip, along with the other video clips in this Event, has a yellowish cast. Although Final Cut Pro analyzed the color balance, you don't see it corrected in your source clip without enabling color balance correction in the Inspector's Video tab.

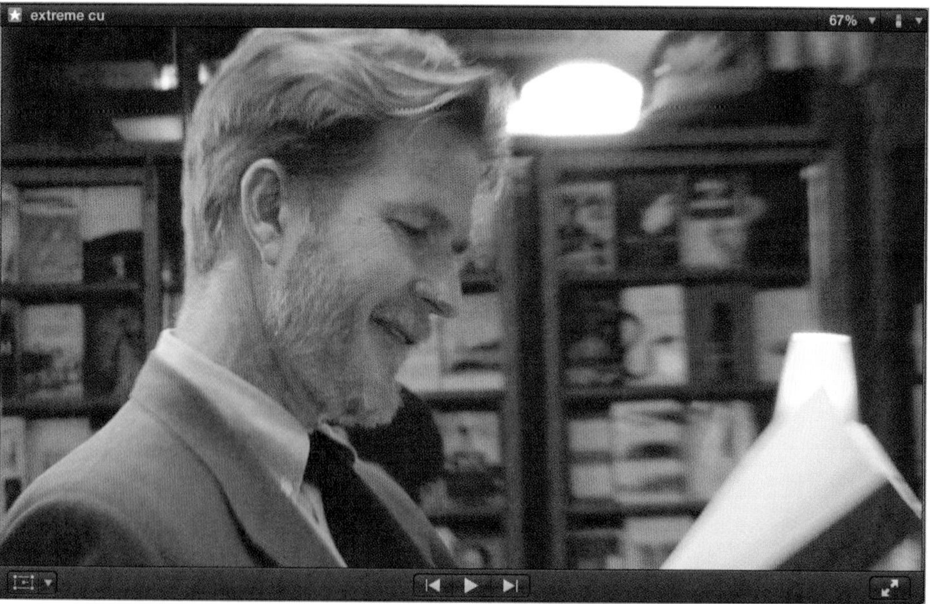

NOTE ▶ After you edit any clip into the Timeline, you can enable color balance for that clip whether or not it was imported with that option selected.

11 Below the Viewer in the toolbar, click the Inspector button. The Inspector will appear to the right of the Viewer.

In the Inspector, you can see how Final Cut Pro is handling your clip, as well as adjust any effects applied to the clip, change the clip's audio volume, and enable corrections to many other functions.

12 At the top of the Inspector, click the Video tab. To enable the color balance effect, select the box next to Balance. Continue to enable and disable this effect to see the color balance change.

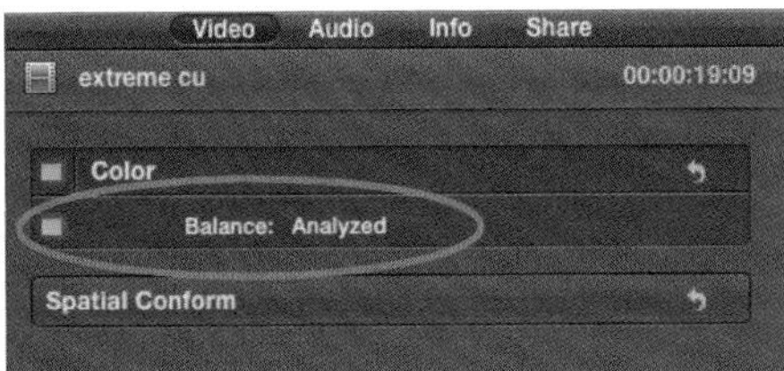

When the color balance effect is enabled, the clip no longer has the yellowish tint. While you may want to tweak these color settings prior to exporting your project, automatic analysis by Final Cut Pro has given you a pretty good start.

13 To close the Inspector window, click the blue Inspector button in the toolbar.

14 In the Event Library, tidy up the area by closing all open disclosure triangles.

NOTE ▶ Color correcting is both a skill and an art. You will learn more about Final Cut Pro color correcting features in Lesson 11.

Transcoding Media Files

The transcoding on import options in Final Cut Pro create media files optimized for better performance during both editing and rendering, and improved color quality for compositing. The transcode process creates copies of your original media files using Apple ProRes digital intermediate codecs while retaining the original media files. By transcoding to an Apple ProRes codec, Final Cut Pro is able to do more work with the same resources. There are two transcode options:

Create optimized media transcodes video media files using the high-quality Apple ProRes 422 codec and still images using JPEG (for images with no alpha channel) and PNG (for images that include an alpha channel). Note that if the format of the original media already provides good editing performance, the option to "Create optimized media" will not be available.

Create proxy media transcodes video to Apple ProRes 422 (Proxy), a lower-resolution and lower-quality format. Proxy files have much smaller data rates and file sizes, allowing older, slower computers to nearly do the work of newer, faster systems. Still images are encoded as PNG or JPEG depending on whether they have an alpha channel or not.

See the Final Cut Pro X Help Guide for more information on using optimized and proxy media.

Importing from a Camera

When it comes to importing or capturing media from a camera, Final Cut Pro can accommodate a variety of capture devices, from built-in FaceTime cameras, to decks, hard drives, and flash cards. This exercise will serve as an introduction to these options by working with a file-based camera card archive. To get started, you will create a new Event.

MORE INFO ▶ You can also confirm your camera or capture device's compatibility by visiting the Apple Final Cut Pro support website: http://help.apple.com/finalcutpro/cameras/en/index.html.

1 In the Event Library, create a new Event on Macintosh HD and name it *Camera Import*. Select the Event, and in the Event Browser, click the Import Media button.

The Media Import window appears. When you previously imported files, you may have noticed that the Media Import window closed automatically. Because you will perform more than one import during this exercise, you can keep the Media Import window open by changing the default behavior.

2 Deselect the "Close window after starting import" checkbox in the lower-left window.

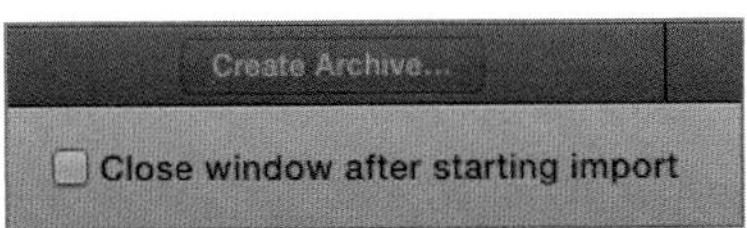

When a supported camera is connected or a camera card is mounted, Final Cut Pro recognizes it and displays it as an import option on the left side of the window under the Cameras heading. In the following steps, you will practice by importing from a disk image of a camera card's contents. This will simulate attaching an SDHC card from a file-based camera to your computer.

TIP To use your own camera for these steps, make sure it's powered on and set to PC Connect mode. If you want to use your own camera card, such as an SDHC card, insert it into the SD card slot of your computer or into a USB card reader and connect that to your computer.

3 Hide Final Cut Pro by pressing Command-H. In the Finder, navigate to the APTS FCP X > FCPX Book Files > Imports folder and double-click the **201107_Flowers.dmg** disk image.

4 Return to Final Cut Pro and select the camera mounted at the top of the sidebar.

TIP The volume that appears is a clone of an SDHC card. It was created with Disk Utility, which is available on every Mac computer.

Final Cut Pro may take a moment to read the files on your camera or camera card. Once the files have been read, the progress circle next to the eject button disappears. As in the Event Browser, controls are available to alter the view between the filmstrip and list view. For this exercise, you'll switch to the filmstrip view.

5 Click the Filmstrip view button.

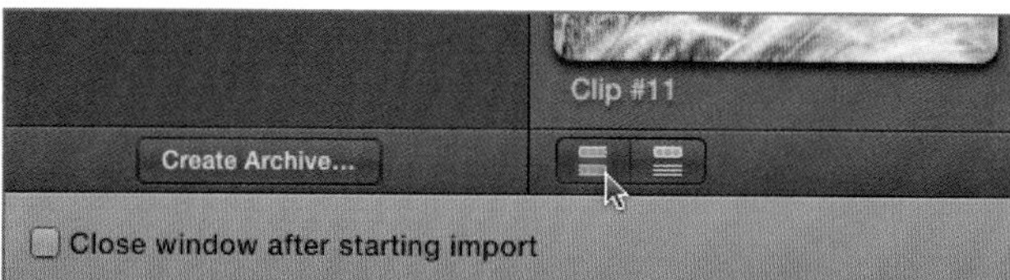

The clips on the simulated SDHC card appear at the bottom of the window, while the selected clip appears in the Viewer at the top of the window.

6 Skim through the clips in the Clip Browser. To play a clip, select it, and press the Spacebar, or use the transport controls beneath the preview area.

After you've reviewed your media, you can decide whether you want to import all the clips or just a few of them.

7 In the Clip Browser, deselect all the clips by clicking in the gray area around the thumbnails, or by pressing Command-Shift-A. Notice that the Import button has changed to Import All.

8 In the clip browser, select **Clip #13**.

You can import more than one clip at a time by using a modifyer key.

9 Command-click **Clip #11** and **Clip #7**.

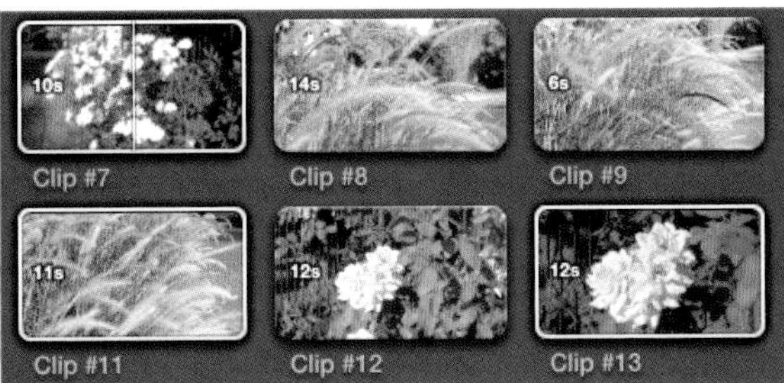

TIP You can Command-click to select noncontiguous clips. Holding down the Shift key while clicking selects all clips between the selected clips.

When you select one or more clips, an Import Selected button appears to import only the selected clips. As you prepare to import, Final Cut Pro tracks your clip selection. When no clips are selected for import, Final Cut Pro will import all the available clips on the device.

10 Click the Import Selected button. In the options dialog, choose to add these clips to the existing Camera Import Event. Then, deselect any other import options, and click Import.

Add to existing event: Camera Import

Create new event:

Save to: Macintosh HD (63.2 GB free)

Organizing: Copy files to Final Cut Events folder
Import folders as Keyword Collections

Transcoding: Create optimized media
Create proxy media

Video: Remove pulldown
Analyze for balance color
Find people

Notice that "Copy files to Final Cut Events folder" is selected and dimmed. Final Cut Pro will copy the media from the SDHC card to the Event folder. If this option was not selected, the clips would be unavailable when you ejected the SDHC card.

So far, you've imported whole clips. However, the Media Import window also allows you to import portions of clips in one import session. These portions can be sections of several clips or more than one section within a single clip.

11 In **Clip #2**, drag the pointer from the beginning of the clip until the camera stops at the top of the flower.

A range is marked for **Clip #2**, identifying the portion of the clip that will be imported. Multiple ranges from different clips may be imported together.

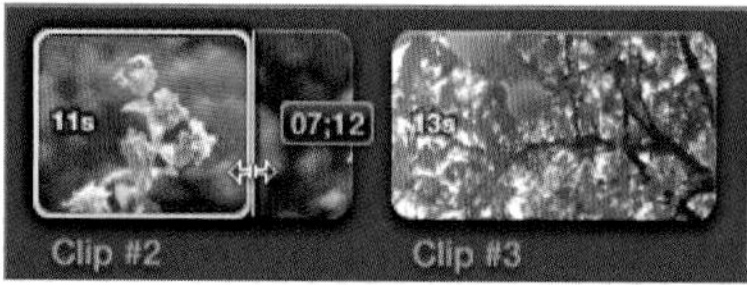

NOTE ▶ If you don't like your initial range selection, you can clear the selected range by pressing Option-X.

12 In **Clip #4**, drag the pointer from the beginning of the clip until the camera tilt-up has stopped.

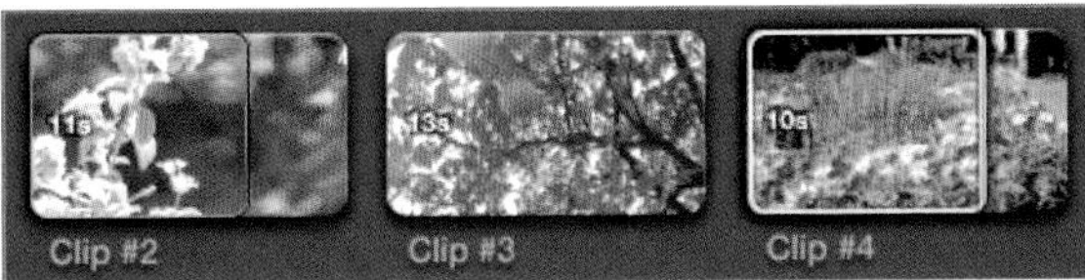

Notice that **Clip #2** retains the range you made a moment ago, but it is not selected, and therefore would not be imported along with the range marked in **Clip #4**. Let's add that range to the current selection.

13 Command-click within the marked range in **Clip #2** to add it to the **Clip #4** selection for import.

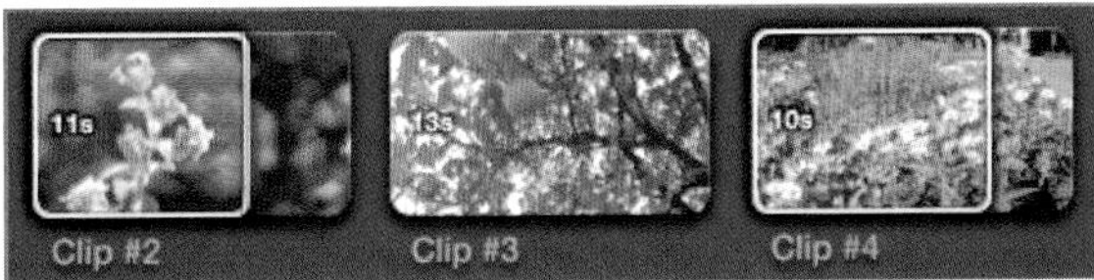

14 With these two clip ranges selected, click the Import Selected button. In the Import dialog, verify that the Camera Import Event is selected, and that all of the analysis options are deselected. Click Import.

15 Close the Media Import window.

TIP If you access a card from which you've previously imported clips, a white line will appear across those clips that have already been imported.

MORE INFO ► The Media Import window is used to import from a tape-based device when the device is connected via a FireWire cable. See the Final Cut Pro X Help guide for details.

► Creating a Camera Archive

Creating a camera archive makes a backup that frees your camera or capture media for reuse, preserves and protects your media for future use, and helps preserve the data structure used by your camera to make it easier to store and access your video files. You may create a camera archive from tape-based or file-based formats.

To create a camera archive in the Media Import window, do the following:

1. Connect the camera or device.
2. Select the source device in the Cameras section, or supported folder copied from a device, and then click Create Archive.

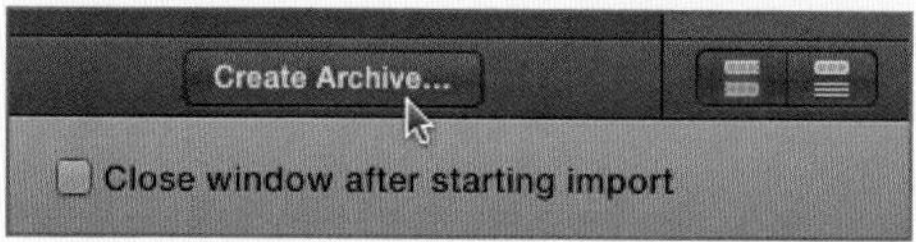

3. Specify a name, select a volume for, and then save the archive.

A new entry appears in the source list under Camera Archives.

NOTE ► It is strongly recommended that you save camera archives to a hard disk different from the one where you store the media files you are using with Final Cut Pro.

Importing from the Finder

You're not limited to importing files through the Final Cut Pro Media Import window, or even the Media Browsers you will work with in later lessons. If you want to start dragging individual media files—or entire folders of materials—directly from the Finder into an Event, you're in luck! Final Cut Pro can import supported media file formats in almost any form they're delivered.

When importing without using the Import Media command, you must set the specific import options—such as media management, Keyword Collections, transcoding video, auto-analysis, finding people, and Smart Collections—*before* you import. You perform this task in the Import tab of the Final Cut Pro Preferences window.

MORE INFO ▶ If you're unsure exactly what kinds of media files Final Cut Pro X can import, refer to the Apple Final Cut Pro support site www.apple.com/finalcutpro/specs. See "Supported Formats and I/O" on the Tech Specs page.

1 To open the Final Cut Pro Preferences window, click the Final Cut Pro menu and choose Preferences, or press Command-, (comma). At the top of the Preferences window, click the Import tab.

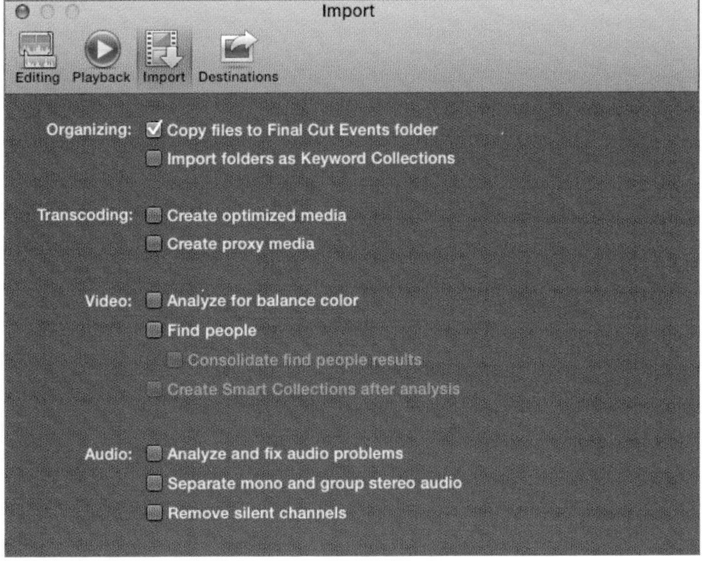

The options in this tab will be familiar; they are the same options you've been working with throughout this lesson. For this exercise, you will drag a folder of still images into an Event and can leave all but the first option deselected.

2 In the Organizing section, make sure that "Copy files to Final Cut Events folder" is selected, deselect the other options, and then close the Preferences window.

Any options you choose here become the default options both for when you import from the Finder to import files, and when you use the Media Import window. The only difference is that when you access the import dialogs, you have a chance to change the options.

3 In the Event Library, create a new Event on Macintosh HD and name it *Baja*. In a Finder window, navigate to the APTS FCP X > FCPX Book Files > Imports > Baja Whales folder.

4 Resize the Finder window smaller and position the windows so you can see the folder you will drag and its destination in the Final Cut Pro Event Library.

5 Drag the Baja Whales folder into the *Baja* Event, but *don't release the pointer.* When the Event is highlighted with a white outline, and you see the green plus (copy) sign on the pointer, release the pointer.

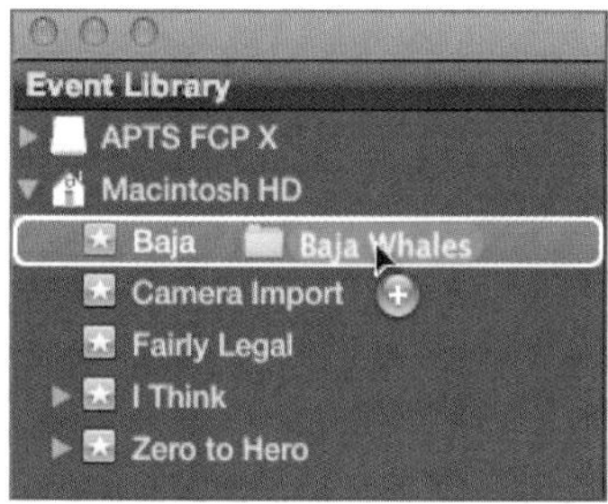

6 Make the Final Cut Pro window active, and check your imported files in the *Baja* Event.

TIP You can also import media files by dragging them directly into an Event.

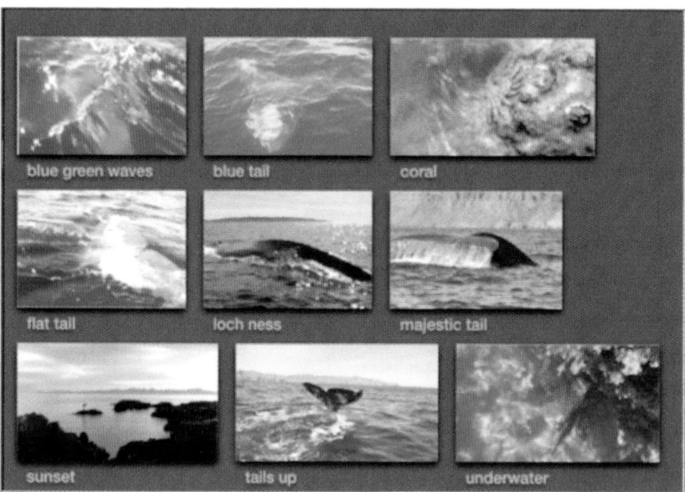

Importing from Other Applications

In addition to dragging content into an Event from the Finder, you can also drag media files from the windows of supported applications such as Aperture, iPhoto, or iTunes. Simply drag the file from the application into an Event.

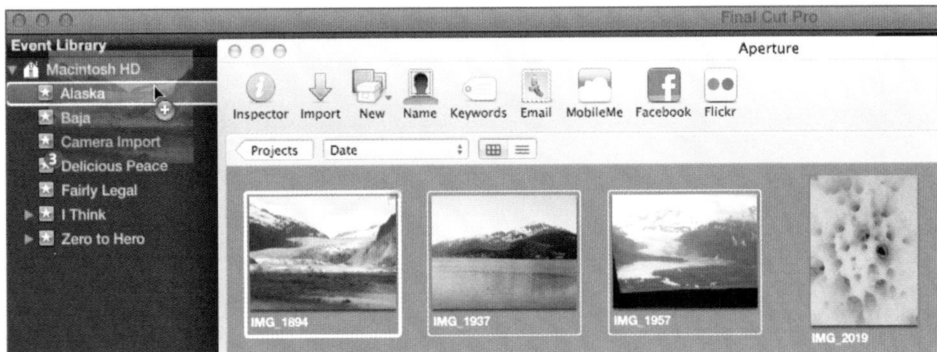

Remember that the Final Cut Pro Import preferences are in effect when dragging files into Final Cut Pro. In the preceding exercises, you chose or utilized the preference for "Copy files to Final Cut Events folder." If you deselect this preference, the pointer becomes a hooked arrow when dragging to import. The hooked arrow reminds you that this operation will only create an alias file in the Final Cut Events folder and will not copy the media to the Event folder.

Editor's Cut

Now that you're thoroughly familiar with the primary importing options, you can apply what you've learned to import the final set of media, Delicious Peace, which is found in the FCPX Book Files folder.

Follow the steps in the very first exercise of this lesson to create a new Event named *Delicious Peace* on Macintosh HD. Then to import and copy all the Delicious Peace clips into the new Event, choose File > Import > Media. Then in the options dialog, select "Copy files to Final Cut Events folder," and deselect all other options.

After the import process has completed (including background tasks), take a moment to delete all of the import practice Events you created on Macintosh HD. These Events will not be used in any other lessons in this book. To delete an Event, select it, and press Command-Delete.

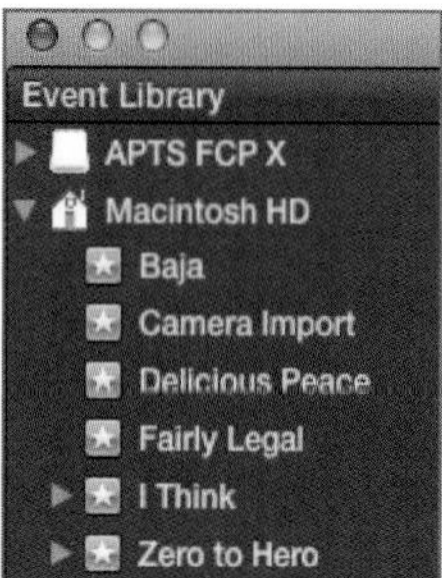

Lesson Review

1. How do you create a new Event?
2. How do you import media files into an Event?
3. What happens if you select the Find People option when importing media?
4. If you select the "Analyze for Balance Color" option when importing media, how do you view the color balance correction?
5. What are the advantages to transcoding your media files?
6. How do you set importing options if you want to drag media files directly from the Finder or another application to an Event?
7. How do you create a Keyword Collection when importing clips from a specific folder?
8. Why would you want to create a camera archive as a backup?

Answers

1. If you don't see the Event Library, click the Event Library button at the lower-left corner of the Event Browser. Choose File > New Event (or press Option-N).
2. Select an Event and click the Import Media button in the Event Browser, choose File > Import > Media, use a keyboard shortcut, or Control-click the Event in the Event Library.

3. The Find People option analyzes images and creates Smart Collections based on the number of faces present and the shot type. After analysis, any of the following keywords are added: One Person, Two Persons, Group, Close Up Shot, Medium Shot, and Wide Shot.
4. In the toolbar, click the Inspector button. Click the Video tab in the Inspector and select the box next to Balance to enable the color balance effect.
5. Final Cut Pro transcoding optimizes media for better editing and rendering performance and improved color quality. The transcode process copies your original media files using the Apple ProRes digital intermediate codecs while retaining the original media files.
6. To import without using the Import command, you set the specific import options before you import. Choose Final Cut Pro > Preferences, or press Command-, (comma). At the top of the Preferences window, click the Import tab and set your options.
7. Make sure that the "Import folders as Keyword Collections" option is selected in the options dialog to create a Keyword Collection for each media folder you import. This is the default option.
8. A camera archive frees your camera or capture media for reuse, preserves and protects your media for future use, and helps preserve the data structure used by your camera to make it easier to store and access your files.

Keyboard Shortcuts

Command-A	Select all items in the current folder or location
Command-I	Open the Media Import window
Option-N	Create a new Event
Command-W	Close an active window
Shift-click	Select a group of contiguous items
Command-click	Select a group of noncontiguous items
Command-4	Open and close the Inspector
Command-9	Open and close the Background Tasks window
Command-, (comma)	Open the Final Cut Pro Preferences window

3

Time This lesson takes approximately 90 minutes to complete.

Goals

Understand metadata

Use metadata to customize Events

Add keywords to clips

Assign multiple keywords to clips

Apply keywords to a clip range

Rate clips and clip selections

Sort and search using metadata

Add notes to clips

Create Smart Collections

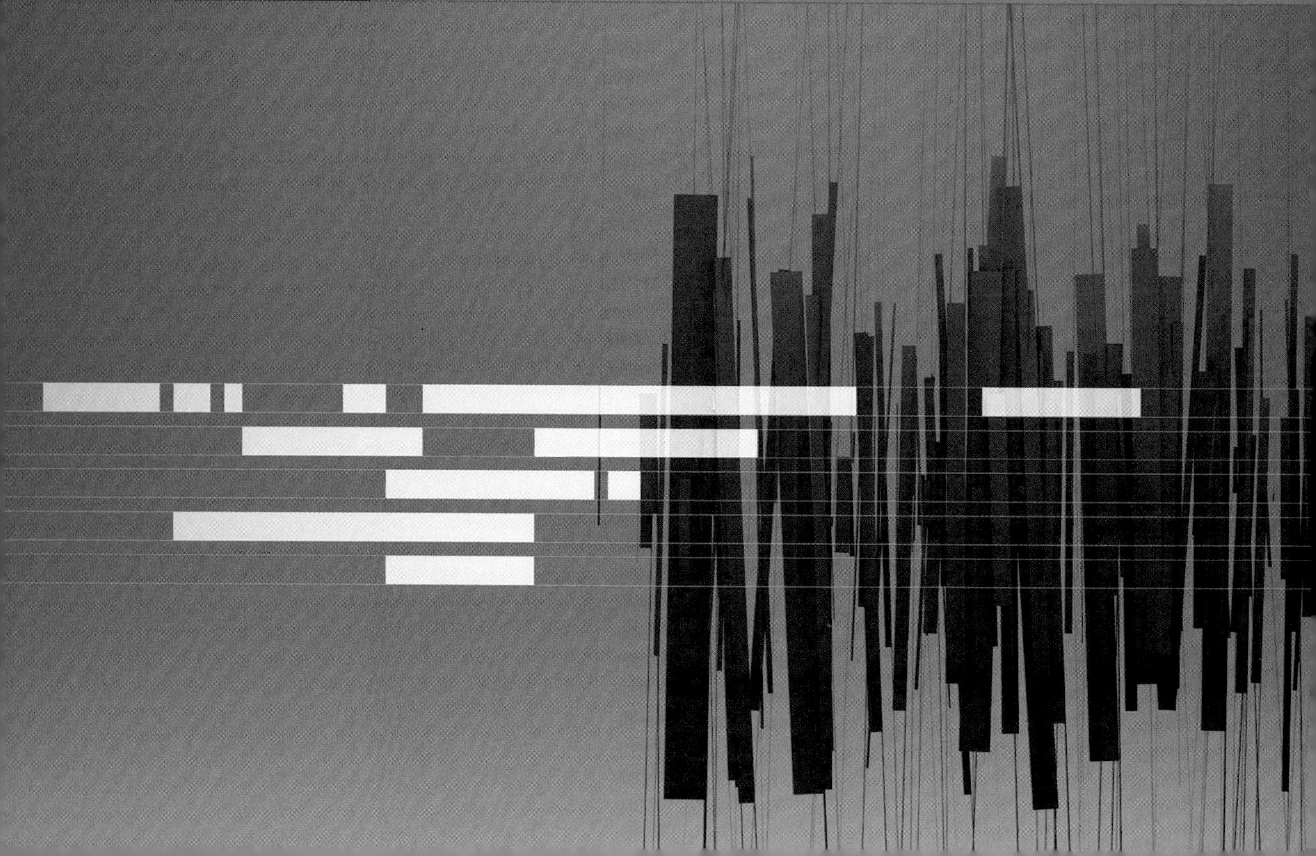

Lesson **3**

Organizing Clips in an Event

After you've imported media, an Event may include hundreds of clips, including wide shots, close-ups, B-roll clips, and interviews. As editor, your task is to review every clip in the most efficient way possible, and select those that you can assemble into an effective story.

In Lesson 2, Final Cut Pro did its part to help you organize clips during import. It followed your instructions for analyzing and fixing certain problems, detecting both people and camera shots, and then organized them into Keyword and Smart Collections. Now it's your turn to enhance your Event management by manually assigning keywords, rating clips, and creating Smart Collections.

A Delicious Peace cooperative member roasts coffee beans over an open fire

Your goal is to arrange and combine the Event clips in an intuitive manner so that you can easily locate them with one click. In the process, you will use the Event Library and Event Browser to organize, sort, filter, and find your media. By the end of the lesson, your media will be prepared and organized, ready to begin your first editing project.

Using Metadata to Customize an Event

Metadata is the foundation of Final Cut Pro media management. But what exactly is metadata? The widely accepted definition of metadata is *data about data*. Or, because *meta* is Greek for *beyond,* it could be defined as data *beyond* data. But what does that tell you? Imagine holding a DVD in your hands that has recorded information but no label. To determine the content, title, length, format, and creator, you would have to take the time to play and watch the DVD.

But if the DVD had a label that listed its contents and other properties, you could quickly decide whether or not to watch it, how long it would take you to watch it, and where to place it in your DVD collection. The written data on the DVD's cover and disc—the *meta*data—tells you about the content on the disc.

Green and blue lines indicate Keyword and Favorite ratings applied to a *Fairly Legal* clip

Final Cut Pro uses metadata in many ways. In fact, you could say that metadata is the language that Final Cut Pro uses to communicate. You've already seen that metadata is automatically logged during import. By tagging keywords to clips, you can assign your own metadata, and find a clip as easily as you would search a word or phrase on Google. By rating clips, you give them your own thumbs-up and thumbs-down values to quickly decide whether or not to use them. You communicate this metadata to Final Cut Pro, and Final Cut Pro responds by organizing it into a structure that is easy to sort, filter, search, and retrieve.

Final Cut Pro includes three categories of metadata:

- Camera metadata—Stored in the camera source files, can include date, clip duration, timecode, frame rate and size, and other information.
- Final Cut Pro metadata—Created by Final Cut Pro by identifying and analyzing media source files, can include people and shot detection, and can identify problems such as audio hum and video instability.
- User metadata—Added to clips by the editor, including keywords, ratings, and log notes, in order to personalize clip organization for a faster and easier workflow.

Perhaps a better explanation of metadata, in the context of Final Cut Pro, is that the presence of metadata gives you a quick look at clip information without having to look at the clip itself. And that saves valuable editing time. Let's see where you can access some of the existing clip metadata in Final Cut Pro.

1 In the Event Library, select the *Delicious Peace* Event from APTS FCP X. Click the List View button to view the clips as a list.

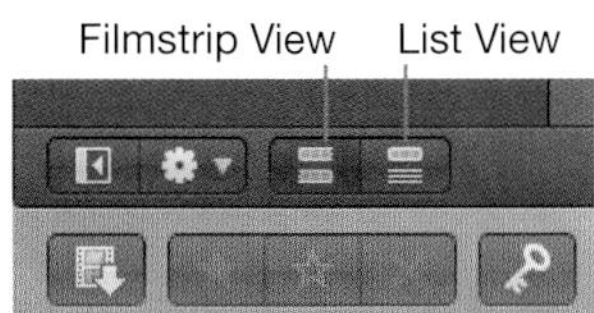

When you view clips as a list, you immediately see the existing clip metadata under each column heading—such as name, start and end timecode, duration, and creation date. The metadata on these clips were collected from the original camera files. Later in this lesson, you will add your own metadata in the Notes column and display additional columns.

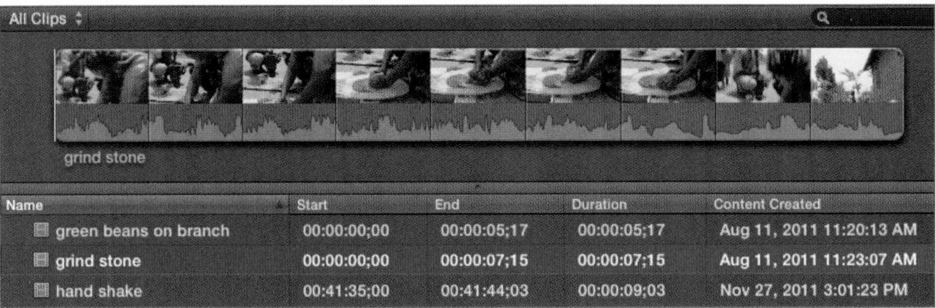

TIP For this exercise, make sure the Event Browser filter at the upper left is set to All Clips. Also choose Group Clips By > None, and sort the list by clicking the Name column header, if necessary.

2 In the Event Library, click the disclosure triangles next to the *I Think* and *Zero to Hero* Events, as well as the I Think > People folder, to see the clip collections listed within those folders.

As you have learned, Events in the Event Library are indicated by a white-starred, purple icon. Each Event is a container that holds imported clips, much like a folder holds documents. Smart Collections are color coded in purple with a purple gear icon. The Keyword Collections are color coded in blue with a blue key.

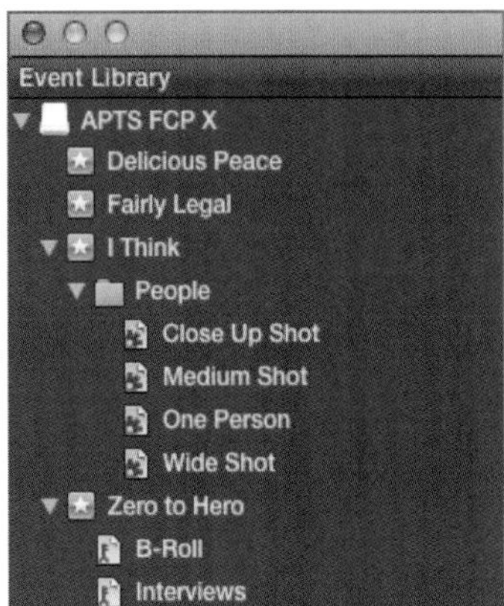

Notice the Keyword and Smart Collections that were created during import. Keyword and Smart Collections group clips that contain specific metadata that you or Final Cut

Pro added to the clips. Because you haven't yet added any metadata, these collections reflect the import options selected in Lesson 2.

3 In the Event Library under the *I Think* Event, select the *One Person* Smart Collection. To see these clips in filmstrip view, click the Filmstrip View button in the lower-left corner of the Event Library.

In the Event Browser, notice that all the clips feature shots of one person and have a horizontal line across the top to indicate an analysis keyword.

Each Smart Collection in the People folder was derived from auto-analysis during import. For example, because you selected the Find People and Create Smart Collection options in the Import dialog, Final Cut Pro automatically collected the clips that contained just one face and placed them in the *One Person* Smart Collection.

4 In the Event Library under the *Zero to Hero* Event, click the *Interviews* Keyword Collection.

Notice that each of the interview clips has a blue horizontal line across the top. This text-based Keyword Collection is named after the Interviews folder you imported in Lesson 2.

Before adding your own metadata to clips, let's set up the Event Browser window, where all organization for Final Cut Pro takes place. For example, the *Delicious Peace* Event has 47 clips. Adjusting the browser options to see all the clip thumbnails at the same time would be helpful. Let's start by making the Event Browser window a little larger.

5 To resize the Event Browser window, place your pointer over the boundary line between the Event Browser and the Viewer. When it changes to the resize pointer, drag right to enlarge the Event Browser. You can also drag the boundary line between the Event Browser and the toolbar.

6 In the Event Library, select the *Delicious Peace* Event. In the lower right-corner of the Event Browser, drag the Clip Duration slider to All to view individual thumbnail images. Click the Clip Appearance button and deselect Show Waveforms; then adjust the Clip Height slider. Resize the Event Browser until you see all the clips in this Event.

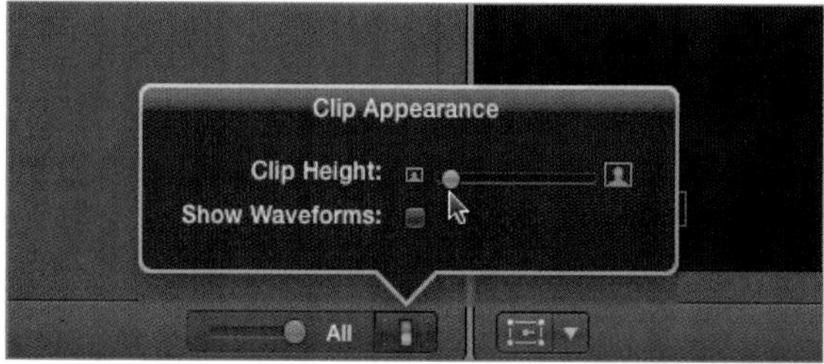

This may look like a lot of media, but when the clips are organized into collections, you can clearly see and access the clips you need.

Notice that a disclosure triangle doesn't appear next to the *Delicious Peace* Event in the Event Library because no Keyword or Smart Collections have been created yet.

In the next exercise, you will add keywords and create Keyword Collections of the *Delicious Peace* clips. First, let's close the Events you won't use right away.

7 In the Event Library, click the disclosure triangle next to the *I Think* and *Zero to Hero* Events.

Adding Keywords to Clips

Of all the work you do in Final Cut Pro, nothing will give you a greater sense of command over your project than using keywords. In fact, keywords form the backbone of the Final Cut Pro organizational structure. A keyword is a descriptive text label you apply to a clip.

Adding keywords is a simple act that has far-reaching benefits in organizing, sorting, and finding your media. Most importantly, it will make your editing workflow faster and easier.

In Lesson 2, you saw the result of having Final Cut Pro add keywords to clips and use them to create Keyword Collections. In this exercise, you will start with a fresh Event and utilize various methods to add keywords to those clips. As you go through the process of tagging clips with keywords, you will see how organization builds in the Event Browser.

1 In the Event Library, select the *Delicious Peace* Event, and then click the List View button. In the Event Browser, click the **beans being hulled** clip.

TIP To improve the filmstrip representation, you can hide the waveforms by choosing View > Hide Waveforms. You can also resize the filmstrip area by vertically dragging the boundary between the filmstrip and the list (above the column headings).

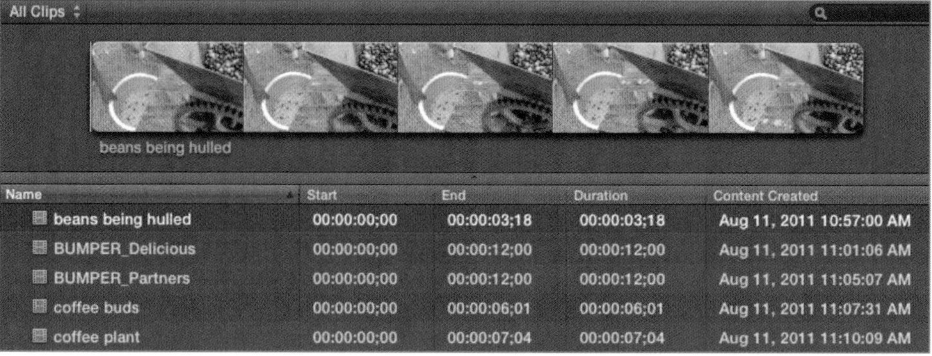

In the *Delicious Peace* Event, you'll see a variety of clips. Some clips document the process of making coffee from growing to roasting. Other clips capture the people and the village where this documentary was shot. It would certainly make your editing life easier if you could collect all the coffee shots into one location for easy retrieval. Let's start by adding a keyword to the first coffee clip. You can do this in the Keyword Editor window.

2 In the Event Browser, click the Keyword Editor button, or press Command-K.

NOTE ▶ The icon for the Keyword Editor button is a key that appears blue when selected, and gray when deselected.

The Keyword Editor opens with the name of the selected clip, **beans being hulled**, displayed in the name area of the window. Any information you type into the Keyword field will be added to this clip.

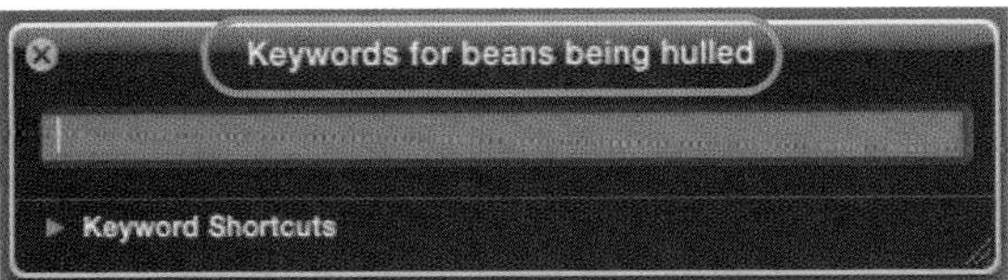

3 In the Keyword field, type *Coffee*. Then watch the **beans being hulled** clip filmstrip as you press Return.

The keyword you entered floats up into a blue horizontal line that is added to the filmstrip. The blue line indicates that a keyword is now attached to the entire clip.

NOTE ▶ Depending on how you arranged your Event Browser, you may not see the same thumbnails shown in these images.

4 Skim through the **beans being hulled** clip. To see the clip information as you skim, choose View > Show Skimmer Info, or press Control-Y. Then skim through the clip again and notice the new keyword.

With Show Skimmer Info chosen, a small transparent flag travels with the skimmer, displaying the clip name, keyword, and current timecode location. The info flag may appear with the skimmer above the filmstrip or below.

In the Event Library under the *Delicious Peace* Event, a new Keyword Collection appears called *Coffee*.

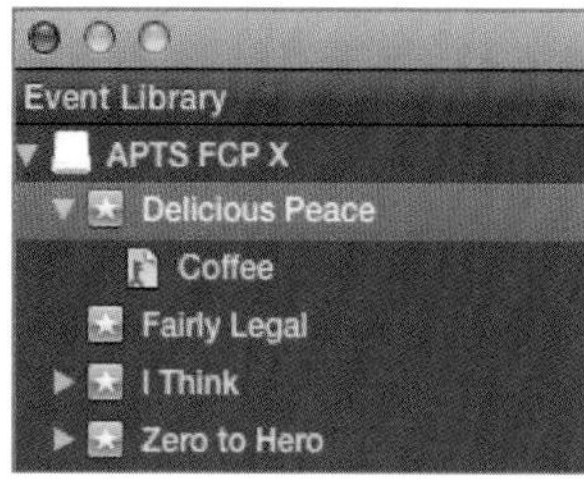

5 In the Event Library, click the *Coffee* Keyword Collection. In the Event Browser, click the disclosure triangle next to the **beans being hulled** clip to reveal the clip's contents.

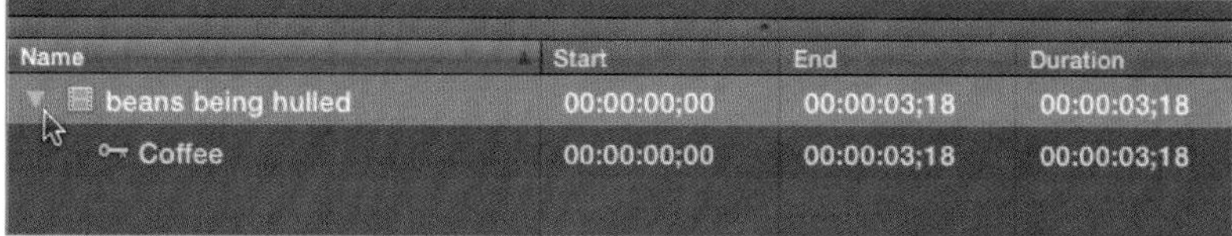

The clip now contains a keyword, as indicated by the blue key icon and the keyword, in this case, *Coffee*. This clip may seem to be a duplicate of a clip in the *Delicious Peace* Event, but it's not. Let's take a look at the original.

6 In the Event Library, select the *Delicious Peace* Event to see all its clips again.

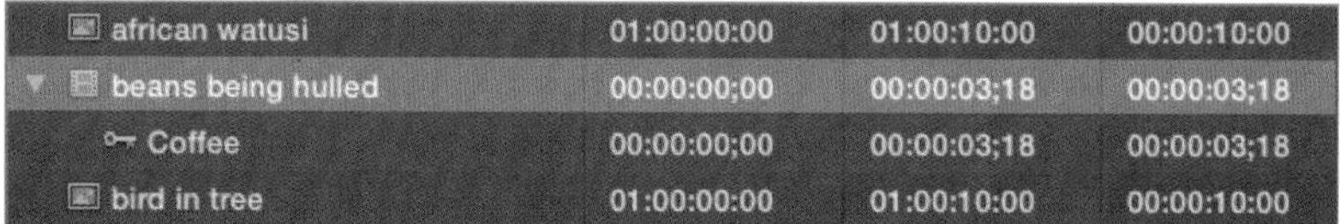

In this Event, this clip is displayed with its keyword contents, just as it was in the *Coffee* Keyword Collection. For organizational purposes, the same clip can appear in multiple collections without duplicating the original clip. Adding a keyword to a clip applies the tag to the original clip within the Event, and also creates a Keyword Collection to group any other clips with the same keyword.

You have more coffee clips to tag. Let's apply a keyword to the second coffee clip using a keyboard shortcut.

7 Select the **coffee buds** clip, and in the Keyword Editor, click the Keyword Shortcuts disclosure triangle to display the Keyword Shortcuts list.

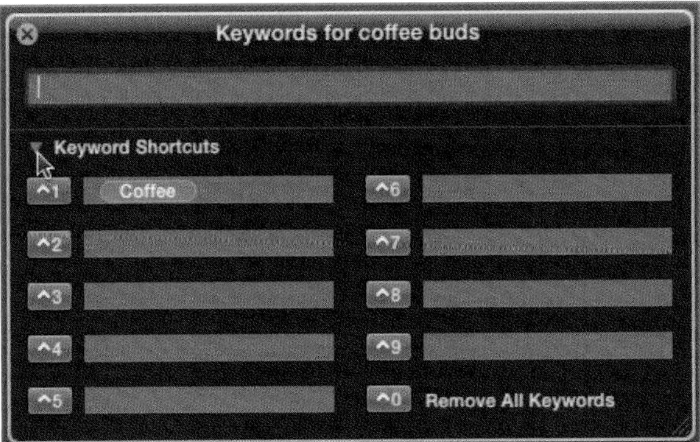

Notice that the keyword field at the top of the Keyword Editor is empty because no keywords are currently assigned to this clip. Notice too that the keyword, *Coffee*, appears in the first keyword shortcut field because it was the first keyword you created.

NOTE ▶ If you previously entered keywords, they may appear here, and the *Coffee* keyword may appear in a different shortcut location. You may want to remove your own keywords to match this exercise.

You have nine keyword shortcuts you can use to apply keywords to clips. Any keyword in these fields can be applied to a selected clip by pressing its corresponding keyboard shortcut.

8 In the Keyword Editor, click the Control-1 (^1) button, and watch the filmstrip as the keyword floats into the **coffee buds** clip's new blue keyword line.

NOTE ▶ You may need to disable or modify the keyboard shortcuts for Spaces or Mission Control to allow Final Cut Pro access to some keyboard commands.

TIP ▶ You can apply keyword shortcuts even when the Keyword Editor is not open.

Notice that the **coffee buds** clip has its own disclosure triangle because it contains a keyword.

Several coffee clips appear directly beneath the **coffee buds** clip. It would make sense to include them in the *Coffee* Keyword Collection. Rather than apply a keyword from the Keyword Editor, however, you can drag a group of clips directly into the Keyword Collection in the Event Library.

9 To select the group of clips, click the **coffee plant** clip, and then Shift-click the **hand shake** clip.

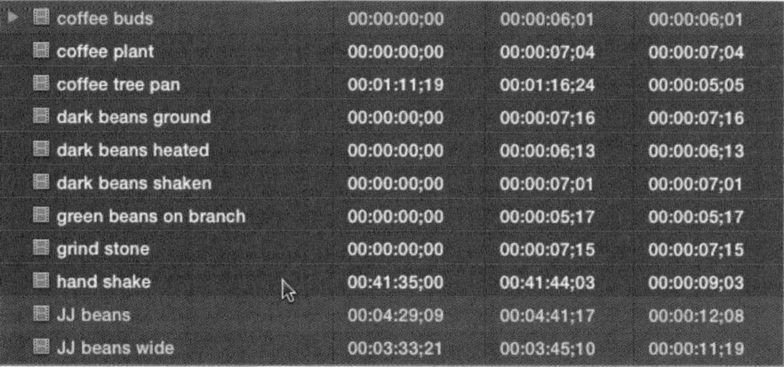

10 Drag the selected group of clips into the Event Library and onto the *Coffee* Keyword Collection. Notice that a transparency of the clip names, as they appear in list view, travels with the pointer.

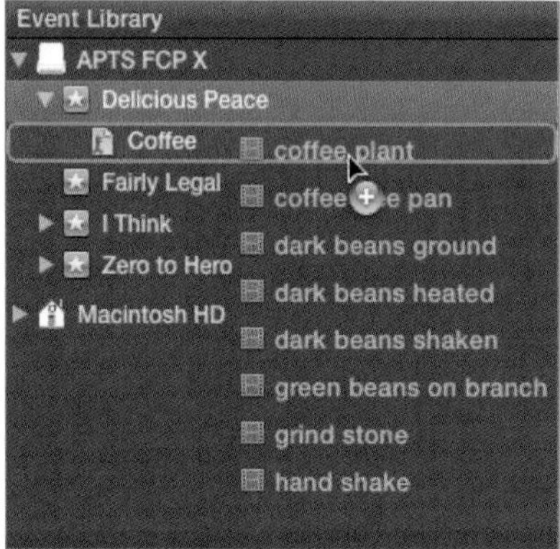

11 In the Event Library, select the *Coffee* Keyword Collection. Now 10 clips with the keyword *Coffee* appear together in the Event Browser.

You can remove a keyword from a clip just as easily as you added it. For example, if a clip isn't really about growing or making coffee, you would want to remove it from the *Coffee* Keyword Collection using the keyword's keyboard shortcut.

NOTE ▶ Remember, creating a Keyword Collection is all about organizing clips in a way that makes the most sense to you and saves you the most time as you search for clips.

12 In the Event Library, select the *Delicious Peace* Event, and in the Event Browser, select the **hand shake** clip and skim it. While the clip does depict the business side of making coffee, it does not pertain to growing or making coffee. In the Keyword Editor, click Control-0 (^0) and watch the filmstrip as the keyword turns into a puff of smoke, and the blue horizontal line disappears.

Without the *Coffee* keyword, you won't find this clip in the *Coffee* Keyword Collection. But it still remains in the *Delicious Peace* Event.

TIP If you want to remove all keywords from all clips, in the Event Browser, press Command-A to select all clips, and then press Control-0.

Assigning Multiple Keywords to Clips

In the previous exercise, you applied a single keyword to one or more clips. But just as a full jacket of information can describe a DVD's contents, so too can a clip have several keywords to detail its contents and make it easier to find. As you tag clips with additional keywords, they will find their ways into more Keyword Collections, and the list of Keyword Collections in an Event will lengthen.

In this exercise, you will apply multiple keywords to several clips using shortcut methods that can save an enormous amount of time, especially if you have lots of media. You will also learn to delete a Keyword Collection. First, you'll change the Event Browser to the filmstrip view to view the clips as thumbnails.

NOTE ▸ In this exercise, you will focus more on the visual aspects of the clips so the skimmer info flag may be distracting. To turn off the skimmer info, choose View > Hide Skimmer Info, or press Control-Y.

1 In the Event Library, select the *Delicious Peace* Event. Click the Filmstrip View button, and then drag the Clip Duration slider to All. If necessary, scroll to find the nine coffee clips (with blue keyword lines) you already tagged.

The filmstrip view is a good choice when you want to locate and skim through clips in an Event. You can also see which clips are missing blue lines, indicating that they haven't been assigned keywords.

TIP ▸ To see the names of the clips as text under each thumbnail, choose View > Show Clip Names, or press Shift-Option-N. If the clips are not arranged in alphabetical order, from the Action pop-up menu, choose Arrange Clips By > Name > Ascending.

2 Press Command-K to open the Keyword Editor, if necessary. Select a few clips in the browser while watching the keyword field at the top of the window.

When you select a clip, its name appears at the top of the Keyword Editor. Any keywords assigned to that clip appear in the Keyword field. If a clip doesn't have a keyword, the field remains empty. Notice that the keyword *Coffee* still appears in the same keyword shortcut position assigned in the previous exercise. In this exercise, you will create new keywords and utilize the additional keyword shortcut fields.

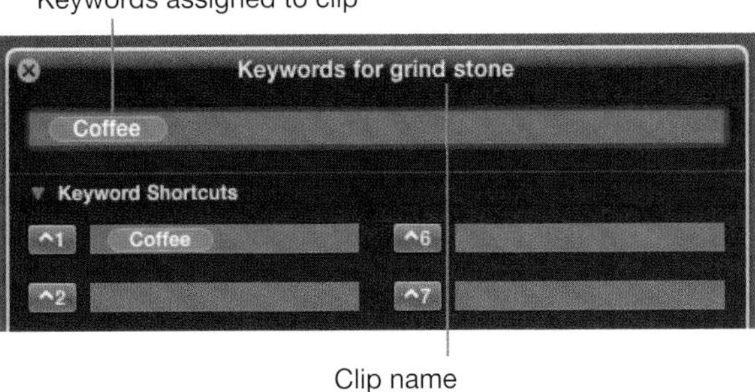

This media features different aspects of making coffee: picking coffee beans, and then sorting, grinding, and roasting them. It includes several clips of JJ, the leader of the cooperative, sorting coffee beans, along with a clip of JJ speaking. Let's create a Keyword Collection of all the JJ clips.

3 Select the **JJ beans** clip, and then Shift-click the **JJ ties bag** clip. In the Keyword Editor window, type *JJ* in the Keyword field, and press Return. (If you're not tired of watching it, follow the new keyword as it drifts into the blue line of the three clips.)

In the Event Library, a new Keyword Collection appears named JJ. Among these clips are three clips of JJ sorting beans. Let's apply a keyword to just those three clips.

4 In the Event Browser, Command-click the **JJ on peace** clip to deselect it and leave the other three JJ clips selected. In the Name field of the Keyword Editor next to the word JJ, type *Sorting,* and press Return.

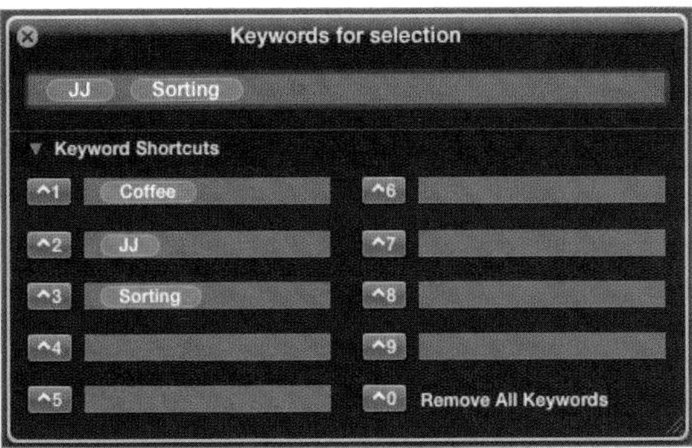

In the Keyword Editor, the keyword *Sorting* appears in the Keyword Editor. In the Event Browser, the keyword is applied to the selected thumbnail images, and in the Event Library, a new *Sorting* Keyword Collection is added to the *Delicious Peace* Event.

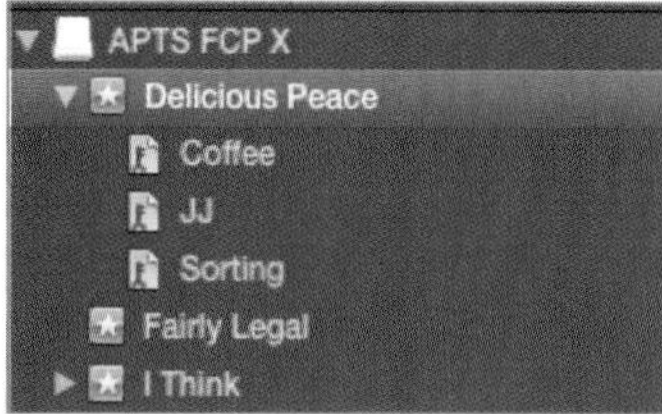

When you assign more than one keyword to a clip, you also create additional Keyword Collections and begin to build an organizational structure that reflects and captures various aspects of your library. Let's take a closer look at the *Delicious Peace* content with an eye toward further organizing this set of clips.

5 Beginning with the second thumbnail clip in the Event Browser, quickly skim several clips while watching them in the Viewer. Look for clips—other than the coffee growing and handling clips—that you may need to embellish the story. These clips could include graphics and maps, narration and music, co-op members talking, and shots of the village and villagers.

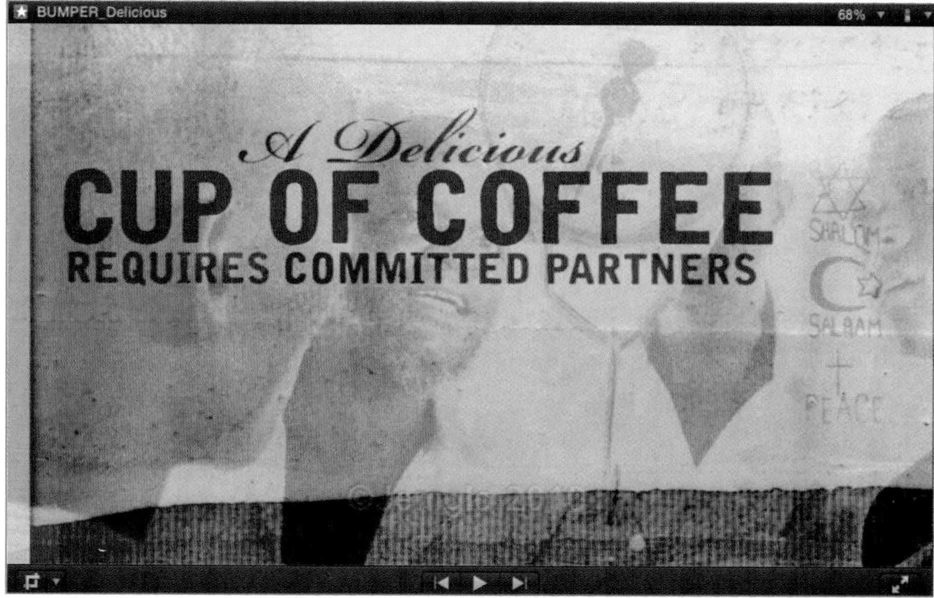

As you review this content, several keywords may immediately come to mind—such as *graphics, maps, narration, music, village, members*, and so on. In fact, to speed up the organizational process, you can actually begin your workflow in the Keyword Editor by entering the nine keywords you know you'll want to use in the shortcut fields.

6 In the Keyword Editor, enter the following keywords into the keyword shortcut fields. Press Tab after each keyword entry to move to the next field.

- Control-4 (^4): *Graphics*
- Control-5 (^5): *Maps*
- Control-6 (^6): *Narration*
- Control-7 (^7): *Music*
- Control-8 (^8): *Village*
- Control-9 (^9): *Members*

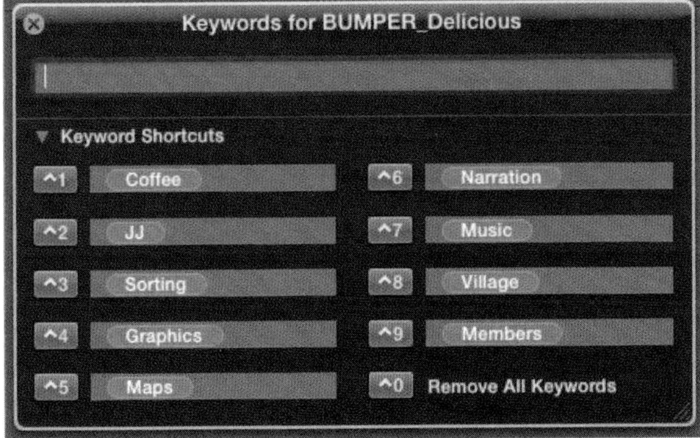

TIP When choosing keywords, use short, specific, and descriptive words or phrases that will trigger memories of shots, people, and sound elements. You can always remove keywords and Keyword Collections if you find that they do not help locate your clips.

7 In the Event Browser, select the **BUMPER_Delicious** clip and Shift-click the **BUMPER_Partners** clip. To assign the *Graphics* keyword to these two clips, click the keyword shortcut button (^4), or press Control-4 on your keyboard.

TIP Do not click *Graphics* in the Keyword Shortcut field. If you do, the field will highlight to add or retype a keyword. Simply click outside this field to leave the keyword unaltered.

8 In the Event Library, select the new *Sorting* Keyword Collection to see these clips. Since these clips are about the coffee-making process, drag them into the *Coffee* Keyword Collection

As you continue organizing clips, you may decide that you no longer want to use a keyword you earlier assigned. Because the *Sorting* Keyword Collection contains only three shots, this collection may no longer be that valuable to you. Before you remove this Keyword Collection, take a closer look at the three clips.

9 To show the skimmer info, choose View > Show Skimmer Info. In the Event Browser, skim through the three clips and notice that three keywords appear in the skimmer info flag: *Coffee*, *JJ*, and *Sorting*.

10 To delete the *Sorting* Keyword Collection in the Event Library, Control-click the collection and choose Delete Keyword Collection from the shortcut menu, or press Command-Delete.

When you delete a Keyword Collection, it removes the collection from the Event Library and also removes the keyword from the clips that were in the collection.

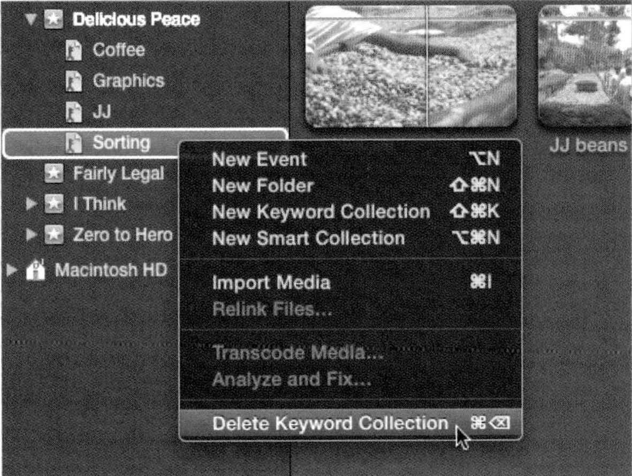

11 In the Event Library, select the *Delicious Peace* Event, and skim through the **JJ beans**, **JJ beans wide**, and **JJ ties bag** clips. Notice that the skimmer info flag indicates only two keywords are attached to these clips: *Coffee* and *JJ*.

TIP Viewing clip information in the skimmer info flag can be helpful at some times and distracting at others. To show or hide the flag quickly, learn its shortcut, Control-Y. Throughout these lessons, you can choose whether or not to view this information as you skim clips.

12 Using one of the methods you've learned, add the *Maps* keyword to the two map clips, the *Narration* keyword to the five VO clips, and the *Music* keyword to the three music clips. Here is a list of the keywords along with the clips that receive each keyword:

- Map: **map of Africa**, **map of Uganda**
- Narration: **VO_07** through **VO_11**
- Music: **music drums**, **music group**, **xylophone music**

Take 2

Just as you finish this task, the director walks into your editing room and sees the Keyword Collections you've created. He wants to put them to use immediately by screening all the coffee clips. But many clips that pertain to coffee growing and making haven't yet been placed in the *Coffee* Keyword Collection. Get to work!

Skim through the *Delicious Peace* Event clips, and using one of the methods outlined in this exercise, add to the *Coffee* Keyword Collection all clips that pertain to growing, picking, and making coffee.

Applying Keywords to a Clip Range

As you skim and play clips, you may find a few great seconds tucked into the middle of an otherwise uneventful shot. You definitely plan to use those few seconds in your project, but adding a keyword to the entire clip wouldn't be helpful. What you really want is a keyword that applies to just that section or range of the clip. In Final Cut Pro, you can identify a range of material within a clip, and then apply a keyword to that range. Assigning range-based keywords refines the organizational process by allowing you to locate just the useful part of a clip. It also prepares a specific section of a clip for editing purposes.

1 In the Event Library, select the *Delicious Peace* Event. Click the List View button, and then select the **rooster beans** clip.

Previously, you added the *Coffee* keyword to this and other coffee clips. In the Keyword Editor, notice that *Coffee* is in the keyword field, indicating that the **rooster beans** clip belongs to the *Coffee* Keyword Collection.

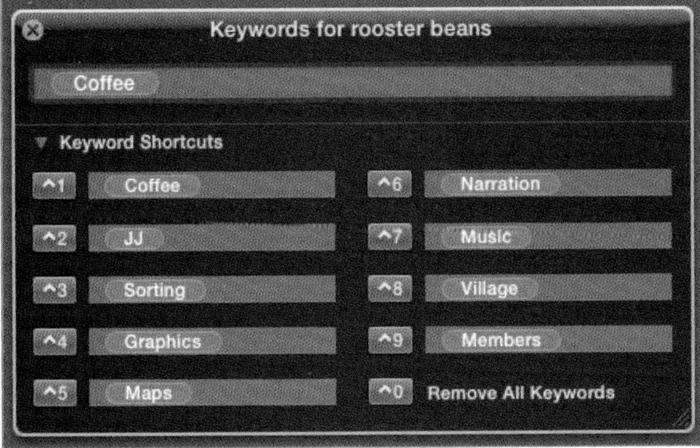

NOTE ▶ Do not delete the keyword from this field. If you do so, the keyword will be removed from the active clip.

Notice also that the keywords you entered in the previous exercise are still present in the Keyword Shortcuts fields. As you organize clips or shift focus from one set of clips to another, your keyword needs will change. You can change the keywords in the shortcut fields to include the keywords you need at present without affecting Keyword Collections.

For example, in this exercise, you will select a portion of a coffee clip that you can use as a sound effect in a project. So let's add the keyword *SFX* (which stands for "sound effects"). And in the next exercise, you will work with the still images in this project, so let's add the keyword *Stills* to the shortcut list.

2 In the Keyword Editor, select *Coffee* in the first keyword shortcut field. Type *SFX*, and press Return. Click in the second shortcut field, type *Stills*, and press Return. You will use these keywords shortly.

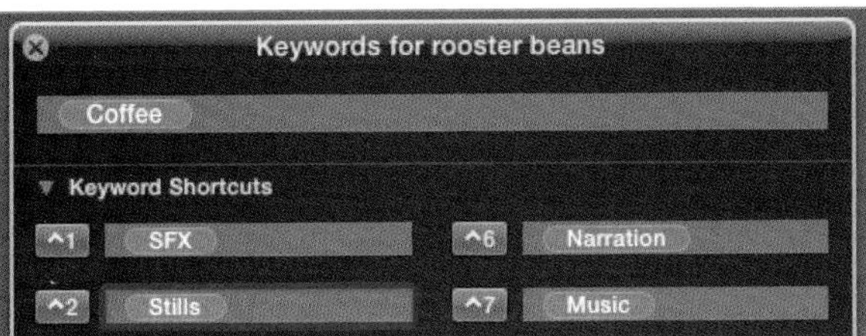

3 In the Event Browser, skim through the **rooster beans** clip, and then click to select it.

Selected clip

When you select a clip, a thick yellow outline appears around it to indicate the *clip range*. The outline can appear around the entire clip, or can be adjusted to select just a portion, or range, of a clip.

4 In the **rooster beans** clip, skim to the point early in the clip—at about 00:47:42:25—where you hear the rooster start to crow. To see a visual reference to this sound in the filmstrip, choose View > Show Waveform.

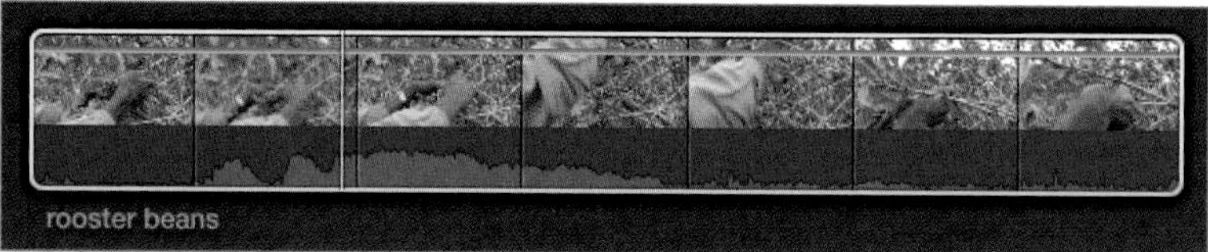

NOTE ▶ As you skim a clip, timecode appears in the Dashboard in the toolbar as well as in the skimmer info flag.

After you identify a specific frame or area in a clip, you can set a range start point and a range end point within the clip.

5 Press I to set the range start at this location. Notice that the clip range now begins at the start point and stops at the end of the clip.

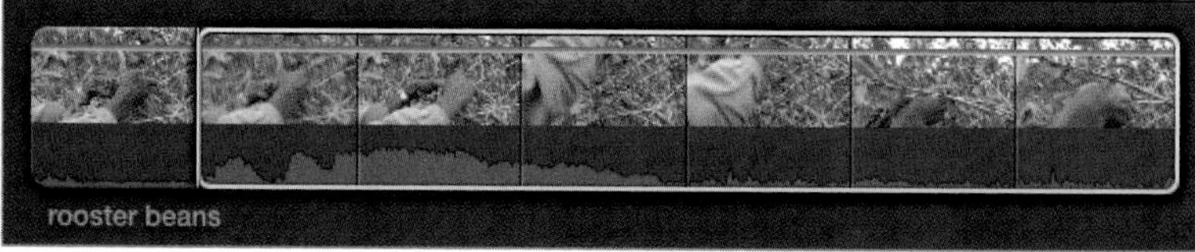

TIP When selecting a range with dialogue, you may want to turn on audio skimming to track the dialogue. When selecting a range within a clip that only has background noise, turning off audio skimming may be helpful. Choose View > Audio Skimming to select or deselect this option, or press Shift-S.

6 Skim the clip to the end of the rooster crow—at about 00:47:44:17—and press O to set a range end. The clip range adjusts to that point, and an outline appears around just the selected portion of the clip.

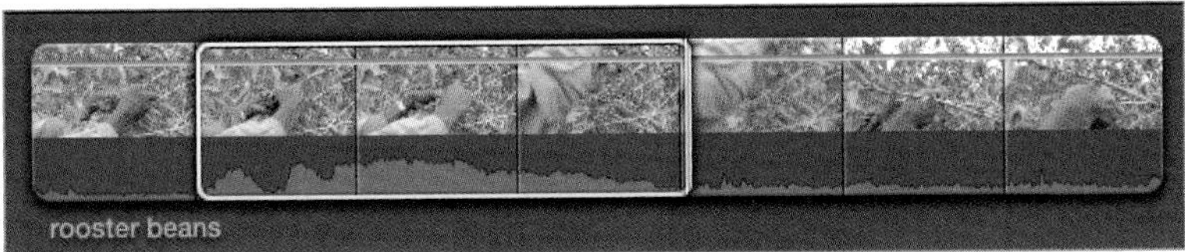

TIP To navigate a clip more precisely, press the Right or Left Arrow keys to move forward or backward one frame at a time, or press the J-K-L shortcuts. To change the Range selection, press I or O, and the start or end of the range moves to that point. To move the playhead to the range start, press Shift-I; and to move it to the range end, press Shift-O.

Now that you selected the range of material you want to use, you can view just that portion of the clip by using a keyboard shortcut.

7 To preview the range from the start to the end points in the **rooster beans** clip, press the slash key (/). Then press the Spacebar to play past the end point to see what happens after the rooster crows.

TIP If you want to repeat or loop the playback of the range, select the Loop Playback option in View > Playback. Press Command-L to toggle the function on or off.

While reviewing the selected range, you might feel that the sound of the rooster ends abruptly. You can add or remove additional clip range frames by dragging the edge of the range selection. Dragging an edge is just like skimming but also moves the start or end point of the selection.

8 In the **rooster beans** filmstrip, position your pointer over the end point of the range selection, and drag right. Listen for the rooster to clearly finish crowing and watch where the waveform of the rooster crow ends, at about 00:47:44:24, and then release

the pointer. Don't forget, you can watch the timecode on the Dashboard as you drag a range boundary.

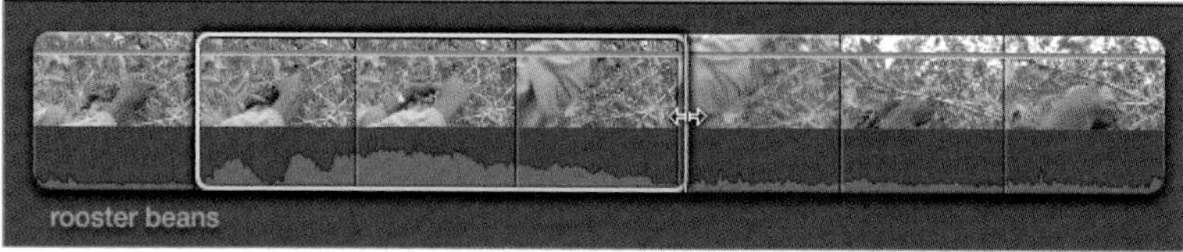

9 In the Keyword Editor, click the first shortcut button to add the *SFX* keyword to the clip. Look at the entry beneath the clip in the Event Browser list.

▼ rooster beans	00:47:42;05	00:47:46;22	00:00:04;17
Coffee	00:47:42;05	00:47:46;22	00:00:04;17
SFX	00:47:42;25	00:47:44;25	00:00:02;00

In the Event Browser list, the new keyword you assigned to the range appears in a separate row. In the metadata columns to the right, the Start, End, and Duration values for the range are different than the full-length clip. You can now preview that range.

10 In the Event Browser list, beneath the **rooster beans** clip, click between the two blue keyword icons, *Coffee* and *SFX*. In the filmstrip, notice the different range for each keyword. Then select the *SFX* keyword icon, and press the Spacebar to play the clip range.

▼ rooster beans	00:47:42;05	00:47:46;22	00:00:04;17
Coffee	00:47:42;05	00:47:46;22	00:00:04;17
SFX	00:47:42;25	00:47:44;25	00:00:02;00
▶ shaking beans	00:00:00;00	00:00:08;18	00:00:08;18

Just the range you identified and tagged with the *SFX* keyword is played back. You can also preview the range in the *SFX* Keyword Collection.

11 In the Event Library, select the *SFX* Keyword Collection. Click the **rooster beans** clip and play it. Just the range you selected is contained in this Keyword Collection. Choose View > Hide Waveforms, and close the Keyword Editor.

By adding keywords and identifying the range, you've readied the content for use in your project by pre-editing it and making it easy to find later.

TIP Setting a range keyword to "pre-edit" a clip does not prevent you from accessing all of the clip's source media at any time in the Event.

Rating, Sorting, and Searching Clips

Editing assignments often come with an enormous amount of media that needs wrangling. In addition to keywords, Final Cut Pro offers a rating system that helps you narrow down the media to a more manageable amount by tagging clips you'll want to use and rejecting those you don't. By rating clips or ranges of clips as Favorites or Rejects, you are giving them your own personal "thumbs up" or "thumbs down." You can sort and filter rated clips to view just those to which you've already given your nod. You can also search clips based on any metadata associated with it.

Restoring Default Settings in the Event Browser

As you begin to apply these search options, it may be helpful to return to the default settings that display all the clips from your Event in the Event Browser:

- Select your Event in the Event Library.
- In the Event Browser, choose All Clips from the Filter pop-up menu.

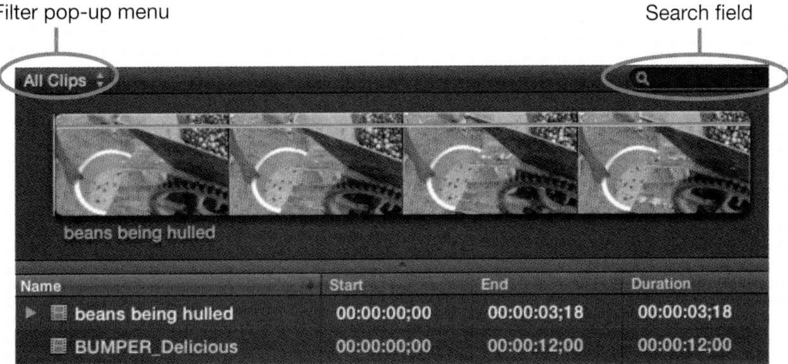

- If any text or icons are present in the upper-right search field, click the reset button (X).
- In the Action pop-up menu, choose Group Clips By > None, and Arrange Clips By > Name/Ascending.

In previous exercises, you added keywords to several clips in the *Delicious Peace* Event. As you work through the organizing process, you may lose track of which clips have been assigned keywords and which haven't. An easy way to refresh your memory is to change the filter option.

1 In the Event Library, select the *Delicious Peace* Event, and click the List View button. In the Event Browser, click the Filter pop-up menu to view the various ways you can filter these clips, and then choose "No Ratings or Keywords." To see a clip filmstrip, select the first clip, **hand shake**.

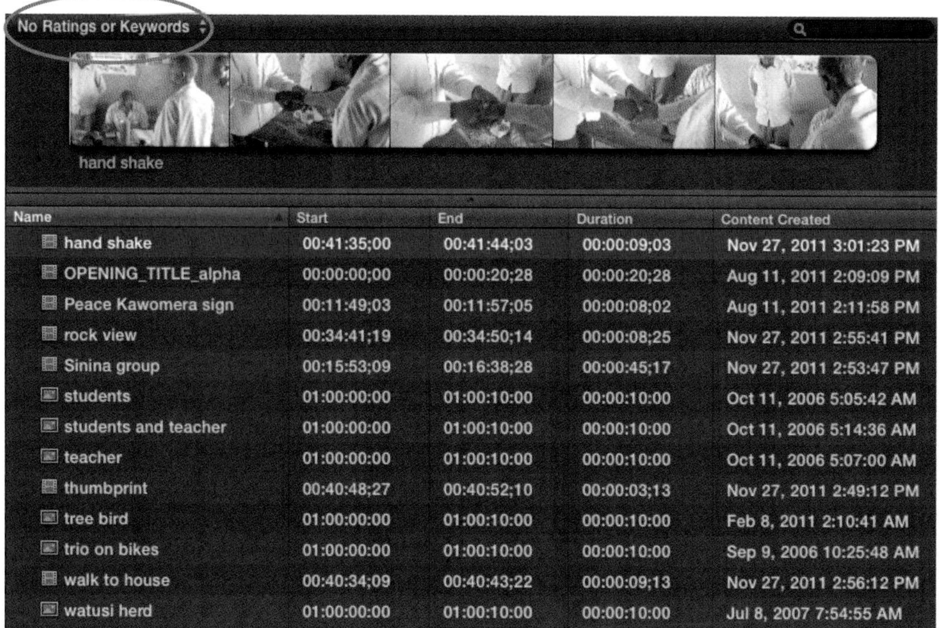

The clips displayed do not have a disclosure triangle because they don't contain any keyword tags or ratings. When you select clips in this sorted list, you won't see any blue keyword lines either. Let's take a closer look at one of these clips.

2 Skim the **Sinina group** clip, then listen to the first part of the clip after the camera finds Sinina, around 16:01:05.

As an editor, you need to keep an eye out for people who contribute to the story or narrative. In this informal interview, Sinina, one of the Peace Kawomera cooperative members, offers an interesting observation on life before the organization was formed. If you made that part of the clip a Favorite, you could quickly isolate and access that portion during editing. To identify the favorite portion, you first select a clip range.

3 Skim to where the camera is focused on Sinina, and just before she says, "We used not to," press I to set the range start. Then play to after she says, "Just to greet each other," at about 16:11:02, and press O to set a range end.

TIP You can also create a range or adjust a range start or end by dragging the range boundary.

4 To rate this range or selection as a Favorite, in the toolbar, click the green-starred Favorite button, or press F.

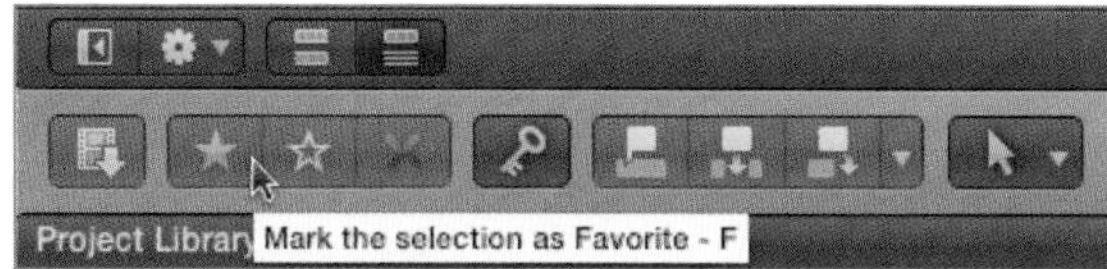

Because the "No Ratings or Keywords" filter is active, the clip you just rated no longer appears in this list. Instead, if you look closely, you'll find two **Sinina group** clips. By skimming these clips, you will see they are the unrated and untagged remnants of this clip from outside the Favorite selection.

5 To see those clips that are tagged as Favorites, from the Filter pop-up, choose Favorites. Select the **Sinina group** clip and play it. It consists of just the portion of the clip you selected and tagged in the previous steps.

In the clip thumbnails, notice the green horizontal Favorite line across the top. Notice, too, that a disclosure triangle appears next to this clip's name in the list.

6 If necessary, click the disclosure triangle next to the **Sinina group** clip to see the added metadata.

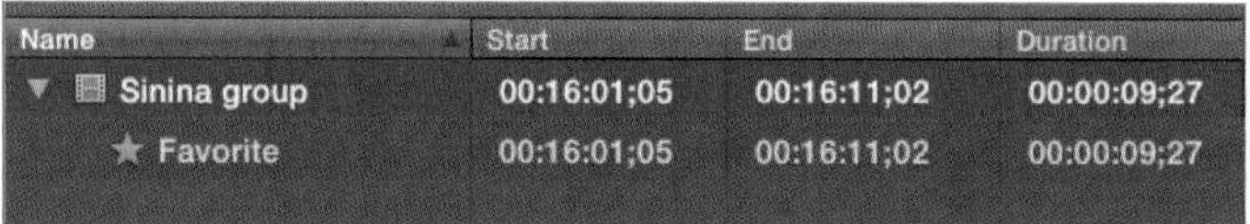

Favorite is listed beneath the clip name. When a clip contains a keyword or rating, a disclosure triangle appears (in list view) so you can hide or reveal that information.

Another way to rate clips is to reject the portion of a clip you don't want to use. To do this, let's find a clip that is not part of a Keyword Collection. If you remember the name of a clip, or even a portion of it, you can easily search for it by entering that information in the Event Browser search field. For example, you might remember a clip with *peace* in the name, but you don't remember anything else about it. Having someone contribute to the story on the topic of peace would be very nice.

7. From the Filter pop-up menu, choose All Clips. In the search field, enter *peace*. Then select the first clip, **JJ on peace**.

NOTE ▶ The text search field is for searching clips using only text from clip names, from markers, or from notes attached to the clips. The text field does not search against keywords. It is the fastest text-based search tool. (You will attach notes to clips later in the exercise.) If you enter a name to search, don't press Return; if you do, the name will be highlighted for the purpose of deleting or replacing it.

Two clips in this Event have the word *peace* in their metadata: **JJ on peace** and **Peace Kawomera sign**. In the **JJ on peace** clip, JJ talks about how he wants other people to copy their peaceful coalition.

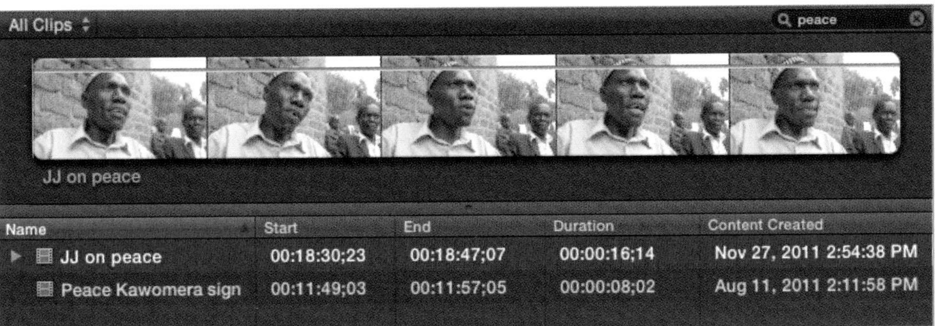

Results of "peace" search

TIP To see a visual representation of what JJ is saying, choose View > Show Waveforms.

8 Play from the beginning of the **JJ on peace** clip and find a clean starting point just before JJ says, "We want other people to copy…." To reject the portion of the clip before that, press O to set a range end, and the first part of the clip is selected. In the toolbar, click the red reject (X) button, or press Delete.

In the filmstrip, a red line appears over the rejected portion of the clip.

In the Event Browser, a new line of metadata is added to the **JJ on peace** clip to identify the rejected portion of this clip.

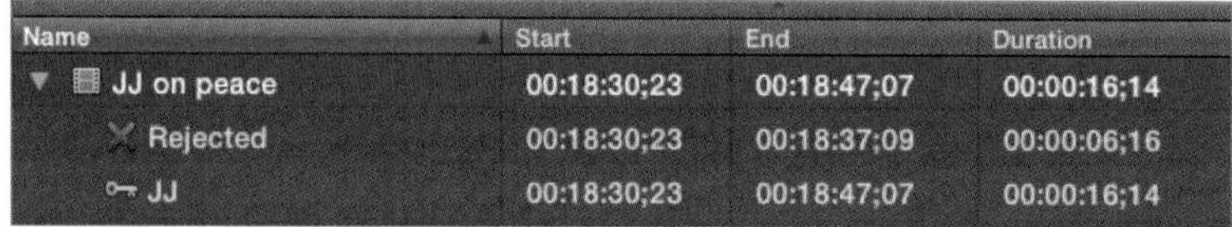

Name	Start	End	Duration
JJ on peace	00:18:30;23	00:18:47;07	00:00:16;14
Rejected	00:18:30;23	00:18:37;09	00:00:06;16
JJ	00:18:30;23	00:18:47;07	00:00:16;14

When you filter rejected clips or portions of clips, it redefines the appearance of the clip in the Event.

9 From the Filter pop-up menu, choose Hide Rejected, or press Control-H. Then select the **JJ on peace** clip and press the slash key (/) to play it. With the rejected portion hidden, this clip now begins with JJ saying, "We want other people to copy…."

In addition to rating, sorting, and searching clips, you can add a note to a clip to identify something you found memorable.

Taking Notes in Editing

Before nonlinear editing, making notes by hand was the traditional method of logging and rating individual shots or "takes" of film or video. Script assistants would start the process on a film or television set, making notes on the script identifying a director's best takes and any other instructions for the editors. Editors would then log their own detailed notes to help them remember, rate, and find shots.

There are still many reasons to use notes in the editing process. While watching a clip, you may want to note the content of an interview, or jot down an idea about how to use a clip in your project. If you're working on a documentary with a voice-over narration, you could attach the portion of voice-over text to the clip or clips you are considering using at that location. You could use the same approach when editing a music video by including lyric lines in notes. By attaching a note to a clip in Final Cut Pro, you can later perform a text search to instantly bring up these clips when you are ready to implement your ideas.

10 From the Filter pop-up menu, choose All Clips. In the search field, click the reset button (X) to clear the field contents. Then select the **grind stone** clip and play the second half of this clip.

As the woman is grinding the roasted coffee beans by hand, you hear her say in the background, "It has a nice smell." This little off-camera statement is a mighty reflection of how happy the workers are when contributing their skills and talents to the cooperative. If you made "nice smell" part of the clip's metadata via the Notes field, you could search for the clip by that phrase and incorporate this aspect of the workers into your story. Although you can apply a note to the entire clip, you can speed up retrieval of this sound bite by assigning the note to a range of the clip that you've marked with a keyword or as a Favorite.

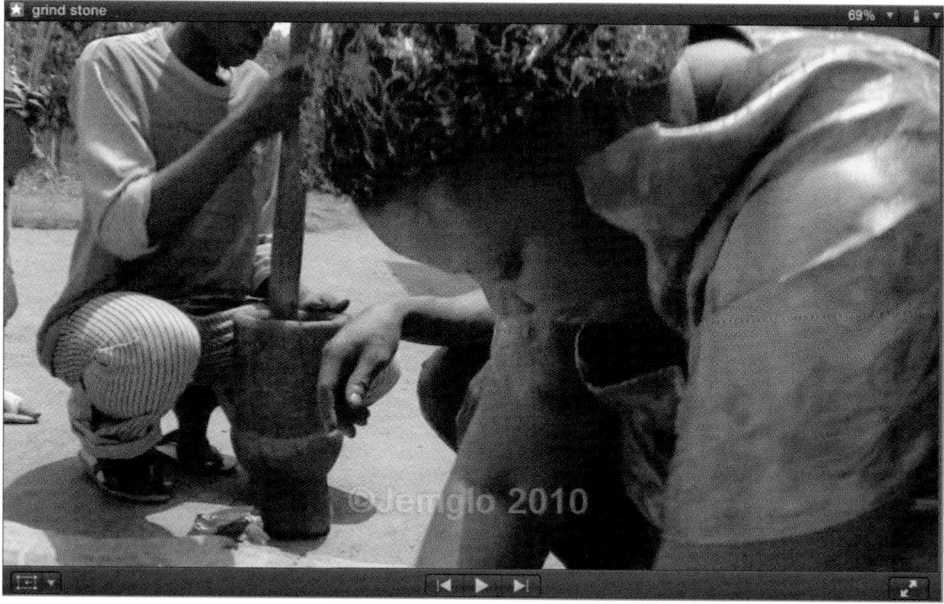

11 Create a range in the **grind stone** clip that includes the statement, "It has a nice smell." Mark this range as a Favorite.

You can add the keywords *nice smell* to the Notes field of the Favorite rating you just created. But first, let's find the Notes column in the Event Browser and position it for optimal use.

12 In the Event Browser, below the clip filmstrip, scroll all the way to the right to bring the Notes column into view. To position this information closer to the Name column, drag the Note column heading to the left and drop it next to the Name column.

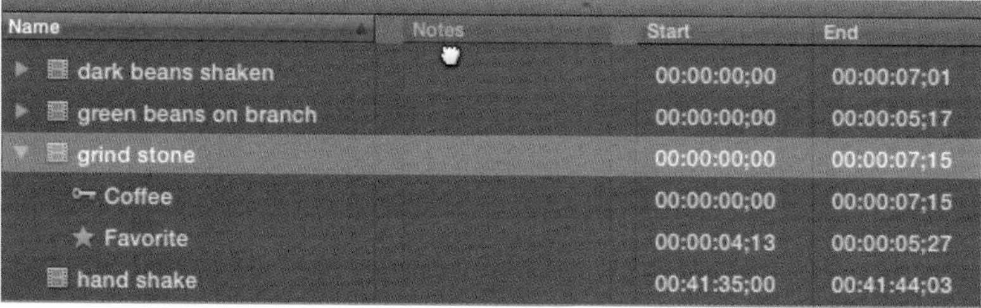

As you drag to the left, the pointer turns into a hand icon, and the other columns shift to the right. You can arrange the metadata column headers in any order, but the Name header cannot be moved from the first column position.

TIP ▶ To change the width of a column, move the pointer over the border between the column headers until it changes to a resize pointer. Drag the column border right or left to make the column wider or narrower.

13 To add a note, select the Favorite that you created in the **grind stone** clip, and then click in the Note column field. When the field becomes active, enter *nice smell*, and press Return.

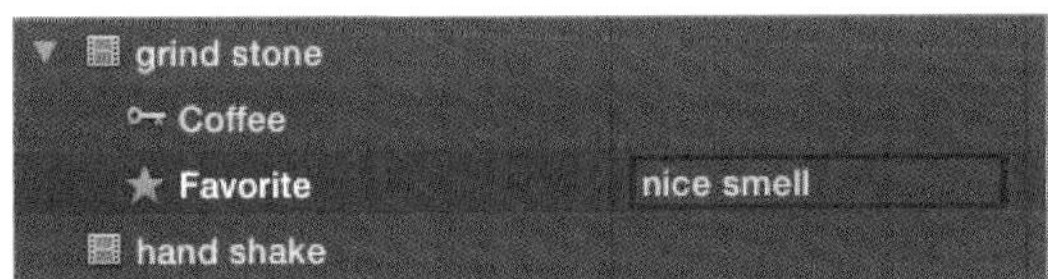

After you've added metadata to a clip, you can use that metadata to search for the clip. For example, while you may not remember the name of this clip, the day the clip was shot, or that you gave it a *Coffee* keyword, you might remember someone saying "nice smell," and you could quickly find the clip by searching for that phrase.

14 In the Event Browser search field, enter *nice smell*. Only the **grind stone** clip appears in the list.

NOTE ▶ You can also change the Favorite label to a more descriptive word by clicking the Favorite text and entering a new name for the selection.

With the powerful rate, filter, and search options in Final Cut Pro X—and, of course, Keyword Collections—the time you spend organizing and pre-editing your media will propel you into the editing stage of your project.

Take 2

Your client suddenly requests to view a sample of the project and you're happy to comply, even though you're under a time crunch. Obviously, you want to show the media in the best possible light, especially if you are the one responsible for shooting it.

TIP ▶ To see all your clips in the Event Browser, click the reset button (X) in the search field to remove the search criteria.

Rather than search and skim every clip in your Event—a potentially frustrating and time-consuming chore for all parties—take a few minutes to rate some clips and ranges of clips as Favorites. When your client arrives, choose Favorites from the Filter pop-up menu and play a collection of only the best clips. Your client can view them quickly, and let you get back to your editing deadline, satisfied that the project is in good hands.

NOTE ▶ As you continue to add metadata to your clips, you will see that a single clip could contain several keywords, different Favorite selections, a rejected selection, and one or more notes.

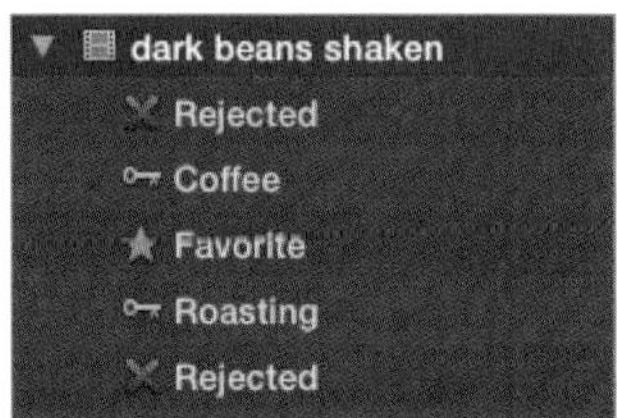

Creating Smart Collections

In Lesson 2, Final Cut Pro analyzed media on import and organized clips into Smart Collections, based on criteria such as number of people in the shot and so on. This was an effective way to automatically sort or filter some of your clips without even screening them first!

But now you've tagged the clips by creating your own keywords, applying ratings, and attaching notes. And you've seen how to search by each criterion individually. Consider how powerful the search function could be if you combined these criteria, such as a keyword *and* a note *only* on Favorite clips.

To perform a more complex search for clips in an Event, you can utilize the Filter window. Here you can choose search criteria and save your search results as a Smart Collection. And because Smart Collections update dynamically, whenever a new clip matches the Smart Collection search criteria, the clip is automatically appears in the Smart Collection in that Event.

1 In the Event Library, click the *Delicious Peace* Event. From the Filter pop-up menu, choose All Clips. Then click the Filmstrip View button and press Shift-Z to display single-frame filmstrips. If necessary, clear the search field.

   When starting a search, it's always a good idea to start with all the clips in an Event as you will narrow the search in the Filter window.

In the previous exercise, you used the search field in the Event Browser to search for clips that had the text "nice smell." But when you click the magnifying glass icon in the search field, it opens a Filter window and the tools to begin a more complex search.

2 In the Event Browser, click the magnifying glass icon to open the Filter window.

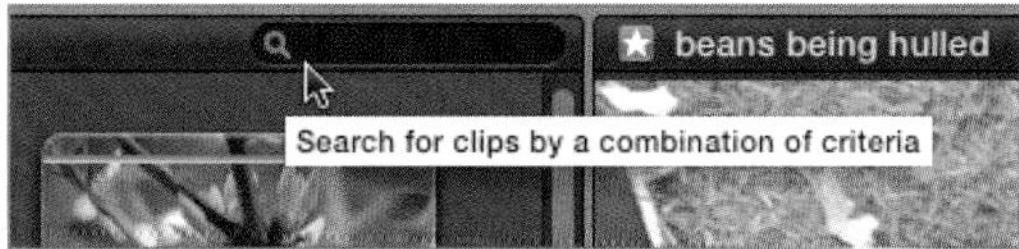

TIP Opening the Filter window is similar to using the Find function in other applications. It even has the same keyboard shortcut, Command-F.

In the Filter window, you can perform a complex clip search, also known as a weighted search. You can use the results of the search to create a Smart Collection based on your chosen criteria.

You can search by text, keyword, type of media, format information, and so on. The default option is to search by text, as indicated by the large red letter T on the first filter line. Next to that red T is a checkbox. When the checkbox is selected, that filter is included as part of the search criteria.

You may want to use some still images in this project as part of a montage to set the scene for your story. Rather than view a lot of individual clips to find the still images, you can use the Filter window to search for them by media type.

3 Next to the Text field, deselect the checkbox to remove Text as criteria for this search. Then click the Add Rule (+) pop-up menu and choose Media Type.

NOTE ▶ Final Cut Pro refers to individual criteria sets as rules. By combining rules, you can focus Final Cut Pro on more specific searches.

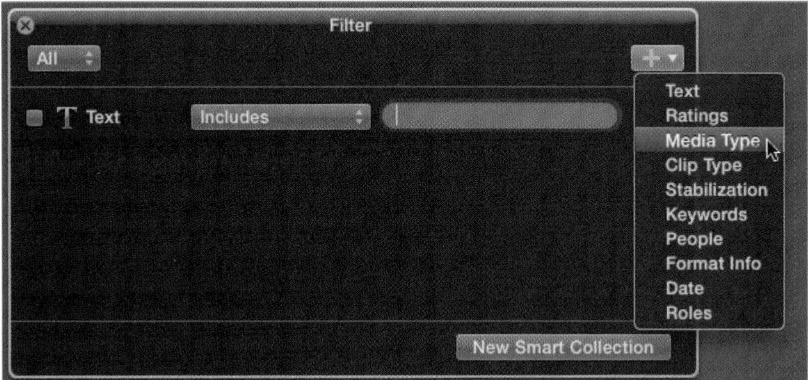

When you select a rule or criteria, such as Media Type, a new filter line appears with available options based on that rule. Notice that the Media filter line contains a pop-up with media options.

If you wanted to search for all the stills in this project, you could simply search for them by media type.

4 Within the Media filter rule, click the second pop-up and choose Stills.

NOTE ▶ Searches that use options such as Includes and Not Includes, or allow you to select and deselect multiple search criteria, are sometimes called Boolean searches because they are based on the Boolean logic of finding and rejecting items based on the concepts of And, Or, and Not.

All the still images from the *Delicious Peace* Event appear in the Event Browser. To create a Keyword Collection of still images, you can select these clips and tag them with the *Stills* keyword. However, another option is to create a Smart Collection, which engages Final Cut Pro to be "smart," and automatically place any newly imported still images directly into this *Stills* Smart Collection without the need to manually tag them.

5 In the Filter window, click New Smart Collection.

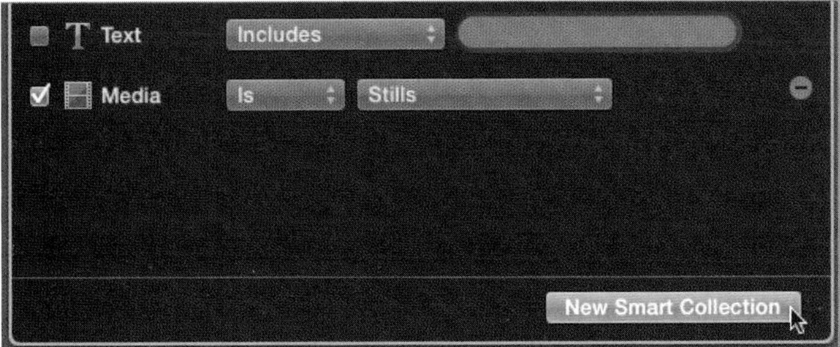

In the Event Library, a new purple-geared Smart Collection appears named *Untitled*.

6 To name the new Smart Collection in the Event Library, verify that its Name field is highlighted and then type *Stills*, and press Return.

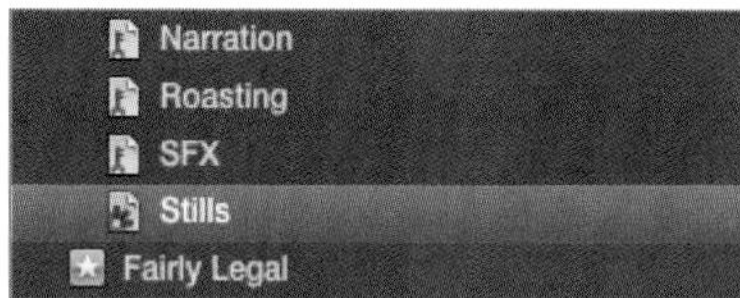

As you begin to edit your project, you may decide you want to fine-tune your Smart Collection. For example, you may not want to include stills of animals with stills of village life. To change an existing Smart Collection, you would open it from the Event Library. But first, tag the clips in this collection that do not include animals.

7 In the Event Browser, select the four clips from the *Stills* Smart Collection that show village life, but not animals. Press Command-K to open the Keyword Editor, and click Control-8 to apply the *Village* keyword to the selected clips.

NOTE ▶ When you click a still image in the Event Browser, a range appears within a portion of the clip, and not around the entire clip. The duration of the range can be changed in the Final Cut Pro > Preferences window. Click the Editing tab, and in the "Still images: Editing duration is" field, choose the duration you want as a default when editing still images.

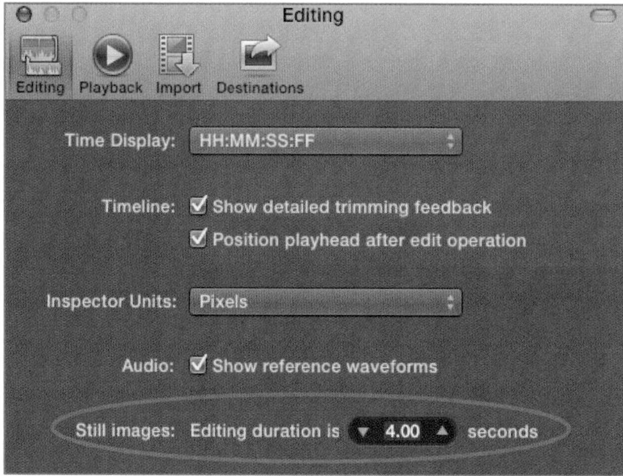

8 In the Event Library, double-click the *Stills* Smart Collection. In the Filter window, click the Add Rules pop-up menu, and choose Keywords.

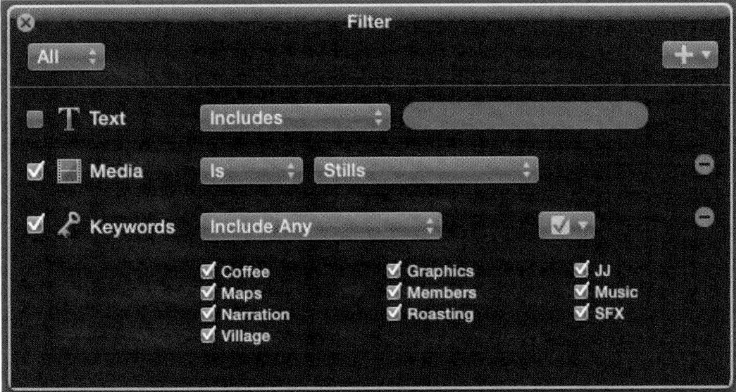

When you add Keywords as a new rule in the search, a list of all the current Keyword Collections appears. Rather than deselect each box individually, you can deselect them all in one step, and then add back only the Keyword Collection you want to include.

9 In the Keywords area, click the pop-up menu that has a checkbox in it, and choose Uncheck All. Then select the check box next to Village to add that keyword to the search. As you perform these steps, watch to see which clips are displayed in the Event Browser.

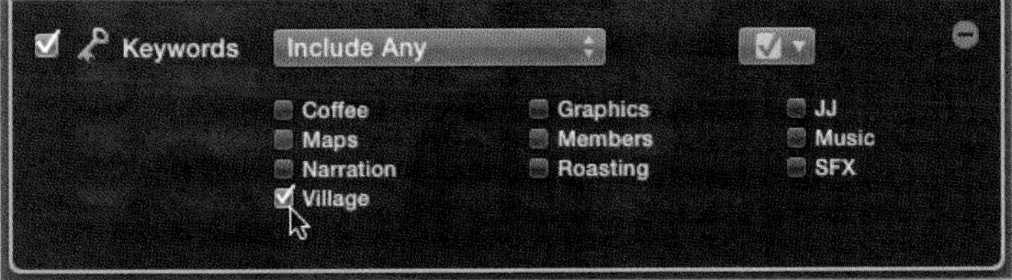

With the *Village* Keyword Collection added to the criteria for the *Stills* Smart Collection, the two animal stills no longer appear.

10 To close the Filter window, click the close button (X) in the upper-left corner, or with the window active, press Command-W.

TIP When you select one or more rules in a search, the rules are represented in the search field as status icons. Make sure that you clear the search by clicking the reset button (X). Closing the Filter window will not clear the search.

Editor's Cut

Editors are often required to start looking at media without knowing much about the project they are about to edit. Even more often, the file names assigned to the media will not consist of descriptive names, but of numbers issued by the camera or cameras that were used.

Using the knowledge of the media you viewed in the first two lessons and the organizational methods and tools you learned in this lesson, skim the clips in the *Fairly Legal* and *I Think* Events to assign keywords and create your own Keyword and Smart Collections. Tagging these clips with your own keywords is not only good practice, it will also help prepare you to edit with these clips in upcoming lessons.

Lesson Review

1. In the Event Browser, what is indicated by a horizontal purple or blue line across the top of a clip?
2. Name three methods that allow you to add a keyword to one or more clips.
3. How do you add a keyword to only the selected clip range?
4. How do you delete a keyword range or multiple keyword ranges from a clip?

5. Describe how to add a note to a clip in the Event Browser.
6. How do you view only those clips that were rated as Favorites?
7. How do you rate a clip?
8. What is the difference between a Keyword Collection and a Smart Collection?
9. How do you create a Smart Collection?
10. How do you search for a clip that isn't part of a Keyword Collection?

Answers

1. A purple line indicates that a clip received a keyword during analysis; a blue line indicates that a keyword was applied to a clip.
2. Select clips in the Event Browser, click the Keyword Editor button, or press Command-K. Then type your keyword, and press Return. If you created a keyword shortcut, you can select clips and press the shortcut. You can also drag clips from the Event Browser to an existing Keyword Collection in the Event Library.
3. Skim a clip in the Event Browser and press I to set a range start and O to mark a range end. Then use one of the three available methods to add a keyword.
4. With the Event Browser set to list view, select the keyword appearing beneath the clip, and then press the Delete key. To remove all keywords applied to a selected Event Browser clip, choose Mark > Remove All Keywords, or press Control-0.
5. Select a clip, click in the Note column field in the Event Browser, enter your text, and press Return.
6. In the Event Library, select the Event you want to search. Choose Favorites from the Filter pop-up menu at the top of the Event Browser.
7. In the Event Browser, select one or more clips. Click the Favorite button in the toolbar, or press the F key, or click the Reject button in the toolbar, or press the Delete key. In the Event Browser, a green line appears at the top of Favorite frames and a red line appears at the top of rejected frames.
8. A Keyword Collection gathers all clips to which you or Final Cut Pro assigned a specific keyword. A Smart Collection gathers all clips that match specified search criteria. Unlike Keyword Collections, which are text based, Smart Collections can be based on camera metadata, such as frame rate or size. Clips can be assigned to multiple Keyword Collections and Smart Collections.

9. Select an Event and use the Filter window to search for clips based on specified criteria. In the Filter window, click the New Smart Collection button. A new, untitled Smart Collection appears in the Event Library. Type a name for the Smart Collection, and press Return.
10. From the filter pop-up menu, choose "No Ratings or Keywords." In the search field, enter the clip name. Only clips with matching text in their names or notes will appear in the list.

Keyboard Shortcuts

Command-A	Select all clips
Command-F	Show the Filter window
Command-K	Show or hide the Keyword Editor
Command-Shift-K	Create a new Keyword Collection
Command-Z	Undo the last command
Command-Delete	Delete or move the selection to the Trash
Option-N	Create a new Event
I	Set the start point for a range
O	Set the end point for a range
Left Arrow	Move the playhead to the previous frame
Right Arrow	Move the playhead to the next frame
Slash (/)	Play the selection
Spacebar	Start or pause playback
Control-F	Show Favorite clips and ranges
Control-H	Hide rejected clips and ranges
Control-Y	Show or hide clip information when skimming in the Event Browser
U	Remove ratings from the selection
Delete	Reject the Event Browser selection

Crafting the Story

4

Time

This lesson takes approximately 90 minutes to complete.

Goals

- Work with projects
- Screen and mark clips
- Use the append edit option
- Arrange clips in the Timeline
- Work with the Magnetic Timeline
- Insert clips
- Use drag-and-drop editing
- Make changes to project clips
- Connect clips to the primary storyline

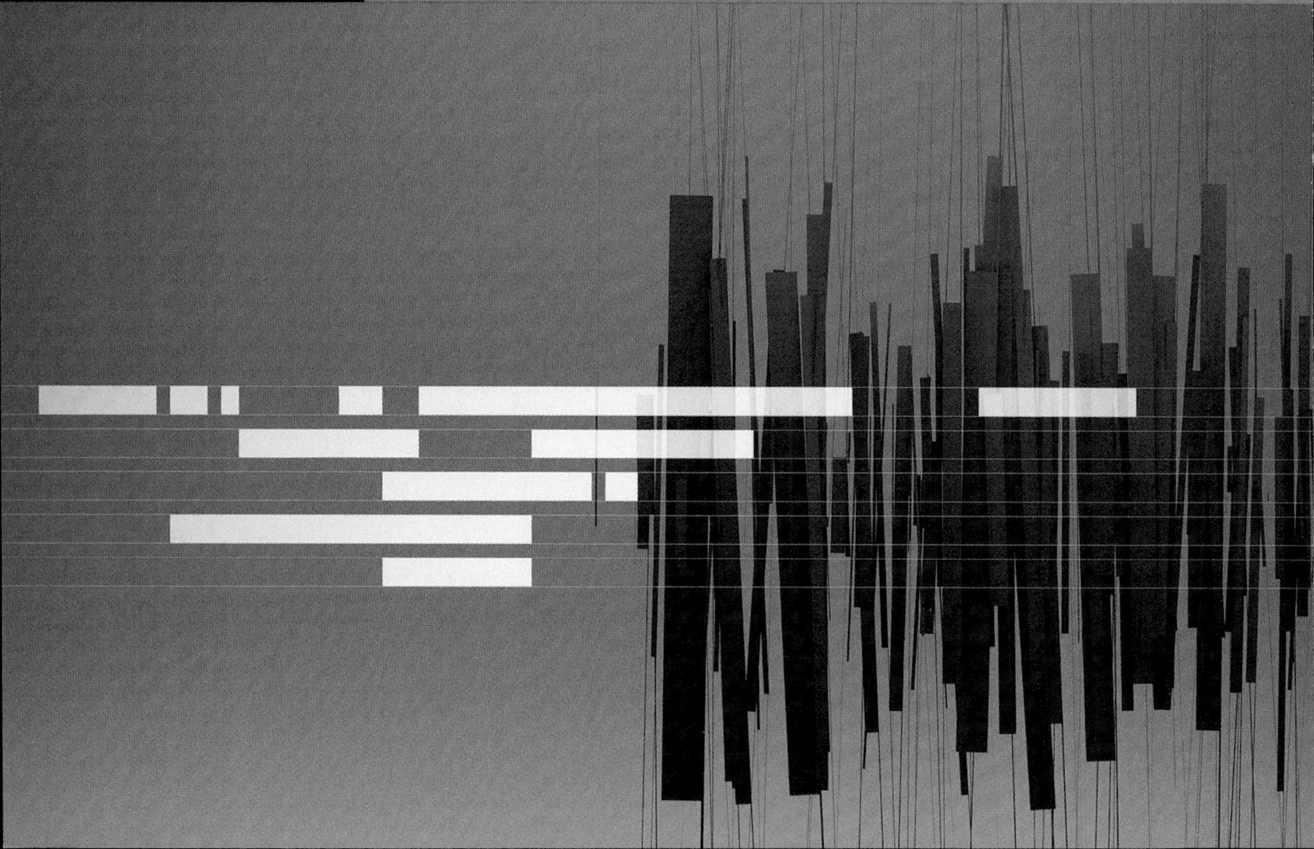

Lesson **4**

Building the Rough Cut

Having imported your media and organized your Events, you are now ready to move into one of the most exciting parts of the editing workflow: building and crafting your story. Why "building" and not "telling?" Because a story needs a foundation, a primary thread—let's call it a storyline—that will take you from beginning to end.

Once you craft the primary foundation or storyline, you can refine it by rearranging some clips and trimming others. You may want to add complementary B-roll visuals to create a secondary storyline, or enhance the story by adding music or narration. This is the real work of an editor, and represents the tasks you will encounter in this very important part of the editing workflow, and in this section of this book.

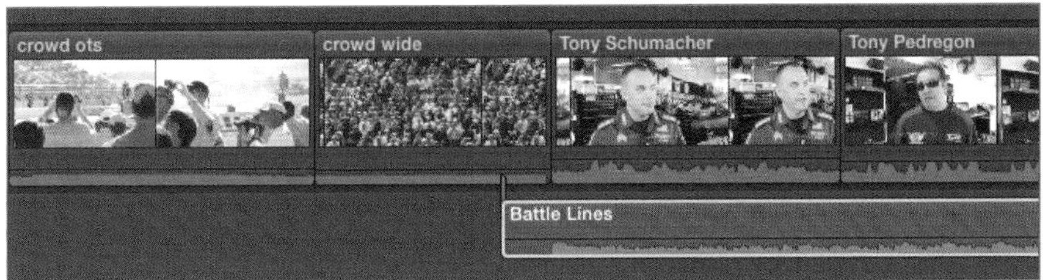

In this lesson you'll build a rough cut using the source media from the Events. To begin, you will create a new project, and mark clips you've placed in Keyword Collections. Then, you'll choose your Favorite clips and edit them into the project to create a primary storyline. Remember, it's a rough cut. It will require trimming, adjusting, and finessing, but all of that will be done in due time.

Creating a New Project

Every story you tell using Final Cut Pro is contained within a project. Projects are created and cataloged in the Project Library. Here you can neatly organize and store your projects until you are ready to refine them or share them with the world.

In this exercise, you will create a new project in the Project Library for the *Zero to Hero* story.

1 If the Project Library is not in view, click the Project Library button in the lower-left corner of the Timeline, or press Command-0 (zero).

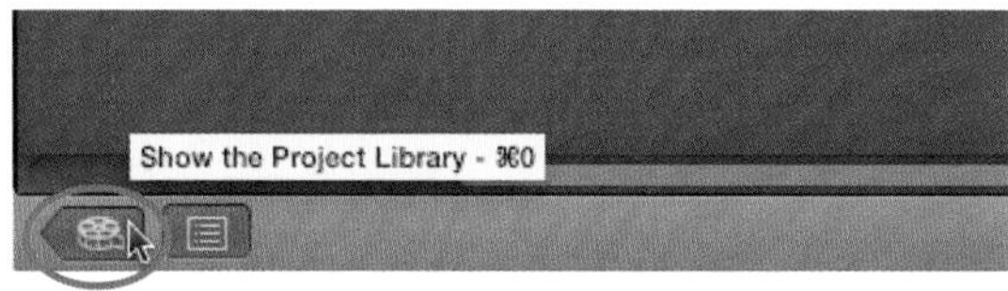

When the Project Library is active, you'll see your internal hard disk along with any external drives connected to your computer. Any projects stored on a volume will appear under that volume's icon.

2 To reveal the projects on the APTS FCP X disk, click its disclosure triangle. To reveal the contents of the Lesson Projects folder, click its disclosure triangle.

The Lesson Projects folder was copied from the DVD and contains project files that you will use throughout the book. One folder has been created for each lesson.

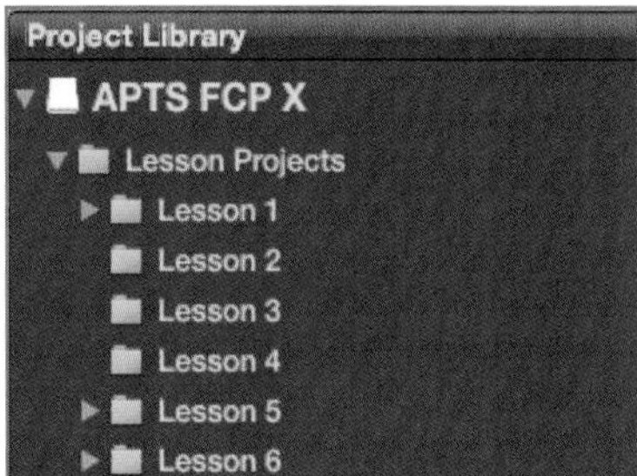

You'll create a new project for this lesson inside the Lesson 4 folder using the *Zero to Hero* Event on APTS FCP X.

3 In the Event Library, select the *Zero to Hero* Event under APTS FCP X. In the Project Library, select the Lesson 4 folder, and click the New Project (+) button.

A project dialog appears asking you to name the new project and the default Event that contains your source media.

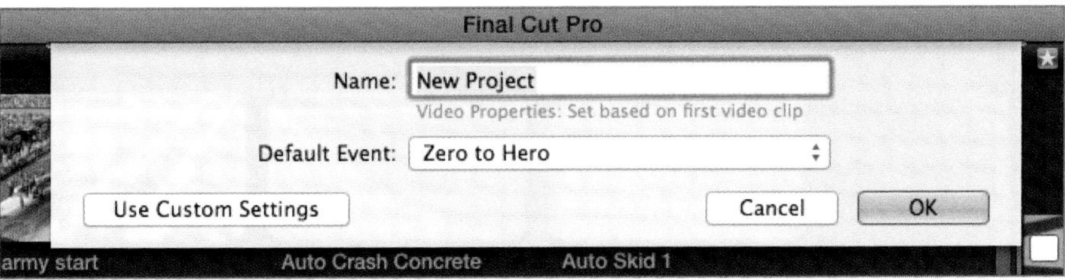

4 In the Name field, enter *Zero to Hero*. From the Default Event pop-up menu, choose the first *Zero to Hero* Event listed.

NOTE ▶ Two *Zero to Hero* Events are listed if you did not delete the Macintosh HD Events created in Lesson 2. The first *Zero to Hero* listed is on APTS FCP X and the second is the Event you created on Macintosh HD.

In the Default Event pop-up menu, Final Cut Pro will display Events stored in the Final Cut Events folders present on any connected hard disk. The current option displayed in the menu simply reflects the Event that was most recently selected in your Event Library. As you edit, however, you can use clips from multiple Events in your project.

By using the default settings, you're allowing Final Cut Pro to create a project using video formats that match the first clip you edit, and audio settings that follow the default audio options.

TIP To customize a project's audio and video properties, click the Use Custom Settings button. For Video Properties, select Custom, and then choose the desired Format, Resolution, and Rate from the pop-up menus that appear. Selecting Custom for the Audio and Render Properties section allows you to select Stereo or Surround sound, the audio sample rate, and the render file format.

5 Click OK.

When you create a new project, it automatically opens in the Timeline window. Notice that the name of the new project is displayed in the upper left of the window.

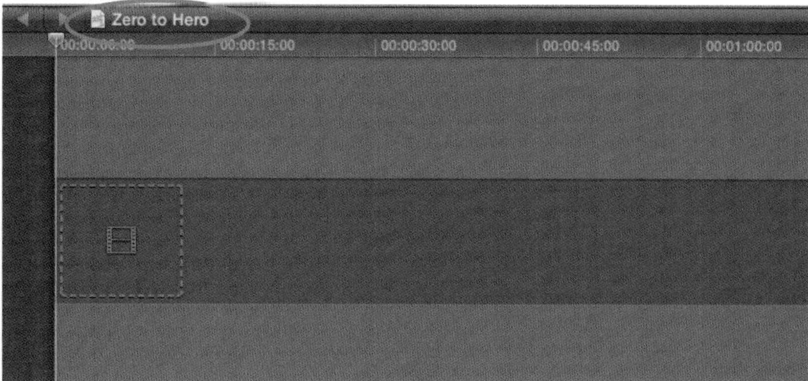

You still have a few more things to organize in the Project Library. For example, to narrow your focus among the many folders, you can bring your Lesson 4 folder front and center, and close the other folders.

6 To return to the Project Library, press Command-0 (zero). For the purposes of this lesson, drag the Lesson 4 folder onto APTS FCP X to bring it to the top level of that folder's hierarchy. Then click the disclosure triangle for the Lesson Projects folder to hide the other lesson folders.

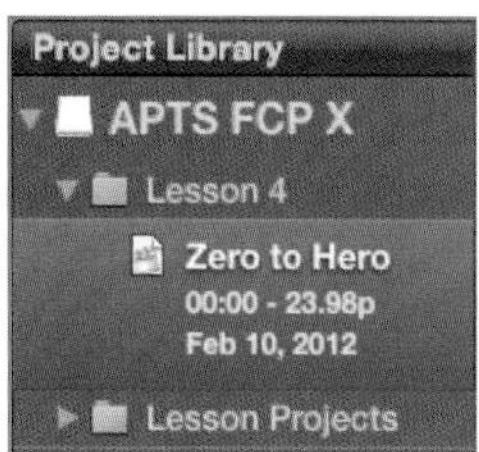

TIP When you create projects, Final Cut Pro creates a Final Cut Projects folder in your Movies folder if Macintosh HD is selected or at the root level of a selected, non-system volume. You can exercise a media management best practice by not manipulating the project or media files in the Finder.

You can have an unlimited number of Final Cut Pro projects, but you can work on only one at a time. Next you'll get started building the project you just created.

7 Open the Lesson 4 folder to reveal its contents. To open the *Zero to Hero* project, double-click its icon. The project opens in the Timeline.

Screening and Marking Clips

If you organized your clips into Keyword Collections, or had Final Cut Pro do it for you on import, you'll have a head start on your editing process. Rather than needing to search through a large group of clips to find the content you want to use, you can select a collection of clips in the Event Library and start editing. In this exercise, you will work with *Zero to Hero* interview clips that were previously imported into a Keyword Collection based on the original folder structure of the media files.

About the Zero To Hero Media

"Zero To Hero" was produced by Pullin Television in partnership with The National Hot Rod Association to create entertainment programming for the professional race teams as well as the grassroots racing community. The series, which was produced and directed by Stephen Pullin, highlights several drag car racing champions and showcases their backgrounds, their passions, and their commitment to racing. Some of the drivers featured in the series are Tony Pedregon, a two-time Funny Car World Champion with 43 career wins and a top speed of 311.49 MPH; Tony Schumacher, a seven-time winner of the Top Fuel Dragster World Championships with 67 career wins and a top speed of 327.03 MPH; Antron Brown, a top fuel dragster driver with 27 career wins, and a top speed of 325.37 MPH; and John Force, a fifteen-time Funny Car World Champion with 132 career wins, and a top speed of 316.23 MPH. The series was broadcast on Fox television and also distributed over the Internet. Each episode was created using a variety of camera sources, including Sony EX3, Panasonic P2, and GoPro for live events, interviews, and field production, as well as additional media from ESPN broadcasts mastered on DVC Pro.

Starting with a Keyword Collection is a good first step for narrowing the choice of clips. But the real craft of editing is to narrow your media choice *within* a clip so you can edit just that selection into your project.

You can do this several ways. In the previous lesson, you used start and end points to define a range, and rated that range as a Favorite. (Final Cut Pro can easily display those Favorites as a group.) But you can also identify a clip range using start and end points and then edit that selection directly into the Timeline. In this exercise, you will view clips and mark the desired ranges you want to edit. You will also adjust the Event Browser to maximize its use for previewing clips before editing.

1 In the Event Library, click the disclosure triangle next to the *Zero to Hero* Event, and select the *Interviews* Keyword Collection. Click the Filmstrip View button.

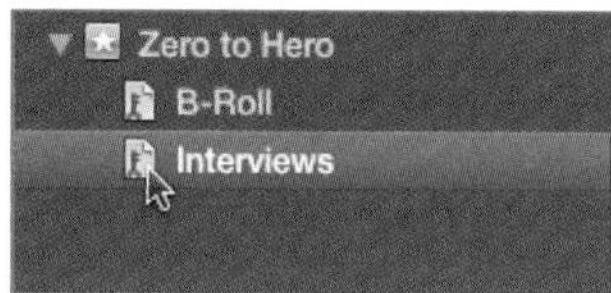

The four people in this Keyword Collection are racers in the National Hot Rod Association (NHRA). They were interviewed on location at their race events.

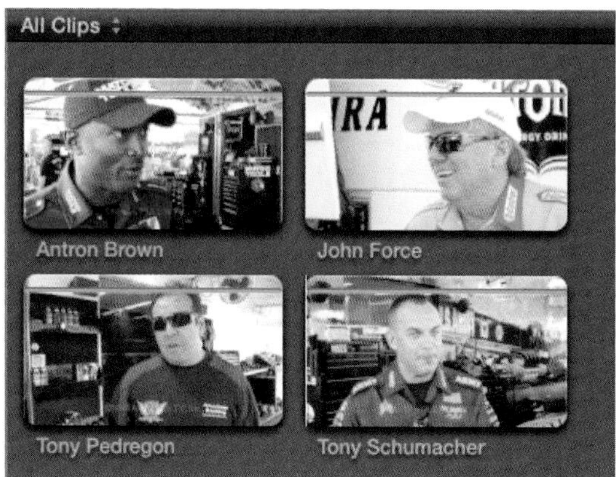

As you've seen, the Event Browser can display clips in several ways. The more familiar you become with the Final Cut Pro editing process, the more you will gravitate to different setups for specific purposes.

2 To optimize the Event Browser for screening and marking selections within these clips, do the following:

- Click the Filter pop-up menu and choose All Clips.
- If text or icons are already in the search field, click the reset button (X) to clear the field.
- In the Action pop-up menu, choose Group clips by > None, and Arrange clips by Name > Ascending.
- To choose a single thumbnail representation, drag the Duration slider right to the All position, or press Shift-Z.
- Click the Clip Appearance pop-up menu, and deselect Show Waveforms, and make the thumbnails as large as possible.
- In the View menu, make sure Skimming, Audio Skimming, and Snapping are chosen.

NOTE ▸ How you view clips in the Event Browser is a personal preference. You can modify your choices as you work through these lessons, but the display setup in step 2 will be reflected in the images in this lesson.

3 To select the first clip, **Antron Brown**, simply click it. Then move your pointer through the clip to skim it.

With a single click, a yellow range selection outlines the entire clip. Notice that you can skim anywhere in the clip, but the white playhead remains positioned at the location where you clicked when you selected the clip.

4 Skim away from the white playhead, and press the Spacebar to play the clip.

TIP ▶ As you play a clip, you may want to fast forward a clip or play it backward slowly to find the beginning of a word or a specific moment. You can press the J-K-L keys to play the clip backward and forward, slow and fast, and use key combinations to move frame by frame.

When you play a clip by pressing the Spacebar or the L key, the clip starts playing from the skimmer location, not the playhead location. This makes it very convenient to skim and play, skim and play, as you seek out editing options. When you're screening a clip for the first time, however, you'll typically want to play from the beginning of the clip.

5 To move the playhead *and* the skimmer to the beginning of the clip, press Shift-I, which moves both skimmer and playhead to the preceding start point. Then press Spacebar to play the entire clip.

NOTE ▶ When the clip finishes playing, you can press the Spacebar to play it again.

To edit a portion of this clip, you will change its selection range. Since Antron begins his comment at the very beginning of the clip, "One day you could be a hero," the current start point is fine. Next you'll set an end point.

6 Play the **Antron Brown** clip from the beginning again and stop after you hear him say, "... you didn't qualify for a race." Press O to set an end point at that playhead location. To play from the start to the end points, press the / (slash) key and watch your selected clip range play in the Viewer.

If the end point isn't exactly what you want—perhaps you caught Antron in the middle of his next word—you can change your range selection by dragging the selection edge, or by remarking the clip. To help you find a specific ending frame, you can also use the J-K-L or Left and Right Arrow keys.

TIP ▶ When audio skimming is enabled, you can hear Antron's audio frame by frame as you skim across the clip. To enable audio skimming, press Shift-S.

7 To move the playhead to the end point, press Shift-O. Press the Left or Right Arrow key to fine-tune the location of your new edit point, frame by frame. Make sure the frame is after Antron says, "…you didn't qualify for a race," but before he begins his next statement. To set a new end point at the playhead location, press O.

TIP Don't worry if your start and end points aren't perfect. Once the clip has been edited into a project in the Timeline, you can later apply trimming techniques to fine-tune the edit points.

With your clip range marked, you're ready to edit it. However, you have more clips to screen. You can rate this marked range as a Favorite for fast retrieval. You will learn more about editing in the next exercise.

TIP You can also press I or O as the clip plays to set a start or end point. Creating edit points in real time is referred to as marking on-the-fly.

8 In the **Antron Brown** clip, rate this portion as a Favorite by clicking the Favorite button, or pressing F.

The green Favorite line appears in the clip over the selected range. This is one way you can always see or easily return to the portion of the clip you liked.

9 In the Event Browser, mark selections for the two following clips. After you mark one clip, remember to save that range as a Favorite so you can return to that portion and later edit it into your project.

John Force—"There's nothing like….greatest feeling in the world." Then press F to save that portion as a Favorite.

Tony Pedregon—"The breed of the drag racer…has no fear." Press F to save this portion as a Favorite.

TIP ▶ Although keywords applied within a clip may overlap, ratings may not. Marking a new Favorite that overlaps a previously marked Favorite results in one big Favorite.

Rating selections as Favorites is a good workflow to preserve and prepare potential sound bites for editing. But another approach is to simply mark one or more selections within a single clip. In Lesson 2, you saw that Final Cut Pro remembers multiple selections while importing from an SD cards. It works similarly while screening and marking a clip in the Event Browser. You'll begin by marking a single sound bite.

10 Play the **Tony Schumacher** clip. Use the I and O keys to mark a range around Tony saying "Nobody wakes up and thinks…average my whole life." Do not press F.

NOTE ▶ Make sure you read through the next few steps before marking a second selection. If you press the I or O key at this point, it would *replace* the previous selection you made, not add to it.

This is a great comment and one you will most likely want to use in the *Zero to Hero* project. But you might find other comments in this clip that are equally useful. As you continue to screen this clip, you can mark another comment without losing this selected range.

11 Continue playing the **Tony Schumacher** clip, and listen for when Tony talks about dreaming of the monster moment. Skim or position the playhead to just before Tony says, "People dream for that massive…."

You've already marked one selection in this clip that you don't want to lose. To add this second sound bite as an additional selection, you must use two modifier keys along with the I or O key.

12 To set an additional range, start in the already marked **Tony Schumacher** clip, and press Shift-Command-I.

TIP Another way to create an additional range selection is to Command-drag the clip's filmstrip or thumbnail.

The start of a second range appears. As expected, this new range automatically extends to the end of the clip. Let's find a more precise end point after Tony's killer statement.

13 Play or skim the clip and position the playhead after Tony says, "…big monster moment." Press Shift-Command-O.

Now you have two range selections within a single clip. Depending on the workflow you choose, you can continue screening and marking other clips before editing either selection. Let's select a different clip and return to this one later.

14 In the Event Browser, select the **Tony Pedregon** clip, and then reselect the **Tony Schumacher** clip by clicking in the middle of the clip between the two selections. Notice that both selections are still present. Click inside the first selection.

Clip selections are persistent. That is, they remain with the clip until you manually remove one or more of them. You can highlight a single range selection by clicking inside it, or select multiple ranges by using a modifier key.

15 Command-click inside the second range to add it to the selection. Command-click the first range to exclude it from the selection. Then Command-click it to add it again. With both range selections active, press F to make these selections Favorites.

Just as you can have multiple selections in a single clip, you can also create multiple favorites at one time from highlighted or active selections.

TIP To remove a range selection, click inside it to select it, and then press Option-X to clear it, or Option-click the range.

Appending Clips in the Timeline

A flexible feature of Final Cut Pro is the ability to mark many Favorites before editing, as you did in the previous exercise. Or, you can mark one clip, edit it into the project, and then you select and mark the next clip, edit it, and so on. Whichever approach you take, you have several methods for editing a source clip into a project.

One option is to simply add or *append* the clip to the end of the storyline immediately after the last clip you edited. When you're building a rough cut, as you're doing in this lesson, adding or appending clips is often the simplest approach to creating your primary storyline. Every project is based on a primary storyline. In this exercise, you will use the append edit option to edit the Favorite portions of the racers' clips you marked in the previous exercise. You'll also take a closer look at some of the Timeline functions.

1 To view just the Favorite selections of the racers, in the Event Browser click the Filters pop-up, and choose Favorites, or press Control-F.

Although just four racers are featured, five clips are displayed. This is because you marked two portions of the **Tony Schumacher** clip as a Favorite. Those two ranges appear separately in this filtered Favorites view.

For now, let's add these clips to the project in the order they appear in the Event Browser. Later you can rearrange them in the Timeline.

2 In the Event Browser, select the **Antron Brown** clip.

Because you are viewing only the Favorites, the portion of the clip you previously rated as a Favorite is selected. To add this clip to your project, you will use the append function.

3 In the toolbar, click the Append button.

The **Antron Brown** clip is edited into the dark gray area in the middle of the Timeline. This is where you will build your primary storyline, which, like the storyline of a book, is the main plot of your project. It drives the story you are telling with video and audio. For now, the append function simply adds the **Antron Brown** clip as the first clip of this story. Now you are ready to add your second Favorite clip to the Timeline.

TIP If you do not choose to use Favorites as part of your workflow, you can mark a range selection within a clip, select that range, and click the Append button to edit that portion of the clip into a project.

4 In the Event Browser, select the **John Force** clip. To review the Favorite portion, press the / (slash) key.

Now let's switch to the Timeline to see where this clip will be edited. As you switch from one window to the next, a few things will change in the interface. Let's examine those changes so you will always know which is the active window.

5 To select the Timeline, choose Window > Go to Timeline, or press Command-2. To select the Event Browser, choose Window > Go to Event Browser, or press

Command-1. Use these shortcuts to continue switching between the two windows and notice the changes in the following areas of the interface:

- Viewer image and name
- Dashboard
- Event Browser and Timeline background color
- Selected range color
- Rating buttons

Rating buttons with Event Browser active

Rating buttons with Timeline active

When the Timeline window is active, the image of the project clip appears in the Viewer along with the project name. The Timeline timecode is displayed in the Dashboard, and the Rating buttons are dimmed. The recently selected clip, **John Force**, remains selected in the Event Browser but the selection outline is now gray and not yellow.

Selected clip in inactive window

When the Event Browser window is active, the **John Force** clip selection outline returns to yellow and appears in the Viewer along with the clip name. The Rating buttons in the toolbar are active. Also, in each case, the active window's background is a lighter gray than an inactive window.

Selected clip in active window

Before you edit the **John Force** clip, let's take a closer look at how the append edit works.

6 To switch to the Timeline, press Command-2, and then press the Home key to move the playhead to the start of the clip. Play the clip from the beginning, but stop playback after Antron says, "take the Wally home." Leave the playhead in the middle of the clip.

NOTE ▸ The Wally is the trophy awarded to winners of an NHRA national event. It's named after the late NHRA founder, Wally Parks.

The toolbar has three edit buttons: Connect, Insert, and Append. Clicking each button performs a different type of edit. When you used append earlier, the function itself did not appear all that special; however, it really is significant. An append edit places the clip at the end of the primary storyline no matter where the playhead is positioned. (You will learn about the other edits later in this lesson.)

7 To edit the selected **John Force** clip to the Timeline, click the Append button in the toolbar, and watch where Final Cut Pro places the clip in the Timeline.

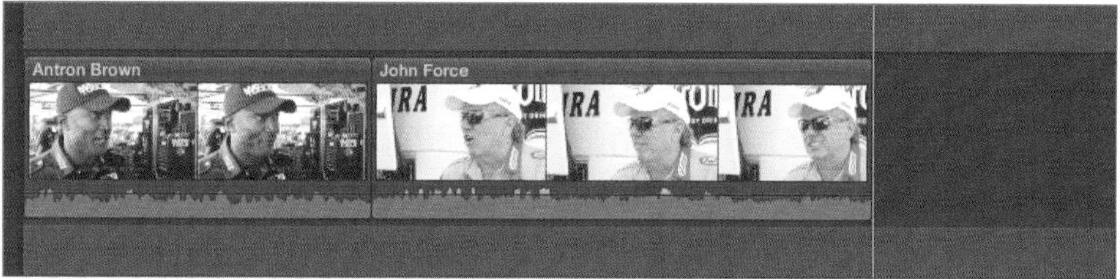

Even though the Timeline playhead was in the middle of the **Antron Brown** clip, Final Cut Pro appended the new clip to the end of the storyline. By using the append edit, you can very quickly add clips to your primary storyline.

TIP ▸ The Append function is further defined as adding source clips to the end of the primary or selected storyline.

Let's add the third clip using the append edit keyboard shortcut.

8 In the Event Browser, select the **Tony Pedregon** clip. To review it, press the / (slash) key. To append the clip to your project, press E.

When you take the time to select a Favorite range in each of your clips, as you've done with these interview clips, you can move the editing process along even faster by appending more than one clip at the same time. In fact, Final Cut Pro can append any number of selected clips, or marked selections, in one step.

NOTE ▶ If you want to change the order of the clips in your project, you can easily rearrange the clips in the Timeline. You will do this later in the lesson.

9 In the Event Browser, drag a selection rectangle around the two **Tony Schumacher** clips to select them. To append these two clips to the storyline, press E.

Both clips are added to the end of the project in the order they appear in the Event Browser. If you Command-click to select multiple clips, they are added in the order that you clicked them.

TIP You can edit multiple range selections from one or more clips in the same way. Select the range selections you want to edit, and then click the Append button, or press E. The selected ranges will be edited in the order they appear.

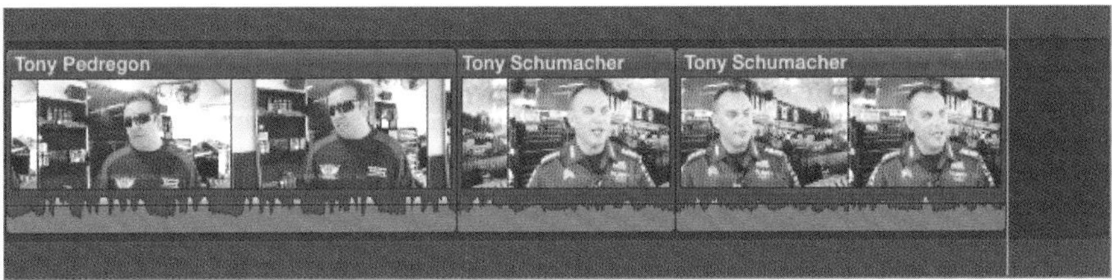

To become more comfortable viewing your current project in the Timeline, let's change the Timeline view and look at some of the Timeline buttons.

10 To fit all the project clips in the Timeline, make the Timeline window active, and press Shift-Z. To play the project, press Home and then press the Spacebar, or the L key. Remember that pressing the Up and Down Arrow keys moves the playhead backward or forward to the beginnings of clips.

Zooming your Timeline with the Shift-Z shortcut is like performing a "Zoom to fit" command. It will either stretch or shrink your clip display so the entire Timeline window is filled with all the clips in the project.

In the upper-right corner of the Timeline, you'll find three buttons that control how you skim through clips, including one that allows you to snap to clips as you skim.

11 Move your pointer *slowly* over the edit point between the **Antron Brown** and **John Force** clips. Notice that the skimmer *snaps* to that edit point. In the upper right of the Timeline, click the Snapping button, or press N, and then move across the edit point once again. Notice that there is no longer a pull toward the edit point.

Snapping selected

With snapping enabled, the skimmer easily aligns or snaps to the edit point and, when at the edit point, turns yellow as a visual cue.

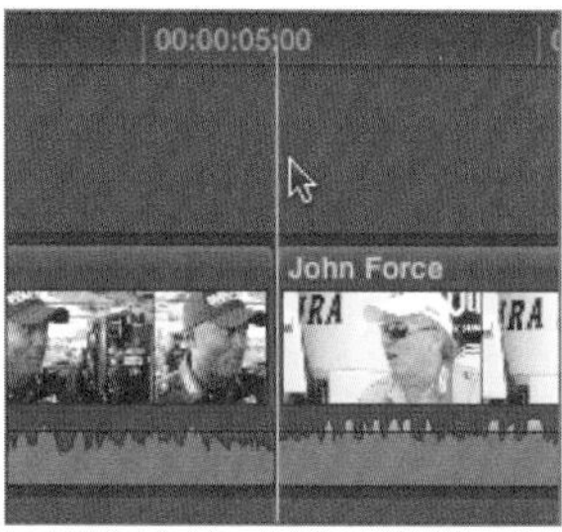

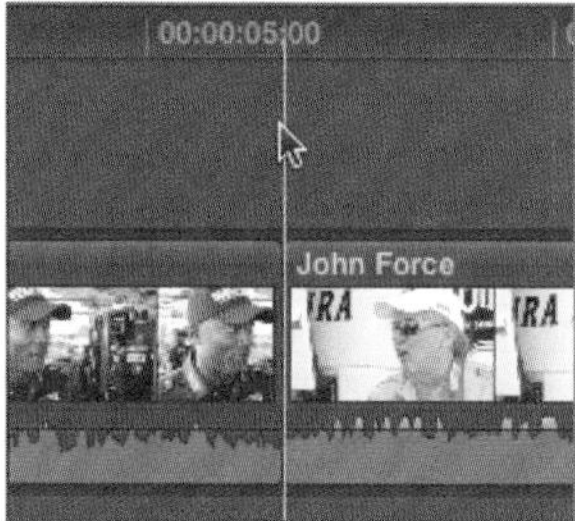

NOTE ▶ The Snapping button also controls snapping in the Event Browser.

Both the Event Browser and the Timeline have a playhead and a skimmer. In the Timeline, the playhead and skimmer produce two different yet overlapping results.

12 Skim through the clips in the Timeline and notice that you are skimming the audio as well as the video. Then drag the playhead from the top of its stem through the clips.

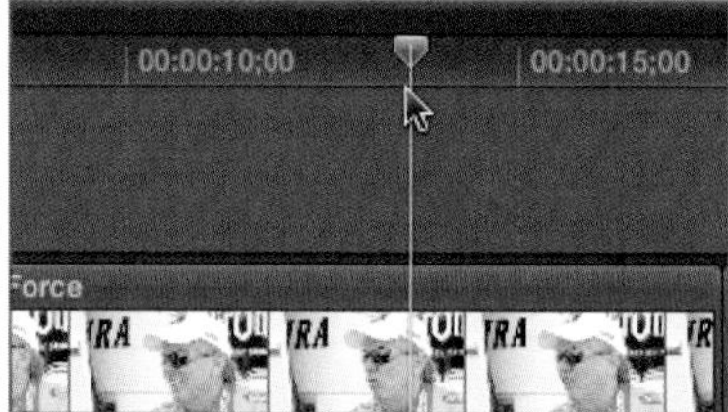

Dragging the playhead through the project does not preview the audio as skimming a clip does.

13 Click the second button, Audio Skimming, to deselect it. Skim through the clips in the Timeline, and then skim through the clips in the Event Browser.

With audio skimming disabled, you no longer hear the clips as you skim through them. Earlier in this lesson, you chose Skimming, Audio Skimming, and Snapping from the View menu. These are the same options controlled by these Timeline buttons. Selecting these options in the Timeline also affects how you view the clips in the Event Browser.

TIP ▶ The third button allows you to solo, or isolate, a clip. You will learn the use of this button in a later lesson.

At times during editing, you may want to edit using only the playhead. If you don't want the skimmer to follow your every move, you can deselect the Skimming button.

14 In the Timeline, deselect the first button, Skimming. When you try to skim through the clips in the Timeline or the Event Browser, you can't. In the Timeline, return the buttons to their active state by selecting all but the third button.

NOTE ▶ When both skimming and audio skimming are enabled, deselecting the Skimming button will deselect audio skimming as well.

Viewing and Arranging Clips in the Magnetic Timeline

Once you've edited clips and viewed their placement relative to each other, you may decide that you can improve your story by changing the clip order. With the Magnetic Timeline, you can easily drag a clip to a different location and let Final Cut Pro automatically create a space for the clip by shifting the other clips. In this exercise, you will change the order of the clips to improve the racing story. You will also employ the Timeline Index to see the list of clips in your project, and learn additional methods to change the way you view clips in the Timeline. Let's start by enlarging the clip thumbnails in the Timeline.

1 In the lower-right corner of the Timeline, click the Clip Appearance button. Click through the six buttons, and then click the fifth button from the left to create larger thumbnails. Drag the Clip Height slider to a middle position.

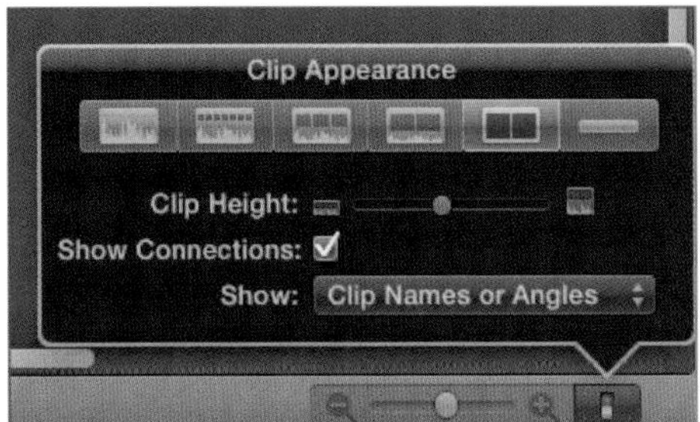

Each time you click a button, the clips in the Timeline change appearance. Sometimes, clip appearance is a personal choice. Depending on where you are in your editing workflow, however, it may be helpful to choose a particular view of your clips. For this exercise, you simply want to see the individual racers clearly, and you're less concerned with audio waveforms.

Before you change the position of the clips in the graphical Timeline layout, let's look at how they appear in a list.

2 In the lower-left corner of the Timeline, next to the Project Library button, click the Timeline Index button, or press Command-Shift-2.

The Timeline Index pane appears to the left of the Timeline. Clips and tags (such as keywords) in the current project are listed here in their order of appearance. The

Timeline Index provides a textual way to navigate your project. A gray highlight bar indicates the clip that is currently selected in the Timeline.

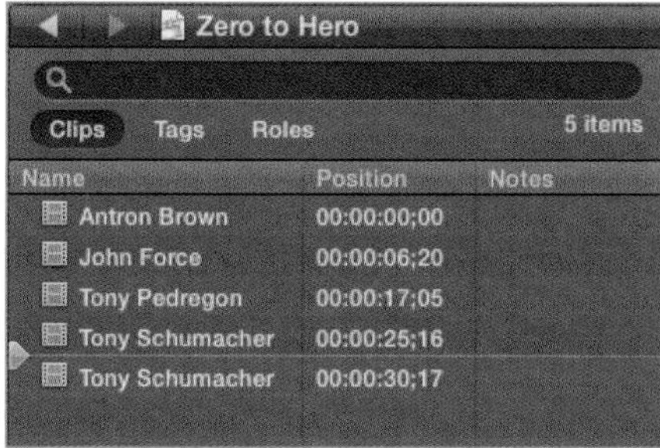

3 At the top of the pane, click Clips, if it's not already selected. Beneath the list of clips, select All. Then select the **Antron Brown** clip at the top of the list.

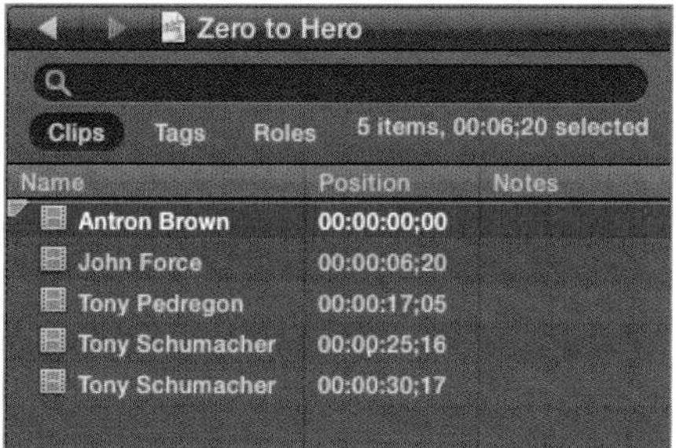

The number to the right of each clip indicates the timecode location in the project where the clip begins. Above the list of clips, you can read the number of items in the project and the duration of the selected item(s).

4 In the Timeline, select the **John Force** clip. In the Timeline Index, notice that this clip is also highlighted. In the Index, select the **Tony Pedregon** clip. In the Timeline, that clip is selected.

TIP If opening the Timeline Index caused some of the clips to go out of view, press Shift-Z again.

The Timeline Index is a great tool to help find clips and other items in your project. Although this project is small, it still provides a good opportunity to see how the Index works.

5 In the Timeline, drag the playhead through multiple clips, and watch what happens in the Index. In the Timeline, drag the playhead between the **Antron Brown** and **John Force** clips.

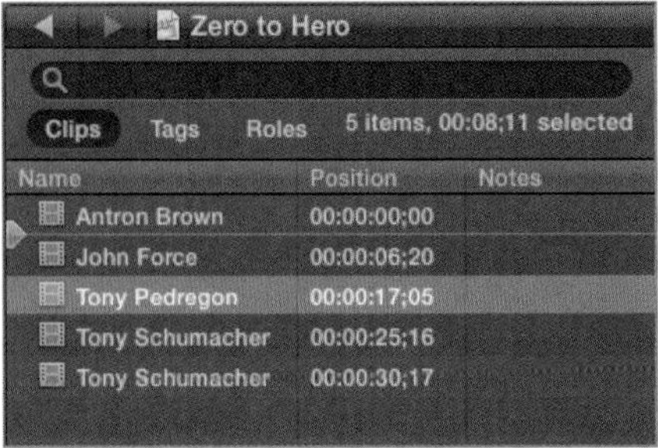

In the Index, the playhead appears horizontally and moves up and down through the clips as you drag the playhead vertically through the Timeline. You can leave the Timeline Index open as you rearrange the clips in the project.

NOTE ▶ You will explore other ways to view the Timeline Index in later exercises.

6 In the Timeline, play the first **Tony Schumacher** clip in which he says, "Nobody wakes up and thinks, 'You know, gosh, I hope I'm just average my whole life.'"

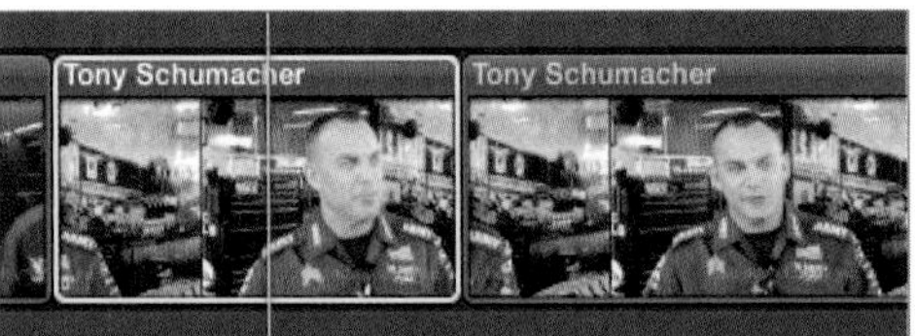

This dynamic line could really kick off the project with a lot of energy. Let's move it to the beginning of the sequence of clips.

TIP ▶ To perform these steps, make sure that the default Select tool is chosen in the tool list.

7 Drag the first **Tony Schumacher** clip left to the head of the project. Before you release it, notice the blue insertion line where you will place the clip. When you see the

remaining clips reposition themselves, release the pointer to place the clip at this location. Then play the first few clips of the project.

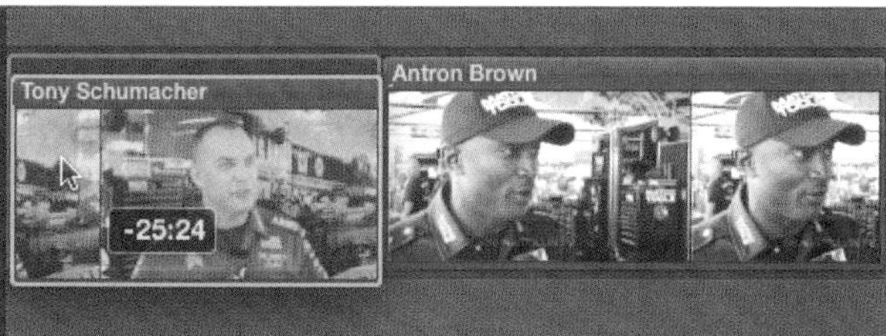

As promised, this clip gives the project a fiery start. In the Timeline Index, notice how the clip appears at the top of the list. Now let's bring Tony Pedregon into the second clip position.

8 Drag the **Tony Pedregon** clip to follow the first clip. When you see the blue insertion line and the other clips scoot aside, release the pointer. Play the first two clips.

When you drag a clip in the Timeline, a numerical value appears, indicating the length of time and in which direction you are repositioning the clip.

While the remaining clips could be reordered in a variety of ways, let's leave them in the order they appear: **Antron Brown**, **John Force**, and the second **Tony Schumacher** clip.

9 To close the Timeline Index, click the Timeline Index button, or press Command-Shift-2.

In the next exercise, you will insert some B-roll racing clips into this project. You may want to create additional room in the Timeline for the new material.

10 In the Timeline, press the Home key to position the playhead at the beginning of the project. Then move the skimmer to the middle of the Timeline. Press Command-- (minus) a few times to zoom out and press Command-= (equals) several times to zoom in to the clips.

The more you zoom in, the wider the clip and skimmer become and the more clip thumbnails you can see. Only the visual representation of each clip changes, not the clip length or duration. Also, the zooming occurs around the skimmer location as long as skimming is enabled. When skimming is disabled, zooming occurs around the playhead position.

You can also zoom in and out of the clips by dragging the Zoom control in the Timeline.

11 In the lower-right corner of the Timeline, drag the Zoom control to the left to zoom out, and then to the right to zoom in on the clips. To prepare for the next edits, settle on leaving about a third of the Timeline empty.

TIP If you are using a mouse with a scroll ball, you can scroll through project clips by moving the scroll ball left or right. You can also swipe two fingers across a Multi-Touch trackpad to scroll through a Timeline.

Inserting Clips into the Primary Storyline

You have added clips to the Timeline to build your rough cut. Like any rough cut, this one is a work in progress. So far, you've laid a strong foundation by editing and then reordering the interview clips that give this project its face, personality, and energy. Now it's time to insert other shots that show or demonstrate more of the racers' story and passion.

But rather than append these clips to the end of the project, you will use the insert edit to place, or insert, them between existing clips in the primary storyline. When you insert a clip, a space for the new clip opens up in the storyline similar to the way the clips opened up when you repositioned them using the Magnetic Timeline.

In this exercise, you will work with media from the *B-Roll* Keyword Collection. In Lesson 2, Final Cut Pro used the existing media folder structure for that project to create a Keyword Collection of clips that were already organized in a B-Roll folder. Let's start by picking three shots to mark and insert into this rough cut.

1 In the Event Library, select the *B-Roll* Keyword Collection. In the Event Browser, from the Filter pop-up menu, choose All Clips. Take a moment to change the thumbnail view so that all clips are visible in the Event Browser.

   When you first select the *B-Roll* Keyword Collection, no clips appear in the Event Browser because the Favorites filter is still active from the previous exercises. By choosing All Clips, you can see all the B-Roll clips in this collection.

NOTE ▶ You may wish to momentarily set the clip height to a smaller setting in order to see all of the clip thumbnails. The Clip Height setting is available by clicking the Clip Appearance button to the lower-right of the Event Browser.

As you look at the clip thumbnails, you will see a few audio-only clips. You won't be inserting audio clips at the moment, so let's hide those audio clips by choosing a media file type in the Filters window.

2 In the search field, click the Filter (magnifying glass) button to open the Filter window, or press Command-F. From the Add Rule pop-up menu, choose Media Type. Then, in the Media Type rule entry, from the Type pop-up menu, choose Video With Audio.

NOTE ▶ You can leave the Text entry selected because the Text field is empty and will not impact the search.

Only those clips that have both video and audio now appear in the Event Browser. In the search field, notice the filmstrip icon that indicates that a search is active based on media type.

To help place your audience at the scene, let's find some racing and crowd shots to insert into this project.

3 Close the Filter window. In the Event Browser, skim the **wall low angle** clip. To select the action portion of this clip, drag a selection from the head of the clip to the point where both cars are out of frame, at about 1:28 in the clip. Use the Viewer as a guide.

TIP ▶ If the entire clip is already selected, deselect it by clicking the selection, and then choose Mark > Clear Selected Ranges, or press Option-X. You can also Option-drag anywhere in the clip to create a new selection.

You could edit this selection immediately, but to preserve the range of this material for later use, rate it as a Favorite.

4 To rate the selected clip range as a Favorite, click the Favorite button, or press F.

TIP ▶ Remember you can press Shift-I or Shift-O to move the playhead to the range start or end points, finesse the range by pressing the Left or Right Arrow keys or J-K-L, and reset the start or end points by pressing I or O.

5 Skim through the **crowd ots** clip. To select the latter part of this clip, press I to set the start point when the red racing lights come on, just before the man with a camera turns. Press F to rate this selection as a Favorite.

When you set a start point by itself, a selection automatically appears from the start point to the end of the clip. Likewise, when you set a single end point, the selection appears from the head of the clip to the end point.

NOTE ▶ OTS stands for *over the shoulder*. It's used to identify a shot that shows a point-of-view perspective, as though you were looking over a viewer's shoulder. In this shot, you are seeing the race track from the crowd's perspective.

6 Skim the **crowd wide** clip. Notice everyone in the crowd moves their heads together at the same time. Mark a start point before the heads turn, and press F to rate the selection from here to the end as a Favorite.

7 To view the Favorites you just created, from the Filters pop-up menu, choose Favorites.

The three Favorite selections you just created appear. Now that they are marked, it's easy to insert them anywhere in the project. To set the stage for this project, let's insert them at the beginning. To do this, you must first specify the edit location.

8 Press Command-2 to switch to the Timeline, and press the Home key to move the playhead to the beginning of the project. Make sure the skimmer is not in a different location.

NOTE ▶ When you press the Home key, it moves both the skimmer and playhead to the beginning of the project. If you skim away from the playhead location into other clips, and make an insert edit, the edit will be performed at the skimmer location.

To review, an append edit automatically places a clip at the end of a storyline no matter where the playhead is located. For insert and connect edits, you must first position the playhead or skimmer where you want to place the clip.

9 In the Event Browser, select the **wall low angle** clip. In the toolbar, click the Insert button. Then play the first few clips.

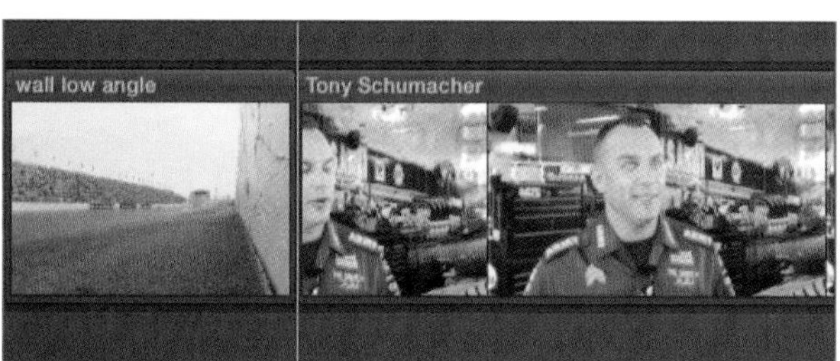

In the Timeline, the **wall low angle** clip now appears before the **Tony Schumacher** clip.

10 In the Timeline, snap the playhead between the first two clips. In the Event Browser, select the **crowd ots** clip, and click the Insert button, or press W.

After you perform any type of edit in the Timeline, the playhead repositions to the end of the newly edited clip. If you want to insert a shot to follow the clip you just edited, the playhead is already in position.

11 To insert the **crowd ws** clip as the third clip, select it in the Event Browser, and press the insert edit keyboard shortcut, W.

TIP As with append editing, you can also insert edit a group of selected clips or marked selections at one time.

Take 2

The producer of your project is old school and remembers the good old days of drag-and-drop editing. She says she doesn't trust an editing system where you can't drag and drop. Although you enjoy the ease of using keyboard shortcuts to make your edits, you know it's also possible to drag a clip from the Event Browser directly into the Timeline at the desired edit point. You ease the producer's worries and perform a drag-and-drop edit by following these steps:

TIP Make sure snapping is enabled for these steps.

- In the Timeline, zoom the project so you can see the last clip.
- In the Event Browser, from the Filter pop-up menu, choose All Clips.
- Select the **smokey banner** clip in its entirety.
- Drag the **smokey banner** clip into the Timeline and snap it to the end of the **Tony Schumacher** clip. Look for the blue insertion line before releasing the pointer.

NOTE ▶ With drag-and-drop editing, you needn't drag the playhead to where you're focused, and click a button in the toolbar. You can simply rely on your eyes to target the new location and manually drag the clip directly to where you want it in the storyline.

Changing Edited Clips

Once you've edited several clips into your primary storyline, you may be distracted by one clip that's too yellow or another clip that's too loud. There are stages during the editing workflow when you will correct all of the color problems or perfectly blend each audio clip. But for now, you just want to view the project without cranking up the volume control or checking to see if you're wearing amber sunglasses.

As you learned in Lesson 2, you can access the Inspector window to view video or audio information about your clip. In this exercise, you will use the Inspector to make a few adjustments that will make viewing your project more pleasant. This is an important part of building a rough cut. Although you aren't making final changes, you are tweaking the Timeline to determine whether or not the clips you've edited are effectively telling your story. Let's start by adjusting the Timeline view.

1 In the Timeline, click the Clip Appearance button and click the third thumbnail button. Then drag the Clip Height control to make the clips taller.

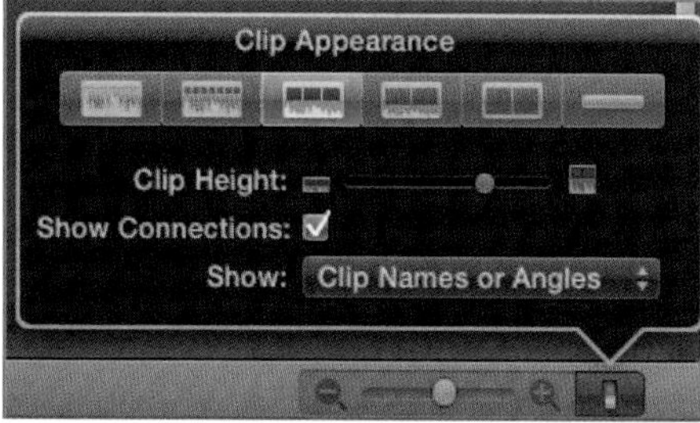

With this clip appearance option chosen, the clip waveform appears beneath the video thumbnails. This makes it easy to see which clips need an audio boost and which are already raising the roof.

TIP Since you will be skimming a few loud clips, you may want to disable audio skimming by deselecting that button in the Timeline, or pressing Shift-S.

2 Skim to the first clip and press Command-= (equals) to zoom in to this area. Then play the first three clips in the project and watch the waveforms as they play.

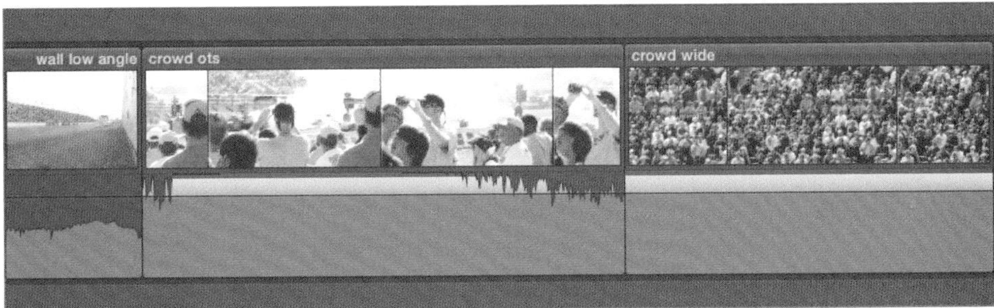

Notice that the first clip's audio waveform is shaded blue and falls safely beneath the horizontal audio volume line. The waveforms of the second and third clips, however, go above the volume line; those portions of the waveforms appear yellow and red. You can easily lower the volume of these two clips in the Timeline.

TIP In the waveforms, yellow indicates audio levels approaching peak levels, whereas red indicates peaked audio. You'll learn more about peaking in Lesson 8; but for now, know that red is too loud.

3 In the Timeline, move your pointer into the **crowd ots** clip and position it over the volume line. When it turns into a vertical resize pointer, notice the 0 dB info flag, and then drag down until the waveform is at a similar level to the first clip.

NOTE ▶ The abbreviation dB means *decibels*, the unit of measurement for audio volume.

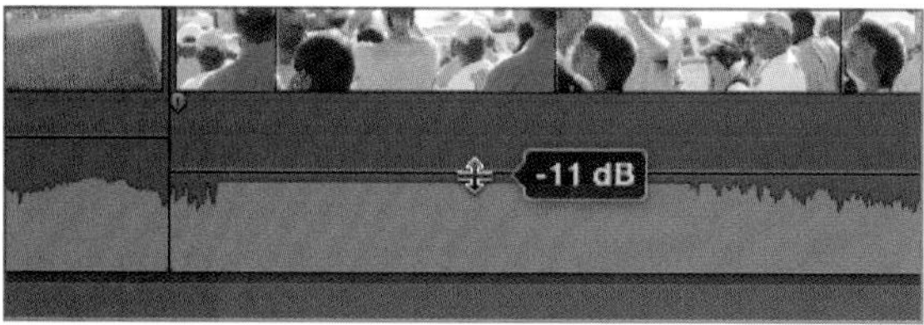

TIP If the skimmer gets in the way of adjusting the volume line, deselect the Skimming button in the Timeline, or press S.

When you lower the volume of the **crowd ots** clip, the waveform no longer displays yellow areas or red peaks. But notice that the top portion of this clip is flat. When the audio was originally recorded at the racing location, the loudness of the race caused the audio to *clip*.

4 In the **crowd wide** clip, drag the volume line down to match the first two clips. Play these clips in the Timeline. To enable skimming again, press S.

NOTE ▶ Remember, the dB number you see in the Level field represents a change of volume up or down relative to the original sound level of this clip.

Now when you play these clips, you can get a better idea of whether their audio content will work in the project.

5 Skim to the fourth clip, **Tony Schumacher**, and play it. Then click above that clip to move the playhead to this location. Notice that the background sounds of the shop are too loud, and the video has a yellow tint. Leave the playhead over the clip so you can see it in the Viewer.

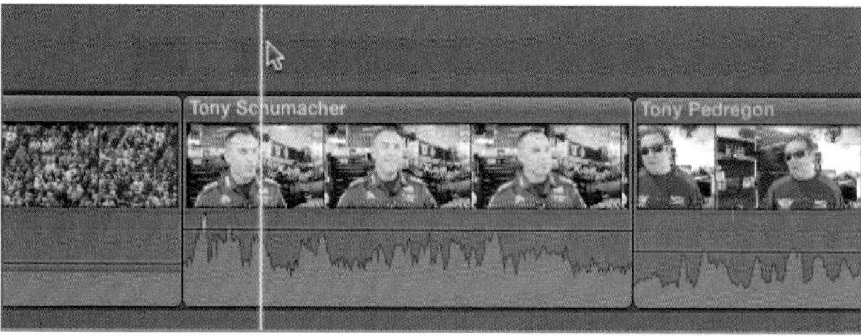

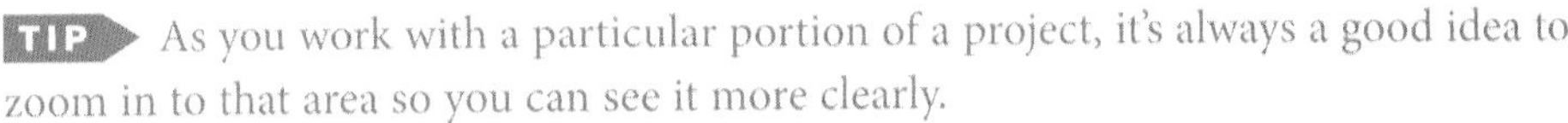
TIP As you work with a particular portion of a project, it's always a good idea to zoom in to that area so you can see it more clearly.

This type of show is often shot under extreme conditions where you have to grab a few minutes with a racer whenever you can, no matter what's going on around him. You may not have time to color balance the camera or ask everyone to leave the shop and reduce the background noise. Final Cut Pro can help in both situations. To get a closer look at this clip's properties, let's open the Inspector.

6 In the toolbar, click the Inspector button, and then click the Video tab at the top of the window. In the Color section, select the checkbox next to Balance, and notice how the clip changes in the Viewer.

By selecting Balance, Final Cut Pro automatically color balances this clip, pulling out the yellow cast, and making it look much more pleasing.

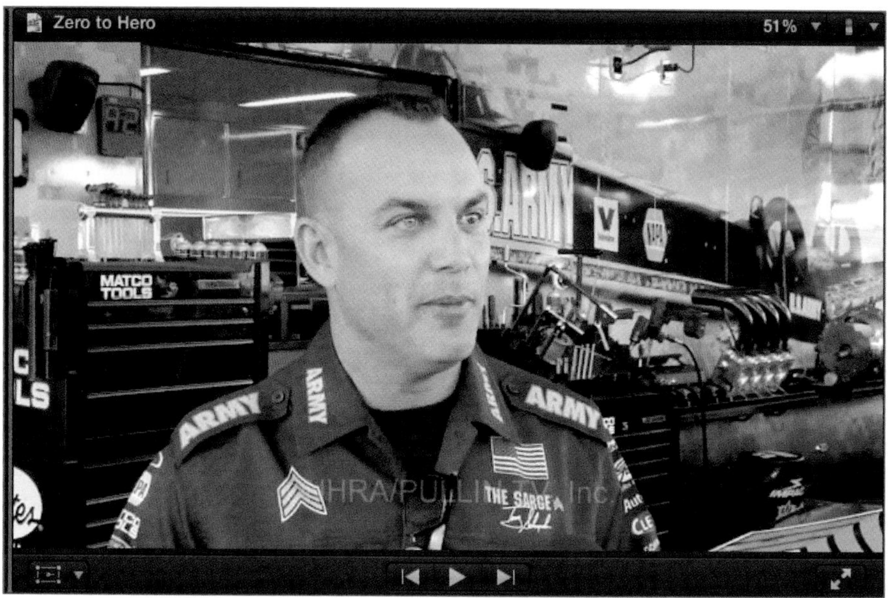

One of the uses of the playhead is to park it to identify a location, like a bookmark, and hold that place while you skim to look for other content. In this situation, it would be nice to compare the **Tony Schumacher** clip you just color balanced with the clip featuring Tony later in the project.

7 With the playhead parked over the first **Tony Schumacher** clip, skim down to the second **Tony Schumacher** clip to compare the clips. Then skim back to the playhead location.

In the Inspector, you can also adjust the volume of the selected clip as well as mute individual channels.

8 In the Inspector, click the Audio tab and look for the Channel Configuration section towards the bottom of the Inspector. Make sure the Channel Configuration area displays four mono channels. If it doesn't, click the disclosure triangle next to the clip's name.

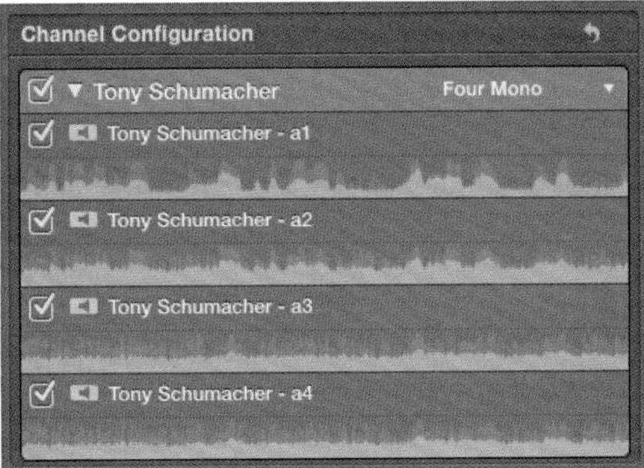

This clip has four audio channels. For this shoot, a lavaliere microphone recorded two channels of Tony's interview, and another microphone recorded two channels of ambient sound from the shop. By deselecting each channel, you can identify which is which.

9 In the Timeline, play the first **Tony Schumacher** clip, and as it plays, deselect the third and fourth mono audio channels in the Inspector window.

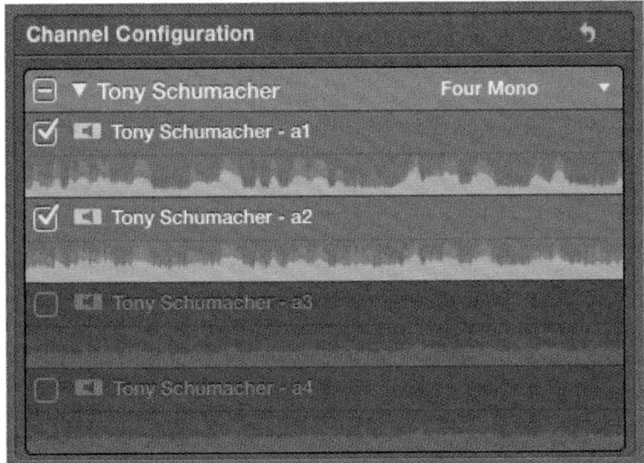

NOTE ► If your pointer is over an audio channel in the Inspector when you press the spacebar, you will hear only that source channel play and not the Timeline clip.

The lower two channels contain the background ambient noise from the shop. By deselecting these channels, you can hear Tony's interview more clearly.

Now let's adjust the clip volume in the Inspector.

10 In the Timeline, click above the **Tony Pedregon** clip and look at the top of the Inspector window to see the clip name change.

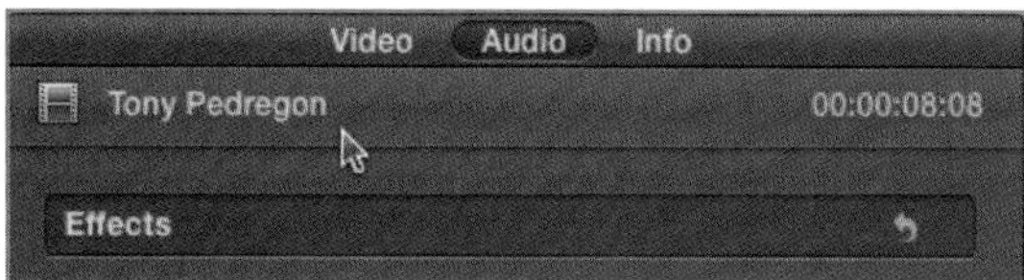

TIP You can also Option-click a project clip to simultaneously select the clip and cue the playhead to that location.

The Inspector window displays the selected clip's properties, whether that clip is from the Timeline or the Event Browser.

11 Play this clip and deselect the third and fourth mono channels. Then select them again.

In this clip, deselecting and turning off these channels leaves the clip sounding a little tinny. Leaving them turned on gives the clip a fuller sound, but also raises the overall volume.

12 In the Inspector window, drag the Volume slider to the left until the clip waveform in the Timeline no longer has yellow areas or red peaks. Then close the Inspector. Now the clip plays at a lower volume.

Connecting Clips to the Primary Storyline

As you build your rough cut, you may find that adding audio—such as narration, music, or sound effects—improves your storyline. For example, it might be nice to add music to help build momentum in the *Zero to Hero* project. But which edit option do you choose? You wouldn't append music to the end of the clips. And you wouldn't insert it between clips. Instead, you use another edit option in the toolbar to *connect* the clip to the primary storyline.

A connected clip could be any clip that is attached to the primary storyline in the Timeline. Connected clips remain attached where you edit them until you move or remove them. In this exercise, you will filter the *Zero to Hero* B-roll clips so that only the audio clips appear, and then connect a music clip to your video sequence and adjust its position in the primary storyline.

TIP If necessary, press Shift-Z to view all the clips in the Timeline.

1 In the Event Browser, from the Filter pop-up menu, choose All. Press Command-F to open the Filter window. From the Media Type pop-up menu, choose Audio Only. Close the Filter window.

TIP You could also open the Filter window by clicking the search field when a search rule, such as the media type icon, is present.

You now see just the audio clips that are part of the *B-Roll* Keyword Collection. Since audio clips have no thumbnails, let's view them as a list.

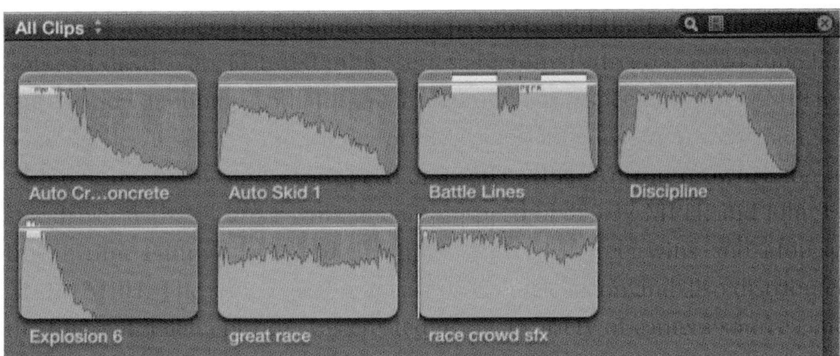

2 In the Event Browser, click the List View button. Then play the first part of the **Battle Lines** music clip. Viewing this clip in list view provides an expanded view of the waveform.

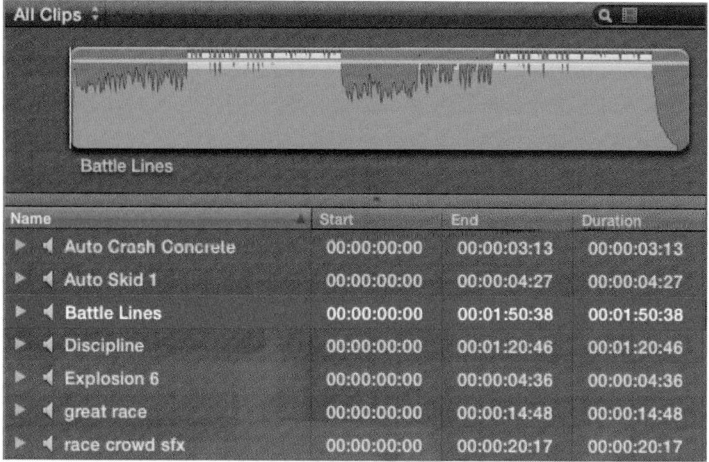

3 To edit the first half of this clip, mark a start point just before the music begins, and an end point after the first series of waveform peaks.

TIP With audio skimming selected, you can press the Left and Right Arrow keys to find the exact music start.

In the clip waveform display, notice that some of the upper parts of the waveform appear yellow and some appear red, indicating that the audio may be peaking at 0 dB. As you know from the previous exercise, you can easily adjust the volume of this clip in the Timeline.

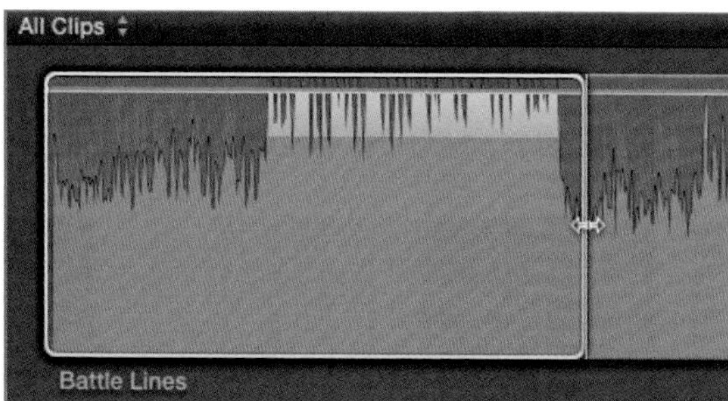

You could start this music at the head of the project. But it might be more fun to let the two race cars zoom by and then begin the music.

4 To make the Timeline window active, press Command-2. Press the Up or Down Arrow key to move the playhead to the beginning of the **crowd ots** clip.

As with the insert edit, when you edit a connecting clip, Final Cut Pro always places the clip at the skimmer or playhead location.

5 In the toolbar, click the Connect button, or press the connect edit keyboard shortcut, Q. In the Timeline, play the first few clips, and then look at the thin vertical line connecting the **Battle Lines** music to the **crowd ots** clip.

By performing a connect edit, you connected the music to the primary storyline at the playhead location. Let's see what happens when you reposition this clip.

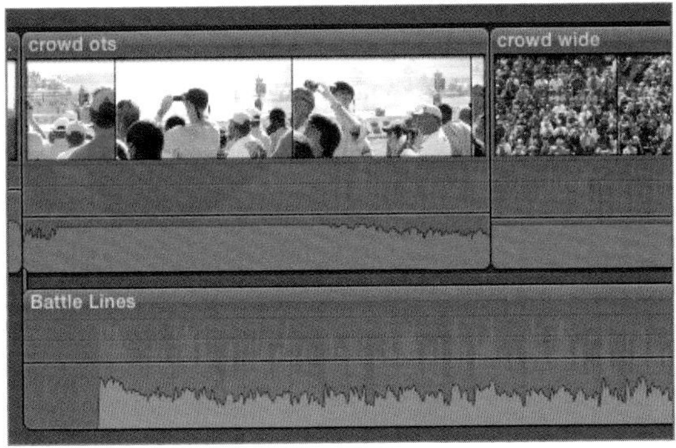

6 Drag the **crowd ots** clip to the right and reposition it after the **crowd wide** clip. Play this arrangement, and then drag the clip back to its original position.

When you move the **crowd ots** clip, the music travels along because it is connected to the clip you're dragging.

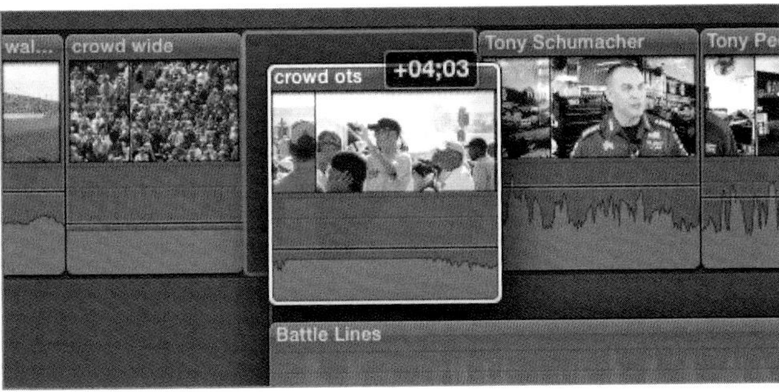

But just because you started a connection with one clip doesn't mean you have to keep that connection. By dragging the music later in the Timeline, you can connect it to a different clip.

7 Drag the **Battle Lines** clip to the right and snap it to the head of the first **Tony Schumacher** clip. Notice that when you snap it to this edit point the playhead turns thick and yellow.

As you drag this connected clip, the thin vertical connection line relinks with another clip in the Timeline, in this case, the **Tony Schumacher** clip.

8 Play the first few clips of the project.

Now the music provides a very dynamic start to the interview clips. However, you are not limited to snapping a connected clip to an edit point. You can also shift the position of the clip left or right. You can do this by using shortcut keys to shift the clip one frame at a time, 10 frames at a time, or by entering a numerical length of time.

9 With the **Battle Lines** clip selected, press the , (comma) key several times to move the clip to the left in one-frame increments. Then press the . (period) key to move the clip to the right in one-frame increments. Press Shift-, (comma) to move the clip to the left 10 frames, or press Shift-. (period) to move it to the right 10 frames.

TIP The comma key shares the Left Angle Bracket key, and the period key shares the Right Angle Bracket key. It may be helpful to think of moving in the direction these keys point.

Sometimes you can successfully finesse clip placement by adjusting it just a few frames. Other times, you may need to move it a specific amount of time, perhaps to allow for another clip you know will be edited later.

10 With the **Battle Lines** clip still selected, enter *–200*. Look at the Dashboard and notice that the number entry has replaced the timecode location. Press Return or Enter.

When you precede a number amount with a + (plus) or – (minus) sign, Final Cut Pro reads that number as a trim or nudge amount, even adding colons every two digits, and moving the selected clip by that amount.

Editor's Cut

You're now familiar with three types of edits, how to mark clips for editing, and how to customize the Timeline and Event Browser. With this arsenal of knowledge, you can create another rough cut using totally different media. Remember, you are still in the rough cut stage of the editing process.

- To work with new media, in the Project Library, create a new project and name it *I Think.*
- In the Event Library, view the *I Think* clips and edit them in whatever sequence feels natural for you.
- You can connect narration and music clips after you have the video clips in place.

NOTE ▸ Although Final Cut Pro editing functions work the same regardless of the media in use, rehearsing them using different types of media is a good way to hone your editing chops and gain greater control over the tools, functions, and shortcuts.

Closing Your Project

Once you finish working in a project, you may want to close it so that you have a clean slate the next time you open Final Cut Pro.

1 In the Project Library, click the disclosure triangle next to the Lesson 4 folder to hide its contents.

2 Drag the Lesson 4 folder into the Lesson Projects folder beneath the APTS FCP X icon.

TIP Closing a project in this way is a good practice to continue when finishing each lesson.

Lesson Review

1. What methods can you use to create a new project?
2. How do you create an additional range selection in the same clip?
3. What four different methods allow you to edit clips into your project?
4. What is an append edit?
5. How can you zoom in or out of an area of the Timeline?
6. How do you change the display size of the clips in the Timeline?
7. How can you view a list of all clips in the Timeline?
8. How can you quickly adjust a clip's volume in the Timeline?
9. How can you mute specific audio channels for a clip in the Timeline?
10. How can you toggle snapping on or off?
11. When you drag clips to rearrange their positions in the Timeline, what visual indicator shows where the clip will be positioned when you release the pointer?
12. How would you connect music or B-roll to the primary storyline in your Timeline?

Answers

1. Click the New Project (+) button; Control-click a folder or drive and choose New Project from the shortcut menu; or select the target location, and choose File > New Project, or press Command-N.

2. Set a range start and end for one section of the clip, then press Shift-Command-I to start a new range, and Shift-Command-O to set the end of the new range. Another method is to press the Command key and drag a range within a clip's thumbnail or filmstrip.
3. To create an edit, click an edit button in the toolbar; choose an editing command from the Edit menu, such as Append; press a keyboard shortcut; drag a clip from the Event Browser, from a media browser such as the Photos Browser, or from the Finder.
4. An append edit adds one or more clips to the end of a project or selected storyline.
5. Press Command-= (equals) to zoom in, and press Command-– (minus) to zoom out. You can also zoom in and out by dragging the Zoom control in the lower right of the Timeline.
6. Click the Clip Appearance button in the lower-right corner of the Timeline. In the Clip Appearance window, drag the Clip Height slider to the left to decrease the clip height, or to the right to increase the clip height.
7. In the lower-left corner of the Timeline, click the Timeline Index button, or press Command-Shift-2. The Timeline Index pane appears to the left of the Timeline and displays clips, roles, and tags (such as keywords) used in the current project in their order of appearance.
8. Position your pointer over the volume line in the Timeline. When the pointer turns into a vertical resize pointer, drag down to lower the volume or drag up to raise it. Audio that approaches peak levels appears yellow in the waveform; audio that exceeds peak levels appears red.
9. Select the clip in the Timeline, click the Inspector button in the toolbar, and then click the Audio tab and deselect the appropriate channels.
10. Click the Snapping button in the Timeline, press N, or choose View > Snapping.
11. A blue insertion line indicates where clips will be placed.
12. Position the playhead in the Timeline where you want to connect one or more clips. Select the clips in the Event Browser. In the toolbar, click the Connect button, or press Q. In the Timeline, a blue connection line for video or a green connection line for audio indicates the connection point.

Keyboard Shortcuts

N	Turn snapping off and on
Command-N	Create a new project
Control-click	Open a shortcut menu
Command-F	Open the Filter window
, (comma)	Move selection to the left 1 frame
. (period)	Move selection to the right 1 frame
Shift-, (comma)	Move selection to the left 10 frames
Shift-. (period)	Move selection to the right 10 frames
Command-0 (zero)	Open the Project Library
Command-1	Go to the Event Browser
Command-2	Go to the Timeline
Command-Shift-2	Open the Timeline Index
Command-– (minus)	Zoom out of the Timeline, Event Browser, or Viewer
Command-= (equals)	Zoom in to the Timeline, Event Browser, or Viewer
Shift-I	Move the playhead and skimmer to the beginning of the range selection
Shift-O	Move the playhead and skimmer to the end of the range selection
Shift-Z	Zoom the contents to fit the size of the Event Browser, the Viewer, or the Timeline
Shift-S	Toggle audio skimming
Up Arrow	Go to the previous item (in the Event Browser) or the previous edit point (in the Timeline)

Keyboard Shortcuts

Down Arrow	Go to the next item (in the Event Browser) or the next edit point (in the Timeline)
S	Toggle video and audio skimming
Q	Connect to primary storyline
W	Insert into primary or selected storyline
E	Append to primary or selected storyline
F	Rate selection as a Favorite
/ (slash)	Play selection
J	Play reverse
K	Stop
L	Play forward
I	Set range start point
O	Set range end point
Spacebar	Play/pause

5

Time

This lesson takes approximately 75 minutes to complete.

Goals

Add markers to project clips

Connect clips to the primary storyline

Replace clips

Overwrite clips

Audition clips

Create and change new storylines

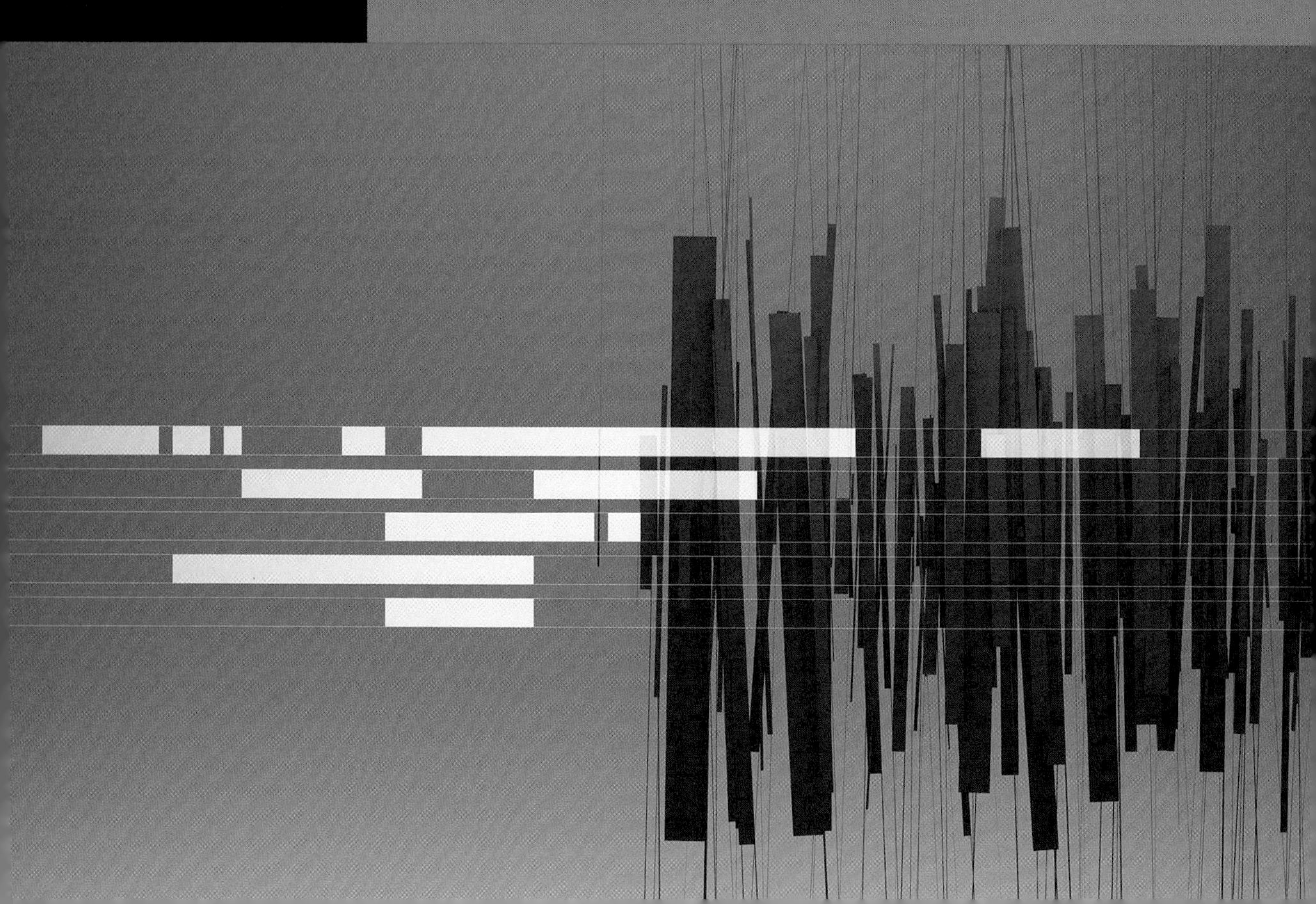

Lesson **5**

Finishing the Rough Cut

Once your primary storyline is under way, you can think about adding material to further develop or finish your story. You may want to connect new clips that refer to, relate to, or synchronize with the clips that are already there. By connecting other visual elements to the primary storyline, you not only create a rich visual fabric, but you weave a more complex and intriguing story.

You can develop and finish your rough cut in several ways, connecting clips to the primary storyline is just one of them. Like a good director, at times you may want to audition clips for a particular section of your project. You could also create additional storylines that connect to the primary storyline.

And if you find that you simply don't like the original clip you edited, you can use the Replace function to remedy the situation. Along the way, you may need to add a gap to improve timing, or mark a project location you want to finesse.

In this lesson, you will explore all of these options as you finish the rough cut you began in Lesson 4. In the process, you will become familiar with new editing concepts and terminology.

Adding Markers to a Project

To tell a story in the most concise way, you often have to edit together one or more *talking head* clips—individuals speaking to the camera—and put them into a logical order. In fact, you already did this while assembling the *Zero to Hero* rough cut in Lesson 4.

But watching the racers talk doesn't paint a complete picture of what racing is like. The solution is to cut away from the racer interviews to show secondary clips of them in action. Clips used in this way are often referred to as *cutaways* and can be found in B-roll collections. In B-roll media, no one talks directly to the camera.

While you have a lot of flexibility when editing B-roll clips, you should also take care to place them strategically so they enhance the primary storyline without covering one of the racers' prime comments, or *sound bites*. In this exercise, you'll begin to define and evoke the world of racing by placing markers to identify B-roll target locations.

1 In the Project Library, display the contents of APTS FCP X, and then display the contents of the Lesson Projects folder. To focus on this lesson's projects, drag the Lesson 5 folder to the APTS FCP X icon. Then click the disclosure triangle next to the Lesson Projects folder to hide its contents.

   TIP Dragging a specific folder onto APTS FCP X is a great way to focus on just those projects in that folder. While studying the lessons in this book, it is a good practice to begin by repositioning a lesson folder onto APTS FCP X.

   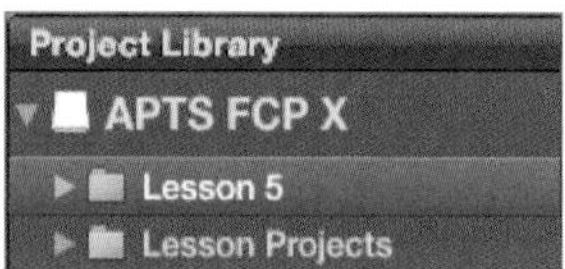

2 Click the disclosure triangle next to the Lesson 5 folder to reveal the projects for this lesson. Double-click the *Zero to Hero* project to open it in the Timeline, and play the first part of the project.

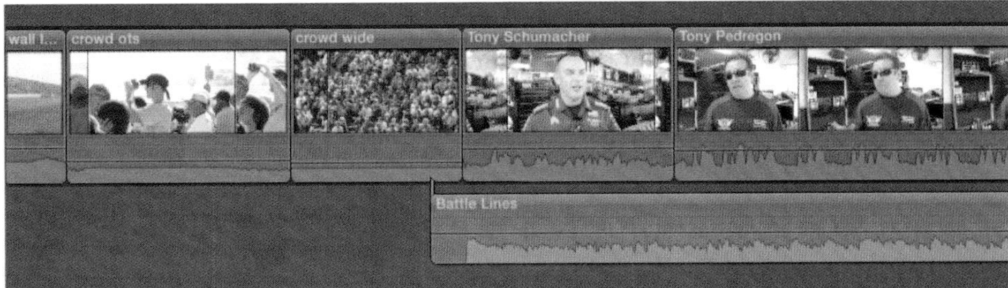

Although the music used here suits this promo, it could distract from the racers' comments. Rather than remove the music, you can leave it in position for now, but disable audible playback.

3 In the Timeline, Control-click (or right-click) the **Battle Lines** music clip and choose Disable from the shortcut menu, or press V. Then play any portion of the music clip.

TIP You could also select the clip and choose Clip > Disable. The Clip menu has additional items you will use throughout the lesson.

The disabled music clip is now dimmed and is not audible. Because this is a temporary state, at any time you can reenable the music by choosing Enable from the shortcut menu, or pressing V.

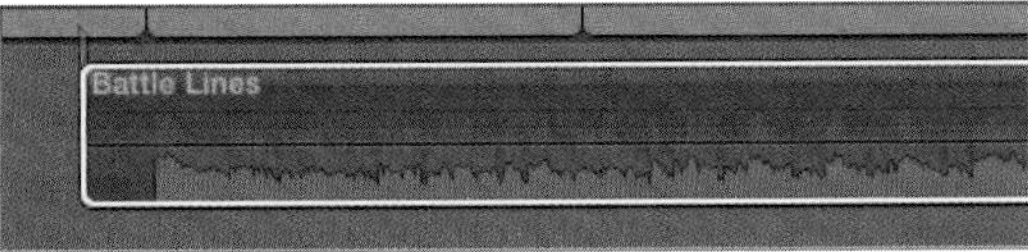

Because the current focus is on the visual aspect of your story, let's set up the interface with a clip appearance that doesn't display clip waveforms.

4 In the lower-right corner of the Timeline, click the Clip Appearance menu and select the fifth clip option. Drag the Clip Height slider to about the middle position, and make sure Show Connections is selected.

5 Listen again to the first portion of the project through the **Tony Pedregon** clip.

As Tony talks about the "breed of the drag racer," it would be nice to see a clip of a drag racer in a personal moment, perhaps getting ready for a race.

NOTE ▶ Remember, you're still working on a rough cut. In Lesson 6, you will trim and tighten your project to improve individual clip timing. For now, make a mental note of the areas you may want to change.

To make Tony's clip easier to identify and locate, you can place a *marker* at its start. A marker is like a bookmark or sticky note you can place on any frame of any clip in your project. Markers have a lot of uses. In this exercise, you will add a marker to mark the spot where you want to add a cutaway.

To snap the skimmer to a precise location, such as the first frame of a clip, make sure snapping is enabled.

6 In the Timeline, verify that the snapping button is blue, which indicates it's in active mode. Then select the **Tony Pedregon** clip, snap the skimmer to the head of the clip, and press M to set a marker.

A blue marker appears at the skimmer location. Markers are given default names such as *Marker 1*, *Marker 2*, and so on. You can customize a marker name to make it even more valuable during your editing process.

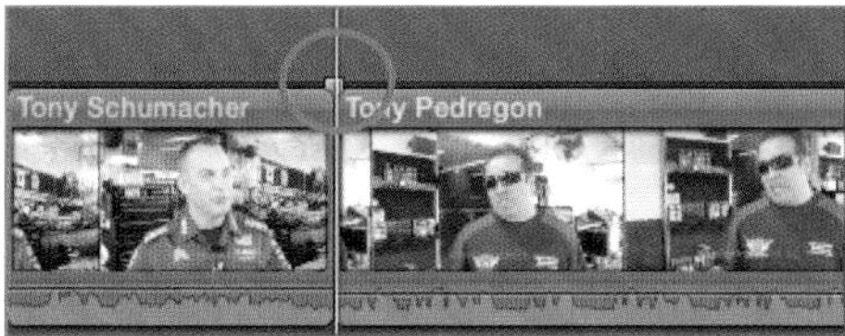

7 To rename this marker, double-click it. In the Marker pop-up window, in the Text field, enter *breed of racer*, and click Done, or press Return.

The Marker window displays the exact timecode of the marker location in the project. It also gives you the ability to create to-do or chapter markers as well as delete a marker.

TIP ▶ You can also apply markers to source clips in the Event Browser, and search for them by name. You will work more with markers throughout this book.

Another good location for a cutaway is when John Force talks about the excitement of pulling up to the starting line. Because you have B-roll material showing that activity, you'll set a marker at the head of his clip as a target for another cutaway.

NOTE ▶ Cutaways are also used to cover edit points when cutting from a person in one clip to the same person in the next clip, or to a similar framing of the same person.

8 Play the **John Force** clip, and then press the Up Arrow once or twice to return the playhead to the beginning of the clip. Press M to set a marker, and then press M again to open the Marker window. In the text field, enter *starting line*, and click Done.

TIP ▶ You can also add a marker by choosing Mark > Markers > Add Marker. Several other marker options are in this menu, such as deleting or nudging a marker.

While this marker indicates a good starting point for a cutaway, you don't want your viewers to miss a line at the end of John's clip, "It's the greatest feeling in the world." Add another marker to flag when John delivers that line.

9 Play the **John Force** clip and skim to a beat before he says, "It's the greatest feeling in the world." This time, to set a marker *and* open the Marker window in one step, press Option-M. In the text field, enter *greatest feeling*, and click Done.

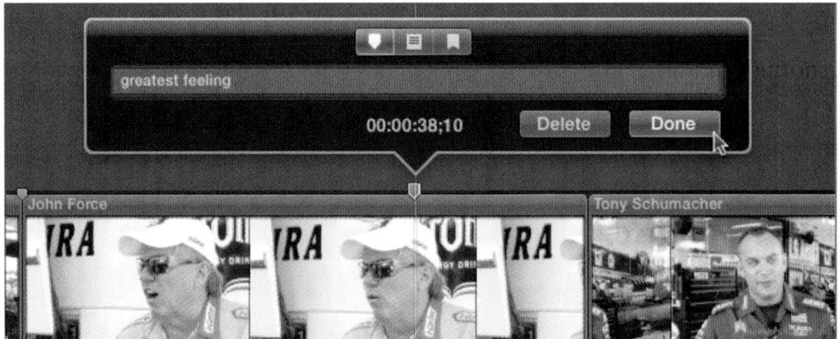

While these three markers are easy to see in this Timeline view, they may not be so clear when you zoom into a different area of the project. You'll open the Timeline Index to view and navigate the markers you just added.

10 In the lower-left corner of the Timeline window, click the Timeline Index button. At the top of the Timeline Index, click Tags. At the bottom of the Timeline Index, click the Show Standard Markers button. Then click each marker in the list and watch as the playhead in the Timeline moves to each marker's location.

11 In the Timeline Index, click the *greatest feeling* marker, and press the Spacebar to play the project from that marker location.

The playhead cues to the marker location in the project and begins playing. This is a great way to quickly review the primary content in this area.

Connecting Clips to the Primary Storyline

In Lesson 4, you were introduced to connecting clips when you edited music to the *Zero to Hero* project. The music was not part of the primary story, but it certainly enhanced it. When you connect a clip to the primary storyline, you are also linking it to the foundation of your project. That is, you can reposition a primary clip, and the connecting clip follows it along. A connecting clip remains attached to and in sync with the primary storyline unless you specifically move it or delete it. In this exercise, you will connect cutaways to the primary storyline at the locations where you added a marker.

NOTE ▶ The *Zero to Hero* rough cut is designed to be a fast-paced promotional piece for a more in-depth story on drag racers. While the sound bites of the racers provide the foundation of the story, cutting to clips of the racers in action will give the audience a preview of what's to come and help build momentum.

1 In the Timeline Index, select the *breed of racer* marker and press the Spacebar to play this area. This time, to return the playhead to the marker, press Control-; (semicolon).

TIP You can press Control-' (apostrophe) to move the playhead forward to the next marker in the project.

The clips you will connect to this project's primary storyline are all in the *B-Roll* Keyword Collection. Once you select that collection, you can close the Event Library to create more room for clips in the Event Browser.

2 In the Event Library, reveal the contents of the *Zero to Hero* Event to see its two Keyword Collections: *Interviews* and *B-Roll*. Select the *B-Roll* Keyword Collection. To close the Event Library, press Shift-Command-1, or click the Event Library button.

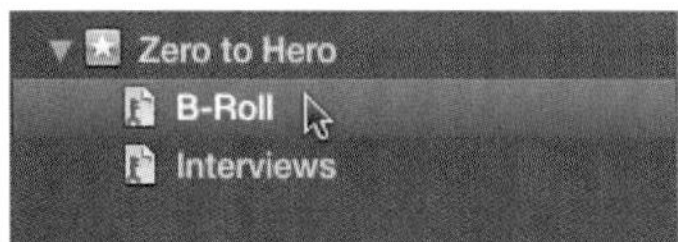

As you've seen, Final Cut Pro offers several ways to view your source clips. In list view, you have access to an alphabetical list of clips, and a wide filmstrip that enables you to select a desired range within each clip.

3 To view the clips as a list, click the List View button. In the Filter pop-up menu, make sure that All Clips is selected, and clear any entries from the Filter search field.

NOTE ▶ Depending on your most recent Event Browser settings, you may want to click the Action pop-up menu and choose Group Clips By > None, and click the Name column to sort the clips alphabetically.

4 In the Name column, select the **driver prep** clip and play it. Then skim to the frame where the man in the black jacket has just passed the camera. Press I to set the selection start point.

You will edit the remaining portion of this clip, which happens to include a man in a white shirt walking past the camera. This one you'll keep for now.

5 To connect the **driver prep** clip to the **Tony Pedregon** clip at the playhead and marker location, click the Connect button, or press Q. Play the clips in the Timeline.

In the Timeline, you'll see several things happen. First, the new clip is placed above or on top of Tony's clip. Second, the playhead automatically relocates to the end of the newly connected clip, as it does when you make an append edit (though this behavior can be disabled in Preferences). And third, a tiny connection line appears between the two clips on the first frame of the clip.

NOTE ▶ When one video clip is stacked on top of another in the Timeline, the clip on top always takes priority and is the clip displayed in the Viewer.

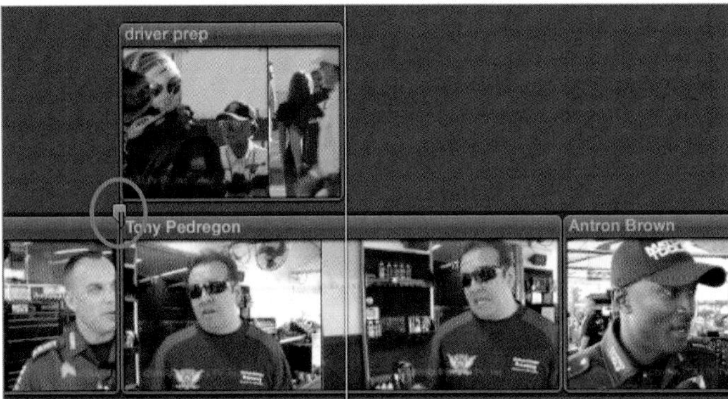

When you edit a clip using a connect edit, you are attaching it to a clip in the primary storyline. Like a truck hauling a boat, wherever you move the primary clip, the connecting clip will follow.

6 Drag the **Tony Pedregon** clip to the right and snap it to the end of the **Antron Brown** clip. Notice that the connecting clip moves with the primary clip. To return the clips to their original positions, press Command-Z.

NOTE ▶ Because the marker is attached to the primary clip, it also moves with that clip.

In this situation, the connection line is difficult to see because the marker is at the same location—the first frame of the clip. Let's reposition this line to make it easier to see.

7 Move the pointer to the middle of the **driver prep** clip, and then Command-Option-click the clip. The connection line will appear wherever you click.

Now you'll add some visual interest where John Force talks about the excitement of being on the starting line. Because this is a slightly longer section, rather than connect only one B-roll clip, you will connect three clips. Before you edit these clips, however, you will lower each clip's volume in the Inspector window so John can be heard above the ambient or background noise.

8 In the Event Browser, play the **flame out** clip. You will edit this clip in its entirety. In the toolbar, click the Inspector button, and then click the Audio tab. Drag the Volume slider to the left until you see –15 (dB) in the numeric field to the right of the slider. Play this clip again.

The lowered volume in this clip adds some natural ambient sound without overpowering John's statement.

TIP ▶ When you edit the entire length of a clip, you do not need to select the filmstrip or drag a selection range. You can simply select the clip in the clip list.

After you've set markers in a project, you can use them as edit points.

9 In the Timeline Index, select the *starting line* marker. To edit the **flame out** clip at this marker location, click the Connect Edit button, or press Q. Play the new clip, and position the playhead at the end of the **flame out** clip.

TIP ▶ One way to remember the keyboard shortcuts for the three primary types of edits (connect, insert, and append) is that the shortcut keys (Q, W, E) appear in a row next to each other in the same order as their buttons appear in the toolbar.

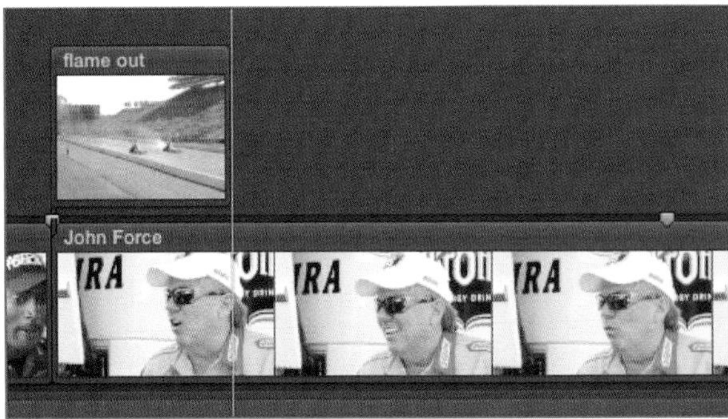

These clips are fairly short, so you can edit two more clips over John speaking. As you proceed, keep your eye on the second marker in this clip to make sure you're protecting John's on-camera line, "greatest feeling."

10 In the Event Browser, play the **race start** clip. Skim to just before the man raises his arm to start the race—at around 18:42:42:00—and press I to set the selection start point. In the Audio tab of the Inspector window, drag the Volume slider to the left to –15 (dB). To connect this clip at the playhead location, press Q.

NOTE ▶ Lowering the audio level by –15 dB on these cutaways may not be the correct level for finishing the piece. But it will reduce the noise of the clip for now so you can focus on the racers talking.

11 For the third cutaway, select and play the **JF in car** clip. In the filmstrip, drag the selection right from the head of the clip until you see a duration of about 2:00 (two seconds) in the range selection information box. To connect this clip at the playhead location, press Q.

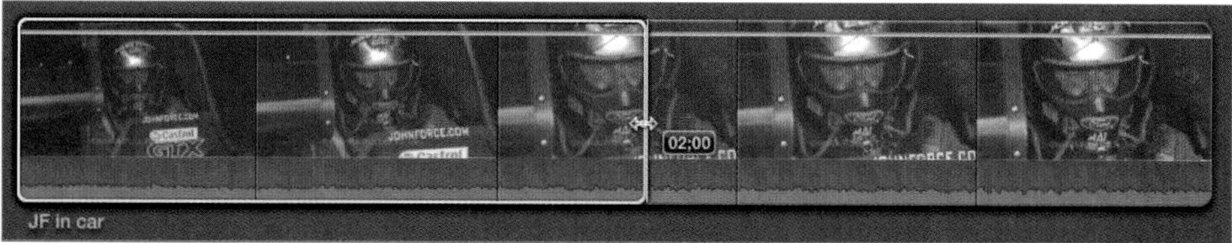

TIP Remember, if you skim through Timeline clips after you've edited them, and the skimmer is at a different location than the playhead, Final Cut Pro will edit the new clip at the skimmer location. If this happens, press Command-Z to undo, position the playhead and the skimmer together, and perform the edit again.

In the Timeline, three connecting clips now appear side by side over the **John Force** clip. Each of the three clips has a connection line that links it to the clip in the primary storyline. And luckily, the clips were short enough to return to John on camera saying, "It's the greatest feeling in the world."

Because all three clips are connected to the **John Force** clip in the primary storyline, they travel with the clip just as the single clip did earlier in this exercise.

12 In the Timeline, drag the **John Force** clip to the right and snap it to the end of the **Tony Schumacher** clip. Play the new clip arrangement. Then press Command-Z to undo this move and return the clips to their original locations.

TIP When pressing Command-Z, if you go back too many steps, you can move forward in your step history by choosing Edit > Redo, or pressing Shift-Command-Z.

Take 2

Your director is a sticky note freak. And although you're not, it's hard to argue with how easy it is to add, view, and navigate markers; and how useful they are for marking places you'd like to fix or change. You're even curious about the To Do button in the Marker window.

To impress the director and help yourself, take a few minutes to add a marker to the two crowd clips at the beginning of this project. Face it, they need trimming, but you're not yet sure what you would do or where you would trim. To add the clips to your editing to-do list *and* marker to-do list, you can select that option in the Marker window.

- In the **crowd ots** clip, skim to where you want to trim this clip, perhaps after the man with the video camera turns. Press Option-M to place a marker and open the Marker window. Enter *trim here*, click the To Do button, and click Done. The red to-do marker appears on the clip.

- Repeat the process for the **crowd wide** clip.
- To see to-do markers in the Timeline Index, click the "Show incomplete to-do items" button at the bottom of that pane.

TIP You can delete a marker by Control-clicking it and choosing Delete from the shortcut menu. You also have other options in the pop-up menu; for example, you can convert a marker to a to-do item.

Overwriting and Replacing Clips

So far, you've edited clips into a project using three methods: append, insert, and connect. In this exercise, you will edit clips using two more edit types. One involves covering up a portion of a project by overwriting it with a new source clip. The other edit involves replacing a *specific* project clip with a new source clip. Let's begin by inserting a new clip into the primary storyline.

1 In the Timeline, play the end of the **Tony Pedregon** clip and the beginning of the **Antron Brown** clip. Then press the Up Arrow to move the playhead to the head of the **Antron Brown** clip, where you will edit new B-roll content.

In these clips, Tony talks about the racer as "someone who has no fear." Then Antron says, "One day you could be a hero…." This section of the project could benefit by showing two clips that represent two sides of the drag racing experience: crashing and winning the Wally trophy.

Rather than cover up what each racer is saying, let's insert the B-roll clip at this location between the two racers.

2 In the Event Browser, play the **TS holds trophy** clip. To select the entire clip, press X. To insert this clip, press W, or click the Insert button on the toolbar. Then play the clip in the Timeline.

NOTE ▶ In an earlier exercise, you changed volume on clips so the racers could be heard. Because this clip is inserted into the primary storyline, it won't compete with the racers' comments.

In this clip, Tony Schumacher and his Army crew have just won the Wally trophy. As sometimes happens during the editing process, you may feel you edited more of this clip than you want or need. Since you want to edit a racing crash in this area, why not overwrite the first part of this clip with the new B-roll content?

3 In the Event Browser, play the **crash** clip. In the filmstrip, skim to around 2:09 and press I to start the clip selection. Skim to just after the two cars collide against the wall at around 5:00, and press O to end the selection.

TIP ▸ To check the timecode of the skimmer location in a clip, look at the Dashboard in the toolbar.

4 In the Timeline, skim to the head of the **TS holds trophy** clip. To overwrite the **crash** clip at this location, press D. In the Timeline, press Command-= (equals) to zoom into this area of the project, and then play the two clips.

By overwriting existing clip material, the new clip can be added without lengthening the project.

NOTE ▸ When you overwrite a clip, such as the trophy clip in this step, it covers part of the clip in the project and thereby shortens the clip without changing the duration of the project.

You now have two clips that demonstrate the highs and lows of racing. But did you edit the best possible clips? If you had coverage of a different racer receiving a trophy, you might consider replacing the **TS holds trophy** clip with one that doesn't look quite so staged.

5 In the Event Browser, play the **JF holds trophy** clip. Find where John raises the trophy, skim back just before that action, and press I to set the selection start point. Then skim to just after he lowers the trophy, and press O to set the selection end point.

TIP ▶ To preview only the selected area, press the / (slash) key.

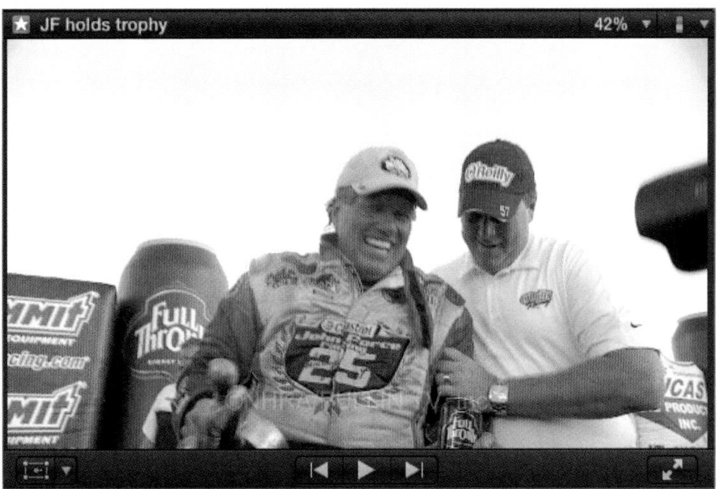

Before you replace the original trophy clip with this clip, you might ask yourself a few questions. Do you want to maintain the length of the original clip? Or use the duration of the new clip? Which is the more important action in this clip: where John raises the trophy at the beginning, or where he lowers it at the end? These are the things to consider when you replace one clip with another. Let's step through these options one at a time.

NOTE ▶ To replace a clip, you can drag the new B-roll source to the project clip in the Timeline. You do not need to position the playhead before making the edit.

6 In the Event Browser, drag the **JF holds trophy** clip into the Timeline and onto the **TS holds trophy** clip. When a white border appears around the project clip, and you see a green circle with a plus sign by the pointer, release the pointer.

7 From the shortcut menu that appears, choose Replace. Notice that the project length changes. Play the new clip.

When you choose Replace, the original clip is replaced by the new one and the project expands to accommodate the new clip's selected range or duration. In contrast to overwrite edits, replacing works on whole Timeline clips only and can change the duration of your project. Let's undo that option and try the others.

NOTE ▶ When the new clip duration is shorter than the original clip, the project contracts to accommodate the difference.

8 To undo the previous step, press Command-Z. Drag the **JF holds trophy** clip onto the **TS holds trophy** clip again and when you see the green plus sign, release the pointer. From the shortcut menu, choose "Replace from Start." Play this clip in the Timeline.

The "Replace from Start" option tips its hat to the originating clip and respects or maintains that clip's duration. Because the previous clip is not long enough to include all the new clip content, Final Cut Pro starts replacing from the beginning of the clip and stops after the duration of the original clip is reached. Let's try one more option.

9 To undo the previous step, press Command-Z. In the Event Browser, drag the **JF holds trophy** clip onto the **TS holds trophy** clip, and when you see the green plus sign, release the pointer. This time, from the shortcut menu, choose "Replace from End."

By choosing this option, you are telling Final Cut Pro to make the end point of the selection range the priority. Knowing the original clip's duration, Final Cut Pro can determine how much of the clip content can be used prior to the end point and replace using that portion of the clip.

TIP You can also replace a clip and add it to an audition. You will audition clips in the next exercise.

10 To return to the previous version of John raising the trophy, press Command-Z, drag **JF holds trophy** over **TS holds trophy**, and from the shortcut menu, choose "Replace from Start."

Auditioning Clips in the Project

Some editing workflows allow you the freedom to experiment with different clip choices and arrangements. Sometimes, that experimentation leads to replacing a clip. But along the way, you may have to view many clips before you know which clip works and whether or not you want to replace it.

Choosing the best take from multiple versions, while creative, can be one of the more time-intensive and tedious editing tasks. You edit a clip, undo the edit, edit another, undo, edit another, and so on. With the Audition feature, you can preview a number of clips within an Audition window without the need to undo any steps.

1 In the *Zero to Hero* project, move the pointer over the **Tony Pedregon** clip and press Command-= (equals) to zoom into this area of the project. Play this clip and notice the activity in the **driver prep** clip cutaway connected to it.

In this clip, the driver in the yellow helmet is being prepped for a race. At the end of the clip, a man walks in front of the camera. While this could be OK, it would be nice to know how a clip of another driver getting ready might look at this location.

2 In the Event Browser, select the **driver prep red** clip and play it.

In this clip, the camera zooms in to the driver in the red helmet, which brings the viewer closer to the action. It could be a better alternative to the yellow helmet driver shot that's currently in the project.

To compare the red helmet racer and the yellow helmet racer shots in the project, you can drag the red helmet clip onto the existing clip in the Timeline to set up an audition.

3 In the Event Browser, drag the **driver prep red** clip into the Timeline, and onto the **driver prep** clip. When you see the green plus sign, release the pointer.

4 From the shortcut menu, choose "Add to Audition."

TIP To add additional clips to this audition, you simply repeat this process.

At first, it looks as though the clip didn't change. You certainly don't see the driver in the red helmet in the clip thumbnail. But if you look closely at the clip name area, you will see a tiny spotlight icon. The Audition icon is one of your entries into the Audition window.

5 To open the Audition window, click the Audition spotlight icon. You can also select the clip and press Y.

In the Audition window, notice that the **driver prep** clip appears under a blue spotlight to indicate the current clip under review. The clip name appears above the clip along with its duration. Below the clip, two indicators represent the number of clips in this audition, just two in this case. A blue star indicates that the first clip is the current *pick*. The second icon represents the *alternate* clip.

NOTE ▶ When you want to apply different effects to the same clip and preview them, click the Duplicate button in the Audition window. You will audition clips with effects in Lesson 11.

You can take a quick peek at the current pick clip by skimming through it in the Audition window.

6 In the Audition window, skim through the **driver prep** thumbnail in the spotlight display. Press the Right Arrow key to switch to the alternate red helmet clip, and skim through its thumbnail display. Press the Left or Right Arrow keys to switch between clips and notice the differences in the Audition window, as well as in the Timeline.

When the second clip moves under the blue spotlight, you see its name above the thumbnail, **driver prep red**, along with its duration, 6:10 (six seconds and ten frames). Notice that beneath the thumbnail the audition clip indicator is blue to indicate it is the current pick (the previous pick is now a gray star).

In the Timeline, as you switch between the clips, you can see that the red helmet driver is actually a few seconds longer than the clip you originally edited at this location.

TIP Although clip length, or duration, plays a role in choosing the most appropriate clip, you can also trim clips to the desired length, as you will do in Lesson 6.

7 To pick the **driver prep red** clip and close the Audition window, navigate to it and click Done, or double-click the clip.

The best way to audition a clip is to play it in real time with its surrounding clips. When using the Audition Preview function, Final Cut Pro will automatically play the audition clip, and continue loop playback as you switch between the current pick and other alternates.

8 To preview the audition clips, Control-click the **driver prep red** clip and choose Audition > Preview from the shortcut menu. You could choose Clip > Audition > Preview, or select the clip and press Command-Control-Y.

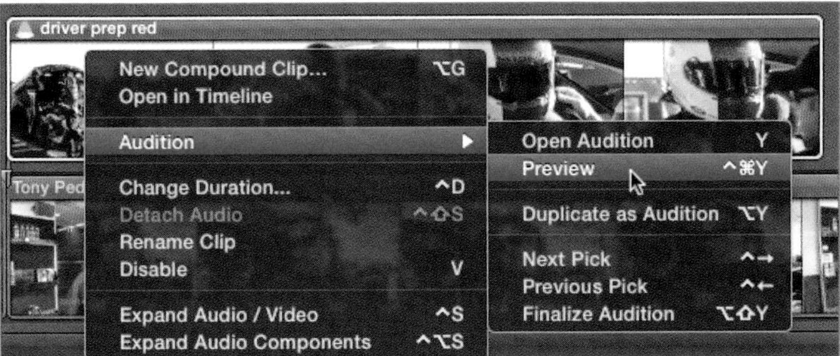

When Preview is chosen, the Audition window opens and the playhead automatically cues to a point before the audition area, plays through the pick clip, and then returns to play it again. Notice that the blue star in the Audition window indicates that the second clip is now the pick.

9 After the preview of the current pick has played a few times, press the Left Arrow to switch the automatic preview loop to the **driver prep** clip. To stop the preview, press the Spacebar.

NOTE ► You can audition clips in the primary storyline. However, if you accept a clip with a different length, the Timeline clips will ripple the change throughout the rest of the project.

By previewing and auditioning clips in this way, you develop a stronger preference for one clip over another. For example, in this situation, you might feel that the yellow helmet clip (with the person walking in front of the camera) is less desirable than the **driver prep red** clip, which holds your attention by staying focused on the driver.

You can also switch between your audition options when you're not in preview mode or inside the Audition window simply by pressing a keyboard shortcut.

10 Select the **driver prep** clip. To switch the pick to the **driver prep red** clip, press Control-Right Arrow, and play this clip.

NOTE ▶ Some shortcuts may require changing the System Preferences shortcuts for Spaces (Mac OS X 10.6) or Mission Control (OS X 10.7 or 10.8).

11 To finalize the audition, Control-click the **driver prep red** clip and choose Finalize Audition from the shortcut menu, or press Shift-Option-Y.

When you finalize an audition, the audition spotlight icon no longer appears next to the clip name. The audition stack is flattened and the clip returns to single clip status.

TIP To create audition clips in the Event Browser, select the clips you want to preview and choose Clip > Audition > Create, or press Command-Y. Then edit the audition clip to the Timeline.

Working with Storylines

When you started the rough cut of the *Zero to Hero* project in Lesson 4, you saw the benefits of working in the primary storyline. For example, you used the append edit to add clips to the project, one after the other, without stopping to reposition the skimmer or the playhead.

In this lesson, you've found reasons to connect clips to the primary storyline so that as you move a primary clip, its connected B-roll cutaway moves with it. By connecting several clips, you have created a secondary video (or audio) story to enhance the primary storyline. Final Cut Pro allows you to join these connecting clips into a secondary storyline, which gives you the ability to move the joined clips as one piece.

In this exercise, you will create a storyline using the John Force trio of clips, and then append two clips to your new storyline. You will also lift two B-roll clips from the primary storyline to create more flexibility editing the soundbites beneath them.

NOTE ▸ As you learn more about editing in Final Cut Pro X, you will find other capabilities of storylines.

1 In the Timeline Index, select the *greatest feeling* marker. Using the playhead as a target, drag the **JF in car** clip to the right, and snap the head of the clip to the playhead location. Play the new arrangement of connected clips.

Connected clips are independent from each other and can be moved or deleted separately. By moving this clip, you created a different arrangement in which you see John *experience* the "greatest feeling," rather than merely hear him say the line on camera.

You may think that the previous arrangement of clips was just fine, so let's return this clip to its original location. When you decide to use a group of clips in a particular configuration, you should consider creating a storyline.

TIP ▸ To allow more room for the project clips, you can close the Timeline Index.

2 To undo the previous step, press Command-Z. With the **JF in car** clip selected, Shift-click the **flame out** clip to complete the selection of all three clips. Control-click one of the clips and choose Create Storyline from the shortcut menu, or press Command-G.

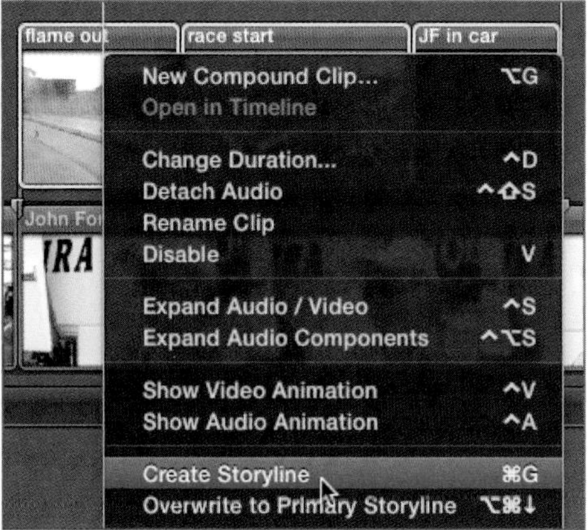

In the Timeline, a shelf appears above the three clips. This is the storyline shelf. You will use this to select and move the secondary storyline. Notice that the vertical connection line still links this storyline to the primary storyline.

3 Click the shelf of the secondary storyline to select it.

4 Drag the secondary storyline to snap the end of the storyline to the end of the **John Force** clip.

Two additional cutaways must be added at the end of the secondary storyline to cover the first part of the **Tony Schumacher** clip with Tony's action clips.

5 In the Event Browser, play the **army prep** clip. Skim to where the nose of the car is pointing toward 5 o'clock, and press I to set the selection start point. Set the end point at about 17:29:33:27. In the Inspector window, drag the Volume slider left to about –15 dB.

When you append a clip, it is automatically placed at the end of the primary storyline. To add the additional clips to the new storyline, you must first select that storyline.

6 To target the new storyline, make sure the storyline is still selected by clicking the storyline's shelf.

7 With the **army prep** clip still selected in the Event Browser, press E to append the clip to the end of this storyline. To deselect the clip, press Shift-Command-A, or click in the gray area of the Timeline.

Without positioning the playhead or skimmer, the clip is automatically added to the end of the selected storyline.

When you deselect the storyline, you can see how the shelf is extended to include the newly appended clip. Let's add one more cutaway in the same way.

8 In the Event Browser, play the **army start** clip and navigate to where the two cars start up and take off. To move back a beat or two, press Shift-Left Arrow two times to move the playhead 20 frames to the left. Press I to set the selection start point. Set the selection end point at around 17:29:47:10. This clip is a little loud, so in the Inspector window, lower the volume to –15 dB.

TIP To navigate a filmstrip, you can skim through it, use the Left and Right Arrow keys, use the Shift-Left Arrow or Shift-Right Arrow keys to move left or right 10 frames, or use the J-K-L keys to play backward or forward.

9 In the Timeline, click the storyline shelf, and press E to append the **army start** clip to the secondary storyline. Play this group of clips.

TIP To change the connection line of a connected storyline, Command-Option-click its shelf.

In addition to creating and adding to a storyline, you can also lift clips from the current storyline. Earlier in this lesson, you edited two clips between Tony Pedregon and Antron Brown. Since you were not covering one of the racer shots, you edited them directly into the primary storyline without connecting them to another clip. But later you may want to adjust the neighboring racer shots to play beneath these B-roll clips.

Lifting these B-roll clips from the primary storyline would allow the racer shots, or perhaps even sound bites, to be edited below the B-roll. Let's select the two clips and bump them up with the other B-roll clips.

TIP Zoom into an area you're working on to narrow your focus and observe more detail of clip names and icons.

10 In the Timeline, to select the **crash** clip a different way, move the pointer over it and press C. Command-click the **JF holds trophy** clip to add it to the selection. Control-click either clip and choose "Lift from Storyline" from the shortcut menu, or press Command-Option-Up Arrow.

In the project, the two clips are lifted from the primary storyline giving you room to adjust the timing from the soundbites below. Beneath each clip, Final Cut Pro has added a black gap clip to fill or hold the space in the primary storyline.

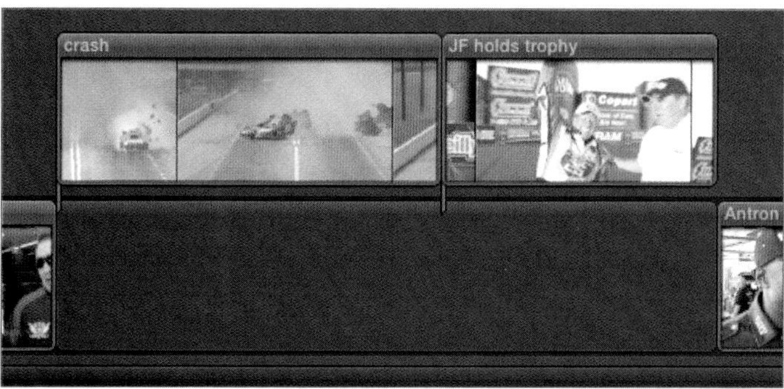

NOTE ▶ Another reason you might want to lift B-roll clips from the primary storyline is to be able to visually scan a project and see at a glance where the B-roll cutaways are located.

11 Click beneath the **crash** clip to select the gap. Press Shift-Command-A to deselect the clip.

Gap clips perform several useful functions within a storyline. Gaps can fill or sometimes create space, locking or flexing the duration of your project. They can also act as generic placeholders that you can later replace with other video clips. In Lesson 6, you will insert them between racers to add dramatic pauses.

You have numerous ways to finish your rough cut in Final Cut Pro. You may find that certain features and options lend themselves to specific types of projects, while other options help you perform better as an editor no matter what type of project you're creating. The most important thing is for you to understand the capabilities of Final Cut Pro and the language and concepts of these new editing functions so that you can apply them whenever you need them.

Editor's Cut

It's not your day off, but the director has left the building. All week long you've wanted to try your hand at editing the *Fairly Legal* and *I Think* material you organized in Lesson 3. The *Fairly Legal* clips give you the opportunity to try your hand at editing dramatic footage. You will work with a rough cut of this scene in Lesson 6 when you learn to trim clips in a project. Also try editing the *I Think* material that is voiceover driven. Unlike the dramatic *Fairly Legal*, the *I Think* material gives you the freedom to arrange (and rearrange) the video clips to tell the story. Begin by creating a new project each for *Fairly Legal* and *I Think* in the Lesson 5 folder, and editing clips from the respective Events. You can review the editing options you explored in Lessons 4 and 5.

Lesson Review

1. How do you add a marker to a clip in the Timeline and name it?
2. How do you find a specific marker in the Timeline?
3. How do you disable a specific project clip?
4. How do you move the connection line for a clip that is connected to the primary storyline without moving the clip?
5. How do you create a to-do marker in the Timeline?
6. How do you replace a project clip with a different source clip?
7. How does an overwrite edit differ from a replace edit?
8. How do you create an audition in the Timeline?
9. How do you utilize the audition feature?
10. How do you create a new storyline that is connected to your primary storyline?

Answers

1. Skim to where you want to create a marker, and choose Mark > Markers > Add Marker, or press M. Double-click a marker to rename it. In the Marker pop-up window, enter a name in the Text field, and click Done. Alternatively, press Option-M to create a marker and open the Marker window in one step.
2. In the lower-left corner of the Timeline window, click the Timeline Index button. In the Timeline Index, click Tags, and then click the Standard Markers button. Click a marker in the list to move the playhead to that marker's location.
3. Control-click a clip and choose Disable from the shortcut menu, or press V. You can also select the clip, and choose Clip > Disable.
4. Position the pointer within the clip to the desired location in the Timeline and Command-Option-click to move the clip's connection line.
5. Skim to the desired location in the Timeline, and press Option-M. In the Marker window, enter a name, click the To Do button, and click Done. The to-do marker appears red on the clip.

6. Drag a clip from the Event Browser to the clip you want to replace. When the clip receives a white outline and a green circle with a plus sign appears, release the clip. From the shortcut menu, choose Replace. This new clip replaces the original clip and the project duration adjusts to accommodate the new clip's range or duration.
7. An overwrite edit overwrites one or more clips in a storyline, starting at a range selection start point or at the playhead or skimmer position. Use an overwrite edit when you want to edit media for a specific span of time. With an overwrite edit, the overall project duration remains the same. Unlike overwrite edits, a replace edit works only on whole Timeline clips and can change the project duration.
8. Drag a clip from the Event Browser to a clip in the Timeline you want to include in the audition. When the clip receives a white outline and a green circle with a plus sign appears, release the clip. From the shortcut menu, choose Add to Audition. A small spotlight icon appears in the clip name area to indicate that the clip is part of an audition. To add additional clips, repeat this process.
9. Click the Audition spotlight icon to open the Audition window. Press the Right or Left Arrow keys to switch to the next alternate clip, and skim through its thumbnail display. Continue to press the Left or Right Arrow keys to switch to alternate audition clips.
10. Select the clips you want to include in the new storyline, Control-click the selection and choose Create Storyline from the shortcut menu, or press Command-G.

Keyboard Shortcuts

M	Set a marker in the Timeline ruler
M	When on a marker, open the Edit Marker dialog
Y	Open audition window
Command-Y	Create audition clips
Command-Control-Y	Preview the audition clips
Shift-Option-Y	Finalize the audition
Command-G	Create a storyline
Shift-Delete	Lift an item or section from the Timeline and leave a gap

Keyboard Shortcuts

Delete	Remove an item or section from the Timeline and ripple the following edits up the duration of the gap
Control-' (apostrophe)	Move the playhead forward to the next marker
Control-; (semicolon)	Move the playhead to the previous marker
Control-M	Delete marker at current playhead location
Double-click	Open a marker's Edit Marker dialog
Command-Shift-1	Show/hide the Event Library
Command-Option-click	Move a clip's connection point

6

Time This lesson takes approximately 70 minutes to complete.

Goals

- Remove selected ranges
- Add gap clips
- Use the Range Selection tool
- Understand trimming
- Ripple trim with the Select tool
- Ripple and roll trim with the Trim tool
- Slip a clip
- Slide a clip
- Extend edit points

Lesson 6

Fine-Tuning the Rough Cut

As an editor, you begin with broad strokes to craft a story. You started a rough cut in Lesson 4 with just four interesting people talking about an exciting sport. In Lesson 5, you completed the foundation by inserting B-roll of the crowd, connecting several cutaways of the racers, and adding another storyline. All of these techniques helped create a more clearly defined story.

Now that you're comfortable with clip placement, you can focus your attention on timing and those smaller fine-tuning adjustments that more precisely make the story what you want it to be.

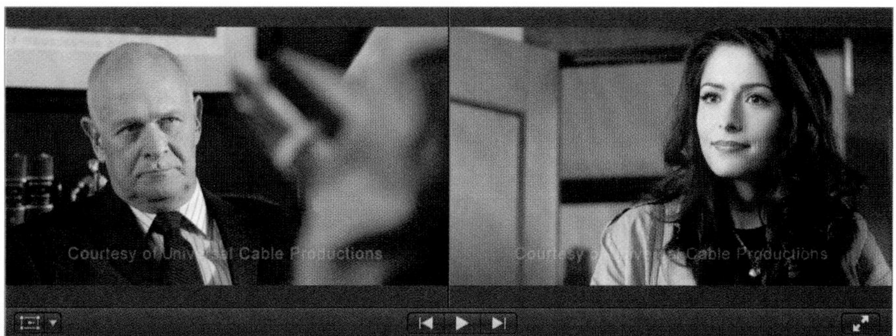

Use the Viewer two-up display to trim two edit points at once.

The process of refining edit points is referred to as *trimming*. In Final Cut Pro, you can trim clips using a variety of methods and tools, including the Trim, Range, and Blade tools. You can also trim with increased control inside the Precision Editor. And numerous shortcuts are designed to help you move through this stage of the workflow quickly and easily.

To see how every project has its own needs and challenges, you will work with three projects in this lesson. Each one provides opportunities to explore the trimming and fine-tuning options in Final Cut Pro.

Duplicating a Project

Before you begin trimming or refining a hundred tiny details in your project, it's a good idea to think about your editorial workflow and ask a few questions. For example, will you ever need to return to the current version of your project? If so, it would be a good idea to duplicate it. Will you need to create shorter and longer versions of the project to show a client? Perhaps duplicating a longer project and whittling it down to create a shorter version would be advantageous. Will you ever want to compare different versions of a project to evaluate your editorial decisions?

Whatever your needs are, duplicating a project before starting down a new editorial path is a valuable step in almost any editing workflow. You duplicate projects in the Project Library.

1 In the Project Library, from the Lesson Projects folder, drag the Lesson 6 folder onto APTS FCP X and reveal its contents. Then close all other project folders.

   In this lesson, you will work with these projects to explore trimming and refining. However, you can't return to your original version (perhaps to try a different approach) unless you first duplicate the project.

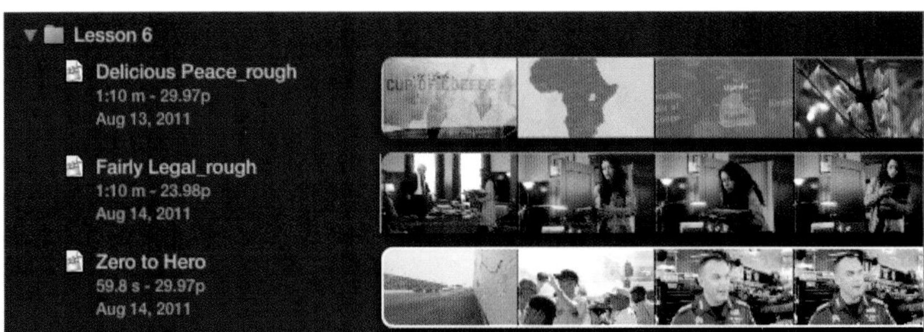

2 Control-click (or right-click) the *Zero to Hero* project and choose Duplicate Project from the shortcut menu.

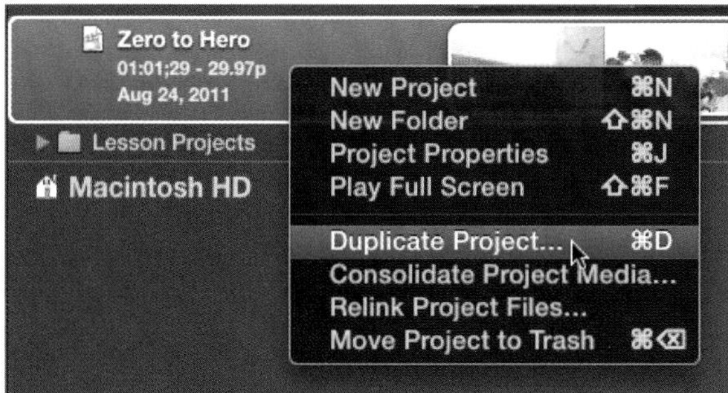

In the Duplicate Project dialog, you have the option to duplicate a project with or without the media contained in its referenced Event. For this lesson, you can utilize the same media the current project references.

3 In the Duplicate Project dialog, choose the location where the project files are currently stored. Rename this project *Zero to Hero_v2*. Select Duplicate Project Only, and deselect Include Render Files. Click OK.

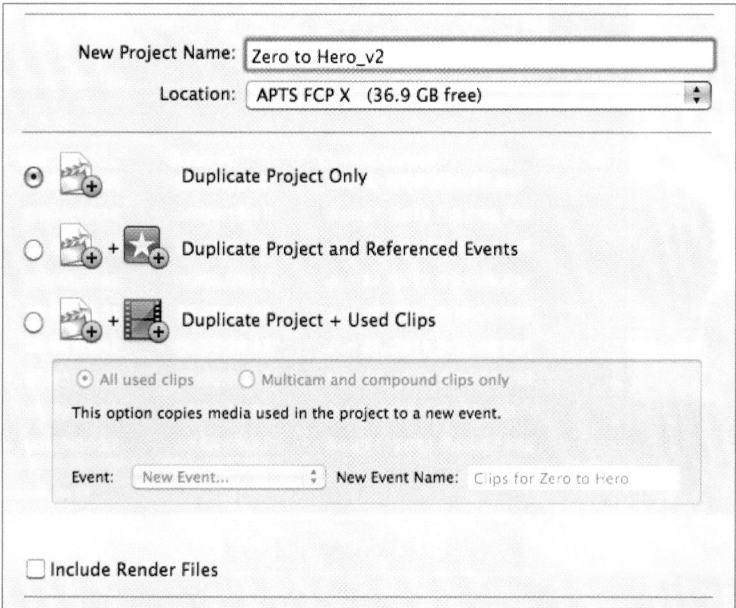

NOTE ▶ You can use a variety of naming conventions when duplicating projects. In Lesson 7, you will add *_BACKUP* to the end of a project name when you duplicate the original version.

4 To open the *Zero to Hero_v2* project with a different method, select the project, and press Return. Press Shift-Z to fit all the project clips into the Timeline.

After you've worked with a project's clips for a while, you are ready to take a closer, more detailed look at edit points or specific areas that need refining. Let's review how to focus into an area of the Timeline.

5 Skim to the edit point between the **crash** and **JF holds trophy** clips. To see this area in more detail, press Command-= (equals) four or five times.

NOTE ▶ Final Cut Pro uses the skimmer as the target location when you're zooming in and out of the Timeline.

As you zoom into an area of the project, a white skimmer *shadow* grows wider and wider. The width of this shadow indicates the width of a frame in the current zoom level. Although this tool is very helpful at times, when you're performing basic trimming and refining, you don't need to dive quite that deep.

6 To zoom out, press Command-- (minus) several times. To see a bird's-eye view of all the project clips, press Shift-Z.

TIP ▶ You can also press Z to select the Zoom tool, or in the toolbar, choose it from the Tools pop-up menu. To zoom into an area of the Timeline, click or drag a box around the area. Option-click to zoom out of the Timeline.

Removing Clip Selections and Adding Gaps

One of the first and most important steps when fine-tuning edits is to adjust the pace and flow of your project. Because the clips in the primary storyline are the engine of your project, you should begin by looking at those clips. Why take the time to trim a cutaway's edit point when you're not happy with the primary clip it supports? To fine-tune the primary clips, you may need to delete a line or divide a clip to add a space between lines of dialog. Doing so can create a dramatic pause or allow an important action to continue. When you create a pause, Final Cut Pro places a *gap* in the project to hold the space between two clips.

In this exercise, you will adjust the pace of the primary storyline in the *Zero to Hero_v2* project by removing a range of material from a few clips, dividing a clip, and adding gap edits as spacers.

The current project represents your combined efforts from the previous two lessons. Recall that you placed markers to flag locations in the second and third clips. Let's take a closer look at those marker areas to see what you can improve.

> **TIP** Check the length of the current project version before making any trims to provide a before-and-after reference. An easy way to do this is to consult the always-on duration beneath the Timeline.

1 To review the content of the *Zero to Hero_v2* project, press the Spacebar to play it. Then skim to the first red marker, and zoom into that area. Make sure snapping is turned on in the Timeline so you can snap the skimmer to the marker.

As you learned in Lesson 5, markers can be used for many purposes. Here, you placed a red to-do marker at a possible trim location because this clip was running too long. The marker can serve as a guide to remove the clip's latter portion, which you no longer need.

NOTE ▶ You can decide whether a clip is too long or too short based on several factors. For this project, you will focus on capturing the action moments in each clip. In this clip, the primary action is when the man with a camera turns his head. Once that action is completed, you no longer need to stay on the clip.

2 With the skimmer on the first red marker, press I to set a start point.

Pressing I or O in the Timeline creates the same results as it does when you use these shortcuts on a source clip in the Event Browser. It creates a range selection that starts or ends at the skimmer or playhead location.

In this case, you pressed I to start a selection at the skimmer that continues to the end of the clip. This is exactly the portion of the clip you want to remove.

3 To remove the selected range of the project clip, press Delete.

When you press Delete, you remove the selected range and reduce the project length by the duration of the selection. Notice that the red marker is no longer present because it was located on the first frame of the selection.

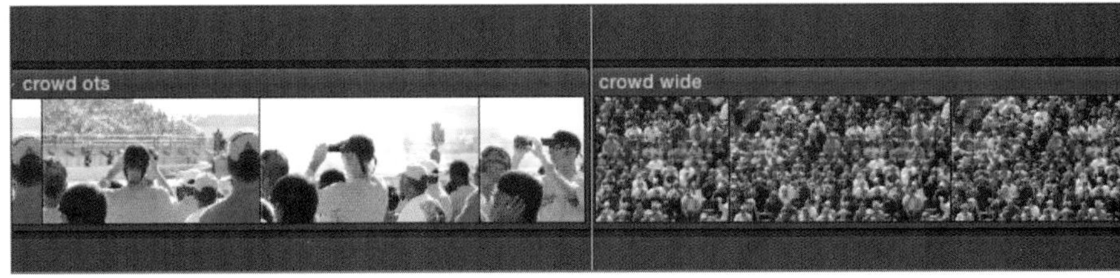

TIP ▶ If you want to remove an entire clip from your project, select that clip and press Delete. You can also set a selection range that includes several clips, and delete all the material within that range.

The next clip also ran long and has a red marker to indicate a possible trim point. You will use the Range Selection tool to select a range in this clip.

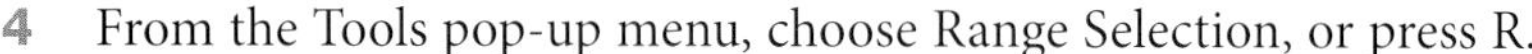

4 From the Tools pop-up menu, choose Range Selection, or press R.

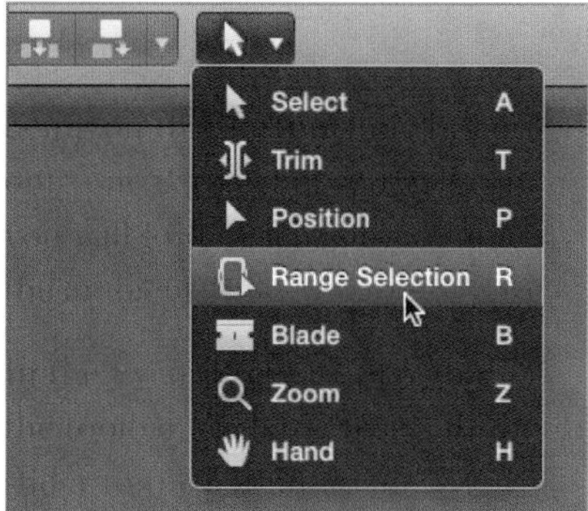

Rather than select an unwanted range from just the crowd clip, let's include unwanted material from the next clip at the same time.

5 Play the first part of the **Tony Schumacher** clip. To set a marker just before he begins his line, "Nobody wakes up," play or skim to that location, and press M.

You've identified a range to remove that starts in one clip and continues into the next.

NOTE ▸ You do not need to set a marker to select a range. In this situation, the marker simply provided a helpful target.

6 To select the unwanted portions of both of these clips, snap the Range Selection pointer to the red marker, and drag the selection to the blue marker. Press Delete, and play these clips. Then press A to return to the Select tool.

You can also delete content by lifting the selection from the clip. When you lift material, the project length doesn't change, but a *gap* clip is left in its place.

In the following steps, you will help Tony Pedregon make his "no fear" point a little faster by lifting a section from the middle of his comments. This time, rather than use the Range Selection tool, you will apply the Blade tool to split the clip into three parts and then lift the part you no longer want.

NOTE ▶ Final Cut Pro can delete or lift whatever is within a selected range, regardless of the tool you used to define the range.

7 Play the first part of the **Tony Pedregon** clip and notice that he stalls a bit before making his point. Skim to just after he says, "the breed." Press B to select the Blade tool, and click at the skimmer location. Skim to just after he says, "drag racer is," and click again at that location. Press A to return to the Select tool.

When you click the Blade tool, it creates a new edit point. The two new edit points in this clip define the clip range you no longer want.

Rather than delete this material as you did in the previous steps, and ripple the change throughout the project, you will replace it with a gap. This gap will allow you to experiment with the timing and placement of the two remaining segments of Tony's statement.

8 Click the middle **Tony Pedregon** clip to select it, and press Shift-Delete. The middle clip is replaced with a gap clip. Play the two clip segments, and then click the black area between the two remaining **Tony Pedregon** clips.

You can delete a gap clip or trim it. You can also overwrite it by repositioning a clip over it. In previous lessons, when you dragged a clip using the default Select tool, you activated the Magnetic Timeline and other clips moved out of its way. When you use the Position tool to drag a clip, you have the freedom to manually place a clip at a specific location without involving any other clips.

9 In the toolbar, from the Tools pop-up menu, choose the Position tool, or press P. Then, drag the second **Tony Pedregon** clip to the left about halfway through the gap clip, and release the pointer. Play the clips in this configuration.

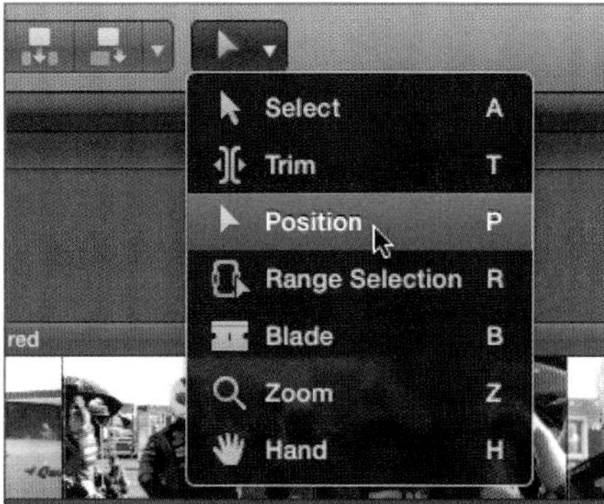

By repositioning this clip closer to the first segment, you hear a more believable delivery of Tony's statement. And because Final Cut Pro places a gap clip in the area the clip vacated, you maintain the project length in the primary storyline.

NOTE ▶ When you use the Position tool to position one portion of a clip over another, other clips will not move out of the way and you will overwrite that portion of the original clip.

10 Press A to return to the Select tool. Press Command-Shift-A to deselect any selected clips or gaps.

Another way to refine a project's pace is to create a dramatic pause. In this project, Antron Brown makes a perfect statement that consists of two extremes about winning a championship and crashing. To first accentuate one point and then the other, you can insert a gap clip. This pause will allow you to visually build on his statement by staying on a cutaway for an extra beat.

11 Play the **Antron Brown** clip. Position the playhead after he says, "take the Wally home." Choose Edit > Insert Generator > Gap, or press Option-W, and notice that the remaining storyline opens up to allow for the new clip. Play through both of these clips.

A three-second gap is placed at the playhead location. This gap creates a placeholder that allows time to visually support what Antron is saying. And like other clips, the gap clip can be trimmed to a desired length.

Take 2

The producer isn't crazy about the timing of the two Tony Pedregon clips. You're sure you can position them to make them work. Using the Position tool, adjust the placement of the second Tony Pedregon clip. If you're going to sell the producer on the cut, you have to make it convincing.

While you're at it, take a closer look at the John Force clip and decide if it might also benefit from a dramatic pause.

Understanding Trimming

Trimming begins to refine your initial editorial decisions. To this point, you've edited rough selections of clip material into your project. Now that you've edited most or all of the clips into your primary storyline, you can consider whether the original start and end points of each clip still represent the best selection of content or placement.

When you play a project in the Timeline, you are seeing only the edited portions of the clips. However, you still have access to all the frames in the original media files. The maximum number of frames you can add to lengthen a clip in an outer direction (head or tail) depends on how much material is available in the original media file. The additional frames outside the marked selection of a clip are referred to as *handles*.

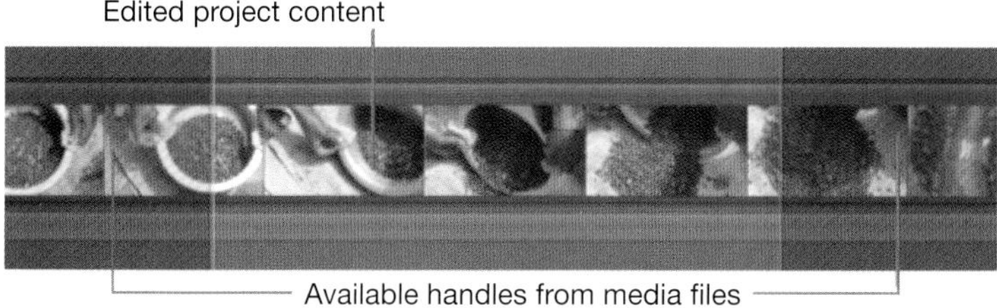

Individual project clips can be opened in a different Timeline view to see available media.

One of the easiest and quickest ways to trim an edit point is to simply drag it using the default Select tool. When you trim an edit point on the primary storyline with the Select tool, Final Cut Pro *ripples* the effect of the trim throughout the rest of the project. For example, when you lengthen a clip, the overall project grows longer by the amount of the trim. When you shorten the clip in the primary storyline, the project becomes shorter.

As long you have media handles on both sides of an edit, you can drag or trim an edit point to the left or the right. Dragging left always moves an edit point earlier in time; dragging right moves it later.

In this exercise, you will use the Select tool to trim edit points in a rough-cut version of the *Delicious Peace* project.

1 In the Project Library, open the *Delicious Peace_rough* project. In the Timeline, play the project. Then skim to the end of the **VO_07** clip, and notice the timecode number in the Dashboard.

While the voiceover ends before the project's one-minute point, the clips in the primary storyline continue well past one minute. Not all projects have to be a specific length, but many projects—such as commercials and programs that fill a broadcast time slot—must have a precise runtime.

In this exercise, you will trim some of the clips in the primary storyline to bring the total project length closer to one minute. But first, let's take a closer look at how Final Cut Pro displays a clip's handles.

2 With the skimmer over the **end of the music** clip, press Command-= (equals) a few times to zoom into that area. In the primary storyline, Control-click the **workers relaxing** clip and choose "Open in Timeline" from the shortcut menu. Press Shift-Z, and then skim across the clip.

When you open a single clip in the Timeline, the marked portion of the project clip is highlighted in milky white, and the available media handles are darkened on either side. This is a good way to review the media content outside the clip selection. For example, in this clip you see a woman in a red shirt prominent in the darkened frames to the right.

In the Timeline history area, next to the project name, you see the name of the currently open clip.

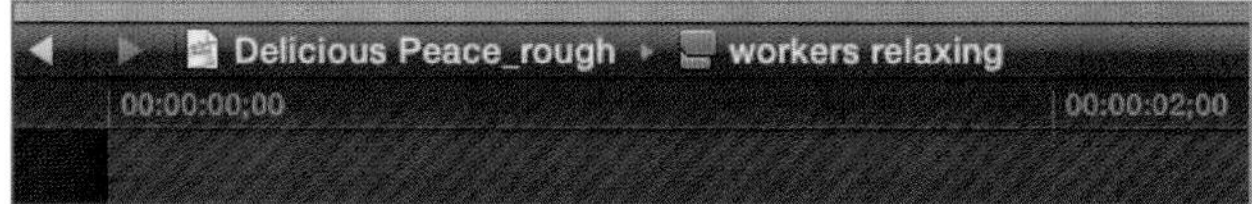

3 To return to the project, click the left History arrow, or press Command-[(left bracket). Find the **woman picks beans** clip, above the **VO_09** clip, and zoom into that area. Play this clip and notice how the woman looks up toward the end of the clip.

With an eye on shaving seconds and frames from the video clips in this project, you might consider removing the portion of the clip where the woman looks up. This would require dragging the end point to the left to end the clip sooner.

4 Move the pointer just to the left of the edit point between the **woman picks beans** clip and the **man picks beans** clip. Click to select the end point.

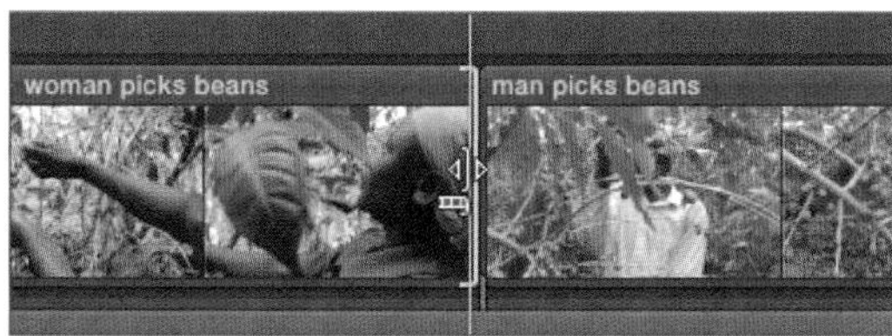

When you position the pointer over an edit point, or click an edit point, the arrow icon automatically changes to the Trim icon, represented by an arrow on either side of an edit point and a filmstrip that indicates the active side. When the filmstrip appears under the left arrow, you could drag to trim the outgoing clip's end point. This is also known as the left edge of the edit point.

5 Without dragging, move the pointer to the right side of the edit point and click the start point of the **man picks beans** clip.

When you position the pointer (or click) to the right of the edit point, the filmstrip appears under the right arrow. Dragging would trim the incoming clip's start point. This is also known as the right edge of the edit point.

TIP ▶ You can use the feet at the top and bottom of the yellow trim highlight as a reminder of which edit point you will adjust. When pointing left, you've selected the outgoing clip's end point; when pointing right, you've selected the incoming clip's start point.

6 Click the **woman picks beans** end point, and drag left until the numerical timecode field reads about –2:00. As you drag, notice that the project clips in the Magnetic Timeline follow along. Notice too that one or more of the voiceover clips change position and begin to bump into a different configuration, changing their spacing. Release the pointer, and press Command-Z to undo this trim.

When you trim a clip in the primary storyline, a ripple effect occurs on all the clips that follow. A trim info flag indicates the clip's new duration and the amount of trim performed since clicking. In this case, the clips were all moved earlier in the project.

NOTE ▶ The minus sign in the trim info flag indicates that you are trimming the edit point to the left. A plus sign indicates that you're trimming to the right.

For this exercise, the goal is to trim the video clips so their combined lengths will better match that of the voiceover clips. To lock in the timing between each VO clip, you can group them into a storyline.

7 To select the voiceover clips, select the first clip, **VO_10**, and Shift-click the last clip in the project, **VO_07**. Or drag a selection rectangle around this group of clips. To convert the selection into a storyline, Control-click one of the selected clips and choose Create Storyline from the shortcut menu.

NOTE ▶ Another way to preserve the current placement of voiceover clips is to create a compound clip from the group. However, because compound clips appear as a single clip, you wouldn't be able to see where each voiceover clip was located or adjust its placement in relationship to the primary storyline.

A storyline shelf appears across the entire group of voiceover clips. Notice that just one connection line connects the voiceover storyline to the first clip in the project.

TIP For greater control when trimming small increments, zoom into the area you're trimming, and turn off snapping.

8 Drag the end point of the **woman picks beans** clip to the left. In the Viewer, watch to see when the woman begins to look up, and release the edit point just before she turns her head.

When you trim this clip, the voiceover clips don't move because they are now part of a storyline that is connected to just the first clip in the primary storyline.

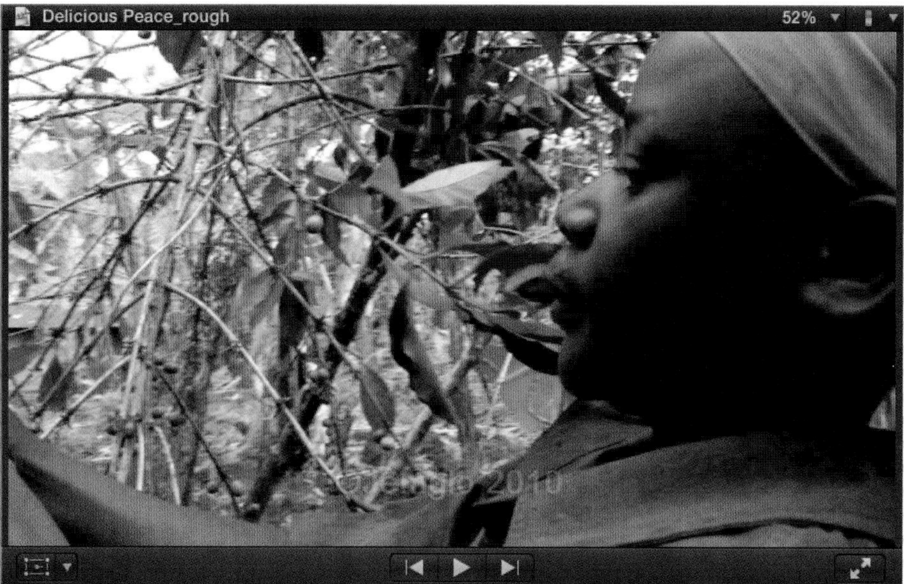

Once an edit point is generally where you want it to be, you can continue to finesse it using keyboard shortcuts. Shortcuts allow you to *nudge* a selected edit point left or right by a single frame, or by 10 frames.

9 To nudge the selected end point later one frame at a time, press the . (period) key several times and watch for the green leaf to come into frame. Press the , (comma) key a few times to nudge the end point back and settle on a frame before the woman turns her head. To deselect the edit point, press Command-Shift-A.

TIP ▶ When you finish trimming, deselect an edit point so you don't change it accidentally.

In the Viewer, the new end frame updates with every trim. In the Timeline, you see the clips that follow move along with the edit point frame by frame.

TIP ▶ To trim in 10-frame increments, press Shift-, (comma) to trim the selected edit point 10 frames to the left, and press Shift-. (period) to trim 10 frames to the right. You can also enter a trim duration in the Dashboard to trim a selected clip. These are the same shortcuts used to nudge the position of a clip when the Position tool is active.

When you've settled on the trim amount, you will want to see how the new clip duration works in your project. To do this, you need to play not just the clip, but also the area around it. Final Cut Pro has a shortcut for this purpose.

10 With the playhead at the end of the **woman picks beans** clip, press Shift-?.

NOTE ▶ For this step, you don't need to wait for the pointer to change to a Trim tool, or to snap the pointer to the edit point.

When you use the Shift-? shortcut, Final Cut Pro notes the current skimmer or playhead location and automatically backs it up by a default amount to play up to and beyond its original position. The length of time it plays up to the set location is referred to as the *pre-roll*, and the time it plays beyond the location is the *post-roll*. You can change these default durations in the Preferences window.

11 Choose Final Cut Pro > Preferences, or press Command-, (comma), and click the Playback tab. Click the Up and Down arrows to set a 3:00 duration in both the Pre-Roll and Post-Roll Duration fields. Close the window, and then press Shift-? to play around the edit again.

TIP Using this shortcut to play around the current skimmer or playhead location is a convenient way to take a quick look at your edit points. By taking the time to customize the pre-roll and post-roll durations, this feature will become even more valuable to you.

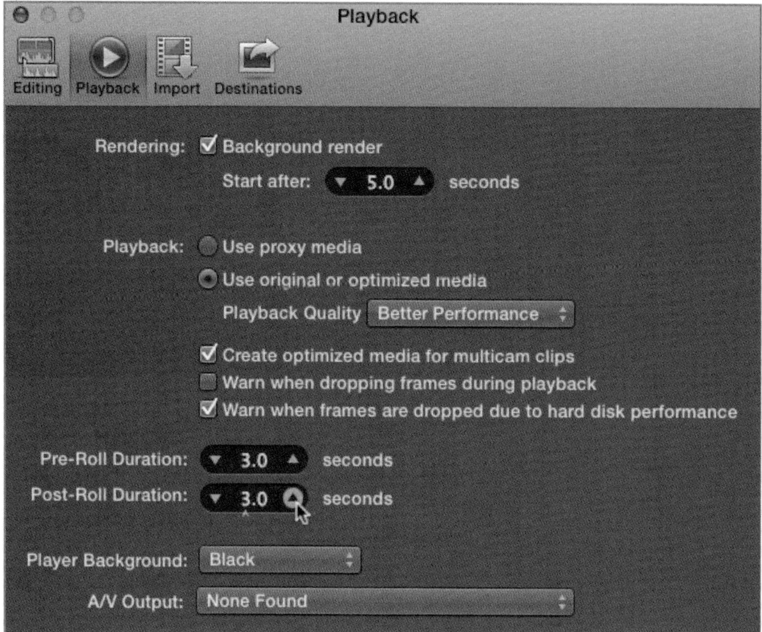

As you fine-tune your project, you'll find that not all clips have handles. When you select an edit point that doesn't have any available media to lengthen a clip, Final Cut Pro displays the edit point selection in red.

12 Move your pointer to the next clip in the project, **man picks beans**. When the filmstrip appears under the right trim arrow, click the start edit point. Try to drag this edit point to the left. Then drag it right and notice that the project clips preceding it move together. Press Command-Z to undo this trim.

TIP If you undo too many steps, you can recover your steps forward by pressing Command-Shift-Z.

Final Cut Pro has several visual indicators to provide feedback as you edit. One indicator that you are trimming the start point of a clip is that all the clips preceding the clip move together. Notice, too, that the Timeline ruler and grid lines also move.

NOTE ▸ When trimming a start point, clips that precede it move with the trim to indicate that type of trim, but do not actually change position in the project.

As you skim through a clip or project, you may see a frame, or even another clip in the project, that you'd like to use as a trim target. With snapping turned on, you can drag an edit point and snap it to another clip or to the playhead location.

13 Skim through the **man picks beans** clip and find where the man starts to lower the beans into the bucket. To set the playhead as the trim target, click above the clip just before this action. Then, drag the start point to the right and snap it to the playhead.

For very fast trimming, an assortment of keyboard shortcuts trim an edit point to the skimmer location or to a range selection without dragging an edit point. When you become familiar with these shortcuts, you will find yourself trimming almost without thinking about it. As with all shortcuts, making them your own takes a little time and practice. For now, let's explore the possibilities.

14 Skim the **dark beans ground** clip, and press Command-= (equals) a few times to zoom into this area. Skim to just before the camera starts to zoom out. After pressing each of the following shortcuts, press Command-Z to undo, and try the next:

- Press Option-] (right bracket) to trim the end point and remove all frames to the right of the skimmer location.
- Press Option-[(left bracket) to trim the start point and remove all frames to the left of the skimmer location.
- Press I and O to set a selection range in the middle of this clip, and press Option-\ (backslash) to trim the head and tail material outside the selection.

You can also use the skimmer location to extend an edit point forward or backward. For example, in an effort to shorten this project, you will probably want to shorten the xylophone music to end with the last voiceover clip.

15 Skim to the end of the **xylophone music** clip, and click its end point to select it. Skim to the end of the **VO_07** clip. To shorten the music clip to this location, press Shift-X. This is known as an extend edit.

NOTE ▶ You can find these keyboard shortcuts listed in the Edit menu.

▶ The Final Cut Pro Magnetic Timeline

As you edit, it's helpful to have as much dynamic visual feedback as possible. In Lesson 4, when you repositioned a project clip in the primary storyline, Final Cut Pro automatically updated other clip positions, providing real-time feedback for your move. When you trim clips in the primary storyline, you will see the same real-time feedback from your current trim operation before releasing the pointer. This is one of the important visual indicators guiding you during the editing process. Here are a few other indicators you will see while trimming:

- As you trim an edit point, the frame being trimmed follows the movement of the pointer, left or right.
- When you see clips to the right of the trim point move, it's a visual indication that you are trimming an end point of a clip.
- When you see clips to the left of the trim point move, it's a visual indication that you are trimming the start point of a clip.
- When trimming the start point of a clip, the Timeline ruler and grid lines move to indicate that they are not being repositioned in time.

Applying the Trim Tool

You can handle a lot of trimming requirements just by using the trim methods and tools you've learned so far. However, Final Cut Pro offers even more trimming methods when you apply the versatile and location-sensitive Trim tool. When you position it on the left or right edge of an edit point, it anticipates that you want to trim just the start or end point of a clip by displaying the Trim icon, which you used in the previous exercise via the

Select tool. Position the Trim icon directly over the edit point, and a Roll icon appears that allows you to adjust both sides of the edit point at the same time. Position the Trim tool over the body of a clip and you can slip the clip content while maintaining the current clip position and duration. And with the use of a modifier key, you can slide one clip between its two neighboring clips.

In this exercise, you will use the Trim tool to finesse additional edit points in the *Delicious Peace_rough* project.

1. In the *Delicious Peace_rough* project, play the two maps toward the beginning of the project and zoom into these clips. Notice that the **map of Africa** clip cuts away before the animation around Uganda has finished. Let's trim the end point later to allow the animation to finish.

   NOTE ▶ In Lesson 7, you will add a transition to this edit point to smooth the flow of one image zooming into the next.

   As an introduction to the Trim tool, you will perform the same type of ripple trim you performed in the previous exercise.

2 From the Tools pop-up in the toolbar, choose the Trim tool, or press T.

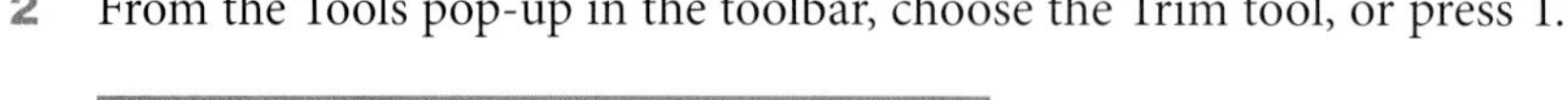

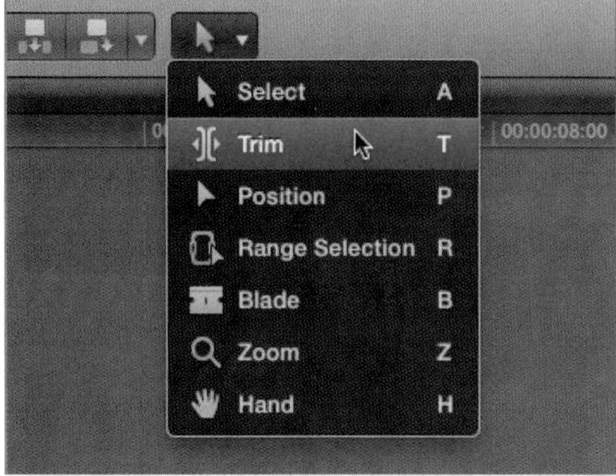

The Trim tool has different modes depending on where it's placed over a clip or edit point.

3 Without dragging, move the Trim tool slowly from one side of the edit point to the other between the **map of Africa** and **map of Uganda** clips. Notice that the icon changes five times. You should recognize two of these icons from the previous exercise.

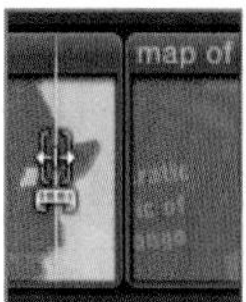

Slip outgoing clip

Trim outgoing clip's end point

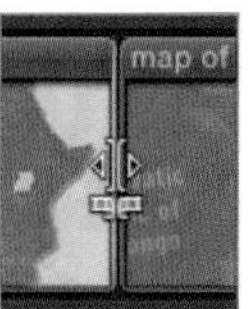

Roll both edit points

Trim incoming clip's start point

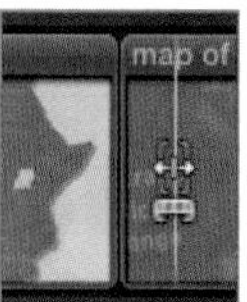

Slip incoming clip

The type of trim the Trim tool performs depends on where it's located on a clip or edit point when you begin to drag. To add more frames to the **map of Africa** clip and complete the animation, you will position the Trim tool at the end of that clip, just to the left of the edit point.

But rather than trim the clip in isolation, Final Cut Pro can display a specialized view to show both clips in the edit point. This view is controlled by an Editing preference.

4 Choose Final Cut Pro > Preferences, or press Command-, (comma). In the Editing pane, make sure "Show detailed trimming feedback" is selected, and close the Preferences window.

5 With the Trim tool positioned over the end point of the **map of Africa** clip, drag right to add about 1.5 seconds to this clip. Before you release the pointer, look at the two-up display in the Viewer, especially the vertical filmstrip in the middle.

With detailed trimming feedback enabled, you see not only the new edit point in the left frame, but the first frame of the incoming clip in the right frame. This reference helps you make better choices about the edit point you're trimming. Notice the vertical filmstrip on the left side of the **map of Uganda** clip, which indicates the first frame of this clip's media file.

TIP The Option key toggles the detailed trimming feedback preference on the fly. If this option is enabled, press the Option key to disable it. If this option is disabled, press the Option key to switch the view between the end point of the left clip and the start point of the right clip.

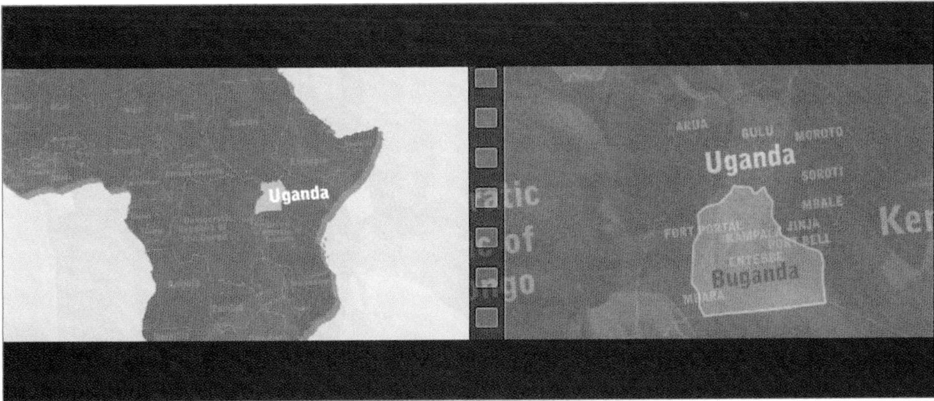

Another way you can use the Trim tool is to roll two adjacent edit points. This type of trim doesn't change the length of the project because it trims the edit points in tandem—whatever it trims from one clip it adds to the other. A roll trim adjusts the outgoing clip's end point and the incoming clip's start point.

6 Position the Trim tool directly over the edit point between the **map of Africa** and the **map of Uganda** clips. When the pointer changes to a bi-directional filmstrip, click to select the edit point. Notice that both sides of the edit point are selected. Try to drag left, and then drag right 15 frames, and play the clips.

TIP You can also use the "nudge" keys here to roll the selected edit points by single-frame or 10-frame increments.

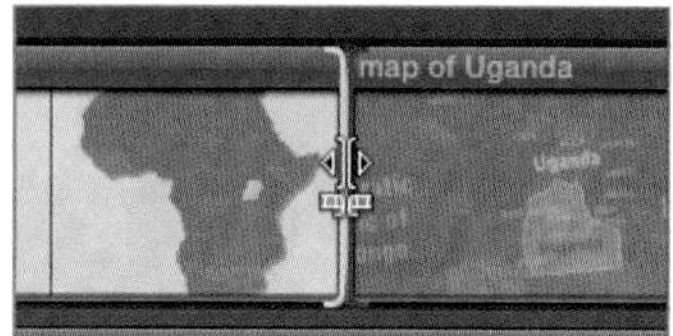

In this situation, because no media is available on the B-side clip, you can't roll to the left. But when you drag right, both edit points roll together. In the Viewer, you can see the new edit points of both clips and can better judge how well they work together. Notice that no clips in the project shift or move because rolling an edit point does not change project length.

7 Play the **grind stone** and **woman sweeps coffee** clips, and zoom into that area of the project. To see a different timing of these clips, roll the edit point left until each clip shows the woman's hand on the grinding stone as she drags it back, about –22 frames. Play the clips.

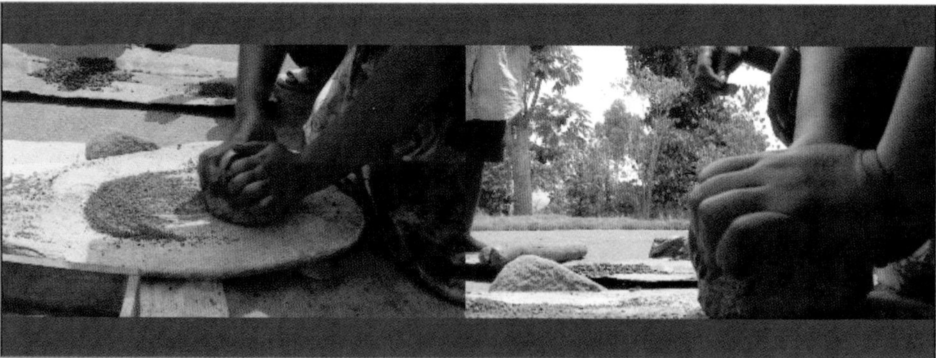

TIP ▶ When you want to finesse a single side of an edit point to match an action, move the Trim tool over that side and drag.

The power of the Trim tool is its ability to trim in four different modes. You've experienced two modes, the ripple and roll modes. The other two trims, *slip* and *slide*, are equally as productive. Like roll, these trims do not change the length of the project because they are trimming two sides of the clip at the same time.

Let's take a closer look at slipping a clip.

8 To fit the project clips in the Timeline, press Shift-Z. Play the third clip from the end, **workers relaxing**. Press Command-= (equals) a few times to zoom into this area.

You may remember that when you opened this clip earlier it contained additional footage of other workers—including a woman in a red shirt—drinking coffee and relaxing together.

Sometimes, a clip may be just the right length and placed in an appropriate location, but it may not be the best selection of source content. Rather than keep the first part of this clip, which features fewer workers, let's slip the content and use a later portion of the clip. To bring later content into the current clip area, you drag the clip left.

9 Move the Trim tool over the middle of the **workers relaxing** clip. When you see the Slip icon, drag left. In the Viewer, watch the left frame and note when the red-shirted woman's arm first appears. Release the clip after slipping it about –4:00 (minus four seconds).

NOTE ▶ When you look closely at the Slip icon, you see it's a bi-directional filmstrip with selection brackets facing inward to indicate that only a single clip is affected. Slipping does not change the project length.

In the Viewer two-up display, rather than seeing an edit point from two different clips as you did in the ripple and roll trims, you see the first and last frame of the *same* clip. The new first frame, or start point, appears in the left frame and the new last frame, or end point, appears in the right frame.

TIP A good way to think about slipping direction is to think of scrolling on an iOS device. If you want to see media that is to the right of the current end point, drag across the clip from right to left as if you were swiping to the left.

10 Press Shift-Z, and then zoom into the **man picks beans** clip and play it.

In the previous exercise, you trimmed a portion of the **man picks beans** clip to shorten it. As you review that clip, you may be comfortable with the shorter clip duration, but less sure about the clip content. For example, at the beginning of the original clip, the man's laugh sets a nice tone.

To slip the clip and bring the laugh back to the head of the clip, you will drag the clip to the right.

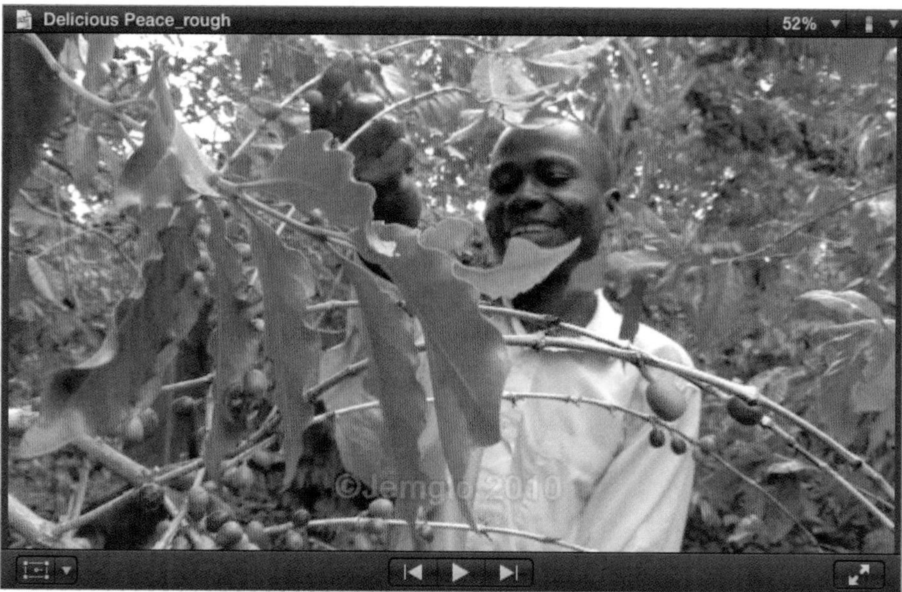

11 Move the Trim tool to the middle of the **man picks beans** clip, and when you see the Slip icon, drag right as far as possible. You will see a red highlighted start point to indicate that you've reached the media limits. Release the clip, and play the new selection.

The fourth mode of the Trim tool, with help from the Option key, slides a clip left or right between the two clips on either side of it. When you slide a clip, you don't change its length or the selection of original source content. You change only its location in the project.

NOTE ▶ If a slip involves a single clip, and ripple or roll trims involve two clips, a slide would involve three clips—with the middle as the clip you slide, and the "bookend" clips changing length to accommodate the move.

12 Skim to the **making coffee** clip, and press Shift-? to play that area. To slide this clip, place the Trim tool over the clip, and then Option-drag to the left. After you start dragging, release the Option key to use the Viewer two-up display as a guide. Position this clip after the woman sweeping beans has completed at least two sweeps. Before you release the clip, look at the slide action in the Timeline, and then in the Viewer two-up display.

TIP You may have to slide to the beginning of the previous clip and count the sweeps forward. If you are not happy with your trim, you can always release the clip and press Command-Z to undo the trim and try again.

In the Timeline, when you hold down Option, the Trim tool icon changes to the Slide icon: two outward-facing selections and two outward-facing filmstrips.

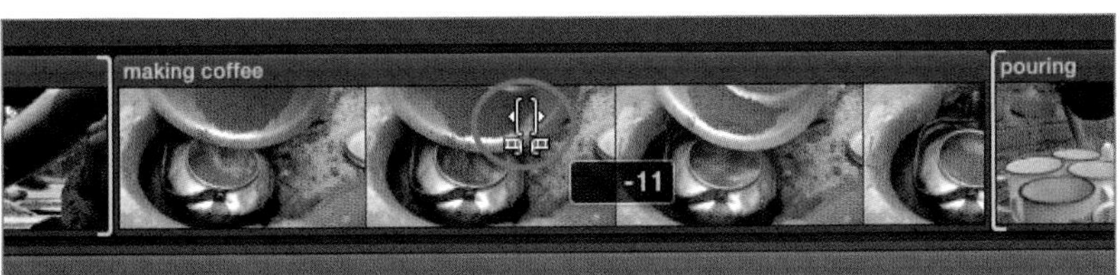

NOTE ▶ Notice that the selection brackets are pointing outward to the two adjacent clips, which change length to accommodate the slide.

After you start Option-dragging, release the Option key as you continue dragging. In the Viewer two-up display, you see the last frame of the first clip on the left side, and the first frame of third clip on the right, which helps you visualize how the new location of the middle clip will look.

Of course, you don't have to wait until you've completed a rough cut to begin using the Trim tool because it's always available. As you continue to work with it, and follow the visual indicators, you will find that trimming and finessing your project can be easily integrated into your editing workflow.

Take 2

The Director of the *Delicious Peace* documentary needs a one-minute promotional piece that PBS and the BBC can use to promote the show. With the trimming methods you've learned so far, trim different clips in the primary storyline to reduce the length to one minute. You may have to be aggressive and delete entire clips. Don't forget that you can create a selection in the Timeline using the Range Selection tool or the I/O shortcut keys, and delete that range. And because the voiceover clips are tucked safely within their own storyline, they won't be affected by the trims.

Trimming with Precision

You may find that certain projects benefit from particular types of trims. In the previous exercise, slipping or sliding the coffee clips helped you achieve the best timing and clip selection. But when you trim and refine material for a dramatic show, such as *Fairly Legal*, your focus is always moving forward in a linear fashion to match the action from one shot to the next. As a result, you are less likely to use the slip and slide trim functions.

In this exercise, you will apply ripple and roll trims with more precision by using the Final Cut Pro Precision Editor. Here, a specialized interface layout allows you to consider and execute your trims quickly and easily. To begin, you will open the *Fairly Legal* project from the Project Library.

1 In the Project Library, from the Lesson 6 folder, open the *Fairly Legal_rough* project and play it in the Timeline. Press A to choose the Select tool.

   As its name indicates, this rough project is obviously not ready for prime time. In fact, it appears as though an assistant editor assembled the clips to save the editor some time.

   Because editing dramatic or narrative content relies heavily on what the actors are saying, it's helpful to view the audio waveforms. And because the project includes only a primary storyline with no connecting clips, you can make the filmstrip thumbnails larger.

2 In the Timeline, click the Clip Appearance button, and from the pop-up menu, choose the fourth icon to make the filmstrip images larger. Play the first two clips and zoom into the edit point between them.

Rather than switch to the Trim tool in this view, it will automatically become available to you in the Precision Editor.

3 To open the Precision Editor, double-click the edit point between the **4A-1_110(A)** and the **4B-3_110(A)** clips. You could also select the edit point, and press Control-E.

The Precision Editor opens, displaying the outgoing clip on the top and the incoming clip below. Notice that the playhead is positioned at the current edit point, and the available media handles of each clip appear darker. In this visual display, you can easily see whether or not it's possible to trim either or both of the edit points and in which direction.

TIP The same shortcuts you use to zoom into an area of the Timeline can be used to zoom in for a closer look in the Precision Editor.

Any time you trim the edit point between two clips, you have three things to consider: the end point of the outgoing clip, the start point of the incoming clip, and the combined timing between them.

Where you place the pointer in the Precision Editor determines what you see in the Viewer.

4 To play the edit point between these two clips, move the pointer over the gray area *between* the upper and lower clip, and press the Spacebar to start and stop playback.

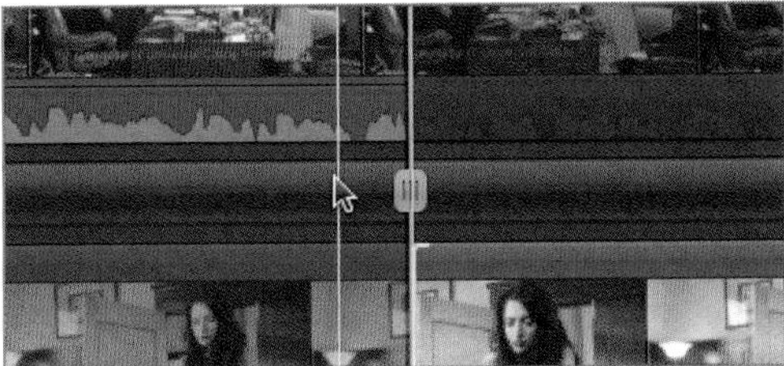

With the pointer sandwiched between the clips, Final Cut Pro defers to previewing the combined edit points.

5 To play the outgoing clip of the judge and view that clip's additional media, move—but don't drag—the pointer over that clip, and then press the Spacebar. Notice that the pointer changes to a hand icon. Then move the pointer over the incoming clip beneath it, and play the area before the edit point.

When you position the hand icon over a portion of the clip that's outside the current selection, the available media becomes brighter.

TIP You can also use the Hand tool in the default Timeline layout to scroll or drag the project horizontally. You can choose the Hand tool in the toolbar from the Tools pop-up menu, or press H.

By watching the different sides of the edit play individually, you get a very clear idea of what your options are. In this situation, you hear the judge deliver the line, "detritus of justice," twice. Let's keep his line on Kate's camera but trim it off the end of the wide shot.

To trim a single edit point in the Precision Editor, you drag the clip filmstrip left or right across the cut point or edit line. As you do this, you can use the audio waveforms as a reference.

NOTE ▶ Dragging a filmstrip in this view may seem somewhat similar to the way old-school film editors used to handle film.

6 Move the pointer onto the outgoing clip, **4A-1_110(A)**. Play the clip and watch the audio waveform as you listen for the judge beginning to say, "detritus of justice." From this point, drag the clip right and release it at the edit point. To play the combined edit points, position the pointer in the gray area between the two clips, and press the Spacebar.

With the outgoing clip trimmed, you can now focus on the incoming clip's edit point. To pick up where the previous clip left off, you will trim the start point of this clip so that it begins where the judge says, "detritus of justice." But rather than drag the edit point, you will use the audio waveform as a reference and simply click where you want to place the new edit point.

7 Move the pointer over the incoming clip, **4B-3_110(A)**, and play from the current start point. Stop playback in the pause after the judge says, "and other." To make this frame the new start edit point, click with the Hand tool. To play both clips, skim to before the edit point in the gray area between the clips, and press the Spacebar.

TIP Once you've finished trimming one edit point, you can press the Up or Down Arrows to view the previous or next edit point in the Precision Editor. You can also press the ; (semicolon) or ' (apostrophe) key to jump backward or forward to the previous or next edit point.

While the judge's audio line now sounds correct, Kate's action in the video doesn't match. You have the ability to roll the edit point in the Precision Editor. Let's see if that will fix this edit.

8 Move the pointer to the edit line handle between the two clips and click it. Notice that both edit points are highlighted. As you watch the Viewer two-up display, drag the edit line handle left about 15 frames to where Kate is holding the book in her arm. Play this edit point.

In this situation, rolling *both* the audio and video edit points will not give you the desired results. Instead, you must roll only the video portion of these two clips without changing the audio, which you just trimmed into place. You can easily roll just the video, but you must first expand the audio and video portions of the clip, which you can do in the default Timeline layout.

9 Press Command-Z and click the Close Precision Editor button in the lower right of the Timeline. You can also press Return.

Because the audio and video of the *Fairly Legal* clips were captured together, Final Cut Pro combines them into a single clip, making each clip easy to edit and move within the project. But at times, such as this situation, you need to adjust the video or audio edit points separately. To do that, you have to expand the audio and video.

10 Control-click the second clip in the project, **4B-3_110(A)**, and choose Expand Audio/Video from the shortcut menu, or press Control-S. Then select the first clip, and press Control-S.

In the Timeline, the two clips display a separate audio clip.

TIP If you want to expand a number of clips at the same time, select them as a group and press Control-S.

To roll just the video edit points, you will use the Trim tool. And because you are no longer in the Precision Editor and it doesn't appear automatically, you have to select it.

11 To select the Trim tool, press T. Move the Trim tool to the edit point between the first two clips, and drag left. In the Viewer two-up display, look for a good match between Kate's actions so she's holding the book in each frame. Press Shift-? to play this edit.

Success! When you look at the clip video and audio edit points in the Timeline, you see that they do not occur at the same place.

Take 2

On her way out of town, the editor of *Fairly Legal* asks if you could take another pass on this scene and get it into better shape. Using the Select tool, Trim tool, and Precision Editor, take a stab at refining the edit points to your liking.

NOTE ► When the Select tool is active, stepping through an edit point in the Timeline (not the Precision Editor) with the Left and Right Arrow keys displays the frames around the current edit point. However, when the Trim tool is active and an edit point is selected, pressing the Left and Right Arrow keys will preview individual frames of available media beyond the edit point of the clip that the pointer is over.

Editor's Cut

While the Final Cut Pro trimming functions work the same regardless of the project, practicing on different projects is a good way to hone your editing skills and gain greater control over its tools, functions, and shortcuts. Since you've worked with dramatic footage in the previous exercise, you may want to apply what you've learned to the *Zero to Hero_v2* project.

Lesson Review

1. How do you remove a single clip from the primary storyline without leaving a gap?
2. How do you insert a gap clip into the primary storyline to act as a placeholder?
3. How do you choose the Range Selection tool to select a range in the a storyline?
4. What happens when you ripple trim the outgoing clip by dragging to the right?
5. Which two sets of shortcut keys allow you to adjust edit points one frame and ten frames at a time?
6. Which two edit points does a roll trim adjust?
7. What happens when you slip a clip?
8. Which clips are altered when you slide a clip, and how are they affected?
9. How do you open the Precision Editor to see an expanded view of the clips on either side of the edit point as well as the clip handles?
10. How do you view the detailed trimming feedback?

Answers

1. Select the clip, and choose Edit > Delete, or press the Delete key. The selected clip is removed from the primary storyline and any clips to the right of the selection ripple to close the region.
2. Place the playhead where you want to insert the gap, and choose Edit > Insert Generator > Gap, or press Option-W. A three-second gap clip is inserted into the primary storyline by default, and you can trim its duration.
3. From the Tools pop-up menu, choose Range Selection, or press R. Then drag in the Timeline to make your selection.
4. Dragging to the right lengthens the outgoing clip, so any clips to the right of the edit point ripple accordingly and increase the project's duration.

5. Press the . (period) and , (comma) keys to nudge right and left one frame at a time. Press Shift-. (period) and Shift-, (comma) to nudge right and left 10 frames at a time.
6. A roll trim adjusts the outgoing clip's end point and the incoming clip's start point without changing the duration of the project.
7. A slip trim adjusts the start and end points of a single clip without changing the duration of the project. This edit is appropriate when you like the clip's length and Timeline location, but want to use a different selection of the media.
8. Sliding affects the position of the middle clip, and the durations of the two surrounding clips. When you slide a clip, you don't change its length or the selection of original content. You change only its location in the project.
9. In the toolbar, from the Tools pop-up menu, choose the Select tool or the Trim tool; and double-click the edit point you want to trim in the Timeline. Alternatively, select an edit point and press Control-E.
10. Choose Final Cut Pro > Preferences, or press Command-, (comma), and click Editing. In the Timeline section, select the "Show detailed trimming feedback" checkbox. The two-up display appears in the Viewer when you use a supported edit type or trim in the Precision Editor.

Keyboard Shortcuts

A	Choose the default Select tool
B	Choose the Blade tool
H	Choose the Hand tool
I	Set range start point
M	Set a marker
O	Set a range end point
P	Choose the Position tool
R	Choose the Range Selection tool
T	Choose the Trim tool
Z	Choose the Zoom tool
Shift-Z	Zoom to fit

Keyboard Shortcuts

Spacebar	Play/pause
Command-Shift-A	Deselect any selected clips
Command-Shift-Z	Redo the last command
Control-S	Expand audio/video
Down Arrow	Go to the next item (in the Event Browser) or the next edit point (in the Timeline)
Up Arrow	Go to the previous item (in the Event Browser) or the previous edit point (in the Timeline)
Option-W	Insert gap clip
Option-] (right bracket)	Trim the end point and remove all frames to the right of the skimmer location
Option-[(left bracket)	Trim the start point and remove all frames to the left of the skimmer location
Shift-Delete	Delete an item or section from a storyline and leave a gap
Shift-?	Play around the skimmer

Completing the Cut

7

Time This lesson takes approximately 60 minutes to complete.

Goals

Apply a video transition

Use the Transitions Browser

Modify a transition

Change parameters in the Inspector

Create a compound clip

Add transitions to a storyline and compound clip

Apply audio transitions

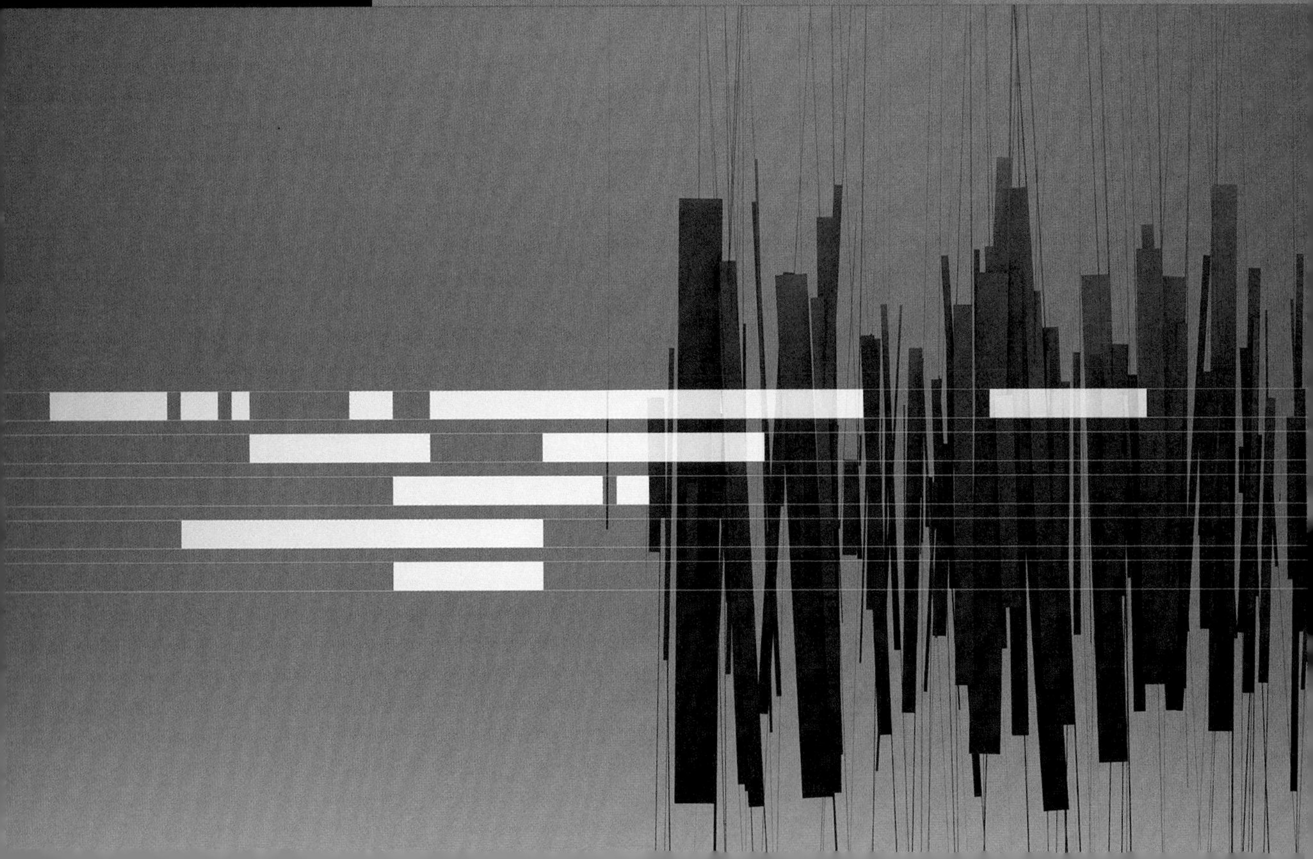

Lesson 7

Applying Transitions

Now that you've fine-tuned your rough cut, the next stage of the editing process is completing your cut. That doesn't mean you'll be ready to ship the final product when you're done. It does mean that you're wrapping up the big things such as adding transitions to refine edit points, mixing audio, and creating opening titles and end credits. Without completing these essential tasks, your project won't be ready for broadcast, a movie theater, or even your soccer league party.

In the next three lessons, you will focus on each of these aspects: adding transitions, mixing sound, and creating titles. Add some special effects, and you are only a few short steps from your final output.

Preparing for Transitions

Not every project requires transitions. Some of the world's greatest films were created with nothing more than a fade-in at the head and a fade-out at the tail. One of the more creative aspects of being an editor is to determine whether transitions will improve the look and sound of your project.

A transition dictates the look of your video and the sound of your audio as it travels from the end of one clip to the beginning of the next. Transitions can smooth an abrupt audio or video edit, convey the passage of time, or create a certain visual style for your project.

Do you want to move seamlessly from one clip to the next? Then a simple dissolve transition might be all that's needed. Does the project's style demand something bolder with color, shapes, and animation? Colorful transitions might enhance your *Zero to Hero* project. Final Cut Pro provides a large number of transitions—from the simple to the complex—for you to consider and explore.

In this lesson, you will apply transitions to video and audio edit points in both the primary and secondary storylines and modify their parameters to suit your style.

1 If you haven't yet done so, return the Lesson 6 folder to the Lesson Projects folder. Drag the Lesson 7 folder onto the APTS FCP X icon. Then click the disclosure triangle of the Lesson Projects folder to hide the other lesson projects.

2 Click the disclosure triangle next to the Lesson 7 folder to reveal its contents.

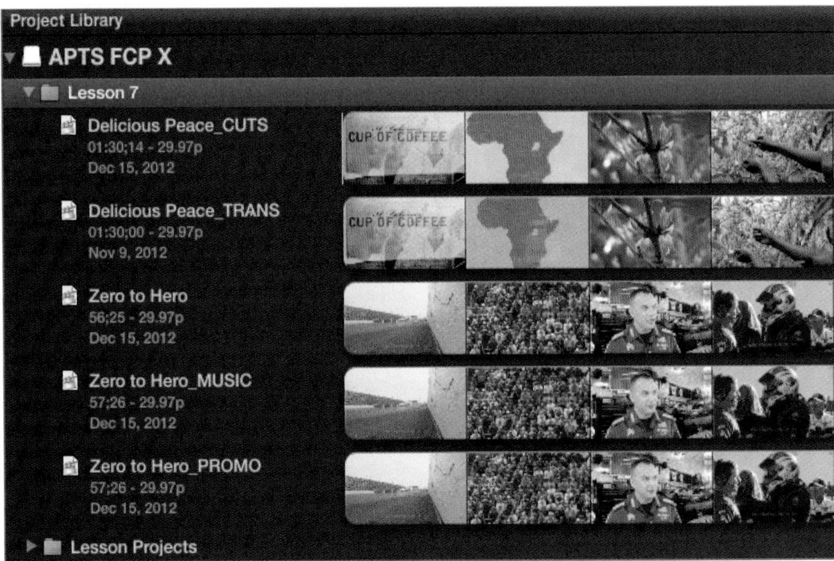

You'll work with five projects in this lesson: *Delicious Peace_CUTS* is a duplicate of the project you viewed in Lesson 1. A second version, *Delicious Peace_TRANS* has transitions applied so you can compare the project before and after transitions. You'll also use three versions of *Zero to Hero* in this lesson.

3 Let's review the *Delicious Peace_CUTS* project. Double-click it to open it in the Timeline, and play the project.

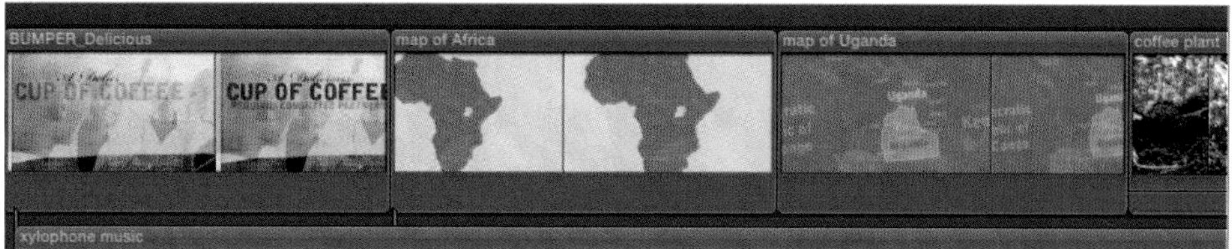

TIP During the next few steps, as you compare one *Delicious Peace* project with another, it might be helpful to adjust the display options in the Timeline so the projects are displayed similarly.

Notice that this project has no transitions. That is, one clip immediately cuts to the next. In addition, the sound of one clip cuts abruptly to the sound of the next. Let's see how transitions might improve this project.

4 To return to the Project Library, press Command-0 (zero), and double-click the *Delicious Peace_TRANS* project. In the Timeline, play the project and see how the project looks with transitions applied.

In this version of the project, cross dissolves were added to edit points between some of the clips. In each case, the dissolve smoothed the audiovisual flow from one clip to the next.

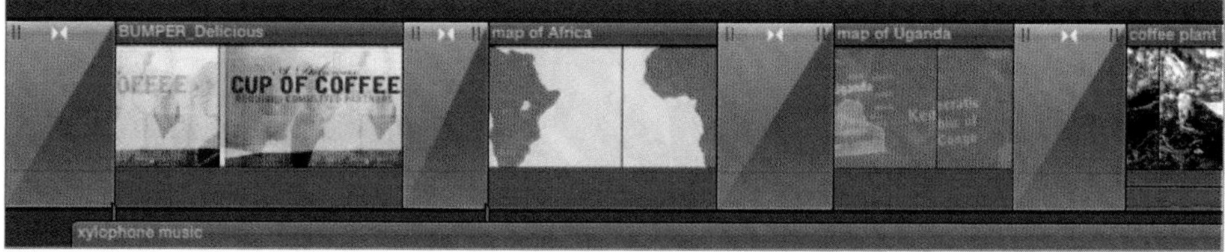

In Final Cut Pro, the default transition is a cross dissolve, and it's frequently used when a clean, simple transition is needed. It blends media from the outgoing clip with media from the incoming clip.

TIP The default duration of any transition is one second unless you change it in the Preferences window.

As you learned in Lesson 6, it's always a good idea to create a duplicate of your project as an unaltered version you can reference or restore if you want to rethink some of your changes. Before you begin to apply transitions to the *Delicious Peace_CUTS* project, let's create a backup.

TIP At the end of this lesson, you may want to experiment with different transition choices. An unchanged duplicate of the *Delicious Peace_CUTS* project gives you a good starting point.

5 In the Project Library, Control-click (or right-click) the *Delicious Peace_CUTS* project, and from the shortcut menu, choose Duplicate Project.

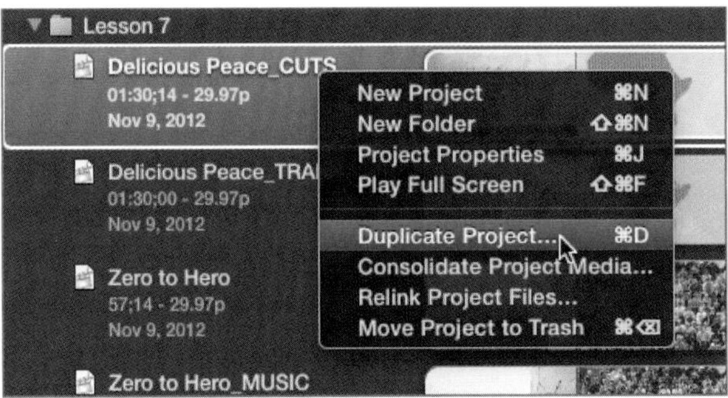

6 In the Duplicate Project dialog, name the project *Delicious Peace_BACKUP*, choose APTS FCP X as the destination location, select Duplicate Project Only, and click OK.

7 To return to the Timeline, click the Project Library button to deselect it, or press Command-0. In the upper left of the Timeline, look for the project name. If you do not see *Delicious Peace_CUTS*, click the left Timeline history arrow to return to that project.

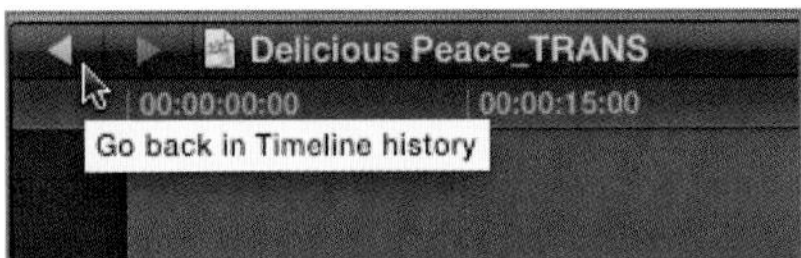

Once you open a project, that project will remain open until you quit Final Cut Pro. When you reopen the app, the project that was active when you quit will be the only open project in the Timeline.

Applying a Video Transition

You can apply transitions to your edit points in different ways. One way is simply to drag it to an edit point; but the easier approach is to select the edit point and then apply the transition with a few mouse clicks or a keyboard shortcut. In this exercise, you will apply a default cross dissolve to *Delicious Peace_CUTS.*

1 In the Timeline, press Shift-Z and then play the first two clips: **BUMPER_delicious** and **map of Africa**. Select an edit point between the two clips.

By selecting the edit point between the two clips, you give Final Cut Pro a target location to place a transition you choose from the menu bar, the Transitions Browser, or by using the keyboard shortcut.

2 Choose Edit > Add Cross Dissolve.

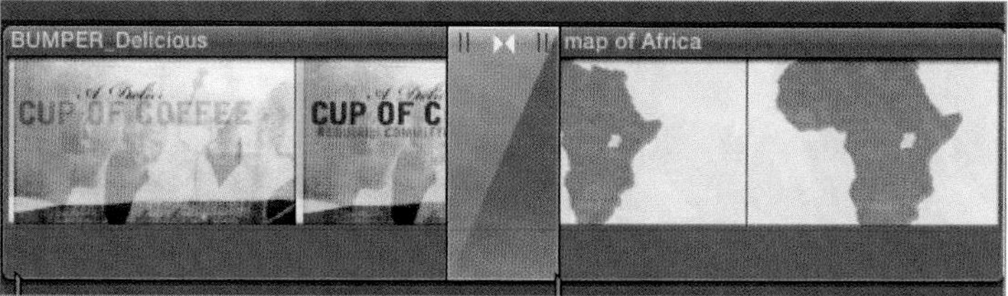

A gray transition icon containing a faint diagonal line appears over the edit point. Note that this transition icon is the graphic representation for all transitions regardless of type.

3 Skim before the transition and then play the new cross dissolve.

In this transition, the outgoing **BUMPER_delicious** clip blends with the incoming **map of Africa** clip. The opacity of the outgoing clip decreases while the incoming clip's opacity increases.

NOTE ▶ An orange bar appears, indicating the impending render of the transition. Final Cut Pro automatically begins a background render as you continue to work. Unless you change this option in the Preferences window, the background render will begin five seconds following the application of the transition or the end of playhead or skimmer movement.

When you work on a long project and want to apply a default transition, using a keyboard shortcut may be faster. The default transition is a cross dissolve.

4 Select the edit point between **coffee plant** and **coffee buds**. To apply a cross dissolve to this edit point, press Command-T. Play the transition.

Final Cut Pro splits the transition's duration over the edit point between the two clips. Again, the two clips blend together, softening the edit. The transition utilizes the extra media at the tail of the outgoing clip and at the head of the incoming clip to create the transition. This extra, available media is known as a *media handle*. Media handles allow a transition to be applied without changing the storyline's duration (and in the case of the primary storyline, the project's duration). Let's undo the transition to see these media handles in action.

5 Press Command-Z. The transition is removed, and the original end and start points of **coffee plant** and **coffee buds**, respectively, are restored.

To take a closer look at how the transition is utilizing the media handles of these clips, let's apply a transition to this edit point inside the Precision Editor.

6 Double-click one of the edges at the edit point between **coffee plant** and **coffee buds** to open the Precision Editor. Alternatively, select one of the edges, and then press Control-E.

As you learned in Lesson 6, the Precision Editor displays the outgoing clip on the top and the incoming clip below. The available media handles are visible as the dimmed section of each clip.

7 With one of the edges still selected, press Command-T to reapply a cross dissolve. Notice how the dimmed sections of each clip have changed.

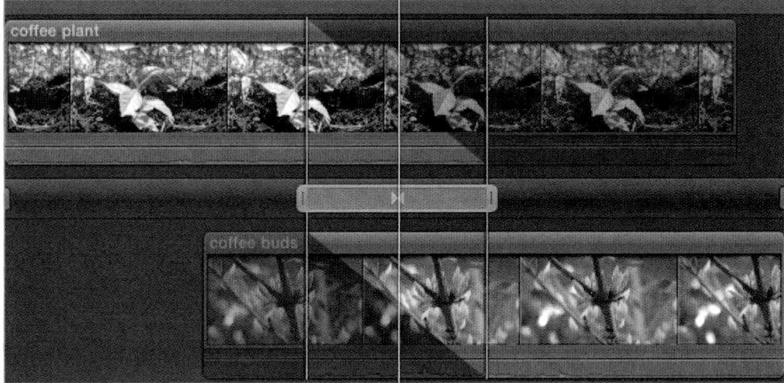

The end and start points of the two clips are altered to create the transition from one clip to the next. Each point is adjusted by half of the transition's duration, which you can see from the diagonal dimmed sections.

NOTE ► Not all the media in a handle may be appropriate for use in a transition. For instance, if a handle contains one second of a show slate, the slate will appear in the transition.

8 Close the Precision Editor, and then play the edit between **woman picks beans** and **man picks beans**. Click the left edge between them and then click the right edge.

As you learned in Lesson 6, the left edge's red bracket indicates that no media handles are available beyond the selected edge while the right edge is yellow, which indicates that a media handle exists. What if an adequate media handle does not exist for one clip? Or both? Final Cut Pro will alert you and offer an optional transition type.

9 To apply a transition to this edit point, press Command-T.

A dialog appears, informing you that not enough media handles exist to apply the transition. You are offered an alternative, an overlap transition.

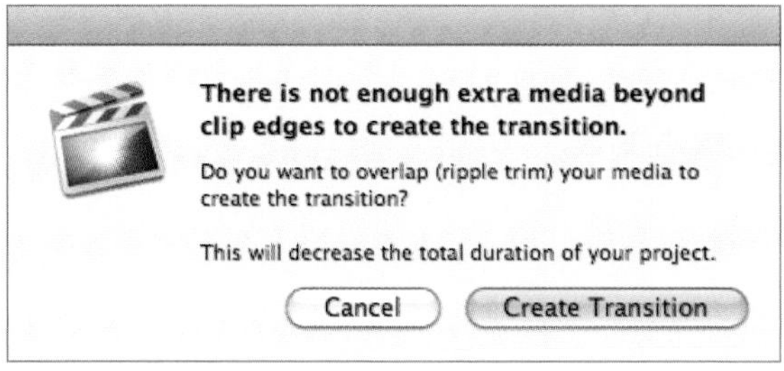

NOTE ► A media handle must have a minimum of two frames to receive a transition and not affect the storyline's duration. In such cases, the transition duration will be shortened to twice the length of the shortest media handle.

10 Note the project's current duration (at the bottom of the interface), and then click Create Transition.

Notice that the project is shortened by one second. The transition overlapped one second of media on *each* side of the edit point even though the incoming clip had a handle.

NOTE ▶ If you were to delete an overlap transition, your project would still be shortened by one second. Final Cut Pro does not restore the media but instead creates a new edit point at the center of the now-deleted transition. To restore the media, you should undo the step by pressing Command-Z.

Applying a transition to both ends of a clip at the same time is easy. Instead of selecting an edit point, you select the clip itself.

11 Play the **man roasts beans** clip. Select the entire clip by clicking in the middle of the clip rather than on the edit point.

12 With the clip selected, press Command-T. A default transition is added to both ends of the clip.

At the bottom of transitions, you can see an audio waveform continuing through the clip. In Final Cut Pro, where audio is attached to video, an audio crossfade is *automatically* added to each video transition, which can save you an enormous amount of time. You will learn more about audio transitions later in the lesson.

Take 2

You walk into the cutting room after a break and see a note from the director: "I want to preview this project with dissolves on every edit in the primary storyline. Back in 5." Since you don't have much time, you think about the fastest approach to applying dissolves to every edit point in the *Delicious Peace* project. Instead of the time-consuming process of applying one transition at a time, you'll probably come up with the following:

- Duplicate the *Delicious Peace_BACKUP* project and rename it *Delicious Peace_ALL*.
- Open the new project, and press Command-A to select all the clips.
- Press Command-T to apply transitions to your storyline clips.

Using the Transitions Browser

Among the various media browsers available in Final Cut Pro X is the Transitions Browser, which opens below the toolbar in the Timeline. Within the browser is a gallery of transitions, many created and animated in Apple Motion. Final Cut Pro organizes transitions into nine categories, with some further organized into subcategories. The transitions provide colorful alternatives to the default cross dissolve.

Each transition in the browser is displayed with a thumbnail image to help you preview and visualize the transition before it's applied. You can also skim the transitions to be certain they represent the exact style you want. In this exercise, you will apply transitions to the *Zero to Hero* project by choosing them in the Transitions Browser.

> **TIP** If you want to save this version of the project before making changes, duplicate the project before continuing. As you continue to create or duplicate new projects, try creating a new folder for each set of footage, such as Delicious Peace, Zero to Hero, and so on. Then drag the individual projects into that folder.

1 From the Project Library, open the *Zero to Hero* project into the Timeline. Play the project.

   Some transitions in the browser might be just the ticket for the fast and colorful racing footage in this project. To begin, you will apply three transitions: Letter X, Lens Flare, and Video Wall.

   > **NOTE** ▶ Since the purpose of this lesson is to expose you to different transition options, you will explore a few wild transitions.

2 In the toolbar, click the Transitions Browser button.

The Transitions Browser opens and displays transition categories to the left and thumbnails of the transitions to the right.

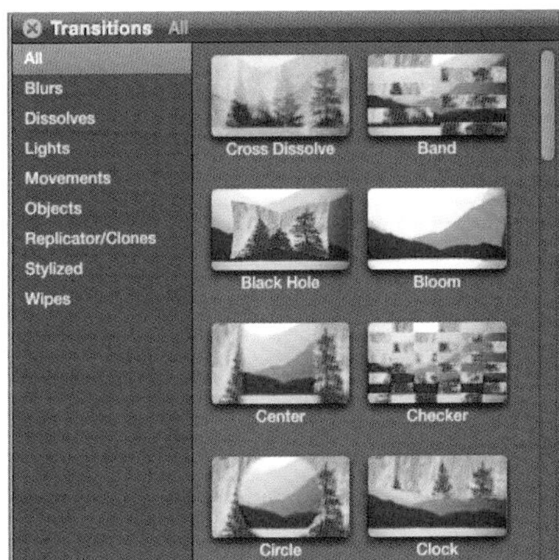

The first time you open the browser, the All category is selected. In the future, the browser will open with the previously viewed category selected. The All category contains every transition; the other eight categories contain the same transitions grouped by type.

3 In the Category pane, click Dissolves. Move your pointer over the Cross Dissolve thumbnail to skim the transition, which appears in the Viewer. Then, skim the Fade To Color transition.

TIP When you move the pointer over a transition thumbnail, you may have to wait a second or two before the skimmer appears.

As you skim the Fade To Color transition, you will see a preview of the transition between two different-colored still images.

4 In the Category pane, select the Stylized category. Notice that the thumbnail images to the right are divided into subcategories according to theme—Boxes, Bulletin Board, Cinema, Comic Book, Film Strip, and so on. Skim through a few transitions to see their behaviors.

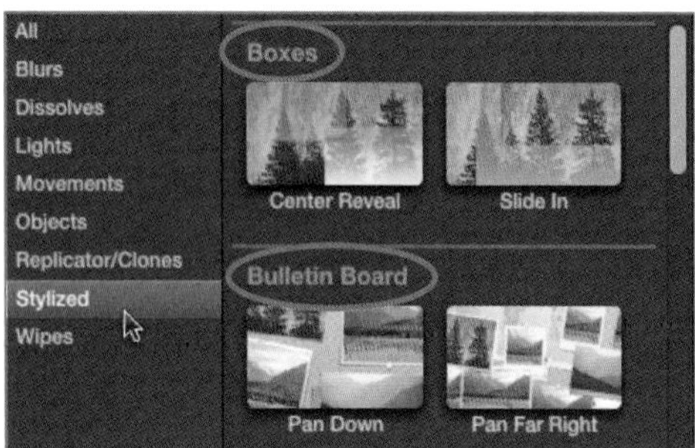

A lot of transitions here look like they'd be fun to explore. To create more space to display the transition thumbnails, let's hide the Category pane.

5 Click the All category again. In the lower-left corner of the Transitions Browser, click the Show/Hide button.

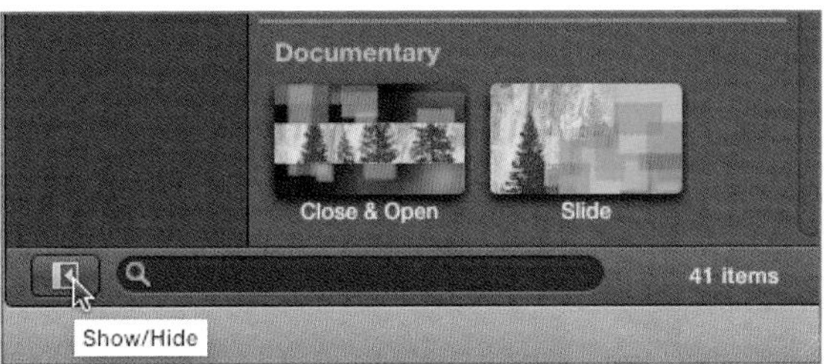

If you quickly want to find a particular transition without looking through several categories, you can search for a category in the search field.

6 In the search field, type *comic book*, which will display the Comic Book subcategory. Click X to clear the field, and type *pan* to find just those transitions with *pan* in their names. Click X to clear the field, and click the Show/Hide button to display the transition categories once again.

Search criteria

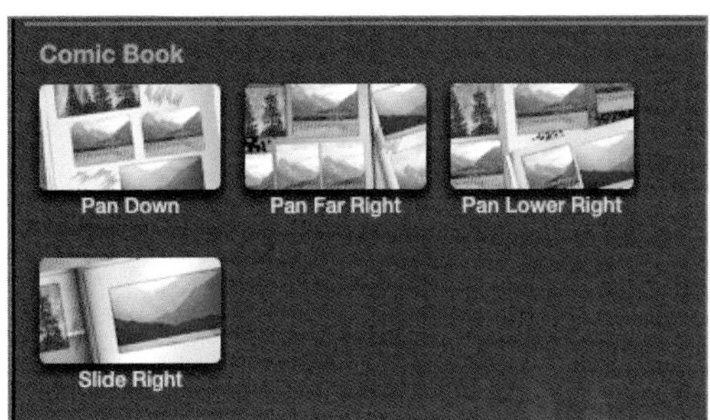

Search results

TIP Be sure to clear the search field before browsing for another transition.

Previewing transitions in the Transitions Browser is a great way to find the look that will be right for your project. And, if you're more into trial and error selection, transitions are easy to apply and delete.

While you can drag a transition from the Transitions Browser to a Timeline edit point, you may find it easier and more efficient to target the edit point and apply a transition with a few mouse clicks.

7 In the *Zero to Hero* project, select the edit point between **army start** and **Tony Schumacher**, around the 47-second mark.

8 In the Wipes category, skim over the Letter X transition to preview it in the Viewer. To apply the Letter X transition to the selected edit point, double-click it in the Transitions Browser. Then, play it in the Timeline.

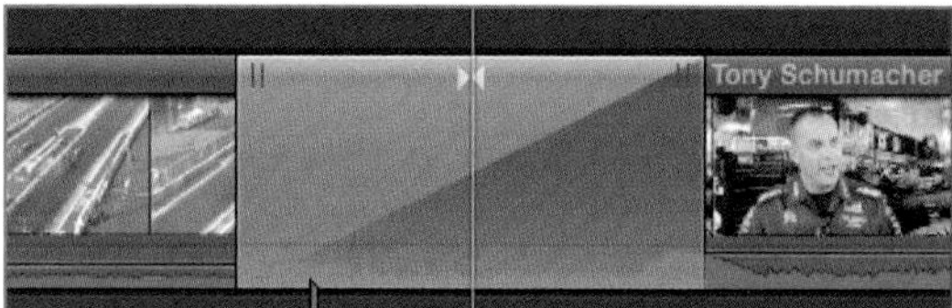

In the Viewer, an X pattern appears to reveal the incoming clip as the outgoing clip disappears. The edges of the X are feathered, and the amount of feather can be adjusted, which you will do in the "Modifying Transitions" section of this lesson.

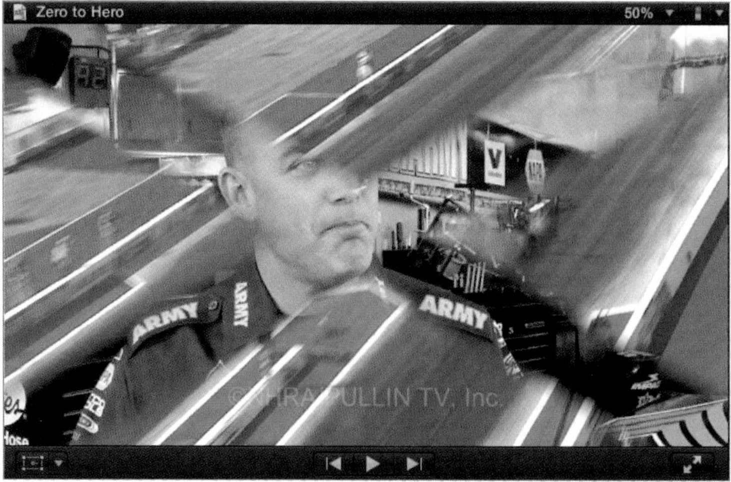

9 Navigate to the second edit point in the project, between **crowd ots** and **crowd wide**, and select it. From the Lights category, skim Lens Flare and then double-click to apply it to that edit point. Play the clip.

The transition makes it seem as if the standing man's camera lens catches the sun's glare and momentarily blinds us.

10 Select the edit point between the sixth and seventh clips, **Tony Pedregon** and **crash**. In the Replicator/Clones category, skim over Video Wall. Then double-click it to add it to the selected edit point.

When you select this transition icon in the Timeline, you will see yellow Timeline pins, which are controls to help you change the frames associated with this transition. You will do this later in the lesson.

Replacing one transition with another is as easy as dragging the new transition from the Transitions Browser onto the Timeline transition you want to replace. Or you can select the current Timeline transition and then double-click a new transition in the browser.

Perhaps you decide that the Lens Flare transition in *Zero to Hero* doesn't quite do the trick. Why not replace it with Bloom, another transition from the Lights category?

11 In the Lights category, drag the Bloom transition into the Timeline and over the Lens Flare transition. When the pointer changes to a green circle with a plus at its center, release the pointer, and play the clips to see the result.

The new transition, Bloom, immediately assumes the same duration as the transition it replaces.

Still not satisfied? It looks as if Lens Flare may be the correct choice here after all.

12 In the Timeline, select the Bloom transition, and then double-click the Lens Flare transition in the browser to restore it.

Use this double-click technique to try placing other transitions between these clips.

TIP As you begin to apply complex transitions, you may see the orange render bar appear more frequently. By default, Final Cut Pro renders in the background, but you can change this option in the Playback pane of the Preferences window. You can always manually initiate a render by selecting the transition and choosing Modify > Render Selection, or pressing Control-R.

Take 2

The director is back, and this time he's steaming. He wants flashier transitions in *Zero to Hero*, and lots of them. See if you can help him out. Don't forget to duplicate the project and then give it a new name, perhaps *Zero to Hero_FLASH!*

Modifying Transitions

Most transitions can be modified beyond just their durations. Would you like to blur the edges of the effect? What about changing the direction of a wipe as it crosses the screen? You can make all these changes easily using a combination of controls in the Timeline and onscreen controls directly in the Viewer.

In this exercise, you will also make use of the Timeline Index, which can help to locate quickly any of your transitions so you can make change after change efficiently. Let's start by changing the transition durations in *Delicious Peace_CUTS*. If you need to return to a recent project, you can use the Timeline history arrows to move from one open project to another. But here's a trick to make it even easier:

1 To reopen *Delicious Peace_CUTS* into the Timeline, click and hold the left arrow at the top left of the Timeline, and choose the project.

If you are working with only two projects and each has recently been opened into the Timeline, you have to click only one arrow or the other to open the second project. If, however, you've opened two or more projects, clicking and holding one arrow or the other will display a project list.

2 In the Timeline, select the first cross dissolve and hover the pointer over the center of either the left or right edge. When the pointer turns into a Trim icon with no filmstrip, drag the transition edge toward the transition's center.

TIP When dragging a transition edge, temporarily turning off snapping (N) will give you greater control over the adjustment, as will zooming in to that area of the Timeline.

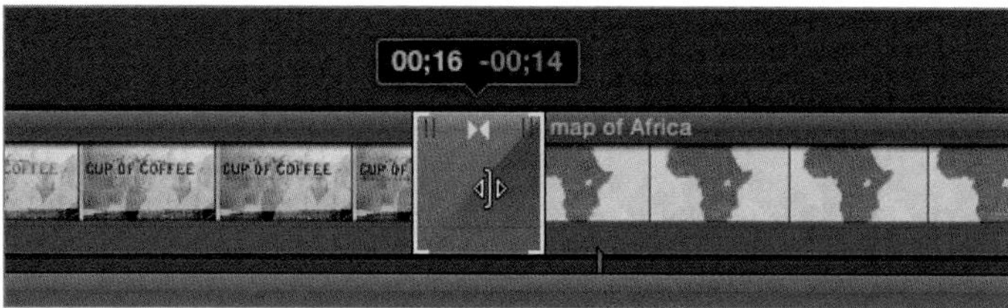

As you drag toward the center, an info flag indicates the transition's new duration and by how much the transition has been shortened.

3 Drag the edge again, but this time drag away from the center to lengthen the transition.

When you cannot drag any farther, you have either reached the limit of the clip's media, indicated by a red bracket, or you've reached the next edit point or transition in the Timeline.

Dragging out and back gives you only a relative amount of change to the duration, such as 12 frames longer or 10 frames shorter. To create a precise length for your duration, you can enter a number in the Dashboard.

4 To give the selected transition a precise duration, Control-click the transition icon and, from the shortcut menu, choose Change Duration, or press Control-D. When the Dashboard is highlighted in blue, type *45* and press Return.

The graphic in the Dashboard indicates you are performing a function that changes the content of the selection—in this case, the duration of the transition.

NOTE ▶ The transition will stop at the maximum duration possible for the underlying edit if you enter a value that exceeds the maximum duration.

As you fine-tune transitions, you may find that a few are not that easy to find. In those cases, you can use the Timeline Index to locate individual transitions throughout the project.

5 In the lower-left corner of the Timeline, click the Timeline Index button to open that pane. Click the Clips button at the top, if necessary, and then choose All from the tabs at the bottom.

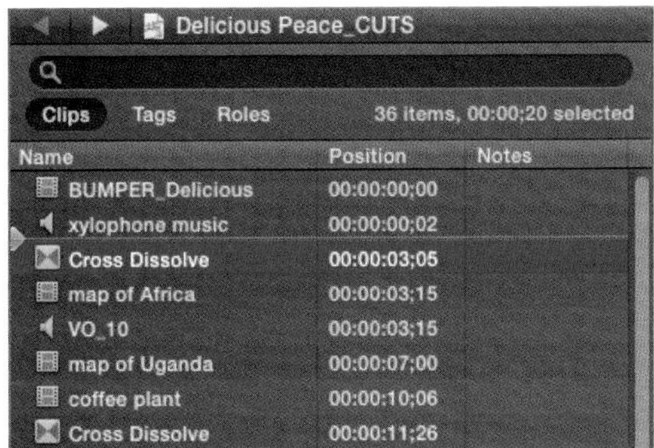

Notice that the cross dissolves in the project are listed with icons to the left that identify them as transitions. They are positioned in the index between the clips to which they were applied in the Timeline, and to the right of each element you can read its precise timecode position.

6 In the Timeline Index, select the cross dissolve at around timecode 22:00. In the Timeline, change the transition's duration at that location to 20 frames. Play the transition.

In the event of a long project or a Timeline with multiple transitions, locating the transition in the Timeline is made easier by using the index. Here you can also search for specific transitions.

7 In the Timeline Index search field at the top of the pane, type *cross*. Click each dissolve that is found, and in the Timeline, notice what happens as you do so.

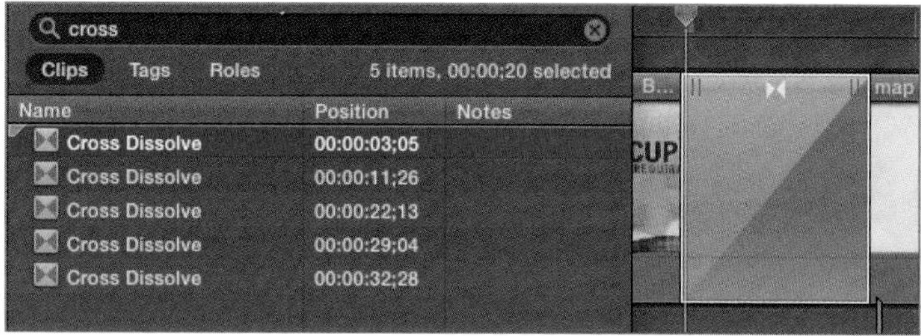

As you select a specific cross dissolve in the index, the playhead in the Timeline moves to the corresponding transition.

TIP All Final Cut Pro searches begin when you type the first letter, so you need to enter only a portion of the transition name to start viewing results.

Most, but not all transition parameters can be modified directly in the Viewer using onscreen controls. Let's return to *Zero to Hero* and modify a few more transitions.

8 To restore *Zero to Hero* to the Timeline, choose it from the Timeline history list. In the Timeline Index search field, type *Letter X* (or just type *let*) and when that transition is listed, select it. Then move your pointer into the Timeline and zoom into that transition.

Selecting the transition in the Timeline Index also selects it in the Timeline. Simply moving the playhead into the Timeline activates the selection.

With the Letter X transition selected in the Timeline, you will notice a set of onscreen controls in the Viewer, including a circle and a line a short distance from the circle with a square at the tip.

TIP If the controls aren't visible, Option-click the transition to select it and cue the playhead over the transition.

9 To see the results of your changes, skim a few frames into the transition where you see both images, and then Option-click to bring the playhead here as a bookmark reference.

Let's change the center position of the Letter X transition.

10 In the Viewer, move your pointer to the circle and drag to move the center of the X. As a target, you can position the X over Tony's nose. Play the transition.

With the center repositioned, the X will now open from Tony's nose. You can also use the onscreen controls to adjust the amount of feathering applied to the Letter X transition.

11 In the Viewer, move your pointer to the square at the end of the control line. Drag outward to make the edges of the X more diffuse. Drag inward to reduce the blur and sharpen the transition. Make the X as sharp as possible.

TIP If you drag the square tip all the way inward until it stops, the edges of the X will all be sharp.

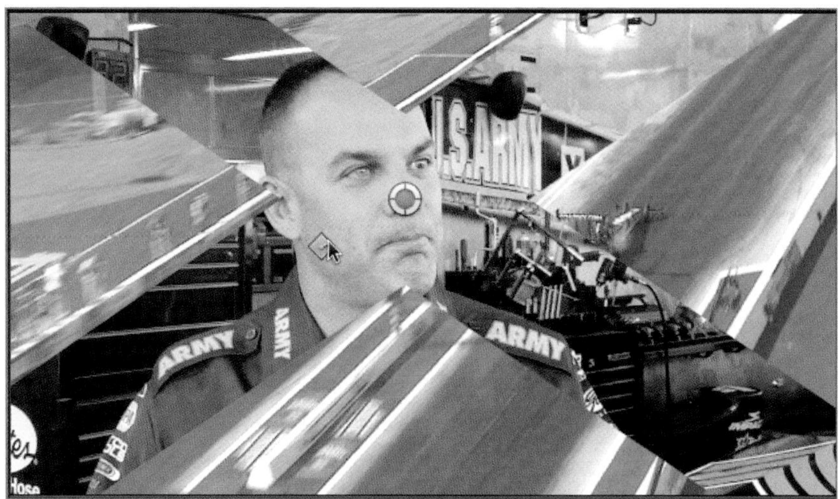

TIP To preview the behavior of the transition frame by frame, press the Right Arrow key to step through it slowly.

Some transition controls appear in the Timeline. In the case of the Video Wall transition, which uses two images from the project, two Timeline pins, represented as yellow numbered circles, can be dragged to replace the current images.

12 In the Timeline Index search field, type *wall* to search for the Video Wall transition. Select it in the list. In the Timeline, Option-click the transition. Notice the two yellow circles numbered 1 and 2.

Each circle is pointing to a specific frame used to fill half the boxes in the Video Wall transition. You can choose a different frame by dragging a pin to any other clip in the project.

TIP ▶ To see more clips from which to choose a frame, press Command-- (minus) to zoom out of the Timeline.

13 Drag pin 1 to the left and onto the **crowd ots** clip. Find the frame where the man with the binoculars has turned to face left. Then drag pin 2 to anywhere in the **crowd wide** clip. Play the transition.

NOTE ▶ The Timeline pins can point to any frame in the primary storyline.

Now the transition displays the two shots of the crowd watching the race, or in this situation, the wreck.

TIP If you want the man with the binoculars to appear in the outer corners of the Video Wall transition, move pin 2 to his frame, and move pin 1 to the crowd shot.

After you apply transitions to your project, you will occasionally need to delete one, some, or all of them from the Timeline. To delete transitions, do the following:

- To delete a single transition, select it in the Timeline or the Timeline Index, and press Delete.
- To delete a few transitions, select one transition in either the Timeline or the Timeline Index, Command-click additional transitions, and press Delete.
- To delete all transitions of the same type, open the Timeline Index. In the search field, type the name of the transition you want to delete. When the transitions are listed beneath the search field, select them all and press Delete.

TIP To immediately recover a deleted transition, press Command-Z.

Changing Transition Parameters in the Inspector

In previous lessons, you used the Inspector to review different aspects of a clip or to change it. The Inspector also provides easy access to all of a transition's parameters, each provided with a slider or numerical field. Although you may choose to modify parameters in the Viewer, some parameters may only be modified in the Inspector. In this exercise, you will modify the Letter X transition in the *Zero to Hero* project, and then add a new transition and modify its color parameter in the Inspector.

1 If necessary, use the Timeline Index to find the Letter X transition in the project. To create more room in the Timeline, close the Timeline Index.

2 Option-click the middle of the Letter X transition. In the toolbar, click the Inspector button, or press Command-4.

TIP If a transition or a clip is not selected in the Timeline, the Inspector will inspect the topmost clip under the playhead. When there is no selection, the Inspector will display "Nothing to Inspect."

The inspector's name appears at the top, in this case, Transition. Beneath the name is a transition icon followed by the name of the selected transition, Letter X. To the right is the transition duration—one second in this case.

The duration field will update to reflect a new duration when you drag an edge of a transition icon in or out in the Timeline. It's a handy aid to choosing a precise duration while dragging.

3 In the Timeline, drag the center of either edge of the Letter X transition and watch the duration change in the Inspector. Then drag to return the duration to 1:00.

You can adjust several parameters in the Inspector, including values you have already modified in the Viewer, such as the Center Point and Border.

NOTE ▶ Below the transition's video parameters are the parameters for the audio crossfade, which is applied automatically with the video transition. You will work with audio transitions in a later exercise.

4 Click the disclosure triangle next to Edge Treatment. From the Edge Type pop-up menu, choose Solid Color. Drag the Border slider to choose an edge thickness. Play the transition.

In the Viewer, the X is now edged with a black border. Its color can be modified in Edge Color, which you will do shortly.

NOTE ▶ Although you often can preview a transition change immediately, you may experience a momentary delay as Final Cut Pro finishes rendering the effect. When the render is complete, the orange bar will disappear.

As you can see, not all parameters are available in the Viewer and Timeline. Color changes must be made in the Inspector.

5 Select the edit point between **John Force** and **army prep**, at around 42 seconds. In the Transitions Browser, click the Movements category, and then double-click to apply the Multi-flip transition. In the Timeline, skim to the midpoint location, and press M to set a marker at this location.

TIP Setting a marker at the midpoint location will make it easier to locate the transition later in this exercise.

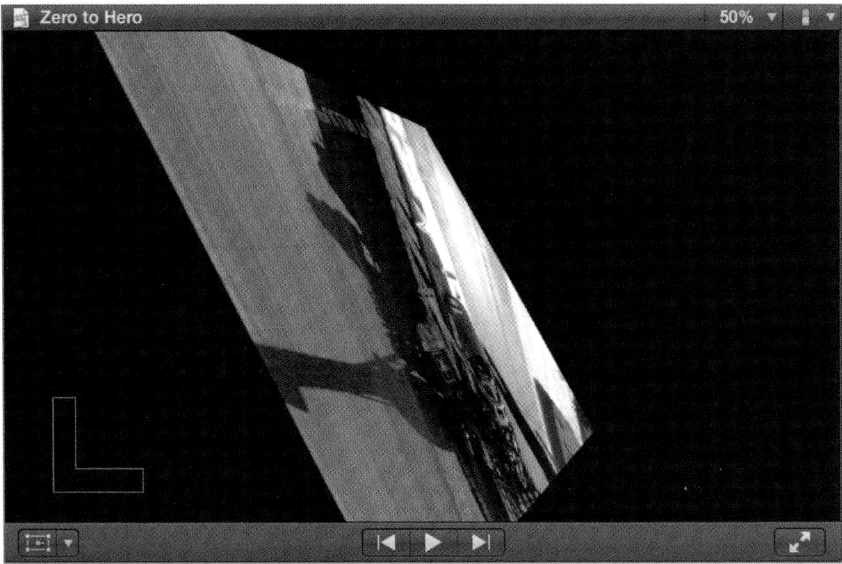

This transition displays the outgoing frame on one side of a rotating wall and the incoming frame on the other side. The default background is black, but you can change that to a different color using the parameters in the Inspector.

6 Option-click the transition you just applied. In the Transition inspector, click the black color well to open the Colors window. If the color wheel appears black, drag the vertical slider all the way up to see the brightest colors.

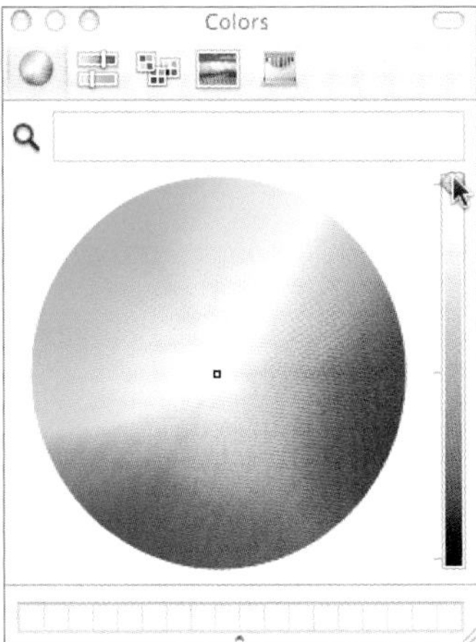

TIP To enter specific values for colors, in the Inspector, click the Color disclosure triangle next to the color well to display those values.

You can choose a color using any of the five color interfaces offered: the color wheel, color sliders, color palette, image palette, or crayons.

7 Click each color interface icon to see the various methods of making color choices. Then choose the color wheel interface and drag your pointer around inside the color wheel.

As you move over a color, that color appears in the horizontal swatch above the color wheel. It also becomes the background color choice for this transition.

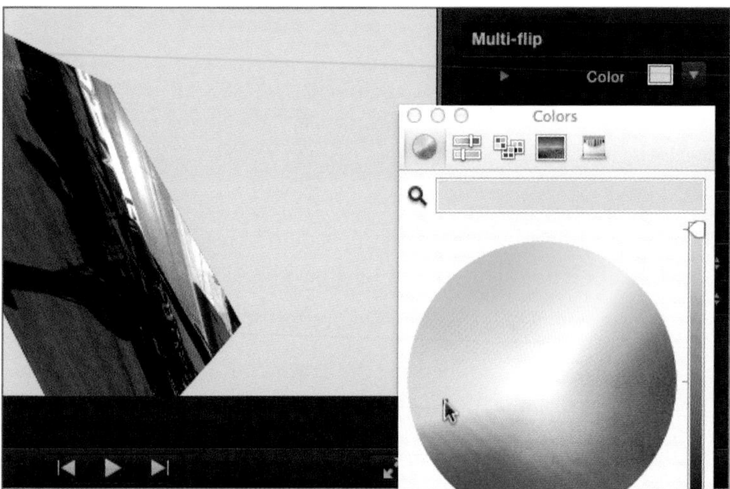

To the left of the color swatch is a magnifying glass. You can use it to select a color from the Viewer display, from a clip in the Timeline, or literally anywhere in your monitor. With a single click, it selects a color, which then appears in the horizontal swatch, the color tile in the Inspector, as well as in the transition background itself.

8 In the Colors window, click the magnifying glass and then click a green color in one of the **John Force** clip thumbnails in the Timeline. Play the transition.

The color is applied automatically to the transition. Each time you click with the magnifying glass, that icon disappears. To select another color, you must click the magnifying glass again.

TIP You can save the color you selected by dragging it from the horizontal swatch down to the small squares at the bottom of the pane. Here you can store a favorite in each of the squares to be saved and available for future use. To store more colors, drag the bottom drawer of the Colors window down to reveal additional color squares.

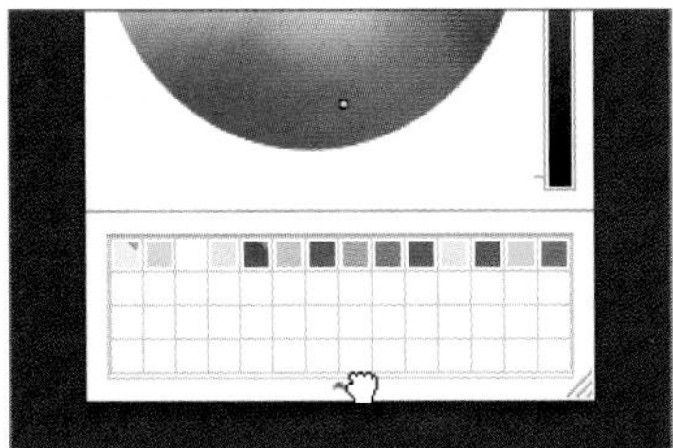

Instead of using color as a background in the Multi-flip transition, you can use an image from the Timeline or even the Event Browser.

9 Close the Colors window, and in the Transition inspector, select Use Image Well. This tells the Inspector to ignore the background color and look for an image to use instead.

The Image Well below the checkbox defines the video frame to use for the background.

10 Click once in the Image Well.

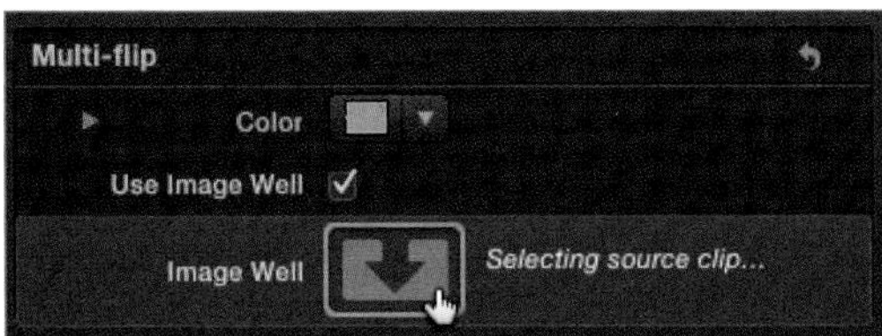

The “Select a Source Clip” window appears in the Viewer. It instructs you to click once on the image you want to use for the background. You can select a frame from any clip in the Timeline or the Event Browser.

Choose a clip that has the "Image Well" you want to use.
Cancel
Apply Clip

11 Click a frame in the **crowd wide** clip, and then click Apply Clip. Return to and play the transition.

The Image Well now contains the clip you selected and displays the source clip’s title. The clip also appears as the background image in the Multi-flip transition.

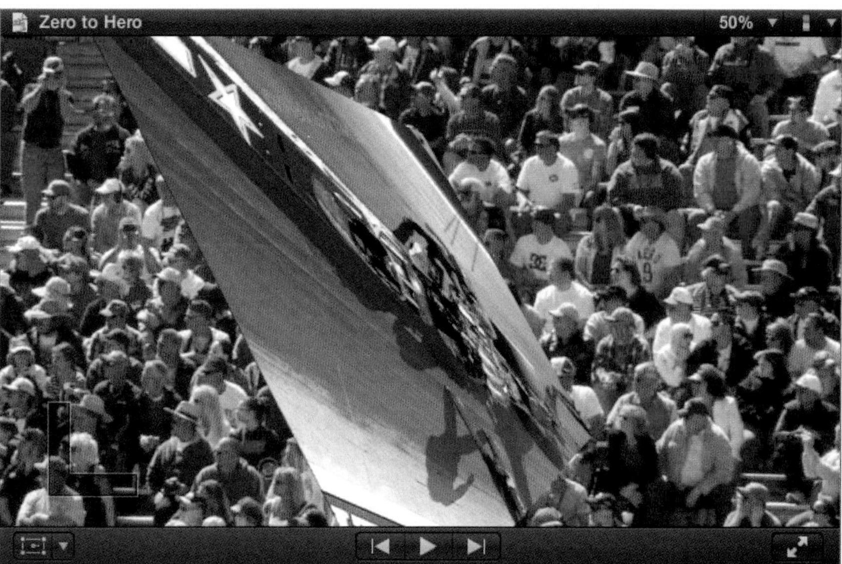
Zero to Hero
50%

Take 2

Oops, the producer and director are arguing about whether or not the Letter X transition is right. Should the edge be feathered as in the default or given a colored edge? You suggest that the colored edge may work best but it shouldn’t be black. While the two of them get yet another cup of coffee, edit the transition to show them a color alternative when they return.

Adding Transitions to Other Storylines and Compound Clips

Many of the projects you've worked with contain clips connected to the primary storyline. You can apply transitions to a connected clip or clips. Final Cut Pro will automatically create a secondary storyline for the connected clip and its transition. You can add additional clips and transitions within the new storyline and modify them just as you would modify transitions in the primary storyline.

As you add transitions, you may want to combine a few individual clips into one group by creating a compound clip. You can incorporate compound clips into an existing storyline and also apply transitions to those clips.

NOTE ▶ A compound clip can consist of clips within the primary storyline, or connecting clips above or below the storyline, that you want to combine or nest together as a set. Once you've created a compound clip, you can move those clips as though they were one clip.

In this exercise, you will work with the *Zero to Hero_PROMO* project and add transitions to a new storyline as well as to a compound clip.

1 In the Project Library, double-click the *Zero to Hero_PROMO* project to open it into the Timeline, and play the project.

TIP As before, it's a good idea to make a backup copy of a project before making major changes.

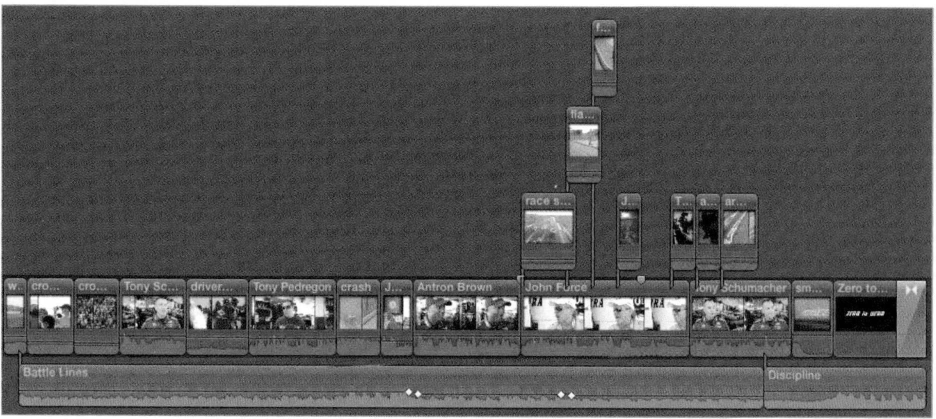

In the Timeline, you can see a grouping of adjacent, connected clips towards the end of the project, all of which could benefit from the addition of transitions.

2 Scroll and zoom in to focus on the three adjacent, connected clips at the end of the project, from **TS holds trophy** through **army start**.

3 Select the edit point between **TS holds trophy** and **army prep**.

Just as you could in the primary storyline, you can add a transition to the edit point between these connected clips.

4 Add the default cross dissolve by pressing Command-T, and then play the clips.

The **TS holds trophy** and **army prep** clips are now contained within a secondary storyline. One connection point connects the new storyline to the primary storyline—rather than two individual clip connection lines—and the two clips are joined by a transition.

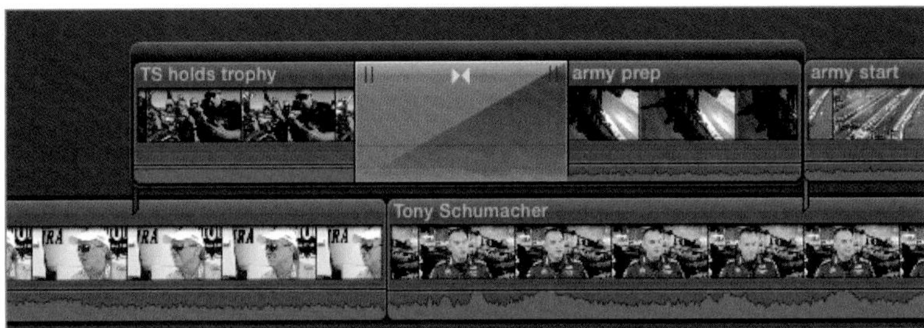

With the aggressive music and fast-paced edit, a cross dissolve may not serve this section. These edits need something fast and with flash. Let's replace the cross dissolve with a transition, conveniently named *Flash*, as the default transition. Then, we can quickly add a white flash between clips.

5 In the Transitions Browser, locate the Flash transition. Skim the Flash transition to preview it. Then Control-click Flash and choose Make Default from the shortcut menu.

Pressing Command-T will now apply a one-second Flash transition to a selected edit point or clip as the new default transition.

6 To exchange the cross dissolve between the **TS holds trophy** and **army prep** clips for the Flash transition, select the existing transition, and then press Command-T.

You can continue this flash theme by adding a Flash transition between the secondary storyline Final Cut Pro created and the next clip. No need to worry about adding the third clip to the storyline first, Final Cut Pro will take care of that automatically.

7 Select an edge between **army prep** and **army start**, and press Command-T.

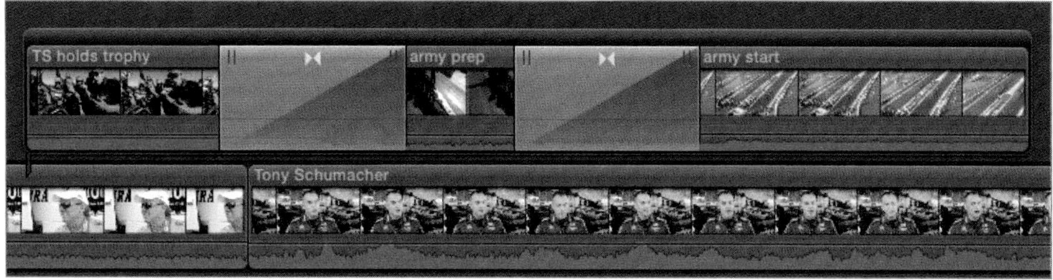

The **army start** clip is added to the previous storyline with a Flash transition. Let's also bookend this series of B-roll clips with the Flash transition.

8 Select the **TS holds trophy** clip, and then Command-click **army start**. Press Command-T to add the Flash transition to the start and end of the storyline.

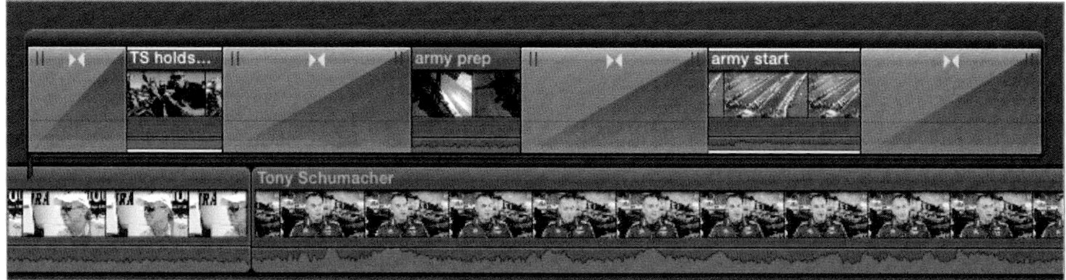

When you review the new transitions, they have flash, but are missing the fast-paced feeling of the footage itself. You can easily change the duration of a group of transitions at one time.

9 Click the first transition, and Command-click the other three to add them to the selection. Control-click any one of the selected transitions, and from the shortcut menu, choose Change Duration, or press Control-D.

TIP ▶ Place your pointer over the middle of the transition to select it. Clicking too close to an edge will select the edge or edges of the transition, preventing you from adding the other transitions to the selection.

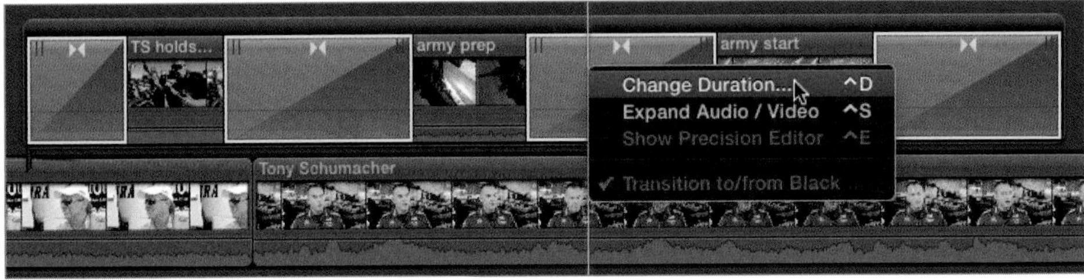

NOTE ▶ When you choose this option for a single transition, the Dashboard displays that transition's duration. With multiple transitions selected, the Dashboard displays 00.

10 Without clicking in the Dashboard, type *10* and press Return.

The duration of each of the four transitions is now 10 frames, making the series of B-roll shots a little snappier.

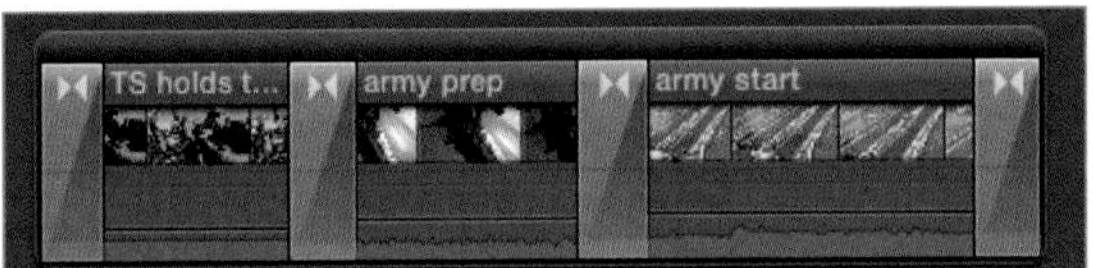

The storyline containing these B-roll shots helped organize them as a group. Look at the four clips connected to the **John Force** clip to the left of the new storyline. These clips provide cutaways for John Force's sound bite. Three of the connected clips overlap vertically: **race start**, **flame out**, and **flame out smoke**. Combining these four cutaway shots into their own storyline would group them together for easy management while reducing the Timeline clutter. This will take a few steps. Let's begin by creating a storyline for the stand-alone **JF in car** clip.

11 Select the **JF in car** clip, and then press Command-G to create a storyline that encapsulates the clip.

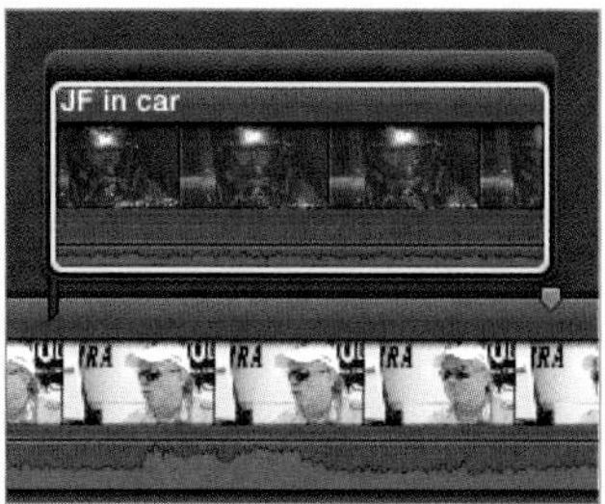

Storylines are easily created with clips that exist in the same horizontal lane of the Timeline. To add the three clips stacked vertically to your new storyline, you must first convert the three into a compound clip.

Compound clips are used to group or nest any combination of clips in the Timeline. You can make a compound clip with either video, audio, or both video and audio components.

12 Select **race start** and then Command-click the **flame out** and **flame out smoke** clips to add them to the selection. Control-click one of the selected clips, and from the shortcut menu, choose New Compound Clip, or press Option-G.

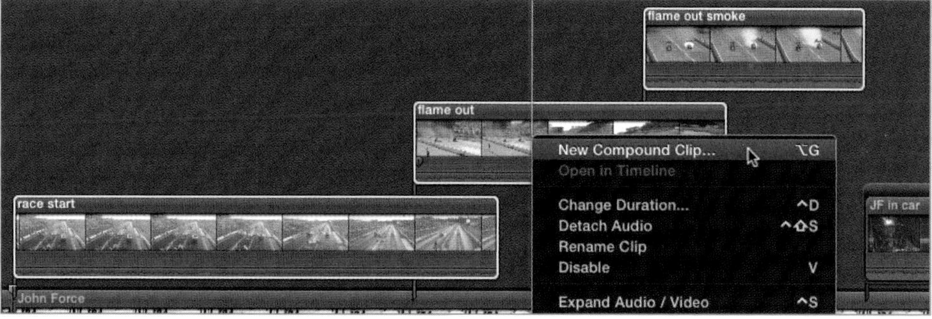

A dialog appears asking you to name the new clip. Compound clips are essentially a project within a project. And Final Cut Pro stores compound clips in an Event for use in other projects.

13 In the Name field, enter *Race_Flame Broll,* and choose Zero to Hero as the Event if it is not already selected.

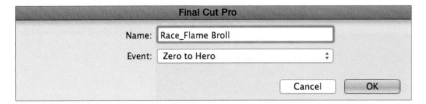

Final Cut Pro
Name: Race_Flame Broll
Event: Zero to Hero
Cancel OK

A new clip called **Race_Flame Broll** is created that combines all three of the individual clips. If you double-clicked the compound clip, the clip would open into its own Timeline for trimming. For now, let's include it in the storyline you just created.

14 Click **Race_Flame Broll** and Command-click the secondary storyline's shelf. Control-click the compound clip, and from the shortcut menu, choose Create Storyline, or press Command-G.

With all the clips in the same storyline, you can add a transition between the first and second clips as though you were transitioning to the in-car camera.

15 Select the edit point between **Race_Flame Broll** and **JF in car**. From the Lights category, drag Static to the edit point or double-click to apply it. When the overlap transition dialog appears, click Create Transition.

Shortening the duration of the storyline by one second exposes more of the **John Force** clip and shortens the duration of the **JF in car** clip. While not wrong, it does create a somewhat abrupt change. Let's add back a second to the end of the cutaway.

16 Using the Select tool, drag the end point of **JF in car** to the right to recover the one second lost to the transition.

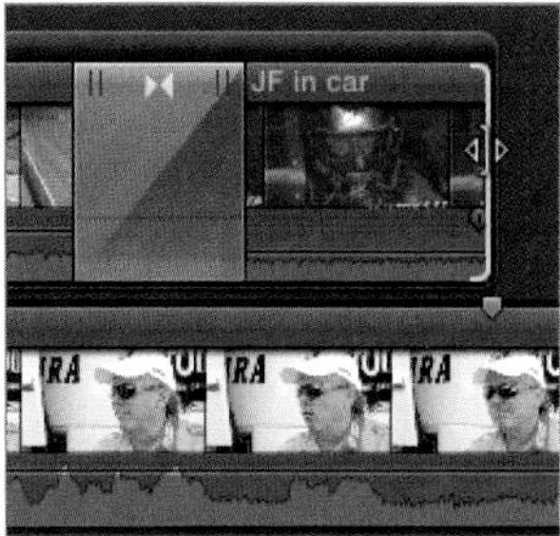

While the Flash and Static transition worked for these edits, they may not work for every edit, so let's reset the default transition to cross dissolve before continuing to edit.

17 In the Transitions Browser, Control-click the Cross Dissolve transition and from the shortcut menu, choose Make Default.

Take 2

The edit bay is getting crowded now because a studio executive has arrived to review *Zero to Hero*. She and the producer and director agree that one more transition is needed between the two connected clips at the end of the project. They leave the choice of that transition up to you. You notice that the ending logo has a little flash to it. Why not enhance the cut to the logo with a fancier transition? Since you're new to this, you decide to make a checklist that looks like this:

- In the *Zero to Hero_FLASH* project, apply a Flash transition to the edit point between the **smokey banner** and logo clips.
- Using the Select or Trim tool, adjust the duration of the transition and trim the logo clip to time the transition to the animation.

Exploring Audio Transitions

As you have seen earlier in this lesson, each video transition automatically includes an audio crossfade transition for audio contained in the video clip. An audio crossfade is the equivalent of a video cross dissolve. So as video media blends or dissolves from one clip to the next, audio from the outgoing clip fades down as audio from the incoming clip fades up. You manually apply audio crossfades to connected, audio-only clips such as music.

As with all transitions, crossfade adjustments can be made in the Inspector. In this lesson, you will smoothly segue between two music clips by adding a transition, trimming the transition edit point, and using fade handles.

1 Open the *Zero to Hero_Music* project. To focus on the audio in this project, click the Clip Appearance button, and from the pop-up menu, choose the third or fourth option. Then adjust the clip height so you can clearly see the video thumbnails.

2 Play the last few clips of this project and focus on the cut between the two music clips, **Battle Lines** and **Discipline**. It should sound a little rough.

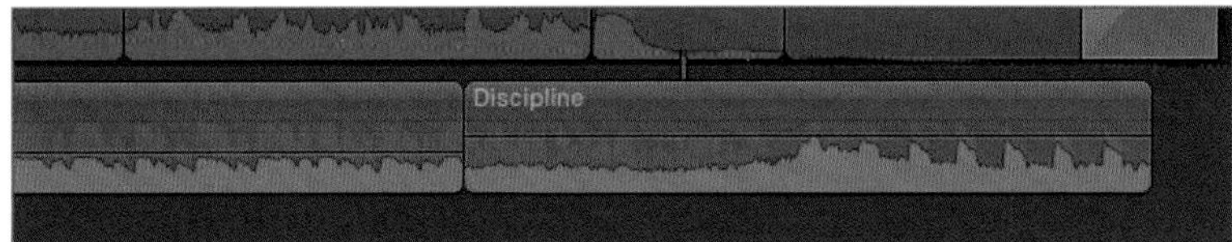

Applying an audio crossfade here would help smooth this edit point.

3 Select the edit point between the two audio clips, and press Command-T to apply the default transition. Play this area of the project.

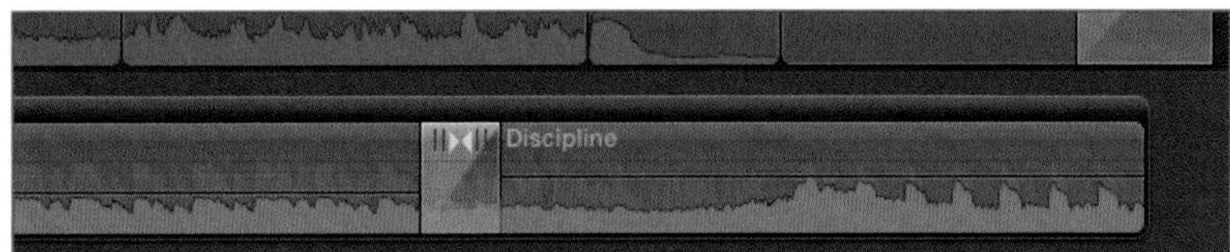

When only audio clips are involved, the default transition is the crossfade. And although adding the default duration helped smooth over the cut, it might be more helpful to make the transition longer.

4 If necessary, zoom into this area and drag either edge of the transition outward to lengthen the transition about 3 seconds. Play this transition again.

NOTE ▶ Remember, the transition will expand only as far as the available clip handles will allow, or until you bump into another edit point. A red edge indicates that you've run out of handles.

Lengthening the duration helped smooth the edit point even further. If you want to adjust the timing of these clips—perhaps to start the incoming music sting a little later—you can roll the edit point beneath the transition.

5 In the transition between the **Battle Lines** and **Discipline** clips, move your pointer over the two white, facing triangles. When the Roll icon appears, drag right. Play through the transition and to the end of the project. Try rolling the edit point a little more right and then left to audition variations of the edit.

With the two audio clips dovetailing nicely, you can focus on how the **Discipline** clip ends the project. It's doubtful that you will want to just stop the music, especially because the video has a nice slow fade to black. Rather than apply a crossfade, let's look at the clip's built-in fade handles.

6 If necessary, trim the music to end with the logo fade-out. With your pointer placed at the end of the **Discipline** clip, the fade control appears at the end of the clip. Drag the fade control left and align it beneath the beginning of the cross dissolve in the last video clip in the primary storyline.

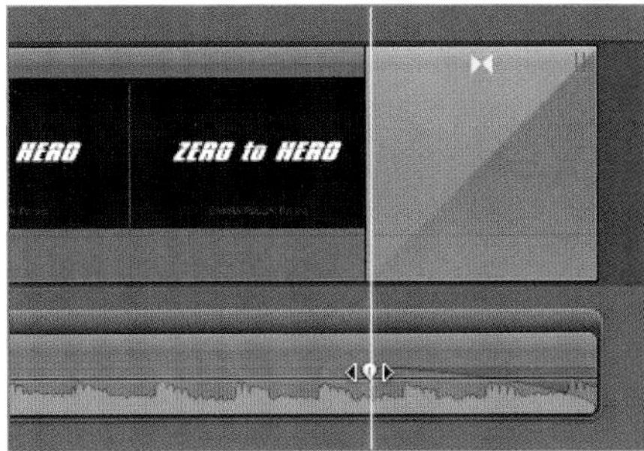

When you drag a fade handle inward, it creates an automatic fade. A fade control appears at the beginning and end of the audio portion of each clip. If you look closely at the audio beneath the video thumbnails, you will find them there as well.

NOTE ▶ This exercise just offers an introduction to these audio handles. In the next lesson, you will learn more about fades and mixing audio.

Editor's Cut

Now that you know how to add and modify transitions, you can duplicate one of the backup projects you created in this lesson and apply a different transition to each edit point. You can also experiment with trimming clips beneath a transition. Don't forget to begin by customizing the clip appearance in the Timeline, which could include selecting a default layout and changing the clip heights.

TIP ▶ Each transition has the trim functions built in. Drag the two parallel gray lines in the upper left or right corners to ripple a clip. Drag the two white, facing arrows in the middle to roll an edit point. Final Cut Pro anticipates what you want to do, and changes the pointer to the appropriate Trim icon.

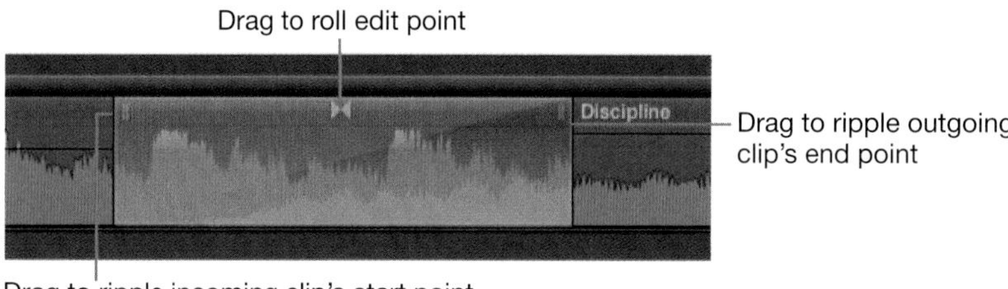

Lesson Review

1. Name three ways to apply a cross dissolve video transition.
2. If you want to apply the same transition to all clips in your project, what must you do first?
3. How can you adjust the duration of a transition in the Timeline?
4. How can you delete all transitions of the same type?
5. How do you change a parameter in the Transition inspector?
6. How do you create a compound clip in the Timeline?

Answers

1. Select an edit point and choose Edit > Add Cross Dissolve, or press Command-T. Alternatively, select an edit point, click the Transitions Browser button, and double-click the Cross Dissolve thumbnail in the Dissolves category.

2. With the Timeline selected but before applying a transition, you must press Command-A to select all the clips in the Timeline.
3. Drag the edge of the transition icon. For more precise control, Control-click the transition icon, and from the shortcut menu, choose Change Duration or press Control-D. When the Dashboard highlights in blue, type a new duration, and press Return.
4. Open the Timeline Index. In the search field, enter the name of the transition type you want to delete. When these transitions are listed beneath the search field, select them all and press Delete.
5. Select a transition, and then in the toolbar click the Inspector button, or press Command-4. The parameters you can adjust depend on the selected transition, but you can adjust parameters using a slider, a numerical field, a menu, an image well, or a color well.
6. Select one or more clips in the Timeline. The selected clips can be any combination of contiguous or noncontiguous clips, compound clips, primary storyline clips, or connected clips. Choose File > New Compound Clip, or press Option-G; or Control-click the selection, and from the shortcut menu, choose New Compound Clip.

Keyboard Shortcuts

Command-T	Apply default transition
Control-D	Change duration
Command-, (comma)	Open Preferences window
Control-R	Render selection
Command-Z	Undo
Shift-?	Play around the skimmer or playhead
Command-4	Toggle Inspector open or closed
Command-G	Create storyline
Option-G	New compound clip

8

Time This lesson takes approximately 75 minutes to complete.

Goals

Monitor and adjust audio levels in the Timeline

Add sound effects and music

Adjust audio levels in the Audio inspector

Apply fades and crossfades

Record voiceovers

Use auditions

Correct audio problems

Add keyframes

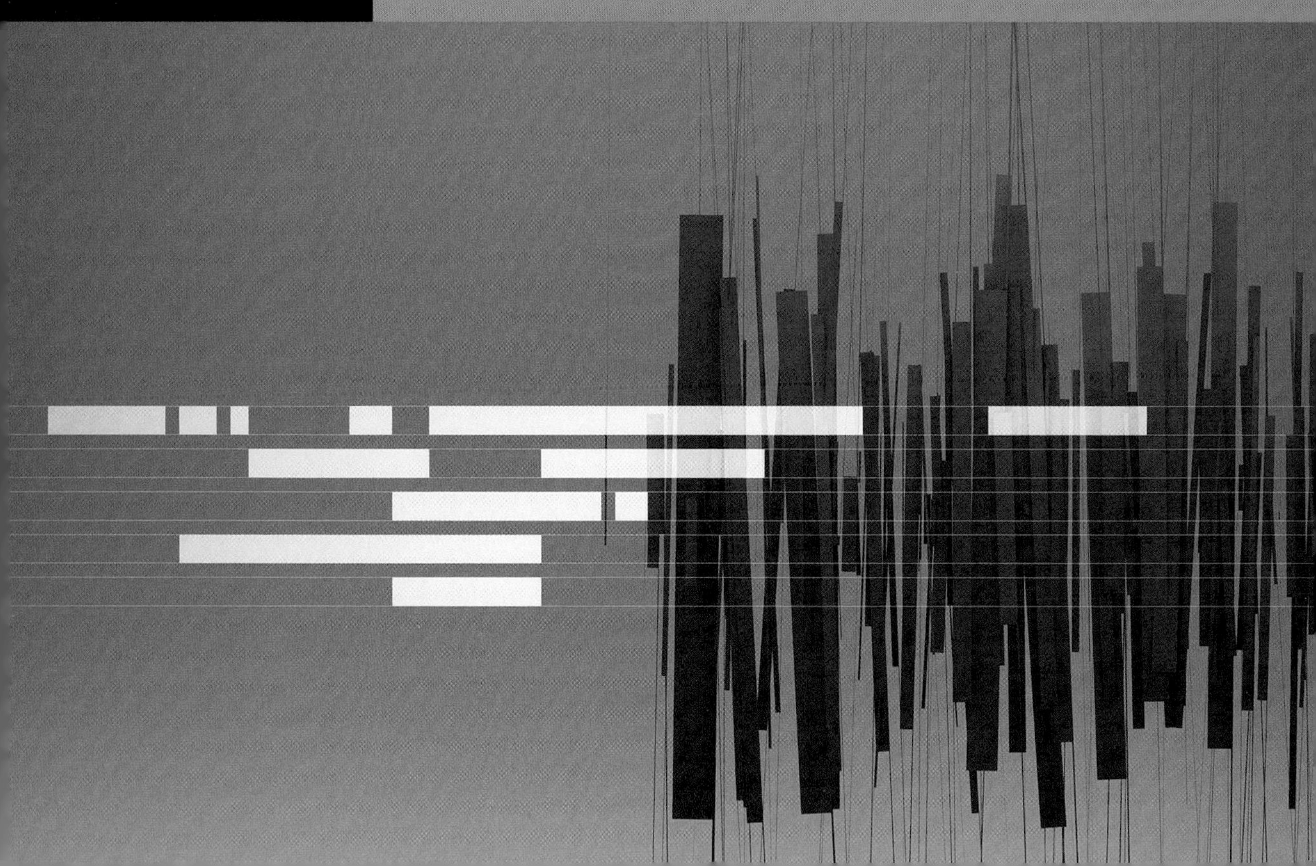

Lesson 8

Working with Sound

A film or video is usually described as something we "watch" or "view." But the importance of film and video sounds should never be underestimated. When dialogue, voiceover, sound effects, and music are properly selected and combined, an audience is pulled into a more immersive experience.

On the other hand, if the sound is too loud, too quiet, or poorly mixed, the audience may become restless and frustrated. A good sound mix not only smoothes out the rough edges of your project, it can actually make or save a project. At its best, a great sound design helps to tell a more complete story and brings your project to life in unexpected ways.

Most projects benefit by the addition of sound effects and music.

In this lesson, you will adjust clip audio levels using several methods. You will navigate the Music and Sound Browser to add music and sound effects. You will also apply fades and crossfades to create more natural-sounding transitions. Then, you will record and audition new narration clips to choose the best vocal performance. Finally, you will correct common audio problems that occur during production.

Monitoring Audio in the Timeline

Before you begin adding and mixing music and sound effects, you should evaluate the current status of the audio in your project. Is it at the proper level? Are the levels consistent from clip to clip? Is the background audio or music too loud to hear the voiceover? Using the Audio meters and clip waveforms as guides, you can correct audio levels in the Timeline. When you have optimized the current settings, it will be easier to determine the next steps in your sound design.

1 In the Project Library, from the Lesson Projects folder, drag the Lesson 8 folder to the APTS FCP X icon. Hide the contents of the Lesson Projects folder, and show the contents of the Lesson 8 folder. Open the *Zero to Hero_mix* project.

   Two Audio meter arrays in Final Cut Pro let you track the audio levels of clips: a small Audio meter in the Dashboard, and a larger Audio meters pane you can open in the Timeline.

2 In the toolbar, to the right of the Dashboard's timecode display, click the small Audio meter icon to open the large Audio meters pane to the right of the Timeline. You can also open this pane by choosing Window > Show Audio Meters, or pressing Shift-Command-8.

   While you don't always need to see the Audio meters pane as you edit, it's essential during sound mixing to display an accurate reference of your audio levels.

3 To increase the size of the Audio meters pane and view your audio channels, position the pointer over the border between the Audio meters pane and the Timeline. When the vertical resize pointer appears, drag left.

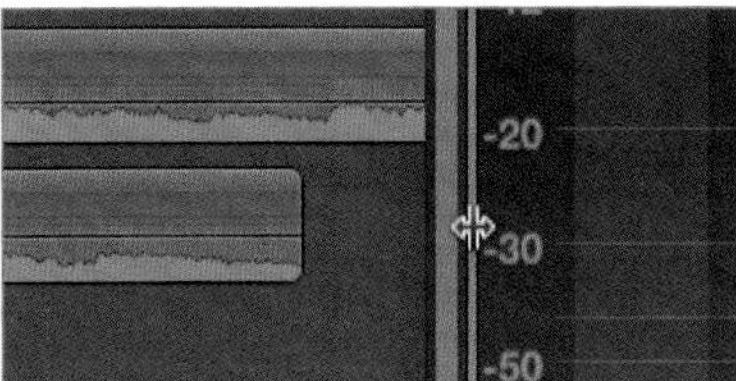

4 In the Timeline, press Shift-Z to see all clips, and then play the *Zero to Hero_mix* project. Watch the Audio meters and notice that at about 20 seconds into playback the audio levels change color according to their decibel (dB) levels.

NOTE ▶ This project is different from other *Zero to Hero* projects you've worked with. It's been edited to demonstrate Final Cut Pro audio functions.

As audio approaches the 0 dB peak, the level color turns from green to yellow. When the audio level exceeds 0 dB, the level color turns from yellow to red. Keep in mind that the levels you see in the Audio meters represent a combined output level of all the clips playing at that point.

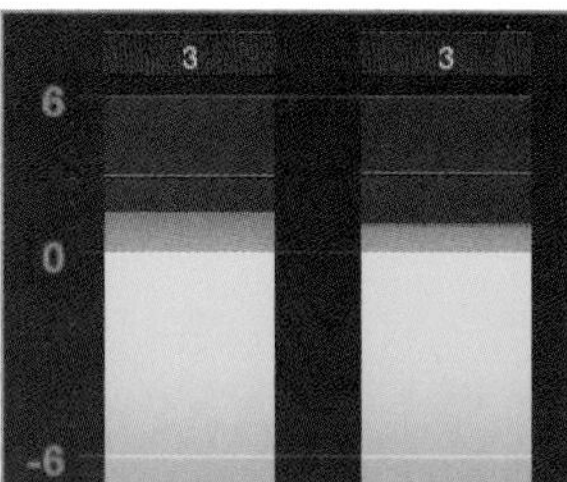

Notice the peak indicators at the top of the Audio meters. One or more peak indicators may turn red, indicating that the level of that audio channel has one or more peaks above the 0 dB level. The decibel level numbers inside each peak indicator box indicate the highest dB currently reached by each channel during playback.

TIP Audio levels are also displayed in the meters while skimming a project in the Timeline, as long as audio skimming is enabled.

This same color-coding system of the Audio meters appears in the Timeline waveforms. To more easily recognize audio level problems in the Timeline, you can adjust the waveform size.

5 In the Timeline, click the Clip Appearance button, and select the second clip appearance from the left, which displays a large audio waveform view and a small reference video view. To more clearly see the waveforms in the Timeline, as well as the reference video, drag the Clip Height slider to the halfway point.

The green audio-only clips and the blue video and audio clips both have yellow and red waveform peaks that indicate where the audio level is near, or above 0 dB. This is the same color code displayed in the Audio meters when peak levels are approaching or are already too "hot." You will adjust these peaks within the Timeline clips in the next exercise.

Setting Decibel Levels

In digital audio, no part of the overall audio signal of the combined clips should exceed 0 dB. When the audio output of your project exceeds 0 dB, the sound will be clipped and distorted.

To avoid exceeding the 0 dB level for your combined clips, set the primary audio clips—such as dialogue and narration—to peak well below that level, perhaps between –12 dB and –6 dB on the Audio meters. Then you might lower the music clip volume on the individual clips to –15 or –18 dB.

These settings allow you to combine the sound clips and achieve an overall level well below the 0 dB peaking level at about –6 to –3 dB. If, however, mixing multiple audio clips causes the overall volume to peak, you will have to adjust your mix accordingly.

The decibel level of the music is obviously too high and will need to be lowered. But the first task of audio mixing is to adjust the volume level of the primary audio clips. In this project, hearing the racers' comments is more important than hearing the music or the audio in the B-roll clips. You have two methods for isolating the interview clips.

When you want to temporarily remove one or two clips from the audio mix, you can select the clips and disable them.

6 To disable the music, select both of the **Battle Lines** music clips. Press V to disable the music clips.

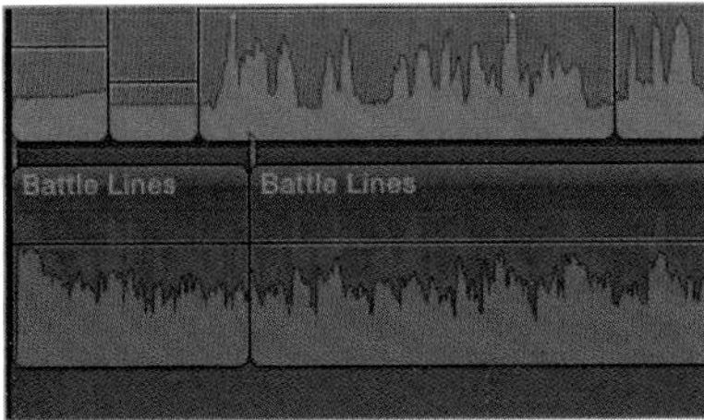

TIP ▶ You can also Control-click the selected clips and choose Disable from the shortcut menu.

Although the clip is still present in the project, the two music clips appear dimmed. Although disabling a clip is effective for momentarily muting the music, disabling many individual clips can become time consuming.

NOTE ▶ Disabling a clip turns off both the audio and video components of a clip.

To isolate the sound bites in the *Zero to Hero_mix*, you would need to select and disable the audio for all the secondary clips. Instead, let's re-enable the music clips and look at a second approach to isolating clips.

7 With both cuts of the **Battle Lines** music selected, press V to enable both of the music clips. Then deselect the clips.

This second method uses an audio function called *soloing*, which mutes audio in all clips in the project other than currently selected clip or clips.

NOTE ▶ Unlike the disable function, the solo function controls only audio monitoring and does not affect the video portion of a clip. Although the term *solo* may suggest that you are affecting only a single clip, you can select and solo several clips at once.

8 Select the three **John Force** interview clips, and choose Clip > Solo, or press Option-S.

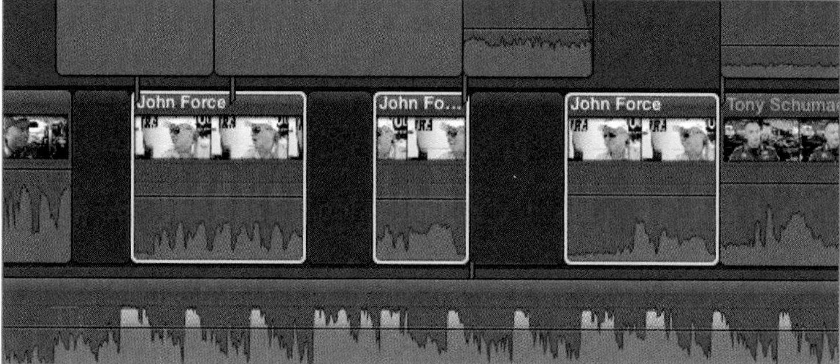

All the project clips surrounding the **John Force** clips turn gray to indicate that the audio of all the other clips has been muted. Also, the Solo button at the top-right of the Timeline illuminates and appears yellow.

9 Play the project. In the Audio meters, notice the current volume levels of the **John Force** clips. The levels of these sound bites are way too low to be intelligible alongside the music and race track audio.

NOTE ▶ As mentioned earlier, the primary audio for this project is the racers' comments. In the next exercise, you will create a sound mix in which the racers' sound bites are easily heard and understood.

10 To return all clips to normal playback, click the Solo button at the top-right of the Timeline, or press Option-S.

TIP A third method for selective monitoring of audio uses Final Cut Pro Roles metadata. More information about the use of roles is available in *Apple Pro Training Series: Final Cut Pro X Advanced Editing* (Peachpit Press).

Adjusting Audio in the Timeline

Now that you know how to isolate clip audio for monitoring, it's time to adjust the audio levels for the project mix. In a documentary or narrative-driven project like *Zero to Hero* or *Delicious Peace*, the spoken words receive the most attention in the final mix. Nonetheless, the audio from cutaways, music, and any sound effects should not be ignored. They are the accents that sustain the momentum of your story and maintain interest.

As the editor, you will devote a lot of time editing video clips that best tell your story. Your audio editing needs to enhance and build upon that story. A sound effect that is too loud or a sound bite that is inaudible will interrupt the flow of any storyline regardless of the video quality.

In this exercise, you'll begin by muting the secondary audio clips and then set the volume level of each sound bite clip. With the sound bite levels set, you will adjust the music and B-roll audio volumes to complement the sound bites.

1 Select the **Tony Schumacher** clip toward the beginning of the Timeline. To solo this clip, click the Solo button at the top-right of the Timeline, or press Option-S. As you play the clip, watch the Audio meters.

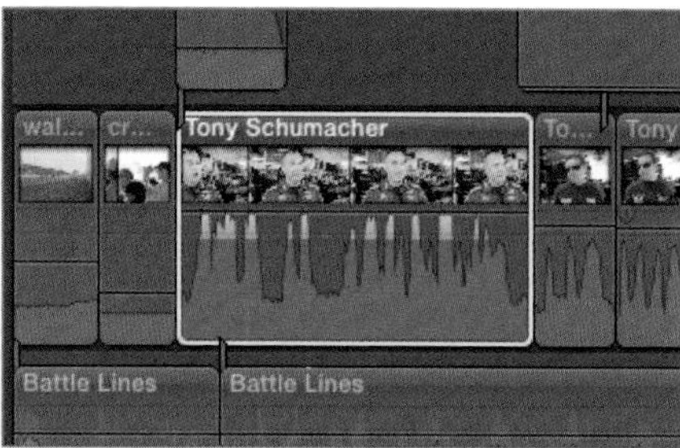

When you are not distracted by the music and cutaway sound, you can hear that Tony's audio sounds OK. However, you can't trust your ears alone during the mixing process. It's essential that you refer to the Audio meters because they show the actual decibel (dB) level. In this case, the Audio meters indicate that the level is too high.

TIP Before adjusting audio levels in the Timeline, you may want to turn off audio skimming by pressing Shift-S.

2 In the first **Tony Schumacher** clip, move your pointer over the horizontal volume control line until it turns into an adjustment pointer. In the dB info flag, the current volume level is 11 dB. Drag the volume control down to 3 dB, and play the clip.

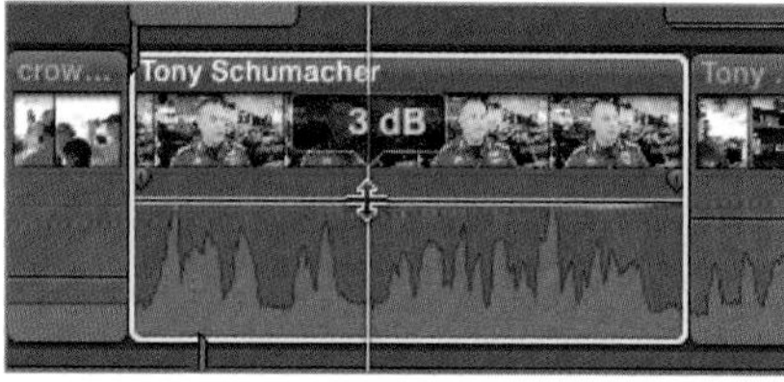

Before level adjustment

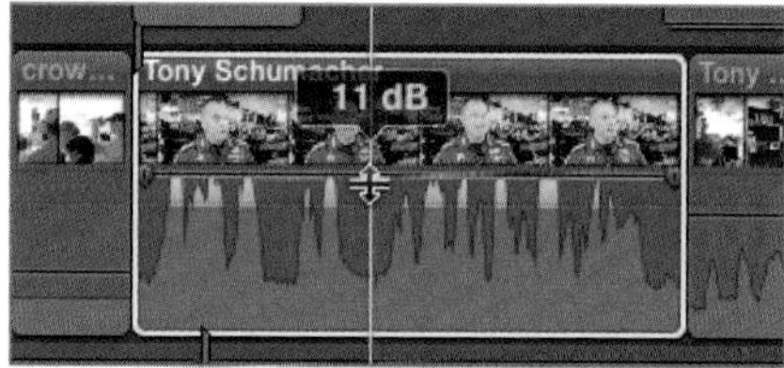

After level adjustment

When you drag the volume control in a clip, you are making a *relative* adjustment to the original volume level. The dB number in the info flag represents the amount of volume change up (*boost*) or down (*attenuate*) compared to the original audio level. You can hear the original audio level of the clip by setting the volume level to 0 dB.

In the Audio meters, the peak audio level for this clip is now between –12 dB and –6 dB, the target range for primary audio.

NOTE ▶ Remember, the levels in the Audio meters reflect the output dB level of the clip.

3 With the **Tony Schumacher** clip selected, Command-click both **Tony Pedregon** clips. To solo these two clips, press Option-S once to restore all clips to normal, then press Option-S again to solo the newly selected clips.

With all three sound bites included in the solo function, you can now compare the volume of one to the others.

NOTE ▶ Pressing Option-S toggles the solo state off or on. You can't add a clip to an existing solo selection. You have to first turn off the state, and then turn it back on for the newly selected clips.

4 Play these three clips as you watch the Audio meters. Note the clips' output level. Then compare the audio waveforms of these clips in the Timeline.

As you monitor their volume levels in the Audio meters, you see that the **Tony Pedregon** clips' volume is lower than the **Tony Schumacher** clips. You can also see this difference reflected in the audio waveforms in the Timeline.

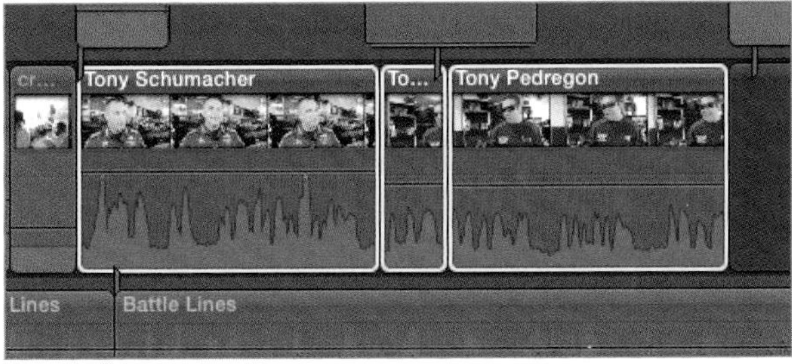

In addition to the volume controls, you can also use a menu command or keyboard shortcut to adjust the volume on one or more clips in the Timeline.

5 Command-click the **Tony Schumacher** clip to deselect it, leaving the **Tony Pedregon** clips selected. Move your pointer over the volume controls to see that the volume level for the first clip is –2 dB and the volume level for the second clip is –3 dB.

6 To raise the volume of the selected clips by 1 dB, choose Modify > Volume > Up, or press Control-= (equals). Move your pointer over the volume controls again to verify that the levels on each clip have been adjusted 1 dB higher.

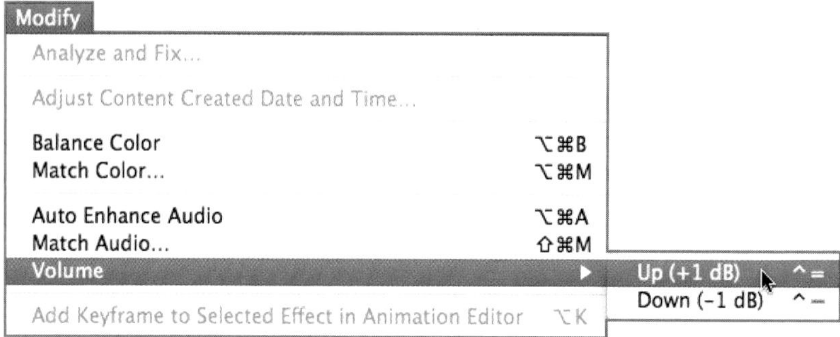

7 Because the audio from these two clips remains low, press Control-=(equals) six more times to raise the volume levels a total of 7 dB leaving new levels of 5 dB and 4 dB, respectively.

So far, you have changed the volume over the entire length of a clip. However, sometimes the audio within a clip is louder at the beginning and softer at the end or vice versa. To set multiple volume levels within a single clip, you create a range within a clip and adjust the volume of that range.

NOTE ▶ When adjusting volume within a range, Final Cut Pro utilizes *keyframes*. You will work more with setting and adjusting keyframes later in this lesson.

8 To return sound monitoring to all clips, press Option-S. Toward the end of the project, select the last **Tony Schumacher** clip and press Option-S to solo it. Play the sound bite.

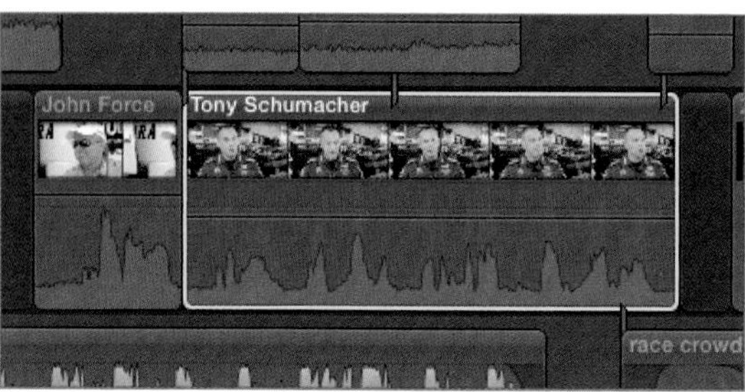

The beginning of the sound bite is a little low compared to the rest of the clip's audio. You may adjust a portion of a clip's audio volume level by first selecting a range within the clip. Marking a selection range in the clip may be accomplished by setting a start point, an end point, or both.

9 Play the beginning of the last **Tony Schumacher** clip and stop just after he says, "People dream." Press O to set an end point and create a range selection from the beginning of the clip to the playhead location.

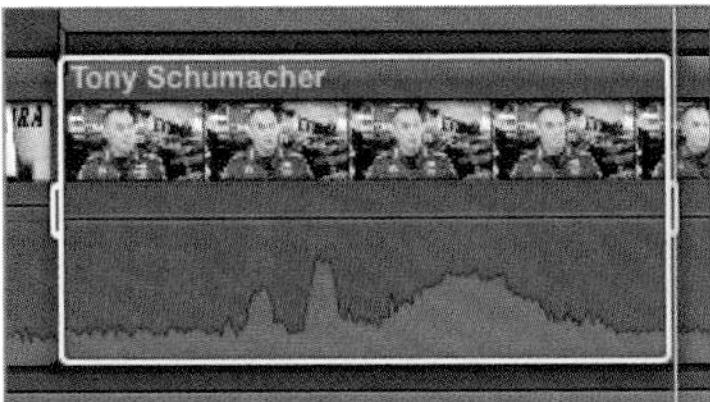

10 Within the range selection, drag the volume control up from 2 dB to 4 dB. Click in the Timeline's gray area to deactivate the range selection, and play the clip.

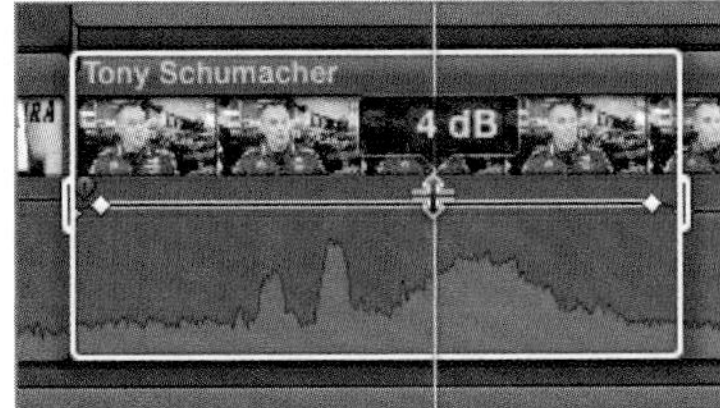

You may notice that the increase in volume sounds very natural. While you raised the volume up only 2 dB, Final Cut Pro created four keyframes (which look like small white diamonds) at the beginning and ending adjustment points. These keyframes create audio ramps that fade the volume over time for a smoother audio transition.

TIP To manually add a keyframe to the volume control line, Option-click the line where you want to place the keyframe. You can drag the keyframe up and down to adjust the volume level or left and right to change its timing. You will learn more about keyframes later in this lesson.

The last sound bite is still a little under a peak of –12 dB. Even after changing volume within a range, a clip's overall volume level still may be adjusted.

11 With the last **Tony Schumacher** clip selected, press Control-= (equals) three times to raise the entire clip's volume level by 3 dB.

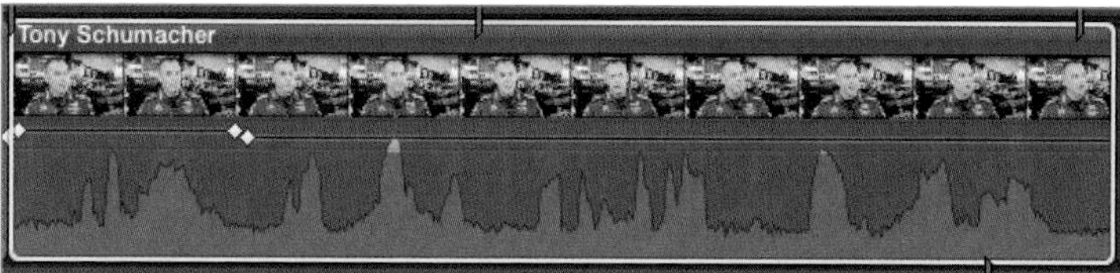

The adjustment is made relative to the existing keyframes and levels over the entire clip.

12 To hear all the Timeline's clips, press Option-S to turn off soloing.

13 Using the methods you learned in this exercise, adjust the following clips in the *Zero to Hero_mix* project by the specified dB levels. Don't forget to solo the sound bite clips so you can get an accurate reading of the audio level without hearing the mix of secondary audio.

- Select and solo the two **Antron Brown** clips. Then lower both audio levels by –3 dB.
- Select and solo the three **John Force** clips and raise their audio levels by 12 dB.
- Select both **Battle Lines** music clips and lower their levels by –10 dB.
- Raise the **Crash** clip level by 10 dB.
- Lower the **JF holds trophy**, **flame out**, and **race start** clips by –15 dB.

TIP When you combine audio clips, it raises the overall volume. Always keep an eye on the Audio meters to ensure that the level of combined audio clips remain within an acceptable range.

When you are finished, play the project and notice the uniform waveforms for the interview clips. You are now ready to add sound effects from the Music and Sound Browser before refining your mix.

TIP ▶ At times you will want to increase or lower the overall audio level of an entire project while preserving each clip's relative volume. You can press Command-A to select all clips, and then press Control-= (equals) and Control-- (minus) to raise or lower clip volumes 1 dB at a time.

Adding Music and Sound Effects

The process of mixing clips—adding music and sound effects, and correcting audio—is often referred to as audio *sweetening*. At no time is that term better understood than when hearing the perfect sound effect bring a video-only clip to life or the majesty of a magnificent orchestra bring tears to your eyes in a rather uneventful dramatic scene. Every project benefits from a little sweetening. In the Music and Sound Browser, you'll find over 1,000 royalty-free music and sound effects files for sweetening your project's audio.

The Music and Sound Browser also includes an iTunes source folder that gives you direct access to your music library. From the source folder, you can drag your iTunes-cataloged production music directly onto the Timeline.

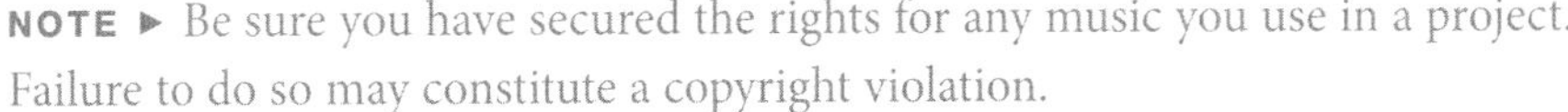

NOTE ▶ Be sure you have secured the rights for any music you use in a project. Failure to do so may constitute a copyright violation.

The *Zero to Hero_mix* project would benefit from the addition of car crash sound effects, as well as a music "stinger" for the end title. For this exercise, you will search for music and sound effects, create a keyword collection for the effects, and edit the clips to your project. These steps will help salvage an uneventful car crash in *Zero to Hero* and end it with a bang.

1 With the *Zero to Hero_mix* project open in the Timeline, and the large Audio meters showing, select the **crash** clip. Zoom into the clip in the Timeline and play it.

   In the **crash** clip, two cars collide and slam into a wall. You might hear a very slight rumble of car engines buried in the music, but the three separate sounds of a car skidding, two cars colliding, and both cars crashing into a wall are missing. The dramatic nature of the clip would be greatly improved by adding these sound effects.

2 In the toolbar, click the Music and Sound button (the musical note) to open the Music and Sound Browser. At the top of the browser, move your pointer over the dimple in the gray bar above the sound files playlist. When the resize pointer appears, drag the bar down about halfway.

   TIP You can also open and close the Music and Sound Browser by choosing Window > Media Browser > Music and Sound.

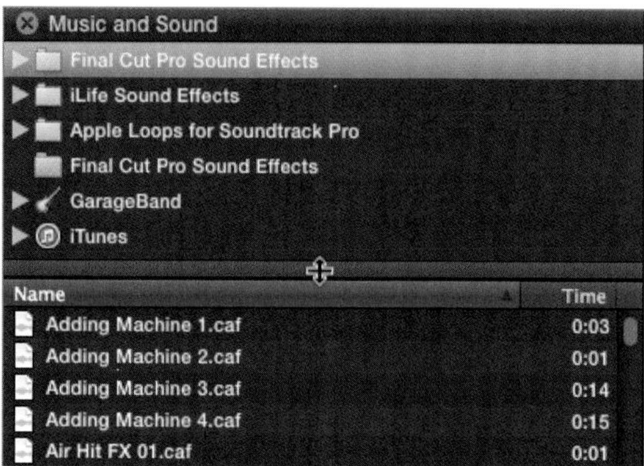

   You can now scroll and search both of the browser's panes. The folders and subfolders in the top pane contain music and sound effects files, as well as source folders for your iTunes Library and GarageBand. When a folder is selected, the audio files inside the folder appear in a playlist in the lower pane.

TIP ▶ Before playing any of the sound effects, you may want to lower your speaker volume. Some of the effects have loud bursts of sound.

3 In the top pane of the Music and Sound Browser window, select the Final Cut Pro Sound Effects folder in the top pane, and in the lower-right corner of the Browser, notice that the folder contains over 1,300 items. Then scroll down to the **Explosion 6.caf** file, and double-click the file to play it.

NOTE ▶ The .caf extension indicates Core Audio Format, an audio container file developed by Apple. It is compatible with OS X v10.4 and higher.

The **Explosion 6.caf** file would work well as the sound effect for both cars hitting the wall. It is one of three sound effects you will add to the **crash** clip. To import all three effects clips and keep them together in the *Zero to Hero* Event, you can create a Keyword Collection for them.

4 In the Event Browser, create a new Keyword Collection in the *Zero to Hero* Event, label it *Crash SFX*, and then drag the **Explosion 6.caf** file from the Music and Sound Browser into the Keyword Collection.

The Music and Sound Browser has a search field next to the Play button arrow. When you enter a word in the field, the effects with that word in their titles are filtered and combined into a list.

TIP ▶ You can also use the search field to locate music, including music from your iTunes library, by typing the name of the artist, album, composer, or song. Any audio clips from the Music and Sound Browser can be previewed during Timeline playback.

5 In the search field, type *auto* to locate the **Auto Crash Concrete.caf** and **Auto Skid 1.caf** sound effects. Click the Play button to play them, and then drag both of them to the *Crash SFX* Keyword Collection.

Now that your additional audio files have been located, imported, and organized, it's time to edit them into the project. Since you no longer need to locate any music or effects, you can close the Music and Sound Browser.

6 Close the Music and Sound Browser by clicking the close (X) button. Then select the *Crash SFX* Keyword Collection in the Event Browser and click the List View button.

As you learned in previous lessons, when you press Q to edit an audio clip into the Timeline, the audio clip is connected to clips in the primary storyline. Because the **crash** clip is placed above the primary storyline, you may move this clip into the primary storyline to clearly see the connection. To hear only your sound effects for now, you will also disable the music clips.

7 In the Timeline, Command-click both **Battle Fields** music clips, and press V to disable them. Then Control-click the **crash** clip, and from the shortcut menu, choose Overwrite to Primary Storyline. When the clip is in the primary storyline, place the playhead on the first frame of the **crash** clip.

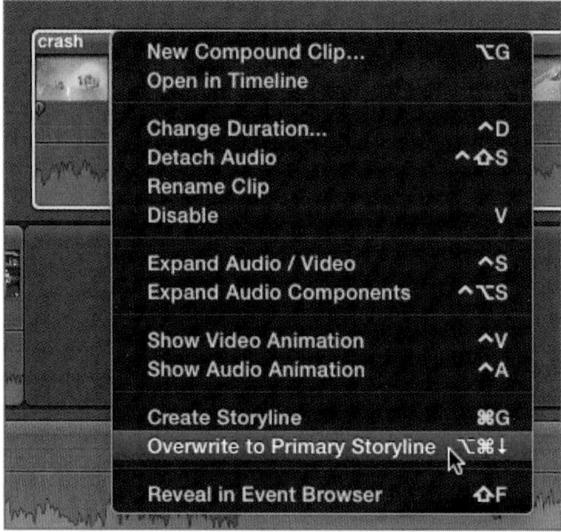

NOTE ▶ Overwriting the **crash** clip to the primary storyline creates a visual of what is known as a J-cut for the Antron Brown clip. The project was already playing the J-cut before as Antron started speaking before you saw him onscreen. After the overwrite, you see the J-cut within the primary storyline.

In the first few moments of the **crash** clip, one car skids before crashing into the other. You will use less than a second of the skid sound effect before adding the crash sound effects.

8 In the Event Browser, select the **Auto Skid 1** clip, drag to select the first 27 frames, and then press Q.

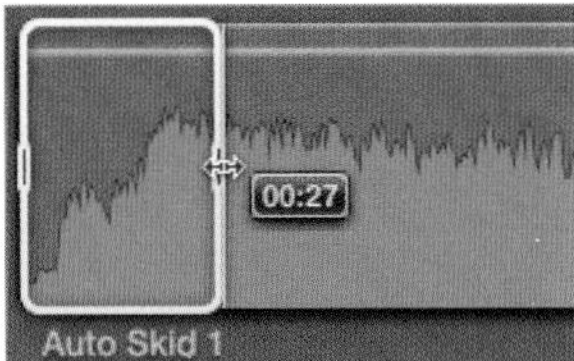

In the Timeline the range selection of the **Auto Skid 1** clip is now below the **Battle Lines** music clip, but it is connected to the beginning of the **crash** clip. The playhead has moved to the end of the edited clip and is in position for the next edit.

TIP You may need to scroll the Timeline view to see both the **Auto Skid 1** sound effects clip and the **crash** clip.

9 In the Event Browser, select the **Auto Crash Concrete** clip, and press Q to connect this entire clip at the end of the **Auto Skid 1** clip.

So far, your two sound effects are in succession, presenting themselves in a linear fashion to viewers' ears. Layering multiple audio clips vertically can add depth and a more natural sound to your mix.

10 In the Timeline of *Zero to Hero_mix,* park the playhead at 12:42, and then in the Event Browser, select the **Explosion 6** clip. Make a range selection around the first 2:00 seconds, and press Q.

The three *Crash SFX* clips are now connected to the **crash** clip and will travel with the clip if it is moved to a different location in the Timeline.

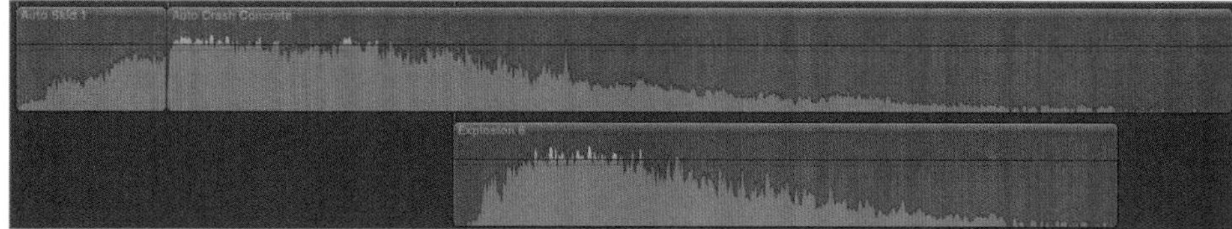

11 In the Timeline, lower the volume controls of all three sound effects clips to –14 dB. Then play the **crash** clip a few times while watching the Audio meters for the peak levels. Also, watch the Viewer to see if the sound effects are synchronized with the video action. Adjust the volume levels or reposition your sound effects as necessary.

You can collect the three sound effects clips into one group by creating a compound clip. Collapsing into one compound clip prevents you from accidentally separating one sound effect from the others and also de-clutters your Timeline.

12 Drag a selection rectangle around the three sound effects clips, and then Control-click one of the clips and from the shortcut menu, choose New Compound Clip, or press Option-G.

13 In the dialog that appears, name the compound clip *Crash SFX* and assign it to the *Zero to Hero* Event.

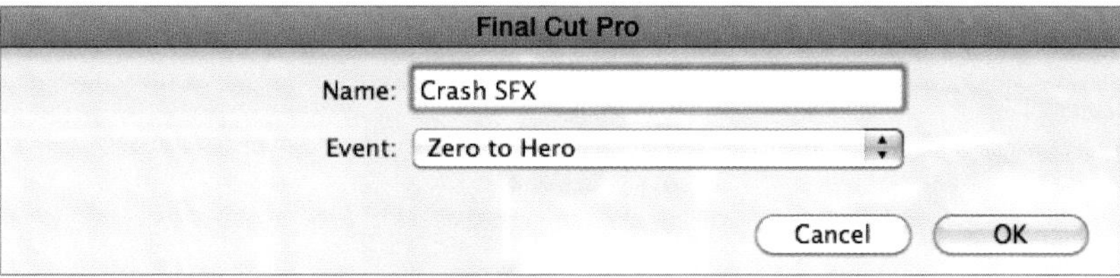

NOTE ▸ When you create a compound clip, Final Cut Pro adds the compound clip to the specified Event. You can view the compound clip in the Event Browser, and use it as a source for editing in this or any other project.

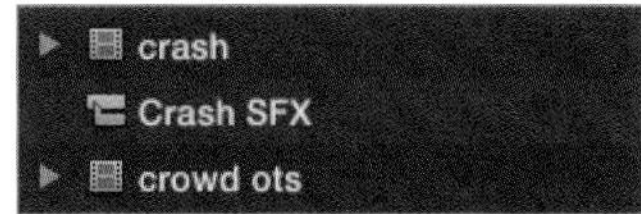

14 Press Shift-Z to fit all clips in the Timeline, and then Command-click both **Battle Lines** clips and press V to enable them.

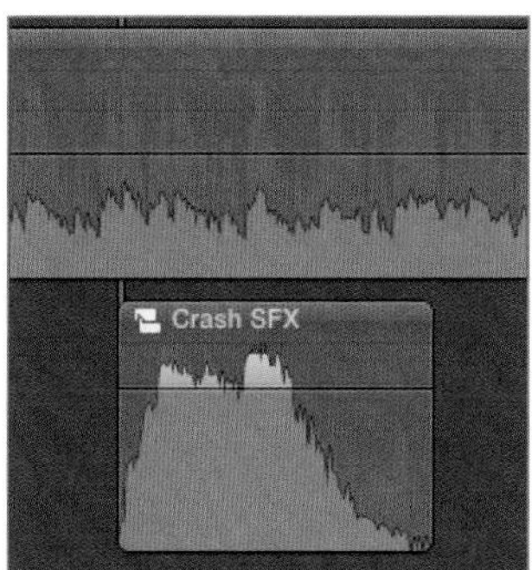

The volume control in the compound clip can adjust all three sound effects equally.

TIP You could have also selected the video clip along with the three sound effects when creating your compound clip. This action would lock the video and audio into one clip.

Your Sound Environment

In an ideal world, sound would always be mixed in an acoustically well-balanced studio environment. All you really need, however, is a good set of speakers and a quiet place to work. Even if you are using your computer's built-in speakers, you can use the following steps to optimize sound before mixing:

In the upper-right corner of your computer's menu bar, click the Volume System Status icon and drag it up to its maximum volume level. The Volume icon looks like an audio speaker with sound waves. The higher the volume, the more sound waves appear in the icon.

To balance your computer's speakers and set volume, choose Apple > System Preferences, and then from the Hardware category, click the Sound option. In the Sound preferences pane, click the Output button, and set the Output volume and Balance using the slider bars.

Return to the Timeline and play the current project. If necessary, lower your computer's audio level using the audio keys on the top row of your keyboard.

If you have external speakers, position them an equal distance on either side of your display, ideally with the tweeters at ear level, and angled toward you away from walls. Set your volume to a comfortable working level while listening to something familiar.

To keep sound levels consistent, try keeping your computer and/or speaker volume at the same level as much as possible. Any volume changes may affect your judgment of sound while mixing.

Adjusting Levels in the Audio Inspector

Blending natural sound with music and narration is a subjective process. In the *Delicious Peace* documentary, gentle xylophone music, professional voiceover, and the sounds of coffee being picked, roasted, ground, and poured, are combined to recreate the experience of "being there." If any one of these sound elements was too loud, or not loud enough, it would no longer enhance the story and the sense of immediacy. As always, it's important to first set the volume of the primary audio before mixing in other sound elements.

In this exercise, you will use the volume controls in the Audio inspector to adjust audio levels in the *Delicious Peace* project.

1 In the Project Library, double-click the *Delicious Peace_mix* project to open it in the Timeline. Make sure the large Audio meters are displayed, and press Shift-Z to fit all clips in the Timeline.

Notice that the audio clips for actor Ed O'Neill's voiceover are located below the **xylophone music** clips. Because the voiceover is the primary audio, let's first adjust the levels for O'Neill's narration.

2 To select all voiceover clips in the Timeline, drag a selection rectangle around all eight clips. Then press Option-S to solo these clips.

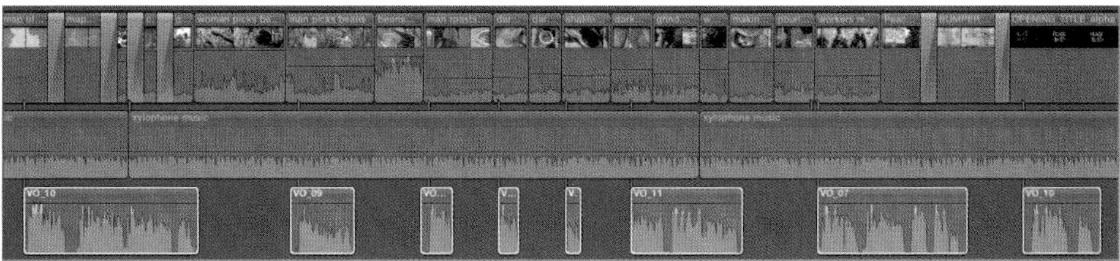

3 Skim to the first clip, **VO_10**, and press the / (slash) key to play it. Monitor the audio levels in both the clip waveforms and the Audio meters.

In the Audio meters, notice that the decibel levels for this clip are peaking above the target output range of –12 dB to –6 dB, and that most of the other voiceover clips have waveforms peaking at about the same level.

In previous lessons, you changed the volume of individual clips in the Timeline. With these clips selected, you can use the Audio inspector controls to set or adjust volume levels to an entire selection of clips at once.

4 In the toolbar, click the Inspector button, and click the Audio tab at the top of the window.

Toward the top of the Audio inspector are Volume and Pan controls. To the right of the Volume slider is a Volume field with a number or dashes in it. When you move your pointer over this number, it turns blue, and arrows appear above and below the number.

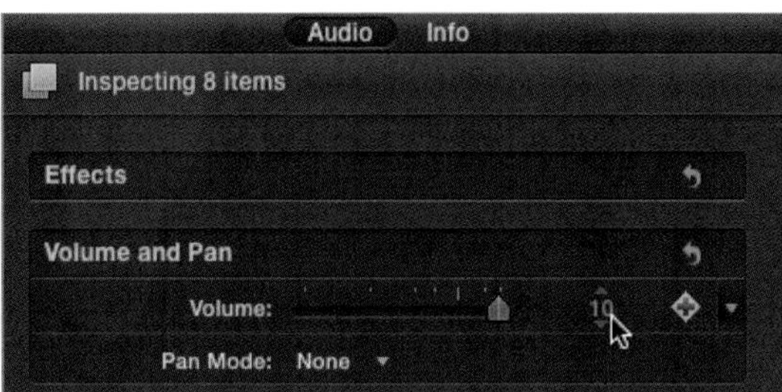

TIP ▶ The Volume and Pan control panel may be hidden. To show the panel, move your pointer to the right side of the Volume and Pan section. Click the Show button, which appears in blue, to open the panel.

5 Double-click the Volume field, and type 6. Then look at the voiceover clip waveforms in the Timeline, and press Return.

NOTE ▶ As you raise or lower the volume of a clip or group of clips, you are not altering the output volume level. You are making relative adjustments to the current clip volume. Here you are raising the volume of the selected clips by 6 dB.

The waveforms have been raised by the 6 dB, the value you entered in the Volume field. Now let's look at another way to adjust volume in the Audio inspector.

TIP You can also use the Audio inspector to adjust the volume of source clips in the Event Browser before adding them to the Timeline.

6 In the Timeline, press Option-S to activate all clips. Then select the second **xylophone music** clip and skim the beginning of the clip.

You will use the Volume slider in the Audio inspector to adjust the volume of this clip while it is playing. Make sure the clip is still selected before you play it so that the Audio inspector for this clip is displayed.

7 In the Timeline, play the second **xylophone music** clip. Click the different areas of the Volume slider, and notice as the dB numbers in the Volume field change. Then drag the Volume slider right and left, and settle on a volume level of –24 dB. Set the other two **xylophone music** clips to the same –24 dB level.

Notice that while dragging the Volume slider to make adjustments on the fly, the other audio clips may cut out. They will become audible again when you stop adjusting the volume.

TIP Another way to adjust audio levels "on the fly" is to drag the volume controls inside a clip during playback.

As you noticed previously, when you move your pointer over the Volume field in the Audio inspector, small up and down arrows appear. You can drag these arrows to raise and lower the clip volume, or to raise or lower relative volume on two or more selected clips.

8 Skim to the **woman picks beans**, **man picks beans**, and **beans being hulled** clips. To zoom into this area, press Command-= (equals), and then select these clips. Skim your pointer over the volume controls in each clip to view their dB info flags.

Although each clip has a different dB level, ranging from –4 dB to 5 dB, the blend between the clips works well. By dragging the arrows in the Audio inspector's Volume field, you can adjust the relative volume levels of all these clips at the same time.

9 With the three clips selected, in the Audio inspector, click the Volume field to activate the arrows, and drag downward until the peak waveforms of the third clip are just below the clip's volume control line. Then press / (slash) to play the clips.

Although this is an imprecise way to adjust volume, dragging the Volume field arrows to adjust a group of clips is another method to preserve the relative volume levels of clips.

TIP To reset clips to their original 0 dB levels, select one or more clips and click the curved arrow icon to the right of the Volume and Pan control panel. You can also click the animation menu to the right of the curved arrow, and from the pop-up menu choose Reset Parameter.

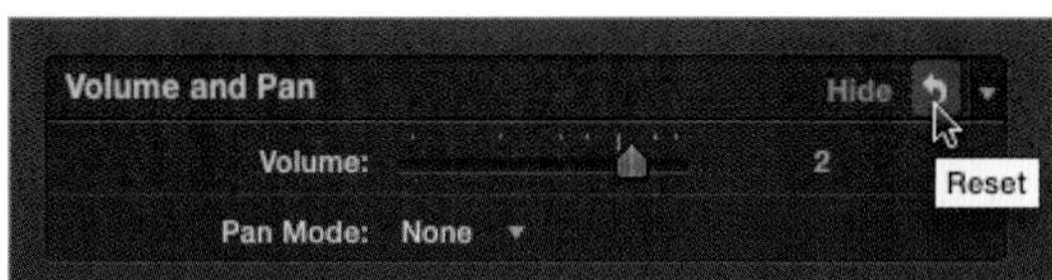

Sometimes, especially when mixing sound effects, it's important to consider where a sound should be heard. Is the car veering off to the left? Should the sound effect be placed to the left to match the visual? Changing the placement of sound is referred to as *panning*. Panning audio in a clip is similar to adjusting the balance knob on a stereo audio device. It steers the sound to the left, center, or right.

Below the Volume slider, a Pan Mode pop-up menu includes a list of stereo and surround presets you can apply to clips to dynamically redirect a sound within your audio environment.

10 In the Audio inspector, click the Pan Mode pop-up menu, and choose Stereo Left/Right.

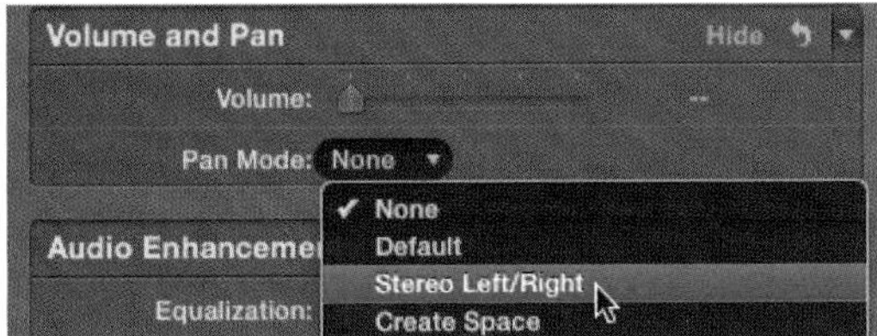

A Pan Amount slider appears, which you will use to pan sound from left to right. Let's create a pan effect so you hear the xylophone music move between your speakers.

11 In the Timeline, press Shift-Z to display all the project clips. Then select the second **xylophone music** clip, and press Option-S to solo it.

In the next step, you will play the **xylophone music** clip while dragging the Pan Amount slider from right to left and observing the changes in the Audio meters.

12 Press / (slash) to play the **xylophone music** clip. In the Audio inspector, click the Pan Mode pop-up and choose Stereo Left/Right, and then drag the Pan Amount slider to the right and left to move the music to each speaker. As you pan from the center to the right, the numbers in the Pan Amount field increase. When you pan to the left, the numbers decrease.

In the Audio meters, notice that the audio levels increase and decrease between the right and left meters, and appear equally in both meters when the slider is positioned at the center point.

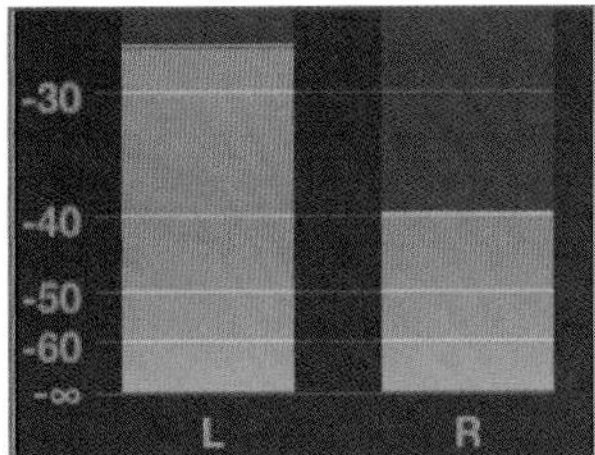

TIP Instead of dragging the Pan Amount slider, you can type a value in the Pan Amount field, or drag the up and down arrows in the Pan Amount field to change the pan value.

13 To the far right of the Pan Amount slider, click the animation menu and choose Reset Parameter to center the Pan Amount. Then, in the Timeline, press Option-S to enable all clips in the project.

TIP To keyframe an audio pan over time, you can set keyframes in the Audio inspector. You can also keyframe volume changes here. To learn more about setting and adjusting keyframes in the Audio inspector, refer to *Apple Pro Training Series: Final Cut Pro X Advanced Editing* (Peachpit Press).

Take 2

The director wants audience members to feel like they are in the fields of Uganda, listening to the grinding of beans and smelling the aroma of coffee being roasted. He tells you that natural sound is very important for this project, but he also wants every word of narration to be clear. Now that you have learned methods for setting and adjusting audio in the Timeline and Audio inspector, you can easily make the necessary volume adjustments to satisfy both of his requests:

- Create a range around the first seven seconds of the first **xylophone music** clip, and raise the audio in the range selection to –14 dB.
- Create a range around the words "with economic development" at the end of the first **VO_10** clip, and raise the level by 5 dB.
- Raise the volume in the **VO_09** clip by 4 dB.
- Raise the volume in the third **VO_08** clip by 6 dB.
- Make a range selection around the words "of peace" at the end of the **VO_07** clip, and make your own audio level adjustment.
- The natural sound in the coffee-picking, roasting, and preparation clips really give you a sense of the daily lives of coffee growers in Uganda. Take a moment to solo these clips and listen to the natural sounds, and then with all clips playing, make any audio adjustments you feel will be beneficial to the mix.

Creating Audio Fades

All sounds can be broken down into a series of four steps: attack, decay, sustain, and release, or ADSR for short. Attack is the speed at which the sound moves from its lowest level (–96 dB) to its peak level, or its loudest point. Decay is the time a sound moves from its initial peak to the sustain level. Sustain is the main duration of the sound, or how long it lasts; and release is the time it takes for the sound to decay back to silence. Even when sounds seem abrupt, like the slamming of a door, this sequence of steps applies.

You can see the ADSR steps in the shapes of waveforms, but when you edit clips, the natural waveform shapes are often cut off at the beginning and the end. To fix the chopped waveforms and meet other sound mixing needs, you can change, or *ramp,* the sound levels by applying fades and crossfades.

1 In the Project Library, open the *Zero to Hero_fades* project. Place the playhead at the beginning of the project, and zoom into this location.

2 Select the first two clips, **wall low angle** and **crowd ots**. Press Option-S to solo them, and then play the clips.

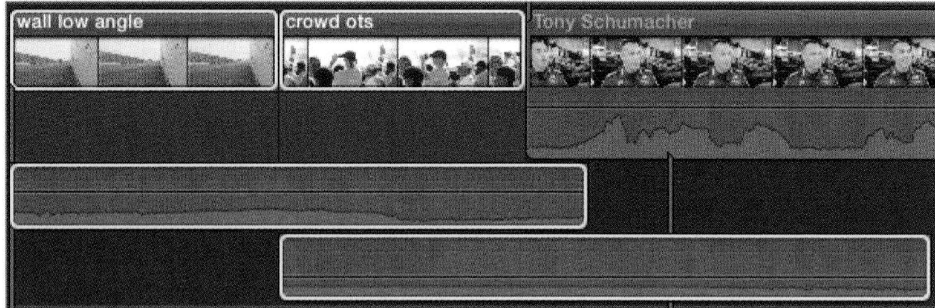

TIP Notice that the audio of each clip has been extended forward in the Timeline, past the video. This type of cut is called an L-cut because the modified clip looks like an L. A J-cut extends the audio so that it precedes the video. It's also referred to as a split edit. When you have split edits in your Timeline, you can quickly show or hide them by choosing View > Expand Audio/Video Clips > For Splits or View > Collapse All Clips.

At the end of the second clip, the sound cuts off. By dragging fade handles, the sound can be adjusted. Fade handles are located in the upper-right and upper-left corners of audio waveforms, and turn white when selected.

3 To select a fade handle, place your pointer over the upper-right corner of the **crowd ots** waveform. When the pointer turns into a cursor with arrows on either side of the handle, drag left until the timecode field above the handle reads –00:00:00:30 frames. Then do the same to the beginning of the clip, creating a 30-frame fade-up.

TIP The farther you drag the handle, the longer the fade duration will be.

4 Repeat the same process to create 30-frame fades up and down for the **wall low angle** clip. Then turn off soloing and play from the beginning of the project through the end of the **Tony Schumacher** clip to hear the smooth fades of the car racing audio.

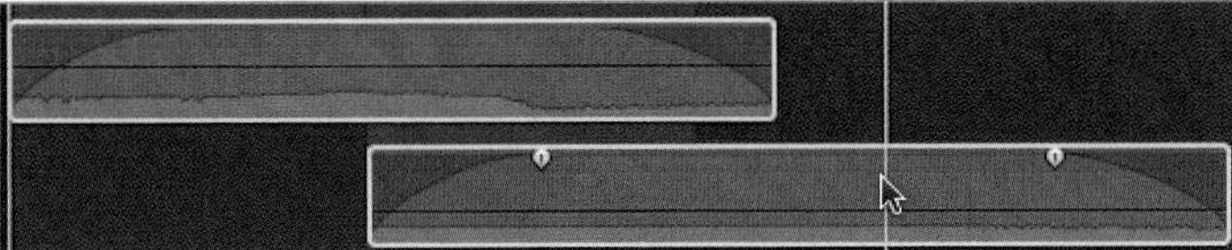

Notice that the two clips to which you just applied fades have curved, shaded edges. The fade shape you used for all four fades is the default +3 dB fade, but you have four fade shapes in all to choose from:

- Linear: The fade changes at a constant rate.
- S-curve: The fade eases in and out with a midpoint at 0 dB.
- +3 dB: The fade starts slowly and then moves quickly to the end. This default fade is the most natural.
- –3 dB: The fade starts quickly and then tapers off at the end. This choice is best used for a quick fade-out.

5 Press Shift-Z to fit all clips in the Timeline. Then select both **Battle Lines** clips, and press Option-S to solo them. Play the last few seconds of the second **Battle Lines** clip while looking at the waveform.

In the clip waveform, the steep-sloping fade cuts into the final strong beat of music, lowering the volume for that beat. You may want to play the clip again to hear the lowered volume created by this fade. You can change this fade shape by clicking the clip's fade handle and opening a shortcut menu.

6 Place your pointer over the clip's fade handle to select it. Control-click it, and from the shortcut menu, choose +3 dB. Then play the end of the clip.

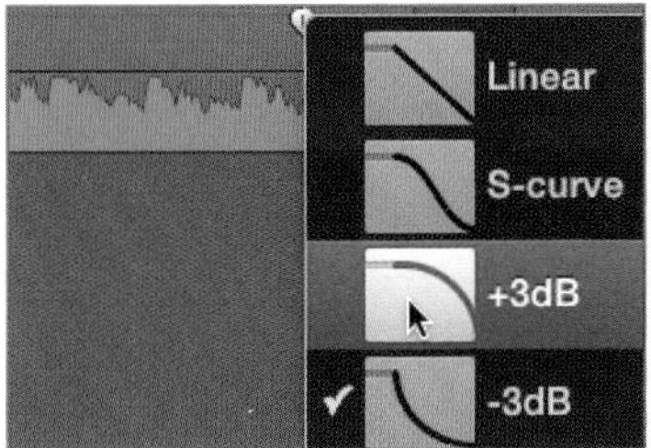

Notice that the last strong beat of music is now at full volume. Try out each choice of fade options for the end of the **Battle Lines** clip, and then return to the +3 dB fade option.

The **Battle Lines** music consists of two clips. By moving your pointer over the volume control lines, you can see an abrupt 8 dB volume level change at the edit point between the two clips. Applying a crossfade would help smooth the transition from one audio level to the next.

NOTE ▸ A crossfade is an audio transition in which the first clip's audio fades down while the second clip's audio fades up. During a crossfade, audio from both clips is heard and can be seen in the waveforms.

7 With the music clips still soloed, play from the beginning of the first **Battle Lines** clip through the edit point to hear the discrepancy in audio levels.

8 Click an edge of the edit point between the two clips. Choose Edit > Add Cross Dissolve, or press Command-T. Play the clips to hear the smooth audio transition. Press Option-S to enable all clips, and listen to the transition again in context.

TIP The default crossfade duration for both audio and video is one second. To change this duration, choose Final Cut Pro > Preferences, or press Command-, (comma) and click the Editing button.

Throughout the *Zero to Hero_fades* project, the music builds in volume and intensity. Earlier in the lesson, you changed audio levels within a clip by using a range selection to create keyframes. You can also change audio levels within a clip by making edits, adjusting volume levels, and applying crossfades.

9 Move the playhead to 5:10 on the Timeline, using the arrow keys to navigate to the exact frame. Press B to select the Blade tool, and click the **Battle Lines** clip at the playhead location. Then move the playhead to 18:40 on the Timeline and use the Blade tool to make an edit point clip at that location. Press A to return to the default Select tool.

Two new edit points are added to the music clip, so you now have a total of four **Battle Lines** music clips.

10 For the new clip that begins at 5:10, drag the volume control down to –13 dB, and for the last clip that begins at 18:40, drag the volume control down to –16 dB.

TIP If you have difficulty dragging a volume control line to a specific dB level, hold the Command key while dragging, or press Control-= (equals) or Control-– (minus) to raise or lower the volume one dB at a time of the selected clip or clips.

You could now crossfade the audio edits individually, but applying all the transitions at once would be faster. Apply transitions to more than one clip at a time only if you want the transition type to be the same for each edit point.

11 From the last three **Battle Lines** clips you created, select the middle of the trio. Press Command-T.

Notice that crossfades are now applied to the edit points between the last three **Battle Lines** clips. You do not need to add a crossfade at the end of the last music clip. The fade you made earlier at that end point of the music will still be there.

TIP Click any audio transition in the Timeline, and then in the Transition inspector, look at the Audio Crossfade controls. Here you can select the same fade options as in the fade handle's shortcut menu.

Recording Voiceovers

As your project nears completion, you may find that you are still waiting for the narration voiceover to be recorded. However, you need a narration clip now to help refine your edit. One solution is to record your own unofficial voiceover, which is sometimes referred to as a *scratch track*, and edit it into your project as a placeholder.

In this exercise, you'll use the Record Audio feature to record several takes of yourself reading a narration for *Delicious Peace*. You can use your computer's built-in microphone for the recordings, or connect your own external mic. Then, using the Audition feature, you will choose the best take.

To prepare for your new scratch clip in the current sequence, let's first disable the voice-over you will be replacing.

NOTE ► If you are using an external microphone for this exercise, connect the device to your computer.

1 To return to the *Delicious Peace_mix* project, click the left Timeline history arrow and choose the project from the open projects list. Make sure the large Audio meters are visible. Then, in the Event Browser, select the *Delicious Peace* Event.

2 In the Timeline, play the **VO_07** clip to become familiar with its content. Then press V to disable the clip.

In this exercise, you will record three takes of this narration, and like any good actor, you will vary each take so you have different interpretations to choose from.

3 To not hear the project audio while you record, turn down your computer and/or external speaker completely. You may need to adjust your position relative to your computer's microphone to realize a proper recording level.

TIP ► As with any recording, refer to the Audio meters while recording a voiceover. If you find that you need to adjust the volume level, you can drag the Gain slider in the Record Audio window.

4 In the Timeline, move the playhead to the beginning of the disabled VO_07 clip, and then choose Window > Record Audio. In the Record Audio window, set the following options:

- Destination: Delicious Peace this is the Event where the recording will be saved.
- Input Device: Choose your recording device. If you are using your computer's microphone, choose Built-in Microphone and Stereo - Channels 1 & 2.
- Gain: If you are using your computer's built-in microphone, you may want to adjust the slider to boost the Input Device Gain to 2 or 3.
- Monitor: Deselect this option so you won't hear feedback during recording.

NOTE ▶ Enable the Monitor option only if you will be wearing headphones to monitor the recording, or if a connected microphone is out of feedback range.

With the options selected, you're ready to record. But before you begin, review the following narration text:

The farmers of Delicious Peace Co-op are a testament to this mutually beneficial relationship, which they have enhanced by adding the requirement of peace.

5 In the Record Audio window, click the Record button and read the narrative text. To stop recording, click the Record button, or press the Spacebar.

In the Timeline, your recording appears as a new **Voiceover 1** clip attached to the primary storyline at the playhead position.

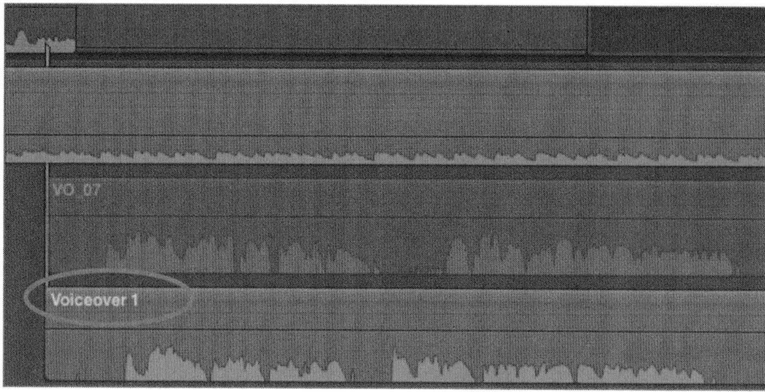

NOTE ▶ If you make a mistake or want to redo a recording, press Command-Z and record the narration again. The playhead will automatically return to the top of the **VO_07** clip.

That may be the perfect take, but let's add two more versions so you can compare them using the Audition function.

6 To record two additional voiceover takes, repeat step 5, changing your emphasis and performance for each take. Close the Record Audio window when you finish.

   Notice that each take of the voiceover narration is recorded as a separate connected **Voiceover** clip, and that each new take is placed below the previous take. Also note that all the takes recorded into the project also appear in the Event Browser. The **Voiceover** clip numbers of the takes may vary, depending on whether you deleted them or recorded more than three.

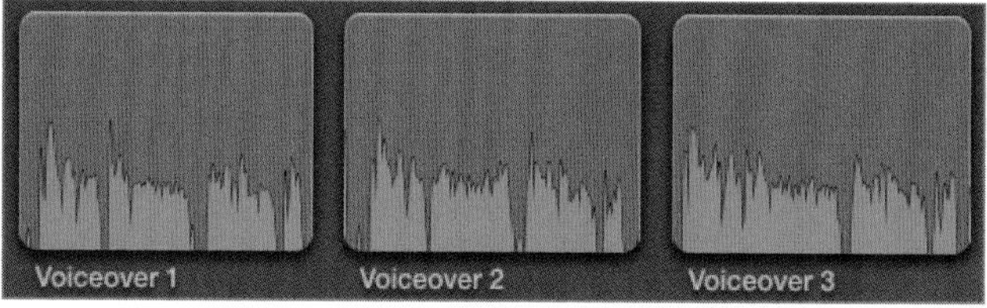

7 In the Timeline, keep the first voiceover you recorded, but select the other two voiceovers, and press Delete.

Although the clips are removed from your project, they are still available in the Event Browser. You will select these clips in the Event Browser to create an audition.

8 In the Event Browser, select the **Voiceover 2** and **Voiceover 3** clips, and then drag them into the Timeline and onto the **Voiceover 1** clip.

9 From the shortcut menu, choose Add to Audition.

In the upper-left corner of the clip, an Audition icon appears that looks like a spotlight shining down, indicating that the clip holds additional audition clips.

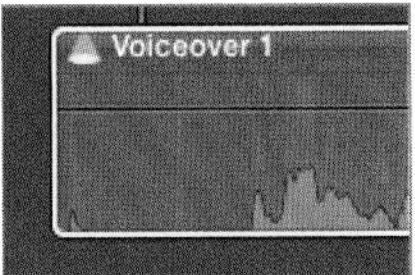

10 Click the Audition icon to open the audition filmstrip, or with the clip selected, press Y.

The **Voiceover 1** clip is the pick and appears highlighted, while the other two clips appear as alternates.

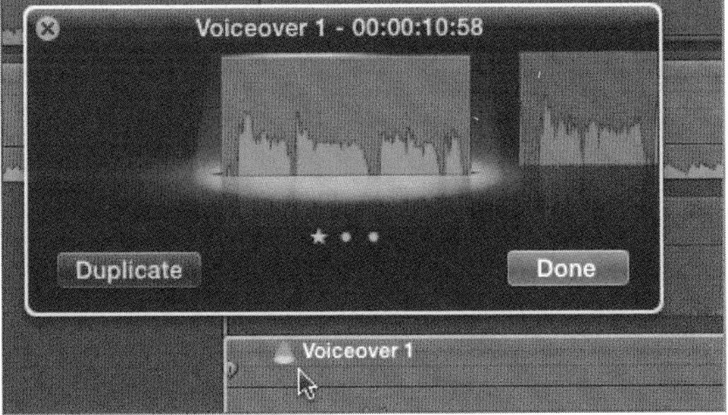

You can scroll through the clips one at a time by pressing the Left and Right Arrow keys. Then turn up your computer's volume and play each clip by pressing the Spacebar. When you click a clip, it plays in place of the current **Voiceover** clip in the Timeline.

11 To audition the **Voiceover 2** clip, press the Right Arrow to highlight that clip, and press the Spacebar to play it. Then audition the **Voiceover 3** clip. Select the audition clip that has your best voiceover take and click Done. The alternate clips remain in the audition.

NOTE ▸ You can edit and adjust volume levels in the selected clip in the Timeline and still keep your audition clips.

12 To finalize your pick, and eliminate the audition and its alternates, Control-click the **Voiceover** clip in the Timeline and choose Audition > Finalize Audition from the shortcut menu, or press Option-Shift-Y.

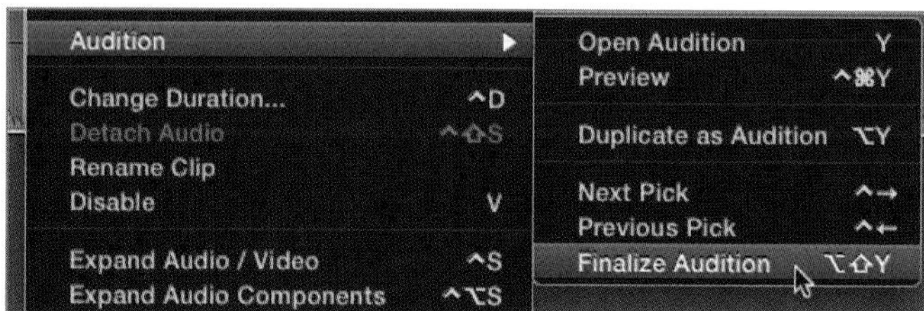

The Audition icon is no longer in the clip in the Timeline. You can now play your voiceover clip and adjust the volume to hear how your voice sounds mixed with the music and natural sound.

TIP Auditioning clips offers an easy way to sample different music and sound effects in your project.

Correcting Problem Audio

From the buzz of an aircraft to an ill-timed cough or faulty sound recording equipment, some of your audio clips will have problems that must be fixed during the postproduction process. You may have already analyzed and fixed some audio problems during import. But with the Audio Enhancement tools, you can finesse audio adjustments and track the changes that Final Cut Pro makes automatically.

In this exercise, you will learn to monitor an automatic correction of a significant hum that overpowers dialogue. You'll adjust a sudden, loud noise using keyframes, and zoom into a waveform to fine-tune an audio sample level. Then you'll compare your adjusted waveform to the original waveform.

For this exercise, you will adjust a project from *Fairly Legal* that could really use some audio intervention.

1 In the Project Library, double-click the *Fairly Legal_hum* project to open it in the Timeline. Make sure the large Audio meters are visible. In the Timeline, click the **4A-2 110(B)_hum** clip and play it.

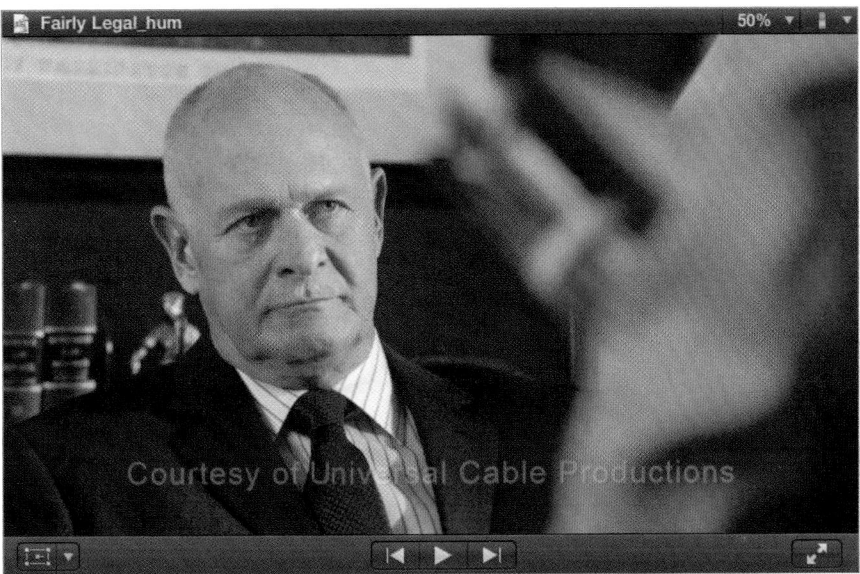

While the audio in this clip may sound normal, the original clip audio contained a loud, distracting hum. Final Cut Pro detected the hum in the clip's audio and then automatically analyzed and removed it. You can listen to the original audio hum and check other properties in the Audio inspector.

NOTE ▸ Final Cut Pro X is very quick to fix an audio problem such as the hum in this clip. If you still hear a hum, however, follow the steps to determine how you can locate and fix the hum yourself.

2 If the Audio inspector is not already open, choose Window > Show Inspector, or press Command-4. In the Channel Configuration parameter, click Show and then click

the disclosure triangle next to the clip name to view the waveform. Skim through the **4A-2 110(B)_hum** clip in the Audio inspector. With the pointer over the waveform, press the Spacebar to play the clip.

When you position the pointer over the Channel Configuration waveform, and then skim or play the clip, you will hear the original, unaltered audio. In this case, you can clearly hear the hum that Final Cut Pro automatically fixed. You can take a closer look at those corrections in the Audio Enhancements section.

NOTE ▶ If you move the pointer outside the waveform and press the spacebar, Final Cut Pro will play the corrected clip audio in the Timeline.

3 In the Audio Enhancements section of the Audio inspector, click Show. Look at the Audio Analysis of this clip. To view this analysis more closely, click the Show Audio Enhancements Inspector button.

TIP To open the Audio Enhancements pane directly, choose Windows > Go To > Audio Enhancements, or press Command-8; or from the Enhancements pop-up menu in the toolbar, choose Show Audio Enhancements.

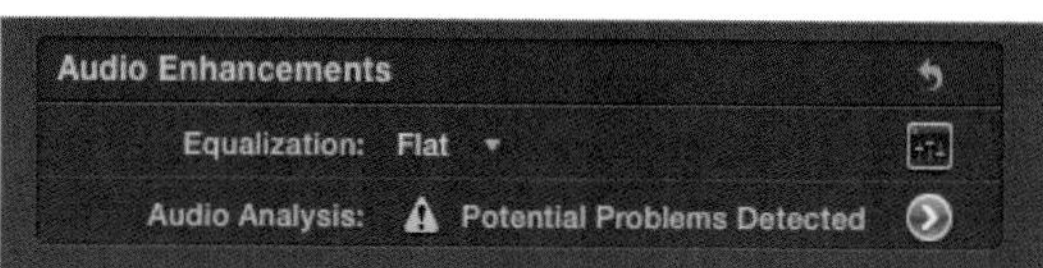

In the Audio Enhancements pane, you see the clip name and duration, and three sections for Loudness, Background Noise Removal, and Hum Removal. Once a clip has been analyzed, a color indicator appears next to each enhancement:

- A red sign indicates severe problems.
- A yellow warning triangle indicates potential problems.
- A green checkmark indicates the clip is OK.

NOTE ▶ If you choose to "Analyze and fix audio problems" during import, Final Cut Pro will correct only severe audio problems. Moderate problems will appear with a yellow warning indicator next to the Audio Analysis in Audio Enhancements section.

Notice that Hum Removal is enabled, indicating this enhancement has been applied to the **4A-2 110(B)_hum** clip.

4 In the Timeline, play the **4A-2 110(B)_hum** clip, and then click the blue Hum Removal enable button to turn it off and then on again. You can also click the Hum Removal icon (that looks like an electrical outlet) to turn the enhancement off and on. As you continue to play the clip, click the button to switch between 50 Hz and 60 Hz, and then leave it on 60 Hz.

NOTE ▶ Removing a dramatic hum such as this one may not result in a perfect audio clip, but it can save a sound bite that may be crucial to your project.

When you switch to 50 Hz hum removal, the hum remains because it is a 60 Hz hum. Final Cut Pro did a pretty good job at removing the hum and enhancing this audio clip. But you can also make manual adjustments to improve the audio quality. For example, you can reduce more hum and make other adjustments using tools in the Audio inspector.

TIP You can also automatically enhance audio by choosing Modify > Auto Enhance Audio, or by choosing Auto Enhance Audio from the Enhancements pop-up menu in the toolbar.

5 In the upper-left corner of the Audio Enhancements pane, click the back button to return to the Audio inspector, and make sure the Audio Enhancements section is open.

Notice the Equalization pop-up menu in which you can choose to automatically correct common audio problems. One choice is to reduce hum. Let's see if it will improve the current clip.

6 Click the Equalization pop-up menu, and see the list of choices to enhance high-end, midrange, and low-end audio. Choose Hum Reduction, and then play the **4A-2 110(B)_hum** clip to notice an additional improvement.

Oftentimes during a relatively smooth sound clip, you will see and hear a spike in the audio level. Because spikes don't represent the entire clip, you can focus in on that small area of sound to fix it.

7 In the Timeline, play the first clip, **4B-1_110(B)**, and notice the audio level when the stack of legal files is dropped on the desk. Navigate to the point on the clip where the sound level is loudest—indicated by a sharp, peaked waveform at around 1:15—and then park the playhead at that point.

You can lower this peak area of the clip by creating three keyframes and then lowering the level of the middle keyframe. This method of using three keyframes creates a smooth and natural way to lower the spike's level.

TIP Turn on snapping when making audio adjustments using the playhead and keyframes.

8 To zoom into the clip, press Command-= (equals) two times. Scroll to adjust the position of the clip in the Timeline so you can clearly see the trough areas before and after the peak wave of the clip.

You will set the first keyframe on the loudest portion of the spike, and then set one additional keyframe on either side of it. You set keyframes manually with the help of the Option key.

9 To set a keyframe on the spike, Option-click at the point where the playhead line and the clip's volume control line intersect. A dB info flag appears with a small white keyframe below it.

A keyframe is assigned to the peak of the waveform. Now let's add two additional keyframes before and after the spike.

10 To add a keyframe after the spike, move the skimmer to 2:05 on the Timeline, and then Option-click the clip's volume control line. To add a keyframe before the peak, move the skimmer back to 1:00 on the Timeline, and Option-click that point on the volume control line.

TIP To remove a keyframe, click the keyframe to highlight it, and press Delete.

With the three keyframes in place, you can now drop the level of the middle keyframe to sharply decrease its volume.

11 Click the middle keyframe, which turns from a solid white diamond into a hollow yellow diamond. Drag the keyframe down until the info flag reads –2 dB. Then play the clip and watch the Audio meters to see that the volume levels for the audio spike have been lowered, and that the transitions are unnoticeable.

By having the two outer keyframes *anchor* the current volume of the rest of the clip, the volume of the middle keyframe can be adjusted smoothly.

To see if the middle keyframe is directly over the audio spike, you can zoom in to the waveform. When you zoom in to an extreme level, you can see the audio sample level, which lasts only a fraction of a second. Here you can make subframe adjustments to the keyframe.

12 Park the playhead on the middle keyframe. Press Command–= (equals) several times until you can no longer zoom in. The peak of the waveform stretches out, and the single white ghost frame that represents one frame fills the Timeline view.

In this view, you can see that the audio spike is flattened, but still visible. You can easily move the middle keyframe right or left to place it directly over the spike.

13 Click the middle keyframe to select it, and then drag the keyframe right or left to position it directly over the audio spike.

TIP You can press Command-Right Arrow or Command-Left Arrow to navigate right or left along the clip at the subframe audio sample level, but you will need to drag the keyframe to move it.

You may have noticed the "ghost" waveforms in the clips. You can compare the adjusted audio levels to normalized waveforms by making a selection in Final Cut Pro Preferences.

14 Choose Final Cut Pro > Preferences, and click Editing. Notice the "Show reference waveforms" preference.

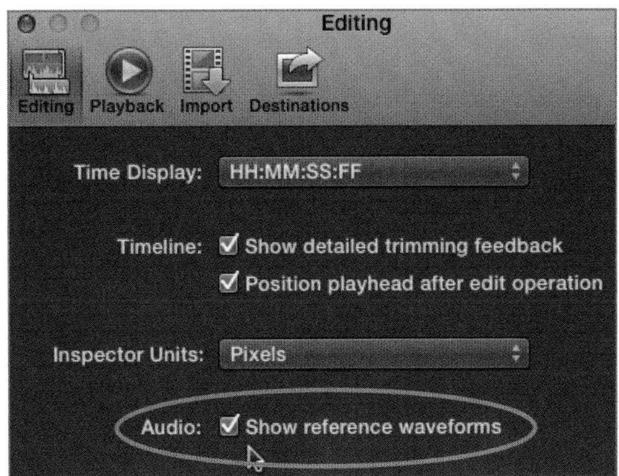

These reference waveforms allow you to see full scale audio waveforms even when the clip's volume control is set to –96 dB.

15 Press Shift-Z to fit all clips in the Timeline and to see the reference waveforms in all the clips.

TIP To hide the reference waveforms, deselect "Show reference waveforms" in the Preferences Editing pane, and then skim the Timeline clips to hide the reference waveforms.

Although not all projects require this fine degree of correction, it's important to know what functions to turn to when these problems emerge.

Editor's Cut

In the last three audio clips in the *Fairly Legal* project, you have found a discrepancy in audio quality. It will take just a few more steps to improve this section of dialogue using one of the most traditional of sound fixes, crossfading audio.

- Command-click to select the last three clips: **4B-1_110(B)**, **4A-2_110(B)_hum**, and **4B-3_110(B)**.
- Control-click one of the clips, and from the shortcut menu, choose Expand Audio/Video, or press Control-S.
- Create a J-cut at the beginning of the middle clip and an L-cut at the end of the middle clip. The duration of the splits should be 10 frames.
- Use the fade handles to fade in/fade out the now stacked audio clips for both edits. Ensure that you do not affect their speech by fading too far.
- Play the three clips to hear a smoother transition between audio edits.

Lesson Review

1. Describe three methods you can use to display the large Audio Meters pane in the Timeline.
2. What do yellow audio meters for a clip indicate?
3. How can you adjust the volume of all Timeline clips at one time while preserving each clip's relative volume?
4. How can you solo one or more clips in the Timeline?
5. How do you preview one of the Final Cut Pro royalty-free sound effects?
6. How do you set a keyframe on the volume control line?
7. How do you adjust the volume of a clip on the fly during playback?
8. How do you create an audio fade-in or fade-out in the Timeline?
9. How do you adjust the fade options in the Timeline?
10. How do you create an audio crossfade between two clips in a storyline?
11. You created an audition to preview several versions of an audio clip. How do you finalize your pick?
12. What tool would you use to automatically correct a clip that includes audio hum?
13. What tool do you use to record your own voiceover, and where do you access it?

Answers

1. In the toolbar, to the right of the Dashboard timecode display, click the Audio meter icon to open the Audio Meters pane to the right of the Timeline; choose Window > Show Audio Meters; or press Shift-Command-8.
2. The audio meters change color according to a clip's decibel (dB) level. As the audio level approaches the 0 dB peak, the meter color turns from green to yellow. When the audio level exceeds 0 dB, the meter color turns from yellow to red.
3. Press Command-A to select all clips, and then press Control-= (equals) or Control-– (minus) to raise or lower clip volume 1 dB at a time.
4. Select one or more clips in the Timeline, and then click the Solo button at the top-right of the Timeline, or press Option-S.
5. In the toolbar, click the musical note button to open the Music and Sound Browser. Select the Final Cut Pro Sound Effects folder, and in the lower section of the Browser, double-click a file to preview it.

6. To manually add a keyframe to the volume control line, Option-click the line where you want to place the keyframe. You can drag the keyframe up and down to adjust the volume level, or left and right to change its timing.
7. In the toolbar, click the Inspector button, and click the Audio tab at the top of the pane. In the Timeline, play a clip. Drag the Volume slider right or left to increase or decrease the volume. While adjusting on the fly, other audio clips may cut out. They will become audible when you stop adjusting the volume.
8. Drag the fade handles that appear when you place the pointer over the upper-left or upper-right corner of the audio waveform. Drag left and right to change its timing.
9. Control-click a clip's fade handle to open the shortcut menu, and choose one of the fade options: Linear, S-curve, +3 dB, or –3 dB.
10. Click the edge of the edit point between two clips, and choose Edit > Add Cross Dissolve, or press Command-T.
11. In the Audition window, select the clip you want to finalize, and click Done. In the Timeline, Control-click the clip and choose Audition > Finalize Audition from the shortcut menu, or press Option-Shift-Y.
12. Select a clip, and then choose Window > Go to Audio Enhancements, or press Command–8. In the Hum category, a red warning sign indicates an electrical hum. To fix it, click the Auto Enhance button at the bottom of the Audio Enhancements inspector.
13. Open the Record Audio window by choosing Window > Record Audio.

Keyboard Shortcuts

Control-= (equals)	Raise the audio level by 1 dB
Control-– (minus)	Lower the audio level by 1 dB
Command-8	Go to the Audio Enhancements inspector
Shift-Command-8	Show or hide the Audio meters
V	Enable or disable a clip for playback
Option-S	Solo selected items in the Timeline
Shift-S	Toggle audio skimming
Option-G	Create a new compound clip

Keyboard Shortcuts

Command-G	Create a storyline from a selection of connected clips
Command-T	Add the default transition to the selection
Y	Open the selected audition
Option-Shift-Y	Finalize an audition
Option-click	Add a keyframe to a clip's volume control
Command-Right Arrow	Move the playhead to the next audio subframe
Command-Left Arrow	Move the playhead to the previous audio subframe

Time

This lesson takes approximately 90 minutes to complete.

Goals

Use the Titles Browser

Add a title and a lower third

Make changes in the Inspector

Import still images to bumper/opens

Work with generators

Explore title themes

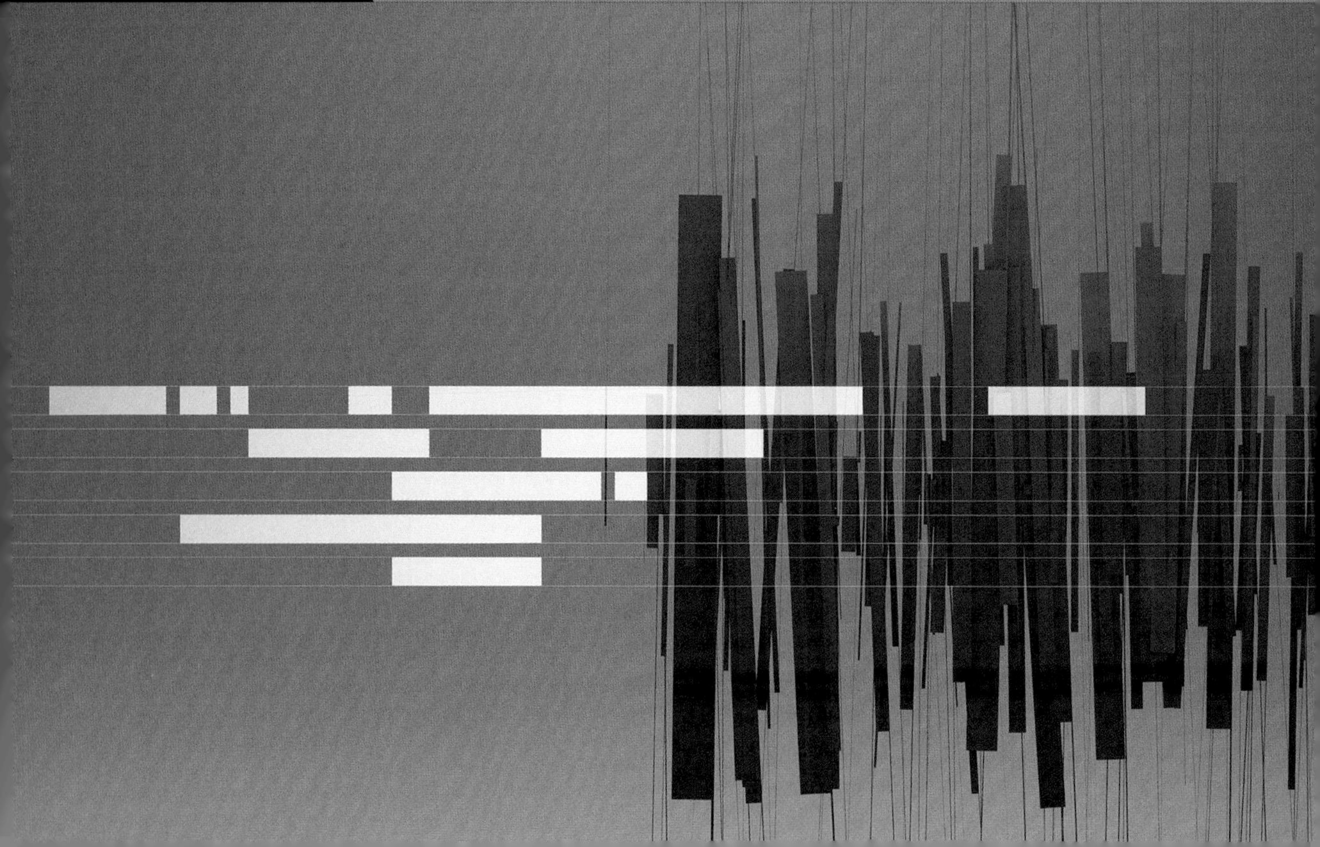

Lesson **9**

Working with Titles, Generators, and Themes

All projects, from the simplest to the most complex, require titles of some sort. Opening titles provide information. What are we about to see? In the case of opening credits, who created what we are about to see? Who is starring? Titles can also be an expression of the film's style. An animated title above a background of colorful, whirling shapes certainly suggests a style of film very different from one with large white text set against a stark black background.

In this lesson, you will work with different kinds of titles, lower thirds to identify stars and a director, end credits to detail the names of filmmakers, a production company bumper, and an opening title to announce what's to come. In addition, you will explore generators created in Motion to provide backgrounds, shapes, or textures. You will also explore themes, which provide a very specific look to your titles. The possibilities are nearly endless.

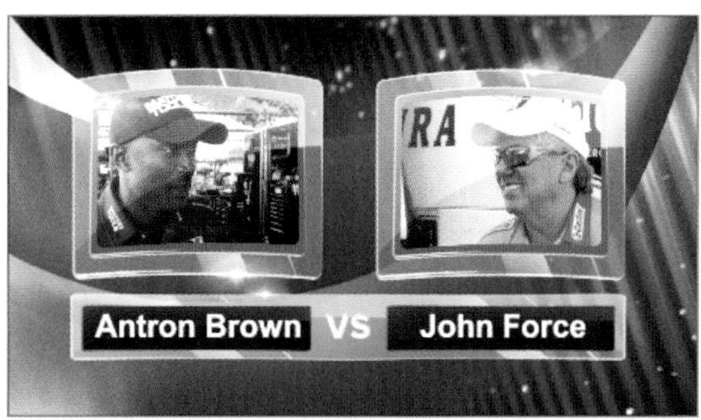

Using the Titles Browser

As it does for transitions and sound effects, Final Cut Pro provides a Titles Browser that contains a collection of preformatted titles created in Motion. These titles come in all shapes and sizes, all of which you can modify to fit your needs. For those with an independent spirit, there is even a custom title to build from scratch on your own. Titles have been sorted into categories and subcategories to make them easier to find. If you know a title's name, you can use the search filter to find it. Whether choosing a Build In/Out, which provides a variety of ways to create text-only credits, or choosing a bumper/opener with colorful, animated backgrounds, the Browser provides what's needed.

Since you are already familiar with the ways to navigate through a Browser, let's take a brief tour of the Titles Browser. Then you will insert an opening title at the beginning of the project, connect a second title to a clip, and change a title's duration in the Timeline.

1 In the Project Library, from the Lesson Projects folder, drag the Lesson 9 folder onto the APTS FCP X icon. Hide the contents of the Lesson Projects folder, and click the disclosure triangle of the Lesson 9 folder to reveal its contents.

   In this lesson, you will work with three projects, *Fairly Legal*, Matthew Modine's *I Think*, and *ZTH_Force vs Brown*. Before you begin making changes to a project, create a backup so you can return to it if necessary.

2 In the Lesson 9 folder, duplicate *Fairly Legal* and name it *Fairly Legal_BACKUP*. Open *Fairly Legal* into the Timeline and play the project.

NOTE ► If the Audio meters are still open from the previous lesson, close them to allow more room in the Timeline to perform the steps in this lesson.

As you can see, important information is missing. You don't know the title of the project. You don't know the names of the actors, and you have no clue as to the name of the director. Let's add a simple opening title to announce the name of the television show and a second with the name of the episode. You will add the actors and director information in the next exercise.

As with transitions, Final Cut Pro sorts titles into categories and subcategories. You can audition them by skimming, and use a search field to locate a specific one.

3 In the toolbar, click the Titles Browser button.

The Browser opens with the All category selected. The lower-right corner shows a total of 176 available items. They have been collected into the general category of All and then subdivided further into five other categories: Build In/Out, Bumper/Opener, Credits, Elements, and Lower Thirds. Titles within categories are listed in alphabetical order.

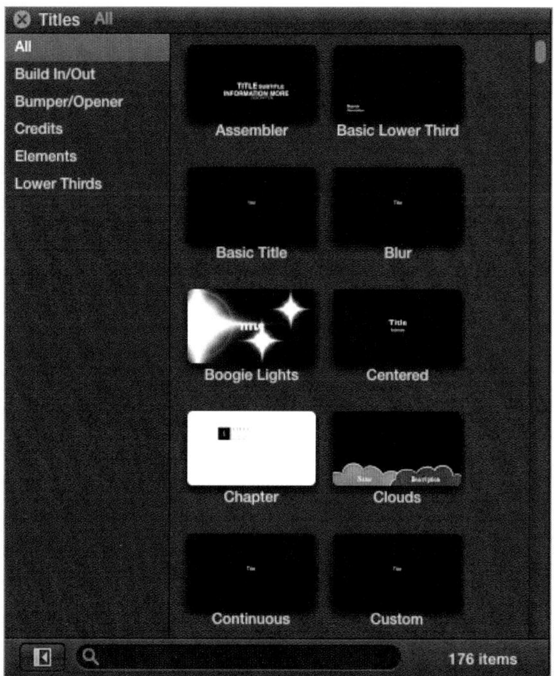

4 Select the Build In/Out category and skim Blur. Then, if it's not visible, type *Far Far Away* in the search field and skim that title. (That should bring back memories. "In a galaxy far, far away...")

TIP ▶ Remember to clear the search field before continuing so that you can view all thumbnails.

Build In/Out offers text (over a black background, by default) to suggest that all these titles come with alpha channels, so you can layer them over another background, either a clip from the Timeline or a background of your own design.

NOTE ▶ An alpha channel is an image channel—in addition to the red, green, and blue color channels—used to store transparency information for compositing. Many of the titles included in Final Cut Pro have alpha channels that make their backgrounds transparent.

Titles can be applied as a storyline clip or as a connected clip. They can be applied as inserts or appends by dragging them from the Browser to be inserted before any clip or appended after the very last clip. The default duration of many titles is four seconds, but you will find that some are much longer. As you learned in a previous lesson, you can easily change duration by dragging inward or outward on the edge of the clip.

5 In the Build In/Out category, find and skim Ornate. To insert it as the very first clip in the project, drag the clip to that location. When you see the blue insertion outline, release clip. Notice that the title clip icon is purple.

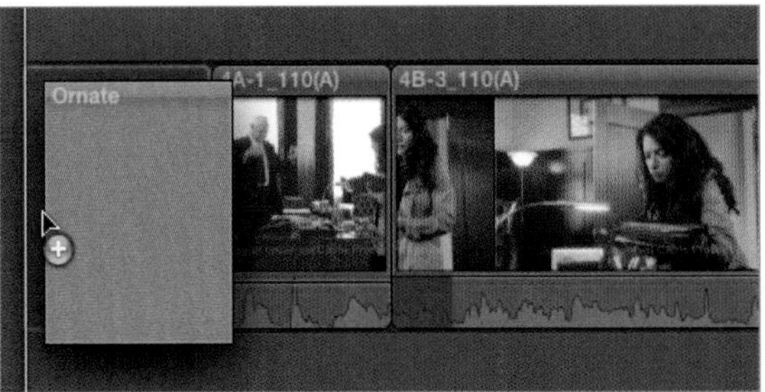

TIP ▶ Another way to insert a title into the primary storyline is to position the playhead at the beginning of the project, select the title in the Browser, and press W.

6 In the Timeline, play the **Ornate** clip, and notice that the animation finishes about halfway through the clip. Then double-click the clip.

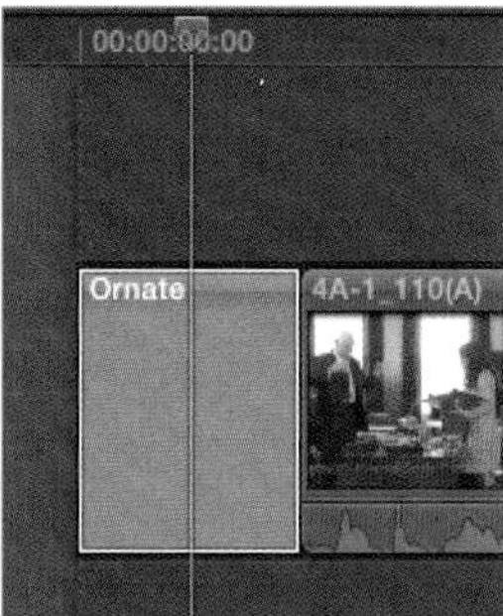

When you double-click a title clip, Final Cut Pro automatically cues the playhead to where the text is fully present on the screen. In this case, it cues to the middle of the clip. Double-clicking a text clip also opens it in the Viewer with the default text automatically selected and awaiting your changes.

Before editing this text, however, let's make sure the title and any accompanying animation fit comfortably within certain boundaries called action safe zones.

7 Choose Window > Viewer Display > Show Title/Action Safe Zones. In the Viewer, two rectangular outlines appear as overlays in the image area. Notice that the **Ornate** clip's outer graphic elements fall just inside the outer outline.

The inner box represents the title safe boundary, and the outer box represents the action safe boundary. The recorded frame size of broadcast video is actually larger than the viewable area of a television monitor. When text is positioned within the title safe boundary, you can be sure the text will appear on any television monitor when the show is broadcast. Likewise, when an important action within a clip appears within the action safe boundary, you can be sure that action is visible to the home viewer.

While some of the animated graphics hug the outer action safe outline, it's clear that the **Ornate** title text fits safely within the title safe zone.

TIP When you want to turn off the safe zone outlines, choose Window > Viewer Display > Action/Title Safe Zones.

Let's type in the title of this television show. You can do this directly in the Viewer. When you double-clicked the clip in the previous step, it automatically selected the default text, so you're now ready to edit it.

8 In the Viewer, where a blue overlay highlights *Title*, type *Fairly Legal*. Press Esc (Escape), and play the clip.

TIP Pressing Esc signals Final Cut Pro that you are done entering text. Pressing Return creates an additional line of text.

The new text appears in the Viewer and, as was the case with transitions, Final Cut Pro may take a few seconds to render the change.

TIP If you decide to change the text, simply double-click either word in the title to restore the blue highlight or, to select the full line of text at one time, triple-click either word. You can also drag to select a word or line, and then type a new title.

Once you've edited the default text to create a new title, you may need to reposition it within the effect. You can easily fine-tune text placement within the Viewer by dragging the text box anywhere within the frame.

9 Move the pointer over the text in the Viewer. A bounding box appears around the text. When you see the pointer with a position tool attached, drag the text box to the left and release the pointer. Press Command-Z to return the text box to its original position.

TIP You can also reposition text while still in the editing mode but before you press Esc. Move the pointer over the position button in the center of the text field, and when the pointer has the position tool attached, drag the position button and release the pointer. You can also drag the position button using the I cursor.

In a previous lesson, you applied a transition by double-clicking it in the Browser. The rule with titles is that double-clicking always results in a connected clip. To apply a title to announce the name of this *Fairly Legal* episode, you will connect it at the playhead position in the Timeline.

10 In the Timeline, position the playhead at about the 00:00:10:07 mark as displayed in the Dashboard. In the Browser, double-click Ornate.

This time, the title is added as a connected clip at the playhead position.

NOTE ▶ As is the case with all connected clips, you can drag the text clip to adjust its position in the project.

11 In the Timeline, double-click the connected **Ornate** clip. In the Viewer, with *Title* highlighted, type *Bridges*, and then press Esc. Play the project through the first two title clips.

Changing the duration of this second clip is an easy task.

12 In the Timeline, click the right side of the second title clip and drag left until the trim info flag reads a duration of 03:00.

Adding a Lower Third

One of the most common titles to add to your project is the lower third, so called because it appears in the lower third of the screen to provide information. It might identify the voice of an unseen narrator, tell you the name of an onscreen reporter, or list the name of the actors in a scene. In each case, the Final Cut Pro X lower thirds provide one or two text fields. Some come with a background, which helps to highlight the text; others come without. Some lower thirds are animated, but you can modify all of them to fit need and style.

In this exercise, you will add lower thirds to identify the two actors in the scene as well as the name of the director. The star of *Fairly Legal* is Sarah Shahi, who plays the lead character Kate Reed. Her frequent guest star and sometime nemesis is a judge played by Gerald McRaney. The director of this episode is Peter Markle.

Let's look at the Lower Thirds category to select one suitable for this project.

1 In the Titles Browser, click the category Lower Thirds and skim Clouds and Echo to see their animated behaviors in the Viewer. Now skim over the Overlap thumbnail and press the Spacebar to play the title animation. Press the Spacebar again to stop it.

Overlap consists of two text fields, one labeled *Name* and the other *Description*. As the title plays, it loops to play again continuously until you press K or the Spacebar to stop it. Overlap is the lower third you will use in this exercise.

2 In the Timeline, position the playhead at about 00:00:15:11, and double-click Overlap to add it as a connected clip. Play the clip.

The Name and Description fields enter from out of the frame, join in the center, pause, and then switch positions to exit again. You will enter information in both fields.

3 In the Timeline, double-click the **Overlap** clip. In the Viewer, replace the highlighted *Name* text with *Starring*. Then double-click the Description field and type *Sarah Shahi*. Press Esc and then play the clip.

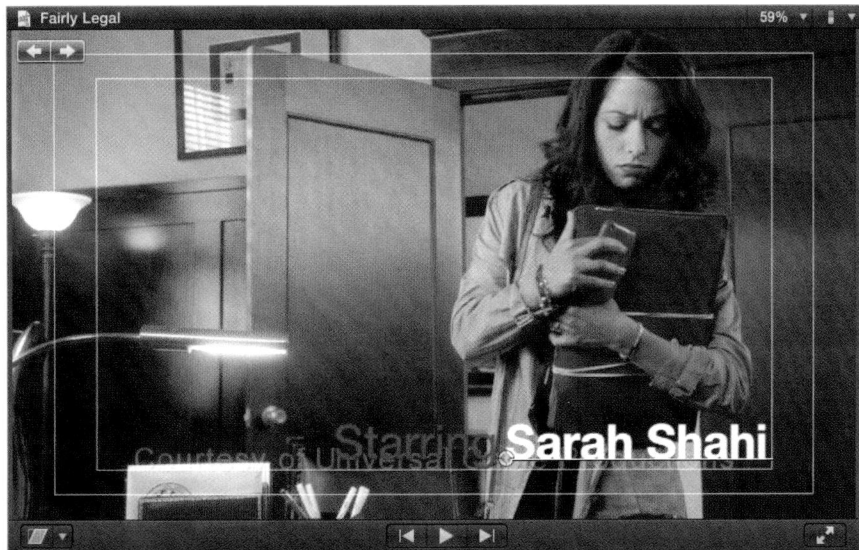

Before making any changes to this lower third, let's add one for the show's guest star. Instead of returning to the Browser to add another Overlap, why not copy and paste the clip that's already in the Timeline?

4 In the Timeline, select the title clip now named **Overlap: Starring** and press Command-C. You can also choose Edit > Copy.

This title is now placed onto a clipboard to be used again and again until a different item is copied to the clipboard and replaces it.

5 In the Timeline, position the playhead at 00:00:20:11 and press Command-V. Then reposition the playhead to 00:00:30:23 and press Command-V again.

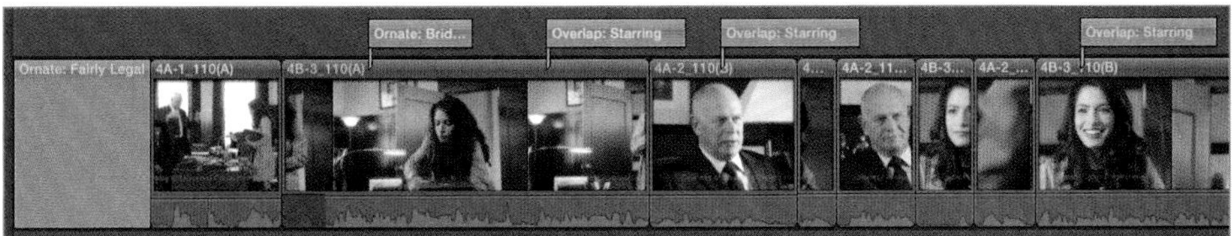

NOTE ▶ What holds true for the opening title holds true for lower thirds as well. You can insert a lower third into a storyline or add it to the end as an append edit.

You now have five title clips in the project. Let's add Gerald McRaney's name to the fourth clip.

6 Double-click the fourth title clip and, in the Viewer, where *Starring* is highlighted, type *Guest Starring*.

The second text box contains two names. If you double-click Sarah, only her name is highlighted. To select both names, or all the text within that text box, triple-click one of the names or select the text you want to change.

7 To highlight Sarah's full name, triple-click it. Type *Gerald McRaney*, and then press Esc.

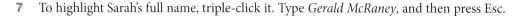

Because the title safe zones are still visible, you can see that McRaney's name does not fit safely within the title safe boundaries. This is an easy correction to make directly in the Viewer.

8 In the Viewer, drag the *Guest Starring* text box to the left and position the text just inside the left title safe boundary.

TIP Hold down Shift while dragging to constrain the movement to one axis.

9 To reposition the *Gerald McRaney* text, drag it until the name just clears the inside right title safe boundary.

Although you will make several adjustments in the Inspector in the next exercise, it's often easy to make initial corrections in the Viewer.

In the next lower third, you will credit the director, Peter Markle.

10 Select the last title clip and, in the first box, type *Directed by*. In the second box, type *Peter Markle*. Play all the lower third clips in the project.

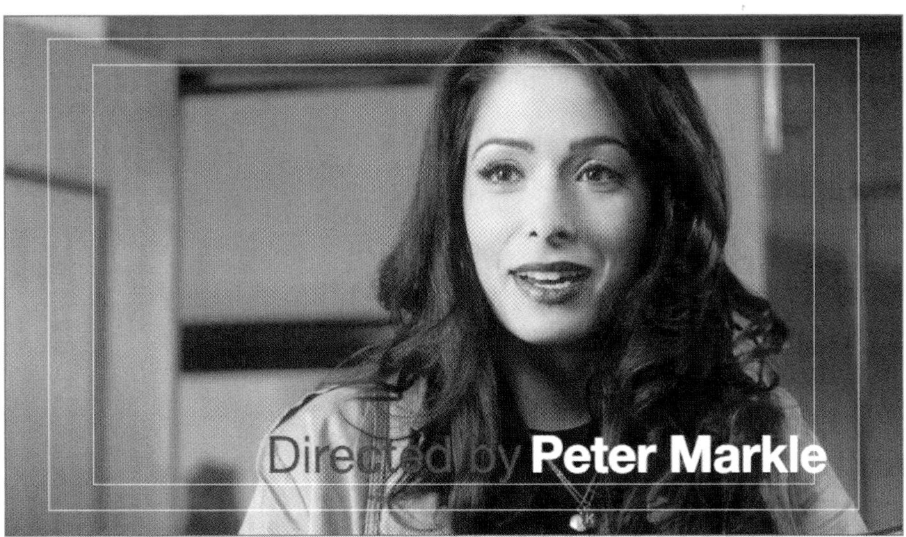

Take 2

Your assistant returns from lunch and points out the fact that Peter Markle's credit isn't quite within the safe zone and he wonders how you will fix it. Why don't you show him? And while you're at it, why not make a new folder inside the Lesson 9 folder and name it *Backups*. As you can see, the Project Library is getting crowded with four projects and their duplicates. Collecting together all the backups might just make for a less cluttered Project Library.

Modifying Titles

Now that you added lower thirds to the Timeline, you will want to adjust them. As you learned earlier in Lesson 7, the transitions chapter, the Inspector has numerical and slider controls to adjust and modify nearly every aspect of the items in a project. In the top of the window are tabs separating different types of parameters as well as blue boxes to toggle parameters on and off so you can view the title with and without any change. Do you want to alter the size and color of the text? Do you want to add a glow or a drop shadow? The Inspector allows you to make these changes and so many more.

Mixing text styles sometimes makes a project look visually uneven. In the previous steps, you added somewhat flowery opening titles followed by rather straightforward lower thirds. It might be a good idea to conform one style to the other for a smoother appearance. In this lesson, you will modify the font in the lower thirds to match the font used in the Ornate title at the beginning of the project. In addition, you will modify the Ornate text to give it some of the color used in Overlap. Finally you will scale the lower third to give prominence to the actors' names.

The first task is to determine the name of the font used in the Ornate title.

1 In the Timeline, select the first **Ornate** title clip. To open the Inspector, click the Inspector button in the toolbar, or press Command-4.

The Inspector opens displaying four buttons at the top: Title, Text, Video, and Info. You will explore three of these inspectors in this lesson and the fourth one in Lesson 10.

2 Click the Title button.

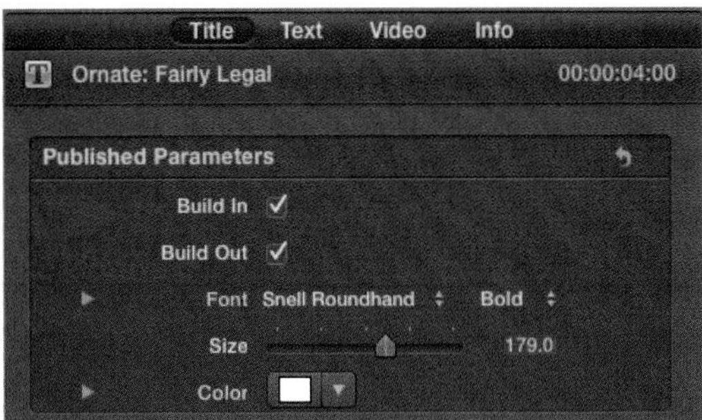

The window reveals the Published Parameters, that is, information supplied by the creator of the title. The title includes both a Build In and a Build Out, which is its movement in and out of frame. Next comes the information we need, that the font is Snell Roundhand, that it is bold, and it has a size of 179. The color is white. Now you know all you need to know to match the font in your lower thirds to this one.

Just as with transitions, the Timeline Index is a handy way to locate a title clip and to send the playhead to its location in the primary storyline.

TIP Titles are easy to delete in the Timeline or in the Timeline Index by selecting one or more and pressing Delete.

3 Open the Timeline Index, and at the top, click the Clips button. At the bottom, click the Titles button. Select the Overlap Starring title, and notice that the playhead jumps to the clip, which is quickly outlined in gray to indicate that it was automatically selected. Close the Timeline Index.

Final Cut Pro correctly assumes that you selected this title via the Timeline Index to make some kind of change. When you close the Timeline Index, the title outline appears yellow.

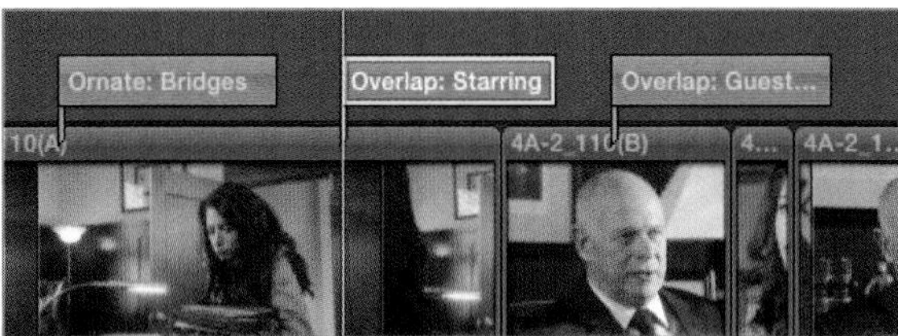

Now you are ready to change the font in this lower third, but first let's examine the options available in the Text and Title inspectors.

4 In the Timeline, double-click the **Overlap: Starring** clip. In the Inspector, click the Text button.

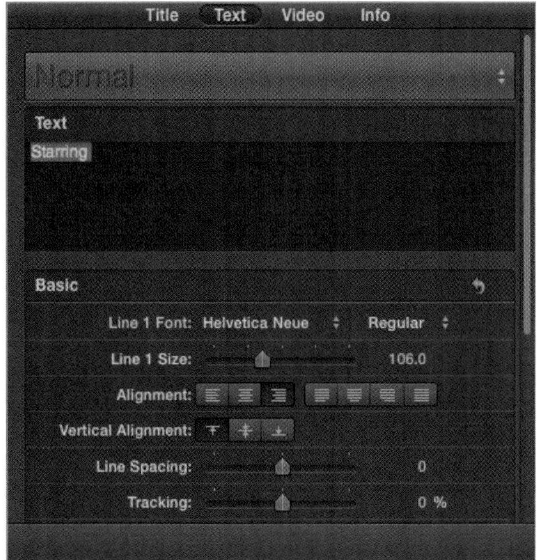

Several parameters are now available. The first parameter is in the Style pop-up menu that reads Normal and is red, reflecting the colored text in the Viewer. This pop-up menu contains a set of stylized fonts.

5 Click the Style pop-up menu and look at the different font options—some in lively colors, some with glow or fill or other effects added. Then click outside the menu to hide it again.

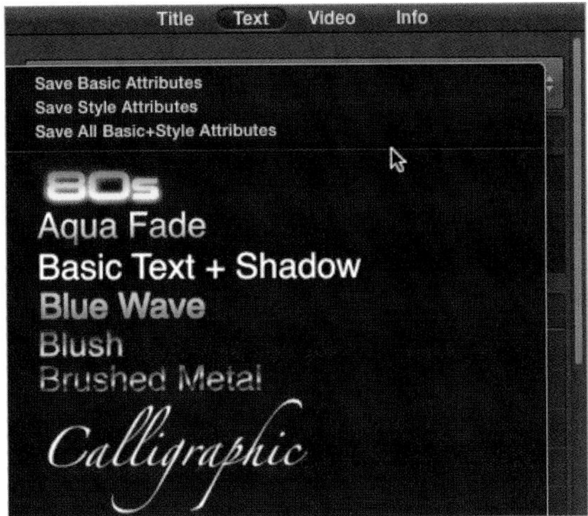

You can draw from this list of stylized fonts when you don't want to create your own. For this exercise, you will modify the parameters yourself.

Below Normal is a Text field. In this case, it reads Starring, text you already entered directly in the Viewer. But you can also enter the text in this field instead.

Each of the remaining parameter categories have Show/Hide buttons that reveal themselves when you move the pointer to the right of the name of a category.

6 If necessary to reveal the parameters in the Basic category, move your pointer to the right side of Basic, and click Show.

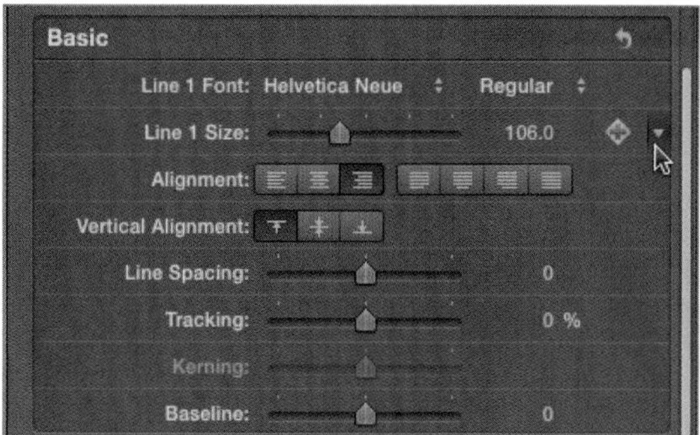

Basic contains the basic building blocks of the text, among them Font, Size, and Baseline, which allows you to move a piece of text higher or lower in the clip. To the far right of each parameter is a Reset button. You can click it and choose Reset Parameter to undo a modification and restore the default.

Although the font parameter appears here in the Text inspector, some title templates allow access to the same parameters in the Title inspector.

7 At the top of the Inspector, click the Title button.

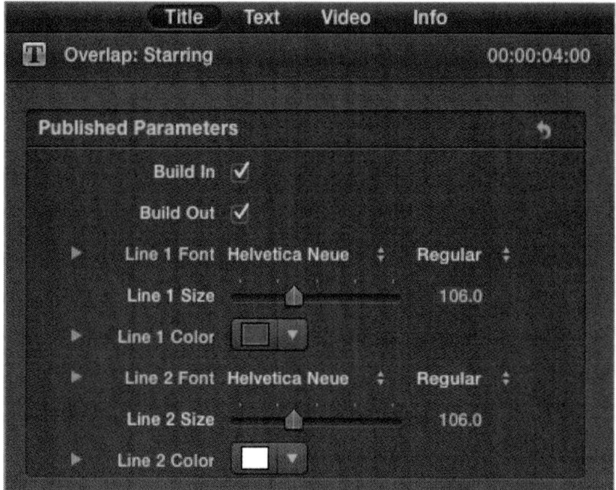

The Title inspector displays the parameters the Apple Motion designer "published" to Final Cut Pro. As you see, this template provides an easy way to change the font and color of each text box as well as disable the animation, if desired. In the next step, you will change the font to Snell Roundhand and make it bold, but leave the size as is for the moment.

TIP Be sure that the action/title safe zones are still visible for these steps.

8 In the Title inspector, click the Line 1 Font pop-up menu. Navigate through the different font options and watch as the first text box in the Viewer displays that font. Then choose Snell Roundhand, and choose Bold from the typeface options to the right of the font.

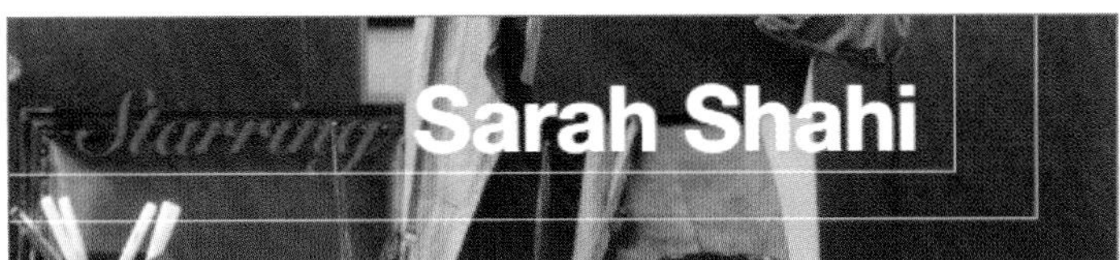

TIP If the typeface options pop-up menu for choosing Bold is dimmed, single-click the text in the Viewer, and then access the typeface pop-up menu.

9 Repeat step 8, but this time change the Line 2 Font for Sarah Shahi's name to Snell Roundhand Bold. In addition, change size to 126. (She is the star after all.) If her name no longer appears within the title safe zone, reposition the text box within the boundary as you did earlier.

Now that the actors' names use the font from the opening title, perhaps the opening title could use a touch of color from the lower third. Although you may change the text color using the Title inspector, you can also change the color, along with other nonpublished parameters such as opacity and blur. You will find these additional parameters in the Face category in the Text inspector.

NOTE ▶ Manipulating nonpublished parameters may have an adverse effect on the title's animation.

10 In the Timeline, double-click the last title. In the Text inspector, show the Face parameters, and click the color tile to open the Colors window.

NOTE ▶ You may have to scroll in the Inspector to see all the Face parameters.

The current red in use appears at the top of the Colors window.

11 To save this color, in the Colors window, drag from the horizontal swatch to a tile in the drawer at the bottom of the window. Close the Colors window.

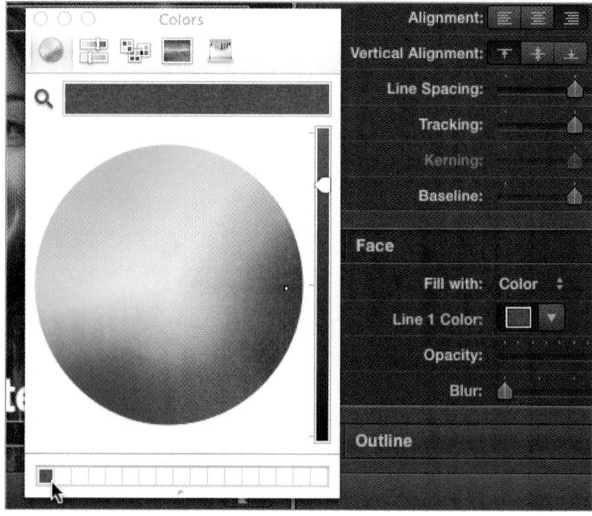

With the color saved, you can now select the text you want to change, in this case just a single letter of the text.

TIP ▶ You can use the Colors window's magnifying glass to sample a color anywhere on the display.

12 In the Timeline, double-click the opening text clip. In the Viewer, drag to select just the first letter, *F*. In the Face parameters, click the color tile to open the Colors window, and click the saved red tile in the bottom drawer.

Now the styles of Overlap and Ornate seem more compatible.

MORE INFO ▸ In the Video tab, you can apply built-in effects to transform, crop, rotate, and distort titles. You will learn about the transform functions in Lesson 10.

Take 2

There is much work to be done to finish the project. You still have to change the *L* in *Legal* to the saved red as well as the *B* in *Bridges*. Otherwise there will be no uniformity of style. That leaves modifying the font of both the guest star credit and the director's credit.

Adding Bumpers and Credits

The Titles Browser includes a separate category for bumpers and openers. You see bumpers often on television since they are brief, stand-alone pieces that start or end the segment of a show. For instance, as a news show goes to commercial, you might see a weather map pop onto the screen with text saying that updates about a coming storm will be next.

Another category in the Titles Browser is for credits, which provides the names of all those involved in the production. It can be pretty exciting to see your own name appear. And given the number of people involved, making changes in a credit roll could be daunting. Final Cut Pro provides a find/replace search engine that will help you out.

In this lesson, you will add a production company bumper to the end of *Fairly Legal*, and make adjustments in the Inspector. Then you'll add a credit named *Scrolling* to the end of the project. Finally, you will use Find and Replace to replace words in your end credits.

1 With the *Fairly Legal* project open in the Timeline, make sure the title safe overlay is still visible.

TIP Another way to turn title/action safe zones off and on is by clicking the Viewer Display Options button, the "light switch," at the top right of the Viewer. Choose Show Title/Action Safe Zones.

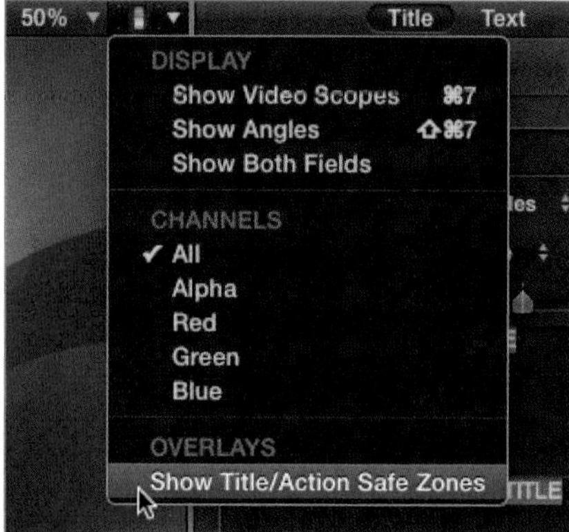

2 In the Titles Browser, select the Bumper/Opener category. Skim one or two to note their behaviors, and then either scroll down or use the search field to locate Slide in the subcategory Cinema. Skim the Slide bumper.

Bumpers are often edited as connected clips with video from the project appearing in an alpha channel area of the bumper. You can, however, use them as Timeline clips.

This bumper will work well to credit the production company that produced the *Fairly Legal* series. Let's append it to the end of this project.

3 In the Titles Browser, select the Slide title, and press E to append the title to the end of the project. Play the clip.

NOTE ▶ If a window other than the Titles Browser is active when you press E, the currently selected clip in the Event Browser will be appended instead of the title clip.

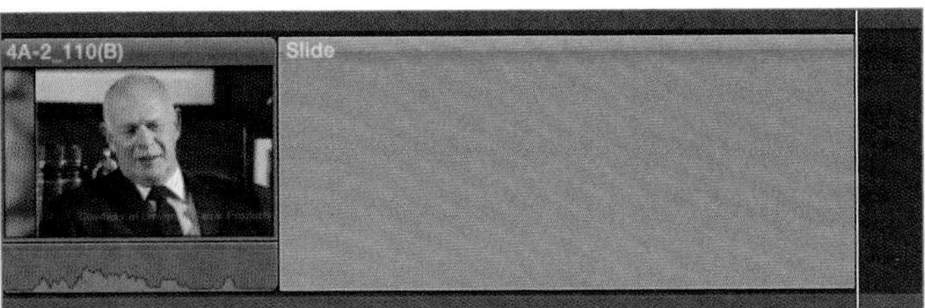

The three text fields in this bumper become visible about three-quarters through the **Slide** clip. When you double-click this clip, Final Cut Pro will cue the playhead to this "all in" text location.

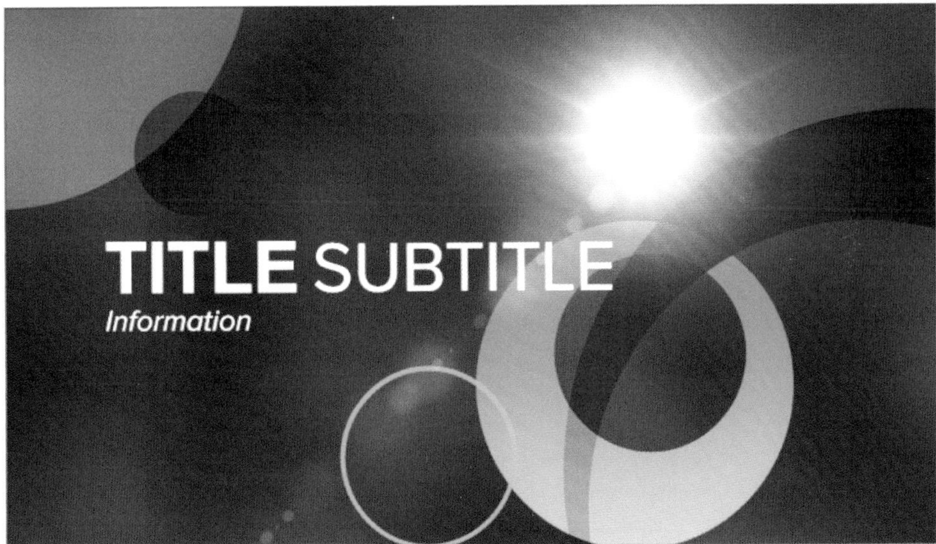

4 In the Timeline, double-click the **Slide** clip. Notice that Final Cut Pro automatically cues the playhead where all three text fields are in view.

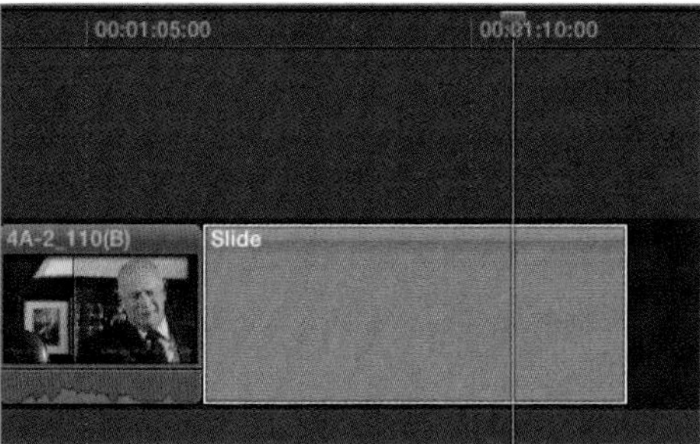

5 In the Inspector, click the Text tab. In the Viewer, type *Universal.* As you type, notice that the text is also entered in the Text field in the Inspector.

The Text inspector provides an additional entry method for titles.

In the Viewer, notice that the text goes beyond the left edge. To correct this, you can use a specialized parameter in the Slide template to position the top two text boxes within the title safe zones.

TIP You can also view all three text fields together in the Title tab of the Inspector.

6 In the Title inspector, drag the Main title alignment slider to the right until the *Universal* text is comfortably within the safe zone's inner rectangle.

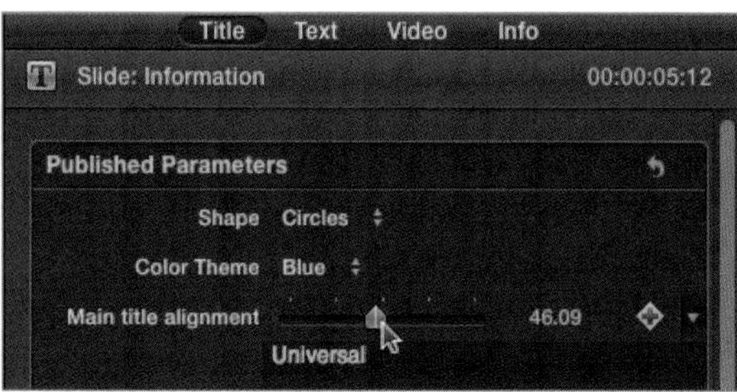

With the text repositioned, let's enter the rest of the title text.

7 In the Viewer, double-click *Subtitle* and type *Cable*. In the lower text box, double-click *Information* and type *Productions*.

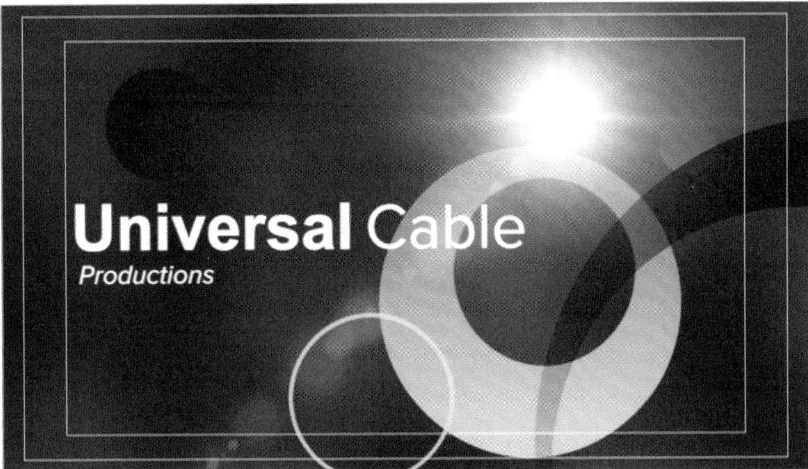

The word *Productions* is a little small. You can use the Text tab in the Inspector to make it larger. Make sure the word is highlighted before taking the next step. You can verify what is selected in the text field of the Text inspector.

8 With the Text inspector showing *Productions* in the text field, drag the Size slider to make the word larger. Try 84. In the Viewer, drag the text position button down to give the larger word more room.

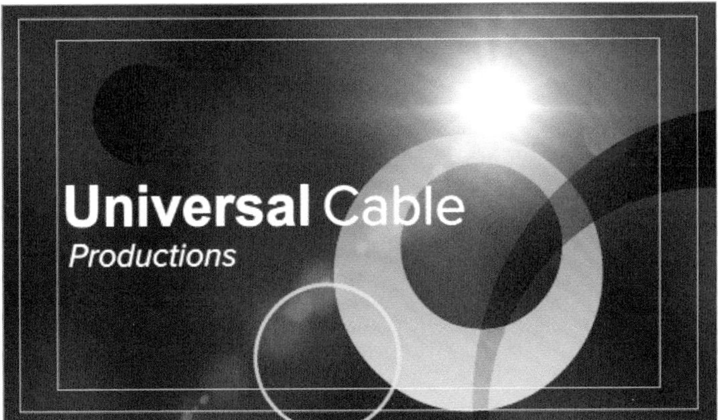

TIP Because many of the titles are animated, be careful not to alter animation behaviors when repositioning text boxes or other template elements. Review the changes you make by screening the entire title clip to ensure that no unexpected animation behaviors are introduced.

Many of the titles have options to change other design elements along with the font parameters. Let's look at some of the options available for the Slide title.

9 In the Inspector, click the Title button. Click the Color Theme pop-up menu, and choose Green. Click the Shape pop-up menu, and choose Squares. Play the clip.

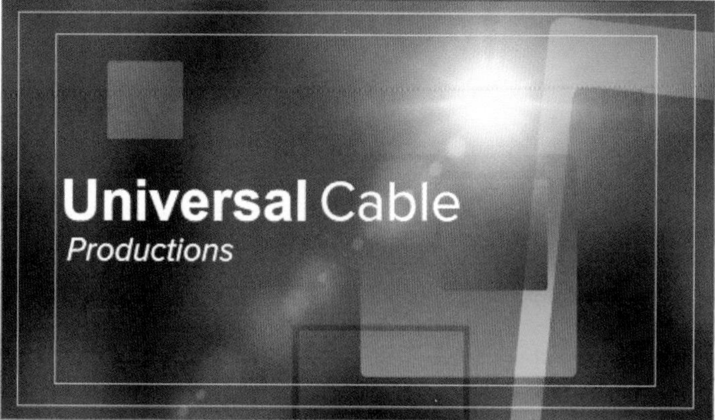

10 After trying different combinations, use the Color Theme and Shape pop-up menus to revert to the Blue Circles.

TIP As with video clips, you can also change the duration of a title clip by trimming it, or by Control-clicking the title clip and choosing Change Duration from the shortcut menu. You can also select it and press Control-D.

The Credits section of the Titles Browser contains just 14 items, some of them with elaborate animations. The one we see on television and in movie theaters most often is Scrolling, the very first item in the category.

Scrolling consists of credits rolling upwards against a black background. This title has an alpha channel so you can place it over any sort of background. In this lesson, you will add Scrolling to the *Fairly Legal* project and, in a later exercise, composite it over a more colorful background.

You will also explore the find/replace search engine, a powerful tool to make your work more efficient.

11 From the Credits category in the Titles Browser, select the Scrolling title. To add this title between the last shot of *Fairly Legal* and the production company bumper, cue the playhead between the two clips, select the Scrolling title in the Browser, and then press W. Play the clip.

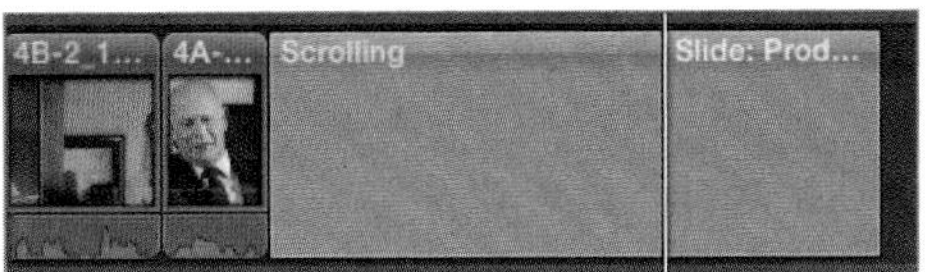

The **Scrolling** clip provides several text fields, but you can add more as needed. You'll change the first three credits, but you'll edit one line at a time.

12 In the Timeline, double-click the **Scrolling** clip. In the Viewer, click in the text box, and then double-click Title to select that single line. Type *Credits*. Change the first name to read *Directed By* and the first description to read *Your Name*. Make the following additional changes in the next two lines.

- Produced By His Name
- Edited By Her Name

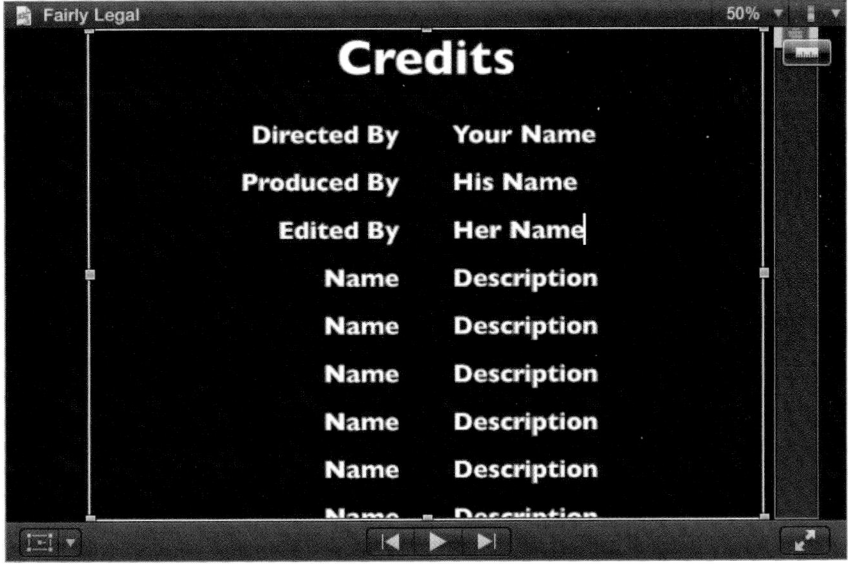

Most of the parameters are open to modification. For instance, in the Text inspector, you can change the font and color. You can also use the Text tab to add additional lines of text if you have more credits to list.

13 In the Text inspector, scroll down to the bottom of the credits list, place your text cursor at the end of the last word, *Description*, and press Return. Press Tab to line up the cursor with the other text, and type *Name*. Press Tab again and type *DESCRIPTION*, all in capital letters.

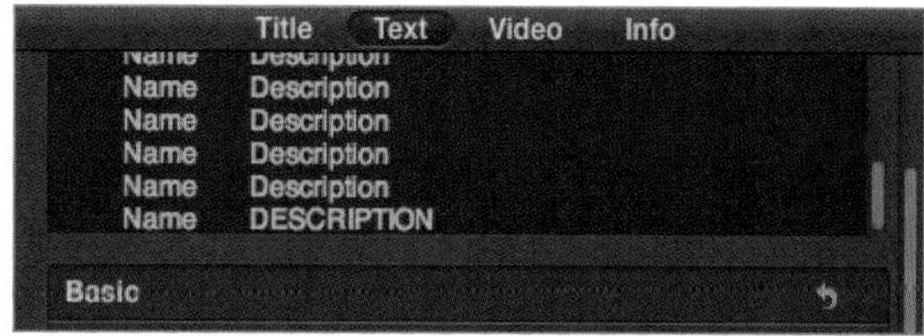

NOTE ▶ You will need DESCRIPTION for the next step.

Now that you have established two additional fields of text, you can highlight and change them just as you did with the first three.

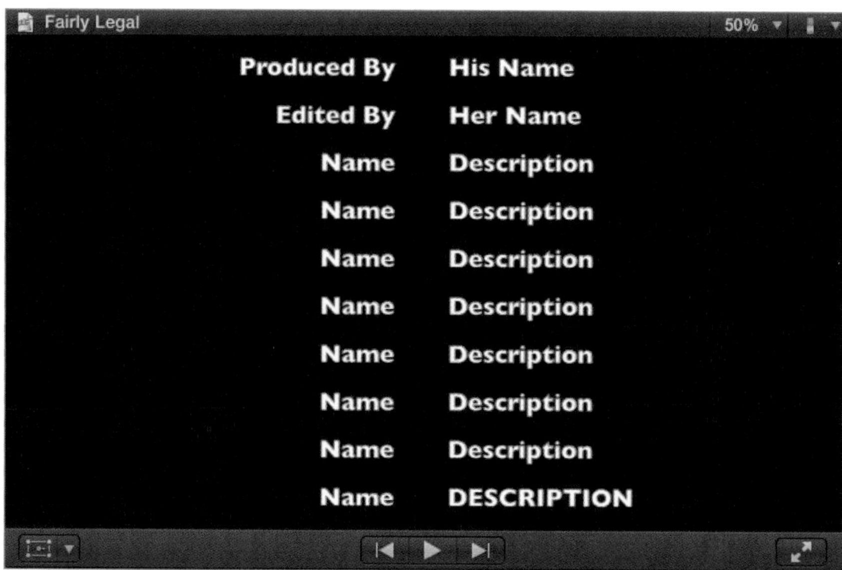

But what happens if you have a long credit roll and need to make text changes? For those who often work in Pages, you will be familiar with the find/replace function.

14 With the **Scrolling** clip still selected, choose Edit > Find and Replace Title Text.

You can search within an entire project, or within a selected clip. Notice the search qualifiers on the right, such as "Match case," "Whole word," and "Loop search."

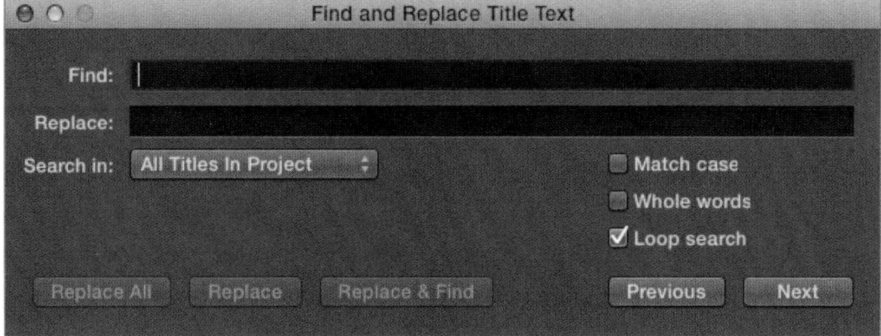

15 In the Find and Replace Title Text window, enter *Description* in the Find field and *My Name* in the Replace field. Click the "Search in" pop-up menu and choose Selected Title. In the search criteria on the right, select "Match case" and "Whole words," and then click Replace All.

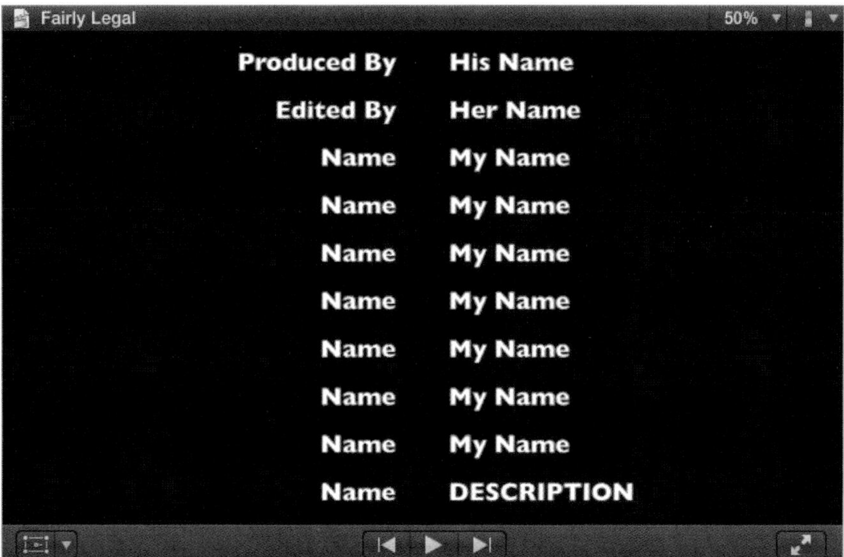

Because you asked Final Cut Pro to match case in its search, each use of the word *Description* has been changed except for the one in all caps.

Working with Video Generators

Generators are special clips created by Final Cut Pro to enhance the video of your project. They are add-ons, if you will, contributing yet another visual layer. Generators have their own separate Browser and, just as with titles, are separated by categories and subcategories. Are credits scrolling up over a black background interesting enough? Or might they benefit from the addition of a generator from the Background category, one with color or one with texture? Do you need a ten-second countdown before the start of your project? What about a timecode generator, to add a timecode overlay to clips? And if the timing of your project has been established but a clip is not yet delivered by your director, you can hold open the space with a placeholder generator and even add details about the content of the scene.

In this exercise, you will add a matte background to the scrolling credits you just created and a ten-second countdown at the start. You will also work with an *I Think* project, adding a timecode overlay and inserting a placeholder to substitute a missing shot.

Let's start by exploring the Generators Browser, which opens in just the same way as the browsers you explored in earlier lessons.

1 In the toolbar, click the Generators Browser button, and choose the All category.

You can see that the Browser contains 41 items in all, categorized further as Backgrounds, Elements, Solids, and Textures. Furthermore, several of the generators offer additional options in the Inspector, after you add the generator to a project.

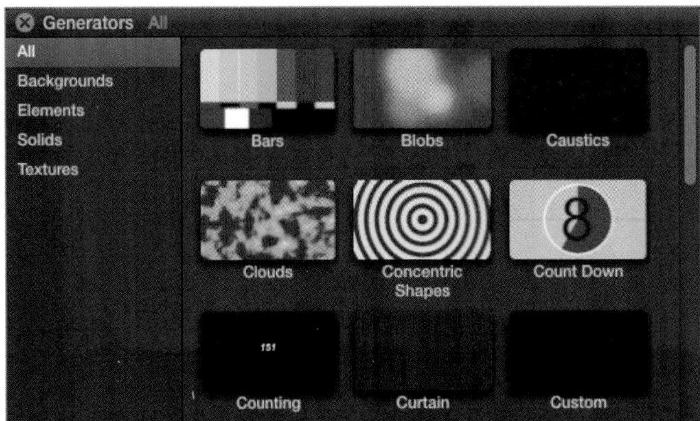

Backgrounds are just what the term implies, something to be used beneath something else, sometimes text but sometimes beneath video with an alpha channel.

The Solids category contains color mattes, which, like backgrounds, are meant to appear beneath something else. This is also true of the 12 items in the Textures category.

Elements offers other kinds of items. Placeholder will behave like a gap clip either in the primary or an alternate storyline. The other three elements are either layered on top of clips or can stand alone in the Timeline. For instance, you could insert Counting before the opening title in *Fairly Legal* to count down from 10 to 1.

2 In the Timeline, press Home to move the playhead to the beginning of the project. To insert a generator into the primary storyline, from within the Elements category, double-click **Counting**.

A generator with a default duration of 10 seconds appears. Notice that the generator clip icon is brown.

NOTE ▶ Because generators are often used as backgrounds, double-clicking a generator clip inserts it into the primary storyline. Double-clicking a title clip, you'll remember, connects it to a primary clip.

Let's adjust this generator in the Inspector so it counts down from 10 to 1.

3 In the Generator inspector, click the color tile and, from the Colors window, choose the red you saved in an earlier step. In the Start field, enter the number *10* and, in the End field, enter the number *1*. Play the clip.

You now have a countdown leading into the project.

Rather than leave the end credits in their stark white on black, a colored or textured matte generator could help to make them pop. For the matte to appear *behind* the credit text clip onscreen or in the Viewer, it must be edited *beneath* it in the project. To do this, you will connect the matte clip beneath the credits as a connected clip.

4 From the Solids category, drag the **Vivid** generator below the **Credits** clip so they are aligned. Play these clips together.

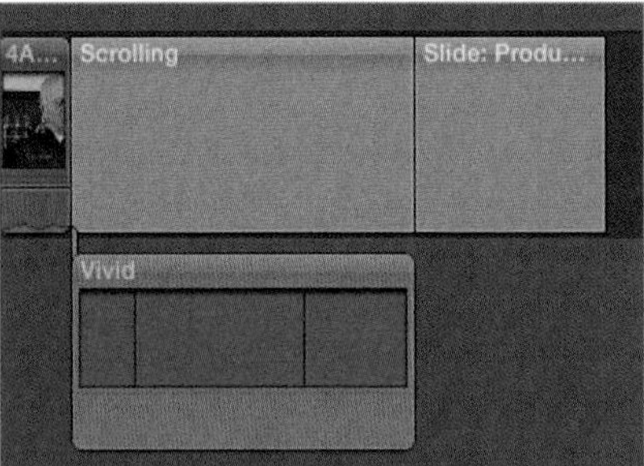

While the durations of the generators differ one from the other, the solids all have a default duration of 10 seconds. Generators can be trimmed just as any other clip.

5 In the Timeline, if necessary, drag the right side of the **Vivid** clip until it's even with **Scrolling**.

Timecode overlays are an invaluable tool. While an editor can simply look at the Dashboard to get the exact timecode of a frame, you will often be asked to show your work to the director or others in a screening room. When a suggestion is made, the timecode overlay will identify the spot where more work is needed. Let's add timecode to the *I Think* project.

6 To return to the Project Library, press Command-0. From the Lesson 9 folder, open the *I Think* project into the Timeline and play it.

About the "I Think I Thought" Media

Matthew Modine wrote, directed, produced, and starred in this sardonically humorous short film co-produced and shot by Adam McClelland and edited by Terence Ziegler.

Joe is a thinker in a world that no longer tolerates analytical thinking. Joe discovers Thinkers Anonymous, where he learns that "we need special people to tell us how to think." "I Think I Thought" (2008) was shot with the Panasonic AG camera in the DVCPRO HD format, in 720p at 23.98 fps. It's available for download from the iTunes Store.

Matthew Modine has phoned the editing room to say he wants to discuss a particular edit. He'll meet you in the screening room. You need to add timecode to the movie version you will screen together. But if you position the playhead and double-click the generator, it will be edited into the project as an insert. Let's drag it instead.

7 From the Elements category, drag the Timecode generator and connect it to the start of the project.

For a visual timecode display to be helpful, it must of course extend across the entire project. Since the default length isn't long enough, let's trim it using the Extend function.

8 Select the end point of the **Timecode** clip, and press End to jump to the end of the project. To extend the end point to the playhead location, press Shift-X. Skim through different areas of the project to see the timecode display.

In *I Think*, a gap clip currently takes the place of a clip the director has yet to deliver, but it gives no information, only the duration. The placeholder, when modified in the Inspector, can tell you whether the clip to come will be an interior or an exterior shot, whether it will be a night or day scene, and it will show you how many people will be in the scene. There is also a space to make specific notes. Let's replace the gap clip in this project with the much more informative placeholder.

9 From the Generators Browser, drag Placeholder to the gap clip in the primary storyline. When the plus sign appears, release the pointer and, from the pop-up menu, choose Replace From Start.

You modify a placeholder clip just as you have modified other clips. Let's say Matthew Modine has sent a note telling you the missing shot is an interior night shot with one person, male. When you open the Generator inspector, you will see fields for all of this information.

10 With the **Placeholder** clip selected in the Timeline, choose the Generator inspector and enter the following.

- Framing: Close-up
- People: 1
- Gender: Men
- Background: None
- Sky: None
- View Notes: Enabled

TIP Be sure to select View Notes in the Generator inspector or you will not see the text you will enter in the following step.

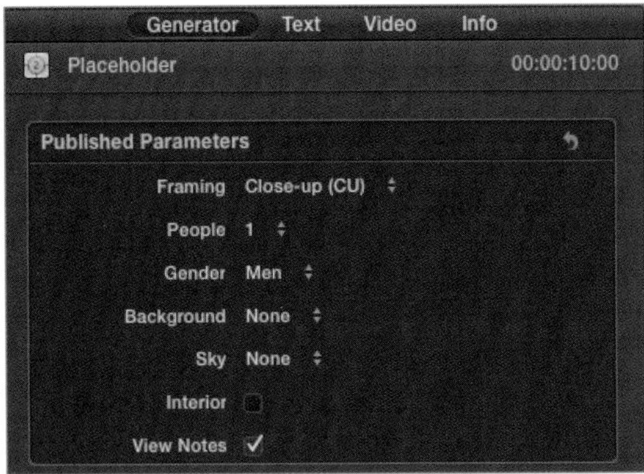

Mr. Modine thinks the missing shot will be another subway clip so it would be helpful to enter that as a note.

11 In the Viewer, double-click the text box, and type *Matt in Sub*.

Notice that all of your changes now appear in the Viewer.

Take 2

The director and the producer and the studio head review *Fairly Legal* and all agree they aren't happy with Vivid. It's just too… vivid. You suggest they replace it with a texture called Grunge. They agree to take a look, and you make the change. In the end, everyone decides the more traditional credits work best, so you delete the background generator to leave the credits over black.

> **TIP** ▶ As with title clips, you can also add a generator to your project by positioning the playhead, selecting the generator, and then pressing the desired edit shortcuts: Q, W, or E.

Using Themes

The Themes Browser contains still more categories of titles. These sometime elaborate clips reflect a very specific theme such as sports, cinema, or a comic book. A theme just might give your project the added personality it needs. If you've filmed a travel documentary, why not use a title containing still images or clips of the place you've been? All sports broadcasts are loaded with thematic titles and graphics.

> **NOTE** ▶ The Themes Browser also contains theme transitions. While you are likely to use the traditional crossfade and fade-in/out when moving from clip to clip, your project on occasion might need a special transition announcing a larger change.

In this lesson you will work with a shorter version of *Zero to Hero* titled *ZTH_Force vs Brown*. This project is about the funny car racing competition between two men: John Force and Antron Brown. It needs an opening title to make clear you're about to see a sports competition.

1. To save a backup of the project before making changes, in the Project Library, duplicate the *ZTH_Force vs Brown* project. Open the original into the Timeline, and play the project.

   This project focuses on just the two racers: Antron Brown and John Force.

2. Click the Themes Browser button.

   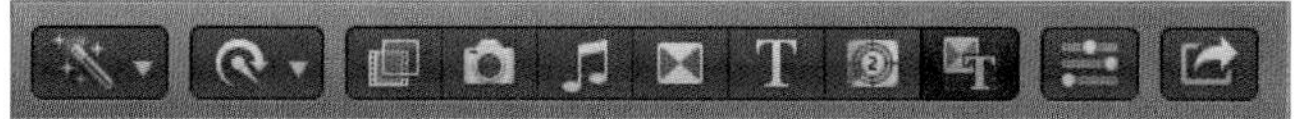

The Themes Browser divides its All collection of 156 items into some 15 other categories. With All selected, notice that the very first group of thumbnails is a collection of 15 or so video generators.

3 In the Sports category of Titles, skim Team and then insert it at the very beginning of the project. Play the clip.

TIP ▶ In the Browser, if you double-click the thumbnail, the title comes in as a connected clip rather than a storyline clip.

You will make several changes to this clip, such as inserting still images in the two drop zones you see in the Viewer, and adding competitor names to the bottom of the screen. But first, let's import two still images of the racers.

4 Choose File > Import > Media, or press Command-I. In the Media Import window, from the Favorites sidebar, select FCPX Book Files. In the file list, navigate to the Imports > ZTH Stills folder, and select the two images. Click the Import button. In the options dialog, choose Zero to Hero from the Add to Existing Event pop-up menu. Select "Copy Files to Final Cut Events folder," and click Import.

The still images are now added to the *Zero to Hero* Event in the Library. A still image icon distinguishes the photos from the other clips.

NOTE ▶ The default selection of an imported still image is four seconds, though you can change it in the Preferences window.

As part of your Event Library, you can edit it to the Timeline just as you would a video clip. Let's open the Inspector to modify the title.

NOTE ▶ Thumbnails of still images have square corners, whereas thumbnails of video clips have rounded corners.

5 In the Event Library, select the *Zero to Hero* Event and scroll to see the two stills you just imported.

You will need to be able to see these two stills in the Event Browser to apply them to the drop zones of the title.

6 In the Timeline, double-click the **Team** clip. Open the Inspector, if necessary, and click the Title Inspector button.

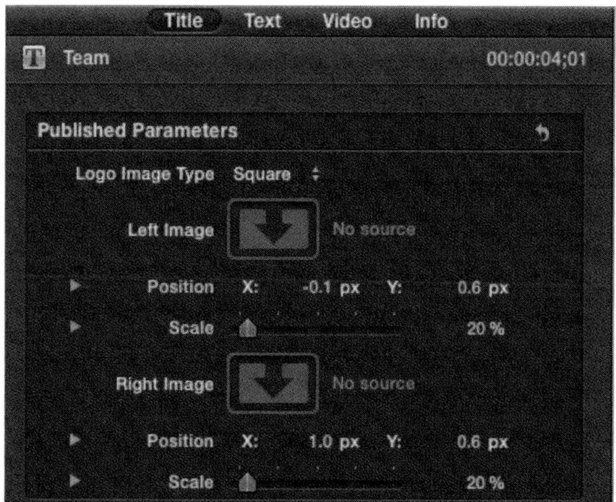

The Title inspector contains two drop zones, or image wells, labeled Left Image and Right Image. An image well can hold either a video clip or a still image. In this case you will add the imported stills of Antron Brown and John Force to the image wells and replace the "Team" text with the racers' names.

7 Click the image well for the Left Image, and then click the still image of Antron Brown in the Event Browser.

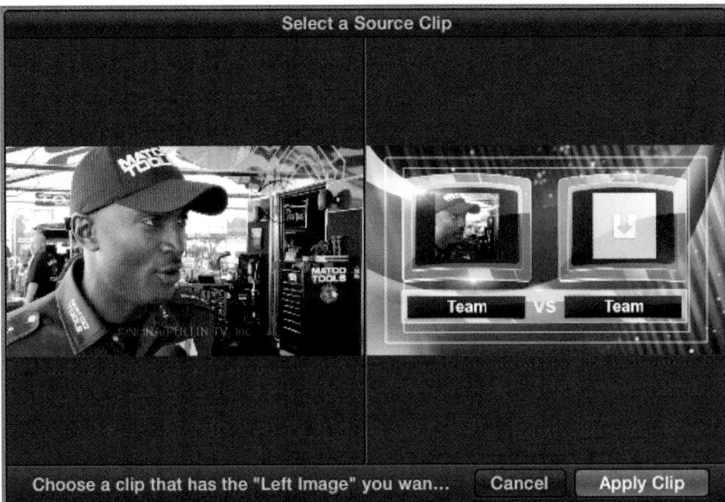

Now the image of Antron Brown appears in the image well in the Title inspector. It also appears in the Viewer split screen, both in the Team graphic to the right of the frame and as the original still image to the left. Without exiting the split screen, let's add the still image of John Force in the Right Image area.

8 In the Title inspector, click the image well for the Right Image. In the Event Browser, click the image of John Force.

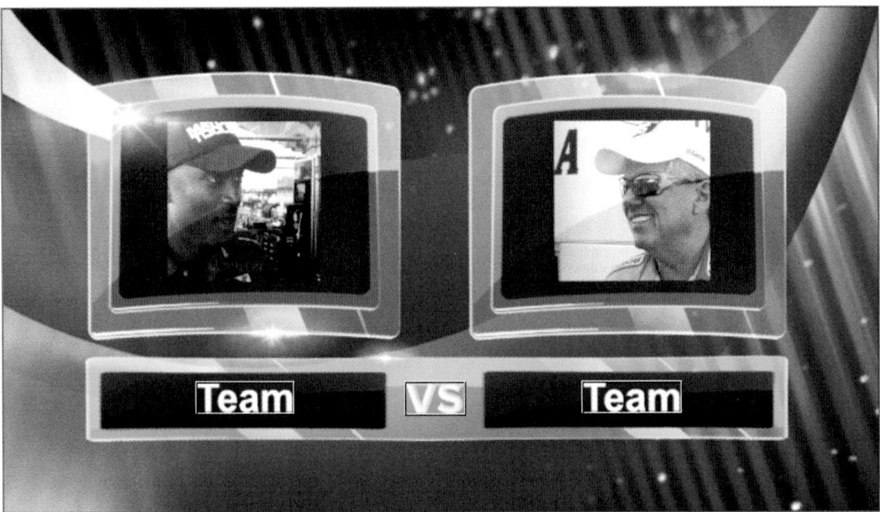

Now both racers appear in the Team graphic. However, if you look closely, you'll see too much empty space between each photo and the edge of the frame that contains it. With a simple parameter change, you can adjust the photos to fill the frames.

9 In the Title inspector, from the Logo Image Type pop-up menu, choose Non-square.

The still images are no longer confined to a square shape, but are used to fill the entire frames within the Team graphic. This is a much better look for this graphic.

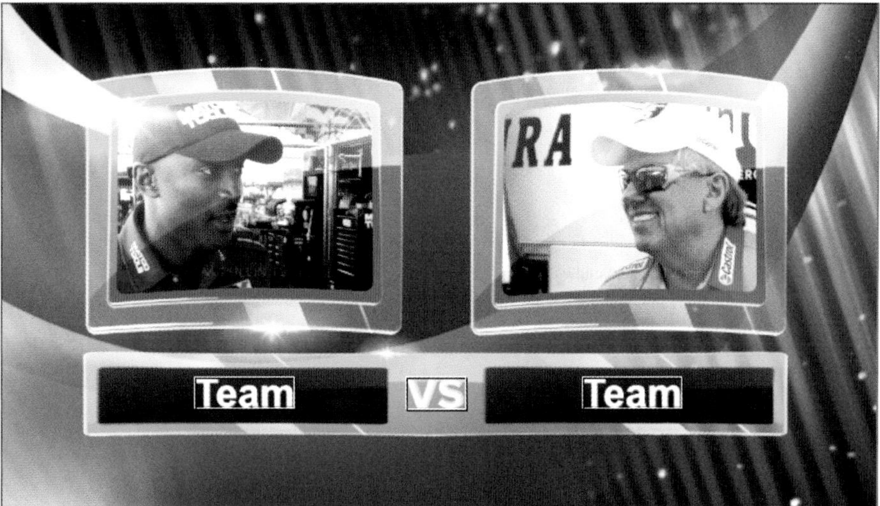

The Viewer is still displaying a split screen with the John Force still image to the left and the Team graphic to the right. To move forward and edit the text, you must indicate which of these you want to continue to work with, the still image or the graphic.

10 In the Viewer, click the right side of the split screen. Notice the background of that split screen turns a lighter gray.

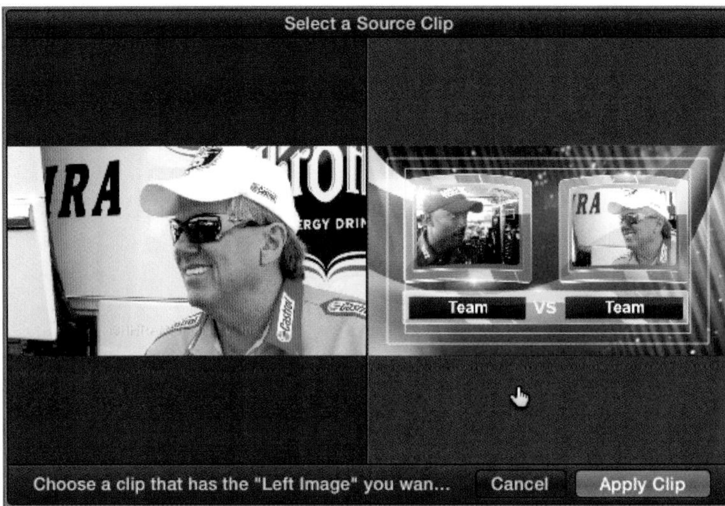

11 At the bottom right of the Viewer, click Apply Clip, and the Team graphic returns to full screen.

Now it's time to identify the racers for your audience. The Team graphic template already has a place for each racer's name. All you have to do is edit this text as you've edited other titles throughout this lesson.

12 In the Viewer, double-click the word *Team* on the left and type *Antron Brown*. Double-click *Team* on the right and type *John Force*. Press Esc when done.

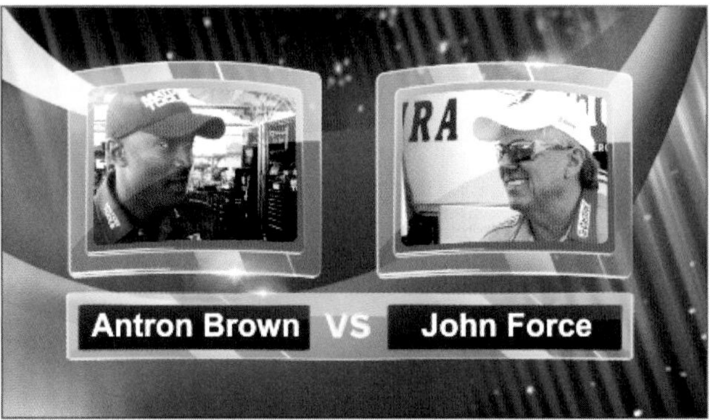

As with all text, you can change font, size, color, and numerous other parameters in the available fields.

Take 2

The director of *ZTH_Force vs Brown* wants to see a final title of John Force raising his Wally trophy. You suggest adding the Sports theme title Push as the last image. He's curious about how you'll do that so you explain to him that you'll first append about two and a half seconds of **JF holds trophy** to the end of the project. Then you will add Push as a connected clip. Finally, you will enter text in the text field identifying the winner.

Using Still Images in Your Project

Still images can be imported into Final Cut Pro directly from your camera, from Aperture, iPhoto, or any place on your Mac hard drive. You can bring in a photo as a single file into an Event you've already created, or you can create a whole new Event just for the still photos. This might be a good idea if, for instance, you are editing a historical piece like Ken Burns' series on the Civil War, in which most of the images come from stills.

Final Cut Pro also provides a Photos Browser. In this Browser, the categories are listed on top rather than to the side, and below are thumbnails of your photos. Instead of "All," you can browse your Aperture and iPhoto libraries. If you click the Aperture or iPhoto disclosure triangles, you'll see a list of all the projects and albums into which you have previously sorted your photo collection. Once you locate the thumbnails of the photos you want in the Browser, it's an easy matter of dragging one or more to an Event or even directly to the Timeline.

Editor's Cut

You added a bumper and a scrolling credit to *Fairly Legal*, and you worked with an abbreviated version of *ZTH_Force vs Brown*. Why not try adding an opening title to the full *Zero to Hero*? In addition, the narrator of *Delicious Peace* is the well-known actor Ed O'Neill. It would be nice to add a lower third so audiences will know who is speaking to them.

Lesson Review

1. How do you open the Titles Browser?
2. How do you insert a title between two clips in the Timeline?
3. How would you superimpose a lower-third title over a Timeline clip in the primary storyline?
4. How do you change the text in a title in your Timeline?
5. How do you display the title safe and action safe zones?
6. How do you adjust the color of a title?
7. How would you reposition a title in the Viewer?
8. What is an easy way to find a specific title in the Timeline?
9. How can you find and replace specific text in a title, for example in a long credit roll?
10. What happens when you double-click a generator in the Generators Browser?
11. Why would you use a placeholder generator instead of a gap clip?
12. How do you assign an image to a drop zone in a theme?

Answers

1. In the toolbar in the upper-right corner of the Timeline, click the Titles Browser button.
2. Drag a title from the Titles Browser to the edit point between the clips. Alternatively, you can insert a title by positioning the playhead where you want to insert the title, selecting the title in the Browser, and pressing W.
3. In the Titles Browser, double-click a title thumbnail. The title is connected over the clip at the playhead position.
4. In the Viewer, double-click to highlight the text. Type your new text and press Esc.
5. Choose Window > Viewer Display > Show Title/Action Safe Zones.
6. Select a title in the Timeline and click the Inspector button in the toolbar. Click the Title button at the top of the pane that appears. Click the color tile to open the Colors window and choose a new color. If the Color parameter is not available under Title, go to the Text inspector Face category where you'll find another color tile.
7. In the Viewer, place the pointer over the text, and when the text box appears, drag the text.

8. Open the Timeline Index and click the Titles button. When the list of titles appears, click the appropriate title. The playhead moves to the title and automatically selects it.
9. Select the clip and choose Edit > Find and Replace Title Text. In the window that appears, enter the text to find in the Find field and the replacement text in the Replace field. In the "Search in" pop-up menu, choose Selected Title, and then click Replace All.
10. Because generators are often used as backgrounds, double-clicking a generator clip inserts it into the primary storyline. This differs from a title, where double-clicking a title clip connects it to a primary clip.
11. A gap clip simply reserves a specific duration in the Timeline. A placeholder lets you enter information about the missing clip such as framing, how many people will be in the scene, the background, whether it is an interior shot, or whether it will be a night or day scene. You can also add specific notes.
12. In the Inspector, click a drop zone and then click the image in the Event Browser. At the bottom of the Viewer, click Apply Clip.

Keyboard Shortcuts

Control-D	Change duration
Command-I	Import file
Command-C	Copy
Command-V	Paste
Command-4	Open/Close Inspector window

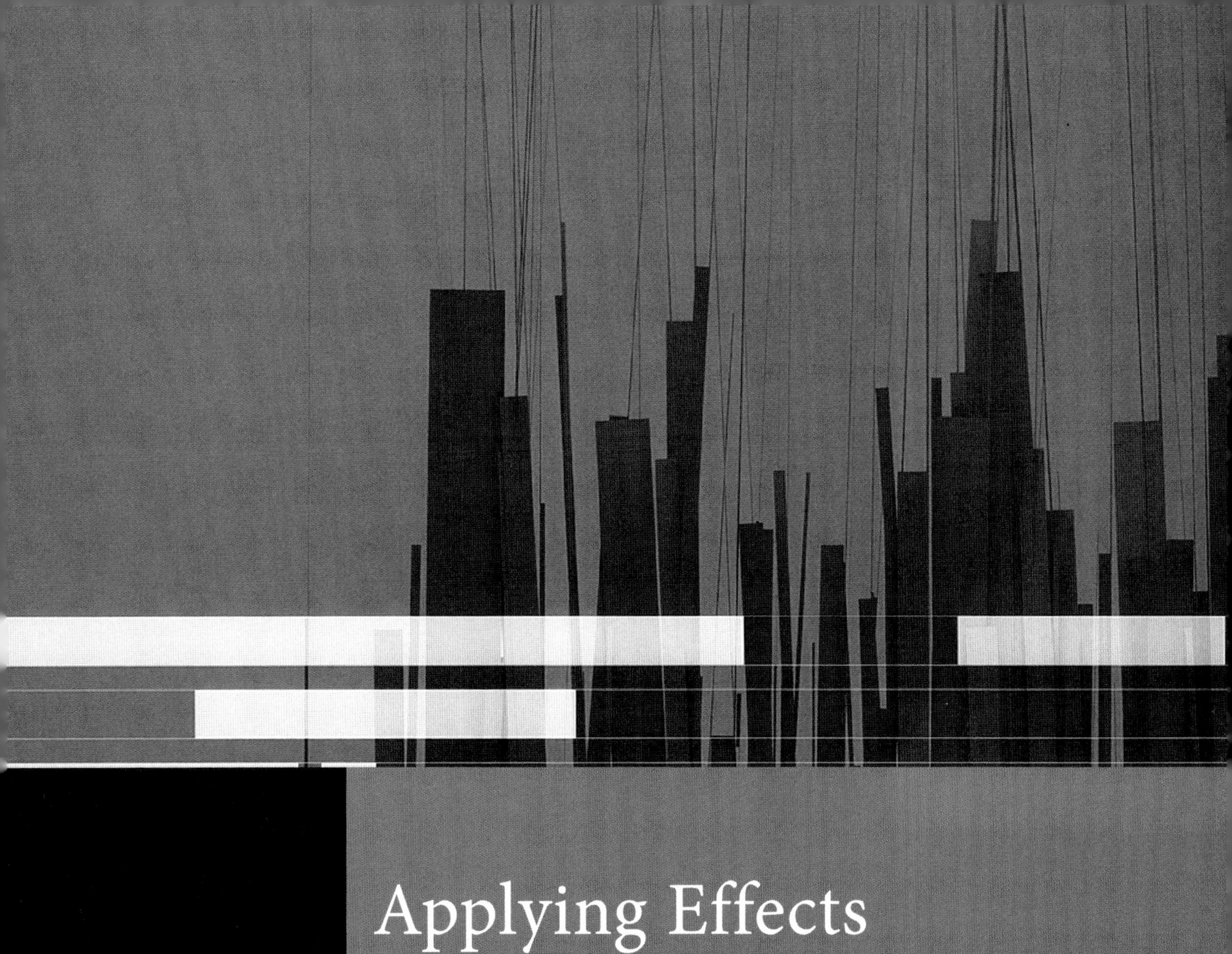

Applying Effects and Finishing

10

Time This lesson takes approximately 60 minutes to complete.

Goals

Understand Final Cut Pro retiming

Reverse clip direction

Change clip speed

Create a hold frame

Add a freeze frame

Apply speed changes to selection

Apply speed presets

Transform and crop clips

Create keyboard shortcuts

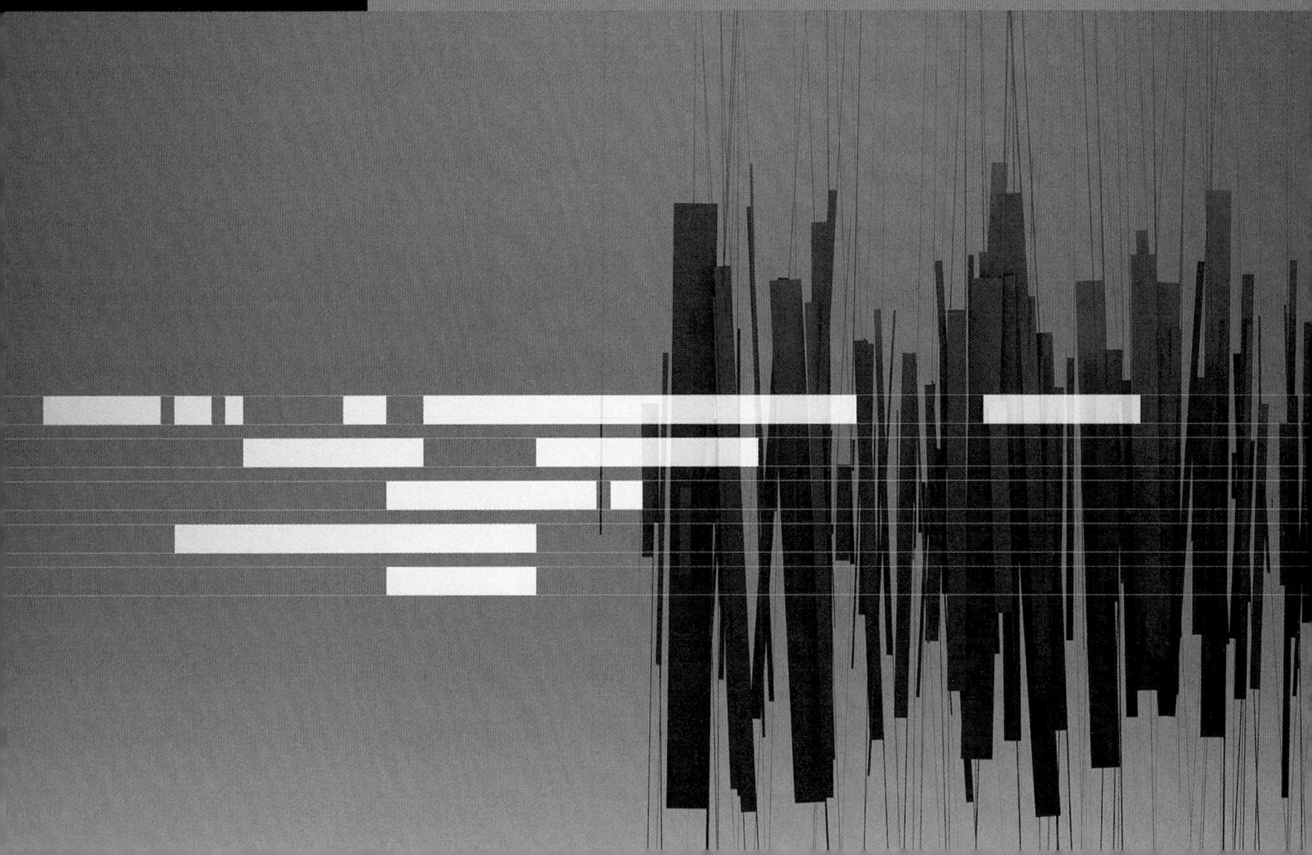

Lesson **10**

Retiming and Transforming Clips

There's something uniquely satisfying about chiseling and crafting a precise project from a relatively rough chunk of media files and clips. But even when your project is complete, you may still find additional needs or even unrealized potential. Among the most enjoyable parts of the finishing process is adding the fixes and embellishments that make your project sparkle.

In this section of the book, you will explore several approaches to finessing a project: Retiming and transforming clips using Final Cut Pro's built-in motion properties, adding clip effects, and perfecting image color. In the final lesson, you will share your fully finished project.

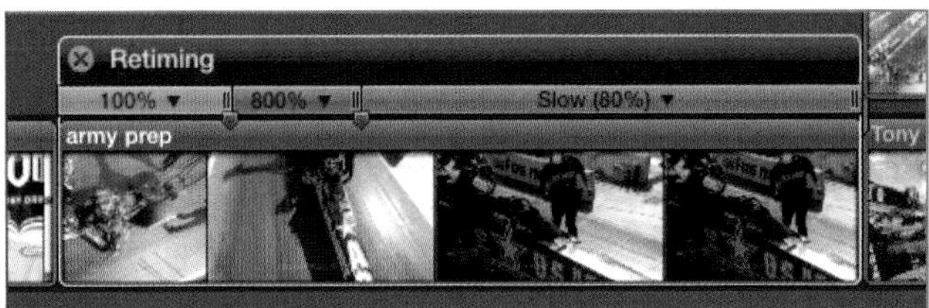

In the following lesson, you will use the Final Cut Pro Retime Editor to alter clip playback speed, hold a frame, add an instant replay, rewind an action, and create a freeze frame clip. Then you will transform and crop clips, and apply the pan-and-scan Ken Burns effect.

Understanding Motion Properties

Before you begin retiming and transforming clips, it will be helpful to preview some of the effects that you will use in this lesson to acquire a visual and conceptual understanding of Final Cut Pro motion properties. To do this, you will take a close look at two *Zero to Hero* projects. Each project contains the same number, selection, and placement of clips; but in the revised project, certain clips were retimed to enhance the original project.

1 In the Project Library, from the Lesson Projects folder, drag the Lesson 10 folder onto APTS FCP X. Hide the contents of the Lesson Projects folder.

2 From the Lesson 10 folder, open the *Zero to Hero_START* project, and play it in the Timeline.

   This is a familiar version of *Zero to Hero*, although red to-do markers are placed throughout the project. As you've seen in previous lessons, you can use markers to tag an area or remind yourself of a location that needs work, such as retiming certain clips.

   To-do markers appear separately in the Timeline Index. You can mark each of them as completed when a task is finished.

3 In the lower left of the Timeline, click the Timeline Index button, or press Command-Shift-2. To see a list of to-do items, at the top of the Index, click Tags. From the Tag options that appear at the bottom, click the "Show incomplete to-do items" button.

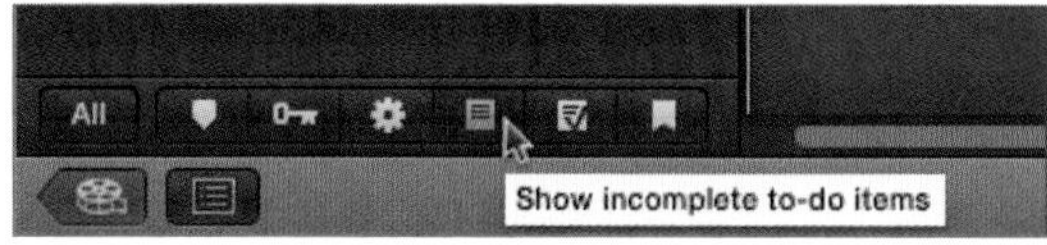

   In the Index, the list of to-do items appears along with the timecode location for each marker in the project.

TIP To move the playhead to a to-do marker in the Timeline, make sure you click the text of the item and not the checkbox. Clicking a to-do marker's checkbox will convert that marker to a completed marker that will no longer appear in this list.

4 In the Index, find the *hold frame* marker, and click its name to move the playhead to that marker. This is the frame you will hold, or *pause*, in an upcoming exercise. Click the *reverse* marker name, play the clip in the Timeline, and imagine this clip played in reverse. Click the *200% both crowds* marker name, and play the clip.

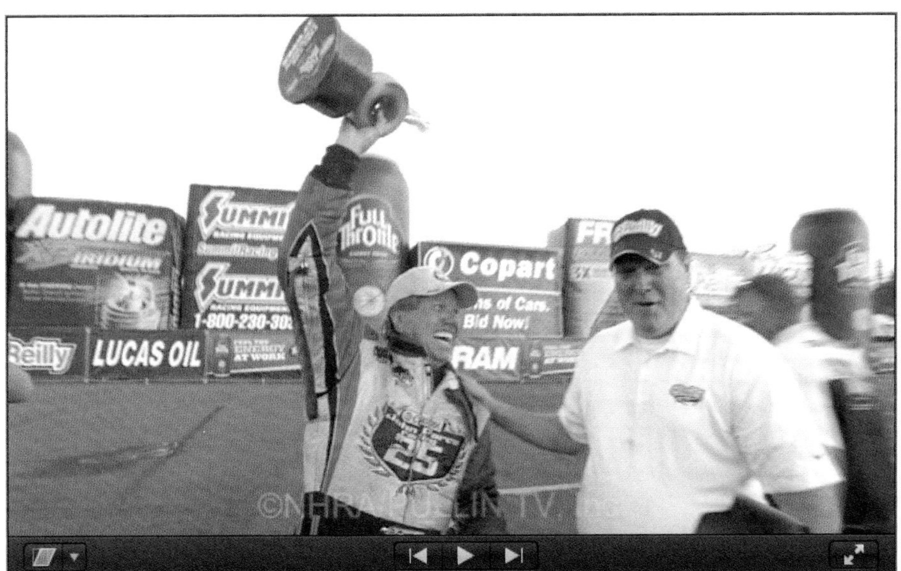

The pacing of this project might be more interesting if a few clips unfolded at a slightly different pace. You can alter clip playback speed in the Timeline using the Retime Editor that is attached to each video and audio clip. When you open the Retime Editor, you can see the current playback speed percentage for each clip and modify that speed.

5 In the Timeline, zoom into the second clip, **crowd ots**, and select it. Choose Modify > Retime, and look at some of the ways to adjust clip playback. Then choose Show Retime Editor, or press Command-R.

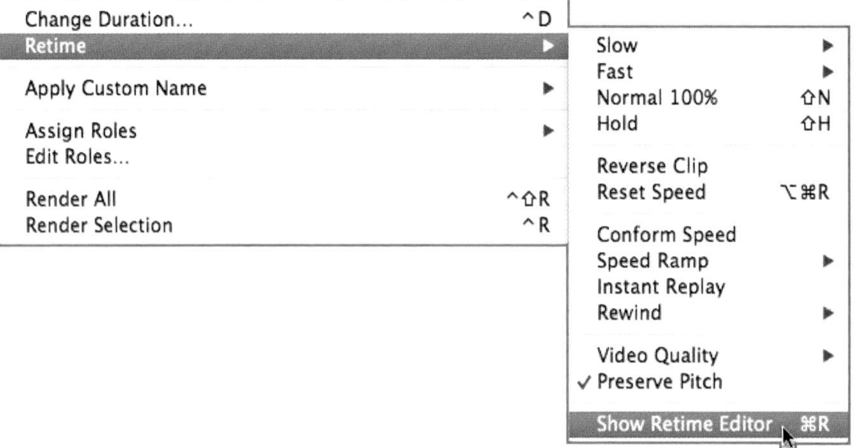

In the Timeline, the Retime Editor appears displaying the current clip speed—Normal (100%)—on a green speed segment bar, which indicates that the playback speed of this clip has not been changed.

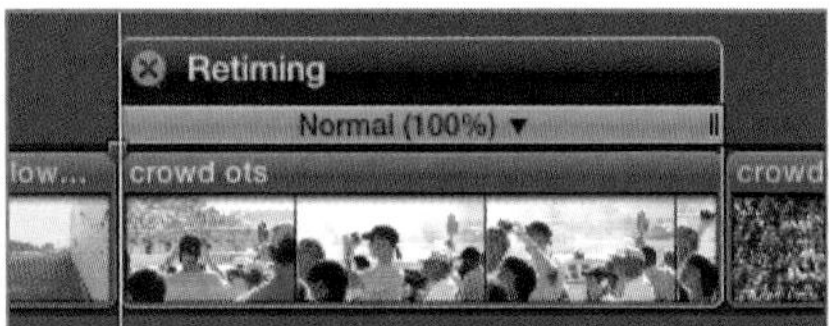

Now let's compare this clip to the same clip in the revised version of this project.

6 In the Lesson 10 folder in the Project Library, open the *Zero to Hero_v2* project, and play the first few clips in the project. In this project, the **crowd ots** clip is shorter and plays faster than in the other project version. Select the **crowd ots** clip, and press Command-R to open this clip's Retime Editor.

The Retime Editor shows that the clip playback speed was changed to 200%, so it plays twice as fast as it was recorded. Also, the speed segment is blue, which indicates increased playback speed.

NOTE ▶ Clips adjusted to play more slowly have an orange speed segment in the Retime Editor.

If you want to quickly review the speed changes in other project clips, select them, and open the Retime Editor.

7 Draw a selection rectangle around the video clips from **flame out smoke** to **army prep** in the *Zero to Hero_v2* project. Then, open the Retime Editor for all the selected clips by pressing Command-R.

Unlike audio or video effects, motion properties such as speed are already a part of every clip in every project. You don't have to *add* a speed effect, you just *change* the motion settings from a normal (100 percent) play speed to a faster or slower playback rate.

8 To see the speed changes, play through the project but notice the speed change in the Viewer when the color of a speed segment changes from the default green to blue or orange. Stop playback.

9 To return to the *Zero to Hero_START* project, click the left Timeline history arrow, or press Command-[(left bracket).

Changing Clip Speed

You've just seen several examples of the way speed changes could improve the *Zero to Hero* project. Speed changes saved some relatively uneventful crowd shots from being cut, paused a priceless moment in time, and added visual interest to otherwise normal-looking clips.

But speed changes aren't only useful for enhancing the pace of your project. You might also consider a speed change to extend a cutaway when it doesn't quite cover a narration clip, or as in some television programming, to create a transition between scenes.

Whether used to add some visual interest or "fix what's broke," speed changes in Final Cut Pro are flexible and easy to implement.

In this exercise, you will learn several methods for changing clip speed, including a more manual approach by changing speed directly on the clip using the Retime Editor.

1 In the *Zero to Hero_START* project, in the Timeline Index, click the *reverse* marker, and play the **driver prep red** clip at that location. Then, zoom the Timeline into this clip.

One of the Final Cut Pro retiming options is to reverse the direction a clip plays. Reversing direction might correct a camera zoom-in that should have been a zoom-out. Or it might simply provide an alternative look, as in this clip. Reversing direction does not change the clip duration.

2 With the pointer over the **driver prep red** clip, press C to select it, and choose Modify > Retime > Reverse Clip. Play the clip.

Because you selected the clip to apply the speed change, the Retime Editor appears automatically. The speed segment is green and displays Reverse Normal (–100%). The minus sign indicates reverse playback, and the green segment bar includes faint arrows that also indicate the playback direction.

As a reminder of how this clip was changed, let's leave the Retime Editor open, and move on to another retiming task, changing clip speed.

Applying a constant speed change greater or less than 100% to a clip affects the clip's duration. Playing a clip faster shortens its duration; playing it slower increases its duration. Let's change the speed of the **JF in car** clip to make it seem more like John Force is in a race.

3 In the Timeline Index, click the *fast driver* marker. After the playhead moves to the marker, play the **JF in car** clip. Notice the clip's length.

4 To change the speed of this clip, select it, and choose Modify > Retime > Fast > 2x, and then play the clip again. When you play this clip twice as fast, it becomes half as long in the project. Notice, too, that a blue speed bar appears, indicating an increased speed.

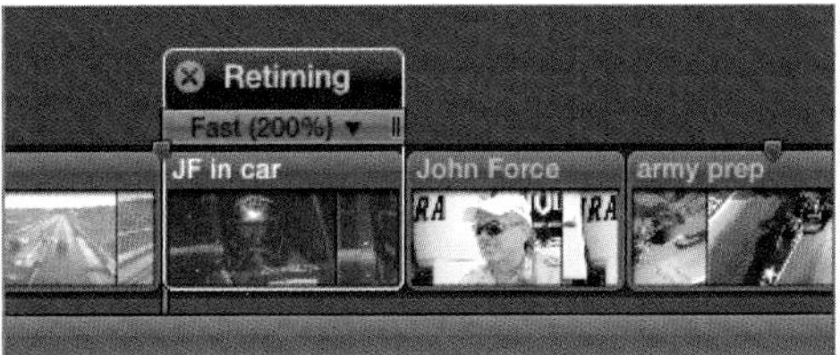

You can also apply a speed change to more than one clip at once, and choose the speed from a Retime pop-up menu in the toolbar.

5 In the Index, click the *200% both crowds* marker, and then play the two familiar crowd clips in the project.

Neither of these clips scream "action," but rather "lazy afternoon." Let's help energize the crowd, and change the speed on both clips at the same time.

6 Select the **crowd ots** and **crowd wide** clips. In the toolbar, click the Retime pop-up menu, look at the available choices, and then choose Fast > 2x. Play the clips and look at the Retime Editor that appears above them.

NOTE ▶ The options in the Retime pop-up menu are the same as those in the Modify menu.

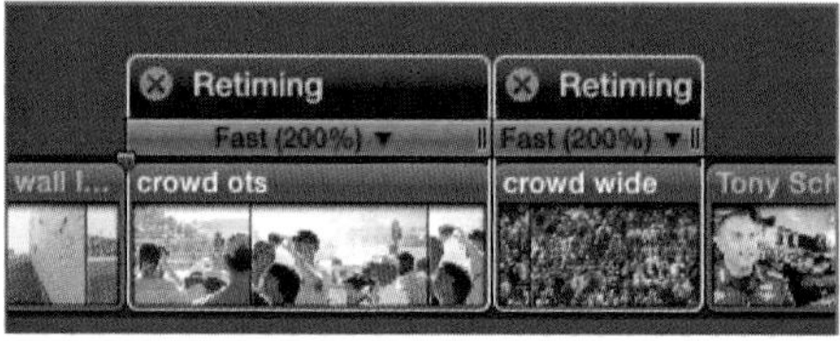

In the Timeline, the two crowd clips now have open Retime Editors indicating current speed settings of 200%. They, too, are now half as long.

NOTE ▶ When you speed up a clip, Final Cut Pro removes frames to make the clip shorter and play faster. When you slow down a clip, Final Cut Pro adds frames to make it play slower. Using the Magnetic Timeline, a project's length will automatically change to accommodate the speed change made to a primary storyline clip.

Although this is a high-action project, slowing down an important action can often add interest. Let's slow the action of a car flaming out, and this time, choose the speed directly from the Retime Editor on the clip.

7 In the Timeline Index, click the *slow down* marker, and zoom into the **flame out smoke** clip at this location. Play the clip. Then select the clip, and press Command-R to open its Retime Editor. From the clip's speed percentage pop-up menu, choose Slow > 50%. Play the clip and notice the change in clip length.

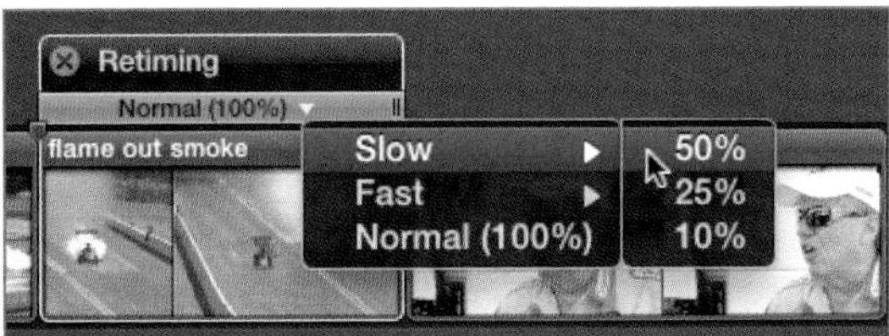

With the clip playing half as fast, it takes twice as long to play. An orange speed segment indicates that a slow-motion effect is applied.

Once you've chosen a preset playback speed for a clip, you can refine that speed by dragging the retiming handle in the Retime Editor.

Because increasing the speed helped to improve the two crowd clips, let's see what slowing the speed will do for the first clip in the project. But first, to keep things organized, let's add a to-do marker to this clip to include it with the others in the Timeline Index.

8 To move the playhead to the beginning of the project, press Home. Press M twice to set a maker at this location and open the Marker window. Name the marker *slow wall*, click the center To Do button, and click Done.

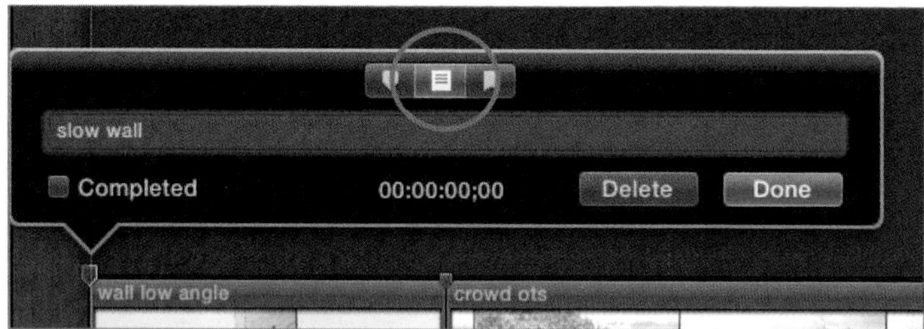

A red marker appears above the clip at the playhead location and the new to-do item appears in the Timeline Index.

9 To change the speed of the **wall low angle** clip, select it and press Command-R to open the Retime Editor. From the clip's speed percentage pop-up menu, choose Slow > 50%. Play the clip.

10 To increase the speed percentage, at the right end of the orange speed segment bar, drag the retiming handle to the left until the percentage reads Slow (70%), and then play the clip again.

By dragging the retiming handle, you can precisely control the speed and the length of the clip.

TIP If you don't like the new direction or speed setting, you can choose Modify > Retime > Reset Speed to reset it. You can also choose this option from the Retime pop-up menu in the toolbar. Keep in mind this option will undo both Reverse *and* speed changes applied to a clip. To return the speed of a reversed clip to normal speed (100%) but maintain the reverse direction, you would choose Reverse Normal -100.

Before continuing with more speed changes, let's check off a few of the to-do items on your list. You can do this in the Timeline Index or directly in the Timeline itself.

11 In the Timeline, double-click the *slow wall* marker. When the marker's information appears over the marker in the Timeline, select the Completed checkbox, and then click Done.

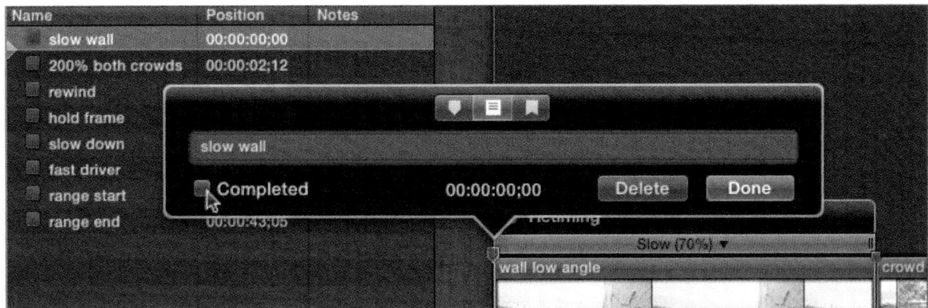

When you select the Completed checkbox, the to-do item is removed from this Index list and placed on the Completed list.

TIP Clicking a to-do marker's checkbox in the Timeline Index is another way to remove it from the to-do Index list and place it on the Completed list.

12 To see the list of completed to-do items, click the "Show completed to-do items" button.

The completed *slow wall* to-do item appears green with a checkmark. In the Timeline, the marker is also green.

NOTE ▶ If you want to place an item back on the to-do list, click the item's green marker checkbox on the Completed list.

TIP After you change the speed of a clip, you can still trim its start or end point, or make other trimming adjustments, using the Select tool or the Trim tool. When you trim to include more frames, those frames play at the current clip speed as shown in the Retime Editor.

Take 2

The director was kind enough to leave you with the original list of eight to-do items you worked on in the previous exercise. To show the director just how much you've accomplished, check off the items you finished. This will also help you focus your work in the next exercise.

- *200% both crowds*
- *fast driver*

TIP As you review your speed changes, you may find that one needs trimming. Look at the **wall low angle** clip, for example. Slowing down this clip made the camera bump more obvious. You can use the Trim tool to shorten the end of the clip to eliminate the bump. Trimming this clip will not alter the reduced clip speed.

Creating Holds and Variable Speed Segments

As you saw in the previous exercise, in only a few steps, you can create a constant speed adjustment across an entire clip. In this exercise, you will create even more excitement in your project by varying the speed *within* a single clip. Perhaps you want to hurry past an uneventful section you can't remove entirely, or hold onto a frame to give it the importance it deserves.

Speed variances within a clip are handled by speed segments. One way to create a speed segment is to identify a speed range using the Range tool. The selected range is used to modify the speed of specified frames within the clip, playing them faster or slower than the clip's other frames. Another way is to create a hold or paused range within a clip. To do so, you target one frame and Final Cut Pro can automatically create a two-second hold segment of that frame.

A championship shot in the *Zero to Hero_START* project is a great candidate for this effect, so let's start by *holding* on to that moment.

1 In the Timeline Index, click the *hold frame* marker, and zoom into the **JF holds trophy** clip. Select the clip, and then snap the playhead at the marker.

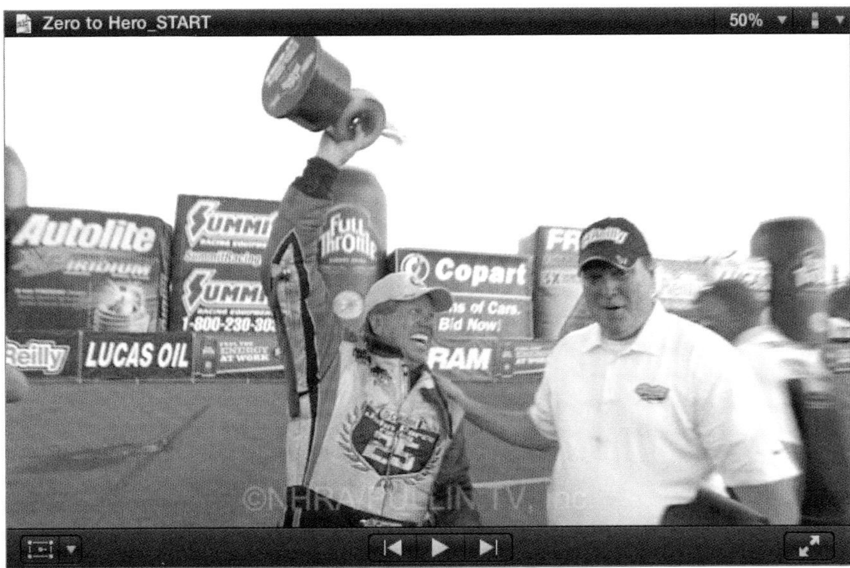

By snapping the playhead to this location, you identify the frame you want Final Cut Pro to hold.

2 In the toolbar, from the Retime pop-up menu, choose Hold, or press Shift-H. Play the new speed settings.

NOTE ▶ Unlike with other speed changes, you cannot select Hold from a clip's Retime Editor.

In the clip Retime Editor, a red speed segment indicates a 0% play speed—or no speed at all. On either side of the Hold is a green Normal (100%) speed segment. Graphically, this shows that the clip begins at normal play speed, stops for the hold (for the default two seconds), and continues playing the remainder of the clip at normal speed.

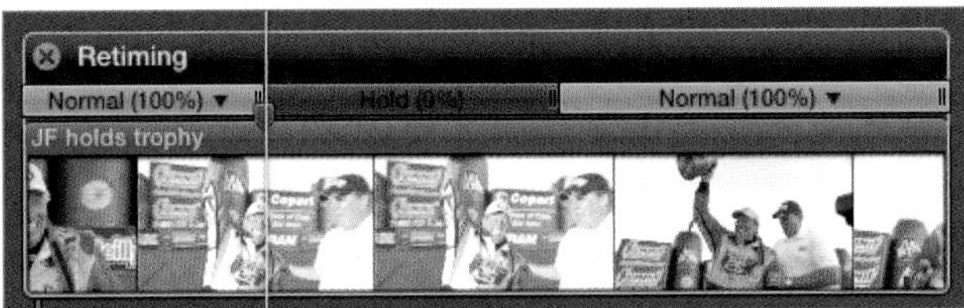

Any speed segment, including a hold, can be adjusted by dragging the retiming handle to the right of the segment. Let's extend this pause to the end of one of Antron Brown's lines.

3 Play the clip again, and stop playback after you hear Antron Brown say, "'Cause you take the Wally home." In the Retime Editor, drag the Hold retiming handle right to the playhead. Play this clip.

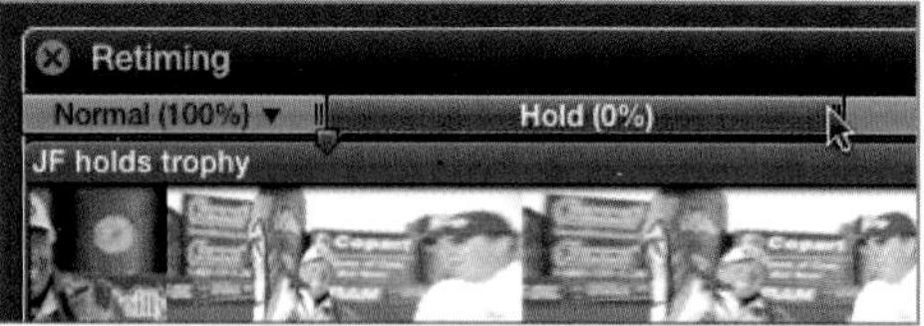

NOTE ▶ Unlike the adjustment you made in the previous exercise, shortening or lengthening the hold speed segment changes the duration but not the speed of the clip.

The remaining portion of this clip is anticlimactic after the hold, so you can trim away the third segment. You've already identified an Antron Brown line, so let's shorten the B-roll clip and return to him speaking.

4 Move the pointer over the end of the **JF holds trophy** clip. When the end point trim icon appears, drag left and snap the edit point to the playhead location. Play the clip.

NOTE ▶ In the next exercise, you will apply a freeze frame to a clip and compare the results to a hold effect.

Another way to add a speed segment within a clip is to select a range using the Range tool.

5 In the Timeline, play the **army prep** clip. Skim to the first marker, and then skim to the second.

In this clip, the camera cranes around from one side of the car to the other. Project time and audience attention is usually limited. To move the action along in this clip, you will change the speed between the two markers by creating a speed segment for the selected frames.

6 To choose the Range tool, press R, and snap the Range tool to the first marker in the **army prep** clip. To select a range, drag right and snap to the second marker. To apply a speed change within the range, choose Modify > Retime > Fast > 8x. Play the clip.

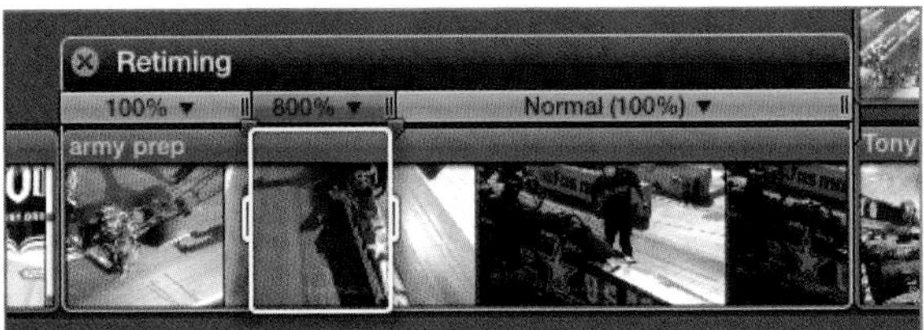

Changing speed in just this range of the clip maintains the overall fast pace of this project. To finesse the effect, you can change the speed segments that were automatically created. Let's slow down the third segment.

TIP You can also use the Range tool to create a selection across several clips in a project, and then apply a speed change. All selected frames will play at the altered speed.

7 In the third speed segment of the **army prep** clip, drag the retiming handle of this segment to change its speed to 80%, and play the clip. The clip now exhibits some personality.

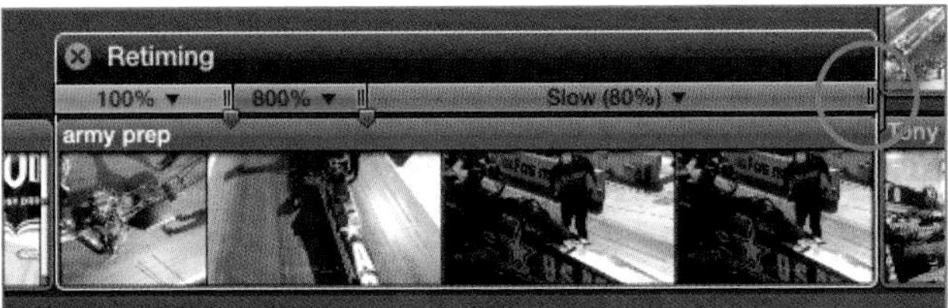

You can finesse a speed segment by dragging a retiming handle, but you can also choose the exact frame on which you want to end a speed segment. In this clip, at the end of the first segment, you may have noticed a man starting to turn. Let's end the first segment before he turns.

8 In the **army prep** clip, skim across the end of the first segment and the beginning of the second. Press the Left or Right Arrow keys, if necessary, to find precisely where the man begins to turn away from the car.

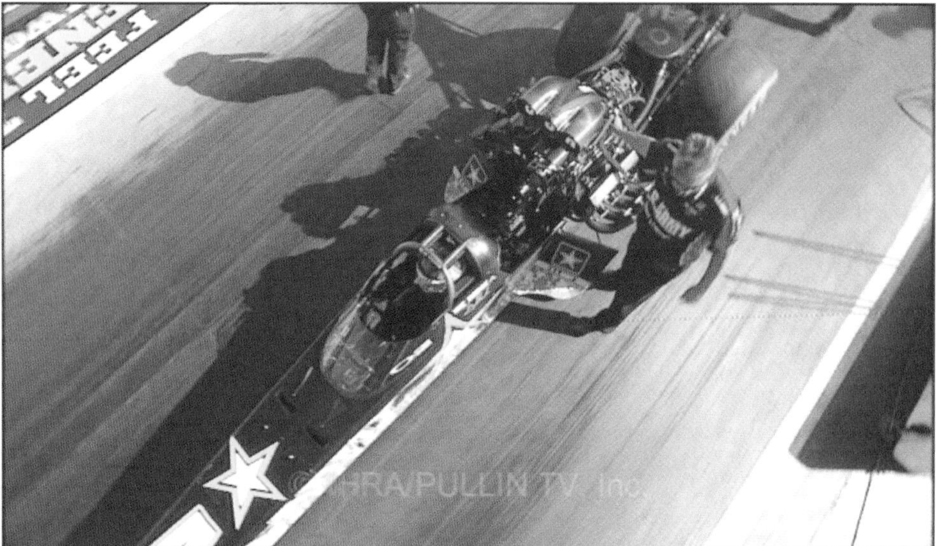

This move could be distracting. It might be better to start the faster speed segment before he turns so it will be less noticeable.

9 In the **army prep** clip's first speed segment, from the speed percentage pop-up menu, choose Change End Source Frame. When the tiny filmstrip icon appears, drag it left or right and watch the Viewer until you see the frame of the man before he turns.

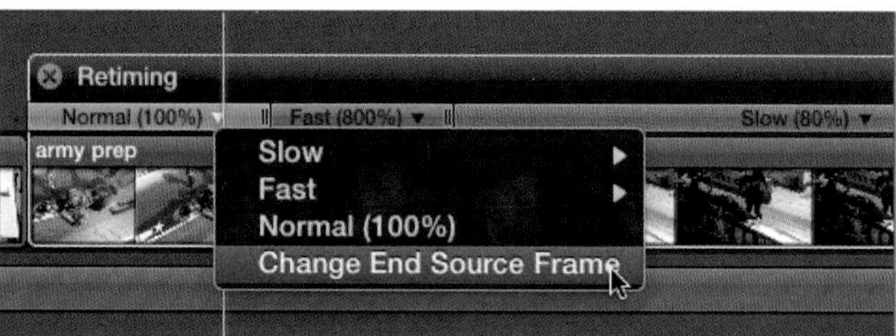

Dragging the end source frame does not change the speed percentage of either segment, but allows you to set the end of one speed segment and the start of the next one. As you change the end source frame, the length of the speed segment on either side will change, causing the overall clip length to change. In the first speed segment bar, notice that the segment length has changed, but the speed has not.

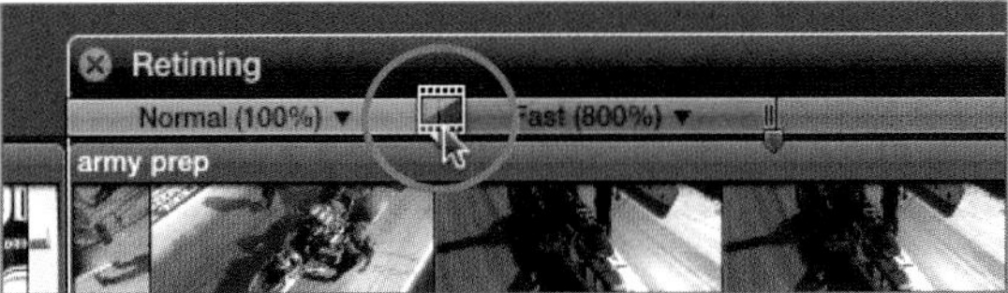

To make these speed changes flow as smoothly as possibly, you can choose a high video quality option called Optical Flow. This option creates the smoothest possible speed change by adding frames.

TIP Many speed changes can be processed using the Frame Blending video quality option.

10 Select the **army prep** clip. In the toolbar, from the Retime pop-up menu, choose Video Quality > Optical Flow, if necessary.

NOTE ▶ Although it takes some time to render, Optical Flow creates the best speed result because Final Cut Pro actually tracks the pixels and builds new frames to smooth the motion. However, in some shots Optical Flow is not desirable, such as when subjects are moving across the screen in both directions.

Applying Preset Speed Effects

Playing clips or clip segments faster and slower, or holding individual frames, isn't the only way you can adjust clip playback and timing in Final Cut Pro.

Additional options have built-in preset actions. For example, rather than jump into a new clip speed, you can ramp in or out of it by applying one of two speed ramp presets. Another preset simulates the automatic rewind of a clip or clip segment; and you can insert an instant replay without creating it manually.

Also, instead of holding a frame within a clip, you can use the freeze frame command that edits the frame into the Timeline as a still image clip.

In this exercise, you will explore these speed presets by applying a speed ramp to enliven a racing clip, an instant replay and rewind effect to relive a car crash, and a freeze frame to preserve a single moment in a crash.

1 In the *Zero to Hero_START* project, play the first clip in the project, **wall low angle**. If the clip Retime Editor is not open, select the clip, and press Command-R.

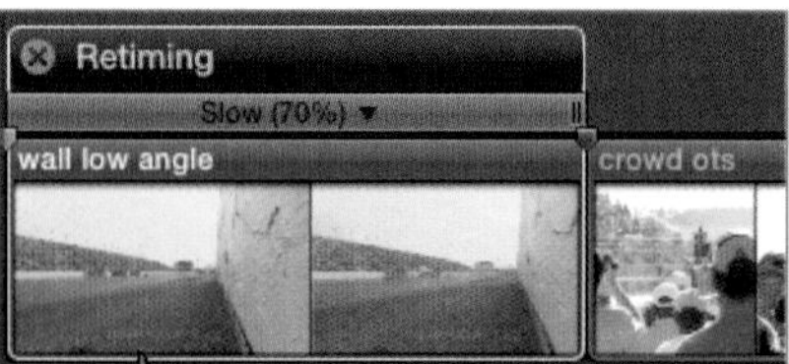

In a previous exercise, you slowed this clip to lengthen it, which allowed the viewer to savor the racing action. To make more of this low angle camera shot, you can apply a speed ramp. Let's apply the "from 0%" speed ramp to start the clip at 0% and accelerate to the current 70% speed.

2 With the **wall low angle** clip selected, click the Retime pop-up menu in the toolbar, and look at the options for Speed Ramp. Then choose Speed Ramp > from 0%, and play the clip.

The clip automatically divides into four speed segments. The first segment begins at 0% and the last segment ends at 70%. Now it appears as though the two cars start farther away because you slowed down that part of the clip the most, almost freezing them in time.

NOTE ▶ When you ramp the speed in a clip, you ease in and out of the speed in a more natural way.

You can also ramp the speed of a clip from its current speed down to 0%. This might be an effective way to look at the car crash.

3 Play the **crash** clip. To open the Retime Editor, select the clip and press Command-R. To apply a speed ramp, from the Retime pop-up menu, choose Speed Ramp > to 0%. Play the clip again.

Once again, four speed segments are created automatically. Each speed segment can be adjusted or changed as you've done in previous steps.

TIP When you change clip speed, it can affect the placement of other clips in the Timeline. Keep an eye on all your project clips, and consider ways you can connect them so they won't be affected. After speed changes, you may need to reposition the added sound effects; however, do not do so for the Speed Ramp you just performed.

This is one approach or treatment for the crash clip. Another would be to hold the frame of the crash itself. Still another would be to apply an instant replay or rewind effect.

4 Press Command-Z as necessary to reset the previous speed change and any repositioning of the sound effects you made. With the **crash** clip still selected, from the Retime pop-up menu, choose Instant Replay. Play the clip.

The instant replay effect literally repeats the clip at its normal 100% play speed. Let's undo that change, and use another approach.

5 To undo the previous speed change, press Command-Z. With the **crash** clip still selected, from the Retime pop-up menu, choose Rewind > 2x. Play the clip.

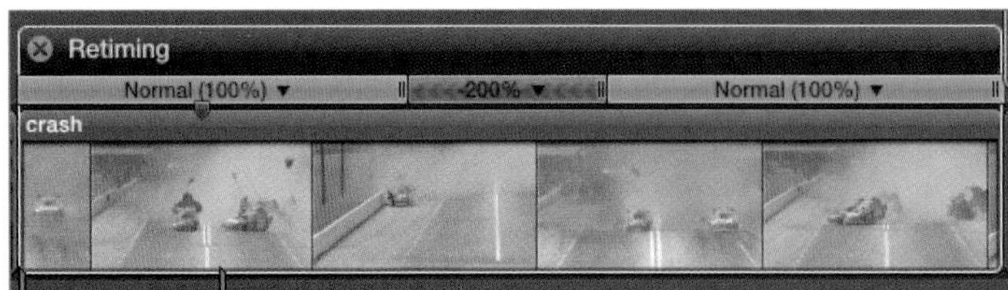

The rewind effect also repeats the clip, but before doing so, it backs up—literally rewinds the clip—before playing it again. Notice the –200% speed segment in the middle of the clip. When you chose Rewind > 2x, you set the speed at which you wanted to back up the cars before they moved forward again.

To customize the automatic rewind effect for this specific clip and project, you can identify the range you want to repeat. As a guide, you can use the marker that's already placed just before the two cars collide.

6 To undo the previous speed change, press Command-Z. This time, press R to choose the Range tool. Snap the Range tool to the marker above the clip and drag to the end of the clip to set the range. From the Retime pop-up menu, choose Rewind > 2x. Play the clip.

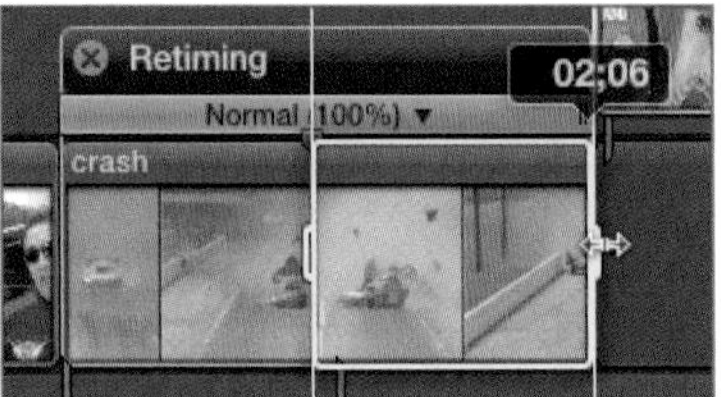

Now the clip plays, but at the beginning of the selection you created, it rewinds to just before the crash. Like all Final Cut Pro effects, applying these effects is simple and straightforward, but additional experience will give you more confidence when customizing them.

These speed effects have an initial automatic setup. But because of the way Final Cut Pro uses individual speed segments to create the effect, you have total freedom to customize each effect. Use the tools you used previously to change individual speed segments or adjust the end source frame, and so on.

NOTE ▶ In the Modify > Retime submenu, Preserve Pitch is selected as a default.

You can also apply the freeze frame effect to stop motion. In the previous speed effects, all the speed changes are contained within the clip itself. But when you apply a freeze to a frame, Final Cut Pro creates a separate individual clip.

7 To undo the previous speed change, press Command-Z. Cue the playhead before the marker where the back end of the race car begins to vertically lift, at around 19:34.

The forces of aerodynamics, along with all the debris, spell trouble for this racer. If you wanted to foreshadow the crash, a hold effect could work perfectly to pause on this frame, and then continue playing to show the car's crash. But if you wanted to use this frame elsewhere, such as the opening title or in a montage of historical crash moments, you might appreciate having a separate clip you could use to re-edit and manipulate on its own.

8 With your playhead cued, choose Edit > Add Freeze Frame, or press Option-F. A four-second freeze frame clip is inserted into the storyline. Notice the timecode number that follows the clip name. This is the location of the freeze frame in the source clip.

NOTE ▶ The default duration for freeze frames can be changed in the Editing tab of the Preferences dialog.

9 Play the three separate **Crash** clips. Notice how the freeze creates a sudden stop and then restarts the momentum just as suddenly, almost with a jolt.

Remember, the freeze frame effect is intended to isolate a single frame from a clip, and make a separate clip from that frame. It's not intended to create a smooth flow of motion. To create a pause smoothly sandwiched between two other speeds within a clip, your best bet is to use the hold function.

TIP You can also create freeze frames from Event Browser clips. In the Event Browser, locate the frame you want to freeze, and choose Edit > Connect Freeze Frame. A freeze is connected to your primary storyline at the playhead's location.

Take 2

You changed speed in quite a few clips in the *Zero to Hero_START* project, and as a result, may have pulled and tugged at some of the important timings, such as the sound effects of the cars crashing, or a beat of music coinciding with an action. Other timings may have been improved. The director notices it, too, and rather than point out each individual adjustment to make, she's going to leave the project to you to finesse. Take a moment to go through this project and improve on as many of those timing issues as possible. When you finish, close the Timeline Index in preparation for the next exercise.

Transforming an Image

Just as every clip in Final Cut Pro has built-in speed properties, each clip has built-in motion properties you can adjust to transform its size, location, image angle, and so on. You might enlarge a clip and then reposition it to hide an unwanted element in the scene, such as a light, microphone, or other piece of equipment. Or you might reduce the size of a clip so additional images can appear on the screen at the same time, creating a split-screen or multiframe effect.

In this exercise, you will transform clips by scaling and repositioning them using a new version of the *Delicious Peace* project. You will also change the opacity of a clip. First, let's look at the motion properties of a finished project.

1 In the Project Library, from the Lesson 10 folder, open the *Delicious Peace_v2* project into the Timeline, and play *just* the first half, focusing on how the clips look in the Viewer. Play that portion again and notice the clip arrangement in the Timeline.

To display two or more clips together onscreen, they must be placed, or stacked, on top of each other in the Timeline. Generally, when you arrange clips this way, you see only the uppermost clip in the Viewer. But when you transform the clip's motion properties by making the clip smaller or moving it to one side, you can also see the clip or clips beneath it.

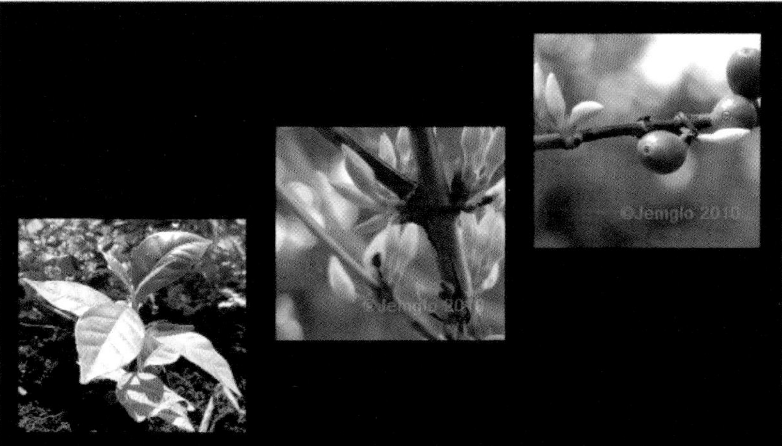

The *Delicious Peace* footage contains several shots showing the stages of growing and making coffee. If you were limited by the amount of time you had to show this process, you might consider combining the images onscreen in a multiframe fashion.

2 Play the second half of the project from around 40:00. Watch the Viewer during the first playback, and then focus on the Timeline while replaying this section.

No two clips appear on the screen at the same time in this section, except during transitions. In the Timeline, no clips are stacked on top of each other except for the ending title credit.

Sometimes you can capture an entire story within a single still image. For example, in the images of the classrooms, the teachers and students look especially engaged and responsive. To highlight individuals in these images, the Ken Burns effect was applied to add movement to these clips, automatically panning and zooming into specific targets, simulating the movement of an active camera operator. You will work with this portion of the project in the next exercise.

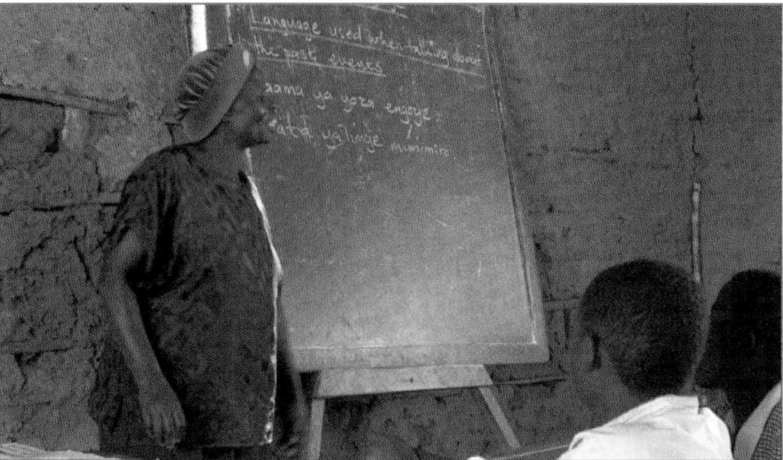

Creating complex multiframe effects, such as you see in this project, takes time and planning and begins with careful image selection during the editing process. It may also require changing the motion properties of certain clips to adjust their durations.

NOTE ▶ In this project, some of the clips were slowed so they would play longer.

3 Return to the Project Library and, from the Lesson 10 folder, open the *Delicious Peace_START* project, and play it.

You can see only the uppermost clip in any stack, and the still images are static.

When you are in an editing stage such as this, where your focus is entirely on the video, it's helpful to consolidate the audio clips so they won't be disturbed or distracting. Let's combine all the audio clips in this project into a single compound clip.

4 In the *Delicious Peace_START* project, drag to select all the audio clips. Control-click any one of the selected clips, and from the shortcut menu, choose New Compound Clip, or press Option-G. Name the compound clip *Soundtrack*, set the Event to Delicious Peace, and click OK.

Now let's look at the Transform controls in the Viewer.

5 In the lower-left corner of the Viewer is a Transform button. Click the pop-up menu next to it to see the other options.

NOTE ▶ The most recently used option will appear on the button. If you used one of these functions prior to this lesson, a different option may appear as the default button.

These buttons represent built-in effects—Transform, Crop, and Distort. You always have immediate access to these controls without opening a window or choosing a menu option.

Let's start with the Transform controls, which allow you to change the size or scale of an image and its position in the image area.

6 In the Timeline, play the first set of stacked clips, then Option-click the **workers relaxing** clip. In the Viewer, click the Transform button, or press Shift-T to select it.

The Transform button is blue when selected; various onscreen controls appear in the Viewer image area, and a thin white solid line appears around the image.

When Transform is chosen, you can drag *any* corner handle to resize the image. By dragging your pointer inside the image area, you can move the image, and there's even a handle extending from the center anchor point to rotate the clip. For now, let's make this clip smaller and position it to the left side of the image area.

TIP If you find it difficult to grab a corner handle, reduce the zoom level percentage in the top right of the Viewer.

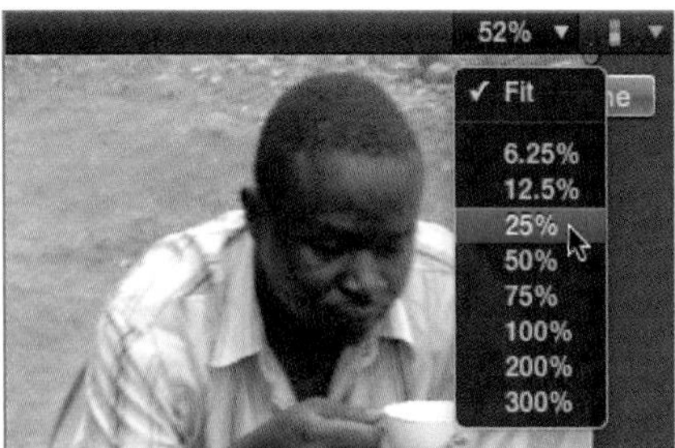

7 Move your pointer to the lower-left corner of the Viewer image area. When you see the diagonal resize pointer, drag the handle toward the center to make the image about half-size.

Dragging a corner handle proportionately scales the image. When you make the upper image smaller, the image beneath it becomes visible.

8 To move the entire image to the left, place your pointer inside the clip's image area, and drag left until the clip is against the left side of the image area.

9 Now click the **walk to house** clip beneath the **workers relaxing** clip. Notice that the Transform button is still active (blue), but the controls now appear around the selected clip. Drag a corner handle toward the center of this image to match the approximate size of the **workers relaxing** clip. Position this clip to the right until you see the man walking on a path toward a house.

NOTE ▶ Transformations are referred to as *persistent* changes because they are live for any clip you select until you toggle off the Transform button or click Done.

Both clips are now visible at the same time, but the effect is not quite finished. You will continue to finesse it in the following steps.

TIP Later in this lesson you will learn how to enter an exact percentage size for an image as well as copy an image and paste its attributes onto a different image.

For the next clip, you will explore ways in which a modifier key can alter how you transform and rotate an image.

10 Cue the playhead over and select the **coffee plant** clip, and drag a corner handle to make the image smaller. Then perform the following operations:

- To squeeze the image, Option-drag one of the edge handles.
- To resize the image proportionally in this aspect ratio, Shift-drag a top or bottom handle.
- To change the proportion dynamically, Shift-drag a corner handle.
- To flip the image horizontally, Shift-drag a corner handle across the image until it reverses.

- To flip the image vertically, Shift-drag a corner handle across the image from top to bottom until it reverses.
- To rotate the image, drag the handle extending from the center like a steering wheel. For more control, drag the handle farther away from the center and drag again.

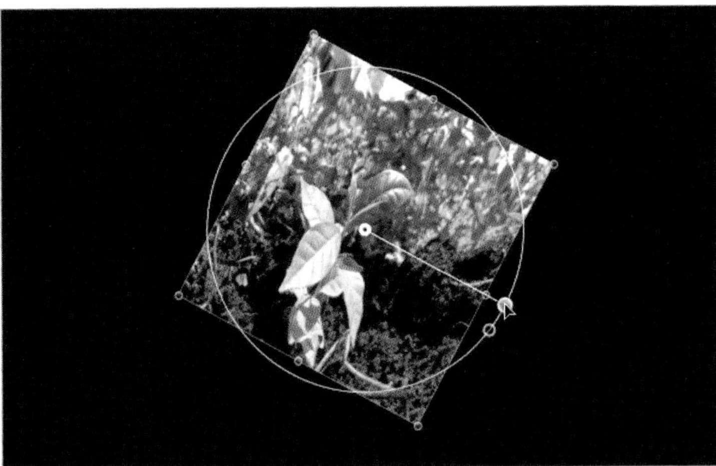

Now that you have experimented with these controls, how can you quickly reset the image to its default, full-screen look? In the Video inspector, you can reset all the onscreen Transform controls.

11 With the **coffee plant** clip still selected, open the Inspector, and click the Video tab. Scroll down if necessary to see the Transform section for this clip. Move the pointer over the Transform line, and when Show appears, click it to reveal the Transform parameters.

The Show button will appear only when the pointer moves over an attribute line.

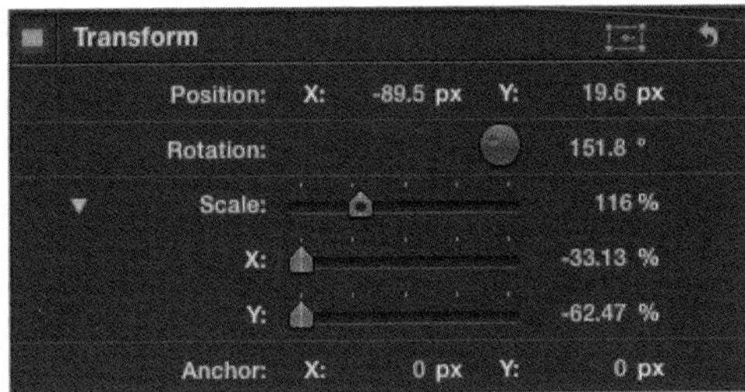

You can also use the Video inspector to transform motion parameters. Here you can drag sliders and enter numerical information for a different kind of control over the image.

TIP The Show button toggles to become the Hide button when the parameters are revealed.

12 To display the Scale percentages, click the Scale disclosure triangle. To reset the Transform parameters, click the Reset button (the curved arrow).

You can use the Viewer and Inspector in tandem to create and refine motion effects. For example, in step 7 you scaled a clip to an approximate size in the Viewer. Now let's enter the precise percentage you want in the Inspector.

13 In the Timeline, select the **workers relaxing** clip, and in the Video Inspector, examine the Scale parameters and the X and Y percentages. Click in the X numerical field, enter *65*, and press Tab. Enter *65* in the Y field, and press Tab. Then, select the **walk to house** clip and repeat these steps.

The two clips are now exactly the same size.

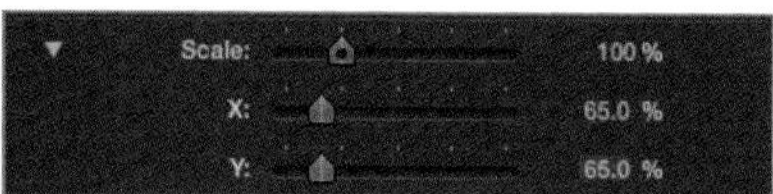

Opacity is another parameter you can adjust when building composite effects. When you change the opacity of a clip, you change its percentage of transparency. As a clip becomes more transparent, the clip beneath it in the Timeline will increasingly show through, thereby creating a superimposition.

In this project, two stacked clips have an image of beans in a silver bowl. It would be nice to dissolve from one image to the next and match the size and position of the two bowls.

14 Move the playhead between the **beans being hulled** clip and the **dark beans heated** clip to see the two silver bowls. Then drag the playhead to the first frame of the **dark beans heated** clip.

15 In the Video Inspector, scroll down to the Compositing section. Drag the Opacity slider to about 50%. Using the lower clip as a reference, resize and reposition the upper clip until it matches the size and position of the lower clip.

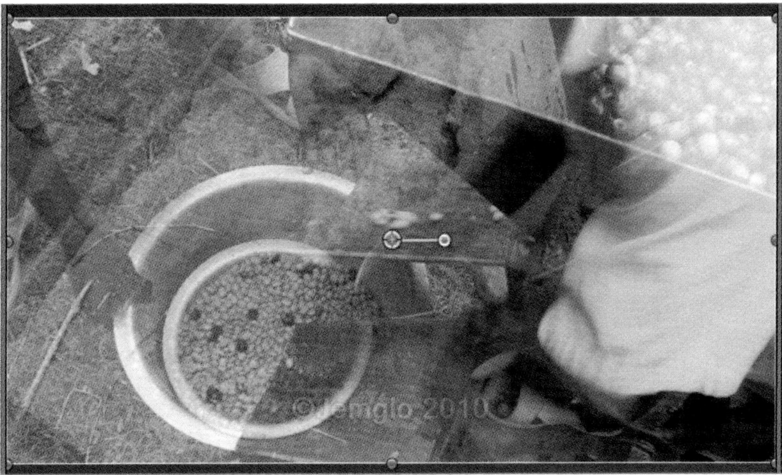

When an upper clip's opacity percentage is lowered, the image beneath it becomes visible.

You can change opacity to align clips or to build a composite of several images.

With the position of the two bowls aligned, you can return the opacity of the upper clip to its default 100% and apply a nice long transition to show off the alignment.

16 In the Video Inspector, drag the Opacity slider to 100%. In the Timeline, select the start of the **dark beans heated** clip, and press Command-T to apply a transition. Drag the edge of the transition to increase the duration to about 1:15 seconds. Play the two clips.

In only a few seconds, you have shown the beans going from being hulled to being roasted. Notice that the Transform button is still active (blue). Keeping it active as you continue to transform your images is a very convenient workflow.

Cropping an Image

Not every pixel of every image is art. But not all projects lend themselves to showing less than full-frame images. Using two of the three crop options in Final Cut Pro, you can remove portions of an image you don't want to see by trimming or cropping the image. Trimming shaves off a portion of an image, whereas cropping uses the original aspect ratio to reframe a section within the image.

In this exercise, you will continue to improve the *Delicious Peace_START* project by using the trim and crop options in the Viewer.

1 Play the first stack of clips in the project, at the **walk to house** clip. Position the pointer about halfway through the clip, and then Option-click the clip to select it and bring the playhead to this location.

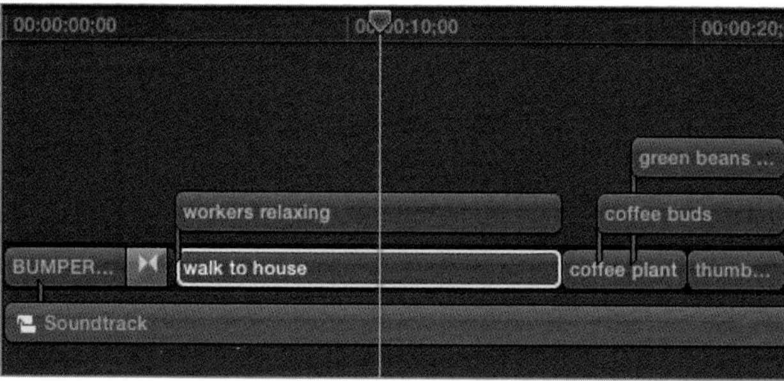

In the Viewer, you can see both images, but they bump up against each other. Since the two images are very different, it might look better to create some space between the two clips. To do that, you can't reposition the clip or you will no longer see the house on the right. Instead, you must trim the left portion of that clip.

2 In the Viewer, from the Transform pop-up menu, choose Crop, or press Shift-C. Three crop options appear beneath the center of the image: Trim, Crop, and Ken Burns. Click Trim if it's not already selected.

The Crop controls around the image are slightly different than the Transform controls. The blue handles are thicker and the white outline is dashed.

TIP The Distort option displays a different look. As you work more with these options, you will recognize the active function simply by the way in which the image is outlined.

3 To trim away the left side of this clip, drag the left handle to the right until you see black space between this clip and the clip on the left. Play the clips.

Similar handles can be found on each side of the clip to trim away excess image from any direction. Also, the image corners allow you to trim two sides at once.

Now that you've taken care of this overlap, you will trim multiple sides of the next clip.

4 Cue the playhead to the **coffee plant** clip at 00:00:16:07, and play this stack of clips.

Each of the three **coffee** clips captures one aspect of coffee growing. Rather than view them one after another, it would be nice to build a composite multiframe image so you can view them together within the same image area. To do that, you will need to trim away all the unimportant portions of each image. Let's start by trimming the first clip so that only the plant remains.

5 Move the playhead to the head of the **coffee plant** clip, and select it. Drag the right-side handle of the image toward the plant leaves in the center. To trim two sides at once, drag the upper-left corner handle down and to the right toward the plant leaves.

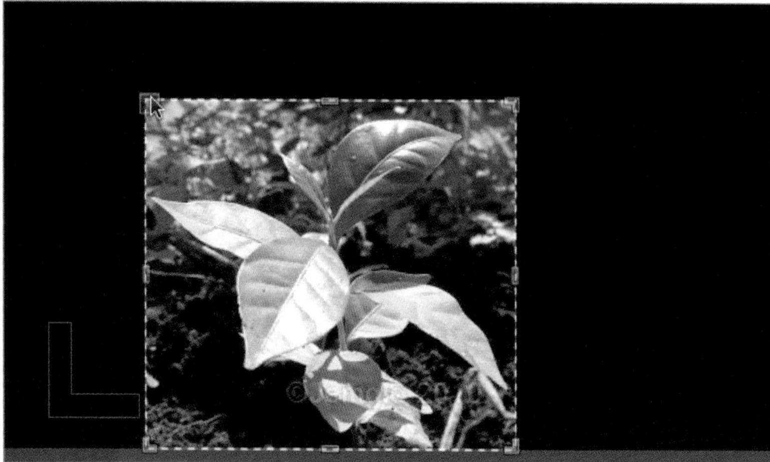

When creating multiframe effects, you often have to bounce between the Transform options. For example, now that you've cropped this clip, you can make it smaller and reposition it to make room for the other two clips in this stack.

6 To switch to the Transform option, press Shift-T. First, reduce the size of the **coffee plant** clip, and then drag it to the lower-left corner of the image area.

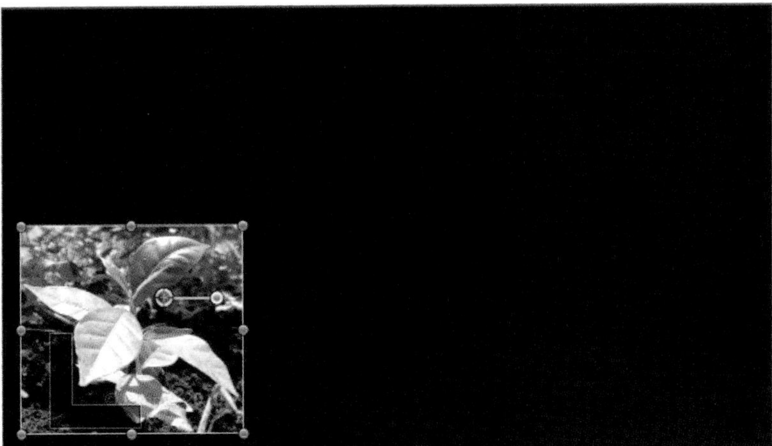

After you've cropped or transformed a clip, you can share specific, altered attributes with another clip. For example, you could apply the attributes of the **coffee plant** clip to the **coffee buds** and **green beans on branch** clips to make them the same size and shape. Rather than do this manually, you can use the Paste Attributes function.

7 In the Timeline, select the **coffee plant** clip, and press Command-C to copy it. Click above the **green beans on branch** clip to move the playhead to that location, and then select the **coffee buds** and **green beans on branch** clips. Choose Edit > Paste Attributes, or press Shift-Command-V.

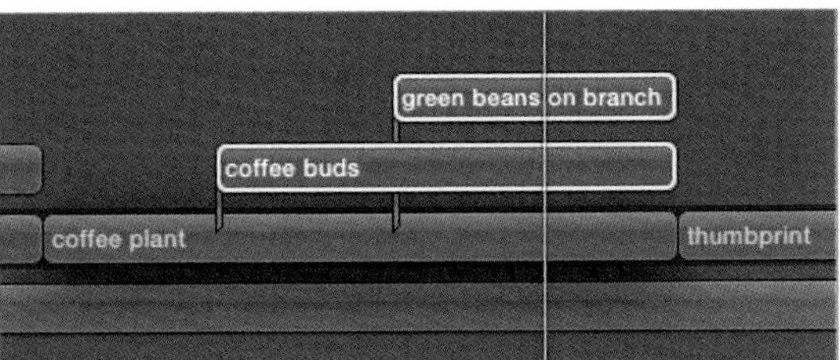

When you press Command-C to copy a clip, you copy everything about that clip. But when you apply the Paste Attributes function, you can choose only those attributes you want to paste from the copied clip.

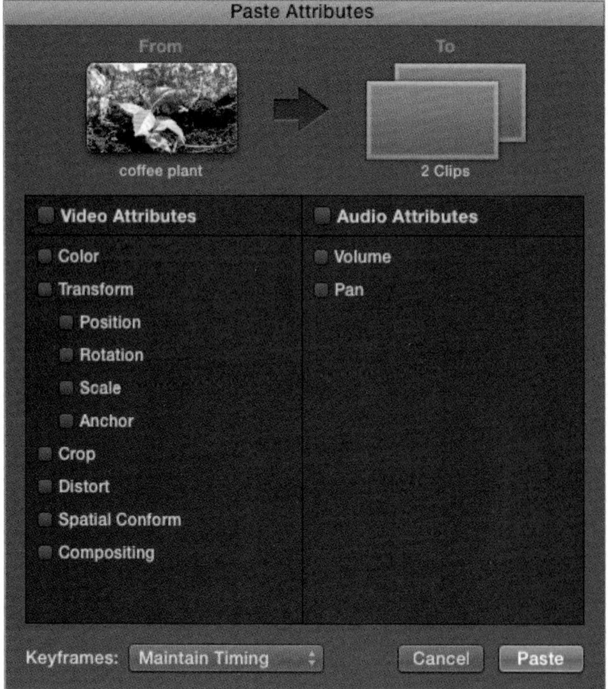

At the top of the Paste Attributes window is a thumbnail image of the source clip from which you copied attributes and the destination clip(s) that will receive those attributes. For this clip, you want to paste from the Transform and Crop sections.

NOTE ▶ You can paste attributes to a single clip or a group of clips, but you can copy attributes from only one clip.

8 In the Paste Attributes window, select the Scale and Crop attributes. Then click Paste, and play the clips.

Both clips are now the same size as the **coffee plant** clip and are cropped the same way. But you see only the uppermost clip because they are stacked on top of each other in the same location. Let's manually reposition the clips.

9 With the Transform button still active (blue), drag the **green beans on branch** clip to the upper-right corner, leaving some black background around it. Then adjust the position of the **coffee buds** clip to the center of the image area. Play this group of clips.

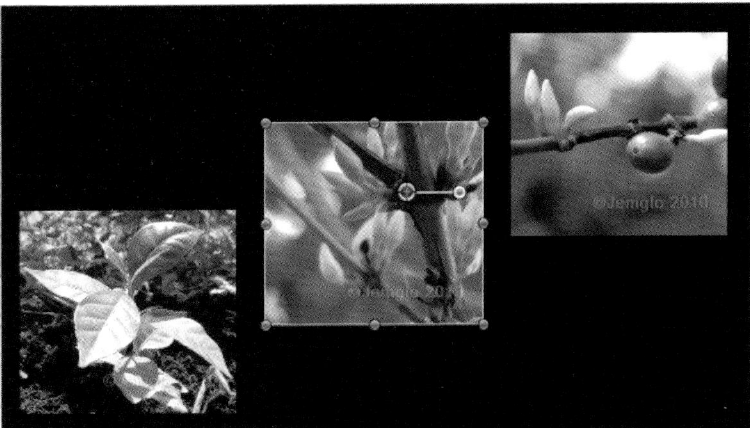

Now let's focus on a different crop option, one that allows you to easily remove unwanted areas of an image while maintaining the aspect ratio of the image. When using this option, rather than drag to remove the portion of the clip you *don't* want, you drag a selection around the portion you *do* want. Whatever portion of the image you select will fill the image area.

10 Play the **thumbprint** clip, and then Option-click in the middle of the clip to select it and bring the playhead to that location.

Notice that the primary activity in this clip is the man placing his thumbprint in the book. If you allow your eye to wander, it could become distracted by the pencils, pens, and notebooks on the table. Your goal is to help the viewer focus on the most important part of the image, but you also want to fill the frame. If you used the trim type of crop, it would leave black around the trimmed edges. Let's try a different method.

11 To change to the crop mode, from the Transform pop-up menu, choose Crop, or press Shift-C. Beneath the image area, click the Crop option. Drag one of the corners toward the center, and then drag within the crop box to position it over the thumbprint portion of the image.

NOTE ▶ When you drag a boundary line while cropping or positioning a clip, you may see a horizontal and/or vertical yellow line appear. These lines are dynamic guides to help you position images relative to the Viewer's image area.

With this method, the selection area retains the aspect ratio of the image but can be sized and positioned around just the portion of the original image you want to see.

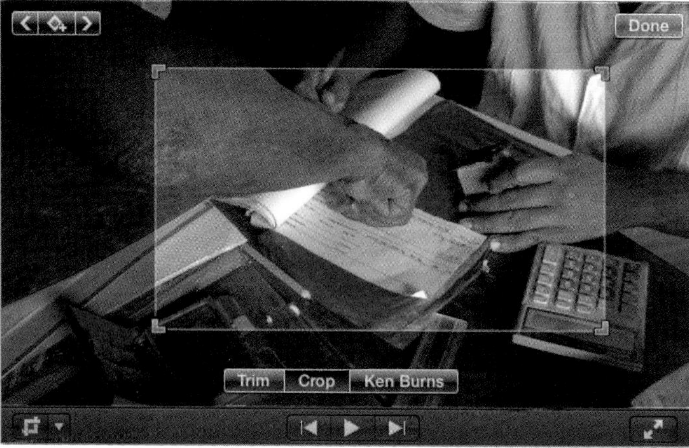

12 When you're finished sizing and positioning the crop box, click Done.

TIP When you've completed applying transformation changes to your clips, you can either click Done or click the blue Crop or Transform button.

Now the selected portion of the clip scales up to fill the image area. By using this crop method, you focus more on what you want to keep, rather than what you want to discard.

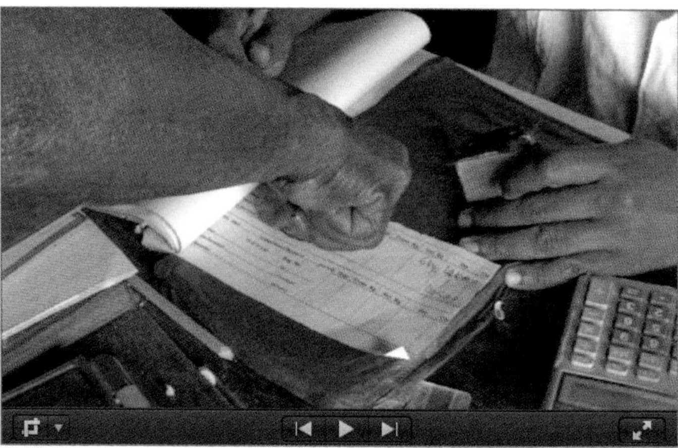

TIP When you make adjustments with the transform and crop controls, Final Cut Pro displays coordinates in the upper left of the Viewer.

Take 2

Once you start incorporating a multiframe style to your project, you will find other opportunities to utilize this approach. But remember, any time you want to see more than one clip in the image area at once, those clips have to be located over each other in the Timeline.

One section in this project has two clips sitting on top of two other clips. This is an ideal section in which to practice applying the transform and crop options to create a split-screen effect. See what you can do with the clips in the following image:

TIP To create a more polished look in the first half of this project, you can apply transitions to the clips you've transformed.

Adding the Ken Burns Effect

In the previous exercises, you discovered that with just a few trims and repositions, you can quickly create some interesting montages and multiframe effects. The third crop option, Ken Burns, combines the power of the Crop controls with the power of animation. You choose starting and ending crop sizes and positions, and Final Cut Pro smoothes and automatically transitions the clip image between those points. Let's apply a Ken Burns crop to the *Delicious Peace* still images.

1 In the second portion of the *Delicious Peace_START* project, play the **trio on bikes** clip at about 40:06. Position the pointer over the middle of the clip, and click to set the playhead at this location.

   Rather than sit on a still image while the narrator talks about the coffee farmers, it might add more life to the image if you could zoom into the faces of these co-op members.

2 In the Viewer, click the Crop button, and choose Ken Burns as the crop type. Two crop selections appear. One selection is green and labeled Start; the other selection is red and labeled End.

Notice that the green start selection found the outer edge of the still image, not the outer edge of the image area. You can drag a crop selection to identify the starting and ending frames for a clip. For this step, you will allow the clip to start at its default size and position. But let's end on a tighter cropping of the three men.

TIP Click the Start or End text labels of the onscreen controls to aid in selecting which part of the animation to adjust. The playhead will cue to the selection.

3 Drag the lower-right corner handle of the red End selection toward the two men on the left. As you drag, an arrow indicates the direction in which the zoom will occur.

4 Now resize and reposition the End selection to include a tight cropping of the three men. To loop playback of the new animation, click the Play button above the left-side of the image. To stop playback, click it again.

TIP If you don't have a good selection of still images to work with, you can create this type of montage and apply these transform and crop options to freeze frame clips–such as the one you created earlier in this lesson.

5 To apply a Ken Burns crop to the next image, Option-click the **students** clip. Select the Ken Burns crop type. The default Start and End outlines appear.

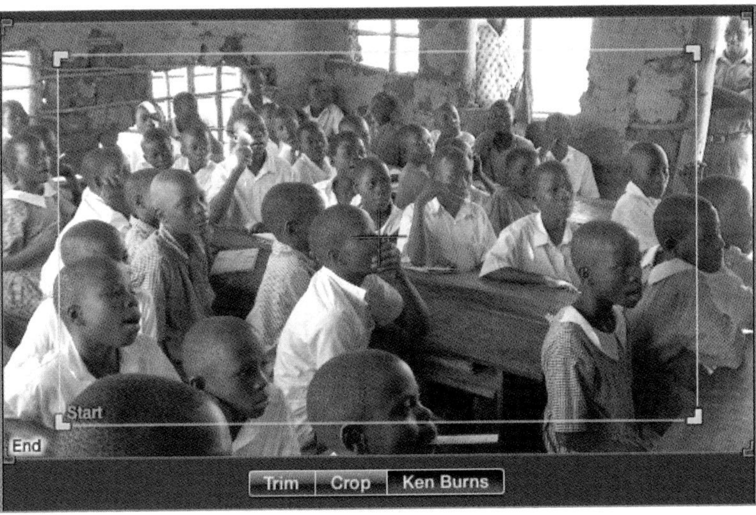

This time, Final Cut Pro offers a default zoom out, from a smaller green Start selection to a wider red End selection. If you don't like the default direction of the effect, it's easy to swap the initial frames.

6 In the upper-left corner of the Viewer, with the Ken Burns Start and End selections active, click the double-arrow Swap button.

Now the End selection is cropped smaller and the zoom will move from a wider Start selection to a smaller End selection.

7 Reframe the red End selection around the children in the middle of the image.

TIP Some still images are vertical or not as wide as the aspect ratio of HD footage. When a still image doesn't fill the frame, you might consider applying a Ken Burns effect to that image.

8 Click Done and review the animation of both clips.

NOTE ▸ When applying Ken Burns to video clips or stills with people analysis, the start and end frames are automatically set around people's faces. Furthermore, when applying Ken Burns to adjacent clips with people analysis, start and end positions are automatically swapped so that zoom in and out behaviors alternate.

Take 2

You've just gotten started with your Ken Burns effects. The producer is very pleased with the results so far and encourages you to continue. Using the *Delicious Peace_v2* project as a guide, add a Ken Burns crop effect to the remaining still images. Then add transitions to the still images.

To finesse the end of this project, view the final stack of clips. You see an opportunity to crop, resize, and position the **OPENING_TITLE_alpha** and **JJ beans** clips so they appear on the screen at the same time above a background clip. One approach would be to reposition the title clip to the right, and then crop and position the **JJ beans** clip so it appears to the left of the title clip. In the next lesson, you will learn how to add a drop shadow effect to the **JJ beans** clip to make it stand out from the background.

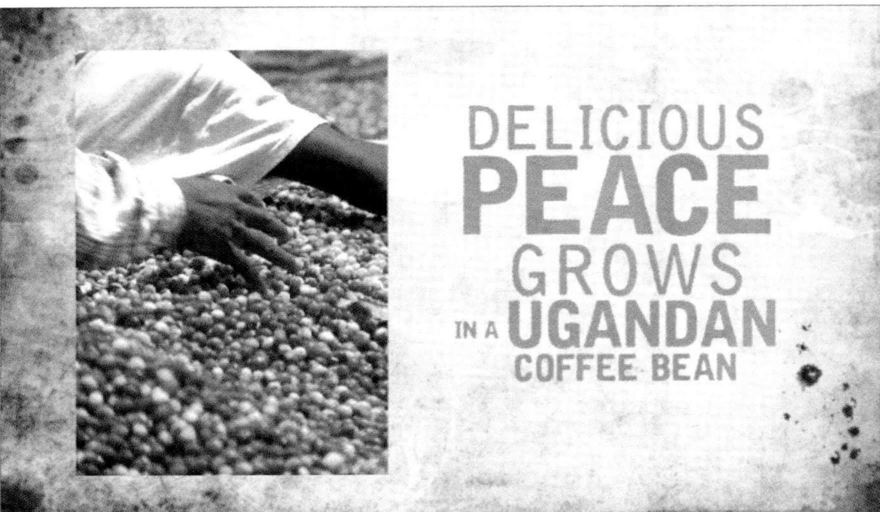

Creating Keyboard Shortcuts

A few times throughout this lesson, having a keyboard shortcut for fast access to a speed or transform command may have been helpful. In Final Cut Pro, you can make changes to the default keyboard layout in the Command Editor. As an introduction to keyboard customization, this exercise steps you through mapping a function to a keyboard shortcut.

1. To open the Command Editor, choose Final Cut Pro > Commands > Customize, or press Command-Option-K.

NOTE ▶ When open, the Command Editor floats over the Final Cut Pro interface, and any other open applications.

The Command Editor includes several sections, most notably the color-coded keyboard. Notice that the Command Groups list also incorporates color coding. For this exercise, you will search for a command by entering it in the search field. Before you begin, however, you must first duplicate the default layout so you won't overwrite any of the original shortcuts.

MORE INFO ▶ For more detail on the Command Editor and customizing the Final Cut Pro keyboard, refer to *Apple Pro Training Series: Final Cut Pro X Advanced Editing* (Peachpit Press).

2 In the upper-left corner of the window, click the Command pop-up menu, and choose Duplicate. When the rename dialog appears, enter your name to personalize the new command set, and click OK.

3 To search for a specific command, such as reverse clip, click in the search field. Enter *reverse clip*.

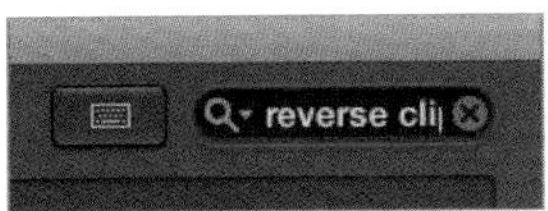

TIP When you enter a command in the search field, and then select it in the Command area, an explanation of the command appears to the right in the Command Details pane.

For this exercise, let's give this command a shortcut that includes the letter R, for Retime.

4 In the keyboard area, click the R key. Notice that on the right side of the window a list appears featuring commands that use the letter R along with the combination of modifier keys.

5 Find an empty slot, such as Command-Control-R, and drag the command from the Command list onto the shortcut's empty slot.

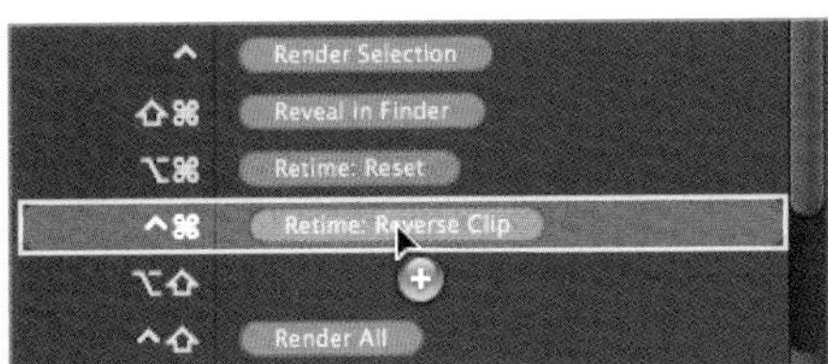

6 To save this layout with your newly created keyboard shortcut, click Save.

7 To test the new reverse clip shortcut, select any clip in the Timeline and press Command-Control-R. To undo this step and return the clip to normal, press Command-Z.

Editor's Cut

Not every project needs the kind of speed and motion adjustments you've made throughout this lesson. But now that you know what Final Cut Pro *can* do and how to do it, apply what you've learned to the *Delicious Peace* project, which you can find in the Lesson 1 folder.

Lesson Review

1. How can you apply a 50% constant speed change to a clip?
2. What indicators show that a clip's speed has been changed?
3. How can you precisely set a custom speed for a clip?
4. How do you reset a speed setting?
5. How do you create a freeze frame vs. a hold?
6. You created a slow-motion segment within a clip. How can you quickly adjust the end frame?
7. How do you automatically ramp down the speed of a clip?
8. Where do you access speed presets such as Instant Replay or Rewind?
9. How do you access the Transform controls?
10. How do you crop a clip while maintaining its aspect ratio?
11. What three crop options does Final Cut Pro offer?
12. How do you apply the Ken Burns effect?
13. How do you open the Command Editor to create custom keyboard shortcuts?

Answers

1. In the Timeline, select a clip. From the Retime pop-up menu in the toolbar, choose Slow > 50%. You can also set the speed option in the Modify menu.
2. A blue speed segment in the Timeline indicates an increased speed while an orange speed segment indicates a decreased speed.
3. From the Retime pop-up menu, choose Show Retime Editor, or press Command-R, to display the Retime Editor above the selection in the Timeline. Drag the retiming handle to set the speed you want.
4. In the Timeline, select a range, a whole clip, or a group of clips. Choose Modify > Retime > Reset Speed.
5. Move the playhead to the frame you want to freeze, and from the menu bar, choose Edit > Add Freeze Frame. To create a speed segment hold, from the Retime pop-up menu in the toolbar, choose Hold, or press Shift-H. You can also select this option in the Modify menu.

6. In the Retime Editor, click the speed percentage pop-up menu, and choose Change End Source Frame. When the tiny filmstrip icon appears, drag it left or right and watch the Viewer until you see the frame you want to use.
7. Select a clip in the Timeline, and from the Retime pop-up menu in the toolbar, choose Speed Ramp > to 0%. The clip is segmented into four parts with different speed percentages. To customize the speed ramp, drag any one of the four retiming handles to set the speed you want.
8. Choose a preset from the Retime pop-up menu in the toolbar.
9. Click the Transform button in the lower-left corner of the Viewer, or press Shift-T.
10. Select a clip in the Timeline, and click the Crop button in the lower-left corner of the Viewer, or press Shift-C. In the upper-left corner of the Viewer, click Crop. Drag the blue handles at each corner of the clip to maintain the original aspect ratio.
11. Final Cut Pro X includes trim, crop, and Ken Burns options.
12. Select a clip in the Timeline. In the Viewer, click the Crop button, and choose Ken Burns as the crop type.
13. Choose Final Cut Pro > Commands > Customize, or press Command-Option-K.

Keyboard Shortcuts

Command-Shift-2	Show/Hide the Timeline Index
Command-R	Show/Hide the Retime Editor
Command-Option-R	Reset speed to clip default
Shift-H	Create two-second hold of the frame at the playhead location
Option-F	Insert or Connect a freeze frame
Command-Option-K	Open the Command Editor
Shift-T	Activate Transform properties in the Viewer
Shift-C	Activate Crop properties in the Viewer

Time

This lesson takes approximately 60 minutes to complete.

Goals

Apply video effects

Modify effects parameters

Audition effects

Animate effects using keyframes

Apply audio effects

Understand color correction

Balance color

Use the Color Board

Match colors

Lesson **11**

Applying Effects and Enhancing Color

Applying an effect in Final Cut Pro is like putting on rose-colored glasses. You see the image in a different way than you might have imagined. Changing the look and feel of a clip is one use of effects. Another use is simply to correct some aspect of the image, perhaps to reverse the direction an actor is facing.

Similarly, Final Cut Pro includes audio effects that can be applied to creatively modify your audio clips—such as turn a normal voice into a robotic or cartoonish one—or to correct, for example, a lack of bass.

In this lesson, you will apply effects to enhance, as well as correct, your video and audio clips. You will copy and paste effects from one clip to another and animate effect parameters. Finally, you will balance, match, and manually alter the color in your Timeline clips.

Applying Video Effects

In previous lessons, you turned to the Final Cut Pro media browsers to help complete your project with transitions, sound effects, titles, and so on. In this exercise, you will explore effects in yet another browser.

Typically, you add effects as enhancements during the finishing stages of a project, after you complete all of your trims, add generators, and adjust your sound. But you may also apply an effect to correct a clip at any time throughout the editing process.

In this exercise, you will open the Effects Browser and add video effects to a few clips in the *Zero To Hero* project.

1 In the Project Library, from the Lesson Projects folder, drag the Lesson 11 project folder onto APTS FCP X. Close the Lesson Projects folder, and show the contents of the Lesson 11 folder.

   In this lesson, you will work with four projects: *I Think*, *Zero To Hero*, *Delicious Peace*, and *Delicious Peace_v3*.

2 In the Project Library, duplicate *Zero To Hero*, and rename it *Zero To Hero_BACKUP*. Then double-click the original to open it into the Timeline.

   This version of *Zero To Hero* has been altered slightly with longer clips to allow you to see applied effects as fully as possible. Because you will focus primarily on video effects, the clip appearance was adjusted to reduce the size of the audio waveforms.

You apply an effect from the Final Cut Pro Effects Browser, which contains over 200 video and audio effects.

3 To open the Effects Browser, in the toolbar, click the Effects button.

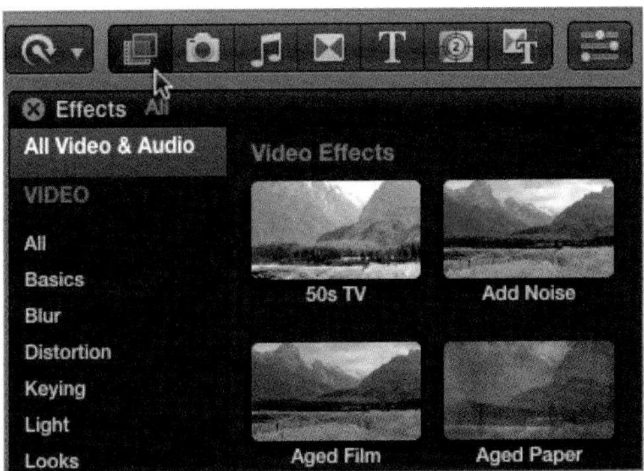

The Effects Browser is organized into eight categories each of video and audio effects. You can view all the video and audio effects, just the video or audio effects, or individual effects categories.

4 At the top of the Effects Browser category pane, click All Video & Audio. Scroll through the effects to see that a video thumbnail or audio waveform represents each effect. Under the Video section, click All. Scroll through these effects.

For this exercise, you will explore just the video categories.

The thumbnails in this browser behave somewhat differently than in other browsers. The thumbnails in other browsers contain a generic image even when skimmed. In the Effects Browser, when you select a video clip in the Timeline and then skim an effect thumbnail, that thumbnail will display your clip, which will also appear in the Viewer.

5 In the Timeline, Option-click the **Crash** clip. In the Effects Browser under Video, select the Stylize category, and then skim Aged Film.

The effect thumbnail displays the car crash with the Aged Film effect applied. In the Viewer, you see a larger demonstration of the effect.

You can apply an effect in one of two ways: Select the clip in the Timeline, and double-click the effect thumbnail to apply it; or drag the thumbnail from the browser to a clip in the Timeline. Let's add the Aged Film effect to the **Crash** clip.

NOTE ▶ As in the other media browsers, you can search for a specific effect by entering its name in the search field.

6 With the **crash** clip still selected, double-click Aged Film to apply that effect. Play the clip.

It now looks as if the crash were filmed in the days before HD cameras.

7 In the Timeline, Option-click the third clip in the project, **crowd wide**. In the Looks category, double-click Night Vision.

This effect gives the clip the appearance of looking through night vision binoculars.

With many of the effects, you can preview the results when you change the effect's primary control. You do this by Option-skimming the thumbnail in the browser. Let's look at some effects using this technique.

8 In the Timeline, Option-click the **driver prep red** clip. In the Effects Browser, select the Distortion category, and then skim Glass Block and Insect Eye to preview their effects. Then Option-skim those same effects.

In the case of the Glass Block effect, the controlling parameters—the scale and number of glass blocks—change from many tiny blocks to fewer, larger blocks. In the Insect Eye effect, Option-skimming displays more (and smaller) or fewer (and larger) hexagonal shapes overlaying the image.

Option-skimming additional effects will give you a variety of results depending on the parameter affected by the skim. With many effects, you can tell right away what the effect does and whether or not you want to use it.

It often happens that a person or an object in a shot is facing in one direction when the shot would make more visual sense if the subject were facing in the opposite direction. By applying the Flipped effect, you can literally turn the subject around to create this illusion.

9 Select the **driver prep red** clip, and make sure the Distortion category is visible. Double-click Flipped to add it to the clip. The driver in the clip now faces in the opposite direction.

TIP You may notice that Final Cut Pro is rendering the effects in the background, but you can still continue to work as the process continues.

Let's add another effect toward the start of the project.

10 In the Timeline, Option-click the second clip, **crowd ots**, and in the Blur category, double-click the Zoom blur.

This adds a swirling sort of blur to the clip. You will animate the amount of the blur later in this lesson.

You can stack multiple effects on any selected clip, but the order in which they are added to the clip is important. Let's add two effects to a single clip.

11 In the Timeline, Option-click the **army prep** clip. In the Distortion category, double-click Tinted Squares. Play the clip.

Gradient squares are superimposed over the image. Now let's add a blur effect on top of the squares.

12 With **army prep** still selected, select the Blur category, and skim the effects to preview them. Option-skim Radial to preview its main control, and then double-click to add it to the clip.

The result of adding the second effect, Radial, is to blur everything that came before, both the image and the Tinted Squares effect.

NOTE ▶ When you apply an effect from the Effects Browser to a clip in the Timeline, you are not changing the media file on your hard disk.

13 Apply the following effects on the listed clips:

- **flame out**: Stylize > Photo Recall
- **army start**: Stylize > Projector
- **Antron Brown**: Stylize > Frame

Modifying Effect Parameters

Sometimes, an effect's default settings or parameters are perfectly suitable for a project. At other times, you must modify those parameters to achieve the desired result. You can modify clips in three different areas of the interface. In the Inspector, you modify effect parameters using sliders, numeric fields, pop-up menu choices, and so on. In the Viewer, for some effects, graphic controls enable a more hands-on approach to changing an effect. And in the Timeline, you can open the Video Animation Editor to raise or lower parameter values or animate values using keyframes.

Let's begin by opening the Inspector and looking at the two effects you just applied to a single clip.

1 In the Timeline, Option-click the **army prep** clip. To open the Inspector, click the Inspector button in the toolbar, or press Command-4. Click the Video tab if it's not already selected.

The clip name and duration are at the top of the pane with the Effects section below. Any effects added to a clip appear in this section in the order they were added. Because you first added the Tinted Squares effect to the **army prep** clip, that effect appears at the top of the Effects list.

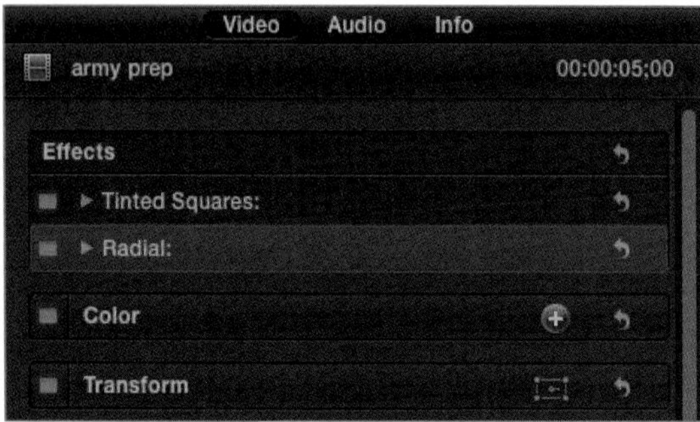

Beneath the Effects section are effects you didn't apply, such as Color, Transform, Crop, and Distort. These are the built-in transform effects you worked with in the previous lesson.

To review each effect separately, you can deselect and select the blue checkbox next to each effect.

2 To turn off the Tinted Squares effect, deselect its blue checkbox and preview the results. Turn on Tinted Squares again by selecting its checkbox, and then deselect Radial and examine the results. Finally, select Radial again, and make sure both effects are enabled.

As mentioned earlier, because you applied the Radial effect after the Tinted Squares, it not only blurs the video of the clip but also blurs the first effect you applied.

Let's compare what happens if you reverse the effects' order, putting Radial first and Tinted Squares second. You can do this by dragging the title bar of the effect up or down and releasing it in a new position.

3 Drag the Radial title bar up until it changes places with Tinted Squares. Then release the pointer.

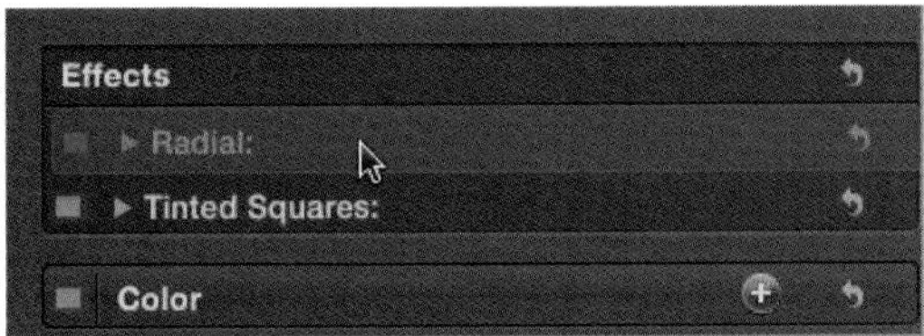

The appearance of the video clip changes dramatically. Radial, as the first effect, now blurs the video in the clip but it does not blur the Tinted Squares effect. Instead, Tinted Squares separates the blurred image into sharply defined squares.

Each effect displays a different set of parameters. Some parameters include specific details of placement or color while others, such as Tinted Squares, offer multiple versions. To change the parameters of the Tinted Squares effect, let's first disable Radial.

TIP To see the parameters of an effect, click the disclosure triangle next to the effect's name.

4 Deselect Radial. In the Tinted Squares parameters, from the Tone pop-up menu, choose B. Skim the **army prep** clip to review this change. Then from the Style pop-up menu, choose C. To preview the results of the combined effects, select the Radial effect.

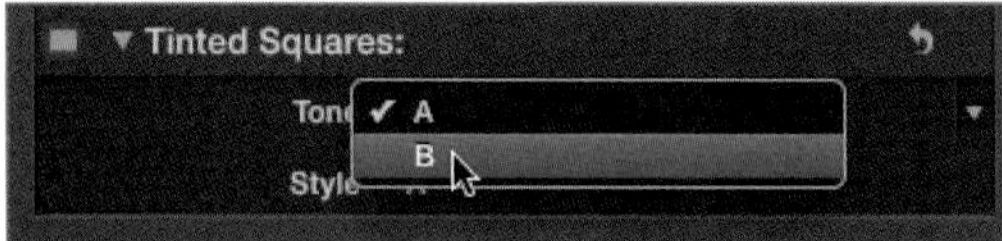

Changing the Tinted Squares parameters has given this effect a more dramatic look.

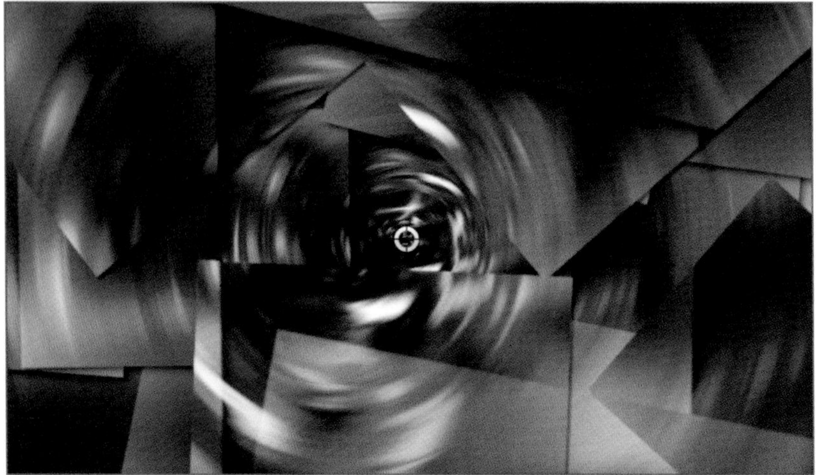

Now let's take a closer look at the Radial effect. As before, the best way to focus on the parameters of a single effect is to disable the others.

5 In the Inspector, deselect the Tinted Squares effect and enable the Radial effect, if necessary. In the Radial effect, drag the Amount slider to the far right, and then far left, all the time previewing the results. To reset this effect to its default parameters, click the Reset button to the right of the effect name.

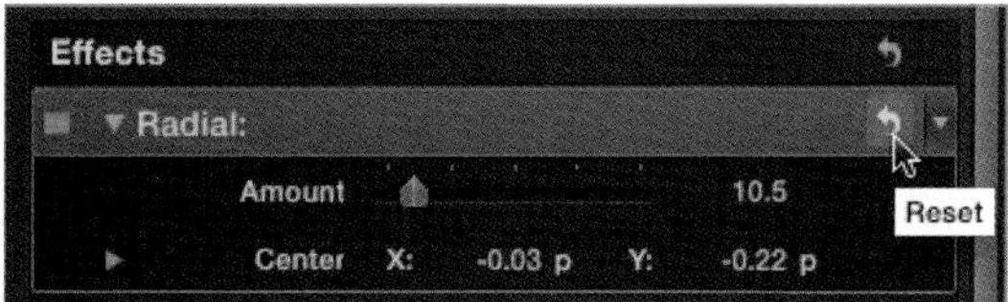

Many effects can be modified directly in the Viewer using graphic controls. To enable the onscreen controls, select the effect in the Inspector.

6 In the Inspector, select the Radial effect. In the Viewer, a center anchor point appears in the middle of the effect. Drag the control to the upper image area over the man standing, and then drag down and to the left to the yellow Army logo and release the pointer. Enable Tinted Squares to see these effects combined.

This onscreen control gives you hands-on ability to change the center point of the Radial blur.

In addition to the inspectors, Final Cut Pro provides an additional way to view and customize the effects you apply to a clip. This alternative, the Video Animation Editor, displays some clip parameters in the Timeline, including some parameters from any applied effects.

7 In the Timeline, Control-click (or right-click) the **crowd wide** clip, and from the shortcut menu, choose Show Video Animation, or press Control-V.

TIP Zoom into this area of the Timeline to see the details of the video animation display.

The Video Animation Editor appears. The title of the first effect is Night Vision: Amount. Amount refers to one of the five parameters you set in a previous step. You can change them directly in the Timeline.

TIP If the Night Vision effect doesn't appear in the Video Animation Editor, deselect Clip > Solo Animation in the menu bar. The Solo Animation command collapses the Video Animation Editor to view only one effect, which is useful when you want to save screen space.

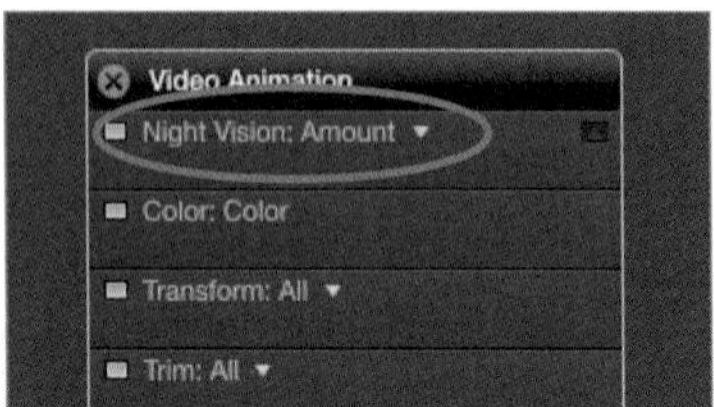

8 To view the other parameters in this effect, click the pop-up menu to the right of the effect title, and make sure Amount is selected.

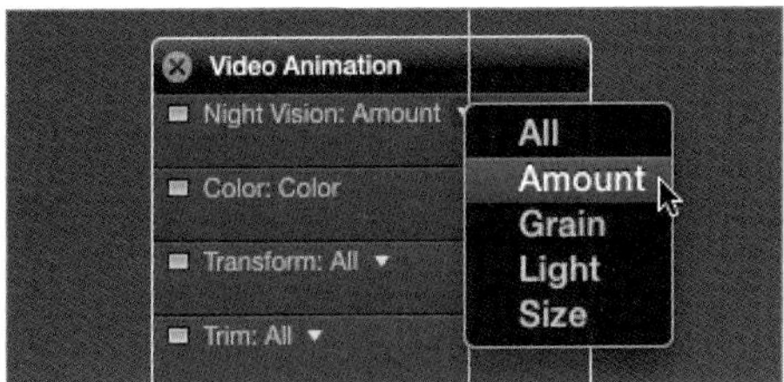

NOTE ▶ The option to change the type of scope doesn't appear in this menu. If you wanted to revert to the binoculars, for example, you would do so in the Inspector.

Some parameters with a single value, such as Amount, can be further expanded. When you do so, the parameter is represented by a black line you can drag up or down to change its value.

9 To the right of the Night Vision bar, click the maximize arrow icon and then drag the black parameter line that appears down to about 97. Exit the Video Animation Editor by clicking the close button.

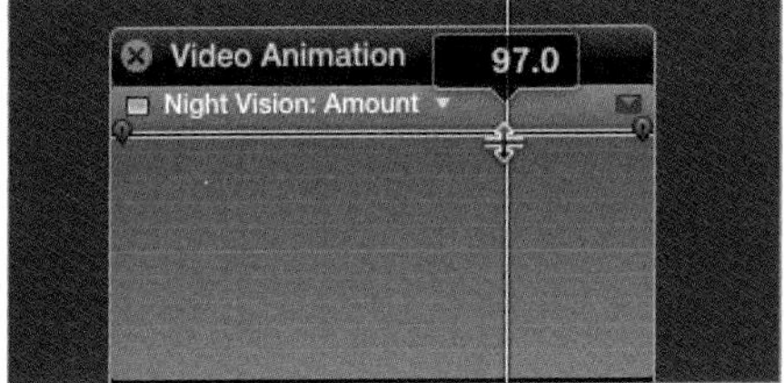

In the Viewer, the area surrounding the telescope lens lightens and you can see some of the crowd appear.

10 Now that you're comfortable applying effects, try different ways to delete one or more effects. After you delete an effect, you can press Command-Z to restore it.

- To remove a single effect, click its name in the Inspector, and press Delete.
- To remove two or more noncontiguous video effects from a clip, select one and Command-click additional ones, and press Delete.
- To remove a group of contiguous effects, click the top effect and Shift-click the bottom to select them all. Then press Delete.

NOTE ▶ Although you've applied two effects to a single clip in this exercise, you can apply any number of effects to achieve your desired result.

Copying Effects Between Clips

After you change parameters in one effect, you may find you want to apply that customized effect to another clip. Rather than apply the default effect to the new clip and readjust the same parameters, you can copy the effect from one clip and paste it to another.

In the previous exercise, you applied the Photo Recall effect to a Timeline clip. In the next few steps, you will customize that effect, copy it, and paste it to a neighboring clip. To see this in action, let's open the Video Animation Editor for the two clips.

1 In the Timeline, select both the **flame out** and the **flame out smoke** clips. Control-click one of the clips, and choose Show Video Animation from the shortcut menu, or press Control-V.

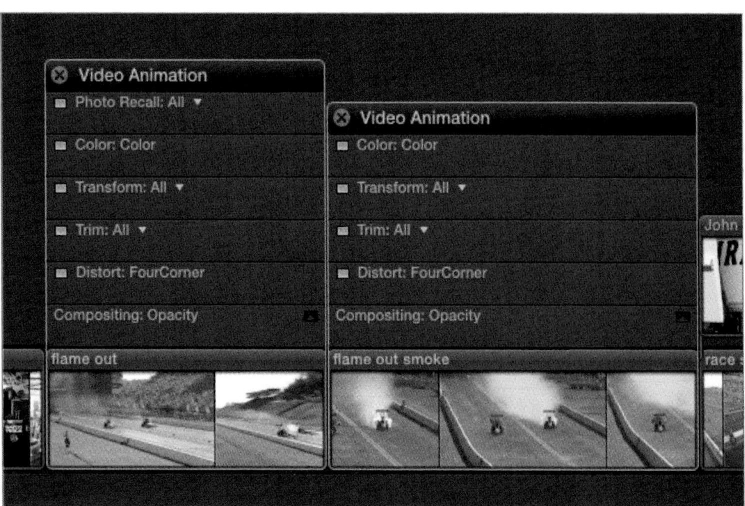

Here you can see that the Photo Recall effect does not yet exist on the **flame out smoke** clip. In the next few steps, you will copy the effect to that clip. But before you do, let's customize the effect by changing some of its parameters.

2 In the Option-click, select the **flame out** clip. In the Inspector, make the following parameter changes:

- Style: Instant
- Blur: 70
- Separation: 100

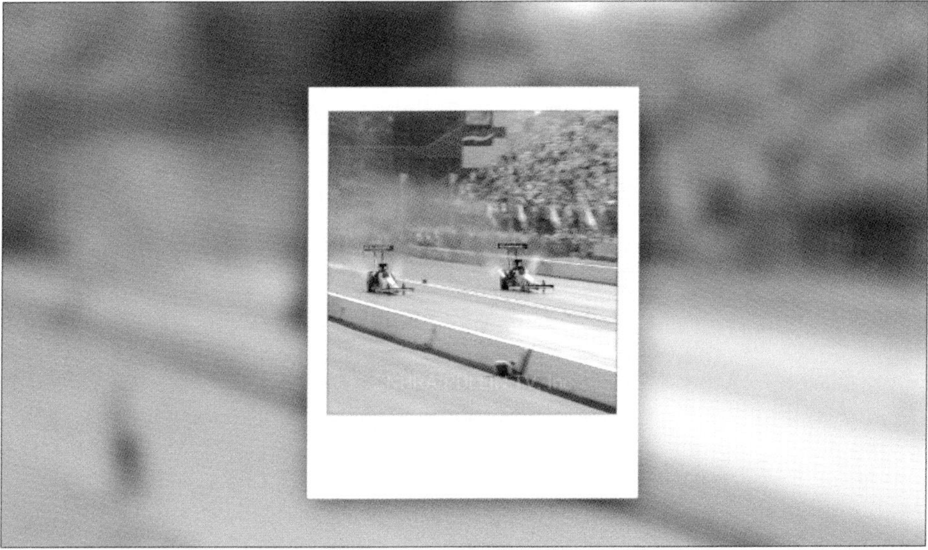

Now you will copy this clip. But rather than paste the contents of the clip, you will selectively paste only the clip's applied effect and its settings.

3 Select the **flame out** clip, and choose Edit > Copy, or press Command-C. Now Option-click the **flame out smoke** clip, and choose Edit > Paste Attributes, or press Command-Shift-V.

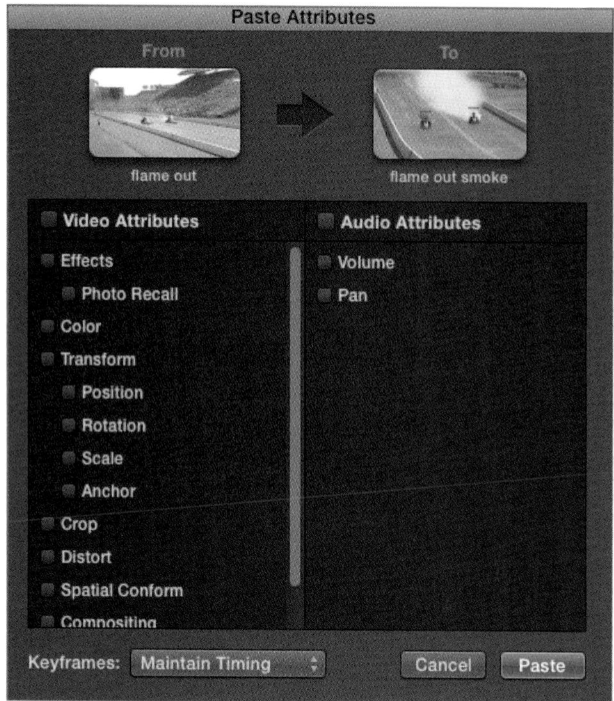

In the Paste Attributes window, you can specify exactly which properties from the copied source clip will be applied to the destination clip. For now, let's focus on the video attributes.

For video, the Paste Attributes window allows you to copy customized effects while ignoring other effects from the source clip. This is handy when, for example, you have a blur effect you want to share with another clip, but want to leave behind the Black & White effect. Also, under the Video Attributes, you'll find options to paste color correction and the transform settings.

NOTE ► In Lesson 10, you positioned images onscreen using the Transform controls. You used the Paste Attributes function to share the same clip size to stack and position a group of clips.

4 Under Video Attributes, select Photo Recall, and then click Paste.

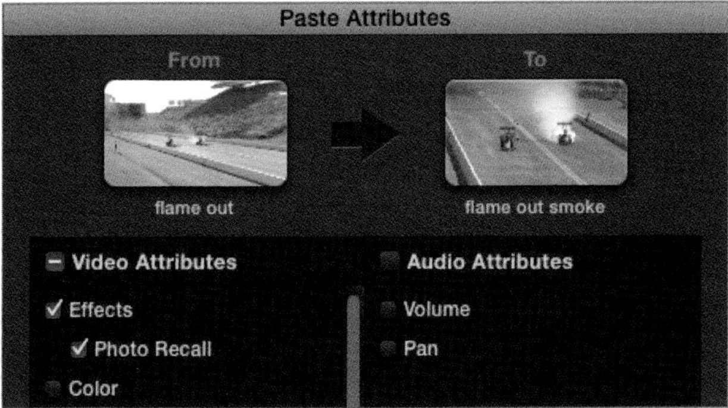

Now the same customized version of the Photo Recall effect is applied to both clips.

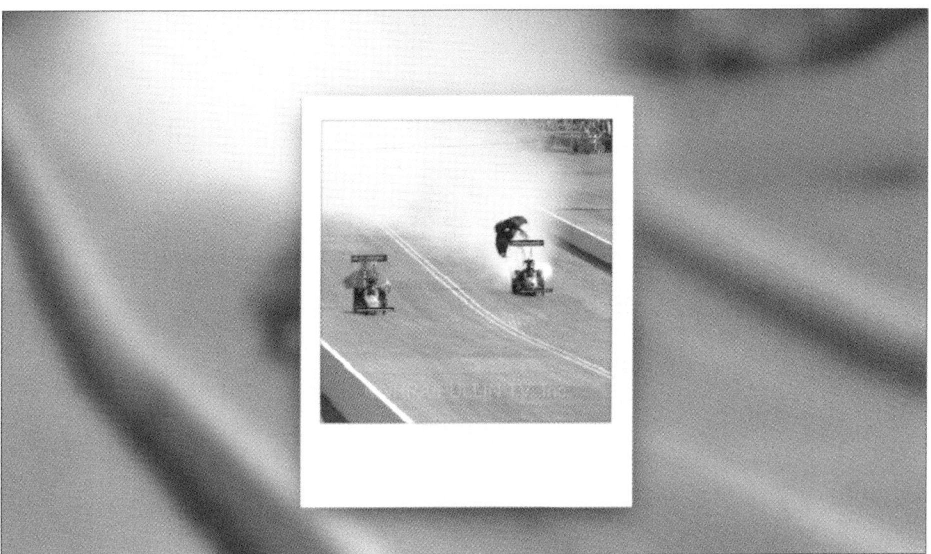

5 To close the Video Animation Editors for both clips, select the **flame out** and **flame out smoke** clips, and press Control-V. You can also click the close button (X) in each Video Animation Editor.

Take 2

The director wants to set the racers apart from the racing action clips. He sees the Frame effect you added to the **Antron Brown** clip, but he isn't impressed. He doesn't realize that effect has several types of frames from which to choose. Take a moment to review the Frame types on the **Antron Brown** clip, pick your favorite, copy the clip, and paste the effect to the other racers. You can paste to a group of selected clips at one time.

Auditioning and Animating Effects

With so many effects, each with a variety of parameters, you may want to preview several options before choosing the best effect for your clip. Rather than apply an effect, delete it, apply another, delete it, you have an easier way to preview effects.

In Final Cut Pro, you can audition effects in the Timeline as you auditioned clips in previous lessons. In this case, you will audition the original clip from the Timeline and duplicates of clips you will create in the Audition window. You can apply an effect to each of the duplicates and navigate from one to the other to see which you would prefer.

1 In the Timeline, play the **JF holds trophy** connected clip. To audition effects on this clip, select the clip, and choose Clip > Audition > Duplicate as Audition, or press Option-Y.

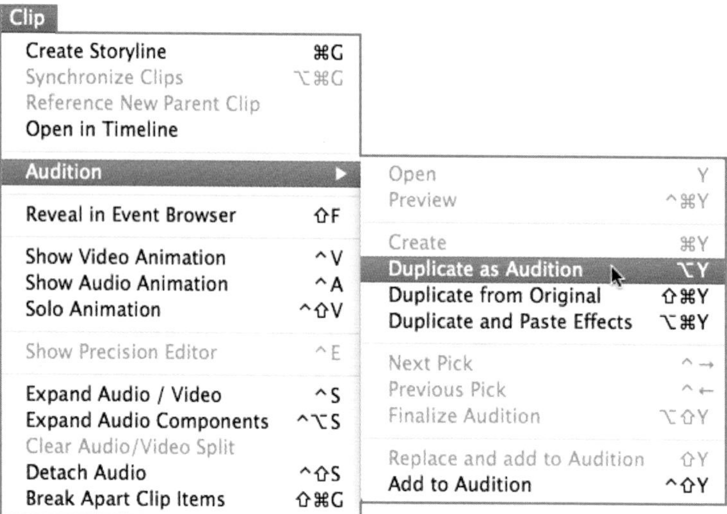

The Timeline clip is now duplicated and placed in an Audition window. In the Timeline, the clip name displays the duplicate clip name: **JF holds trophy - copy 1**.

You can apply effects to a clip inside the Audition window.

2 To open the Audition window, Control-click the **JF holds trophy** clip, and from the shortcut menu, choose Audition > Open Audition, or click the Audition icon next to the clip name.

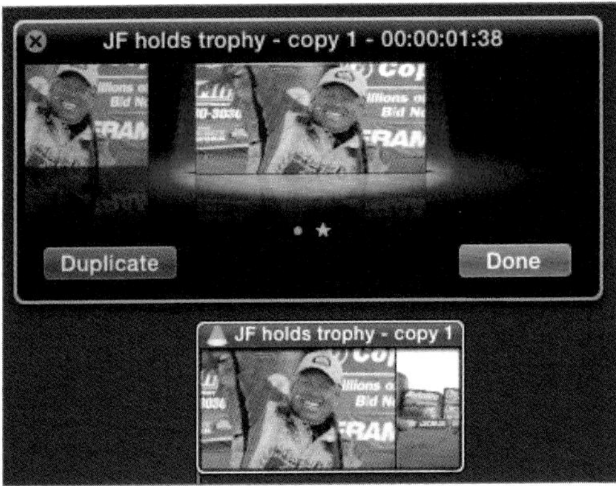

The Audition window opens with the newly created duplicate selected. If you want to audition several effects, you will need to create more copies of the original clip. You can duplicate the clip directly in the Audition window.

3 In the Audition window, click the Duplicate button twice. Notice the dots and star beneath the thumbnail.

You now have the original clip represented by the first dot beneath the thumbnail; the first duplicate clip, which is the current pick (represented by a star); and two alternates (third and fourth dots).

Now you can navigate to each alternate clip and apply a different effect.

TIP ▶ As with auditions created using clips from the Event Browser, you navigate through the Audition window by pressing the Right and Left Arrow keys, or clicking the thumbnails to the sides of the pick. You can also scroll through the audition thumbnails.

4 Navigate to the second thumbnail, the pick of the audition, and in the Distortion category, double-click Water Pane. Remember, to see the effect in the Viewer, you must skim through that thumbnail in the Audition window, and not the clip in the Timeline.

NOTE ▶ When you move your pointer out of an alternate thumbnail in the Audition window, the Viewer reverts to the original clip.

5 Navigate to the second alternate, and apply Stylize > Camcorder. Navigate to the third alternate, and apply Style > Bad TV. Skim through the various effect options in the Audition window.

NOTE ▶ As you navigate through the audition clips, a fresh Inspector window appears with each alternate displaying the alternate's effect.

You now have three effects applied to the same clip and can navigate through each one to see whether you prefer one of the three effects you just added, or no effect at all. Let's use the Water Pane effect.

6 Select the alternate with the Water Pane effect, and click Done. Play the clip in the Timeline. Then select the clip and look at the effect in the Inspector.

The Water Pane effect has several interesting parameters worth exploring. The default overlay appears as a vignette with soft borders. You can adjust the Size and Falloff values of the vignette using the onscreen controls in the Viewer. The sliders in the Inspector will reflect the changes you make in the Viewer. Let's change two of the Inspector parameters.

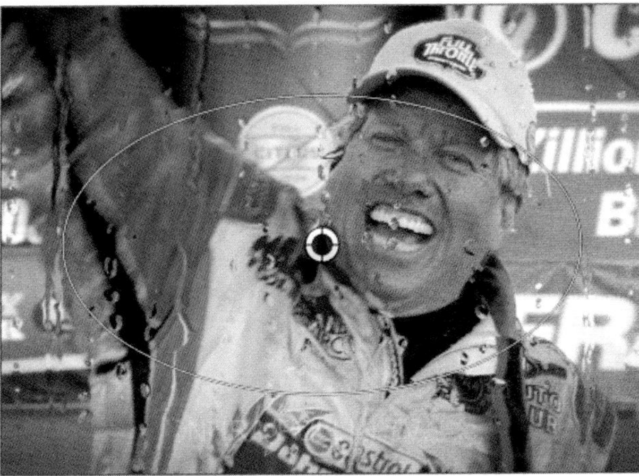

TIP Within the Stylize category, you will find a stand-alone vignette effect. This effect was originally applied to the entire *Zero to Hero* final project to give every clip the look of being in the spotlight.

7 With the **JF holds trophy** clip selected, in the Inspector, drag the Refraction Amount slider to 100, and change Refraction Softness to zero. With this adjustment, the raindrops appear more boldly outlined.

TIP ▶ With an Audition window open, if you move to a different project, the window remains open. This allows you to compare your current clip and its alternates to other clips in other projects.

Effects don't have to appear static or unchanged throughout an entire clip. Many parameters can be changed or animated over time. Television shows often cut in and out of a segment or episode by starting the scene in black and white, and moments later, transforming to full color saturation.

Similar to animating volume, Final Cut Pro provides built-in fade handles on certain effect parameters. These handles can be adjusted quickly for a smooth effect.

NOTE ▶ You can also add keyframes manually as you did when correcting audio problems in Lesson 8.

8 In the Timeline, play the **crash** clip to review the Aged Film effect you applied in a previous exercise. Then Control-click the clip, and from the shortcut menu, choose Show Video Animation.

At the top of the editor is the parameter Aged Film: Amount. You will use this parameter to animate the Aged Film effect.

9 On the right end of the Aged Film animation bar, click the Maximize button, and move your pointer into the adjustment area beneath the parameter value line. Look closely at the far right and left for the fade handles positioned at either end of the parameter line.

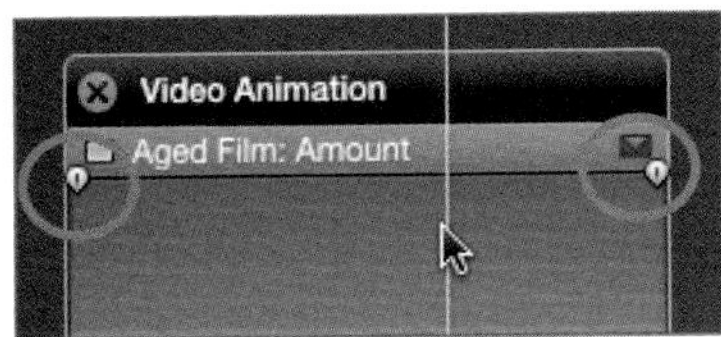

As when creating an audio fade, these fade handles allow you to ramp the parameter's values. Let's see what it looks like to fade out this effect during the second half of the clip.

10 Drag the end fade handle to the left toward the middle of the parameter value line. Watch the information box to see when you've moved about two seconds from the end of the clip, and then release the pointer. Play this clip.

By adjusting the fade handles on this parameter, Final Cut Pro ramps the Amount parameter down to the end of the clip.

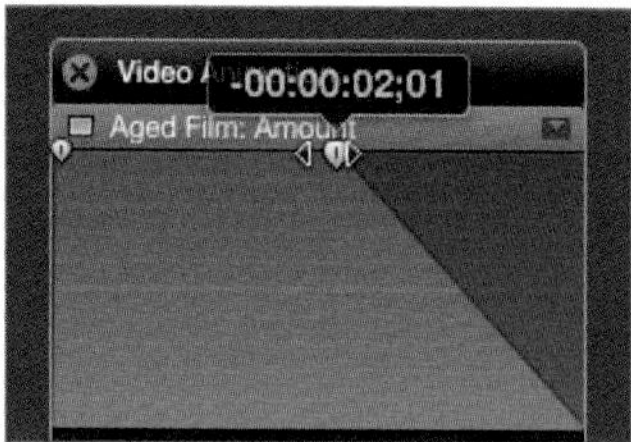

But what if you want to fade out the Aged Film effect sooner and maintain the clip's pristine HD quality before leaving it? To do this, you must manually add keyframes to the parameter value line. Although this approach requires a few extra steps, manually adding keyframes gives you the most control when animating parameters.

For this effect, you will need to create two keyframes. You will place the first one in the middle of the clip, and the second one between that keyframe and the end of the clip.

11 Press Command-Z to undo the previous move. To set the first keyframe, position the playhead onto the Aged Film: Amount parameter line around the middle of the **crash** clip. Option-click the parameter line, or press Option-K. To set the second keyframe, position the playhead over the parameter value line between the first keyframe and end of the clip, and press Option-K.

NOTE ▶ The first keyframe is where the Amount parameter begins to change, and the second keyframe is where the change ends.

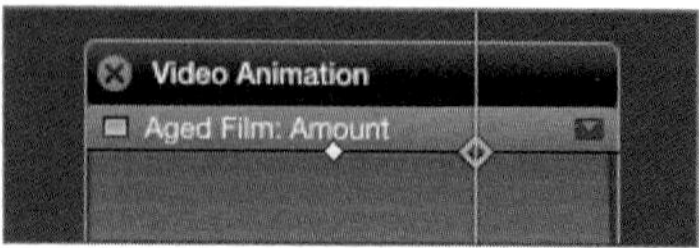

Notice that the selected or active keyframe appears yellow, while all other keyframes appear white.

12 To reduce the Aged Film effect to zero at this location, drag the second keyframe all the way down, and play the clip to see the results. Exit the Video Animation Editor.

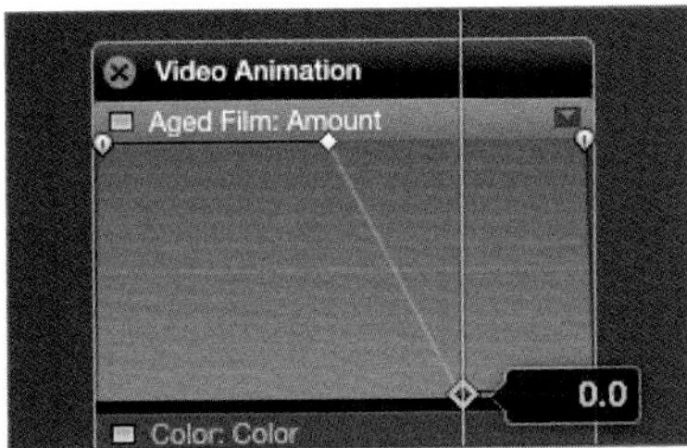

TIP With current keyframes displayed as white diamonds, any keyframes previously applied to another parameter will appear dark gray. Double diamonds indicate two parameters keyframed at the same point.

Take 2

The producer wants to kick off this project with a visual bang! You've already applied a Zoom blur to the **crowd ots** clip. But to really grab the audience's attention, you suggest increasing the amount of the blur and animating the center point to move from right to left across the screen to follow the cars racing by. Experiment with animating the effect to realize the director's vision.

Applying Audio Effects

Once the audio clips of your project are mixed, they often go unnoticed until the final output. But at times you will need to improve or correct a clip's sound or add an audio effect before putting the project to bed.

In this exercise, you will add different audio effects to the narration of actor Ed O'Neill in the *Delicious Peace* project. Audio effects are applied in the same way as video effects so you are already familiar with the process.

1 In the Project Library, duplicate the *Delicious Peace* project and add *BACKUP* to its name, and then open the original project into the Timeline. Play the project.

   While some audio effects are added to make serious corrections, some are just fun to use. It's time for fun.

2 In the Effects Browser, scroll down to the Audio section, and click the Voice category.

   When you scroll in any Audio category, you will find that Final Cut effects are listed first. Further down are those effects derived from Logic. At the bottom, you will find the Mac OS X effects. In this exercise, you will work with the Final Cut audio effect named Robot.

   As is the case with most browser items, you can also preview audio effects. To preview an audio effect, select the clip in the Timeline and the audio thumbnail in the browser. Then play the thumbnail by pressing the Spacebar. The effect will loop until you stop playback.

   NOTE ▸ The Ed O'Neill narration clips are labeled VO for voiceover, followed by a number.

3 In the Timeline, select the first voiceover clip, **VO_10**. In the Voices category, in the Final Cut section, select Robot. With the pointer placed over the effect, press the Spacebar to start and stop the preview.

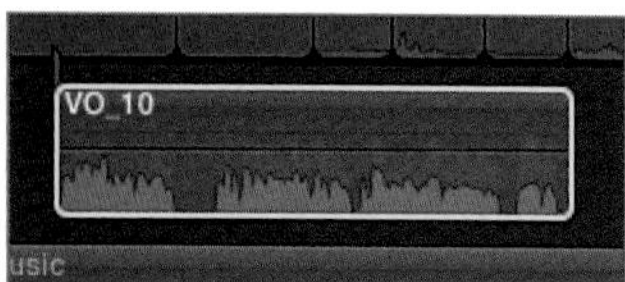

Ed O'Neill's voice is transformed to give it a robotic quality. You may apply an audio effect just as you applied a video effect, by dragging the effect to the clip, or double-clicking the effect thumbnail.

4 With **VO_10** still selected, double-click the Robot thumbnail to apply it to the clip, and then play that portion of the project.

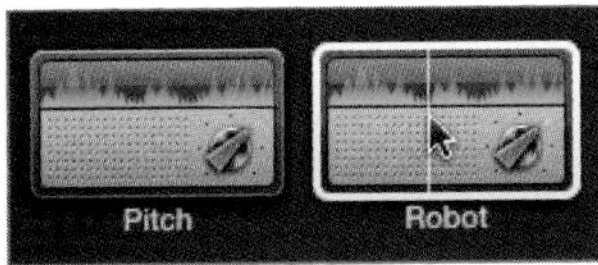

Like video effects, audio effects have parameters that can be modified in the Inspector. Some parameters offer preset options you can choose from a pop-up menu, while others require you to enter a numeric value or drag a slider.

5 With the **VO_10** clip selected, in the Inspector Effects section, from the Preset pop-up menu, choose Android. Drag the Amount slider to 9.0. Play the result.

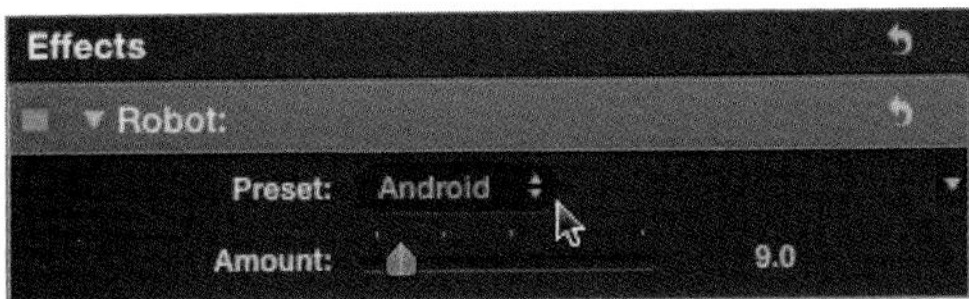

You can copy and paste audio effects from one clip to another. Let's copy the new effect to the next audio clip, **VO_09**. This time you'll use the Copy and Paste Effects commands. Paste Effects is a fast way to paste all the attributes of the source clip to a destination clip.

6 In the Timeline, select **VO_10**, and press Command-C. Select **VO_09**, and choose Edit > Paste Effects, or press Command-Option-V. Play the **VO_09** clip.

Let's find more effects from the Voice category to preview and apply to the narration.

7 Select **VO_11** in the Timeline, and then select the Cartoon Animals effect in the Effects Browser. With the pointer over the effect, press the Spacebar to preview the effect with this clip. To apply the effect to the selected clip, double-click the effect.

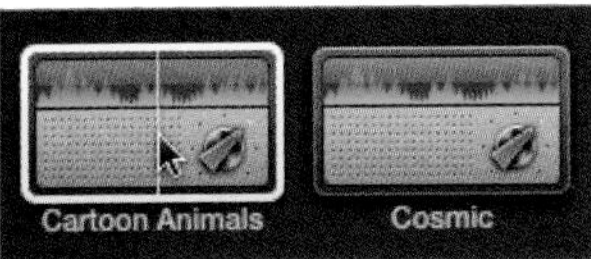

NOTE ▶ As you preview audio effects, keep in mind that Final Cut Pro will preview the effect beneath the pointer in the Effects Browser.

8 In the Audio inspector, from the Preset pop-up menu, choose Squirrel. Then play the clip in the Timeline. Change to the Mouse preset, and play the clip again.

A commonly used effect is Telephone, which simulates a voice heard over phone wires. It's a staple of film and television. Let's apply this effect to another voiceover clip in the project.

9 Select the final voiceover clip in the project, **VO_10**. In the browser, in the Distortion category, select Telephone, and press Spacebar to preview it. To apply it to the selected clip, double-click the effect. Play the clip.

It sounds as if Ed O'Neill is an on-the-scene reporter calling in his narration via a phone line. Let's change some of the parameters in the Audio inspector.

10 In the Telephone section, from the Preset pop-up menu, choose Cellphone Earpiece. Change the Amount to 25, and play the clip.

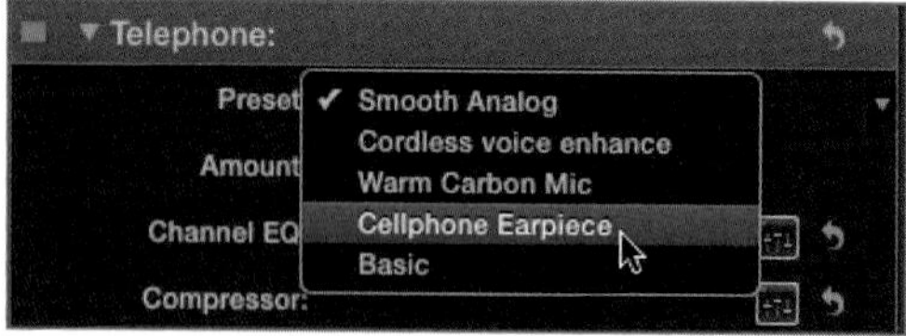

NOTE ▶ In the Timeline, you can access the Audio Animation Editor to delete or animate audio effects, just as you accessed the Video Animation Editor earlier in the lesson.

Deleting audio effects is just like deleting video effects. Select and delete one or more effects in the Inspector, or select and delete effects from the Audio Animation Editor.

Take 2

The producer of "Pluto-The Wannabe Planet" wants some ideas on how to make an alien character's voice sound interesting and convincing, especially when the character is on a spaceship. What other effect could you add to the Robot effect you've already applied? Let the Ed O'Neill voiceover clips stand in for the alien character and experiment with adding a second audio effect to the first clip. (Hint: You might try Spaces > Spaceship.)

Enhancing Color in Final Cut Pro

While some productions have the time to meticulously set and adjust lights to ensure a high-quality video image, others must shoot on the fly with very little, if any, camera setup or lighting support. In these situations, you often have to capture the existing media and worry later about improving its video quality.

With the color enhancements in Final Cut Pro, however, "fixing it in post" has gotten a lot easier. You have three primary ways to improve image color. The first option can be used early in the editing workflow when you allow Final Cut Pro to automatically color balance your clips on import, as you did in Lesson 2. Second, you can easily match color balance from one clip you like to another. And finally, you can manually adjust color attributes using the Final Cut Pro Color Board. In addition, you can apply a variety of color presets to your project.

▶ Understanding Color Basics

Video is an additive color system, meaning that all colors added together create white. So your reference to what is white in your image is very important. For example, if you white-balance your camera for indoor lighting, and then shoot outdoors, the outdoor footage won't be color balanced because the camera's indoor reference to white will not match the white in the outdoor scene. If your white balance is off, the overall balance of colors in the image will also be off. When you have too much of any one color in your video, it's referred to as a color cast.

One aspect of color is the *hue* or actual color of the image, which is always a mix of the three primary video colors: red, green, and blue. Combinations of any two of these colors produce a set of secondary colors: yellow, magenta, and cyan.

Continues on next page

Understanding Color Basics *(continued)*

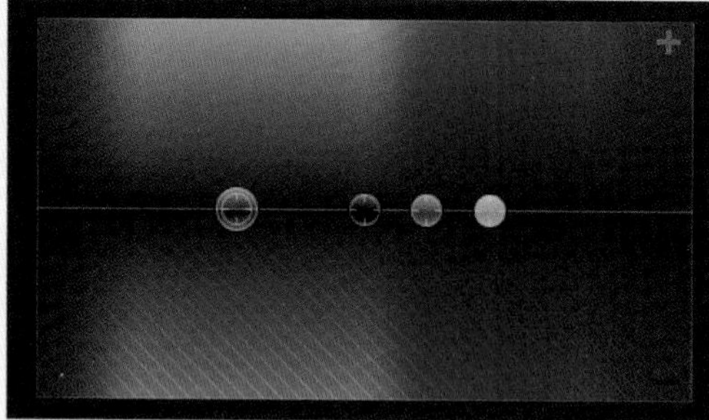

Final Cut Pro's Color Board for Controlling Hue

The amount of color that's present in a clip or image is referred to as *saturation.* For all colors, 0 percent saturation shows white. If red is fully saturated at 100 percent the result is fire engine red. Decrease the saturation to 50 percent and you will get rose. Decrease it to 25 percent and you will get pink. Each of these colors is part of the red family in that they share the same hue or color but not the same level of saturation.

Images have varying amounts of lightness and darkness, sometimes referred to as brightness or luminance levels, that can be adjusted similar to a camera's exposure settings. In Final Cut Pro X, you can raise or lower the amount of brightness for specific pixel groupings, such as darker pixels or shadows, midtones, or brighter pixels or highlights.

1 In the Project Library, from the Lesson 11 folder, open the *I Think* project. In the Timeline, skim through each clip and notice a yellow color cast.

The yellow cast in these clips indicates the camera was not white balanced before shooting. One of the easiest color corrections to make is to have Final Cut Pro balance the color within a clip.

2 In the Timeline, Option-click the first clip, **subway passing**. In the Video inspector, in the Color section, notice that Balance is not enabled, and that the current Balance status is Not Analyzed. To color balance this clip, select the Balance checkbox.

With Balance enabled, you instantly see the results of the analysis: the yellow color cast is successfully removed from the selected clip, which returns to a more natural-looking color.

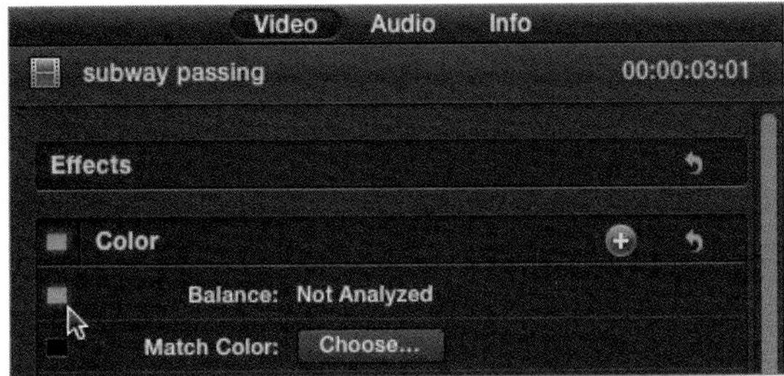

Rather than select each clip individually and select Balance, you can select the effect for a group of clips. And rather than select Balance in the Inspector, you can toggle the results in a menu.

3 To select the remaining clips in this project, drag a selection rectangle from the third clip to the last clip. To enable the color balance on these clips, choose Modify > Balance Color, or press Command-Option-B. Skim through the clips again and notice that the yellow color cast has been removed on every clip.

TIP When you want Final Cut Pro to analyze and fix color balance on clips after they've been imported, select the source clips in the Event, and choose Modify > Analyze and Fix.

While the automatic color balance has certainly improved these clips, you may want to make additional manual adjustments. You can do so in the Final Cut Pro Color Board.

4 In the Timeline, Option-click **book shelves**. To access the Color Board, in the toolbar, click the Enhancements button, and from the menu, choose Show Color Board.

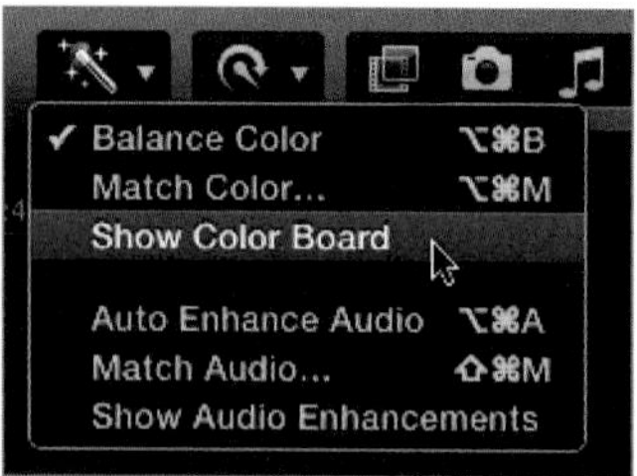

As described in the "Understanding Color Basics" sidebar, you can adjust three color components in your clips: hue, saturation, and brightness. These components are represented in the Color Board by Color, Saturation, and Exposure buttons. You control or correct one component at a time. Let's start with Exposure.

TIP The professional workflow for adjusting color is to always start with the luminance or exposure levels, and then move on to color and saturation, in that order.

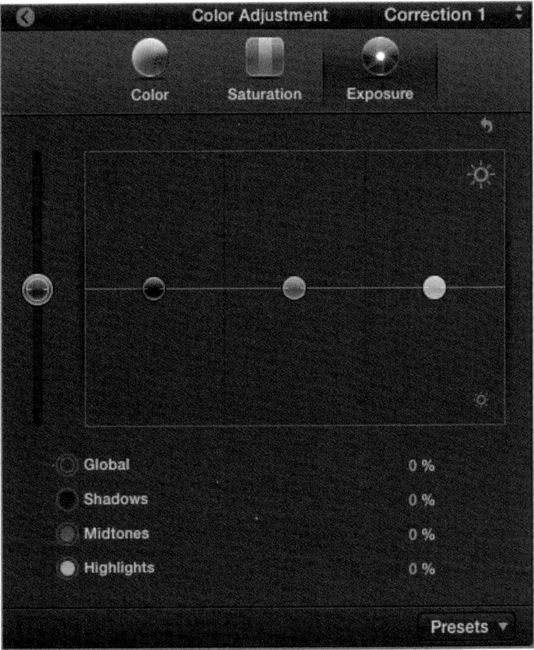

To better see the results of your color changes, you can use the video scopes, which allow you to view or monitor your image in ways that help you measure such image aspects as luminance and chrominance.

5 To open the video scopes, choose Window > Viewer Display > Show Video Scopes, and then adjust the width of the Event Browser, if necessary, to see a larger representation of the scopes. In the upper right of the window, from the Settings pop-up menu, choose Waveform.

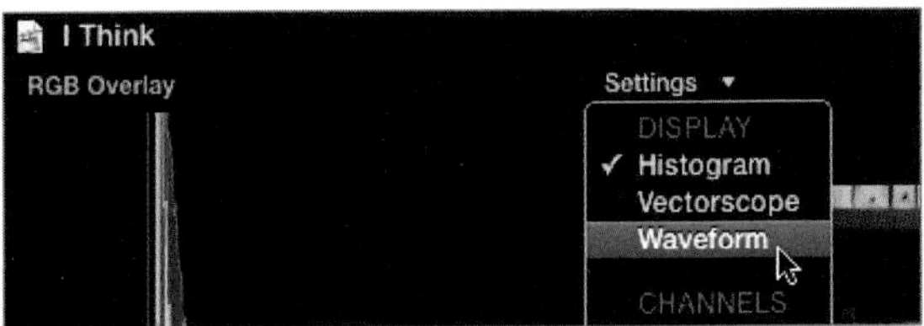

TIP With video scopes open in the Viewer, you can also adjust the boundary between the scopes and the image to make one or the other smaller or larger.

The Waveform Monitor shows the brightness or luminance values of the current frame. Broadcast standards specify a maximum luminance level of 100 percent for any video, as displayed in the Waveform Monitor.

TIP Even when your projects aren't intended for broadcast, it is still good practice to use the video scopes to monitor the image levels.

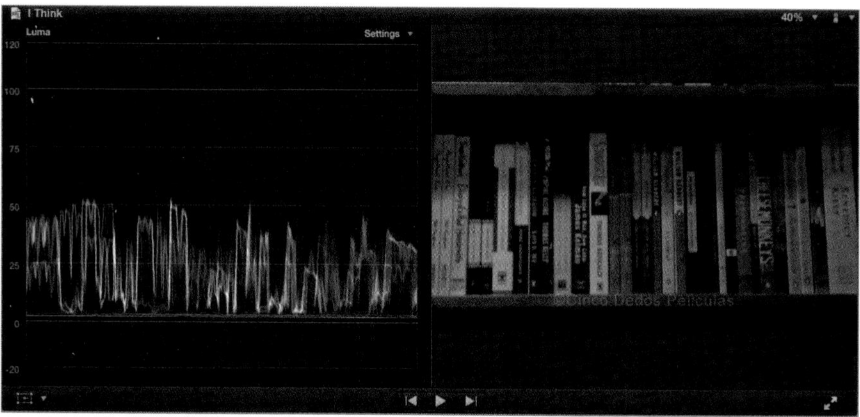

Now that the waveform display is in place, let's change the brightness for all the pixels in the image at one time by making a global adjustment.

6 In the Color Board, click the Exposure button, and drag the Global control on the far left slider all the way up and then down to raise and then lower the luminance of the clip. Notice the changes in the Global percentage and the other control percentages. In the waveform, watch as the pixels of the image change.

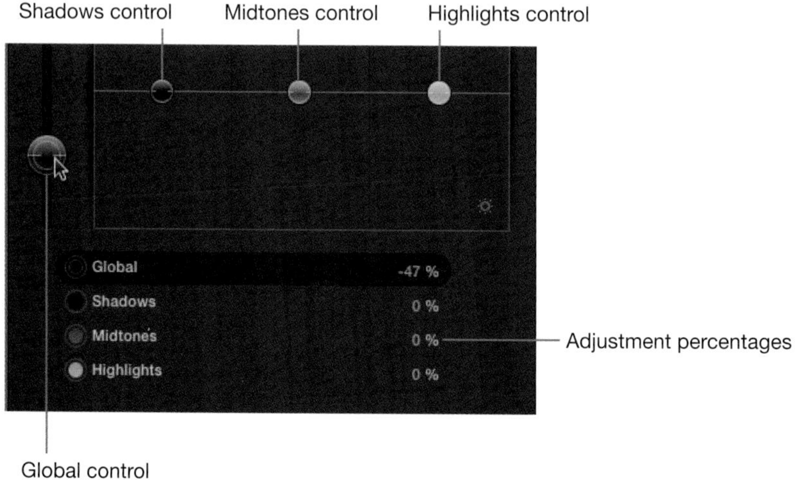

The Color Board has four sets of controls that change or alter pixel color and brightness:

- **Global**: Changes all the pixels in the image
- **Shadows**: Changes the darkest pixels of the images
- **Midtones**: Changes the midrange pixels of the image
- **Highlights**: Changes the brightest pixels of the image

Sometimes making a global change will correct an image to your liking. But with Exposure, you typically need to change the individual pixel ranges. In this image, changing the image midtones will improve it.

7 To reset the global change you just made, select the Global slider control, and then press Delete, or click the Exposure Reset button. Then drag the Midtones control down to about –6%, and play the **book shelves** clip.

TIP Adjusting the midtones is a good way to bring out more detail in an image that is dark or underexposed, or to improve a washed-out, overexposed image.

Another way to improve this clip is to raise the saturation level so that the clip looks more colorful. Rather than adjust saturation in any particular group of pixels, you will make a global saturation change.

8 In the Color Board, click the Saturation button. In the Saturation control area, drag the Global slider to about 22%. With increased saturation, this clip stands out more.

When you have some clips in the project that are properly corrected along with others that still require correction, you can utilize the Match Color function. You choose a clip that needs correcting and then skim to a frame in a different clip with a color balance you want to match. You can preview any number of match options before selecting one.

9 In the Timeline, skim to a later frame in the **corner reveal** clip, and Option-click to set the playhead at this location. To return to the Video inspector, click the return button in the upper-left corner of the Color Board. In the Color section, select the Match Color checkbox.

NOTE ▶ When you first select the Match Color checkbox, only half of the box is solid. When you apply a match to this clip, it turns solid.

When you select the Match Color function, the Match Color window appears with a two-up display. The window instructs you to skim clips and click to preview the color balance of that frame applied to the target image to the right.

10 Skim different clips and click various frames to preview the color changes on the target clip. Then click a frame in the **book shelves** clip, and click Apply Match. To see the clip with and without the new color adjustment applied, in the Inspector, select and deselect the Match Color checkbox.

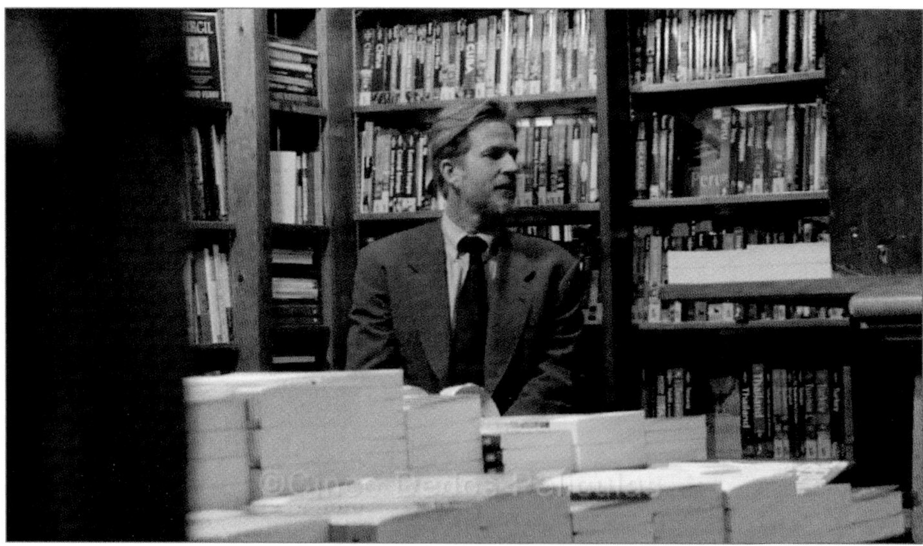

TIP To move to the Color Board from the Video inspector, click the Show Correction button to the right of Correction 1. To add another correction to a clip, click the Add Correction button in the upper right of the Color section, next to the Reset button.

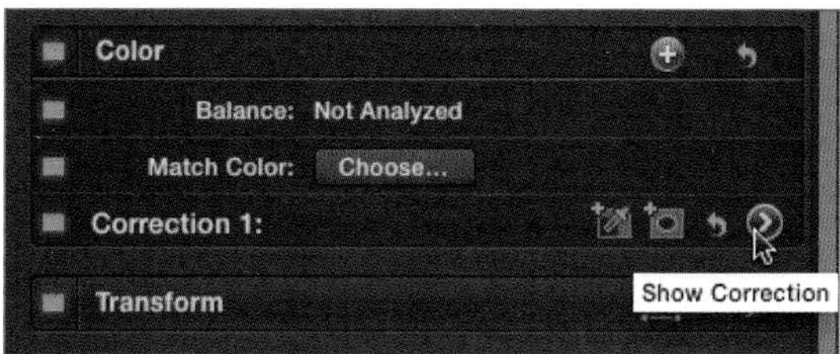

TIP You can also select a clip and choose one of several color presets found in the Presets pop-up menu in the lower-right corner of the Color Board pane.

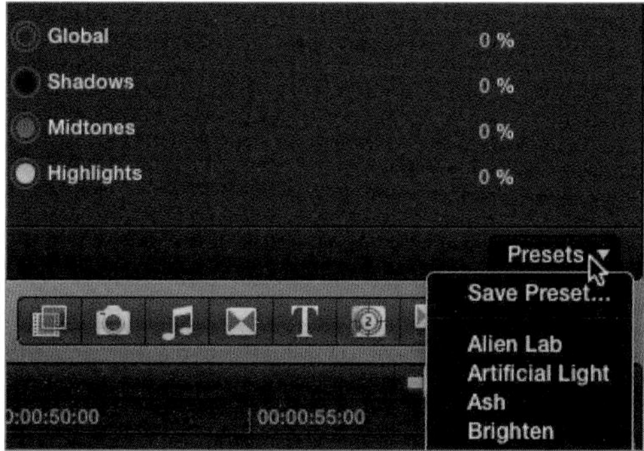

Editor's Cut

Although applying effects isn't hard, getting comfortable with the parameters and learning to animate them may take some time. To help develop your skills in this area, from the Project Library, open the *Delicious Peace_v3* project. Review the last stack of clips at the end of the project. Then adjust the drop shadow already applied to the **JJ beans** clip. Use either the Inspector or the Video Animation Editor to make changes.

TIP You can find the Drop Shadow effect in the Effects Browser > Stylize section.

Lesson Review

1. Describe two ways to apply a video or audio effect.
2. How do you view and disable effects applied to Timeline clips?
3. How do you modify the priority of effects applied to project clips?
4. How do you delete one or more effects from a project clip?
5. How do you copy a customized effect from one clip to one or more clips in the Timeline?
6. How do you activate the onscreen controls in the Viewer to modify an effect?
7. How do you create duplicates of a clip so you can audition multiple versions of effects?
8. How can you quickly fade an effect in or out?
9. How do you add keyframes in the Video Animation Editor?
10. How do you automatically color balance multiple clips at once?
11. How do you ensure that all scenes depicting the same location have the same color balance?

Answers

1. Select one or more clips in the Timeline. Then, in the Effects Browser, double-click an effect thumbnail. You may also drag an effect from the Effects Browser to modify one clip at a time.
2. Select the clip in the Timeline. Click the Inspector button in the toolbar, or press Command-4. Click the Video tab, if necessary. To disable an effect, deselect the blue checkbox next to the effects you don't want to view.
3. With the clip selected in the Timeline, in the Video inspector, drag the effect title bar above or below another effect.
4. To remove a single effect, click its name in the Inspector, and press Delete. To remove contiguous effects, click the top effect, Shift-click the bottom effect, and press Delete. To remove two or more noncontiguous effects, click one effect, Command-click the additional effects, and press Delete.
5. Select the clip with the custom effect, and choose Edit > Copy, or press Command-C. Now select one or more clips in the Timeline, and choose Edit > Paste Attributes to select from a list of parameters and effects that are on the source clip.
6. Option-click the clip in the Timeline, and then in the Video inspector, select the effect you want to adjust. Onscreen controls will appear in the Viewer that allow you to adjust parameters such as center point.

7. Select the clip in the Timeline, and choose Clip > Audition > Duplicate as Audition, or press Option-Y. Then click the Audition spotlight next to the clip name to open the Audition window.
8. In the Video Animation Editor, click the disclosure triangle to expand the parameter you want to adjust. Fade handles appear at either end of a parameter line. Drag right or left to fade an effect in or out.
9. In the Video Animation Editor, click the Maximize button to expand the parameter you want to adjust. Position your pointer on the parameter line where you want to start or end a change, and then Option-click the parameter line, or press Option-K, to create a keyframe.
10. Select the clips in the Timeline, and choose Modify > Balance Color, or press Command-Option-B.
11. In the Timeline, Option-click to set the playhead at a frame you want to correct. In the Color section of the Video inspector, select the Match Color checkbox. Find a frame with the color balance you want to match, and click to preview that balance applied to the selected clip. To match the current color balance, click Apply Match in the Match Color window.

Keyboard Shortcuts

Command-4	Open Inspector
Command-6	Go to Color Board
Command-7	Show/hide video scopes
Command-C	Copy
Command-Option-B	Balance color on selected clip(s)
Control-A	Show/hide Audio Animation Editor
Control-V	Show/hide Video Animation Editor
Option-Y	Duplicate as audition
Command-Shift-V	Paste attributes
Y	Open audition

12

Time — This lesson takes approximately 75 minutes to complete.

Goals

- Adjust audio peaks
- Conform video levels for broadcast
- Share a Master file
- Export an audio file
- Publish to iTunes and Apple devices
- Publish to YouTube and other video sharing sites
- Modify destinations in the Share menu
- Export a still frame
- Burn to discs and create a disk image (.img) file
- Back up projects and Events

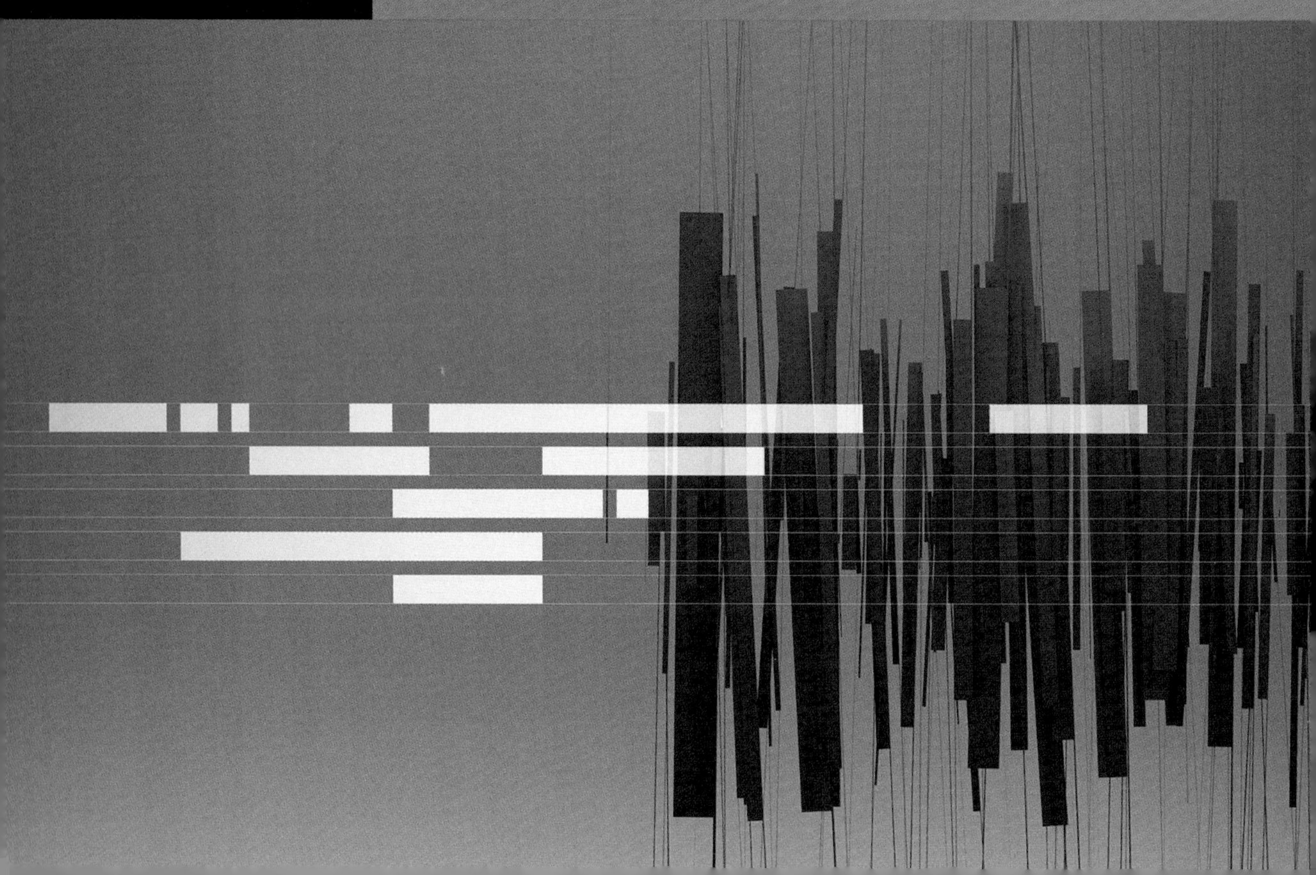

Lesson 12

Sharing Your Project

In previous lessons, you worked closely with clips, from refining edit placement to applying transitions and effects. Now with your project finally finished, you're prepared to share it with others. Whether you want to distribute your movie for playback on a mobile device, submit it to a network, or publish it to YouTube, the export process begins with the Final Cut Pro Share command.

Before you send your movie on its way, however, take a 10,000-foot view of your project to make sure the video and audio meet the highest standards. This final check isn't just for "good looks," although your project's appearance is important. It's also to ensure that your project meets the broadcast standards for audio and video. Meeting those standards is not just a legal broadcast requirement, it also gives your project the professional polish it deserves.

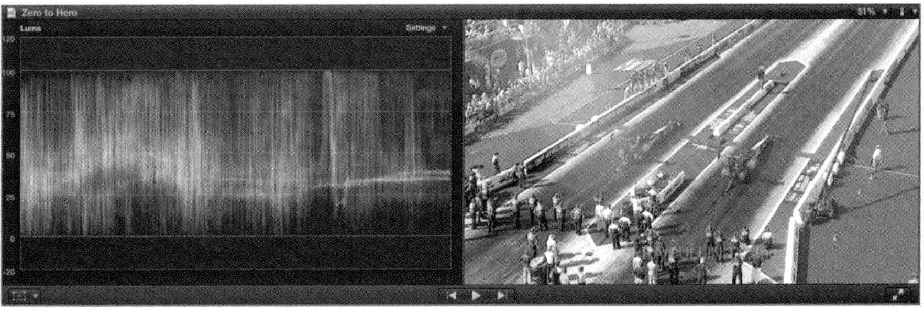

Luma level readings in the Waveform Monitor graphically represent the brightness levels of the trackside camera.

After finishing and sharing, you'll archive your Events and projects for easy-access viewing and future use. This simple and practical content "insurance policy" will give you peace of mind that your media and edits are safely preserved.

Preparing a Project for Sharing

For any given project, you may have gathered clips from a variety of audio sources, such as narration recorded in a studio, ambient sound recorded in the field, sound on tape, and music from iTunes or CDs. Likewise, the video may also have multiple sources. Some footage may have been shot indoors, some at night, and some outside in bright sunlight.

While you may have mixed audio and adjusted color to your liking, the human eye and ear can't always detect the "hot spots" that spell trouble. A clip that looks perfectly color-balanced to the eye may have brightness levels exceeding the 100% limit for luma. Audio may sound perfectly pleasant, but may actually be peaking into the red zone, past the 0 dB limit. Fortunately, Final Cut Pro has scopes and visual indicators that make these problems easy to identify, and includes solutions to fix them on the spot.

NOTE ▶ As you've done throughout these lessons, bring this lesson's folder forward and hide the other lesson projects.

1 In the Project Library, in the Lesson 12 folder, double-click the *Zero to Hero* project to open it in the Timeline. Press Shift-Z to see the entire project, and then play some of the project. Notice that the connected B-roll clips you edited in previous lessons now appear in the primary storyline next to the racers.

This version of *Zero to Hero* contains changes and additions you applied in previous lessons—mixed audio clips, transitions, effects, color corrected clips, and so on. One of the changes applied for you to prepare this project for sharing was to overwrite all connected clips into the primary storyline.

To more closely examine the audio in this project, it is helpful to view the Audio meters and evaluate the audio waveform peaks in the Timeline.

2 To display the Audio meters, click the right side of the Dashboard, or press Command-Shift-8.

3 Play the *Zero to Hero* project from the beginning and watch both Audio meters. Then play the area around the **Tony Pedregon** clips and notice that the audio levels peak above 0 dB, displaying red peak indicators at the top of the Audio meters.

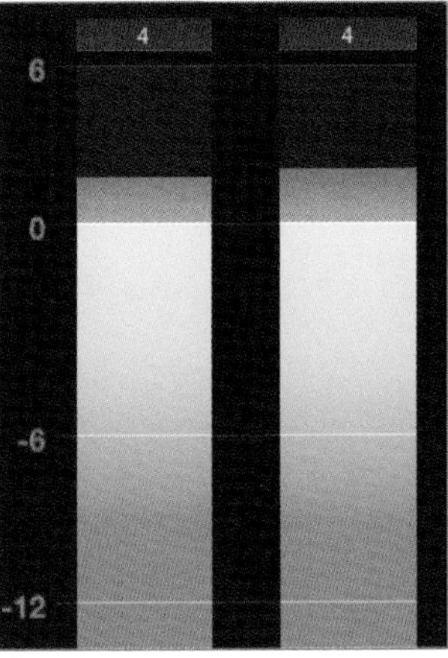

To target this hot spot, let's adjust the clips' appearance in the Timeline.

TIP In digital audio, distortion occurs when the combined audio level of all clips is above 0 dB. When mixing sound, the primary audio should peak at –12 dB, and music and other background audio should peak at –18 dB. The combined audio level of all clips should peak at –6 dB or less.

4 In the lower-right corner of the Timeline, click the Clip Appearance button. Click the first clip icon, and drag the Clip Height slider to the middle. In the Timeline, notice which clips display yellow- or red-tipped waveforms.

With the larger waveform appearance, you can easily see where clips peak and by how much. This large waveform clip display does not include video thumbnails, only a name reference at the top of each clip.

NOTE ▶ You also may have noticed the numerous split edits, or J and L cuts, throughout the project.

5 In the **Tony Pedregon** clip, drag the audio level overlay down so that no red peaks appear in the waveforms. Touches of yellow are acceptable, but not red peaks. Then adjust any other project clips that display audio that peaks too high.

TIP In some clips, the peaking may occur across only a few frames. Rather than lower the volume of the entire clip, Option-click the volume control line to create keyframes that allow you to adjust that specific section of the clip.

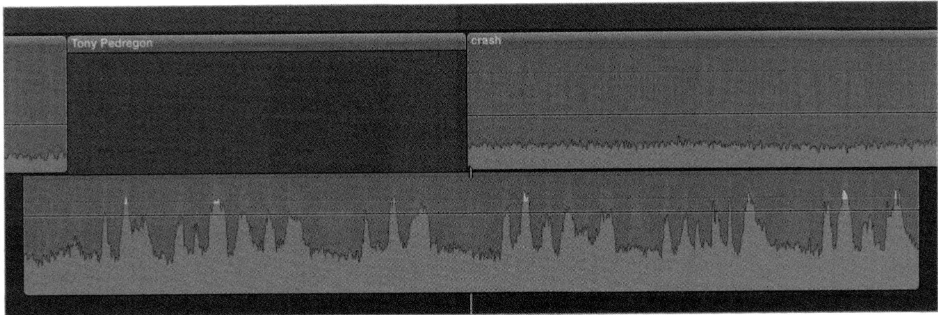

TIP ▶ Lowering audio peaks in one clip can affect the overall mix of sound in that area if other clips are present. Before sharing your project, review each changed section to make sure that you maintained the quality of your audio mix.

Now that the audio is at the proper level, you can focus on correcting video problems. To do that, you will change the Timeline appearance to feature the video clips and use the video scopes to view the luminance, or luma, levels of the clip.

NOTE ▶ *Luma* is an abbreviation for luminance, which describes the brightness of a video image. A luma channel is a grayscale image showing the range of brightness across an entire clip.

MORE INFO ▶ In previous lessons, you explored the Color Board, a powerful tool that supports a wide variety of manual color corrections. In this exercise, you will address a common problem, video levels that are too bright. However, in addition to correcting the entire image, you can correct only a specific color, draw a mask to correct a specific area, or apply multiple color corrections to a single clip and use shape masks in combination with a color mask. To learn more about the advanced features, please see *Apple Pro Training Series: Final Cut Pro X Advanced Editing* (Peachpit Press).

6 Below the Timeline, click the Clip Appearance button and select the fifth clip icon to show only the video display. If necessary, adjust the clip height to see all the clips in the Timeline.

In this view, the video displays as large thumbnails. Below the images are thin green audio strips with name references but no audio waveforms.

7 To view the project clips in video scopes, choose Window > Viewer Display > Show Video Scopes, or press Command-7. The Viewer splits into two areas, with a smaller Viewer on the right and the video scopes to the left.

A video scope can display the video signal in several ways. You used some of these in the previous lesson. To check for broadcast-safe video levels, you should view the luma levels in the waveform display.

Broadcast-Safe Video

One of the most common problems with video levels is that the whites, or luminance levels, are sometimes too bright. The FCC mandates that no video intended for broadcast can have a luminance level over 100 IRE, which is the broadcast-safe level. (IRE is a unit of measurement in video named for the organization that created it—the Institute of Radio Engineers.)

Continues on next page

Broadcast-Safe Video *(continued)*

If video luminance exceeds 100 IRE, the video level clips during broadcast, which can cause audio interference or noise. Some networks or facilities may reject projects that are not deemed broadcast-safe, and choose not to air them at all. This is why it's always a good practice to double-check luminance levels before sharing a project.

8 In the upper-right corner of the video scopes window, from the Settings pop-up menu, choose Display: Waveform. Then, from the Settings pop-up menu, choose Channels: Luma.

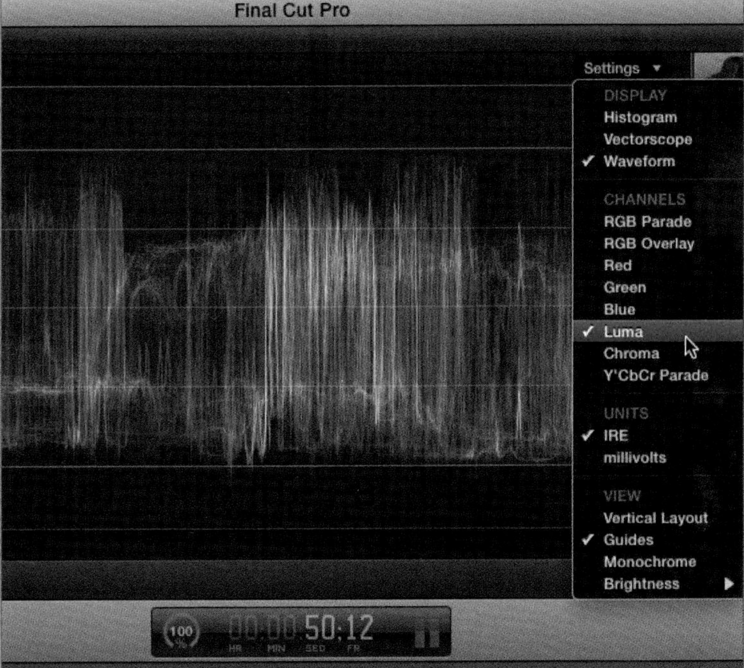

9 While looking at the waveform display, select and skim the **Antron Brown clip**, noting where the luma levels appear on the scope.

The levels in this clip appear above the 100% line in the waveform display. To manually lower the luminance level of this clip, you use the Color Board color correction tool.

10 To open the Color Board, in the toolbar, click the Enhancements button, and choose Show Color Board, or press Command-6. In the Color Board, click the Exposure tab.

TIP Because you will often use the Color Board in conjunction with the video scopes, remember their adjacent keyboard shortcuts: Command-6 and Command-7, respectively.

In the Exposure tab, you can alter a clip's luminance level, by adjusting the darkest pixels, the midrange pixels, the brightest pixels, or the entire luma range. In the **Antron Brown** clip, the brightest pixels in the background seem to boost the video level out of range.

11 In the Exposure tab, drag the Highlights control down to lower the clip's luma level to just under 100%. Use the waveform display as a guide.

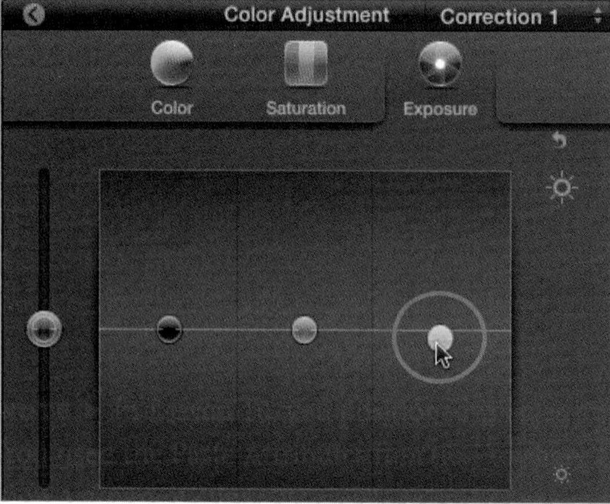

Under the Color Board, Highlights shows a negative percent value, which reflects the percentage of luminance you lowered the clip.

12 Skim the *Zero to Hero* project and look for any other clips that have high luminance. To make them broadcast-safe, reduce their luma levels to just below 100%.

TIP In addition to manually adjusting a clip's luma level in the Color Board, you can also apply a Broadcast Safe effect from the Effects Browser. When applied, this effect automatically adjusts the luminance level of a clip.

13 Press Command-4 or click the Inspector button in the toolbar, to close the Color Board. To close the video scopes, choose Window > Viewer Display > Hide Video Scopes, or press Command-7.

TIP Another way to prepare your project for output is to add visual timecode, found in the Elements category of the Generators Browser. As you learned in Lesson 9, doing so displays the project's timecode in every frame, making it easier to locate specific places in the project with other team members. If desired, add the visual timecode before beginning the sharing steps.

Sharing a Master File

Now that you have tweaked the audio and video levels into their appropriate zones, you can move on to the primary goal of this lesson: creating a single movie file of your project. In the following exercises, you will discover several ways to export and distribute your project, creating files suitable for the Internet, email, iOS devices, and other platforms. Of all the choices, however, perhaps the most important is the master File. It's a stand-alone file of the highest-quality output for your project, and makes an excellent archive of your finished video.

1 In the *Zero to Hero* project, press Option-X to remove any marked ranges in the Timeline.

You may share an entire project, an entire Event clip, or a range from either. Unless you want to export just a portion of a project, a good practice is to press Option-X in the Timeline to clear any marked ranges before beginning to output.

TIP Sharing a project from the Project Library exports the entire project regardless of any marked range inside the project.

2 Near the right-end of the toolbar, click the Share button, and look at the destinations listed in the pop-up menu.

Final Cut Pro includes several export presets, called destinations, configured for many popular online and device formats. Later in this lesson, you will learn how to customize this list for your workflow. Notice that Master File is noted as the default. Master File is the high-quality, big-file output destination from a mastering and an archiving perspective.

TIP If the Share button is dimmed, click the Timeline window to activate it, or select the project in the Project Library.

3 In the Share pop-up menu, choose Master File. In the Master File Share window, skim the video screen to confirm that this is the project, range, or clip you want to export.

TIP Although the shortcut is not listed in the Share pop-up menu, you can open the Master File Share window by pressing Command-E.

A wealth of information is presented in the Share window, gleaned either from the metadata you provided or what Final Cut Pro detected about this project and its media. This metadata will be included with the shared movie file. Some of the metadata in this window can be customized to better fit your project. For example, let's change the title to identify this promotional video in the series.

NOTE ▶ If you see the "missing or offline" dialog instead of the Share window, click Cancel, and return to the Project Library to modify the Event References for the project. See the Final Cut Pro Help Guide for more information.

4 In the title field, click at the end of the "Zero to Hero" text, and append this text with – *Adrenaline*. Press Tab to advance to the next field.

TIP The title here is the name that appears in the QuickTime Player title bar; that is, it's the movie title a viewer will see. In a moment, you will save the movie file under a different filename for organizational purposes.

5 To continue customizing this file's metadata, enter the following text in the appropriate data fields. Remember to press Tab to jump to the next field after data entry. In the Tags field, press Return after entering each "token."

- Description: *NHRA racers describe what makes them put it on the line to take home the Wally.*
- Creator: <your name>
- Tags: *NHRA, Racing, Antron Brown, John Force, Tony Pedregon,* and *Tony Schumacher*

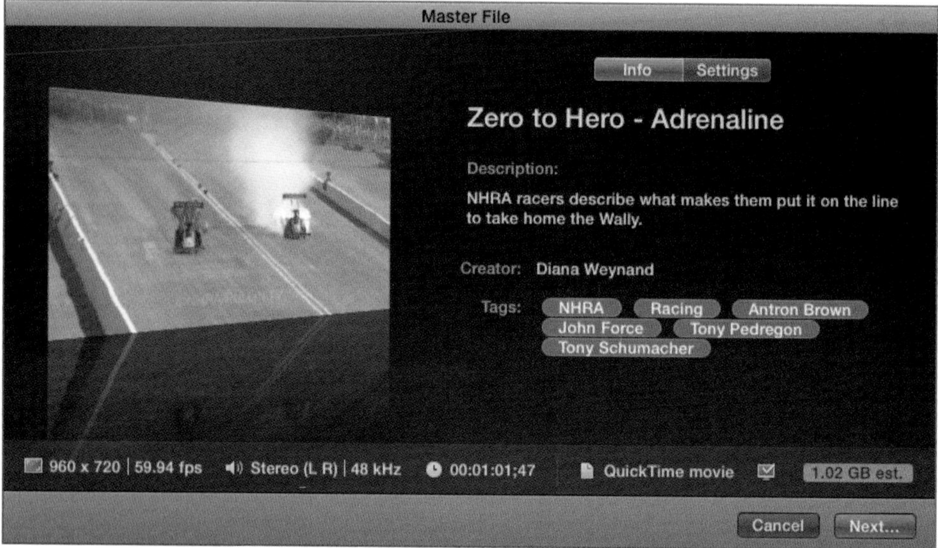

Now that you have customized some of the metadata, let's look at the movie's properties.

6 Click the Settings button to review the properties of the movie file you are creating. Be sure the Format option is set to Video and Audio.

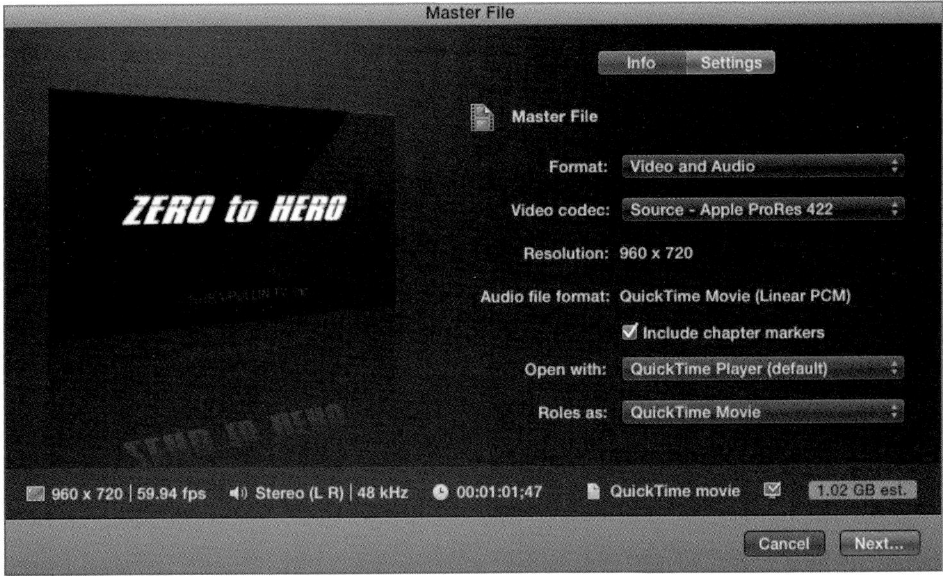

In this section, you can review the default settings that will produce a high-quality file. Let's examine a few of the options you may want to apply to your exports.

7 From the "Video codec" pop-up menu, choose Source – Apple ProRes 422 (the default).

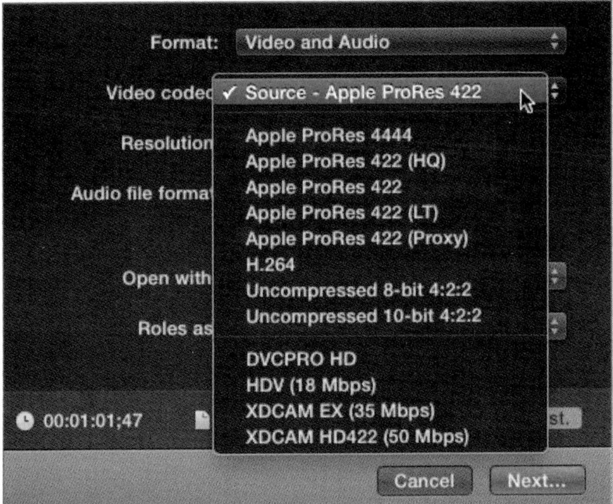

With Source chosen, you will export a movie file using the same format as the project's render settings. The default render and project codec is Apple ProRes 422, which produces a very high-quality file—up to a 10-bit, 5K resolution—but at a large file size. When you want to export the highest-quality file for mastering or archiving, the Source option is the best choice.

You have a few other options available in this dialog. You can choose an application (QuickTime or Compressor, for example) in which to open the exported movie, and you can identify whether you want to export video and audio together, separately, or a combination based on assigned roles.

TIP If you added chapter markers to your movie, and want those to be included in the master file, enable "Include chapter markers" if it's not already selected. For more information about setting and utilizing Roles, see *Apple Pro Training Series: Final Cut Pro X Advanced Editing* by Michael Wohl, Alexis Van Hurkman, and Mark Spencer (Peachpit Press).

8 To open your exported movie automatically in QuickTime, from the "Open with" pop-up menu, make sure "QuickTime Player (default)" is selected.

At the bottom of the window is a summary of the new file's properties. There are a couple of key items to observe.

9 At the center of the summary bar, notice the duration of the file and, at the far right of the summary bar, the estimated file size.

10 To the left of the file size, place your pointer over the Compatibility icon to activate the pop-up menu.

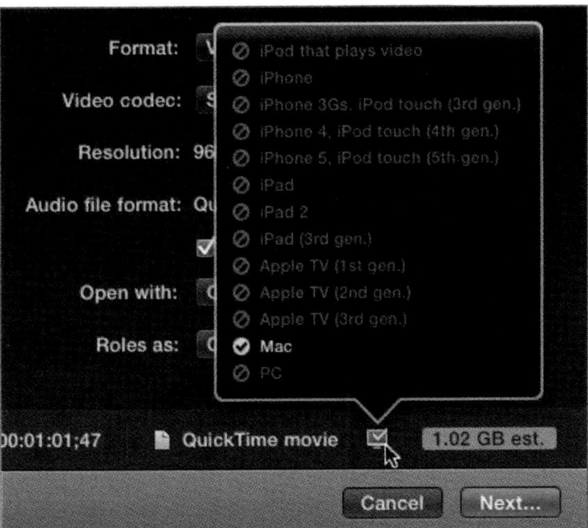

The pop-up menu shows which devices can play the file you are about to create. Since this is a Master file, you won't be able to play it on an iOS device such as an iPhone or iPod. (We'll explore the Share commands for iOS devices later in this lesson.)

11 In the lower right of the Share window, click Next. In the Save As field, enter *Zero to Hero – Promotional 1_MASTER*. If necessary, click the expand arrow to display the full Finder window.

In the Save As field in this dialog, you can create a filename that conforms to your project's organizational structure. Because there are two places where you can customize the name in the share process, it might be helpful to first name the movie for viewing purposes, which you did earlier in this exercise, and then name it for archival purposes.

TIP To consolidate your exported movie files into a single location, create a target folder on your internal or external hard disk. In the FCPX Book Files folder, an Exports folder was created for your use in this lesson.

12 In the left sidebar, select the APTS FCP X volume, and then navigate to the FCPX Book Files > Exports folder. Click Save.

In the Dashboard, the Background Tasks button displays the progress of the export. Sharing is a background process which allows you to continue editing this or other projects while the share is in progress. When the share has completed, the movie file will automatically open in QuickTime Player.

13 In the QuickTime movie window, click the Play button, or press the Spacebar, to start and stop the movie. Notice the quality of the image. Then, in the QuickTime Player, choose Window > Show Movie Inspector, or press Command-I to open the Inspector and display the metadata you entered in the Share window.

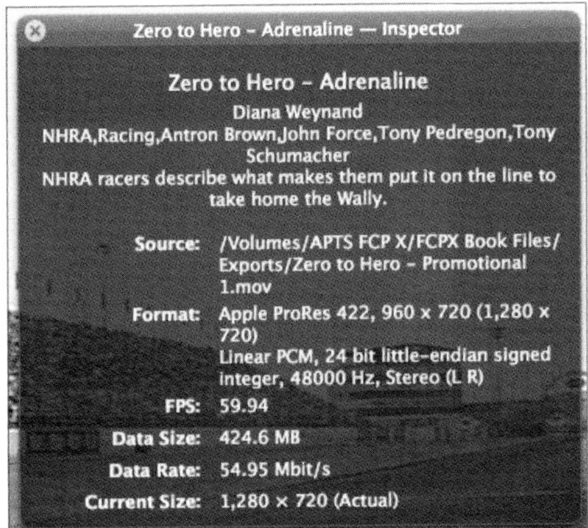

Notice that the title in the Inspector, and the movie's title bar, is the title you entered for the shared movie and not the filename you entered in the Save As dialog to archive the file.

NOTE ▶ Using Final Cut Pro to embed metadata into your shared files is a great way to prepare your movies for online viewing, especially when search engine optimization is essential for getting your video discovered. As you continue to create more movies, you can utilize the metadata as the basis for your archive catalog.

14 To exit QuickTime Player, choose QuickTime Player > Quit.

15 In Final Cut Pro, press Command-0 to return to the Project Library. Notice the Share icon displayed next to the project name.

The Share icon indicates that the project has been exported, or published. This icon also appears next to the project name in the Timeline.

If a project is altered in any way, an alert triangle appears next to the Share icon. To bring the Share icon up to date, you will need to re-output the project.

Each project also has a Share inspector that tracks the metadata along with the destinations you have used for the project. Let's take a quick look.

16 With the *Zero to Hero* project selected in the Project Library, press Command-4 to open the Inspector, if necessary. Click the Share button at the top of the Inspector.

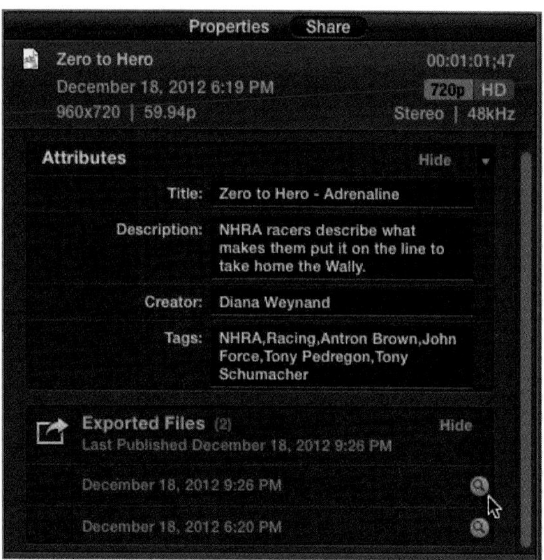

The metadata you previously entered appears as part of the project's attributes. In the lower section, you see a list of exported versions. (In this case, two versions were exported for demonstration purposes.) Each export is date/time stamped. Clicking the magnifying glass at the far right will perform a reveal in Finder.

Sharing Your Project as an Audio File

You can create and export a single audio file that contains only a mix of your project's audio. Click the Share button, and choose the Master File destination. In the Share window's Settings section, from the Format pop-up menu, choose

Continues on next page

Sharing Your Project as an Audio File *(continued)*

Audio Only. You may then choose an audio file format from the pop-up menu that appears. Select an application from the "Open with" pop-up menu to automatically open the exported audio file, if desired. Click Next, assign the file a name, navigate to where you want to save the file, and click Save.

Publishing a Project to Apple Devices

The widespread popularity of mobile devices means that you can now show your completed project to anyone, anywhere, at any time. You may want to share it with friends, show it to a producer for feedback, or just carry it around and watch it yourself. By publishing your project to Apple devices, you can share your finished movie on an iPad, iPhone, iPod, Mac, PC, Apple TV, or all the above. When you choose one or more of these devices, Final Cut Pro automatically transcodes your project to the optimum file size and format for each device.

When outputting to an Apple device, the default behavior is to export to iTunes.

1 In the Project Library, select the *Delicious Peace* project. Click the Share button, and locate the two Apple Devices options: Apple Devices 720p and Apple Devices 1080p. For this exercise, choose the Apple Devices 720p destination.

The Share window you saw during the previous exercise appears asking for metadata.

NOTE ▸ You don't have to memorize which preset is suitable for each device. After you choose a preset, you can access the Compatibility pop-up menu in the Share window to view compatible devices.

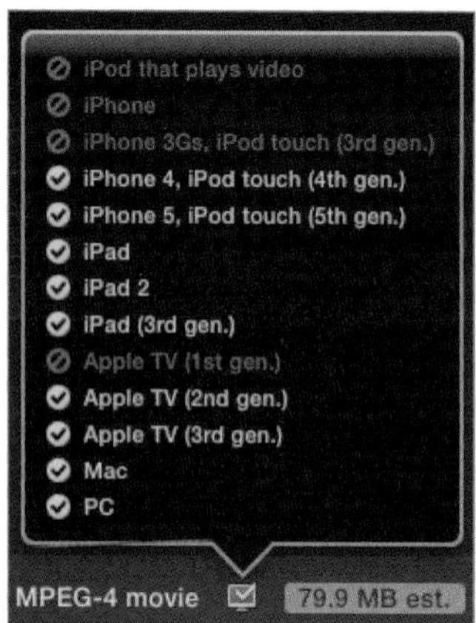

2 In the Share window, click the Settings button.

You'll see available options you did not see in the Master file output from the previous exercise. For example, in this preset, you can change the frame size.

3 Click the Resolution pop-up menu. As your project is 1280 x 720, the 1920 x 1080 frame size is dimmed. If not already selected, choose 1280 x 720.

NOTE ▸ Both Apple Devices presets, 720p and 1080p, automatically select the resolution closest to your project's frame size.

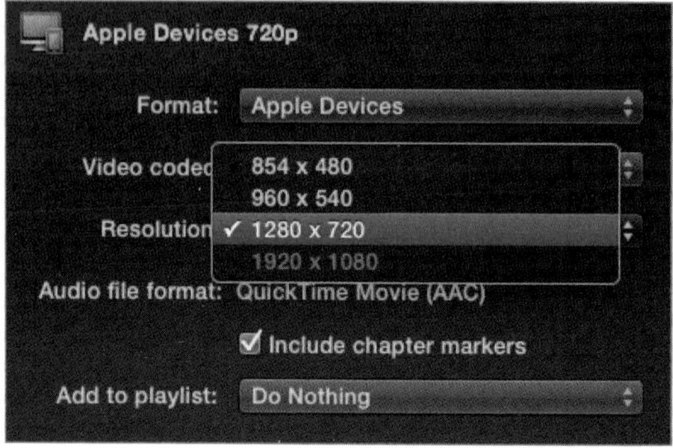

The last pop-up menu allows you to set an automated action for Final Cut Pro to perform after processing the project. This is known as a post-transcoding action or *post-action*. These optional actions enhance the Share function by automating tasks such as delivering the processed file to iTunes for syncing to your iOS device.

4 Click the post-action pop-up menu, located beneath the "Include chapter markers" checkbox, to view the current default on your system and any additional options.

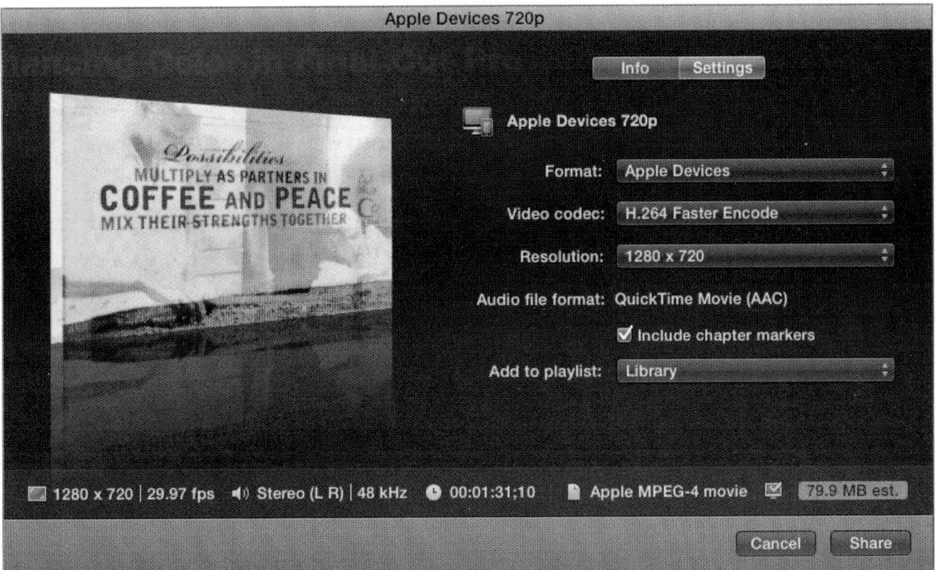

NOTE ► Depending on your computer's software configuration and any prior selections made in the menu, you may see different Settings options in your Share window than the images in this exercise.

The post-action options can range from the simple "Do Nothing" to a more complex set of actions that include delivering to a third-party application for automatic delivery to an FTP site with an email notification. The label of the pop-up menu and the button at the bottom right of the window will change depending on the chosen action.

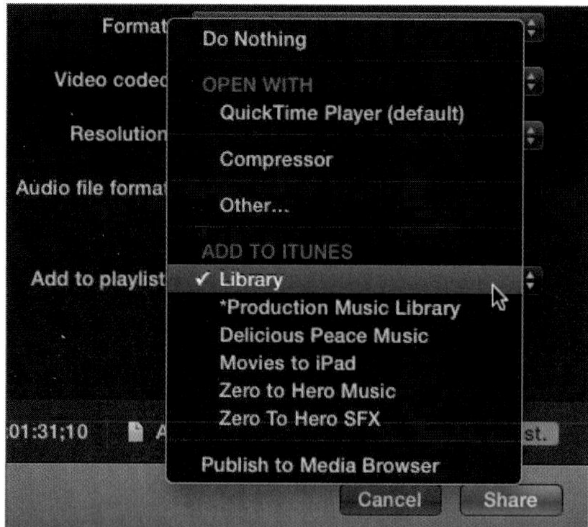

If you are using iTunes on your computer, the default action is Library. If you have created playlists in iTunes, those playlists will appear in the Add to iTunes section for you to choose from. The Share button will appear at the bottom right of the window to place the processed file in iTunes.

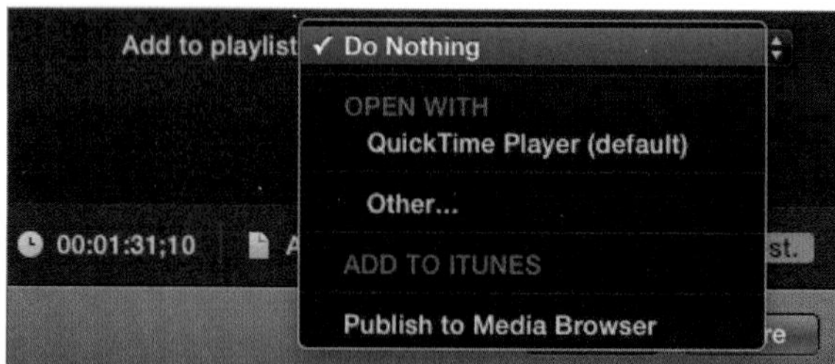

If you are not using iTunes on this computer, the action Do Nothing or QuickTime Player is selected depending on your software configuration or prior selection. The Next button that becomes available when either is selected will open a Save As dialog for you to specify a name and location for the processed file.

TIP To update the button and post-action label, make a selection and the interface will update.

5 If QuickTime Player is not listed or you would like to select another application, choose Other, and then navigate to the application in the Browser that appears. Select the application, and then click Open.

The chosen application will now appear in the post-action list.

6 Click Cancel to exit this Share window.

Publishing a Project to Video Sharing Sites

Video sharing sites are the fastest way to get your finished project into the world. They're free, and expose your movie to a wide audience, including filmmaking peers who can give you feedback and spread the word to others. You may already have accounts at one or more of the four video sharing sites in the Share menu—Facebook, Vimeo, YouTube, and CNN iReport.

In this exercise, you will prepare a project to publish to a YouTube account, and then compare similarities with Vimeo.

1 In the Project Library, select *Delicious Peace*, click the Share button, and then select the YouTube destination. In the YouTube video display, skim the project to verify the correct project version.

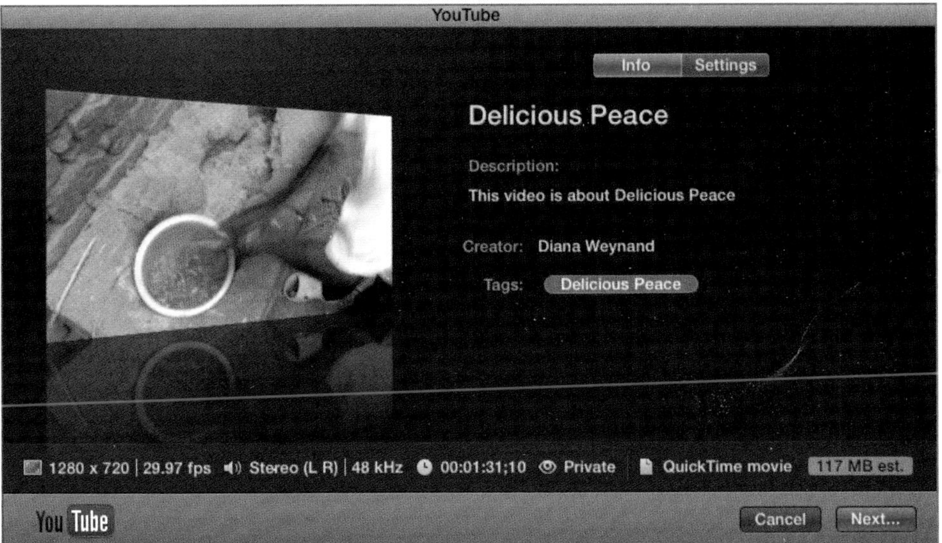

In the title field, you can enter the name of the movie as you want it to appear on YouTube. Because *Delicious Peace* is the name of this project, that title has been entered automatically. Let's personalize it.

2 In the title field, enter *My Delicious Peace.* Then enter a description along with some tags that will help users search for this movie or subject matter after you make it public.

One description might be: *Despite their religious differences, coffee growers in Uganda unite to promote peace and fair trade in this documentary narrated by actor Ed O'Neill.* Tags might include *Uganda, coffee, peace, fair trade, Uganda cooperative*, and so on. Remember to press Return after entering each tag.

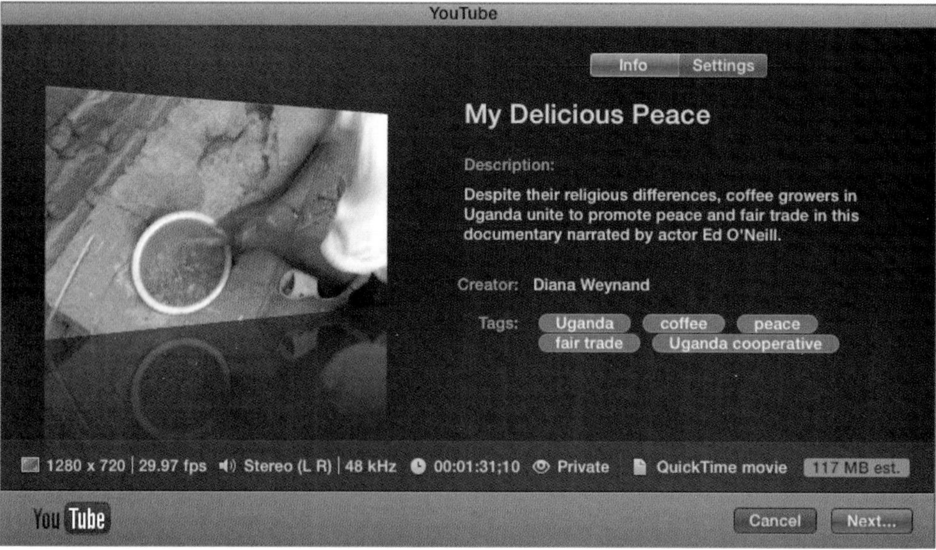

TIP If you want a general audience to find your movie, don't make it private; and enter a compelling description to help sell your movie. Descriptive tags will help your audience search for and discover your movie.

Now that the metadata for the video has been entered, you will look at the movie properties in the Settings section.

3 Click the Settings button.

The Settings section of the Share window includes fields for YouTube account login, output options for file size and compression method, privacy, and video category.

TIP To create a free YouTube account to publish your own movies, visit www.youtube.com

For the purposes of this exercise, you will not enter your login credentials. But let's examine some of the project settings and information options.

4 Click the Resolution pop-up menu to choose the frame size you want to upload. Here again you see that 1080p is dimmed because the project is set to 1280 x 720 resolution.

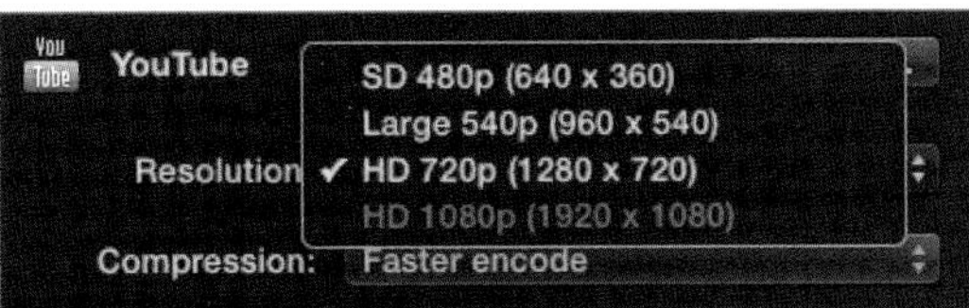

5 In the Resolution pop-up menu, choose different settings while keeping an eye on the estimated file size above the Next button. Then return the Resolution to HD 720p.

When you make resolution changes, the summary information at the bottom right of the window flashes yellow as it updates the estimated file size.

Not only do you see the estimated file size change in the summary bar, you also see the frame size and the privacy indicator change as you update those respective setting parameters.

6 In the Compression pop-up menu, leave the default "Faster encode." Select "Make this movie Private," and watch for "Private" to flash yellow on the summary bar.

When you select "Make this movie Private," only contacts that you specify in your YouTube account settings can see your movie.

7 From the Category pop-up menu, choose Nonprofits & Activism.

8 Click Next. If you did not previously provide your YouTube account credentials, the sign-in dialog reappears. For this exercise, you don't need to enter your credentials.

If you were to sign in at this stage, a YouTube Terms of Service dialog would appear and you would click Publish to continue the export and automatic upload to YouTube.

TIP During an upload, you can click the Background Tasks button in the Dashboard and monitor the progress in the Background Tasks window. You may continue editing this or other projects while Sharing continues to process in the background.

9 In the YouTube dialog, click Cancel to close the credentials or Terms of Service dialog, and in the Share window, click Cancel.

NOTE ▶ Keep in mind that the material used for these exercises is copyrighted and should not be posted to any site.

The Vimeo destination requires the same type of account and password information, and the Resolution and Compression pop-up menus are also the same. The only difference is the "Viewable by" pop-up menu, which offers three options for your target Vimeo audience.

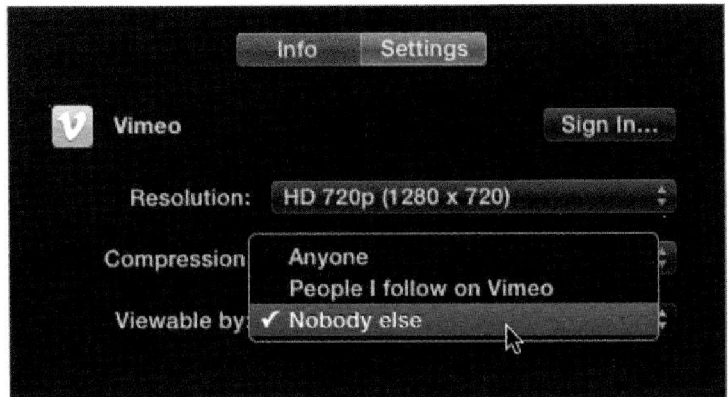

TIP ▶ To create a free Vimeo account to publish your own movies, visit www.vimeo.com.

Customizing the Destinations Menu

In addition to the destinations you've seen on the Share pop-up menu, Final Cut Pro has several other built-in destinations for your convenience. For example, you might need to create a Blu-ray disc, upload a movie to a popular news site or send video in an email. Or when you need to send the same project to more than one site, you might want to create and customize a bundle of destinations.

In this exercise, you will add to and customize the destinations in the Share pop-up menu, and create a bundle of target destinations.

1 Close the Share window, and press Command-0 to access the Project Library. Select the *Delicious Peace* project.

NOTE ▶ Remember, a project may be shared from the Project Library as well as the Project's Timeline. Whenever you export from the Library, the project's entire duration is exported.

2 On the toolbar, click the Share button and choose Add Destination.

Choosing this option opens the Final Cut Pro Preferences window. Here you can add, delete, and modify the presets in the Destinations pop-up menu. Notice the list of current destinations on the left side of the window, and the additional destinations to the right.

TIP You can also access this destination list by choosing Final Cut Pro > Preferences, and then clicking the Destinations tab at the top of the window.

Let's remove DVD as a destination and replace it with Blu-ray.

3 On the left side of the Destinations window, select DVD. At the bottom of the window, click the Remove (–) button to remove this destination.

TIP Another way to delete a destination from this list is to Control-click (or right-click) the destination icon in the left column, and choose Delete from the shortcut menu, or press Command-Delete.

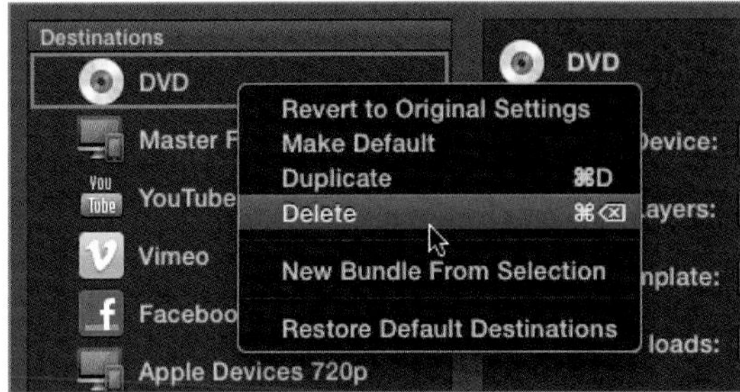

While DVD is removed from the Destinations list, it remains available with the other presets to the right. You will return it to the Destinations list later in the lesson.

Adding destinations to the list is just as easy.

4 From the group on the right, drag the Blu-ray destination to the Destinations list, but don't release the pointer until you see a blue insert bar between the Master File and YouTube destinations.

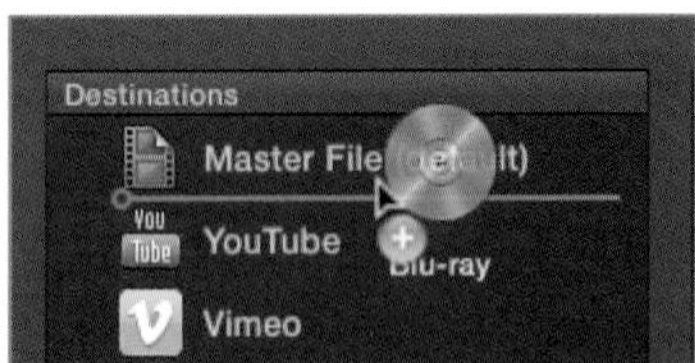

Not only can you delete and add destinations, you can control their order of appearance within the pop-up menu.

TIP You can position a destination as you first drag it into the list, or release it into the list and then drag it into position.

5 At the bottom of the list, click the Add (+) button to display the available destination presets. Drag the Email destination to the list.

When you release a preset into the list, the destination's parameters appear on the right.

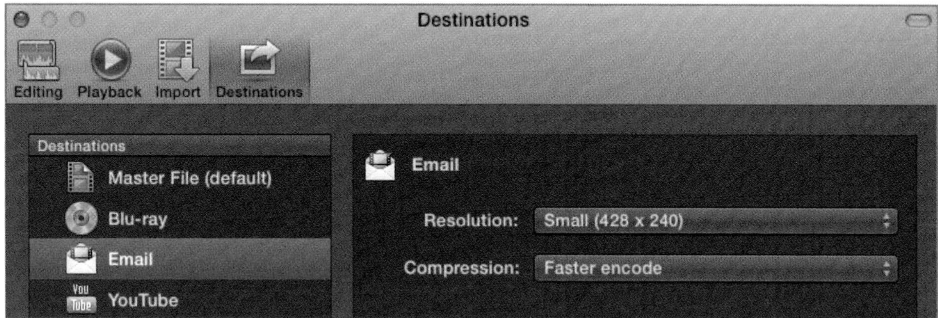

As you experienced in other Share options, the Resolution pop-up menu presents the possible frame sizes for the video file you're sending to this destination. Beware that some email systems are unable to handle the resulting file size from choosing a higher resolution. The Compression pop-up menu allows you to choose between one-pass processing (Faster Encode) and two-pass processing (Better Quality).

6 Click the Add (+) button again, and add the Save Current Frame preset to the Destinations list. You will use this destination in a later exercise.

When you want to share to multiple destinations at once, you can combine those destinations into a bundle. For example, let's say you're working on a video series and are asked to distribute three file types: a high-quality Master file, a file uploaded to YouTube, and a file that is iOS-compatible. Placing these three destinations in a bundle will give you a "one in, many out" workflow that will save time.

7 Drag the Bundle preset to the bottom of the Destinations list. To name this bundle, click in the bundle's name field to select the text, and rename it *Share Pack: DP* to indicate this is the bundle for Delicious Peace exports.

Dragging a bundle into the Destinations list

Renamed bundle

The next step is to simply drag the desired destinations into the folder or bundle container. However, once you include a destination in a bundle, you no longer have independent access to that destination. To keep the Destination list intact, *and* add an existing destination to a bundle, you can duplicate the destination before placing it in the bundle. Let's add the step of first duplicating the destinations you want to include in this bundle.

8 In the Destinations list, Control-click the Master File (default) destination and, from the shortcut menu, choose Duplicate. Repeat this process by duplicating the YouTube and Apple Devices 720p destinations.

TIP Another way of duplicating a destination is to select it in the list, and press Command-D.

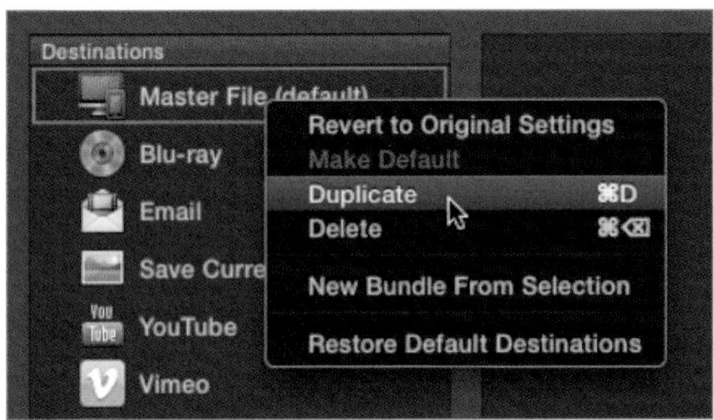

9 To add the Master File copy destination to this bundle, drag it down and release it on top of the Bundle folder. Then drag the YouTube copy destination into the bundle, and finally the Apple Devices 720p copy destination.

Now the three (copied) destinations are contained in the *Share Pack: DP* bundle, while the original destinations remain in the Destinations list for independent access.

TIP Just as you customized the name of the bundle, you can customize the destination names by clicking the name text, and entering a new name, such as Master File DP. You can also reorder the bundled destinations.

There is a keyboard shortcut that opens the default destination. By making the new bundle the default, you can have even faster access to sharing a project.

10 Control-click the *Share Pack: DP* bundle, and choose Make Default. Close the Preferences window.

Let's take a look at how this bundle works when sharing the Delicious Peace project.

11 With the *Delicious Peace* project still selected, press Command-E to share using the default destination. In the lower left of the Share window, click the navigation arrows to cycle through the destinations in this bundle. Notice that the Info section applies the same metadata to all destinations.

12 Click the Settings button, and then click the navigation arrows to cycle through the different destinations. Notice the changes in the Settings section are different for each destination.

13 Click Cancel to close the Share window.

> **TIP** ▶ In all the destinations, just a few parameters allow tweaking of the exported file. If you need to customize additional parameters, such as bit rate or an odd frame size, you must use Compressor to create destinations with specific settings. Compressor is an additional application available in the Mac App Store.

Take 2

The producer walks in just as you are posting the finished project to YouTube for all the fans to see. That's fine, he says, but can you spread the word to his contact list? And can you email a copy of the movie to his sister? Final Cut Pro offers two email options, one to share a link of a published movie, and the other to share the movie itself.

- ▶ To announce the newly published movie to the producer's contacts, with the project selected in the Project Library, show the Inspector, and click the Share button at the top of the Inspector. Click the pop-up located to the right of the published project, and choose Tell a Friend. An email message appears with a link to the published project and a subject.

- ▶ To email the movie to the producer's sister, select the project and click the Share button to select Email from the Destinations list. In the Share window, in the Settings section, choose a resolution and compression from the pop-up menus and click Share. When an email message appears with the movie attached, compose a message and click Send.

> **NOTE** ▶ If your email application is not configured, you will not be able to perform this Take 2 exercise.

Exporting an Image from Your Project

You may want to select and save single images from your project for DVD covers or movie posters, film festival websites or magazine articles, and even for bumpers or titles. Good still images from your project are always in demand, especially when marketing and publicizing a project.

In addition, some video sharing sites, such as Vimeo, allow you to include still images from your movie on their website, which is a good opportunity to entice an audience with a preview of things to come.

Final Cut Pro can export still images in several formats. You might send a TIFF file to a graphic artist who needs to create printed material. Or you could export a smaller JPEG file and email to a producer for review. In this exercise, you will save a single image JPEG file from your project that is suitable for email.

1 In the Lesson 12 folder in the Project Library, double-click the *Fairly Legal* project to open it in the Timeline.

2 Click the Timeline Index button. In the Timeline Index, click the Clips and All buttons to display all the clips in the Timeline. Select the second instance of **4B-3_110(B)**.

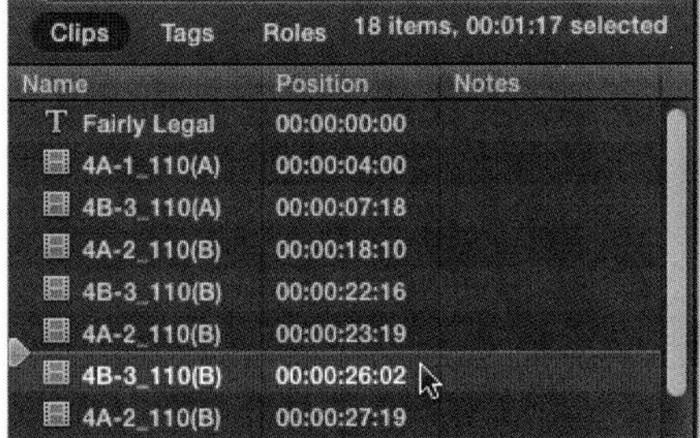

In the Timeline, the playhead moves to the first frame of the selected clip, a close-up of the star of *Fairly Legal*, actress Sarah Shahi.

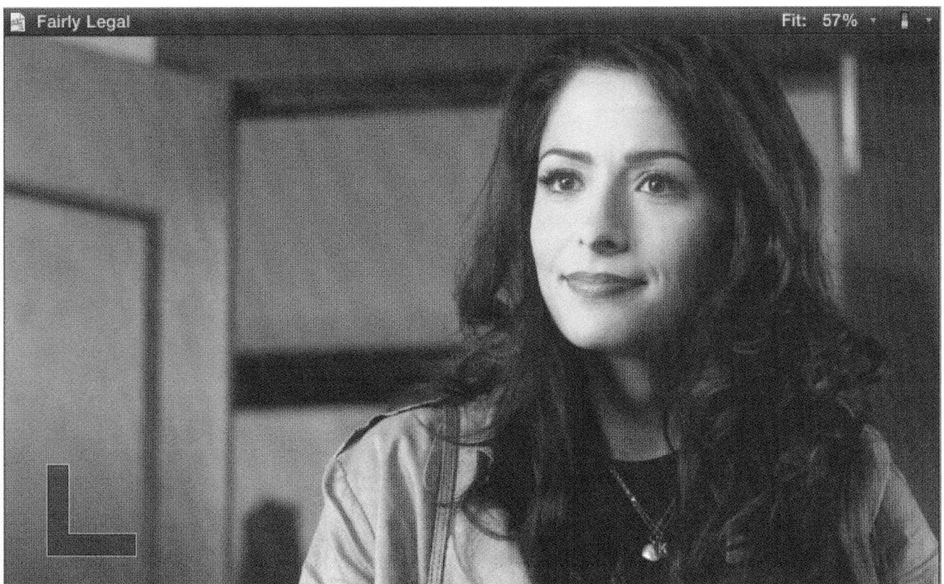

3 Press the Left and Right Arrow keys, or the J-K-L keys, to move through this clip and choose a favorite frame of Sarah. Then set the playhead on that frame to target it for output.

4 In the toolbar, click the Share button, and choose the Save Current Frame destination.

The Share window appears with the chosen frame on the left side.

5 In the Settings section, click the Export pop-up menu, and look at the list of image file formats.

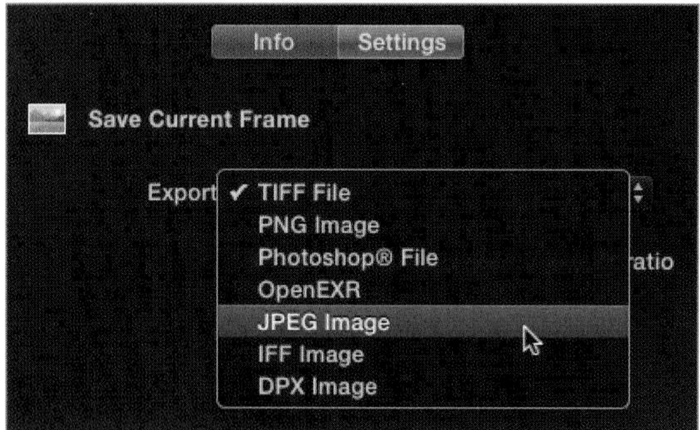

You choose a file format based on how the still image will be used. To create a compact file you can email, JPEG is a good choice.

6 From the Export pop-up menu, choose JPEG Image, and then, if necessary, select "Scale image to preserve aspect ratio."

Because of the difference in pixel shapes between still images and video images, if you don't select "Scale image to preserve aspect ratio," the JPEG file image may be distorted.

7 Click Next. In the Save As field, enter *Sarah Shahi*. Navigate to FCPX Book Files and select the Exports folder as the file destination. Then click Save.

The Background Tasks button shows the quick progress of the export.

8 When the process is completed, return to the Project Library and, with the project selected, go to the Share inspector. Click the magnifying glass to the right of the Exported Files entry.

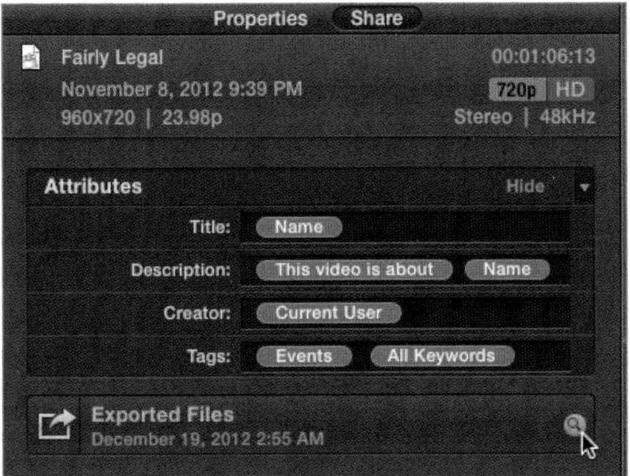

A Finder window opens revealing the shared still image file.

9 Select the **Sarah Shahi.jpg** file. To see it in QuickView, press the Spacebar, and then press the Spacebar again to return to the Finder.

In the preview area of the Finder, notice the image format (JPEG) and its size (approximately 140 KB). This file size is easily small enough to send as an email attachment.

Take 2

The publicity department for a film festival just emailed you a request for two stills from your film for the festival website. No problem, you can grab a couple of stills and email them back. Using the steps you learned in this lesson, select and save two images from this project, and make sure the images are small enough to email.

Exporting for Blu-ray Disc, DVD, or Disk Image

Most of your exporting activities may create movie files to post or play on computers and other devices. Some situations, however, may require a hard copy of your project in the form of a DVD or Blu-ray disc. But if a hard copy *is* required, and you don't have the specific equipment to create it, you can create a disk image (.img) file. This is a useful way to share a project, and a convenient way to preserve and archive it as well.

While you can create a disk image for either DVD or Blu-ray disc, the Blu-ray disc output offers a few more ways to enhance the finished project, such as applying special animated menu templates. It also allows you the option to play the disc in most AVCHD-compatible players. In this exercise, you will explore these options by creating a Blu-ray disc image of your project.

NOTE ▸ DVD burners and players use a red laser, while Blu-ray burners and players use a blue laser. The blue laser has a shorter wavelength, which allows more data to be stored on Blu-ray discs than on DVDs.

1 In the Project Library, select the *I Think* project, and then click the Share button and choose the Blu-ray destination. In the Share window, click the Settings button.

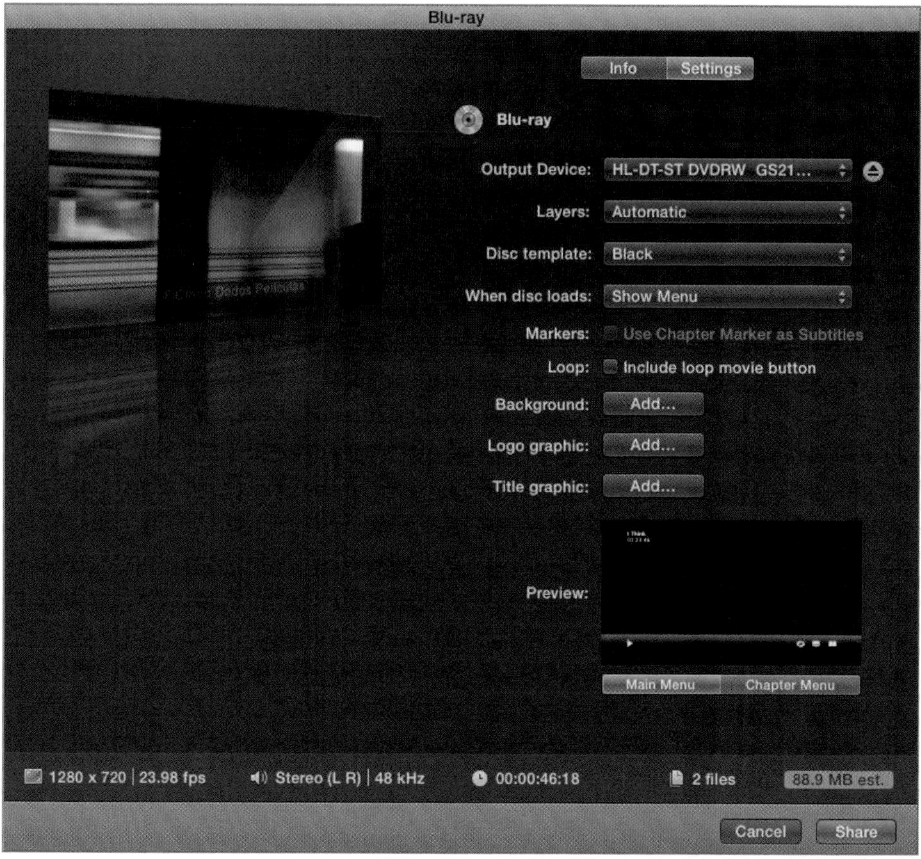

2 Click the Output Device pop-up menu. Review the choices, and then choose Hard Drive (Blu-ray) to create a disk image (.img) file you can archive or transfer to a different computer to burn a disc at a later time.

NOTE ▶ If you have a Blu-ray burner connected to your computer, that device will also appear in the Output Device pop-up menu.

NOTE ▶ When you've chosen to create a Blu-ray disc, choosing a DVD-R as the output device will burn an AVCHD file onto a DVD disc. When creating a DVD disc, choosing DVD-R as the output device will burn a standard-definition DVD.

3 Click the Layers pop-up menu to view the options, and leave Automatic chosen.

By choosing Automatic, Final Cut Pro automatically detects whether the inserted disc is single- or double-layered. When Hard Drive is selected as the output device, Final Cut Pro creates a single-layer disk image.

You can choose from several options to customize your output, including a variety of templates, backgrounds, title graphics, and so on.

NOTE ▶ Two buttons are located beneath the video display in the lower portion of the dialog: Main Menu and Chapter Menu. To see the templates in the steps that follow, ensure that Main Menu is selected.

4 Click Main Menu. Then from the "Disc template" pop-up menu, choose Street.

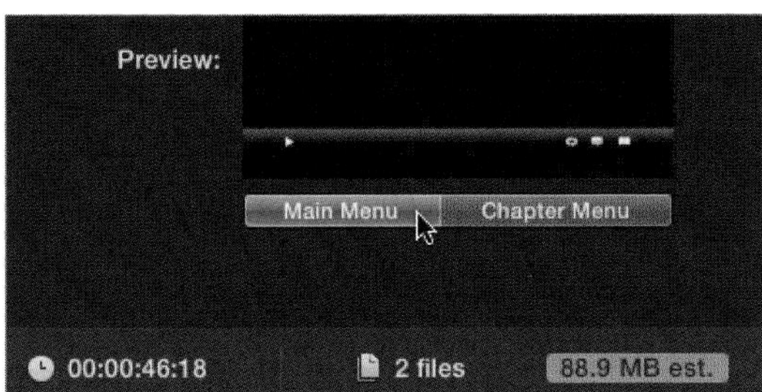

Five themed template options are available for Blu-ray output: solid black, solid white, and three templates with animated backgrounds. When you choose a template with an animated background, the background will animate as a continuous video loop.

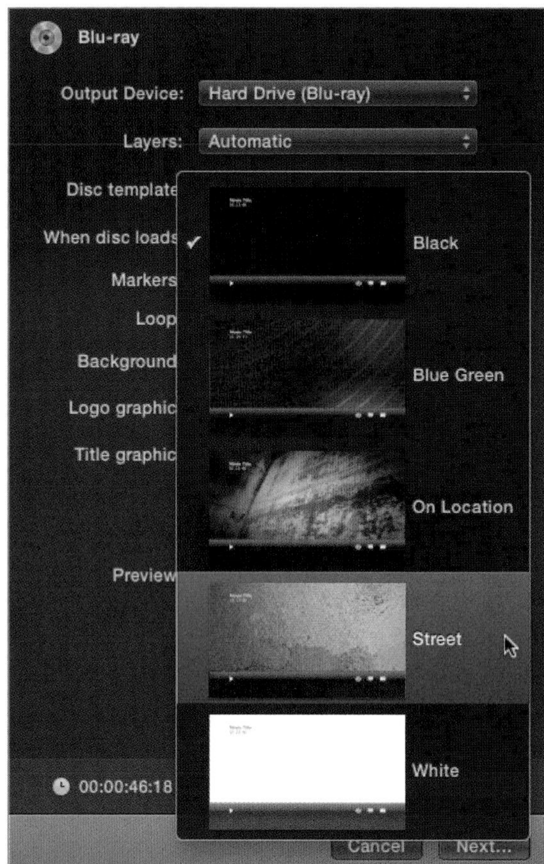

You can choose other options for adding customized backgrounds and graphics, looping the playback, and automatically playing the disc when loaded. Choose these options based on the needs of your project. For now, let's create the disk image.

NOTE ► Often a disc is made for one-time use as a "screener" or work-in-progress. In that instance, you may want the movie to automatically play when the disk is inserted into the player without showing a menu. The loop option is good for occasions such as a convention where a looped video is a common occurrence, but this option is not available for all disc templates.

TIP When you select a graphic, logo, or title, it appears in the Main Menu video display. If you want to try a different choice, click the reset button (X) to the right of the parameter and click Add again.

5 Take a look at the summary bar along the bottom of the Share window. Notice that two files are exporting: one for audio and one for video.

6 To create a disk image, click Next. In the Save As field, enter a name, and navigate to the Exports folder as the save location. Then click Save.

7 To view the disk image, navigate to the Exports folder, and select the *I Think* disk image.

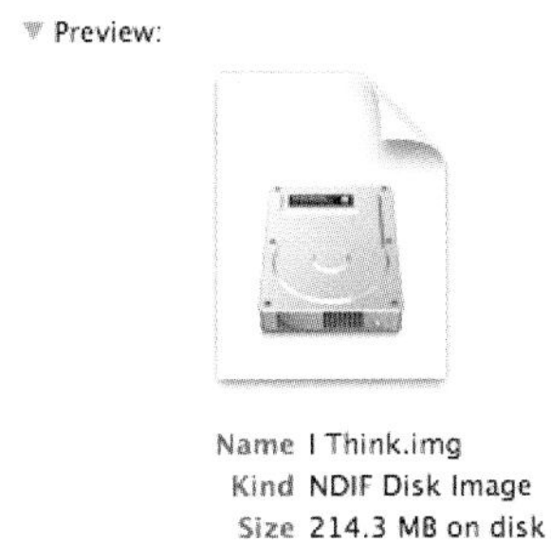

You can now transfer this file to another computer to create a Blu-ray disc, or simply save it as an archive.

Backing Up Projects and Events

The sense of satisfaction that comes from delivering a finished project to a client is something that every editor anticipates and enjoys, even if you are your own client. As you bask in your accomplishment, however, don't forget that backing up your files is an important responsibility that will save you time in the long run because old projects are often revisited, altered, and used for new purposes.

Periodic backups of projects, Project Library contents, and Events is not only an essential part of your editing workflow, it's an insurance policy against wasted time and lost files.

This exercise provides a step-by-step guide to backing up a project and its associated Events to an external drive.

1 Connect an external hard disk or other storage device to your computer. Otherwise, in the Finder, navigate to the APTS FCP X volume. There you will find a disk image named Archive. Double-click it.

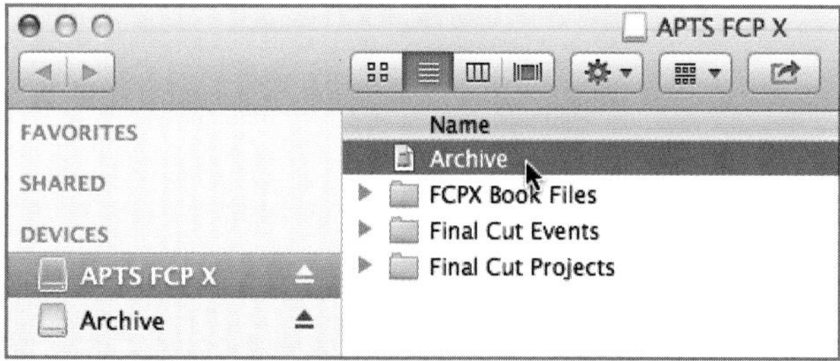

2 Open a Finder window and, in column view, select the storage device from the sidebar.

Before you begin the backup process, verify that the hard disk has sufficient available space to store the Event and project files.

TIP The virtual Archive drive is included in the "hard disk" reference for the rest of this exercise. The use of a disk image is a great way to collect Events and projects into one container for sharing with collaborators. Disk images also serve as containers for gathering associated projects and Events into one location for archiving and backing up on the same volume as other projects.

3 With the hard disk selected, press Command-I. In the Info window, notice the amount of free space in the drive information.

Capacity: 8.54 GB
Available: 8.51 GB

4 Return to Final Cut Pro, and press Command-0, if necessary, to view the Project Library. In the Lesson 12 folder, Control-click the *I Think* project and, from the shortcut menu, choose Duplicate Project.

The Duplicate Project window opens with various options to duplicate this project, each option preceded by buttons for projects, Events, and clips.

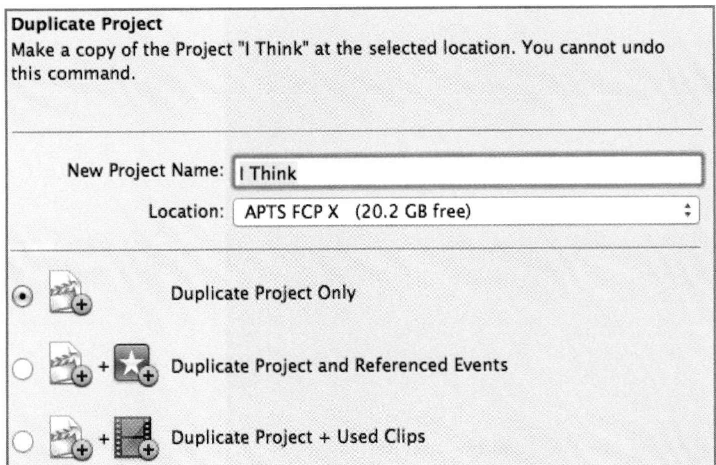

5 From the Location pop-up menu, choose the connected storage device you want to use for the backup. If you are using the disk image from the DVD, choose Archive.

In previous lessons, you duplicated a project using the default option: Duplicate Project Only. When you back up a project, however, you also need to duplicate the files used to create that project. You can consider two options for this task:

- Duplicate Project and Referenced Events: Duplicate the project and all the media in the referenced Events. All unused media is included.
- Duplicate Project + Used Clips: Duplicate the project and only the media used in the project. When this option is selected, a new Event is created, and you need to enter a new name in the field below the option.

6 To create a complete backup of all your media files, choose "Duplicate Project and Referenced Events." Then deselect Include Render Files, if selected.

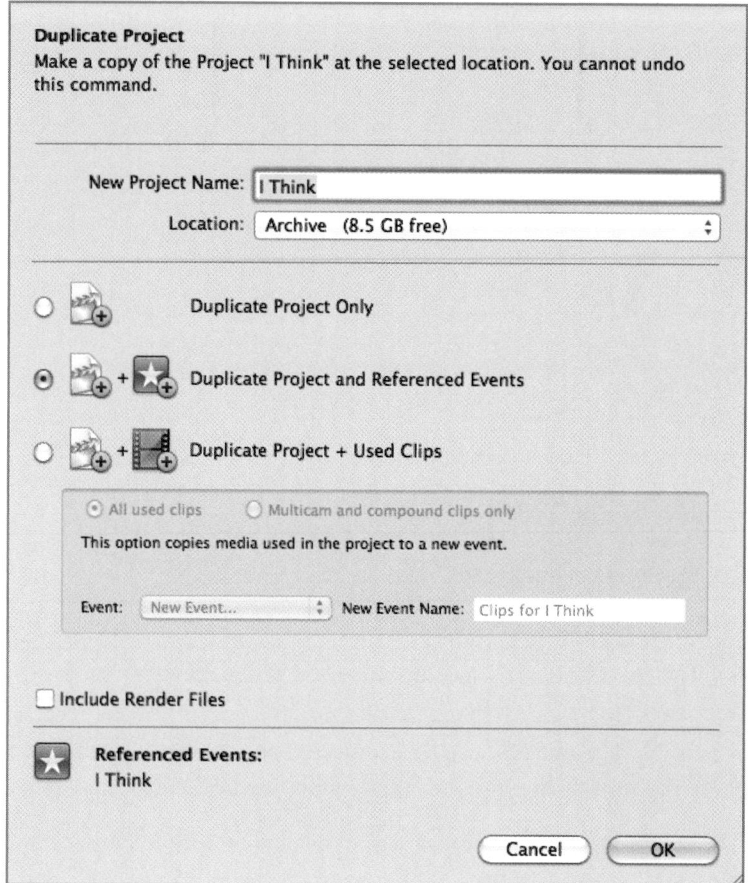

NOTE ▸ It's not essential that you duplicate render files. If you choose not to duplicate them, Final Cut Pro will create new ones.

7 Click OK.

You probably noticed that this process happened very quickly. In the target drive location, Final Cut Pro creates Final Cut Events and Final Cut Projects folders (if they don't already exist) and places a copy of the Event and the project files into the appropriate location. Whether the source media files were copied at this point depends on whether you copied files into the Event folder during import. Don't worry if you don't remember what you did during import. Final Cut Pro has a simple command to ensure that all source media is copied into the Event folder for safekeeping.

8 In the Event Library, select the *I Think* Event on the Archive volume. Make sure that the Event is highlighted in blue (and not in gray, which indicates the Event Browser is active).

9 Choose File > Organize Event Files. In the dialog that appears, click Continue to permit the externally referenced files to be copied into the Event.

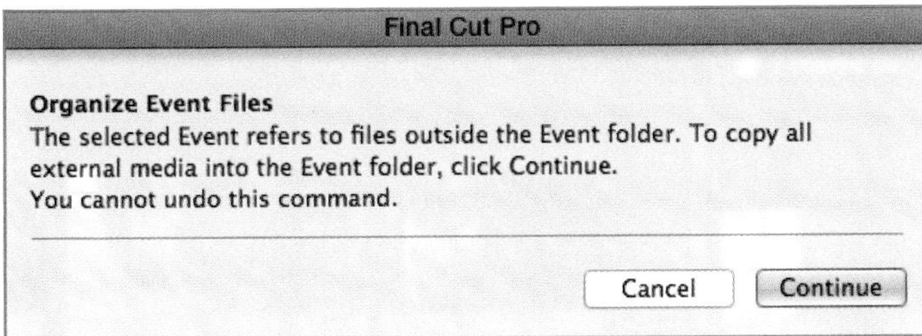

This time the background tasks take a little longer as the source media files are copied to the Archive volume. It is safe to run this command on the Archive drive whether or not the source media files were copied during import.

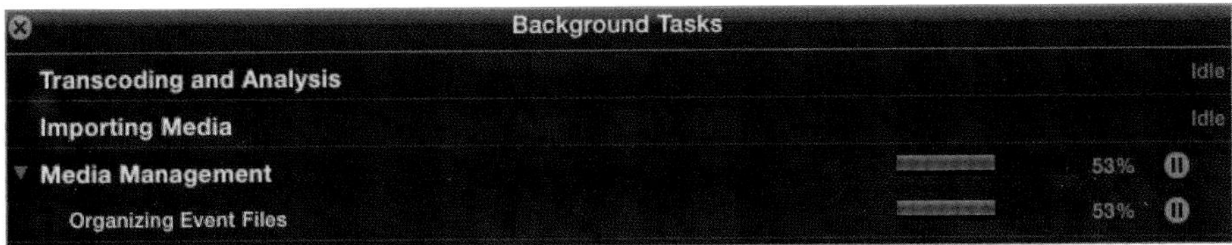

If at any time you want to view or edit these backup files, just connect the storage device to your computer or mount the disk image of the Events and project. The backed-up project and Events automatically connect to Final Cut Pro and can be located in the Event and Project Library.

Editor's Cut

In the Project Library, choose your favorite project from the Lesson 12 folder and take the project through a top-to-bottom finishing and exporting process. Start by checking and fixing the luma and audio levels. Then use the Share function to export the Timeline to several destinations, including emailing the project to yourself (but remember the copyright rule and don't post them to a public site). Use the Background Tasks window to follow the details of the processing.

Finally, duplicate the project onto the Archive disk. The more familiar you are with the steps in the finishing process, the more likely you are to include them as part of your personal workflow.

Now that you have completed the lessons in this book, you have the skills at your fingertips to create an exciting array of projects. Happy editing!

Lesson Review

1. How would you correct an audio clip that displays red peak indicators for only a few frames?
2. How do you set the Timeline appearance to display video clips as large thumbnails without any audio waveforms?
3. How can you display the video scopes to determine whether an image falls within the broadcast-safe range?
4. How do you view the luma levels in the waveform display to check for broadcast-safe video levels?
5. How do you open the Color Board to prepare your project for output?
6. What does the Share icon in the Project Library indicate?
7. How do you track the progress of an export?
8. How can you post a project on YouTube?
9. How do you set who can view a movie you post on Vimeo?
10. How can you export a still image from a project?
11. How can you create a backup that includes only the content that was used in the project?
12. How can you email a copy of a movie?
13. Why would you want to create a disk image of your project or Event?

Answers

1. Option-click the volume control line in the Timeline to create keyframes that allow you to adjust that specific section of the clip.

2. Below the Timeline, click the Clip Appearance button, and select the fifth clip icon to show only the video display. If necessary, adjust the clip height to see all the clips in the Timeline.
3. Choose Window > Viewer Display > Show Video Scopes, or press Command-7. The Viewer splits into two areas, with a smaller Viewer on the right and the video scopes to the left.
4. From the Settings pop-up menu in the video scopes window, choose Display > Waveform. Then, from the Settings pop-up menu, choose Channels > Luma.
5. In the toolbar, click the Enhancements button, and choose Show Color Board, or press Command-6. In the Color Board, click the Exposure tab.
6. The Share icon next to the project name indicates that the project has been shared. This icon also appears next to the project name in the Timeline.
7. After you click Share, Publish, or Save, click the Background Tasks button in the Dashboard to display the export progress.
8. In the Project Library, select the project you want to share, and from the Share pop-up menu, choose the YouTube destination.
9. In the Vimeo Settings section of the Share window, the "Viewable by" pop-up menu offers three options to set who can view your movie on Vimeo.
10. After adding the Save Current Frame destination to the Share pop-up menu, move the playhead to the frame you want to export, and from the Share pop-up menu, choose Save Current Frame.
11. In the Project Library, Control-click the project, and choose Duplicate Project from the shortcut menu. Select "Duplicate Project + Used Clips" to copy the project and only the media used in the project. When this option is selected, a new Event is created, and you must enter a new name for the backup. After the duplication is finished, select the copied Event, and choose File > Organize Event Files to copy all media into the Event folder.
12. Select the project, and choose the Email destination for Sharing. In the Share window, choose a movie size and compression from the menus, and then compose a message and send it.
13. A disk image (.img) file is a useful way to archive Events and projects within a container that simulates a volume from a hard disk. With good media management practice in Final Cut Pro X, the disk image should contain everything necessary for editing those projects.

Keyboard Shortcuts

Command-D	Duplicates a selected destination in the Share window.
Command-E	Opens the Share window for the default destination
Command-Delete	In the Share window, removes the selected destination from the active list.
Command-7	Show/hide Viewer video scopes

Glossary

#

16-bit A standard bit depth for digital audio recording and playback.

16 x 9 The standard display aspect ratio of a high-definition television set.

24-bit A video image with three channels—red, green, and blue—each with 8-bit resolution.

32-bit A four-channel image with each channel 8 bits deep. Typically, a CGI image includes a red, green, blue, and alpha channel.

4 x 3 The standard display aspect ratio of a standard-definition video.

4:2:2 A digital compression scheme. For every four samples of luminance, two samples are taken for each of the color difference signals.

4:4:4 A digital compression scheme. For every four samples of luminance, four samples are taken for each of the color difference signals.

64-bit Final Cut Pro X is a 64-bit application, which dramatically speeds up numeric calculations and other tasks.

A

action safe The area that is five percent smaller than the overall size of the video frame. Most of the time, anything in your video image that's outside this border will not display on a video screen.

AIFF (Audio Interchange File Format) The native uncompressed audio file format created by Apple for the Macintosh computer, commonly used for the storage and transmission of digitally sampled sound.

alpha channel Grayscale image channel in addition to the red, green, and blue color channels that is used to store transparency information for compositing. In Final Cut Pro, black represents 100 percent transparent, and white represents 100 percent opaque.

anamorphic An image shot in a widescreen format and then squeezed into 4 x 3 frame size.

anchor point A point that is used to center changes to a clip when adding effects such as a rotation. A clip's anchor point does not have to be at its center.

animation The process of changing any number of variables such as color, audio levels, or other effects over time using keyframes.

append edit Adds one or more clips to the end of the primary or selected storyline.

Apple ProRes 422 This codec creates high-quality files optimized for efficient editing. Apple ProRes 422 provides better performance, faster rendering, better color quality, and faster exporting compared to many standard video codecs.

Apple ProRes 422 (Proxy) Files transcoded to this codec are smaller than the original file in data size, yet can retain the original frame rate and aspect ratio. Proxy media files speed your offline editing workflow and save storage space.

aspect ratio The ratio of the width of an image to its height on any viewing screen. Standard TV has an aspect ratio of 4 x 3; HDTV is 16 x 9.

attributes All of the unique settings that have been applied to either audio or video clips.

Audio Animation Editor The Audio Animation Editor adjusts effect parameters, creates fades, or animates effects over time using keyframes.

Audio meters A graphic display of the audio level (volume) of a clip. Used to set incoming and outgoing audio levels and to check for audio distortion and signal strength.

audio mixing The process of adjusting the volume levels of all audio clips in an edited project, including the production audio, music, sound effects, voice-overs, and additional background ambience, to turn all the sounds into a harmonious whole.

audio peaks The highest audio levels in a track. Peaks that exceed 0 dB will be clipped, or distorted.

audio sample rate The rate or frequency at which a sound is sampled to digitize it. 48 kHz is the standard sampling rate for digital audio; CD audio is sampled at 44.1 kHz.

audio waveform A graphical representation of the amplitude (loudness) of a sound over a period of time.

audition You can organize related clips into auditions, from which you can choose one clip to use. Create an audition of different clips to try multiple takes, or with multiple versions of the same clip to preview different effects. Auditions appear in the Event Browser and Timeline as clips with an Audition icon.

axis An imaginary straight line (horizontal, vertical, 3D diagonal) along which an object can move or rotate in space.

B

Background Tasks window The Background Tasks window shows the progress of importing, transcoding, analyzing, rendering, and other tasks occurring in the background while editing continues. The window allows for pausing or terminating individual tasks or categories of tasks.

Bezier handle The "control handles" attached to a Bezier curve on a motion path that allow you to change the shape of the curve.

black level The measurement of the black portion of the video signal. In analog television, this should not go below 7.5 IRE units. In digital television, black may be 0 units.

blanking The black border around the edges of a raw video image, created by the video camera CCDs. These black pixels should be cropped out of your image if you plan to composite over other footage.

Blend mode The Blend Mode menu in the Compositing section of the Video inspector offers many methods to combine two or more images.

broadcast safe The range of color or luminance that can be broadcast free of distortion, according to the NTSC standards, with maximum allowable video at 100 IRE units and digital black at 0 IRE, or analog black at 7.5 IRE units.

B-roll A term used to describe alternate footage that intercuts with the primary footage used in a program to help tell the story, or to cover flaws. B-roll is usually referred to as cutaway shots.

C

cache An area of a computer dedicated to storing still images and digital movies in preparation for real-time playback.

chroma The color information contained in a video signal consisting of hue (the color itself) and saturation (intensity).

clip Media files that may consist of video, audio, graphics, or any similar content that can be imported into Final Cut Pro.

clipping Distortion during the playback or recording of digital audio due to an overly loud level.

codec Short for compression/decompression. An algorithm used to compress and decompress data such as audio and video files.

color balance Refers to the overall mix of red, green, and blue for the highlights (brightest), midtones, and shadow (darkest) areas in a clip. The color balance of the three areas can be adjusted using the Color Board.

Color Board Lets you manually adjust a clip's color properties to add or subtract a tint, and control the intensity and brightness of the video. In addition to an overall control, each pane has individual controls for the highlights, midtones, and shadows.

color correction A process in which the color of clips used in an edited program is adjusted so that all shots in a given scene match.

color depth The possible range of colors that can be used in a movie or image. Higher color depths provide a wider range of colors but require more disk space for a given image size. Broadcast video is generally 24-bit, with 8 bits of color information per channel.

color matte A clip containing a solid color created as a generated item.

compositing The process of combining two or more video or electronic images into a single image. This term can also describe the process of creating various video effects.

compound clip Compound clips group clips in the Timeline or Event Browser, and nest clips within other clips. Compound clips can contain video and audio components, clips, and other compound clips. Each compound clip is a mini project, with its own distinct project settings. Compound clips function just like other clips: you can add them to your project, trim or retime them, and add effects and transitions.

compression The process by which video, graphics, and audio files are reduced in size. The reduction in the size of a video file through the removal of redundant image data is referred to as a lossy compression scheme. A lossless compression scheme uses a mathematical process and reduces the file size by consolidating the redundant information without discarding it. See also *codec*.

connect edit A type of edit that lets you attach clips to primary storyline clips in the Timeline. When you edit clips by dragging, you can connect video clips below the primary storyline or audio clips above the primary storyline.

connected clip Connected clips are attached to clips in the primary storyline in the Timeline. They are useful for cutaways, superimposed or composited images, and sound effects, and remain attached and synchronized until you explicitly move or remove them. Connected clips interact only with primary storyline clips, not with other connected clips.

connected storyline A group of clips connected to the primary storyline. Clips within a connected storyline can interact with each other similarly to clips in the primary storyline. Use connected storylines for the same purposes as connected clips (such as creating cutaways, compositing titles and other graphics, and adding sound effects and music).

contrast The difference between the lightest and darkest values in an image. High-contrast images have a large range of values from the darkest shadow to the lightest highlight. Low-contrast images have a more narrow range of values, resulting in a "flatter" look.

crossfade A transition between two audio clips where one sound is faded out while the other is faded in. Used to make the transition between two audio cuts less noticeable.

cut The simplest type of edit where one clip ends and the next begins without any transition.

cutaway A shot that is related to the current subject and occurs in the same time frame; for instance, an interviewer's reaction to what is being said in an interview or a shot to cover a technically bad moment.

D

dashboard Provides a timecode display as well as icons showing audio levels and the status of background tasks.

data rate The speed at which data can be transferred, often described in megabytes per second (MB/sec) or megabits per second (Mb/sec). The higher a video file's data rate, the higher quality it will be, but it will require more system resources (processor speed, hard disk space, RAM, and throughput). Some codecs allow you to specify a maximum data rate for a movie during encoding.

decibel (dB) A unit of measure for the loudness of audio.

decompression The process of restoring a video or audio file for playback from a compressed video, graphics, or audio file. Compare with compression.

de-interlace The process to convert video frames composed of two interlaced fields into a single unified frame: for example, a still image of an object moving at high speed. In Final Cut Pro X, the process is set using the Field Dominance Override setting in Inspector > Info > Settings View.

desaturate To remove color from a clip; 100 percent desaturation results in a grayscale image.

dissolve A transition between two video clips where the first one fades out at the same time the second one fades in.

drop frame timecode A type of timecode that skips two frame numbers each minute, except for minutes ending in 0, so that the end timecode total agrees with the actual elapsed clock time. Although timecode numbers are skipped, actual video frames are not skipped. Drop frame timecode is a reference to real time.

drop shadow An effect that creates an artificial shadow behind an image or graphic.

dynamic range The difference, in decibels, between the loudest and softest parts of a recording.

E

edit point (1) Defines what part of a clip you want to use in your project, such as a start point, which specifies the beginning of a range of a clip, and an end point, which specifies the end of a range of a clip. (2) The point in the Timeline where the end point of one clip meets the start point of the next clip.

effects A general term used to describe all the Final Cut Pro capabilities that go beyond cuts-only editing. See *filters*, *generators*, and *transitions*.

Effects Browser A media browser in Final Cut Pro that contains video and audio clip effects.

end point The point where an edit will end.

Event When you import or record into Final Cut Pro, your source media files are stored in Events. An Event is similar to a folder that holds video, audio, and still images. Each Event in the Event Library refers to a folder on a hard disk with the original source media or references to external source media, any render files, and a database file that tracks everything.

Event Browser Displays the clips for the item selected in the Event Library. You can select clips or mark ranges of clips in the Event Browser for use in a project, and sort by a variety of clip metadata such as creation date, date imported, reel, scene, clip duration, and file type. You can also view clips as filmstrips or in a list.

Event Library The Event Library holds and organizes the Events with your imported media. When you select an Event in the Event Library, the media appears as clips in the Event Browser. The Event Library also stores Keyword Collections and Smart Collections, a powerful method to organize media using keywords and persistent search filters.

F

fade An effect in which the picture gradually transitions to black.

Favorite A way to tag and subsequently sort preferred clip content. Press the F key or click the Favorite button in the toolbar to mark a clip or range as a Favorite.

field Half of an interlaced video frame consisting of the odd or the even scan lines.

field dominance The choice of whether field 1 or field 2 will be displayed on the monitor first. See *interlaced video*.

Filter pop-up menu Use this menu in the Event Browser to quickly locate individual clips by rating, or the absence of ratings and keywords.

Filter window This window performs complex searches for clips or clip ranges, also known as a weighted search. Search with a wide variety of criteria, including clip name, rating, media type, excessive shake, keywords, the presence of people, format information, and date.

finishing The process of fine-tuning the audio and video levels and preparing the project for output.

FireWire The Apple trademark name for the IEEE 1394 standard used to connect external hard drives and cameras to previous generation Macs. It provides a fast interface to move large video and audio files from an external hard disk to the computer for processing.

frame A single still image from either video or film. For video, each frame may be made up of two interlaced fields (see interlaced video) or a single frame (see progressive video).

frame blending A process of inserting blended frames in place of frames that have been duplicated in clips with slow motion, to make them play back more smoothly.

freeze frame An effect that edits a four-second (default) clip into the Timeline using a single source frame from an Event Browser or Timeline video clip.

frequency The number of times a sound or signal vibrates each second, measured in cycles per second, or hertz.

G

gain In video, the level of white in a video picture; in audio, the loudness of an audio signal.

gamma A curve that describes how the middle tones of an image appear. Gamma is a nonlinear function often confused with "brightness" or "contrast." Changing the value of the gamma affects middle tones while leaving the whites and blacks of the image unaltered.

gap clip A placeholder clip with blank video and silent audio you can adjust to any duration. The industry term for this is *slug*.

generators Clips that are synthesized by Final Cut Pro. Generators can be used as different kinds of backgrounds, titles, and elements for visual design.

gradient A generated image that changes smoothly from one color to another across the image. The change can occur in several ways: horizontally, vertically, radially, and so on.

green screen A solid green background placed behind a subject and photographed so that later the subject can be extracted and composited into another image.

H

Hand tool The editing tool that allows you to scroll in the Timeline. You select the Hand tool by pressing the H key.

head Either the very beginning of a clip or a marked range within a clip.

histogram A window that displays the relative strength of all luminance values in a video frame, from black to super-white. It is useful for comparing two clips in order to match their brightness values more closely.

hold A retiming attribute applied to a Timeline clip that creates a pause in action. The length of the pause can be adjusted in length.

hue A specific color or pigment, such as red.

I

incoming clip The clip that is on the right side, or B-side, of a transition or cut point.

Info inspector Displays metadata about a clip or group of clips in the Event Browser or the Timeline. Displays different combinations of metadata about your clips, such as codecs, media start and end times, reel, scene, take, EXIF information, and IPTC information. You can also use the Info inspector to change the metadata for a selected clip or group of clips, and create custom sets of metadata to display using the Metadata Views window.

insert edit A type of edit that places a clip into the Timeline while automatically moving or rippling the following clips (or remaining frames of a clip) to the right to make room. An insert edit does not replace existing material.

inspectors Let you view and change the attributes of selected items. For example, adjust video effects and apply color corrections in the Video inspector. Other inspectors include the Audio, Audio Enhancements, Info, Transition, Title, Text, Generator, Properties, and Share inspectors. Inspectors appear in the Inspector pane in the upper-right corner of the Final Cut Pro main window.

interlaced video A video scanning method that first scans the odd picture lines (field 1) and then scans the even picture lines (field 2), which merges them into one single frame of video. Used in standard-definition video, some formats may reverse the scanning order. Interlaced formats are often notated with the letter "i".

IRE A unit of measurement for luminance in an analog signal established by the Institute of Radio Engineers (IRE).

J

JPEG (Joint Photographic Experts Group) A popular image file format that lets you create highly compressed graphics files. The amount of compression can vary. Less compression results in a higher-quality image.

jump cut A cut in which an abrupt change of the content in time, space, or framing occurs between two sequential shots.

K

keyframe In Final Cut Pro, a point at which a parameter, effect, or audio level is specified. At least two keyframes representing two different values for the same parameter are required to show a change.

keying The process of dropping out a specific area of an image, such as its background, so that the image can be composited with another. You can key out information in a clip based on brightness and darkness, or color. See *mask/matte*.

Keyword Collection When you apply a keyword to a clip, a Keyword Collection is automatically created in the Event Library. Select the Keyword Collection to display each clip tagged with that keyword. You can also create Keyword Collections from folder names during import.

keywords Keywords add descriptive information to a clip or a section of a clip to organize, sort, and classify media. You can add keywords automatically during import or manually in the Event Browser.

kilohertz (kHz) A measure of audio frequency equal to 1000 hertz (cycles per second).

L

letterbox An effect that can mask video to appear in a variety of widescreen aspect ratios. This typically results in a black bar at the top and bottom of the picture.

lower third Lines of text used to identify a person, place, or thing in a clip typically appearing in the "lower third" of the frame.

luma Short for luminance. A value describing the brightness part of the video signal without color (chroma).

luma key An effect used to isolate a luminance value, creating a matte based on the brightest or darkest area of an image. See *keying* and *mask/matte*.

M

markers Reference points that can be placed on a clip to help you find a specific location while you edit. You can also use markers for task management. Markers are classified as standard informational markers (blue), to-do items (red), completed to-do items (green), and chapter markers (orange).

mask/matte An effect using an image, clip, or shape to create areas of transparency in another clip. Alternatively, an effect that creates areas of transparency within a clip based upon selected gray scale, color value, or a shape. Similar to an alpha channel.

master shot A single long shot or wide shot of some dramatic action or scene. It is often used to establish a new scene.

media browsers Media imported into Events is accessed from the Event Library and Event Browser, but media browsers let you access effects, titles, and transitions as well as media in other applications. For example, the Photo Browser can access video and images in your iPhoto or Aperture libraries. The Media Browser pane appears in the lower-right corner of the Final Cut Pro main window.

media file A generic term for imported or acquired elements such as QuickTime movies, sounds, and pictures.

media handles The remaining clip media before a marked start point and after a marked end point that is utilized during trims and transitions.

midtones The middle brightness range of an image. Not the very brightest part, nor the very darkest part.

mono audio A single channel of audio, typically output to both the left and right channels.

motion blur An effect that blurs any clip with keyframed motion applied to it, similar to blurred motion recorded by a camera.

MPEG (Moving Picture Experts Group) A group of compression standards for video and audio.

Music and Sound Browser A media browser that lets you access iTunes content as well as sound effects and loops from Final Cut Pro and iLife.

N

natural sound The ambient sound used from a source videotape.

non-drop frame timecode A type of timecode in which frames are numbered sequentially and run at 30 fps. NTSC's frame rate, however, is actually 29.97 fps; therefore, non-drop frame timecode is off by 3 seconds and 18 frames per hour in comparison to actual elapsed time.

noninterlaced video The standard representation of images on a computer, also referred to as "progressive scan." The monitor displays the image by drawing each line, continuously one after the other, from top to bottom.

nonlinear editing (NLE) A video editing process that uses computer hard disks to randomly access the media. It allows the editor to reorganize clips very quickly or make changes to sections without having to recreate the entire program.

nonsquare pixel A pixel whose height is different from its width. An NTSC pixel is taller than it is wide, and a PAL pixel is wider than it is tall.

NTSC (National Television Systems Committee) Standard of color TV broadcasting used mainly in North America, Mexico, and Japan, consisting of 525 lines per frame, 29.97 frames per second, and 720 x 486 pixels per frame (720 x 480 for DV).

O

offline editing The process of editing a program at a lower resolution to save on equipment costs or to conserve hard disk space. When the edit is finished, the material can be reimported or relinked to a higher quality.

opacity The degree to which an image is transparent, allowing images behind to show through.

outgoing clip The clip on the left side of the cut point or the A-side of a transition.

overwrite edit A type of edit where the clip being edited into a project replaces an existing clip or a portion of an existing clip. The duration of the project remains unchanged.

P

PAL (Phase Alternating Line) The European color TV broadcasting standard consisting of 625 lines per frame, running at 25 frames per second, and 720 x 546 pixels per frame.

pan To rotate a camera left or right without changing its position.

Parade scope A modified Waveform Monitor that breaks out the red, green, and blue components of the image, showing them as three separate waveforms. Useful for comparing the relative levels of reds, greens, and blues between two clips, especially in a graphics situation.

peak Short, loud bursts of sound that last a fraction of a second and can be viewed on a digital audio meter that displays the absolute volume of an audio signal as it plays.

phase An attribute of color perception, also known as hue.

pixel Short for "picture element," one dot in a video or still image.

pixel aspect ratio The width-to-height ratio for the pixels that compose an image. Pixels on computer screens and in many high-definition video signals are square (1:1 ratio). Pixels in standard-definition video signals are nonsquare.

playhead A navigational element that indicates the current frame in the Timeline. You move the playhead by dragging or clicking in the Timeline. You use the playhead to scrub, or move through your project and play back from different locations. The playhead appears as a gray vertical line. See also *skimmer*.

postproduction The phase of film, video, and audio editing that begins after all the footage is shot.

post-roll The amount of time that the playhead continues to roll past the playhead's current location or after previewing an audition clip, typically between 2 and 5 seconds.

poster frame The representative still frame of a clip that is the thumbnail image.

Precision Editor An expanded view that displays the upper-left outgoing clip above the lower-right incoming clip along with the media handles, if any, of each clip. Use this window to adjust the edit point between two clips or the individual edit points very precisely.

pre-roll The amount of time that the playhead cues up before the playhead's current location or before previewing an audition clip, typically between 2 and 5 seconds.

primary storyline The main sequence of clips that you build to create your movie in the Timeline. Establishes sync for a project.

progressive video A video scanning method that begins the scan at the top of the image and proceeds sequentially line-by-line to the bottom of the image to complete one single frame of video. Used in high-definition video, some video formats expose the entire camera sensor at one time, similar to film. Progressive formats are often notated with the letter "p".

project Build a project by adding and editing clips in the Timeline. A project is also defined by its video, audio, and render properties. In most cases, Final Cut Pro manages project settings automatically based on the properties of the first clip you add to a project.

Q

QuickTime The Apple cross-platform multimedia technology. Widely used for editing, compositing, web video, and more.

QuickTime streaming The Apple streaming media addition to the QuickTime architecture. Used for viewing QuickTime content in real time on the web.

R

RAID (Redundant Array of Independent Disks) drive A method of formatting a group of hard disks to act as a single large storage volume with built-in redundancy for data protection.

range A selection in the Event Browser or project you adjust by changing the selection start or end point. In contrast to clip selections, which include entire clips, range selections allow you to select a portion of a clip or a portion of a project. A range selection has handles you can drag to adjust the selection.

real-time effects Effects that can be applied to clips in an edited project and played back in real time, without requiring rendering first. Real-time effects can be played back using any qualified computer.

Redo A feature that allows you to redo the last edit or trim command.

render To process video and audio with any applied effects, such as transitions or effects. Effects that aren't real time require rendering in order to play back properly. Once the effects are rendered, they can play in real time.

render file The file produced by rendering a clip to disk. Render files are stored with your Final Cut Pro project files.

replace edit Allows you to replace an existing shot in a project with a different shot.

reveal This command matches the Timeline clip at the playhead to the source clip in the Event Browser by putting a selection border around it. This is useful to duplicate a clip in your project or add the same clip to a different project.

RGB An abbreviation for red, green, and blue, which are the three primary colors that make up a color image.

ripple A type of trim that modifies the start or end point of a project clip, and repositions (or "ripples") subsequent clips, while lengthening or shortening the entire project when performed in the primary storyline.

roll A type of trim that modifies the shared edit point of two clips. The end point of the outgoing clip and the start point of the incoming clip both change, but the overall duration of the project stays the same.

S

sampling The process whereby analog audio is converted into digital data. The sampling rate of an audio stream specifies how many samples are captured. Higher sample rates yield higher-quality audio. Examples are 44.1 kHz and 48 kHz.

saturation The purity of color. As saturation is decreased, the color moves toward pastel and then toward grayscale.

scale An adjustable value that changes the overall size of a clip. The proportion of the image may or may not be maintained.

SECAM (Séquentiel Couleur à Mémoire) The French television standard for playback. Similar to PAL, the playback rate is 25 fps and the frame size is 720 x 546.

selection rectangle The rectangular lasso that the pointer generates as it is dragged in the Event Browser or Timeline to select items.

Show reference waveforms This preference sets the background of a clip's audio to show the maximum visual resolution of the actual audio waveform. By factoring out loudness, reference waveforms let you view the sound's shape more clearly. When the actual waveform changes shape (for example, it diminishes when a clip's volume is low), you can continue to view its reference waveform in full for easy reference.

skimmer Previews clips in the Timeline, Event Browser, or Project Library, without affecting the playhead position. The skimmer appears as a pink vertical line as you skim or freely move the pointer over the clip. If snapping is turned on, the skimmer turns orange when it snaps to a position. When present in the Timeline, the Skimmer overrides the playhead for most edit functions.

slate A small clapboard, placed in front of all cameras at the beginning of a scene, which gives basic production information such as the take, date, and name of scene. A slate or clapper provides an audio/visual cue for synchronization of dual-system recordings.

slide A type of trim in which an entire clip is moved, along with the edit points on its left and right. The duration of the clip being moved stays the same, but the clips to the left and to the right of it change in length to accommodate the new positioning of the clip. The overall duration of the project and of these three clips remains the same.

slip A type of trim in which the location of both start and end points within a clip are modified at the same time, without changing the location or duration of the marked media. The result is a change of the clip's content.

Smart Collection When you search for clips in an Event using the Filter window, you can save the results in a Smart Collection that displays clips matching the search criteria. Whenever a clip that matches the criteria is added to the Event, the new clip is automatically shown in the Smart Collection. Clips that appear in Smart Collections are not duplicates. Smart Collections filter clips to help you focus on the clips you need to use for a specific task.

SMPTE (Society of Motion Picture and Television Engineers) The organization responsible for establishing various broadcast video standards like the SMPTE standard timecode for video playback.

snapping A setting in the Timeline that affects the movement of objects such as the playhead, clips, and markers. With snapping enabled, when dragging these objects close together, they "snap," or move directly, to each other to ensure frame accuracy.

solo An audio monitoring feature in which audio clips may be isolated for listening. When turned on, the Solo button in the Timeline turns yellow. Clips outside the solo selection appear black and white, making the soloed clips easy to identify.

SOT Sound on tape.

sound bite A short excerpt taken from an interview clip.

split edit An edit in which the video or the audio component of a clip ends up being longer than the other component. For example, the sound may be longer than the video at the head of the clip, so it is heard before the video appears. Also referred to as an J-cut. The reverse, having the audio lag the video edit, is referred to as an L-cut.

square pixel A pixel that has the same height as width.

start point The edit point that determines where an edit will begin.

stereo audio Sound that is separated into two channels, one carrying the sounds for the right ear and one for the left ear.

storylines The Timeline contains a primary storyline, which is your main sequence of clips. A connected storyline is a sequence of clips connected to the primary storyline. You can use connected storylines for the same purposes as connected clips (such as creating cutaways, compositing titles or graphics, and adding sound effects and music).

straight cut An edit in which both the video and audio components are cut together to the Timeline.

streaming The delivery of media over an intranet or over the Internet.

superimpose A visual composite created by placing two or more clips in a vertical stack in the Timeline, often used to overlay titles onto a clip below.

super-black Black that is darker than the levels allowed by the CCIR 601 engineering standard for video. The CCIR 601 standard for black is 7.5 IRE in the United States, and 0 IRE for PAL and for NTSC in Japan.

super-white A value or degree of white that is brighter than the accepted normal value of 100 IRE allowed by the CCIR 601.

sweetening The process of creating a high-quality sound mix by polishing sound levels, re-recording bad sections of dialogue, and recording and adding narration, music, and sound effects.

sync The relationship between the image of a sound being made in a video clip (for example, a person talking) and the corresponding sound in an audio clip. Maintaining sync is critical when editing dialogue.

synchronized clip Final Cut Pro can automatically analyze and sync clips into a synchronized clip in the Event Browser. Final Cut Pro looks for sync points such as markers you added, timecode, file creation date, and audio content. If no sync points are found, clips sync at their respective starting points.

T

tail Either the very end of a clip or the end of a marked range within a clip.

three-point editing The traditional process of creating an edit by setting three edit points that determine source content, duration, and placement in the project. When a range is marked within a project, the default is to ignore the end point of the Event Browser clip unless backtiming an edit.

Thunderbolt A connection technology developed by Intel and Apple to provide extremely fast throughput between the newest generation Macs and external hard disks, displays, networks, and video ingest devices all in a simple cable and small connector. Thunderbolt allows dual-channel communication on a single connector at speeds up to 10 Gbps per channel.

TIFF (Tagged Image File Format) A widely used bitmapped graphics file format that handles monochrome, grayscale, and 8- and 24-bit color.

tilt To pivot the camera up and down, which causes the image to move up or down in the frame.

timecode A numbering system of electronic signals laid onto each frame of video that is used to identify specific frames of video. Each frame of video is labeled with hours, minutes, seconds, and frames (01:00:00:00). Timecode can be drop frame, non-drop frame, or time of day (TOD) timecode, or EBU (European Broadcast Union) for PAL projects.

Timeline A window that displays a chronological view of an open project. You can use the Timeline to edit and arrange a horizontal sequence of clips. The vertical order of the clips in the Timeline determines the layering order when you composite multiple video clips. Changes you make in the Timeline are seen when you play back in the Viewer.

time remapping The process of changing the speed of playback of a clip over time. The equivalent of varying the crank of a film camera.

Title Browser A media browser that provides access to all the title effects included with Final Cut Pro or custom titles published from Motion.

title safe Part of the video image that is guaranteed to be visible on televisions. The title safe area is the inner 80 percent of the screen. To prevent text in your video from being hidden by the edge of a TV set, you should restrict any titles or text to the title safe area.

transition A visual or audio effect applied between two edit points, such as a video cross dissolve or an audio crossfade.

Transitions Browser A media browser in Final Cut Pro that contains video transitions.

trimming To precisely add or subtract frames from the start or end point of a clip. Trimming is used to fine-tune an edited project by carefully adjusting many edits in small ways.

U

undo A feature that allows you to cancel the last edit or trim command used. You are unable to undo many interface adjustments and most media management commands.

V

variable speed Speed that varies dynamically within a clip among a range of speeds, in forward or reverse motion.

Vectorscope A window in Final Cut Pro that graphically displays the color components of a video signal, precisely displaying the range of colors and measuring their intensity and hue.

video level The measurement of the level (amplitude) of a video signal. It is measured using a Waveform Monitor.

video scopes Tools you can use to evaluate the color and brightness values of video clips. Video scopes display an analysis of the video frame located at the skimmer or current playhead position.

Viewer The Viewer is where you play back your Events, projects, or individual clips within the interface, in full-screen view, or on a second display.

VU meter (Volume Unit meter) An analog meter for monitoring audio levels.

W

Waveform Monitor A window in Final Cut Pro that displays the relative levels of brightness in the clip currently being examined. Spikes or drops in the displayed waveforms make it easy to see where the brightest or darkest areas are in your picture.

white balance The reference to the shade of white that is made during recording. This reference can be changed within Final Cut Pro, correcting or improving it in order to display true white.

white level An analog video signal's amplitude for the lightest white in a picture, represented by IRE units.

widescreen An aspect ratio such as 16:9 or 2.35:1 that allows for a wider image, suitable for widescreen television or film projection.

window burn Visual timecode and keycode information superimposed onto video frames. It usually appears on a strip at the bottom or top of the frame, providing code information to the editor without obscuring the picture.

wipe A type of transition that uses a moving edge to progressively hide the current clip to reveal the next clip.

X

x axis Refers to the x coordinate in Cartesian geometry. The x coordinate describes horizontal placement in motion effects.

Y

y axis Refers to the y coordinate in Cartesian geometry. The y coordinate describes vertical placement in motion effects.

YCbCr The color space in which digital video formats store data. Three components are stored for each pixel—one for luminance (Y) and two for color information, Cr for the red portion of the color difference signal and Cb for the blue color difference signal.

YUV The three-channel PAL video signal with one luminance (Y) and two chrominance color difference signals (UV). It is often misapplied to refer to NTSC video, which is YIQ.

Z

z axis Refers to the z coordinate in Cartesian geometry. The z coordinate describes perpendicular placement in motion effects, which includes zooming toward or away from the viewer, or rotating an image in space.

zoom To change the magnification of your image or Timeline.

Index

B

C

D

E

U

V

Downloading Lesson Files

Thank you for purchasing *Apple Pro Training Series: Final Cut Pro X, Second Edition*. If you have purchased the digital version of the guide or your Mac does not have a DVD drive, you have access to the lesson and media files by following the steps below:

TIP The lesson files are approximately 4 GB in size and may take some time to download. Before attempting to download the files, we suggest you update your browser to the latest version and make sure Java is enabled; quit other applications; and set your energy settings to prevent your computer from going to sleep during the download.

1. Go to this URL:

   www.peachpit.com/ebookfiles/013340921X

2. Download the sparseimage and ReadMe file using the "Download All" link in the upper-left corner to prevent the download session from ending prematurely.

3. Follow directions for use in the ReadMe file included in the download.

NOTE ▶ Due to copyright restrictions, you may not use this footage for any purpose other than completing the exercises in this book.

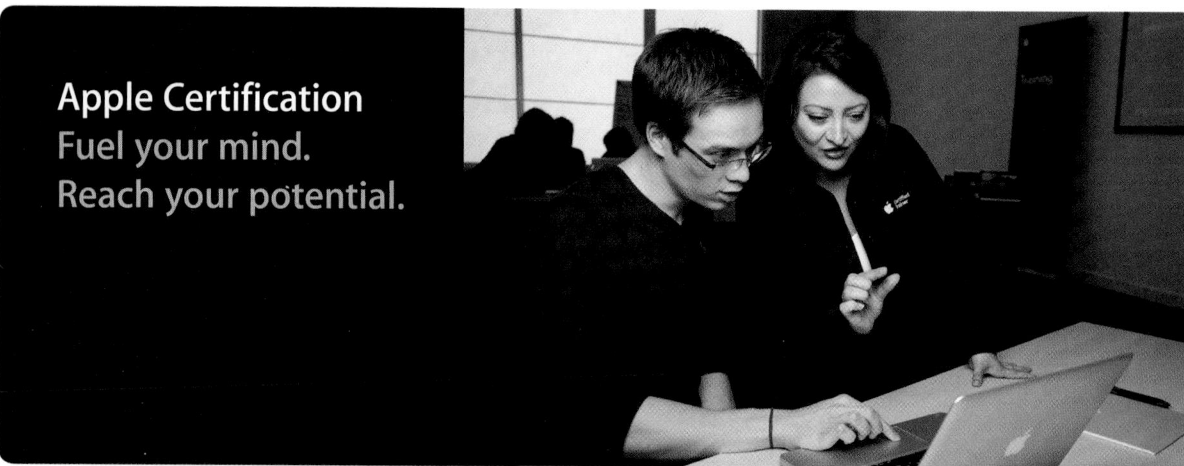

Gain recognition for your expertise by earning Apple Certification to validate your Final Cut Pro X skills.

This book prepares you to earn Apple Certified Pro—Final Cut Pro X Level One status at an Apple Authorized Training Center (AATC). Level One certification attests to essential operational knowledge of the application. If you prefer to validate entry-level skills, you can take the Associate Level exam online from the comfort of your home or office.

How to Earn Apple Certified Associate Status

For exam details,visit training.apple.com/certification/proapps. To take the Associate Level exam online for $65.00 USD, please follow these steps:

1 Visit http://training.apple.com/certification/onlinecert for system requirements.

2 Log on to ibt.prometric.com/apple, click Secure Sign-In and enter your Prometric Prime ID. If you don't have an ID, click First-Time Registration to create one.

3 Click Continue to verify your information.

4 In the Candidate Menu page, click Change Domain on the left and set the Domain to IT&ProApps. (If you don't see this option, skip to the next step.)

5 Click Take Test.

6 Enter FCPXASCPP in the Private Tests box and click Submit. The code is case sensitive and only valid for one use.

7 Click Take This Test.

8 Read and Agree/Accept the Certification Program Agreement.

9 Click Continue to skip the voucher and enter your credit card information.

10 Click Begin Test at the bottom of the page.

Reasons to Become an Apple Certified Pro

- **Raise your earning potential.** Studies show that certified professionals can earn more than their non-certified peers.
- **Distinguish yourself from others in your industry.** Proven mastery of an application helps you stand out from the crowd.
- **Display your Apple Certification logo.** Each certification provides a logo to display on business cards, resumes and websites.
- **Publicize your Certifications.** Publish your certifications on the Apple Certified Professionals Registry to connect with schools, clients and employers.

Training Options

Apple's comprehensive curriculum addresses your needs, whether you're an IT or creative professional, educator, or student. Hands-on training is available through a worldwide network of Apple Authorized Training Centers (AATCs). Self-paced study is available through the Apple Pro Training Series books, which are also accessible as eBooks via the iBooks app. Video training and video training apps are also available for select titles. Visit training.apple.com to view all your learning options.

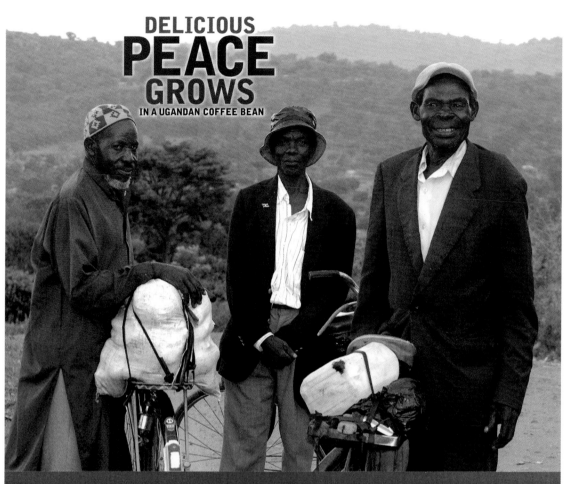

DELICIOUS PEACE GROWS

IN A UGANDAN COFFEE BEAN

JEWISH, CHRISTIAN AND MUSLIM UGANDAN COFFEE FARMERS FORMED A FAIR TRADE COOPERATIVE TO BUILD PEACE & ECONOMIC PROSPERITY.

U.S. COFFEE CONSUMERS ARE MIRRORING THEIR MODEL.

A DOCUMENTARY NARRATED BY ED O'NEILL

PRODUCED BY **JEMGLO PRODUCTIONS** | DIRECTOR **CURT FISSEL** | PRODUCER **ELLEN FRIEDLAND**

MOTION AND GRAPHIC DESIGN **LORI NEWMAN** | POST-PRODUCTION TECHNICAL SUPPORT **3SOURCE MEDIA**

WWW.DELICIOUSPEACETHEMOVIE.COM

SALAAM SHALOM PEACE

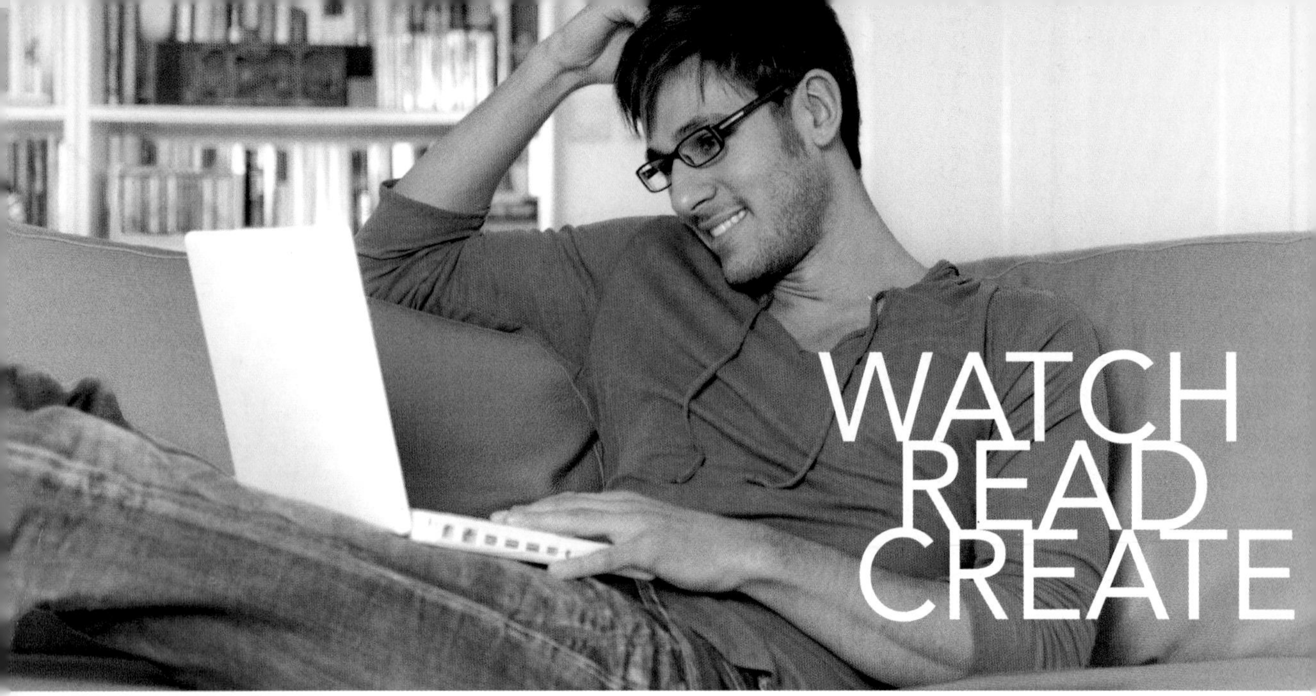